A BILINGUAL TEXT

Education in Contemporary Japan
-System and Content-

バイリンガル・テキスト

現代日本の教育
〈制度と内容〉

Yokuo Murata and Mitsuru Yamaguchi
村田翼夫 & 山口 満
［編著］

東信堂

目　次

はしがき……………………………………………………………… 8
執筆者一覧 (16)

第Ⅰ章　日本の教育の背景・展望と基本原則……………… 21

1　日本の教育の背景・展望 (22)
2　教育の基本原則 (32)

第Ⅱ章　教育の概要…………………………………………… 51

1　生涯学習社会と教育改革 (52)
2　学校制度 (56)
3　特別支援教育制度 (100)
4　社会教育制度 (128)

第Ⅲ章　教育行財政・経営の現状と課題………………… 145

1　日本の政治機構 (146)
2　教育行政の基本的原理 (148)
3　国レベルの教育行政 (154)
4　地方レベルの教育行政 (166)
5　中央と地方教育行政の関係 (178)
6　学校経営 (184)
7　教育財政 (196)
8　教育行財政・経営の課題 (210)

Contents

Preface ··· 9

Contributors (17)

I. The Background / Perspective and Basic Principles in Japanese Education ·· 21

    1   The Background and Perspective of Education in Japan (23)

    2   The Basic Principles of Education (33)

II. The Outline of Educational System ·· 51

    1   Lifelong Learning Society and Educational Reform (53)

    2   School System (57)

    3   Special Needs Education System (101)

    4   Social Education System (129)

III. The Conditions and Issues of Educational Administration, Finance and Management ·· 145

    1   Political Structure in Japan (147)

    2   Fundamental Principles of Educational Administration (149)

    3   Educational Administration at the National Level (155)

    4   Educational Administration at the Local Levels (167)

    5   Relationship between the Central and Local Institutions of Educational Administration (179)

    6   School Management (185)

    7   Educational Finance (197)

    8   The Issues in Educational Administration, Finance and Management (211)

第Ⅳ章　教員制度の現状と課題……………………………221

1　日本の教職員の特徴（222）
2　教員養成・採用・研修（232）
3　教員人事（246）
4　教員団体（258）

第Ⅴ章　国際教育の展開……………………………265

1　教育の国際交流・協力の拡大（266）
2　学校教育の国際化（282）
3　国際教育行政の発展（304）
4　教育の国際化・グローバル化の課題（312）

第Ⅵ章　教育内容・方法の概要……………………………323

1　教育課程（324）
2　学習指導要領（328）
3　教科書（338）
4　学校暦・時間割（340）
5　授業（346）
6　教育評価（354）

第Ⅶ章　教科教育等の特色……………………………363

1　国語（364）
2　社会科（380）
3　算数・数学（400）
4　理科（422）
5　生活（446）

IV. The Conditions and Issues of Teachers 221

    1 Characteristics of Japanese Teachers and Staff (223)

    2 Pre-Service Training, Adoption
       and In-Service Training of Teachers (233)

    3 Personnel Affairs of Teachers (247)

    4 Teachers' Organization (259)

V. Development of International Education 265

    1 Expansion of International Relations
       and Cooperation in Education (267)

    2 Internationalization of School Education (283)

    3 The Development of International Educational Administration (305)

    4 Main Issues Concerning the Internationalization
       and Globalization of Education in Japan (313)

VI. Outline of Curriculum and Teaching Method 323

    1 Curriculum (325)

    2 Course of Study (329)

    3 Textbook (339)

    4 School Calendar and Timetable (341)

    5 Class Hour (347)

    6 Educational Evaluation (355)

VII. The Characteristics of Courses 363

    1 Japanese Language (365)

    2 Social Studies (381)

    3 Arithmetic and Mathematics (401)

    4 Science (423)

    5 Life Environment Studies (447)

6　芸術（450）

　　　　（1）音楽（450）

　　　　（2）図画工作・美術・工芸（462）

　　　　（3）書道（470）

　　　7　家庭科、技術・家庭科（476）

　　　8　体育、保健体育（496）

　　　9　道徳教育（512）

　　　10　外国語活動、外国語（542）

　　　11　総合的な学習の時間（564）

　　　12　特別活動（576）

　　　13　職業教育（600）

　　　14　ＩＴ教育（624）

　　　15　生徒指導（634）

第Ⅷ章　教育内容・方法の課題……………………………………661

　　　1　学校週五日制と教育課程・方法（662）

　　　2　学力問題とカリキュラム（666）

　　　3　「総合的な学習の時間」に関する問題（670）

　　　4　教育内容・指導方法の一貫性・接続性（676）

　　　5　体験活動の充実（678）

　　　6　少人数教育と少人数指導（682）

　　　7　キャリア教育（686）

あとがき……………………………………………………………692
索引…………………………………………………………………696

装幀　田宮俊和

6 Arts (451)

(1) Music (451)

(2) Arts and Handicrafts, Fine Arts and Craft Production (463)

(3) Calligraphy (471)

7 Homemaking, Industrial Arts and Homemaking, and Home Economics (477)

8 Physical Education, Health and Physical Education (497)

9 Moral Education (513)

10 Foreign Language Activities and Foreign Language (543)

11 Period for Integrated Study (565)

12 Extracurricular Activities (577)

13 Vocational Education (601)

14 IT Education (625)

15 Student Guidance (635)

Ⅷ. The Issues of Educational Contents and Methods ⋯⋯⋯⋯⋯⋯ 661

1 The Five-day Week School System and Curriculum/Method (663)

2 The Issues of Scholastic Ability and Curriculum (667)

3 The Issues of Period for Integrated Study (671)

4 Consistency and Articulation of Educational Contents and Teaching Methods (677)

5 Enhancement of Hands-on Activities (679)

6 Small Class Education and Small Class Teaching (683)

7 Career Education (687)

Postscript ⋯⋯⋯⋯⋯⋯⋯⋯⋯⋯⋯⋯⋯⋯⋯⋯⋯⋯⋯⋯⋯⋯⋯⋯⋯⋯⋯⋯⋯ 693

Index ⋯⋯⋯⋯⋯⋯⋯⋯⋯⋯⋯⋯⋯⋯⋯⋯⋯⋯⋯⋯⋯⋯⋯⋯⋯⋯⋯⋯⋯⋯⋯ 703

はしがき

■人々や情報の国際交流が盛んになり、教育の国際化、グローバル化が進展する現代にあって、多くの国の人々の間で日本の教育に対する関心が高まっている。近年、来日する留学生、研修生、研究者、日本から外国へ出かける留学生、教員、研究者が増えるとともに、彼らが日本の教育理解を深めたり、外国の人々にそれを深めてもらったりしようとする時に、英語で書かれた適当なテキストや参考書がなくて困っている姿が頻繁にみられるようになった。他方、日本の学校に子どもを通学させる外国人父母も増え、彼らも日本の学校教育の理解に悩んでいる。このような問題状況をみて、外国人および日本人に「現代日本の教育」の現状と課題を理解していただくのに役立てばと思い、本書の「現代日本の教育―制度と内容―」と題するバイリンガル・テキストを編集した。

■本書は、当初、主に1980年から始まった大学における外国人教員研修留学生プログラムのテキスト用に作成したものである。1989年に筑波大学において『バイリンガル・テキスト日本の教育―現状と課題―』と『―教科教育―』の2冊本とし、高倉翔、村田翼夫編で筑波大学教育研究科から発行した。その後、学習指導要領の改訂、教員免許法の改正、教員の初任者研修制度の施行、外国人児童生徒の増加などがあり、教育制度と教育内容が改革された。そのため、1998年に、読みやすいように1冊にまとめて同テキストの改訂を行うことにして内容の刷新を図った。対象者も一般の外国人留学生、研修生、研究者、ならびに国際交流・協力に関係する日本人の留学生、教員、研究者等に広げて想定した。書名は、『バイリンガルテキスト日本の教育―制

Preface

■ At present, the international exchange of persons and information is increasing and the education in many countries is in the process of being internationalized and globalized. As a result, many foreigners have become more interested in the education of Japan. In recent years, the number of students, trainees and researchers who come to Japan have increased considerably. At the same time, Japanese students, teachers and researchers who visit foreign countries have also increased. While the foreigners want to deepen their understanding of the education in Japan, the Japanese on the other hand, want to help and make foreigners understand Japanese education. Both have frequently been confronted with the difficulty of finding adequate textbooks and reference books about Japanese education that are written in English. The foreign parents whose children are enrolled in Japanese schools have increased and they feel difficulty in understanding the education in those schools. In order to remedy this problem, this bilingual text, "Contemporary Education in Japan- System and Content -" has been written and published with the hope that it will give foreigners and Japanese a better understanding and insight of the present condition of education in Japan.

■ Originally, this textbook was intended for participants of the In-Service Training Program for Overseas Teachers which started at some national universities in 1980. In 1989 a bilingual text was published composing two volumes. The first covers fields of educational systems under the theme of the Present Situation and Problems in Japanese Education. And the second one described the contents and teaching method of all the teaching subjects in school education. These texts were edited by Prof. Sho Takakura and Assoc. Prof. Yokuo Murata. It was published by the Graduate Dept. of Education, University of Tsukuba. After that, there were revisions made to the national standard on primary and secondary school curricula - "Course of Study" -, the reform of

度と課題・教科教育―』としてつくば国際教育研究会編(高倉翔・村田翼夫代表)で学習研究社から発行してもらった。同本は比較的好評で、現在は絶版になっているが、今も購買希望者がみられる。そこで、新しい項目を加えるとともに新たな研究者に執筆者として加わってもらい、現代日本の変化する教育状況に対応したテキストにしようと再度の改訂を試みた。

■本テキストの特色として、次の4点をあげることができるであろう。
①和英対照のバイリンガル・テキストとして、日英両語で学習できるようになっている。
②日本の教育制度を主な図表を入れながら記述し、学校制度、特別支援教育、教育行財政、学校経営、社会教育、教員制度、国際教育などに関してその現状と課題が理解し易いように工夫している。
③小学校、中学校、高等学校等において展開されている学校生活、カリキュラムおよび各教科等の内容・教育方法、ならびにそれらの特色、最近の動向および課題について統計や時間表などを入れながらわかり易く説明している。特に、2008年、2009年改訂の学習指導要領の内容も考慮した。
④取り上げている事項は、現代日本の教育の原則・枠組みを知る上で必要な基本的なものが中心となっている。さらに、学校教育を中心にして、その制度や内容・方法を簡潔に示すように編集した。

このような工夫が試みられている点で、従来の教育制度中心の「日本の教育」に関する教材より外国人にとって分かりやすくかつ利用しやすいもの

teacher's certificates system and, the implementation of in-service training for new teachers. Moreover, foreign students entering Japanese primary and lower secondary schools had increased. Considering these reforms and changes, the Bilingual Text was revised in one book renewing the contents which became easier to read. The readers of the book were broadly expected to be general foreign students, trainees, researchers and Japanese students going abroad, teachers, researchers who were concerned with international exchange and cooperation. The name of the book was "A Bilingual Text: Education in Japan-Present System and Tasks/Curriculum and Instruction". It was edited by the Tsukuba association for International Education Studies with Prof. Emeritus Sho Takakura and Prof. Yokuo Murata as editors in chief. The Gakken Co., Ltd published the revised text. The text book became rather popular. Though it was out of print, many people wanted to buy it. Therefore, we tried to revise the Text again in order to correspond to the educational changes in contemporary Japan, adding new items and asking some researchers to become new contributors.

■ The features of this text are shown as follows:

① As this text is written in two languages, anyone can study its contents either in Japanese or in English.

② This textbook describes the education system in Japan complete with figures and tables and the present situation and problems in the fields of school system, special needs education, educational administration and finance, school management, teacher's conditions, as well as social and international education.

③ The school life, curriculum, and the contents and teaching method of every teaching subject in primary, lower secondary, upper secondary education and so on, as well as those characteristics, recent trends and issues are explained in an understandable way using statistics, charts and timetables of the schools. Particularly, we have considered new contents of the Course of Study revised in 2008 and 2009.

④ This book deals with the fundamental matters which are necessary to learn the principals and frameworks of education in contemporary Japan. And

になっていると思う。また、日本人が外国人に対して「日本の教育」について説明したり教えたりしようとする時の有益なテキスト、参考書になり得るものと確信している。ただし、日本の教育の制度や内容・方法をより詳しく学習したい方は、本書を手掛かりとしてより専門的に書かれた文献や資料を活用していただきたい。

■国際教育交流が促進されるとともに、日本の外国に対する教育協力・援助も増加する今日、本書が、日本のみならず外国においても広く利用され、「現代日本の教育」の理解増進と国際交流・国際協力援助に役立つことになれば編者、執筆者の最も喜びとするところである。

■また、日本は近代化を進めた初期の時代から、欧米諸国の進んだ科学技術、社会制度、教育文化等の吸収に努めてきた。こうした先進国の情報文化の受け入れに腐心する国家は、情報受信型国家と呼ばれる。一方、今日の日本では、特色ある科学技術、社会制度、教育文化等を外国の人々に伝え理解してもらうことが非常に重要になっていると多くの識者が指摘している。例えば、「日本の教育経験」を見直し、その特色・長所を外国における教育改善に活用しようとする動きもみられる。いうなれば、日本は情報発信型国家に転換することが求められている。そのような観点からみて、このテキストが情報発信型国家として発展して行くための一助となり得れば、誠に意義深い出版と考えられよう。

■本書の改訂版作成にあたり、執筆者各位および編集作業を援助いただいた上田学教授および堤正史教授に対し御礼を申し上げる。また、大部分の翻訳

the education system and teaching contents and methods used in school are described concisely.

It is hoped that with these features, foreigners may find this textbook as a more comprehensible and useful reference material in their study of Japanese education compared with the former ones which focused on the education system. In the same light, Japanese educators may find this textbook of great value when explaining and teaching the many aspects of Japanese education to foreigners. We hope that people who want to study the education systems, teaching contents and methods in more detail would refer to more specialized books and materials with reference to this text.

■ Nowadays, international exchange in education has been promoted and the Japanese educational cooperation with and aid to foreign countries have increased. Furthermore, it will be our great pleasure if this textbook could be an effective tool in the promotion of understanding contemporary Japanese education, international exchange programs, cooperation and aid in education, not only in our country but also in foreign countries.

■ Moreover, Japan has tried so far to absorb the advanced science, technology, social system and educational and cultural knowledge from European and American countries since the beginning of the Modern Period. Countries which possess such a character are called "Information Recipient Nations". Today in Japan many knowledgeable people have recognized that it is very important for us to let other people know and understand the Japanese social system, education and culture. For example, there is a present trend to reconsider the characteristics and merits of "educational experiences in Japan" and to apply those to the improvement of education in foreign countries. With this in mind, Japan should become "An Information Providing Nation". Therefore, the editors and authors are pleased that this Bilingual Text will be able to help Japan become an "Information Providing Nation".

■ Our deep thanks should be given to authors, Prof. Manabu Ueda, and Prof. Masashi Tsutsumi who have supported our editing of this revised textbook.

にあたってもらった Mr. Steve Jugovic（びわこ成蹊スポーツ大学）および山本充恵さんに感謝する次第である。さらに、翻訳に加え図表作成等の作業を手伝ってもらった京都女子大学院生の平阪美穂さん、水森ゆりかさん、中村友里さん、翻訳を部分的に行ってくれた京都女子大学院生の人見麻紀さん、学部生の南増美さん、内藤麻理恵さんにも感謝する。最後に、本書の出版を快く引き受けていただいた東信堂の下田勝司氏（社長）に厚く御礼申し上げる次第である。

2010年1月

村田　翼夫（京都女子大学教授、筑波大学名誉教授）
山口　満（筑波大学名誉教授、びわこ成蹊スポーツ大学名誉教授）

We are thankful to Mr. Steve Jugovic (Biwako Seikei Sport College) and Ms. Mitsue Yamamoto who translated most of the Japanese articles into English. Moreover, we appreciate the contribution of Miss Miho Hirasaka, Miss Yurika Mizumori and Miss Yuri Nakamura, graduate students of Kyoto Women's University who translated the Japanese articles into English and helped with the works of making figures, tables etc. We also express thanks to Miss Maki Hitomi, a graduate student, and Miss Masumi Minami and Miss Marie Naito, undergraduate students of Kyoto Women's University who have partly assisted in the translation. Lastly, we gratefully acknowledge the favor by Mr. Katsuji Simoda, the president of the Publisher, Toshindo who has kindly accepted the publication of this Bilingual Text.

January, 2010

    Yokuo Murata, Professor, Kyoto Women's University,
        Professor Emeritus, University of Tsukuba
    Mitsuru Yamaguchi, Professor Emeritus, University of Tsukuba,
        Professor Emeritus, Biwako Seikei Sports College

執筆者一覧

村田翼夫（京都女子大学、筑波大学名誉教授：はしがき、第Ⅰ章－1、第Ⅲ章、第Ⅴ章）

山口　満（筑波大学名誉教授、びわこ成蹊スポーツ大学名誉教授：はしがき、第Ⅵ章、第Ⅶ章－5, 11、第Ⅷ章）
高倉　翔（日本高等教育評価機構、筑波大学名誉教授：第1章－1, 2）
上田　学（京都女子大学：第Ⅰ章－2、第Ⅱ章－1, 2）
渋谷英章（東京学芸大学：第Ⅱ章－1, 2, 4）
中田英雄（筑波大学：第Ⅱ章－3）
米田宏樹（筑波大学：第Ⅱ章－3）
野口晃菜（筑波大学大学院生：第Ⅱ章－3）
堀井啓幸（山梨県立大学：第Ⅲ章）
秋川陽一（倉敷市立短期大学：第Ⅲ章、第Ⅳ章－1, 3）
猿田真嗣（常葉学園大学：第Ⅳ章－1, 2, 3, 4）
浮田真弓（静岡大学：第Ⅶ章－1）
江口勇治（筑波大学：第Ⅶ章－2）
磯田正美（筑波大学：第Ⅶ章－3）
畑中敏伸（東邦大学：第Ⅶ章－4）
長洲南海男（常葉学園大学、筑波大学名誉教授：第Ⅶ章－4）
桂　直美（東洋大学：第Ⅶ章－6 音楽）
山野てるひ（京都女子大学短期大学部：第Ⅶ章－6 美術）
服部鋼資（東京福祉大学短期大学部：第Ⅶ章－6 美術）
四方康子（聖母短期大学：第Ⅶ章－6 書道）
木村範子（筑波大学：第Ⅶ章－7）
松本格之祐（桐蔭横浜大学：第Ⅶ章－8）
堤　正史（大阪成蹊大学：第Ⅶ章－9）

Contributors

Yokuo Murata (Kyoto Women's University, Prof. Emeritus, University of Tsukuba: Preface, I -1, III, V)

Mitsuru Yamaguchi (Prof. Emeritus, University of Tsukuba, Prof. Emeritus, Biwako Seikei Sports College: Preface, VI , VII - 5, 11, VIII)

Sho Takakura (Japan Institution for Higher Education Evaluation, Prof. Emeritus, University of Tsukuba: I - 1, 2)

Manabu Ueda (Kyoto Women's University : I - 2, II - 1, 2)

Hideaki Shibuya (Tokyo Gakugei University: II - 1, 2, 4)

Hideo Nakata (University of Tsukuba: II - 3)

Hiroki Yoneda (University of Tsukuba: II - 3)

Akina Noguchi (Graduate Student, University of Tsukuba: II - 3)

Hiroyuki Horii (Yamanashi Prefecture University: III)

Yoichi Akikawa (Kurashiki College: III , IV - 1, 3)

Shinji Saruta (Tokoha Gakuen University: IV -1, 2, 3, 4)

Mayumi Ukita (Shizuoka University: VII - 1)

Yuji Eguchi (University of Tsukuba: VII - 2)

Masami Isoda (University of Tsukuba: VII - 3)

Toshinobu Hatanaka (Toho University: VII - 4)

Namio Nagasu (Tokoha Gakuen Universitiy, Prof. Emeritus, University of Tsukuba: VII - 4)

Naomi Katsura (Toyo University: VII - 6, Music)

Teruhi Yamano (Junior College, Kyoto Women's University: VII - 6, Fine Arts)

Kosuke Hattori (Junior College, Tokyo University of Social Welfare: Fine Arts)

Yasuko Shikata (Seibo Junior College: VII - 6, Calligraphy)

Noriko Kimura (University of Tsukuba: VII - 7)

Kakunosuke Matsumoto (Toin Yokohama University: VII - 8)

Masashi Tsutsumi (Osaka Seikei University: VII - 9)

奥村真司（湘南短期大学：第Ⅶ章－10）
柴沼　真（大阪成蹊大学：第Ⅶ章－11）
林　尚示（東京学芸大学：第Ⅶ章－12, 15）
安井一郎（獨協大学：第Ⅶ章－13）
宮本友弘（聖徳大学：第Ⅶ章－14）

Shinji Okumura (Shonan College: Ⅶ - 10)
Makoto Shibanuma (Osaka Seikei University: Ⅶ - 11)
Masami Hayashi (Tokyo Gakugei University: Ⅶ - 12, 15)
Ichiro Yasui (Dokkyo Universiy: Ⅶ - 13)
Tomohiro Miyamoto (Seitoku University: Ⅶ - 14)

第Ⅰ章

日本の教育の背景・展望と基本原則

The Background / Perspective and Basic Principles in Japanese Education

中学校の入学式　Entrance Ceremony of Lower Secondary School

1. 日本の教育の背景・展望

■日本の教育を規定してきた大きな要因として、自然的・文化的・社会的背景、及び特に明治維新によって近代国家が成立して以来の歴史的な背景が考えられるであろう。
■日本は極東アジアに位置しており、本州・北海道・九州・四国の四つの主な島と、小さな多くの島々から成る南北に長い列島である。地理的には温帯に属し、春夏秋冬の四季の区別が比較的はっきりしている。伝統的には農耕民族で一毛作の稲作に依存し、「結い」と呼ばれる地縁的な共同作業の形態や、米を中心とする独特の食文化を形成してきた。

■人種的には日本民族が大多数を占め、単一民族国家に近く、諸外国に多い複合民族国家ときわだった対照を示している。言語的には、日本語が国語として定着しており、学校などすべての教育機関の教授用語となっている。宗教的には仏教徒が多いが、一般的に宗教に対する固執性が強くはないため、宗教や宗派の違いによる争いは、ほとんどみられない。以上のような自然的・文化的背景が、日本人の民族意識や行動様式などに影響を及ぼしてきた。

■近代の教育発展では、明治時代以降、3つの主要な教育改革が行われている。明治時代初期における第1の教育改革では、政府は江戸時代の教育遺産（藩校、寺子屋、私塾など）の上に立って、1872年（明治5年）の学制や1879年（明治12年）の教育令などの公布により、統一的な国民教育制度の確立を図りつつ近代学校の普及に努めた。1892年（明治31年）に小学生の就学率は69%に達し、1908年（明治41年）に義務教育は4年から6年に延長し実施された。

1. The Background and Perspective of Education in Japan

■ Possible main factors forming education in Japan are natural, cultural and social backgrounds, and especially historical since the modern regime was established by the Meiji Restoration.

■ Japan is a crescent - shaped island country lying from north to south in Far East Asia. It consists of four main islands (Honshu, Hokkaido, Kyushu, Shikoku) and many smaller islands. Japan has a temperate climate, and has four seasons. Traditionally, agriculture has been the main industry of Japanese people, so they have relied on a rice crop, and have created their typical cooperative working system in a community called "yui" and food culture characterized by rice.

■ Most of the Japanese are Asian Mongoloid race. Ethnically, Japan is almost a mono-racial country, and forms a remarkable contrast with other multi-racial countries. Linguistically, the Japanese language is used as a national language, and is used in all educational institutions including schools. Religiously, many Japanese are Buddhists. As Japanese are quite tolerant of religion generally, they have almost no conflict caused by the difference of religion or sect. The above-mentioned natural/cultural backgrounds have affected national consciousness or behavior patterns of Japanese people.

■ In the process of modern educational development, three main educational reforms have been conducted. In the first educational reform done in the beginning of Meiji Period the government stressed the dissemination of modern schools while trying to establish a uniform national education system by means of promulgations of the Educational Ordinance (Gakusei) in 1872 and the Education Order in 1879. It took advantage of the educational legacy of the Edo period, evidenced by the hanko (schools of the feudal domains), terakoya (small private schools), and shijuku (private tutoring schools). The primary school enrollment ratio reached 69% in 1892, and the term of compulsory education was extended from

■第2次世界大戦後における第2の教育改革により、学校制度は6-3-3制、義務教育は9年制となった。2008年度において9年間の義務教育は6歳から15歳までの年齢層の100％、それに続く高等学校進学者も97.8％とほぼ100％に近い。大学や短期大学への進学者も52.9％に達している。

■第2次世界大戦後、急速に男女平等が実現されており、教育の領域でみるかぎり男女不平等は完全に一掃されている。しかし、職業選択の面などで、男女の実質的な平等の実現が今後の課題とされている。

■1960年代以降、高度経済成長と科学技術革新のテンポが早く、その結果、産業構造に急速な変化がみられる。2005年の国勢調査結果により日本の産業構造を就業者数からみると、第1次産業は4.8％、第2次産業は26.1％、第3次は69.1％を占めている。このような状況が、特に高等学校教育及び大学教育に影響を及ぼしている。

■明治維新による近代国家の成立以後の歴史的な推移をみると、後発国として近代化の道を歩んだ日本は、長い間、教育を含めて欧米先進諸国への「追いつき追い越せ」政策を採用してきた。その結果、中央集権的教育行政と画一的な教育内容・方法がとられてきた。このような状況は、第2次世界大戦後の学校制度及び教育行政制度の改革を経ても、かなりの程度継続してきたのである。

■日本の伝統的な教育方法として、児童生徒が集団を形成して各種の教育活動や学校行事を行ってきた。それにより、集団への帰属意識や協調性、礼儀、集団規律なども培われた。特に、会合、授業、学校行事等における時間厳守

four years to six years in 1908.

■ As part of the post-WW II educational reform which was the second one, the school system became 6- 3- 3 and the term of compulsory education was extended to nine years to cover children aged 6–15. As of 2008, the enrollment ratio for the term of compulsory education was 100% . Further, of those graduating from lower secondary schools, 97.8% continued on to upper secondary schools, while 52.9% of the upper secondary school graduates continued on to university or junior college.

■ After WW II, equality between the sexes has been realized rapidly, and at least in the field of education, inequality between the sexes was completely eliminated. Yet, in other fields, problems still remained; for example, substantial equality in employment.

■ Since the 1960s, as a result of the rapid economic and technological development, the Japanese industrial structure has changed drastically. The Japanese industrial structure can be understood from the number and status of workers in the national census of 2005. The ratio of workers in the primary, secondary, and tertiary industries was 4.8% , 26.1% , and 69.1% , respectively. This condition, in particular, affects the education of upper secondary schools and the universities.

■ By examining Japanese historical movement after the establishment of the modern regime after the Meiji Restoration, it is clear that Japan, which pursed modernization as a follower did adopt the "catch-up policy" in every field including education for a long time to overtake European countries or the U.S.. Consequently, the centralized educational policies, homogeneous education and standardized educational method have been adopted. Such situation continued for a long time even after the reform of the school system and political system of education after WW II.

■ In the Japanese education system, traditionally, students form groups to carry out various educational activities and to take part in school events. Consequently, group consciousness, cooperativeness, manners, and discipline have been

が強調されてきた。
　新教育基本法も強調しているように、国民が上述のような伝統文化の長所を保持しつつ21世紀の社会に適応するとともに国家社会の発展に寄与することが望まれる。

■「追いつき追い越せ」政策に終止符を打ち、21世紀をめざした第3の教育改革を実現するために、1984年に内閣総理大臣の諮問機関として「臨時教育審議会」が設置され、1987年に最終答申が出された。答申は、集権よりも分権を、画一よりも多様性を、硬直よりも柔軟をモットーに、(1)「個性重視の原則」、(2)「生涯学習体系への移行」、(3)「変化への対応(国際化対応、情報化対応、高齢化対応など)」の3つを改革の基本的な視点としている。その後、この答申に示された改革の方向に沿って、具体的な第3の改革が進められてきている。

■これからの日本社会は、臨時教育審議会や中央教育審議会の答申でも指摘されているように、国際化・グローバル化社会、情報化社会、少子高齢化社会、知識基盤社会になるであろう。そのような社会に適応し能力を発揮できる人材を育成することが21世紀教育の主要課題である。

■異文化の人々が交流し合う国際化・グローバル化社会では、異文化を理解し多文化の人々と共存・共生していく生き方を学ぶ必要がある。それは英語教育の振興にとどまらない。また、従来、日本は欧米諸国の国家社会制度をモデル視してそれら諸国の知識技能を受容する受信型国家を目指してきた。今後の社会においては、日本の伝統文化、発展経験の中から特質・長所を学んでそれらを世界に発信していくことも重要である。国民は発信型国家の成員として活躍できる能力を身につけなければならない。

cultivated among the students. Particularly, punctuality in meetings, classes, and school events has been emphasized.

As highlighted in the new Basic Act on Education, while maintaining the virtues of the above-mentioned traditional culture, there is a need for the Japanese public to adapt to the 21st century society and to contribute to the development of the nation and the society.

■ To put an end to the "catch-up policy" and to realize the third reform of education toward the 21st century, the 'National Task Force for Educational Reform' was established in 1984 as a consultative body for the Prime Minister. In 1987, the final report was submitted. In it, under the mottoes of "decentralization rather than centralization", "variety rather than uniformity" and "flexibility rather than rigidity", three fundamental points of reform, i. e. (1) the principle of putting emphasis on individuality, (2) shifting to a lifelong learning system, (3) coping with various changes (internationalization, information society, etc.) are suggested. In line with the direction indicated in this report, the basis of third reform is on going.

■ As pointed out in the reports of the National Task Force for Educational Reform and the Central Council for Education, Japan will soon become an internationalized, globalized, information-oriented society, and a knowledge-based society with a low birthrate and an aging population. A prime issue facing education in the 21st century is the fostering of human resources that can adapt to such a society and capitalize on their skills.

■ In an internationalized and globalized society where people with different cultural backgrounds interact with each other, it is essential to understand different cultures and learn how to coexist in a multicultural environment. Further, this goes beyond the promotion of English education. Traditionally, Japan has seen the national social system of Western countries as a model, and has aimed to be a receiver country that receives knowledge and skills from the West. It is vital for Japan to find characteristics and virtues from its traditional culture and development experience, and to exhibit the wealth to the world. The

■情報化社会では、情報処理能力を養い、多様な情報の中から適切なものを選ぶ能力が要請される。学校では、情報環境を整備し、情報リテラシーを高める教育の充実が図られなければならない。

■少子高齢化社会においては、生涯にわたって学び続ける力の育成が重要であり、生涯学習の確立が課題となっている。その際、学校教育の発展は生涯にわたる学習の基盤を形成する。特に義務教育段階において質の高い教育を提供し、子ども一人ひとりの個性や能力を伸ばし生涯にわたって力強く生きていく基礎を培う必要がある。それとともに、学校外教育、社会教育の発展、学社融合の工夫も見逃せない。具体的には、保護者や地域住民の学習活動、教育機関運営への参加を保障しつつ、幼児教育機関、社会教育機関、高齢者向き大学等の拡充が求められよう。

■工業社会から変化するとされる知識基盤社会では、中央教育審議会の「新しい時代の義務教育を創造する（答申）」（2005年10月）や学習指導要領の改訂（2008年3月）においても重視されたように、基礎的知識・技能を中心に確かな学力を身につけることが優先課題である。また、同社会においては、各種の競争と技術革新により知識は絶えず日進月歩するので、幅広い知識とともに柔軟な思考力、判断力も求められる。さらに、国際競争が加速する中で、各国・各地域間の教育・文化・経済など多方面にわたる協力、ならびに開発途上国の自立を促す協力援助も必要とされる。それらのことを実現していくためには、人々の各種の創意工夫や協調的態度が要求されるであろう。初等・中等教育では、学校が主体性と創意工夫によって教育の質を向上し、児童生徒一人ひとりが自立した個人として変化の激しい社会をたくましく生き抜き、創造性、協調性を発揮しながら社会に寄与する能力を育成することが不可欠

Japanese people must obtain an ability to be active members of a transmitting country.

■ In the information-oriented society, it is essential to be able to choose adequate information from among the diversified information available by developing information-handling abilities. In schools, information literacy must be enhanced by improving the informational environment.

■ In an aging society with fewer children, it is important to foster an ability to continue learning throughout life and establishment of a lifelong learning system is a task to be tackled. Development of school education forms the base of lifelong learning. As such, education received at school must be of a high quality, particularly during the compulsory education period, to develop each child's individuality and abilities, and build a foundation so that the child is able to live its life with strength and dignity. At the same time, the development of out-of-school education and social education, and school-social integration are no less important. Specifically, while ensuring the participation of guardians and local citizens in educational activities and daily operations of educational institutions, expanding the institutions of pre-school and social education, and the universities for the elderly are required.

■ In a knowledge-based society that is said to be derived from an industrial society, fostering solid academic capabilities, mainly basic abilities and skills, is a priority issue. This is emphasized in the report "Creating compulsory education in the new era" issued by the Central Council for Education in October 2005 and the Course of Study revised in March 2008. In addition, not only flexible thought and judgment but also broad knowledge are required in a knowledge-based society as knowledge would constantly advance, owing to the continuing competition and technical innovation. Moreover, in the midst of accelerating global competition, cooperation among countries and among communities in wide ranging areas including education, culture, and economy is needed. Cooperation and assistance to promote the self-sustainability of developing countries are also required. To accomplish these tasks, people have to be inventive and cooperative.

である。高等教育においても、世界的な水準の教育研究を行う機関を設立し発展させることが期待される。

昼休み、楽しい学校生活　Enjoyable School Life

In primary and secondary education, it is vital that schools take initiative and use their creative ingenuity to improve the quality of education so that their students can have capabilities to survive in a rapidly changing society as independent individuals, and to contribute to society while being creative and cooperative. Further, in higher education, institutions providing world-class education and conducting world-class research need to be established and developed.

楽しい運動会　Fun Sports Day

2. 教育の基本原則

■第2次世界大戦前の教育が、教育令という天皇の命令によって規定され、中央集権主義に従い文部省や内務省が学校を管理していた。学校制度は複線型が採用され、小学校（6ヶ年）修了後は、大学まで進めるコースと進めないコースに分かれていた。女子の生徒・学生に対する教育機会も制限されていた。学校では国家主義を原則として、皇国民の育成が目標になっていた。

■第2次世界大戦後は、アメリカ合衆国の影響を受け教育制度の民主化を基本原則として大きな改革が行われた。国の教育事項は、国会で議決された法律によって規定されることになった。都道府県や市町村に教育委員会が設置され、地方分権主義にそって直接学校を管理することになった。学校制度は単線型となり、能力と適性にしたがって上級レベルの学校へ進学できることになった。その結果、多くの女子学生も高等教育を受けることができるようになった。

■日本国憲法は、国家の教育に関する基本原則、政策を規定した。第26条には「すべて国民は、法律の定めるところにより、その能力に応じてひとしく教育を受ける権利を有する。すべて国民は法律の定めるところにより、その保護する子女に普通教育を受けさせる義務を負う。義務教育は、これを無償とする。」と規定され、第23条では、「学問の自由は、これを保障する。」と規定された。

■1947年に制定された教育基本法は、憲法の精神に則り、教育の目的と原則をより細かく規定した。その内容には、教育の機会均等、義務教育、男女共学、公教育、社会教育、政治教育、宗教教育、教育行政に対する不当な支配の禁止などの原則がうたわれた。

2. The Basic Principles of Education

■ The prewar education was prescribed by the Emperor's order which was called "Education Order". The Ministry of Education, or the Ministry of the Interior managed schools based on the principle of centralization. The school was organized under a multi-track system. After common elementary school (6 years), it was divided into two courses; one led to university education and the other did not. The opportunity of education for female students was limited. The schools aimed to train the people to have obedience to the Emperor, influenced by the strong nationalism.

■ In postwar days, the great reform was made as the basic principle to democratization of the education system influenced from the U.S.A.. The law which is approved by the Diet prescribes the educational affairs in Japan. The board of education was established in the metropolis, prefectures and municipalities. The school was managed directly through decentralization of power. The education system then became a one track type. The students were able to enter higher education school according to their ability and aptitude. As a result, many female students were able to go on to higher education.

■ The Japanese Constitution prescribed the basic principles and policies of education. Article 26 provides that: "(1) All people shall have the right to receive an equal education correspondent to their abilities, as provided for by law. (2) All people shall be obliged to have all boys and girls under their protection receive ordinary education as provided for by law. Such compulsory education shall be free". Article 23 states that "Academic freedom is guaranteed".

■ The Fundamental Law of Education which was prescribed in 1947 provided educational purposes and principles more explicitly according to the spirit of constitution. The contents are the following principles; equality of educational opportunity, compulsory education, coeducation, public education, social

■教育基本法が制定されて以来、何回となく改革論議が展開されてきたが、2006年12月に改正された。今回の教育基本法の改正は、2000年（平成12年）に首相の私的諮問機関として設置された「教育改革国民会議」において「新しい時代にふさわしい教育基本法を」という一項が盛り込まれたことがその端緒であった。

このような流れのなかで、文部科学大臣は2001年（平成13年）11月に中央教育審議会にたいし「教育振興基本計画の策定と新しい時代にふさわしい教育基本法の在り方について」諮問した。その後2003年（平成15年）3月に答申を出した。これを受けて2006年に政府案が国会に上程され、同年12月の国会で改正が決定されるにいたった。

■改正された教育基本法の特色として、①信頼される学校教育の確立、②「知」の世紀をリードする大学改革の推進、③家庭の教育力の回復、学校・家庭・地域社会の連携・協力の推進、④公共の精神に基づき主体的に社会の形成に参画する意識や態度の涵養、⑤日本の伝統・文化の尊重、郷土や国を愛する心と国際社会の一員としての意識の涵養、⑥生涯学習社会の実現、⑦教育振興基本計画の策定などがあげられる。

education, political education, religious education and prohibition of the improper control over educational administration. The last part of this section states in full the Fundamental Law of Education.

■ After the enactment of the former Fundamental Law of Education, a lot of trials to revise it had been taking place and it was revised in December of 2006. The movement of replacing it with the completely new one started just after the proposal of National Conference for Educational Reform and was organized as the advisory committee under the Prime Minister in 2000 proposing the new Fundamental Law of Education fit for the new era. Accordingly the Minister of Education, Culture, Sports, Science and Technology consulted the Central Council for Education as to the promotion of the basic program for encouraging education and the legislation of new Fundamental Law of Education. The Central Government decided to present the bill to the National Diet in 2006 and it was approved as the Basic Act on Education in December of that year.

■ The purpose of this revision is said to realize the following; ① to establish reliable education in school, ② to promote the reform of higher education which leads the intelligent society, ③ to encourage the sound environment around the children's development at home and to cooperate the close relation between school, family and local community, ④ to develop the willing attitude for participating in various activities of society based on the public spirit, ⑤ to bring the natural feeling to respect Japanese tradition and culture and to be conscious as a member of the international community, ⑥ the lifelong education as a whole, and finally, ⑦ to promote the basic program for encouraging education.

(参考) 新教育基本法
　　　　 2006 年改正　法律第 120 号

　我々日本国民は、たゆまぬ努力によって築いてきた民主的で文化的な国家を更に発展させるとともに、世界の平和と人類の福祉の向上に貢献することを願うものである。

　我々は、この理想を実現するため、個人の尊厳を重んじ、真理と正義を希求し、公共の精神を尊び、豊かな人間性と創造性を備えた人間の育成を期するとともに、伝統を継承し、新しい文化の創造を目指す教育を推進する。

　ここに、我々は、日本国憲法の精神にのっとり、我が国の未来を切り拓く教育の基本を確立し、その振興を図るため、この法律を制定する。

第1章　　教育の目的及び理念

　第1条（教育の目的）教育は、人格の完成を目指し、平和で民主的な国家及び社会の形成者として必要な資質を備えた心身ともに健康な国民の育成を期して行われなければならない。

　第2条（教育の目標）教育は、その目的を実現するため、学問の自由を尊重しつつ、次に掲げる目標を達成するよう行われるものとする。

　一　幅広い知識と教養を身に付け、真理を求める態度を養い、豊かな情操と道徳心を培うとともに、健やかな身体を養うこと。

　二　個人の価値を尊重して、その能力を伸ばし、創造性を培い、自主及び自律の精神を養うとともに、職業及び生活との関連を重視し、勤労を重んずる態度を養うこと。

　三　正義と責任、男女の平等、自他の敬愛と協力を重んずるとともに、公共の精神に基づき、主体的に社会の形成に参画し、その発展に寄与する態度

Basic Act on Education

Revised in 2006 (Act 120)

We, the citizens of Japan, desire to further develop the democratic and cultural state we have built through our untiring efforts, and contribute to the peace of the world and the improvement of the welfare of humanity.

To realize these ideals, we shall esteem individual dignity, and endeavor to bring up people who long for truth and justice, honor the public spirit, and are rich in humanity and creativity, while promoting an education which transmits tradition and aims at the creation of a new culture.

We hereby enact this Act, in accordance with the spirit of the Constitution of Japan, in order to establish the foundations of education and promote an education that opens the way to our country's future.

Chapter . Aims and Principles of Education

(Aims of Education)

Article 1

Education shall aim for the full development of personality and strive to nurture the citizens, sound in mind and body, who are imbued with the qualities necessary for those who form a peaceful and democratic state and society.

(Objectives of Education)

Article 2

To realize the aforementioned aims, education shall be carried out in such a way as to achieve the following objectives, while respecting academic freedom:

(1) to foster an attitude to acquire wide-ranging knowledge and culture, and to seek the truth, cultivate a rich sensibility and sense of morality, while developing a healthy body.

(2) to develop the abilities of individuals while respecting their value; cultivate their creativity; foster a spirit of autonomy and independence; and foster an attitude to value labor while emphasizing the connections with career and

を養うこと。
　四　生命を尊び、自然を大切にし、環境の保全に寄与する態度を養うこと。
　五　伝統と文化を尊重し、それらをはぐくんできた我が国と郷土を愛するとともに、他国を尊重し、国際社会の平和と発展に寄与する態度を養うこと。

　第3条（生涯学習の理念）国民一人一人が、自己の人格を磨き、豊かな人生を送ることができるよう、その生涯にわたって、あらゆる機会に、あらゆる場所において学習することができ、その成果を適切に生かすことのできる社会の実現が図られなければならない。

　第4条（教育の機会均等）すべて国民は、ひとしく、その能力に応じた教育を受ける機会を与えられなければならず、人種、信条、性別、社会的身分、経済的地位又は門地によって、教育上差別されない。

　2　国及び地方公共団体は、障害のある者が、その障害の状態に応じ、十分な教育を受けられるよう、教育上必要な支援を講じなければならない。

　3　国及び地方公共団体は、能力があるにもかかわらず、経済的理由によって修学が困難な者に対して、奨学の措置を講じなければならない。

practical life.

(3) to foster an attitude to value justice, responsibility, equality between men and women, mutual respect and cooperation, and actively contribute, in the public spirit, to the building and development of society.

(4) to foster an attitude to respect life, care for nature, and contribute to the protection of the environment.

(5) to foster an attitude to respect our traditions and culture, love the country and region that nurtured them, together with respect for other countries and a desire to contribute to world peace and the development of the international community.

(Concept of Lifelong Learning)
Article 3
Society shall be made to allow all citizens to continue to learn throughout their lives, on all occasions and in all places, and apply the outcomes of lifelong learning appropriately to refine themselves and lead a fulfilling life.

(Equal Opportunity in Education)
Article 4
Citizens shall all be given equal opportunities to receive education according to their abilities, and shall not be subject to discrimination in education on account of race, creed, sex, social status, economic position, or family origin.

(2) The national and local governments shall provide support in education to persons with disabilities, to ensure that they are given adequate education in accordance with their condition.

(3) The national and local governments shall take measures to provide financial assistance to those who, in spite of their ability, encounter difficulties in receiving education for economic reasons.

第2章　教育の実施に関する基本

第5条（義務教育）国民は、その保護する子に、別に法律で定めるところにより、普通教育を受けさせる義務を負う。

2　義務教育として行われる普通教育は、各個人の有する能力を伸ばしつつ社会において自立的に生きる基礎を培い、また、国家及び社会の形成者として必要とされる基本的な資質を養うことを目的として行われるものとする。

3　国及び地方公共団体は、義務教育の機会を保障し、その水準を確保するため、適切な役割分担及び相互の協力の下、その実施に責任を負う。

4　国又は地方公共団体の設置する学校における義務教育については、授業料を徴収しない。

第6条（学校教育）法律に定める学校は、公の性質を有するものであって、国、地方公共団体及び法律に定める法人のみが、これを設置することができる。

2　前項の学校においては、教育の目標が達成されるよう、教育を受ける者の心身の発達に応じて、体系的な教育が組織的に行われなければならない。この場合において、教育を受ける者が、学校生活を営む上で必要な規律を重んずるとともに、自ら進んで学習に取り組む意欲を高めることを重視して行われなければならない。

Chapter . Basics of Education Provision

(Compulsory Education)
Article 5
Citizens shall be obligated to have children under their protection receive a general education pursuant to the provisions of other acts.
(2) The objectives of general education, given in the form of compulsory education, shall be to cultivate the foundations for an independent life within society while developing the abilities of each individual, and to foster the basic qualities necessary for those who form our state and society.
(3) In order to guarantee the opportunity for compulsory education and ensure adequate standards, the national and local governments shall assume responsibility for the implementation of compulsory education through appropriate role sharing and mutual cooperation.
(4) No tuition fee shall be charged for compulsory education in schools established by the national and local governments.

(School Education)
Article 6
The schools prescribed by law shall be of a public nature, and only the national government, local governments, and juridical persons prescribed by law shall be entitled to establish them.
(2) The schools set forth in the preceding paragraph shall, in order to fulfill the objectives of education, provide a structured education in an organized way suited to the mental and physical development of the recipients. It shall be carried out in a way that emphasizes instilling the recipients with respect for the discipline necessary to conduct school life, and strengthening their own motivation to learn.

第7条（大学）大学は、学術の中心として、高い教養と専門的能力を培うとともに、深く真理を探究して新たな知見を創造し、これらの成果を広く社会に提供することにより、社会の発展に寄与するものとする。

2　大学については、自主性、自律性その他の大学における教育及び研究の特性が尊重されなければならない。

　第8条（私立学校）私立学校の有する公の性質及び学校教育において果たす重要な役割にかんがみ、国及び地方公共団体は、その自主性を尊重しつつ、助成その他の適当な方法によって私立学校教育の振興に努めなければならない。

　第9条（教員）法律に定める学校の教員は、自己の崇高な使命を深く自覚し、絶えず研究と修養に励み、その職責の遂行に努めなければならない。

2　前項の教員については、その使命と職責の重要性にかんがみ、その身分は尊重され、待遇の適正が期せられるとともに、養成と研修の充実が図られなければならない。

　第10条（家庭教育）父母その他の保護者は、子の教育について第一義的責任を有するものであって、生活のために必要な習慣を身に付けさせるとともに、自立心を育成し、心身の調和のとれた発達を図るよう努めるものとする。

(Universities)
Article 7
Universities, as the core of scholarship activities, shall cultivate advanced knowledge and specialized skills, inquire deeply into the truth and create new knowledge, while contributing to the development of society by broadly disseminating the results of their activities.
(2) University autonomy, independence, and other unique characteristics of university education and research shall be respected.

(Private Schools)
Article 8
Taking into account the public nature of privately established schools and their important role in school education, the national and local governments shall endeavor to promote private school education through subsidies and other appropriate means, while respecting school autonomy.

(Teachers)
Article 9
Teachers of the schools prescribed by law shall endeavor to fulfill their duties, while being deeply conscious of their noble mission and continuously devoting themselves to research and self-cultivation.
(2) Considering the importance of the mission and duties of the teachers set forth in the preceding paragraph, the status of teachers shall be respected, their fair and appropriate treatment ensured, and measures shall be taken to improve their education and training.

(Education in the Family)
Article 10
Mothers, fathers, and other guardians, having the primary responsibility for their children's education, shall endeavor to teach them the habits necessary for life,

2　国及び地方公共団体は、家庭教育の自主性を尊重しつつ、保護者に対する学習の機会及び情報の提供その他の家庭教育を支援するために必要な施策を講ずるよう努めなければならない。

第11条（幼児期の教育）幼児期の教育は、生涯にわたる人格形成の基礎を培う重要なものであることにかんがみ、国及び地方公共団体は、幼児の健やかな成長に資する良好な環境の整備その他適当な方法によって、その振興に努めなければならない。

第12条（社会教育）個人の要望や社会の要請にこたえ、社会において行われる教育は、国及び地方公共団体によって奨励されなければならない。

2　国及び地方公共団体は、図書館、博物館、公民館その他の社会教育施設の設置、学校の施設の利用、学習の機会及び情報の提供その他の適当な方法によって社会教育の振興に努めなければならない。

第13条（学校、家庭及び地域住民等の相互の連携協力）学校、家庭及び地域住民その他の関係者は、教育におけるそれぞれの役割と責任を自覚するとともに、相互の連携及び協力に努めるものとする。

encourage a spirit of independence, and nurture the balanced development of their bodies and minds.

(2) The national and local governments shall endeavor to take necessary measures supporting education in the family, by providing guardians with opportunities to learn, relevant information, and other means, while respecting family autonomy in education.

(Early Childhood Education)
Article 11
Considering the importance of early childhood education as a basis for the lifelong formation of one's personality, the national and local governments shall endeavor to promote such education by providing an environment favorable to the healthy growth of young children, and other appropriate measures.

(Social Education)
Article 12
The national and local governments shall encourage education carried out among society, in response to the demands of individuals and the community as a whole.
(2) The national and local governments shall endeavor to promote social education by establishing libraries, museums, community halls and other social education facilities, opening the usage of school facilities, providing opportunities to learn, relevant information, and other appropriate means.

(Partnership and Cooperation among Schools, Families, and Local Residents)
Article 13
Schools, families, local residents, and other relevant persons shall be aware of their respective roles and responsibilities regarding education, and endeavor to develop partnership and cooperation.

第14条（政治教育）良識ある公民として必要な政治的教養は、教育上尊重されなければならない。

2　法律に定める学校は、特定の政党を支持し、又はこれに反対するための政治教育その他政治的活動をしてはならない。

第15条（宗教教育）宗教に関する寛容の態度、宗教に関する一般的な教養及び宗教の社会生活における地位は、教育上尊重されなければならない。

2　国及び地方公共団体が設置する学校は、特定の宗教のための宗教教育その他宗教的活動をしてはならない。

第3章　　教育行政

第16条（教育行政）教育は、不当な支配に服することなく、この法律及び他の法律の定めるところにより行われるべきものであり、教育行政は、国と地方公共団体との適切な役割分担及び相互の協力の下、公正かつ適正に行われなければならない。

2　国は、全国的な教育の機会均等と教育水準の維持向上を図るため、教育に関する施策を総合的に策定し、実施しなければならない。

3　地方公共団体は、その地域における教育の振興を図るため、その実情に応じた教育に関する施策を策定し、実施しなければならない。

4　国及び地方公共団体は、教育が円滑かつ継続的に実施されるよう、必要な財政上の措置を講じなければならない。

(Political Education)
Article 14
The political literacy necessary for sensible citizenship shall be valued in education.
(2) The schools prescribed by law shall refrain from political education or other political activities for or against any specific political party.

(Religious Education)
Article 15
The attitude of religious tolerance, general knowledge regarding religion, and the position of religion in social life shall be valued in education.
(2) The schools established by the national and local governments shall refrain from religious education or other activities for a specific religion.

Chapter . Education Administration

(Education Administration)
Article 16
Education shall not be subject to improper control and shall be carried out in accordance with this and other acts; education administration shall be carried out in a fair and proper manner through appropriate role sharing and cooperation between the national and local governments.
(2) The national government shall comprehensively formulate and implement education measures in order to provide for equal opportunities in education and to maintain and raise education standards throughout the country.
(3) The local governments shall formulate and implement education measures corresponding to regional circumstances in order to promote education in their respective regions.
(4) The national and local governments shall take necessary financial measures to ensure the smooth and continuous provision of education.

第17条（教育振興基本計画）政府は、教育の振興に関する施策の総合的かつ計画的な推進を図るため、教育の振興に関する施策についての基本的な方針及び講ずべき施策その他必要な事項について、基本的な計画を定め、これを国会に報告するとともに、公表しなければならない。

2　地方公共団体は、前項の計画を参酌し、その地域の実情に応じ、当該地方公共団体における教育の振興のための施策に関する基本的な計画を定めるよう努めなければならない。

第4章　　法令の制定

第18条　この法律に規定する諸条項を実施するため、必要な法令が制定されなければならない。

(Basic Plan for the Promotion of Education)
Article 17
In order to facilitate the comprehensive and systematic implementation of measures for the promotion of education, the government shall formulate a basic plan covering basic principles, required measures, and other necessary items in relation to the promotion of education. It shall report this plan to the Diet and make it public.
(2) Local governments, referring to the plan set forth in the preceding paragraph, shall endeavor to formulate a basic plan on measures to promote education corresponding to regional circumstances.

Chapter . Enactment of Laws and Regulations

Article 18
Laws and regulations necessary to implement the provisions stipulated in this Act shall be enacted.

幼稚園　Kindergarten

高等学校　Upper Secondary School

第Ⅱ章

教育の概要

The Outline of Educational System

小学校　Primary School

中学校　Lower Secondary School

1. 生涯学習社会と教育改革

■日本の学校教育の普及率は、世界でも有数である。9年間の義務教育機関の就学率はほぼ100％であり、義務教育後の高等学校への進学率も98％に達している。さらに、大学、短期大学に専修学校を加えれば、中等後の教育への進学者は7割近くにまでなっている。いわば、学校化された社会というのが日本の特徴といえよう。しかし、この学校教育の普及によって、どの学校を卒業したかでその人の一生が決定されると考えられる傾向が強まるとともに、子どもたちの生活は学校中心となり、家庭や地域の教育力の低下が叫ばれるようになってきている。その一方で、平均寿命の延伸や少子化などによるライフサイクルの変化や、日常生活や職業生活上の変化によって、学校教育を修了した後にも人々が学習活動に参加する必要性が高まってきている。

■このような状況において、単に学校教育を普及し社会教育の機会を充実するだけではこれらの変化に対応することが不可能であり、人々のライフサイクルやライフスタイルに応じて学校、地域そして家庭における教育機能を有機的に連携させた生涯学習社会の実現にむけた施策が展開されつつある。具体的には学校が子どもの教育の唯一の場であるとするのではなく、家庭での教育や地域社会で組織されるさまざまな教育活動と連携を保ちながら、子どもの教育の一部分を学校が分担するべきであるとされる。また、これからの日本の子どもに対しては学校教育で学習が終了するのではないということを前提に、生涯学習の一時期として、成人した後にも主体的な学習が継続できるような学校教育のあり方が求められている。さらに、成人に対しては、多様な学習要求に応じたきめ細かな学習機会が提供されるとともに、国際化・グローバル化社会、情報化社会、少子高齢化社会、知識基盤社会など、今後の日本の進むべき方向に応じた、人々の意識の啓発や行動変容を目的とする学習の組織化が取り組まれつつある。そして、学校と社会教育さらには福祉、労働、産業、文化などの行政組織や、民間企業、そして市民団体などとの達

1. Lifelong Learning Society and Educational Reform

■ The Japanese school enrollment rate is the highest in the world. The enrollment rate in the nine years of compulsory education is almost 100 % and that of the upper secondary education is over 98 %. More than 70 % of upper secondary school graduates proceed to universities, junior colleges, or special training schools. Because of the high enrollment rate, however, the name of the school and university which one graduated from becomes important in deciding one's future, and the life of a child has become school-centered while family and community play less an important role in providing education to the child. Also, the changes in life-cycle, caused by longer life expectancy and fewer children, as well as the changes in daily and vocational life, make it necessary for those who had completed school education to join learning activities.

■ In this situation, not only educational opportunities in the field of school and social education should become rich, but a new educational policies has been undertaken to realize a lifelong learning society which includes the educational function of schools, communities, and families according to the changes of life-cycle and life-style of the people. Basically, school is no more the sole educational institution, but shares its educational function with local communities and families. Then, as completion of school education takes place, this does not mean the end of education, but education for kids should be provided in school, as a part of lifelong learning, considering that learning in school continues after they become adults. Furthermore, various learning opportunities should be provided for adults based on their different needs, and the educational reforms which try to organize their learning in order to adapt to people's way of thinking and patterns of behavior for the future of Japanese society, which is going to be an internationalized and globalized society, an information society, a low birthrate and aging society, and a knowledge-based society. Various local governments

携のもとに生涯学習を推進する生涯学習推進体制が、地方自治体で整備されてきている。

■時代の進行とともに社会から要請される学習内容に変化が生じ、また学習形態も従来の学校中心から多様な教育機会の提供に移行しつつある。このような中で、中央政府は教育を含む幅広い政策変更を試みてきている。「地方分権」、「規制緩和」、「民営化」などがその具体的な方向である。

are in the process of eatablishing a lifelong learning system with the cooperation among school and social education, administrative agencies of welfare, labor, industry and culture, private industries, and NGOs.

■ Thus, the contents of learning has been changing according to the social climate, and the learning style also has changed to adjust to the diversity of learning motivation of people from that based on school centered learning. In this circumstance, the central government has attempted to improve various policies including that of education. The major key words of them can be summarized as "decentralization", "deregulation", and "privatization".

2. 学校制度

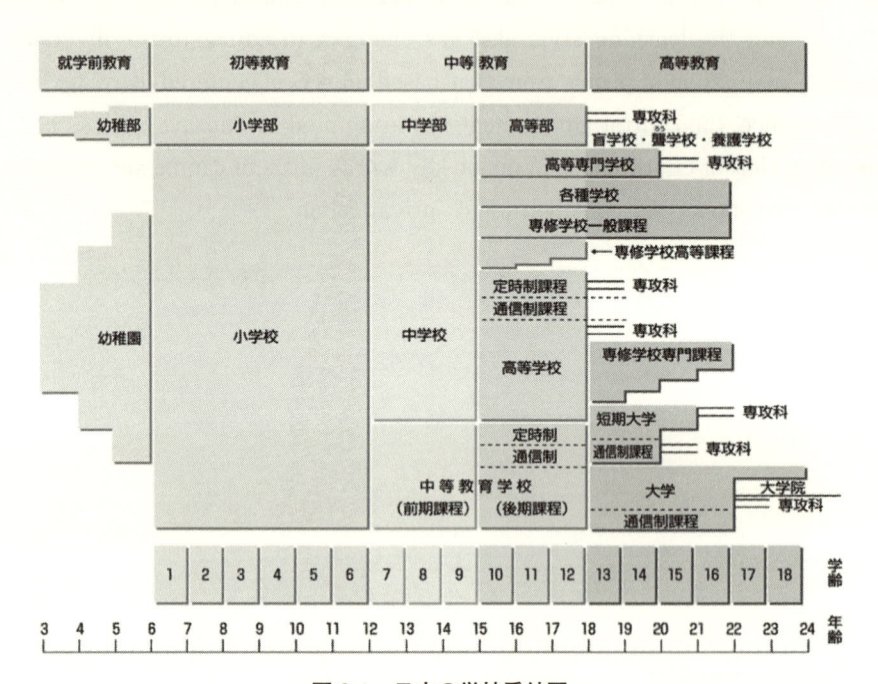

図 2-1　日本の学校系統図
出典：文科省ホームページ、2009 年

（1） 6・3・3・4制

■日本の学校制度は、第2次世界大戦後の教育改革期において制定された教育基本法および学校教育法によって6・3・3・4制が導入され、それを基本的な枠組みとして現行制度が構成されている。近年では1999年から中学校と高等学校を連結した中等教育学校が新しく登場している。現行の学校制度は、図2-1に示される通りである。「学校」という言葉は日本においては

II. The Outline of Educational System   57

2. School System

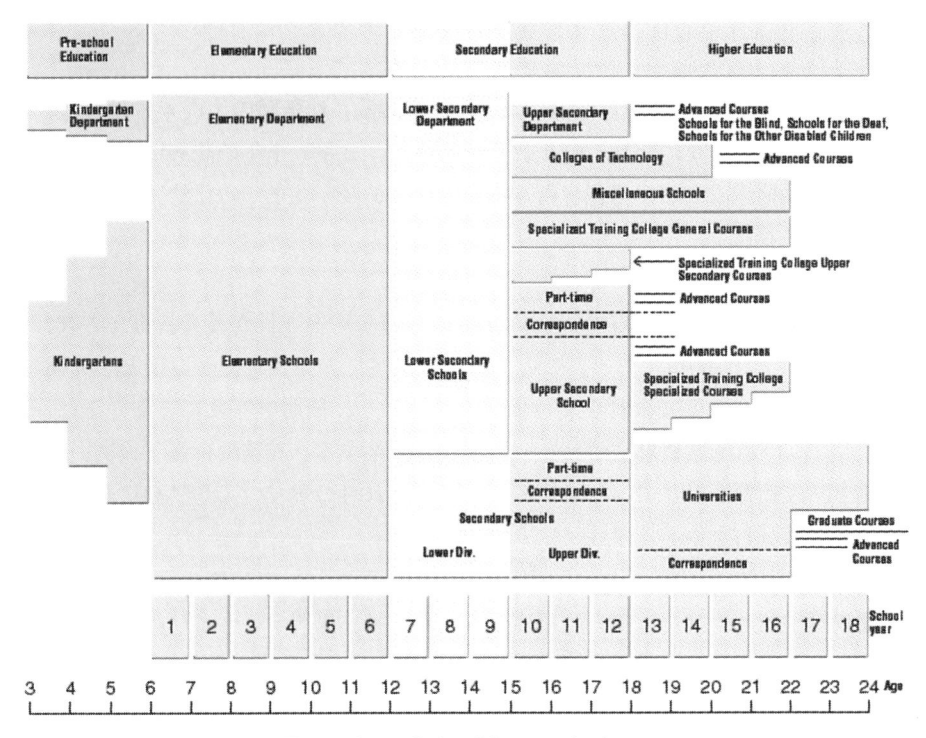

Figure 2-1   School System in Japan
Resource: Home Page of the Ministry of Education, Culture, Sports, Science and Technology, 2009

(1) 6-3-3-4 School System

■ Since the Education Reform after World War II Japan has adopted the 6-3-3-4 school system. The fundamental organization of this school system based on the Fundamental Law of Education and the School Education Law in 1947, has been maintained. The current school system is illustrated in Figure 2-1. Although the term "school" is used extensively in Japan, "the school" prescribed

幅広く用いられているが、厳密には学校教育法第1条に定める幼稚園、小学校、中学校、高等学校、中等教育学校、特別支援学校、大学、高等専門学校が該当する。その他、学校に類似する教育機関として、同法第124条に定める専修学校、134条の各種学校がある。

■就学前教育を行う学校としては幼稚園がある。幼稚園の入園年齢は3歳、4歳、5歳であり、それぞれ6歳までの3年、2年、1年の課程がある。この他に福祉施設としての保育所があり、0歳から6歳までの乳幼児の保育を行っている。

■小学校と中学校に相当する6歳から15歳までの9年間が義務教育とされ、就学率はほぼ100％である。この段階ではすべての児童生徒が原則として同一のカリキュラムで教育を受ける。これに対し、後期中等教育段階からは、カリキュラムや履修形態が異なった学校が併存する。義務教育修了後に引き続き学校教育を受けようとする場合には、これらの学校の入学試験に合格しなければならない。

■高等学校はカリキュラムの相違から、普通科、専門学科および総合学科に分けられている。専門学科は農業、工業、商業、水産、家庭、看護、情報、福祉科などに分類される。また、履修形態は全日制、定時制、通信制に分けられる。全日制の修業年限は3年であり、定時制、通信制の修業年限は3年以上とされている。さらに、学年制をとらない単位制高等学校も開設されている。なお、このような学科や課程の違いにかかわらず、いずれの高等学校を修了してもその卒業資格は同等である。

■この他に、5年制の課程で、後期中等教育と高等教育の一部を合体させた高等専門学校がある。高等専門学校は、基礎的な能力を身につけた中堅の職

in Article 1 of the School Education Law includes kindergarten, primary school, lower secondary school and upper secondary school, secondary school, special needs school, university and technical college, as its basic part of the system. In addition, there are other educational institutions, specialized training colleges (Art. 124) and miscellaneous schools (Art. 134), which are prescribed in Article 1 of the School Education Law.

■ As for pre-school education, there are kindergartens. The entrance age to a kindergarten is 3, 4 or 5 years old. Three, two or one year courses, respectively, are adopted in each of these, all of which end at the age of six. In addition, there are day care centers also considered as welfare institutions and children from zero to six years old are taken care of there.

■ Nine years of compulsory schooling, from 6-year-old to 15-year-old, consist of 6 years of primary school and 3 years of lower secondary school. The school enrollment rate is approximately 100%. At this stage, in principle, all students receive education on the same curriculum. In contrast, from the upper secondary schools, curriculum and types of courses vary. Those who want to receive school education after the compulsory stage have to pass an entrance examination to the upper secondary schools and so on.

■ The upper secondary schools are classified as general courses, specialized vocational courses and comprehensive courses according to the curriculum. The specialized vocational courses consist of agriculture, industry, commerce, fishery, home economics, nursing, information technology, social welfare and so on. The schools are classified as full time, part time and correspondence courses. Full-time courses span for 3 years, and part time and correspondence courses take 3 or more years. Furthermore an upper secondary school credit system without a grade-based framework has been established. Yet, the graduate certificate is the same with other secondary schools despite the wide variety of courses and curricula.

■ There are technical colleges which provide both the upper secondary education and higher education for five years. These technical colleges were

業技術者を養成するために、1962年に設置された。現在は、機械、電子、情報、電気、環境などの工業系学科が主流となっている。なお、高等専門学校の第3学年を修了した者は高等学校卒業と同等の資格を有し、卒業者は短期大学卒業者と同等であるため、一般的には高等教育機関として位置づけられ、四年制大学への編入も可能となっている。

■また、専修学校の高等課程（高等専修学校）や一部の各種学校も後期中等教育段階の教育機関である。専修学校はかつてすべて各種学校とされていたもののうち一定の水準のものに付与される名称で、1976年からこの制度が発足した。これらの学校は職業に関する実務的な教育や生活上の実際的知識を与えることを目的としている。

■なお、文部科学大臣の認定を受けた一部の高等専修学校や各種学校を修了した者にも大学入学資格が与えられている。そのほか、外国の学校で原則として12年の学校教育を修了した者、文部科学大臣認定の在外教育施設修了者、大学入学資格検定試験や国際バカロレア試験合格者などにも、大学入学資格が認められている。

■高等教育機関には、大学、短期大学、前述の高等専門学校、文部科学省以外の省庁の所管のものがある。大学の修業年限は一般学部が4年、医学系学部が6年である。短期大学は、現行の学校制度が発足した当時は暫定的なものであったが、1964年にはその役割の独自性から恒久的な高等教育機関として位置づけられた。短期大学の修業年限は、その専攻によって2年のものと3年のものがある。いずれも、全日制のほか夜間制、通信制のものがある。これ以外に学校教育法に基づかない文部科学省以外の省庁の所管の学校などがあり、一定の水準を満たす大学校の卒業者には大学卒業者と同じ学士の学位が授与される。

introduced in 1962 in order to supply middle-level technicians with basic abilities. They generally provide technical departments, such as mechanical engineering, electronics, information technology, electrical engineering and environmental civil engineering. Students who completed grade 3 are equivalent to the graduates from upper secondary schools, while graduates from technical colleges have the same qualification as graduates from junior colleges. That is the reason why the technical colleges are considered to be higher educational institutions and also the leavers are qualified to be accepted into university courses.

■ Upper secondary courses in specialized training colleges and some miscellaneous schools are also included in upper secondary education. Miscellaneous schools which satisfy certain requirements were sanctioned as special training schools. This system started in 1976. The purpose of these schools is to provide students practical vocational education and useful knowledge for life.

■ Graduates from certain upper secondary courses in special training schools and miscellaneous schools approved by the Ministry of Education, Science and Culture like those who have completed 12 years of school education outside Japan, and those who have passed the Qualifying Certificate Examination or International Baccalaurea are qualified to enter universities in Japan.

■ As for institutions of higher education, there are universities, junior colleges, technical colleges and higher institutes established by Ministries other than the Ministry of Education, Culture, Sports, Science and Technology. The length of courses in universities leading to a bachelor degree is usually four years for general faculties and six years for the faculty of and pharmacy. Although junior colleges were tentatively set up when the present school system was established, they became permanent institutions for higher education in 1964 because of their importance and necessity. The length of courses in junior colleges is two or three years according to their majors. In both, there are evening courses and correspondence courses in addition to full-time courses. Apart from the higher institutes under the control of the Ministry of Education, Culture, Sports, Science

■大学教育よりも高度な学術の教授研究を行う機関として、大学院がある。大学院には修士課程と博士課程があり、修業年限はそれぞれ2年、5年とされている。ただし、博士課程を前期課程2年、後期課程3年に分け、前期課程を修士課程と同等に扱うこともある。修士課程は高度の専門性を要する職業人の養成、博士課程は専門的研究者の養成を主たる目的としている。なお、入学に当たっては学士号を取得していることが基本的要件であるが、優秀な学生に対し大学の第3学年修了で入学できる特例もある。

■特別支援教育に関しては、それぞれの障害の種類に応じた学校が、各教育段階に応じて設置されている。1979年以降は、障害をもつ子どもの受ける教育も義務化された。障害児を対象とする学校の名称は2007年から「特別支援学校」に統合されることになった。

■以上の学校は、その設置者により、国によって設置される国立学校、地方公共団体によって設置される公立学校、学校法人によって設置される私立学校に分類される。ただし、特別支援学校および幼稚園についてはその設置者は学校法人に限定されない。学校が公的な性質を有しているという理由から個人立の私立学校の設立は認められていない。しかし、近年の制度改革の結果、放送大学学園法人（放送大学）や2002年から構造改革特別区域法が制定されたことによって会社、NPO法人も学校の設置主体として認められるようになった。このように学校の設置者は次第に多様化してきている。義務教育段階では公立学校が大半を占めるが、幼稚園、大学、短期大学については、私学に依存する率が高い（図2-2参照）。

and Technology, there are other types of higher Institute under other Ministries, and graduates of these institutes obtain a bachelor degree as well.

■ For those who have completed university, there are graduate schools where education and research on a higher academic level are conducted. There are two-year master's courses and five-year doctoral courses. Some doctoral courses are divided into two stages: the first stage of two years can be treated equal to a master's course; and the second stage of three years can be treated as a doctoral course. Graduate schools for Medical Science extend for four years. The objective of the master's course is to educate individuals to have advanced professional ability in their respective fields. The objective of the doctoral course is to educate individuals to be research scholars. In order to enter graduate schools, a bachelor's degree is in principle required but as an exception for excellent students, it is possible to proceed to graduate schools after third grade of undergraduate education.

■ As for the education of children with disabilities, schools have been set up according to their disabilities and educational levels. In addition to schools for the blind and schools for the deaf, schools for mentally & physically handicapped children have been compulsory since 1979 and the name of such school was integrated as the special needs schools from 2007.

■ The schools described above can be classified according to their establishing body: state schools by the central government, municipal schools by a municipal or a local government, and private schools by a school corporation. The private schools cannot be established by individuals because the schools have some public characteristics. However, special needs schools and kindergartens do not have to be established by a school corporation. Furthermore, according to the recent reform, the provider of schools has enlarged to the corporation of the University of Air, non-profit organizations and limited liability companies. The percentage of private institutions is high in the kindergartens, universities, and junior colleges while most schools for the period of compulsory education are public. (See Figure 2-2).

■現在の学校制度は戦後の学制改革の産物であり、すでにこの制度が成立して 60 年以上が経過している。その基本的枠組みは大きく変容するまでにはいたっていないものの、1970 年代以降、学校制度に対して積極的な改革の取り組みがなされてきている。1971 年の中央教育審議会の答申「今後における学校教育の総合的な拡充整備のための基本的施策について」は、社会の急激な変化、学校教育の急激な膨張などを背景として、幼児期の教育と小学校教育の統合、6 年一貫の中等教育の実現、中等教育と前期高等教育の統合など従来の 6・3・3・4 制の変更を視野に入れた「先導的試行」への着手を提言した。さらに、1984 年 9 月には臨時教育審議会が発足し、21 世紀に向かっての成熟化、情報化、国際化等の日本社会の変化への対応をめざし、個性重視の原則、生涯学習体系への移行、変化への対応を基本的な考え方とする改革が提示された。これ以後はこの答申の内容に沿った改革が推進されている。

■ The present school system is an outgrowth of the postwar educational reform, and has been in its existence for more than 60 years. This does not mean, however, that the reform of the system has not yet been discussed at all. In 1974, the report of the Central Educational Council, "On the Basic Policy for Overall Expansion and Improvement of Future School Education", aimed to reform postwar education corresponding to the rapid social changes and rapid expansion of school education. Some changes have also been introduced as a "pilot study" aiming to change the existing 6-3-3-4 system, suggesting for example, integration of infant education with primary school education, establishment of six year secondary schools and, integration of upper secondary education with the first stage of higher education. In September 1984, the National Task Force for Educational Reform was organized. The National Task Force recommended education respecting individuality, transformation to a lifelong learning system, and responding to changes for the Japanese society in the 21st century, to ensure a mature, information and international society. The current educational reform is following the recommendations of this Task Force.

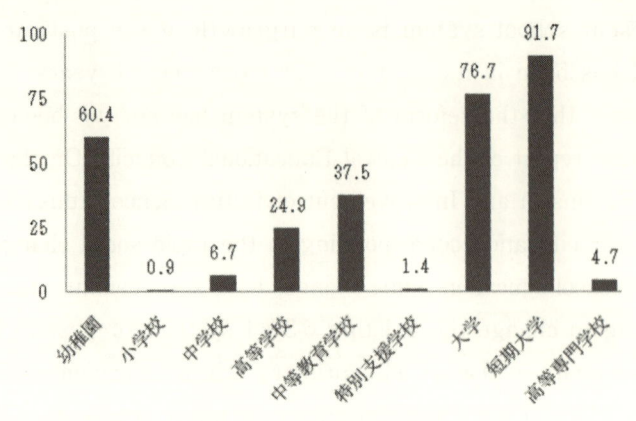

図2-2　私立学校の割合

(幼稚園 60.4、小学校 0.9、中学校 6.7、高等学校 24.9、中等教育学校 37.5、特別支援学校 1.4、大学 76.7、短期大学 91.7、高等専門学校 4.7)

（2）幼児期の教育の現状

■小学校へ入学する前の幼児を対象とした教育機関として、幼稚園が設置されている。幼稚園には3歳からの3年保育、4歳からの2年保育、5歳からの1年保育というように小学校の就学年齢である6歳までの保育を行うクラスがあるが、どのクラスを設置しているかは幼稚園ごとに異なる。幼稚園は「幼児を保育し、幼児の健やかな成長のために適当な環境を与えて、その心身の発達を助長することを」を目的とする。そこでの保育は、1．生活習慣の養成と身体諸機能の調和的発達、2．集団生活を通じての家族や身近な人への信頼感の深化、自主・自律、協働精神と規範意識の育成、3．社会生活や事象に対する正しい理解と態度の養成、4．言語の正しい使い方と相手の話を理解する態度の育成、5．音楽、身体表現、造形等を通じた完成と表現力の育成、をその内容としている。したがって、幼稚園の教育課程は健康、人間関係、環境、言葉、表現の5領域で構成され、毎学年の教育週数は39週以上、1日の教育時間は4時間が標準とされている。

■一方、母親が就労している場合には、福祉施設としての保育所がある。保育所は「日々保護者の委託を受けて、保育に欠けるその乳児または幼児を保育する」ものとされており、その「保育に欠ける」状態とは、母親の居宅外労働、家事以外の居宅内労働、母親のいない家庭など、母親による育児が不可能な場合を指す。したがって、保育所における保育内容は、家庭における

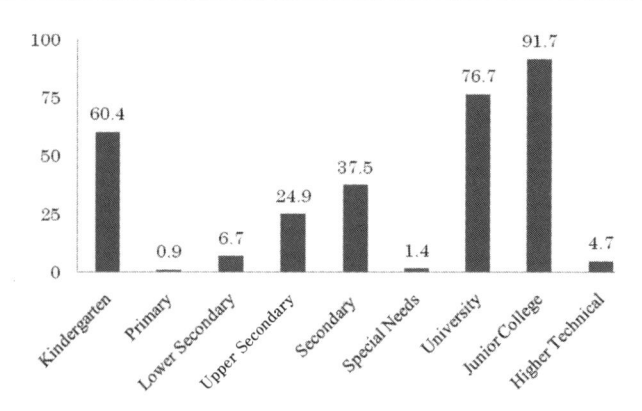

Figure 2-2　Percentages of Private School

(2) Present Condition of Infant Education

■ Kindergartens have been established for infants who have not yet entered primary school. In kindergartens, children are educated until the age of six. The kindergarten education consists of the three-year course from three years old, the two-year course from four years old, and the one-year course from five years old. Not every kindergarten has all courses. Kindergartens, while aiming to nurture very young children, also promote their physical and mental sound development, cultivate healthy habits for everyday life, develop sociability among children, foster independence, cultivate skills and interest in language culture, and ability for creative representations in music, performance and formative arts. Thus, the courses in kindergartens consist of five fields: health, human relations, environment, language, and expression. The standard number of class days for each level is more than 39 weeks a grade, and the standard number of daily teaching hours is four hours.

■ For working mothers, nursery services are available. Day care centers aim to take care of children who have been entrusted by their parents or guardians to the institutions for reasons such as: mother's employment obligations both inside and outside the home, and no one to take care of the baby at home. Thus, the contents of nursery schooling are substitutes for home education. Day care

育児の代替であり、母親の出産休暇が明ける8週間後から6歳までの乳児・幼児を預かる。そして開所日数も母親の就労日数に対応し、1日の保育時間も8時間以上が一般的である。

■このように現在の日本では、就学前の幼児に対して、文部科学省の所管であり「学校」としての性格を備えた幼稚園と、厚生労働省の所管であり家庭での保育を補完する福祉施設としての保育所が並存する幼保二元体制が特徴とされる。そして、施設・設備や園具・教具の基準、教職員の資格や勤務条件、教職員一人あたりの幼児数など、さまざまな点で両者の違いがみられる。幼稚園の教職員は教育職員免許法に基づいた幼稚園教諭免許状を所持していなければならない。この免許状を取得するためには、課程認定を受けた大学、短期大学あるいは文部大臣の指定した教員養成機関に少なくとも2年以上在学し、所定の単位を修得しなければならない。

■一方、保育所の職員は保育士と呼ばれるが、厚生労働大臣の指定した養成機関を卒業した者か、高等学校卒業以上で保育士試験に合格した者に保育士資格が与えられる。また、公立の機関については、幼稚園教諭には教育公務員特例法が適用されて研修の機会が保障されているが、保育士は一般の公務員と同等である。さらに、幼稚園では4時間であるが保育所では8時間という保育時間の差や夏休みなどの長期休業の有無などが指摘される。ただし、1990年の保育所保育指針では、保育所においても4歳以上の幼児については幼稚園教育要領に準じた教育を実施することが定められ、また1998年から幼稚園と保育所の施設の共用化が認められ機能を統合した認定子ども園などが開設されるなど、次第に両者の格差を解消する傾向が見られる。このような傾向は第一に幼児の数が減少してきたため、幼稚園と保育所が共同して保育にあたることが効率的であるとの考えが受け入れられてきたこと、第二に、就労する女性の数が増加してきたため、子どもを早期から預かる施設への需要が高まってきたことなどが、その背景にあると考えられる。

centers are available for infants and babies after eight weeks when the maternity leave of the mother expires and until the age of six. The number of attendance days in a nursery institution corresponds to the number of working days of the mother. Daily nurture hours usually consist of more than eight hours.

■ As seen in the discussion above, the dual system is a special feature of infant education in Japan: kindergartens have characteristics of 'school' within the jurisdiction of the Ministry of Education, Culture, Sports, Science and Technology; and day care centers cover the lack of child care in families as a welfare institution under the Ministry of Health, Labour and Welfare. There are different standards between these two institutions in their facilities and equipment, their teaching materials, qualifications and working conditions of their staff, and ratio of infants per staff. Kindergarten teachers must possess a kindergarten teaching certificate approved by the Educational Personnel Certification Law. To obtain it, one must complete a two-year course and earn credits at a university, a junior college or a teacher training institution recognized by the Ministry of Education, Culture, Sports, Science and Technology.

■ Staff at day care centers are called "hoikushi" and their qualifications are provided by certain institutions authorized by the Minister of Health, Labour and Welfare, or graduates of upper secondary schools can be certified after passing the qualification test. In the public kindergartens, teachers are guaranteed to get in-service training, as provided for by the Law for Special Regulation Concerning Educational Public Service Personnel. However, day care center staff are not given this chance because their status is equal to the general municipal service personnel. The working conditions of kindergarten teachers and nursery staff are different. The number of working hours in kindergarten is four hours while in day care centers it is eight hours. Also kindergarten has summer, winter and spring vacations, but day care centers are open almost all weekdays. As the 1990 guideline of nursing in day care centers stipulates, infants more than four years old in day care centers should be given the education equivalent to that in kindergartens. Moreover, as new types of institutions such as autholized kids

■近年の出生率の低下による少子化傾向は、一つには、幼稚園教育は私立に大きく依存するなかで幼児数の減少による幼稚園の経営難という事態を引き起こし、閉園に至る幼稚園の増加をもたらしている。その一方で、数が少ない子どもに対する親の期待が高まり、多額の教育費支出が可能となったことから、幼児期から文字、数や英語の学習を開始する教育投資の早期化の傾向もみられる。さらに、「ひとりっ子」の増加により家庭や地域における子ども同士の接触の機会が減少したことにより、幼稚園や保育所における集団保育の重要性が高まってきているといえる。

(3) 義務教育の現状

■1886年（明治19年）の「小学校令」により、4年間の尋常小学校とその上に4年制の高等小学校が設置され、父母及び後見人に対して尋常小学校に児童を就学させる義務を課したのが、わが国における義務教育の始まりである。その後1900年（明治33年）の「小学校令」の改正により、就学義務規定が明確化され、就学年限4年、満6歳入学、授業料徴収の原則的禁止、学齢児童雇用の禁止などが定められた。1872年（明治5年）の学制発布の直後には就学率は30％程度であったのに対し、1900年当時には88％にまで上昇した。さらに1907年（明治40年）には義務教育年限が6年に延長されたが、その時点で尋常小学校の就学率は約98％にまで到達していた。1941年（昭和16年）には戦時下の状況に対応し、「国民学校令」が公布され、小学校は国民学校となった。

■第2次世界大戦後の教育改革では6・3制が導入され、初等教育の小学校6年と前期中等教育の新制中学校3年の9年間が義務教育とされた。それ以前には、国民学校修了者に対しては、エリート養成のための男子のみの中学

centers are trying to integrate both functions of kindergarten and nursery school since 1998, and differences between the two types of infant education are gradually disappearing. The declining birth rate in recent years, and the necessity of effective management and the increasing needs for nursing, particularly among the young working mothers has encouraged this trend.

■ Because of the decline in the birth rate, and because a majority of kindergarten schools are private, a number of kindergartens have encountered management difficulties and closed down. As the number of children in a family is decreasing, parent's expectation toward their children's future is intensifying, and they can afford to spend much for their child's education, such as teaching Japanese letters and characters, arithmetic and English in early infanthood. The increase of 'single child families' results in less contact among children in families and communities, so that group activities in kindergartens and day care centers have become more important.

(3) The Present Condition of Compulsory Education

■ As provided for by the Primary School Ordinance in 1886, the general primary course of four years and advanced primary course of four years were established. The first four years was made compulsory by requiring parents and guardians to send their children to primary school. With the amendment of the Primary School Ordinance in 1900, the provision for compulsory school attendance was defined: four years of attendance, six years old as entrance age, prohibition of school fees and employing of school-age children. The percentage of school enrollment increased from 30% in 1872 to 88% in 1900. In 1908, the length of compulsory education was extended to six years, but school attendance remained at 98%. In 1941, during the wartime, the National School Ordinance was proclaimed, and primary schools were converted to national schools.

■ The educational reform after World War II introduced the 6-3 system of compulsory education; six years of primary education and three years of lower secondary education. Before this reform, several types of secondary schools

校、高等女学校、実業学校、国民学校高等科などの進路があったが、この改革によって、初等教育修了者はすべて単一の中学校に進学することになった。現行の学校教育法では、小学校の目的は「心身の発達に応じて、義務教育として行われる普通教育のうち基礎的なものを施す」こととされ、中学校の目的は「小学校における教育の基礎の上に、心身の発達に応じて、義務教育として行われる普通教育を施す」とされている。日本の義務教育は普通教育のみを施し、職業準備教育は実施されていない。

■小・中学校の1学級の児童生徒数は、小学校設置基準および中学校設置基準により40人以下と定められている。また、小学校、とくに低学年では、学級担任の教師がその学級ですべての教科を教える全科担任制がとられ、中学校では教師が1つの教科について複数の学級で教科指導を行う教科担任制がとられるのが普通である。

■わが国における義務教育の原則は、就学義務、学校設置義務、就学援助義務、避止義務の4つの要素でなりたっている。就学義務とは憲法第26条および教育基本法第5条に示されるように、国民がその保護する子女に9年の普通教育を受けさせる義務を負うとするものであり、子どもが満6歳から満15歳に達するまでの9年間が義務教育の期間とされる。学校設置義務とは、市町村がその区域内の学齢児童・生徒を就学させるのに必要な小学校・中学校を設置する義務である（学校教育法38条）。就学援助義務とは、経済的理由により就学が困難な児童・生徒の保護者に対して市町村が必要な援助を与えなければならないとするものである（学校教育法19条）。避止義務とは、子女を使用するものは義務教育への就学を妨げてはならないとするものであり、子女の雇用者の義務である（学校教育法20条）。これらの義務教育の原則に従って、現在まで60年以上もの間、義務教育の就学率は99.9％以上を維持してきている。

existed such as, boys' middle schools, girls' high schools (Koto jo gakko), vocational schools and advanced courses of national primary schools. With this reform, however, all graduates of primary schools were made to proceed to a single type of lower secondary school. The School Education Law states that primary school "aims to give all primary students a common education necessary for their physical and mental development", and a lower secondary education "on the foundations of the primary education, the general secondary education should be provided according to students' physical and mental developmental levels". Thus, compulsory education in Japan provides a common general education, not a vocational education.

■ Class size in primary and lower secondary schools should be less than 40 students according to the Standard of the Primary School Establishment and the Standard of the Lower Secondary School Establishment. In primary schools, especially in the lower grades, one teacher is assigned to teach all the subjects, while in the lower secondary school one teacher is assigned to teach one subject to several classes.

■ The four principles of compulsory education are: compulsory school attendance, compulsory school establishment, obligation of assistance to school attendance, and compulsory prohibition of learning obstruction. Compulsory school attendance means that people are required to send their children to school for 9 years, as stated in the 26th article of Japanese Constitution and the fifth article of the Basic Act on Education. Compulsory establishment of schools refers to establishing bodies such as cities, towns, and villages which are obliged to establish schools for compulsory education for children within their area, as stated in article 38 of the School Education Law. Obligation of assistance to the guardians of school attendance means that the establishing bodies provide the necessary assistance to the guardians of students who cannot go to school for economic reasons, as stated in article 19 of the School Education Law. Compulsory prohibition of learning obstruction means that the employers should not employ children within the compulsory education age, so as not to

■しかし、わずかの例外を除いてすべての日本国民の子どもが小・中学校に在学するという状況の中で、学校生活に適応できずに長期に欠席する児童・生徒の存在、すなわち「不登校」が問題となってきている。従来「不登校」はその児童生徒本人に原因があると考えられる傾向があったが、最近では学校における人間関係や生徒指導のあり方、さらには学校そのものの特性をも再検討するなかで、その解決が模索されつつある。また、「校内暴力」や「いじめ」の発生も深刻な問題となってきている。

■このような不登校児童生徒やいじめに苦しむ子どもにたいし適切な教育機会を提供するために、指定された校区外の学校への通学が認められるようになった。また1992年からは、学校以外の施設で学習支援を受けているような場合には、そこでの出席状況を義務教育日数としてカウントするなどの柔軟な対応策がとられるようになった。これとは別に、このように子どもたちの心をめぐる問題が次第に深刻になってきていることを踏まえ、1995年にはスクール・カウンセラーを学校に配置し、相談や助言等を行うことにより、揺れ動く青少年の精神面の指導の充実をはかるようになってきた。
■2000年から実施された総合的な学習の時間は、地域や子どもの実態に応じた身近な素材を扱うことによって、特定の教科ではなく教科の枠をこえて子どもの認識や経験の幅を広げていくことをそのねらいにしている。これを円滑に実施するために学校から地域住民や保護者に支援を要請し、また地域住民や保護者がこれに協力するという連携が広くみられるようになってきた。これとは別に学校行事に住民が積極的に参加し、また登下校時の子どもを見守る活動が住民や保護者が行うなど、両者の連携・協力体制が築かれつつある。
■これとは別に、家庭と学校とが連携して子どもの成長を支援し、地域に開かれた学校づくりを進めるという観点から、2000年に校長の求めに応じて

obstruct their chance of school attendance, as provided in article 20 of the School Education Law. With these provisions for compulsory education, the percentage of school attendance at the compulsory level has been maintained at about 99.9% for more than 60 years.

■ While all Japanese children from the age of 6-15 are attending primary or lower secondary schools, some children, unable to adapt to school life, take prolonged absences. This problem, which is called 'Fu-toko' (truancy), has become a serious problem. Previously it was considered that the cause of 'Fu-toko' lies in the children themselves, but recently, factors such as human relationships, student guidance, and characteristics of school education have come to play a part in solving this problem. Additionally 'school violence' and 'bullying' are also serious problems in school education.

■ Thus, the Central Government decided to alter the school catchment area so that kids who suffer from truancy or bullying are provided with an alternative opportunity to enjoy their school education. Also, the kids who attend alternative organizations in which their individual learning is supported apart from the formal school, could be recognized as regular attendance from 1992. Additionally, as such numbers of kids has been increasing, a new policy was introduced in 1995 to allocate a professional school counselor in school to assist and to advise such kids under serious situations.

■ The period of integrated study which started from 2000 aims to spread knowledge and experience of kids over the framework of subjects by integrating the materials of local circumstances or their daily life. In this context, it has been observed that schools are likely to ask parents of local communities to support this programme and join them as much as possible and vice versa. Apart from this, local people as well as parents positively join the school events or assist the school, and from this the relations between school and local community can be seen as much more cooperative than ever before.

■ On the other hand, the new system called "School Council" was introduced in 2000 which aims to give advice to the principal according to his/her request.

学校運営に意見を述べるために学校評議員が置かれるようになった。このように学校が地域住民や保護者の意向を反映させ、地域の実情を踏まえて運営されるというこの制度は、日本の教育界において初めて取り入れられた。現在までのところ、全国の公立学校の82％でこれが実施されている。しかしこの制度は校長が評議員になる人物を推薦すること、評議員は個人的な意見を述べるだけの役割に限定されているなど、地域住民や保護者による学校運営への参画が実現されているとはいえない状況にある。

■地域住民や保護者による学校運営への本格的な参画を実現する方策として、2005年から学校運営協議会制度が発足した。これは地域住民や保護者が一定の権限と責任をもって学校の運営に直接参加する組織であり、地方当局が既存の公立学校を指定してそこに協議会を置くというものである。具体的には、校長による教育課程の編成方針の承認と、教職員人事への具申を行う権限をもっている。このように学校運営協議会は保護者や住民の学校経営への参画を制度的に保障するものであり、教育委員会や学校教員のみで運営されていた学校を外部の参加によって、より地元や保護者のニーズに近いやり方を取り入れることの重要性を実行しようとするものといえる。
■また義務教育学校をめぐって、いわゆる学校間連携がはかられ、子どもたちの指導と教育が円滑に進むような政策も実行されつつある。それは第一に、幼稚園から小学校への接続を図る局面である。幼稚園では子どもたちの自発的な活動を中心に教育活動が展開されているのに対し、小学校に入学すると教科学習が主流となり、授業時間も厳格に守られるとともに、学校規模が大きくなり、子どもたちに学校での生活環境は大きく変化する。同じことは小学校から中学校への進級の際にも指摘できる。小学校での授業は一部に専科教員が配置されている場合があるが、多くは一人の学級担任が全教科を教えるという形式をとっている。しかし中学校では教科ごとに担当教員が変わるため、このような仕組みに慣れていない新入生はこれに戸惑うだけでなく、英語が新しく教科に加わり、学習内容も次第に高度化していく。また多くの場合二ないし三つの小学校から一つの中学校に進級するため、新たな人

This policy can be understood by listening to the public opinion of local people more positively regarding school management and is the first case in recent Japanese education. At the moment, such council has accepted nearly 82% of state primary and secondary schools. However, there are a couple of problems, for example the members of council are nominated by the principal him/herself and opinions against the school policy are not reflected at all and the opinion of members of the council are accepted as personal ones, etc. As a result, it is far from an optimal system to collect opinions widely, and to reflect them to the school management.

■ In addition, the school management board system was introduced in 2005 to allow the local people and parents be involved in the school management. This is the new organization consisting of representatives of parents and other people to have the competence to approve the curriculum submitted by the principal and to propose the personnel plan to the local authority. This could be recognized as the new policy to reflect local opinions and the needs of parents to the school management whereby schools should be operated not only by the board of education and school teachers but to follow external views as far as possible.

■ Furthermore, the policy to fill the gap of school stages has been reinforced in recent years for the smooth transition from the lower to the higher stage. The first one is observed from kindergarten to primary school. Although kids are encouraged to be active in kindergarten, when they come to primary school, they are expected to follow the timetable and the curriculum. In this circumstance they are likely to be embarrassed and such a situation affects the attitude to the learning and their achievement by and large. Such drastic change of the learning circumstance can be seen when they go to lower secondary school as well. Almost all the classes are in charge by one teacher in primary school, but at lower secondary school, teachers take charge of one subject respectively and this means kids have to attend their classes under different teachers. Additionally, English learning starts from that stage and again the learning standard of each

間関係を作るのに戸惑いを感じる子どももいる。新しい環境に速やかに適応できない子どものなかには次第に学習意欲が減退し、学校になじめないことなどが背景となって「不登校」となっていく場合もある。これらのことから幼稚園の頃から小学校の見学や、小学校高学年の児童との交流などを行い、小学校そのものに慣れさせるための「幼小連携」や、小学校と中学校の教員がお互いに情報を交換し、また授業交換を行うなど、教員間の理解を深めだけでなく、小学生による中学訪問と見学などを通して円滑な適応をはかる試みが行われてきている。

（4）後期中等教育の普及と問題点

■義務教育を修了し中学校を卒業した者の95％以上が、高等学校あるいは高等専門学校に進学する。高等学校は、通常3年間の課程で、「中学校における基礎の上に、心身の発達に応じて、高等普通教育及び専門教育を施すことを目的とする」ものである。高等専門学校は1962年度から設置された5年制の学校であり、「深く専門の学芸を教授し、職業に必要な能力を養成することを目的」とする、後期中等教育と高等教育の一部を統合した教育機関である。高等学校は昼間に教育が行われる全日制と働きながら勉学する生徒を対象にした定時制とがある。後者の割合は高校教育がまだ十分に普及していなかった60年前では、13％であったが、現在では約2％の生徒が通っているに過ぎない。図2-3に高等学校への進学率の推移を示した。

■第2次世界大戦後の教育改革では、普通教育と職業教育を統合した総合制、通学区を小規模にする小学区制、そして男女共学という「高校3原則」をスローガンとして、新制公立高等学校の整備がめざされた。しかしながら、設置当初からこの原則が完全に守られたわけではなく、その後の社会状況の

subject becomes higher. A lot of kids become embarrassed in this complete change of learning circumstance, and as a result some of them decline the active attitude of learning and their achievement falls down gradually until it finally reaches truancy. To avoid such serious situations, some attempts have tried to fill the gaps between kindergarten and primary and between primary and secondary respectively. For example, information regarding the actual situation for kids and of the difference of learning atmosphere has been shared among each stage of schools and also, visiting schools in advance before students enter is encouraged.

(4) Increased Attendance of Upper Secondary Education and its Problems

■ Most of the students who finished compulsory education go on to upper secondary schools or technical colleges. The percentage of enrollment of upper secondary schools and technical colleges is currently more than 95%. The upper secondary schools aim at "giving higher general education or specialized vocational education according to students' mental and physical development on the foundation of the lower secondary education" usually for three years. The technical colleges were established in 1962 as a five-year educational institution that aims at "teaching the deep technical learning and cultivating the ability needed for the students' future occupations". Upper secondary school is divided into two types. One is full time school in which students attend their school at day time, and the other one is to provide education for them after their work and mainly takes place in the evening. The percentage of the latter used to be 13% when upper secondary school was not so diffused nearly 60 years ago, but at present it decreased to only 2%. Figure 2-3 shows the trend of students' ratio going to upper secondary school.

■ Due to the educational reform after World War II, upper secondary school was re-organized with the 'three upper secondary principles'; comprehensive courses with integrated general education and vocational education, the small-school district system, and co-education. However, these principles were not realized

変化に応じて、普通科と職業学科の並立と、中学区制、大学区制割が一般的になってきていた。高等学校等への進学率は、1950年には42.5％であったものが1975年には91.9％に達し、2007年では97.7％にまでなっている。また、1970年頃までは普通科と職業学科の生徒数の割合はそれぞれ60％、40％であったが、その後普通科の割合が増加し、平成18年では普通科の生徒数が72％を占めている。

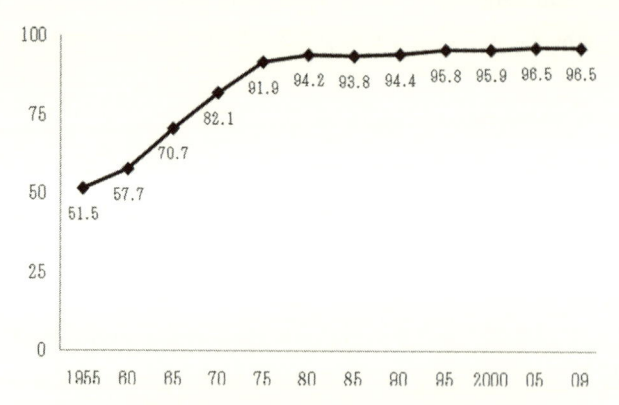

図2-3　高等学校への進学率の推移（通信制を除く）
出典：『文部科学統計要覧・平成20年度版』p.54より作成

■このように高等学校教育が義務教育に準じるほど一般化している中で、学習者のニーズの多様化と教育水準の維持をどのようにはかるか、また特色ある学校づくりなどが重要な政策課題となってきている。例えば、従来からある普通科、専門学科に加えて1994年から新たに「総合学科」が設置されるようになった。その趣旨は普通教育と専門教育を選択履修できるようにし、高校生の個性と卒業後の進路に柔軟に対応できるようにすることにある。なお、学科別の高等学校数を図2-4に示しておいた。

一方、高校教育が準義務化するにともない、一貫した課程のもとで学習できる環境を提供し、生徒の個性と関心に応じた教育を行うことを目的として、1999年から中学校と高等学校を連結した「中等教育学校」という新しいタイプの学校が作られるようになった。このような学校は2009年度には42校

from the beginning, and according to latter changes in the social conditions, coexistence of the general course and the vocational course and the larger school district system became widespread. Enrollment in upper secondary schools was 42.5% in 1950, but reached 91.9% in 1975, and 97.7% in 2007. The enrollment ratio of the general education course was 60%, while vocational courses was 40% up until 1970, but the ratio of general education courses has been increasing since then, currently reaching 72%.

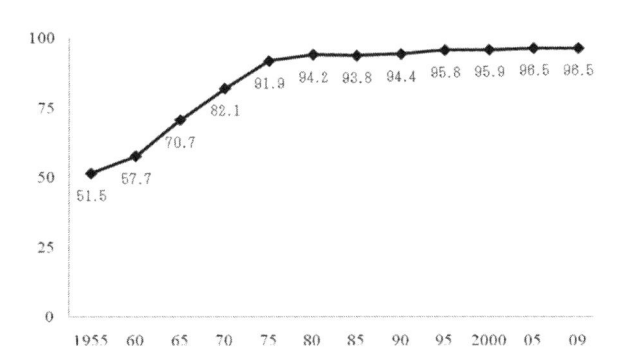

Figure 2-3 Trend of Students' Ratio Going to Upper Secondary School
(not including the case of correspondance courseand schools)
Cit. from "Statistical Abstract of the Ministry of Education, Science, Sports and Culture, 2008 edition", p.54

■ Thus, upper secondary school education has become universal topic like semi-compulsory education, and it is urgently required to provide diverse education according to the needs and standards of achievement and to keep the quality of education at a certain level. Also it has been discussed regarding the necessity of originality of a school which is distinguished from other schools nearby. For example, a new course called "integrated studies" was launched in 1994 apart from the ordinary and vocational course. Its purpose is just to provide students with the possibility of choosing any subject from both the ordinary and vocational course depending on the policy of respecting the diversity of students' aptitude and providing students ease in choosing their destination after leaving school. The number of upper secondary school by courses, 2007 is shown in Figure 2-4.

となっている。

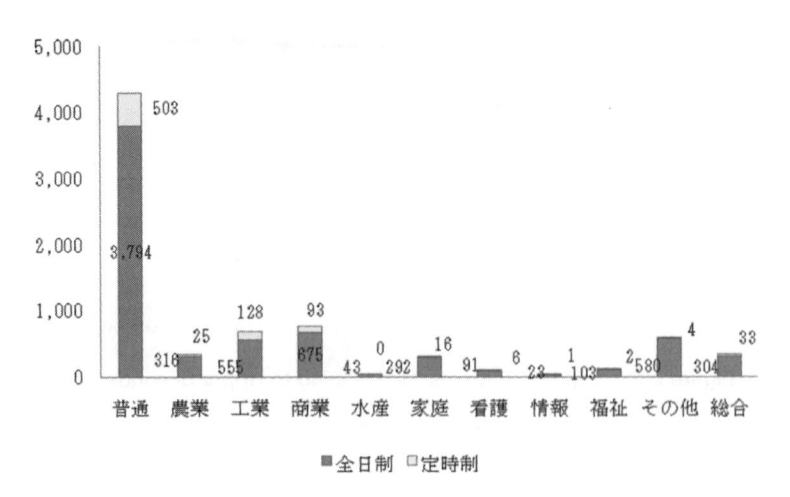

図 2-4　学科別高校数（2007 年度）
出典：『学校基本調査速報・平成 20 年度』より作成

■一方、高等学校は義務教育ではないため、入学するためには入学試験を受けそれに合格しなければならない。高等学校の入学試験は、公立高校については都道府県ごとに、国立学校及び私立学校については学校ごとに実施される。従来、選抜の方法は受験生の中学校での学業と行動の記録を報告する内申書と、高校側が課す学力試験の結果をもとにして入学者が決定されるのが通例であった。そして、内申書と学力試験の結果をどのように調整するか、学力試験にどの学科を課するかなどは、各都道府県あるいは学校に任されて

On the other hand, another kind of secondary school containing six year courses was founded in 1999 which incorporates lower secondary school with upper secondary school education. In this school, kids need not to prepare for the entrance exam during the second half of lower secondary school stage and they can enjoy a relaxed atmosphere. It also means that they are able to concentrate on learning or playing school sports if they wish. At present, this kind of school numbers 42 in total.

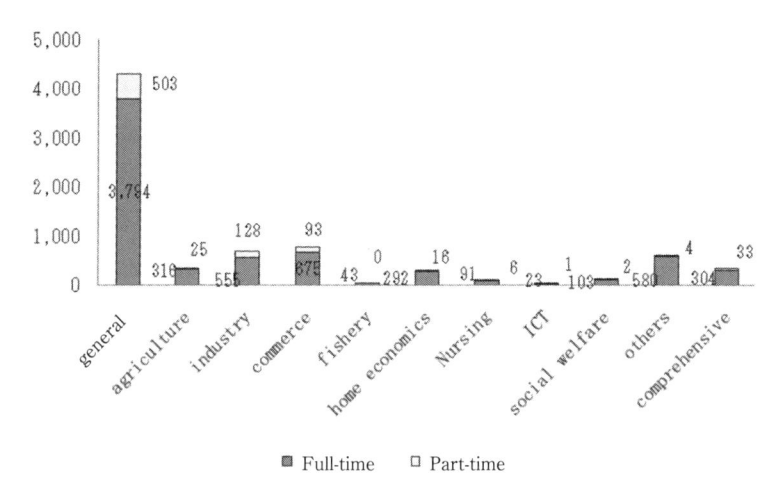

Figure 2-4　Number of Upper Secondary School by Courses, 2007
Resource: "Spot News of the School Basic Survey, 2008"

■ There were also critical reforms regarding entrance examination. In order to enter upper secondary school, one must pass an entrance examination. The entrance examination for public schools is carried out by each prefecture, while that of national and private schools is carried out by each school. Admissions are generally determined according to the school transcripts received from the lower secondary school and the result of the entrance examination that is a scholastic achievement test. It is left to each prefecture or school, to decide the

いる。しかし、高校への進学が当然のようになってきているという風潮のなかで、志願者の学業成績と進路の適性や個人の希望などを加味して、適切な進路を提供することは至難の問題となってきている。そのため文部科学省は、進路指導が生徒の能力・適性、興味・関心などに基づいて行われるべきこと、生徒自身が自己の能力・適性、興味・関心、将来の希望を考え、主体的に進路を決定することという進路指導の方針を示した。そして、進路指導の充実のために中学生の高等学校の訪問・見学、体験入学の実施や勤労体験学習、奉仕活動への参加などが奨励されている。

(5) 高等教育の多様化と大衆化

■第2次世界大戦後の教育改革により、それまでの高等学校から大学へという6年間の課程と3～4年の課程の専門学校が並立する高等教育制度は、1949年に大学、短期大学、および大学院に再編成された。また、同時に新制大学の発足により師範学校も大学の教育学部あるいは学芸学部として位置づけられた。その後、1962年には高等専門学校が、1975年には専修学校制度が発足した。また、水産大学校、気象大学校、防衛大学校、海上保安大学校等の文部科学省所轄以外の高等教育機関も存在する。

■大学は「学術の中心として、広く知識を授けるとともに、深く専門の学芸を教授研究し、知的、道徳的及び応用的能力を展開させる」ことを目的とした4年制（医歯薬学系は6年）の機関である。一方、短期大学は「深く専門の学芸を教授研究し、職業又は実際生活に必要な能力を育成する」ことを目的とし、修業年限は2年ないし3年であり、学部ではなく学科を置き、実際的・職業的教育に重点を置く点が大学と異なる。短期大学は当初は暫定的な

ratio of the school transcripts and examination results as well as the examination subjects. However, while people took it for granted that students enter upper secondary school, it was very difficult to provide appropriate student career guidance considering students' scholastic achievement, suitability of career and individual desire. Therefore, the Ministry of Education, Culture, Sports, Science and Technology provided a guideline that guidance should be based on students' ability, aptitude, interest, and desire in future life, and it is the students themselves that should decide which school they should try to enter considering their own ability and other factors. Now, it is recommended that lower secondary school students have an opportunity of school visits and participation of classes in upper secondary schools, as well as learning through work experience and voluntary activities in lower secondary schools.

(5) Diversification and Popularization of Higher Education

■ The education reform after World War II changed the parallel system of higher education with six-year education from upper secondary schools to universities and that with three to four year professional schools. It was reorganized into universities, junior colleges, and graduate schools in 1949. At the same time, when the new university system was established, normal schools were organized as a faculty of education, or a faculty of art and science in the university. Technical colleges were started in 1962, and special training schools in 1975. National Fisheries University, Meteorological College, National Defense Academy, and Japan Coast Guard Academy are also provided by Ministries other than the Ministry of Education, Culture, Sports, Science, and Technology.

■ The university is a four-year institution (medical science and pharmacy is six-year) which aims at "not only teaching broad knowledge but also studying professional learning and developing intellectual, moral, or applied ability." In contrast, a junior college, which consists of two or three-year courses, aims at "studying professional learning, and cultivating the ability necessary for vocational or actual life". In such cases, it is usually the departments not the faculties that put

機関であったが、1964年に恒久化された。なお、両者ともに全日制のほか夜間制、通信制の課程を置くことができる。大学は教育研究組織として学部を置くことを通例とし、大学の運営にあたっては大学の自治、そして実際には学部自治が基本的前提であった。しかしこの点に関する見直しが行われ、学部を置かずに研究組織と教育組織を分離した筑波大学が1973年に開学した。1978年からは、教員の現職教育を主たる目的とする大学院修士課程を持つ新教育大学が相次いで開設された。一方、生涯学習の機会の充実をめざして、1985年にはテレビ、ラジオ等のマスメディアを利用した放送大学が開設されている。

■大学および短期大学は、その設置者によって国立、公立および私立に分けることができる。2009年の統計によると、大学部門では国立が87（11.1％）、公立が92（11.9％）であるのに対し、私立大学は全体の77％にあたる595校となっており、大半が私立であることがわかる。短期大学も同様の傾向を示しており、私立は全体の93.1％（378校）となっており、圧倒的に私立が優勢となっている。（表2-1参照）。

　国立大学は研究の高度化や社会のニーズに迅速に対応し、また大学ごとの個性に応じた柔軟な運営ができるようにするため、2004年からそのすべてが大学法人として再スタートすることになった。具体的には、①大学ごとに法人格を与え、自律的な運営を行うことを可能にしたこと、②大学の管理運営組織を改め、民間的な経営手法を導入したこと、③大学の独善を排し、社会のニーズをふまえるために学外者を運営に参画させるようになったこと、④大学の教職員を公務員とは異なるカテゴリーとし、能力・業績に応じた人事管理を行えるようにしたこと、⑤第三者評価制度を導入したこと、などである。

　またこれに併せて全国にある公立大学も設置者である地方自治体の判断で、公立大学法人に移行することが可能となった。2009年度には公立大学全体の48％にあたる45大学がこの制度の下で運営されている。

stress on practical and vocational training, which is different from the university. The junior college was a provisional institution when it was established, but it became a permanent one in 1964. Both university and junior college can provide not only full-time but also part-time and correspondence courses. The university usually consists of faculties, and for the management of the university, the basic prerequisite is autonomy. In fact, autonomy of a university lies with the faculty. Hence, reform of this situation was considered. The University of Tsukuba which has no faculty system and separates research institutes and educational colleges was established in 1973. Since 1978 new universities of education with master courses were established whose main purpose is in-service training of teachers. In order to promote the opportunity for life-long education, the University of the Air which utilizes mass media, like television and radio, was established in 1985.

■ University and junior college is classified into three parts according to the character of providers; firstly by national university cooperation, formerly by the central government, secondly-by prefectures or municipal corporations and finally private-by the private school corporations. As far as the four years' university is concerned, the number of state universities include 87 (11.1%), local 92 (11.9%) and private 595 (77.0%), the last of which can be recognized as the largest of them in 2009. The similar percentage is found in the case of junior colleges. And the number of private institutions is 378 (93.1% of total ones). It is apparent that most of higher institutions are private. (See Table 2-1).

State universities were reorganized as those provided by the university cooperation from 2004 to make them easier to correspond to the social needs and the development of research. By this reform, state university is permitted to manage autonomously and replaced the former bureaucratic organization by the system of private enterprise. At the same time this new system can accept the external personnel to be involved in the university management. On the other hand, academic and clerical staff is evaluated by their performance and aptitude under such new system and university itself is assessed by an external examiner.

This trend affects the local government. They are able to transfer the

さらに 2002 年の構造改革特区制度の導入により、従来認められてこなかった会社立の大学が認可されるようになった。このタイプの大学は私立のカテゴリーに含まれるが、2007 年に 6 大学が経営を行っている。

表 2-1　設置者別に見た高等教育機関（2009 年度）

	設置者	学校数	学生数（千人）	女子学生の割合
大学（含大学院）	国立	86	622	
	公立	92	137	40.7
	私立	595	2,087	
短期大学	国立	2	0	
	公立	26	10	89.1
	私立	378	151	
高等専門学校	国立	55	53	
	公立	6	4	15.7
	私立	3	2	

出典：文部科学省『学校基本調査・平成 21 年度』速報より

■大学、短期大学への進学率は 1955 年には 10％程度であったが、その後の日本の経済成長や高等学校の普及などを背景に徐々に上昇し、1970 年代後半から始まる少子化傾向のなかでさらに加速し、2009 年度には 53.9％にまで上昇している。またこれに専門学校への進学者を含めるとその比率はなんと 68.1％に達する。男女別にみた大学・短期大学への進学率の推移は、図 2-5 の通りである。

university provided by prefecture or municipal cooperation to that like the state university cooperation if they wish. At present there are 45 universities (48%) which changed in the governing organization from being provided by the prefecture or municipal corporation to the new one.

Furthermore, the university organized by a joint stock company was approved for the first time by the Government policy of admitting exceptional treatment by the local authority in recent years. As of 2007 this new type of private university numbered six.

Table 2-1 Trend of Higher Education Institutions (2009)

	provider	number of institutions	number of students	percentage of girls' student
university (inc. graduate school)	state	86	622	
	local authority	92	137	40.7
	private	595	2,087	
junior college	state	2	0	
	local authority	26	10	89.1
	private	378	151	
technical college	state	55	53	
	local authority	6	4	15.7
	private	3	2	

Resource: The Ministry of Education, Culture, Sports, Science and Technology "Spot News of the School Basic Survey, 2009"

■ The percentage of students going on to university or junior college was approximately 10% in 1955, and it had increased because of the rapid economic growth after 1960's and of the nation-wide diffusion of upper secondary schools. In addition this trend had more accelerated by the declining rate of birth afterwards. In 2009 it goes to 53.9% and such percentage including number of students to go to the specialized training colleges (specialized courses) reaches to 68.1%. Figure 2-5 shows the percentage of students by sex to the universities and junior colleges.

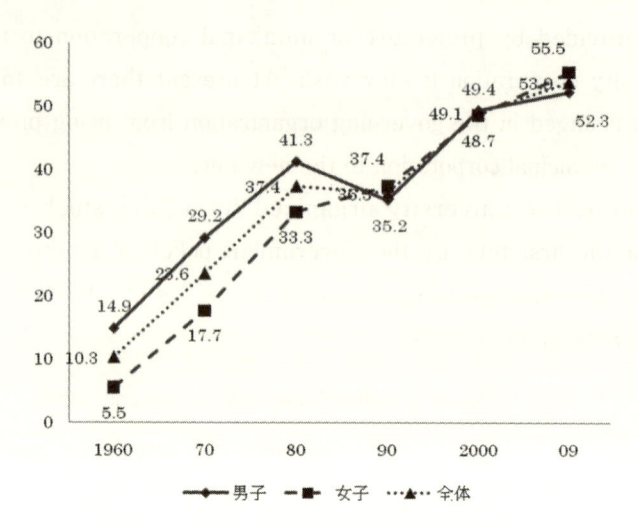

図 2-5　大学・短期大学への進学率の推移
出典：文部科学省『学校基本調査』各年版より作成

　このような高等教育の普及の一方で、18歳人口が逓減していくという少子化傾向なかで、大学ごとの個性や特色を出して、多様な学生層のニーズだけでなく社会から大学に寄せられる期待に対応していく必要性が生じてきている。そのため現在の高等教育の直面する問題として、もはや量的拡大ではなく質的向上が重要となってきている。1991年の大学審議会答申では、大学の教育機能の強化、世界水準に達する教育研究、生涯学習への対応が質的充実の方向として示され、この答申を受け同年に大学設置基準が改正された。その結果、各大学が独自にカリキュラムを編成することが可能になった。またそれと同時に、各大学が教育と研究に関して自己点検、自己評価を行い、常に改善へ向けての努力を払うべきことが規定された。図2-6に大学・短期大学の専攻分野別の学生比率を示した。

II. The Outline of Educational System 91

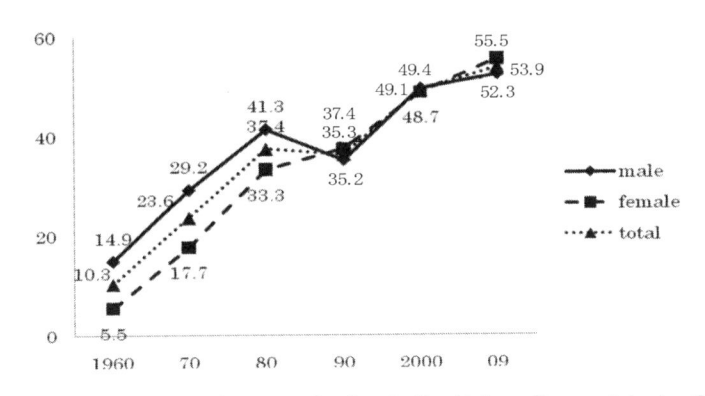

Figure 2-5 Percentage of Students by Sex to the Universities and Junior College
Resource: The Ministry of Education, Culture, Sports, Science and Technology
"The School Basic Survey, each year"

On the other hand, it becomes so urgent for the universities to provide the demands of different types of students and of the society with the distinction and the feature from others to attract candidates whose number has been declining very quickly. From this, it can be considered that the higher education has become more important not to provide much more institutions but to improve its quality according to the wide demands of students. In fact the University Advisory Council recommended in 1991 to reinforce the educational function of university, to advance the quality of research to the global standard, and to correspond to the learning society and the criteria for establishing universities was revised according to it. Then it became possible to provide individual curriculum by the effort of each university and also they were asked to evaluate the performance both of education and research to make their own effort to improve them. The percentage of students' study area is shown in Figure 2-6.

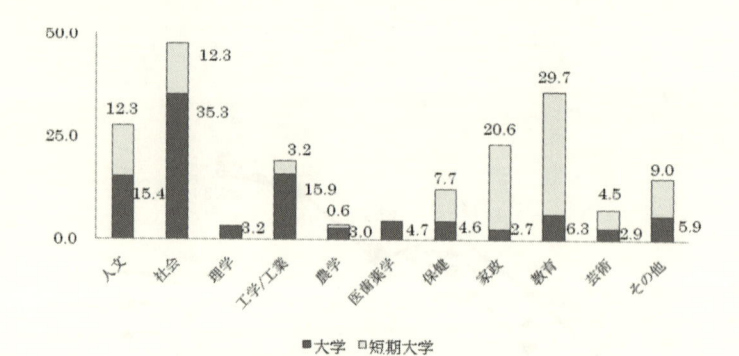

図 2-6　専攻分野別の学生比率
出典：文部科学省『学校基本調査・平成 21 年度版』速報から作成

■高等教育への進学者の増加や各大学での改革の進展は、大学入学者選抜制度の改善を促している。1979 年から実施されたすべての国公立大学を対象とした統一試験である共通一次試験は、1990 年度入学者からは一部の私立大学を加えた大学入試センター試験へと変更され、参加大学は増加しつつある。その一方で、受験機会の複数化や選抜方法の多様化、推薦入学の導入、AO 入試、社会人や帰国子女などを対象とした特別選抜の実施などが進められている。

　これと関連して大学での諸活動を高校生に広く知ってもらい、大学も高校での学習に一定の理解を持つことが重要であるという観点から、高大連携という試みが始められ、また大学側が積極的に受験生に情報を流す試み、たとえば教員が高等学校に出向いて大学紹介を兼ねた講義を実施したり、受験生に大学見学を奨励するなども行われるようになってきている。

Ⅱ. The Outline of Educational System

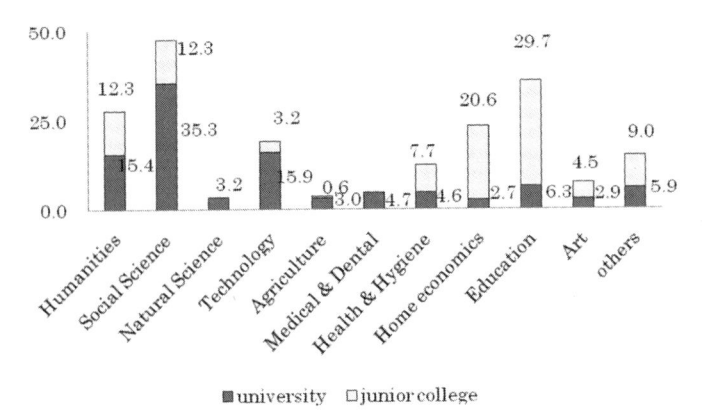

Figure 2-6 Percentage of Students'Study Area
Resource: The Ministry of Education, Culture, Sports, Science and Technology
"Spot News of the School Basic Survey, 2009"

■ The increasing number of the students and the result of the reform in each university has promoted the system and methods of entrance exam. The common entrance exam which was introduced in 1979 for all candidates to state and local universities was replaced by the newly planned exam by Entrance Exam Center in 1990 and the number of universities to join it has increased including private universities. On the other hand, each university has improved its entrance exam system by own effort according to own circumstance, for example expanding opportunity to candidates to have, to develop a various kinds of exam, introducing admission by recommendation from the principal of upper secondary school and selection to which admission office is involved, and admission of adulthood and Japanese students returning from abroad and so on.

Furthermore, a new plan called coordination of upper secondary school and university, has been developed by universities to promote understandings concerning activities among students of upper secondary school and on the other aspect of it, academic staff of the university visit upper secondary schools to give information regarding entrance exam and curriculum positively or to give introductory lecture for them.

■このような動向とは別に、大学がこれまでのように社会の動きとかかわらずに孤高を守るといういわゆる「象牙の塔」という考え方を脱し、社会や地域の発展に貢献することが要請されるようになってきた。具体的には地域を支える人材の育成、例えば教員、医師その他地場産業を担う技術者などの人材育成を地元大学が担い、一定数を輩出することが期待されてきている。また大学で開発される多様な知識や技能を地元社会に還元するような試みとして、講義等の公開、講演会や公開講座の開催、講演会・研修会などへの大学から専門的人材の派遣、施設の地域住民への開放などがその事例としてあげられる。

■他方、国際化が急速に進展する社会にあっては学生だけでなく研究者の交流が盛んになっていく。このような状況のなかで大学の国際競争力を高め、国際的な研究の推進が求められてきている。また国際的に通用する人材の育成が従来に増して要請されてきている。これを受けて近年、海外の大学と交流協定を締結する大学が1万件を超え、留学生の受け入れ数も2008年には12.4万人を超す勢いとなっている。また海外での修得単位を国内の大学で読みかえる措置や、外国から高度な研究者を招へいして採用するなどの仕組みが開発されつつある。

■さらに大学の国際化を推進するため、「国際化拠点大学」計画や、国際的に通用する高い水準の教育・研究を展開し、科学技術の発展と国際貢献を目指して留学生を30万人に増やすという計画も進行しつつある。また、海外に拠点を設け、現地における共同研究や学術交流だけでなく、現地における日本人の支援や日本への留学を希望する学生への情報提供なども行われてきている。このような多角的な活動は日本ではまだ緒に就いたばかりであるが、今後は先進国なみに展開されることが期待される。

■大学院は「学術の理論及び応用を教授研究し、その深奥をきわめ、又は高

■ Thus, the university has been expected to contribute the development of local community and social progress which has not been so dominant particularly among the tradition of university. Such trends used to be called the "ivory tower", isolated from the actual situation of society. For example, local universities can train primary or secondary teachers, medical staff and technological staff who has a possibility to develop it. On the other hand, universities are likely to cooperate the local society to provide knowledge or skills to the local people and organizations by sending staff concerned to meeting, workshop, and hold the open meeting for local people just like the university extension.

■ On the other hand, exchange of students as well as academic staff has been developed in this borderless society and it becomes urgent to raise the standard of research and ranges of learning in this situation to compete with other countries. At the same time it has been expected to train the bright and excellent persons to work on the international stage effectively. In this context, the number of universities which has contracted universities abroad to develop the exchange scheme has become more than ten thousand and the number of students from oversees has reached more than 124 thousand in 2008. Also, under the new system which has been launched, credits which the student attained at the foreign university can be recognized formally and highly regarded scholars can be invited and employed.

■ Additionally, a new project has been undertaken recently to approve some universities as the base to promote internationalization, to improve academic standards comparable with international levels, and to increase the number of foreign students studying in Japan to 300,000 for the scientific and technological progress and contribution to other countries. Apart from this, some universities have tried to provide a branch abroad in order to give useful information to the students who are going to visit Japan. These various movements have just started but it is expected to continue and expand until reaching a level comparable with advanced countries.

■ Graduate schools aim at "studying the theory and application of learning,

度の専門性が求められる職業を担うための深い学識及び卓越した能力を培い、文化の進展に寄与すること」を目的としている。大学院には研究科をおくことになっており、通常は大学の学部の上に設けられるが、必要がある場合には学部を置くことなく、単独で大学院のみを開設することもある。また夜間大学院や通信制による大学院の存在も認められている。大学院は2年制の修士課程と5年制の博士課程があり、原則として両者とも大学卒業を入学要件としている。これまで大学院は、「広い視野に立って精深な学識を授け専攻分野における研究能力又は専門性を要する職業等に必要な高度の能力を養う」修業年限が2年（ただし優れた業績をあげた者は1年以上）の修士課程と、「専攻分野について研究者として自立して研究活動を行うに必要な高度の研究能力及びその基礎となる豊かな学識を養う」ことを目的とする5年制の博士課程（ただし優れた業績をあげた者は3年以上）によって構成されていたが、1993年からは社会人を対象とした博士課程の夜間開講が認められると同時に、「高度に専門的な業務に従事するために必要な高度の研究能力」の養成がその目的に加えられた。この夜間開講の実施と博士課程の目的の改定は、職業上の知識・技術のリフレッシュや新たな習得を目的とする職業人のためのリフレッシュ教育機関として大学院が位置づけられた。また、時代の要請にこたえるために先端的、学際的な分野の専攻・研究科や、学部を持たずに大学院のみで運営される独立研究科・大学院大学なども認められるようになり、多様な形態で大学院教育が展開されてきている。このように大学院が多様化していくなかで、入学要件も弾力化されてきた。具体的には大学に3年以上在学あるいは外国で15年の課程を修了した者で、大学院が所定の単位を優れた成績で習得したものと認めた者も大学卒業者と同等以上の学力があるとされ、また1学年の「飛び級」が認められて大学院入学が認められるようになった。

■このような既存の大学院とは別に、2003年から科学技術の進展や社会・経済のグローバル化に伴う、社会的・国際的に活躍できる高度専門職業人養成へのニーズの高まりに対応するため、高度で専門的な知識・能力を備えた

deepening the knowledge, cultivating aptitude which contributes to undertaking a higher standard of career and contributing to cultural development". Graduate schools consist of five years for a doctorate degree and two years for master's courses. Usually it is provided as a base of the undergraduate schools, but it can be organized independently as necessary. Also, part time graduate courses mainly held in the evening or via correspondence are permitted. In principle, the qualification to enter them is graduation from university. Two years master's course (one year for those who attain excellent results) aims to "deepen learning in a broad vision, and cultivate the high ability necessary for research of major specialized fields". The five years course (three years for those who attain excellent results) aims to "cultivate the high ability necessary for conducting research as an independent scholar of a major specialized field" according to the criterion for establishment of graduate schools in 1974. From 1993, evening courses for doctorate degrees was approved for employed people, and an additional purpose of it was implemented for cultivating the advanced research ability to undertake professional jobs. Introduction of evening courses and the amendment of the purpose of doctorate courses means that the role of the graduate school includes the renewal and acquisition of vocational skills and knowledge. Similarly, according to the social needs, various types of graduate school education has been developed, for example, highly advanced or interdisciplinary departments, independent graduate schools which has no accompanied undergraduate course as the basic organization and so on. In this trend, the qualification for admission to graduate school has loosened for the candidates who completed 15 years of school education abroad, and those who are educated in undergraduate courses more than three years and certified by the graduate school including those with similar or distinguished ability. In comparison graduates from university can skip one year from the formal course and be accepted to the graduate course.

■ Similarly, according to the evolution of science and progress of international trade, a new type of graduate school was introduced to train human resources with highly developed aptitude to make activities in such a borderless society

高度専門職業人を養成することを目的として、専門職大学院が創設された。当初は法科大学院から始まったが、時間の経過とともに会計、ビジネス・技術経営、公共政策、公衆衛生等の様々な分野で大学院の設置が進み、2008年からは実践的指導能力を備えた教員を養成する教職大学院が開設し、専門職大学院が設置された。このような専門職大学院では研究者ではなく、高度で専門的な職業能力を有する人材を養成することが目的とされ、理論と実務を架橋した高度で実践的な教育を行うことが期待されている。そのため在来型の大学院とは異なり、社会人の在学率が高くなっているという特色がある。2008年度ではこのタイプの大学院に2.3万人が在籍し、その40％を社会人が占めている。

from 2003. At the very beginning of launching such new schools, only the law school started, but after that various types of new graduate schools such as business, management, public policy, hygiene had been introduced gradually, and from 2008 graduate schools for the teaching profession opened to raise the teaching skills and quality of teachers. In this type of school, the aim is not to train academic research staff, but to encourage professionalism and from this the percentage of people who had left school and worked already, is higher than usual graduate school. In 2008 the total number of this type of school reached 23,000 and about 40% is occupied by those who left school and worked already.

3. 特別支援教育制度

(1) 障害児教育パラダイムの転換と特別支援教育

■2007年4月1日、「学校教育法等の一部を改正する法律」の施行により、日本の障害児教育は特別支援教育へと制度転換した。特別支援教育では、従来の障害児教育（＝特殊教育）の対象児に加え、学習障害（LD）、注意欠陥多動性障害（ADHD）、高機能自閉症（HFA）等の障害のある児童生徒にまで、その対象が拡大された（図2-7）。特別支援教育は、障害等により生活上、学習上の困難を有する「特別な教育的支援を必要とする児童生徒」一人ひとりの教育的ニーズを把握し、その子どもの持てる力を高め、生活や学習上の困難を改善又は克服するために、適切な教育を通じて必要な支援を行うものであり、これらの児童生徒の自立や社会参加に向けた主体的な取組を支援するものである（特別支援教育の在り方に関する調査研究協力者会議，2003年）。

■障害児教育から特別支援教育への転換は、障害種別の教育サービスから個別のニーズにもとづく教育サービスへのパラダイムの転換である。このパラダイムの転換は、主に、①盲・聾・養護学校在籍児童生徒の障害の重度・重複化への教育的対応の必要性、②通常学校・学級において学習上、生活上の困難を有している児童生徒への教育的対応の必要性、③教育的対応を担う特別支援教育担当教員の専門性を担保する教員免許制度の必要性、の3つの理由から必要となった。

3. Special Needs Education system

(1) Paradigm Shift in the Education for Children with Disabilities and Special Needs Education

■ The partially amended School Education Law was enacted on April 1^{St}, 2007. With this amendment, Education for Children with Disabilities shifted to Special Needs Education. In Special Needs Education, children with Learning Disability (LD), Attention Deficit Hyperactivity Disorder (ADHD) and High-Functioning Autism (HFA), who were not targeted to receive special support traditionally, are to receive special support based on the fact that they have specific needs as well (Figure 2-7). Special Needs Education aims to identify the educational needs of each "child with special educational needs" who have difficulties in school and in their everyday lives because of their disabilities. Its goal is to help each child reach his or her fullest development by providing support through appropriate education so that the child can fully participate in schools and in everyday life, as well as supporting the child to actively participate in society (Special Needs Education Research Committee, 2003).

■ The shift from the Education for Children with Disabilities to Special Needs Education is effectively a paradigm shift from providing educational service corresponding to children's different types of disabilities to a service based on the needs of the individual. There are three main reasons for this shift: ① To meet the educational needs of students with severe or multiple disabilities studying at Special Schools for the Blind, Schools for the Deaf and Schools for Children with Intellectual Disabilities, Physical/Motor Disabilities and Health Impairments, ② to meet the educational needs of students at regular schools struggling to cope with school and daily life, and ③ to meet the need to develop a system of certifying teachers that ensures Special Needs Education teachers have the expertise and specialist skills to respond to children's special needs.

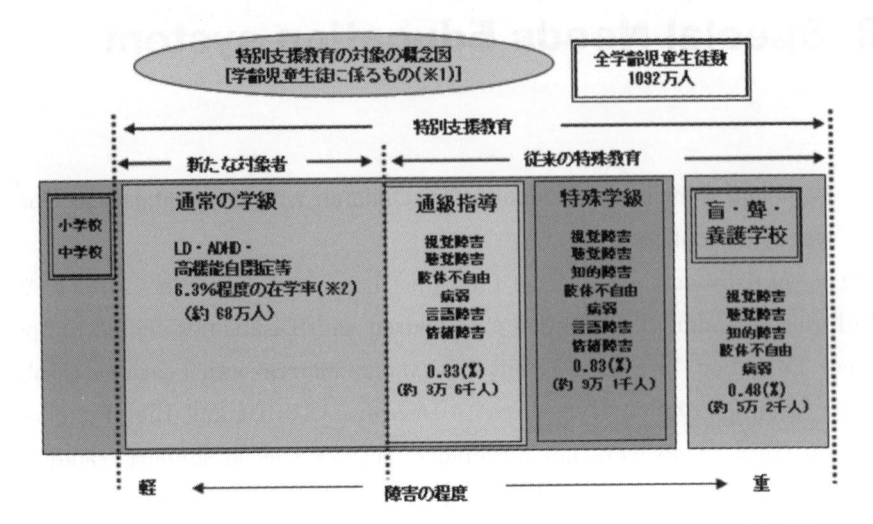

図2-7 特別支援教育の対象の概念
出典:「特別支援教育を推進する制度のあり方について（答申）」2003年、参考資料1．

■①児童生徒の障害の重度・重複化への対応としての特別支援学校

　盲・聾・養護学校の在籍児童生徒数の推移をみると、知的障害養護学校の在籍児数が大きく増加した一方で、その他の学校はほぼ横ばいである（表2-2）。また、近年は、在籍児の障害の重度・重複化の傾向がみられ、盲・聾・養護学校小・中学部全児童生徒数に占める重複障害学級在籍者の割合が増加し40%台となっている（表2-3）。特に重複障害児の在籍率が高く、その増加が著しいのは肢体不自由養護学校であり、最も重複障害児の在籍率が低いのは聾学校である（表2-3）。

II. The Outline of Educational System   103

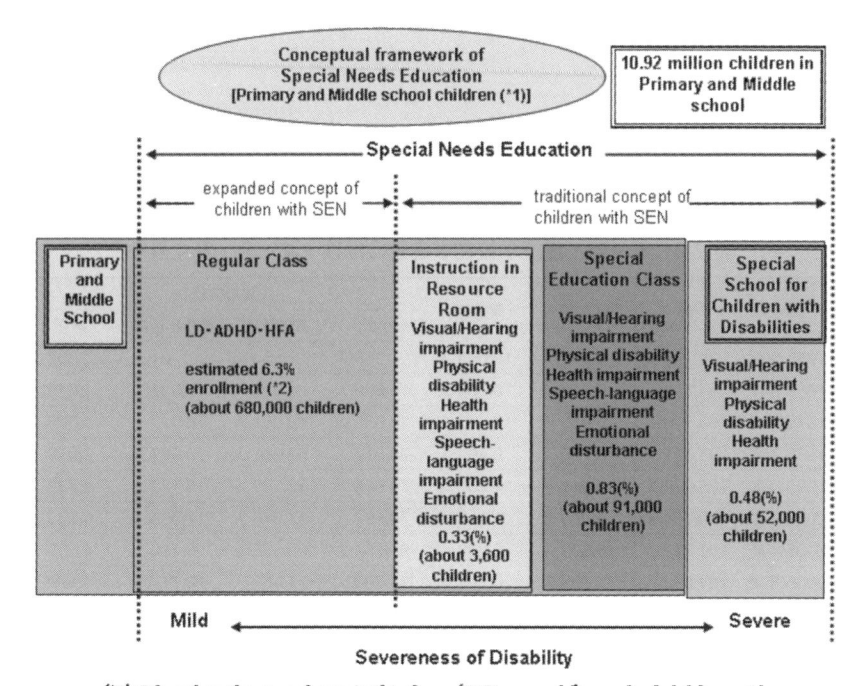

```
           Conceptual framework of              10.92 million children in
           Special Needs Education              Primary and Middle
           [Primary and Middle school children (*1)]    school
```

◄─────────────── Special Needs Education ───────────────►

◄── expanded concept of   traditional concept of ──►
    children with SEN   ◄──   children with SEN

| Primary and Middle School | Regular Class LD·ADHD·HFA estimated 6.3% enrollment (*2) (about 680,000 children) | Instruction in Resource Room Visual/Hearing impairment Physical disability Health impairment Speech-language impairment Emotional disturbance 0.33(%) (about 3,600 children) | Special Education Class Visual/Hearing impairment Physical disability Health impairment Speech-language impairment Emotional disturbance 0.83(%) (about 91,000 children) | Special School for Children with Disabilities Visual/Hearing impairment Physical disability Health impairment 0.48(%) (about 52,000 children) |

Mild ◄─────────────────────────► Severe

Severeness of Disability

(*1) Other than the ages shown in this figure(6-15 years old), preschool children with disabilities and students with disabilities in high schools are to be included in the SNE system as well.
(*2) This number is based on the answers obtained from surveys for teachers in regular classrooms. Thus, it is not based on doctors' opinion.

Figure 2-7   Conceptual Framework of Special Needs Education
Source: Committee to research the state of special needs education: "The Future Direction for Special Needs Education (final report)," 2003

■① Special Needs Schools as a response to the increasing severity of children's disabilities and increasing incidence of multiple disabilities

The changes in the number of students at "Special Schools" show that although the number of students at Schools for Children with Intellectual Disabilities have greatly increased, the number of students at other types of Special School have remained roughly the same (Table 2-2).

Furthermore, the proportion of students with multiple disabilities in the elementary and middle school division of Special Schools has increased, and now

表 2-2　盲・聾・養護学校在学者数の推移－国・公・私立計－

区分	計	盲学校	聾学校	養護学校			
				小計	知的障害	肢体不自由	病弱
1955年度	28,142人	9,090人	18,694人	358人	60人	61人	237人
1965年度	44,316人	9,933人	19,684人	14,699人	4,923人	7,931人	1,845人
1975年度	63,548人	9,015人	13,897人	40,636人	19,081人	16,927人	4,628人
1985年度	95,401人	6,780人	9,404人	79,217人	52,061人	19,937人	7,219人
1995年度	86,834人	4,611人	7,257人	74,966人	52,102人	18,131人	4,733人
2000年度	90,104人	4,089人	6,818人	79,197人	57,078人	17,886人	4,233人
2005年度	101,612人	3,809人	6,639人	91,164人	68,328人	18,713人	4,123人
2006年度	104,592人	3,688人	6,544人	94,360人	71,453人	18,717人	4,190人

出典：文部科学省初等中等教育局特別支援教育課「特別支援教育資料（平成18年度）」2007年
http://www.mext.go.jp/a_menu/shotou/tokubetu/material/013/001.pdf

表 2-3　重複障害学級在籍状況の推移（特別支援学校小・中学部）

区分	1985	1990	1995	2000	2001	2002	2003	2004	2005	2006
総計（％）	36.6	38.3	43.8	45.1	44.6	43.4	43.5	43.3	43.1	42.8
盲学校（％）	26.6	30.9	35.4	41.9	43.3	43.8	42.3	44.5	46.4	46.0
聾学校（％）	12.7	12.7	15.7	17.9	17.4	17.9	17.9	18.4	19.4	18.8
知的障害養護学校（％）	34.1	34.0	37.2	37.6	36.7	34.9	34.9	34.3	34.3	34.3
肢体不自由養護学校（％）	53.9	59.9	71.4	75.0	74.9	74.4	74.8	75.3	75.4	75.3
病弱養護学校（％）	33.3	33.0	31.4	32.5	34.1	35.9	37.9	38.5	39.5	39.3

出典：文部科学省初等中等教育局特別支援教育課「特別支援教育資料（平成19年度）」2008年
http://www.mext.go.jp/a_menu/shotou/tokubetu/material/020/002.htm

■②通常学校における障害児教育の対象の拡大と特別支援教育

　第2次世界大戦後の日本の学校教育を規定している学校教育法（1947年制定）においては、小・中学校に特殊学級を置くことができる旨の規定がなされ、中軽度の障害児の教育は、その障害区分（弱視・難聴・肢体不自由・病弱

Ⅱ. The Outline of Educational System   105

stands at over 40% (Table 2-3). This increase in the proportion of students with multiple disabilities has been particularly marked at Schools for the Children with Physical/Motor Disabilities, while it has been least noticeable at Schools for the Deaf (Table 2-3).

Table 2-2 Changes in the number of school children at "Special Schools"

	Total # of children	School for Children with Visual Impairments	School for Children with Hearing Impairments	School for Children with Intellectual Disabilities, Physical/Motor Disabilities and Health Impairments			
				Total	Intellectual Disabilities	Physical Disabilities	Health Impairments
1955	28,142	9,090	18,694	358	60	61	237
1965	44,316	9,933	19,684	14,699	4,923	7,931	1,845
1975	63,548	9,015	13,897	40,636	19,081	16,927	4,628
1985	95,401	6,780	9,404	79,217	52,061	19,937	7,219
1995	86,834	4,611	7,257	74,966	52,102	18,131	4,733
2000	90,104	4,089	6,818	79,197	57,078	17,886	4,233
2005	101,612	3,809	6,639	91,164	68,328	18,713	4,123
2006	104,592	3,688	6,544	94,360	71,453	18,717	4,190

Source: Ministry of Education, Culture, Sports, Science and Technology, Office of Primary and Secondary Education, Special Needs Division: "Special needs education materials for 2006 academic year", 2007
http://www.mext.go.jp/a_menu/shotou/tokubetu/material/013/001.pdf

Table 2-3 The proportion of pupils with multiple disabilities in the primary and middle school division of "Special Schools"

	1985	1990	1995	2000	2001	2002	2003	2004	2005	2006
Total (%)	36.6	38.3	43.8	45.1	44.6	43.4	43.5	43.3	43.1	42.8
Schools for Children with Visual Impairments (%)	26.6	30.9	35.4	41.9	43.3	43.8	42.3	44.5	46.4	46.0
Schools for Children with Hearing Impairments (%)	12.7	12.7	15.7	17.9	17.4	17.9	17.9	18.4	19.4	18.8
Schools for Children with Intellectual Disabilities (%)	34.1	34.0	37.2	37.6	36.7	34.9	34.9	34.3	34.3	34.3
Schools for Children with Physical Disabilities (%)	53.9	59.9	71.4	75.0	74.9	74.4	74.8	75.3	75.4	75.3
Schools for Children with Health Impairments (%)	33.3	33.0	31.4	32.5	34.1	35.9	37.9	38.5	39.5	39.3

Source: Ministry of Education, Culture, Sports, Science and Technology, Office of Primary and Secondary Education, Special Needs Division: "Special needs education materials for 2007 academic year", 2008
http://www.mext.go.jp/a_menu/shotou/tokubetu/material/020/002.htm

■ ② The increased number of children with disabilities receiving education at regular schools and the new system of Special Needs Education

The School Education Law (1947), which has regulated school education in Japan since the end of World War II, allowed special classes to be established in

および身体虚弱、言語障害、情緒障害、知的障害）ごとに、学籍を固定して小集団における発達段階に応じた特別な教育課程や指導法により、特殊学級（現、特別支援学級）で行うものとされた（表2-4）。しかし、中軽度の障害児の教育は、固定式の特殊学級への措置のみで解決されるものではなかった。

表2-4 特殊学級数及び特殊学級在籍児童生徒数の推移－国・公・私立計－

区分	学級数			児童生徒数		
	小学校	中学校	合計	小学校	中学校	合計
1955年度	930学級	242学級	1,172学級	20,497人	3,983人	24,480人
1965年度	5,485学級	3,044学級	8,529学級	51,450人	30,221人	81,671人
1975年度	13,313学級	7,260学級	20,573学級	84,204人	48,165人	132,369人
1985年度	15,095学級	6,938学級	22,033学級	69,629人	34,363人	103,992人
1995年度	15,125学級	7,167学級	22,292学級	43,850人	22,189人	66,039人
2005年度	23,706学級	10,308学級	34,014学級	67,685人	29,126人	96,811人
2006年度	24,994学級	10,952学級	35,946学級	73,151人	31,393人	104,544人

出典：文部科学省初等中等教育局特別支援教育課「特別支援教育資料（平成18年度）」2007年
http://www.mext.go.jp/a_menu/shotou/tokubetu/material/013/001.pdf

■1990年、文部省に「通級学級に関する調査研究協力者会議」が設けられ、1992年3月には「通級による指導に関する充実方策について（審議のまとめ）」が出された。この報告書では、1988年10月1日現在、全国の公立小・中学校の特殊学級で非在籍児童生徒12,793人が指導（通級による指導）を受けていること、さらに、その中には、当該特殊学級を設置している学校とは別の学校に在籍している児童生徒も7,536人含まれていること（他校通級）、非在籍の傾向は障害種別では言語障害、難聴、弱視、情緒障害に強くみられることが説明された。そして、「通級」が「各教科等の指導は主として通常の学級で受けながら、心身の障害の状態等に応じた特別な指導を特殊学級等で受けること」と規定され、通級の担当教員が対象となる児童生徒がいる学校に

regular schools. Students with mild to moderate disabilities were to be taught in a Special Class (now called Special Needs Class) according to their disabilities (low vision, hard-of-hearing, physical/motor disabilities, health impairments, speech/language disorders, emotional disturbances, intellectual disabilities) and based on their intellectual development, using special curricula and teaching methods (Table 2-4). However, simply putting students with mild to moderate disabilities in self-contained Special Classes did not solve the problem of how to provide quality education.

Table 2-4　Number of Special Classes and children enrolled in Special Classes in regular school

	# of Classes			# of Children		
	Primary School	Middle School	Total	Primary School	Middle School	Total
1955	930	242	1,172	20,497	3,983	24,480
1965	5,485	3,044	8,529	51,450	30,221	81,671
1975	13,313	7,260	20,573	84,204	48,165	132,269
1985	15,095	6,938	22,033	69,629	34,363	103,992
1995	15,125	7,167	22,292	43,850	22,189	66,039
2005	23,706	10,308	34,014	67,685	29,126	96,811
2006	24,994	10,952	35,946	73,151	31,393	104,544

Source: Ministry of Education, Culture, Sports, Science and Technology, Office of Primary and Secondary Education, Special Needs Division: "Special needs education materials for 2006 academic year", 2007
http://www.mext.go.jp/a_menu/shotou/tokubetu/material/013/001.pdf

■ In 1990, the Ministry of Education established the "Research Group Conference Regarding Instruction in Resource Rooms", the findings of which were presented in a report entitled "Strategies for improving Special Needs Support in Resource Rooms (Conclusion of the Conference)". The study found that as of October 1st 1988, there were 12,793 students across the nation who were not officially enrolled in Special Class but were receiving some instruction in Special Class. This total included some 7,536 students who were enrolled in different schools. The report went on to explain that students not enrolled in Special Classes, but who were receiving some instruction in Special Classes, tended to have the following disabilities: speech/language disorders, hard-of-

行って必要な指導を行う場合等についても、通級の一形態として考えるのが適当であるとされた。これを受けて、1993（平成5）年1月28日に「学校教育法施行規則の一部を改正する省令」（文部省令第1号）が公布され、同年4月1日に施行され、通級による指導が制度化された。定められた対象は、言語障害者、情緒障害者、弱視者、難聴者、その他心身に故障のある者で通級による指導が適当なものであった。

■その後、2001年10月に「特別支援教育の在り方に関する調査研究協力者会議」が設置され、2003年3月に「今後の特別支援教育の在り方について（最終報告）」が示された。この最終報告の中で、注意欠陥多動性障害[1]と高機能自閉症[2]の定義と判断基準（試案）、指導方法が提示され、これをもって、学校が通常学級で困難を抱える児童生徒の障害を学習障害、注意欠陥他動性障害、高機能自閉症と判断するための基準と手続きが整えられた。また、同じく2003年3月に、「通常の学級に在籍する特別な教育的支援を必要とする児童生徒の全国実態調査」の結果が公表され、学習障害、注意欠陥他動性障害、高機能自閉症を含む特別な教育的支援を必要とする児童生徒が、約6.3%の割合で通常学級に在籍している可能性があることが示された（文部科学省, 2006, 2）。そして、2004年1月には文部科学省より『小中学校におけるLD（学習障害）ADHD（注意欠陥／多動性障害）高機能自閉症の児童生徒への教育支援体制の整備のためのガイドライン（試案）』が出された。

hearing, low vision, and emotional disturbances. "Instruction in Resource Room" was defined as when students "receive education regarding academic subjects in a regular class, while receiving special instruction according to their specific physical and mental condition in a Special Class or other equivalent class." It was also considered appropriate as one of the ways to provide Special Needs Support in Resource Rooms when a Resource Room teacher goes to the school where the child is enrolled to provide special instruction. In response to these reports, on January 28th, 1993, the Ministry of Education issued "Ordinance on Partial Revision of the Regulations to Implement the School Education Law" (Ministry of Education Ordinance No.1), which systematized the Special Needs Service in Resource Rooms from the beginning of the next academic year (April 1, 1993). The Special Needs Support in Resource Rooms was deemed to be suitable for the education of students with speech/language disorders, emotional disturbances, low vision, students who are hard-of-hearing and students with other difficulties.

■ In October 2001, the "Research Group Conference on the Future Direction of Special Needs Education" was held, and a final report entitled "The Future Direction for Special Needs Education" was issued in March, 2003. This final report included a definition of both Attention Deficit Hyperactivity Disorder (ADHD)[1] and High Functioning Autism (HFA)[2], as well as a tentative proposal on how to recognize these conditions and techniques for teaching students who had them. It established standards for determining whether students who were having difficulties in regular classes had LD, ADHD or HFA, and procedures to provide appropriate support for them. In March 2003, the results of the Ministry of Education, Culture, Sports, Science and Technology's "National survey of pupils in regular schools having special educational needs" (2006, 2) were issued. These results indicated that around 6.3% of all students in regular classes have special educational needs because they had conditions such as LD, ADHD or HFA. In January 2004 the Ministry of Education, Culture, Sports, Science and Technology published a proposal entitled "Guidelines to Develop a Support System for Elementary and Middle School Pupils with LD, ADHD or HFA."

■このように種々の状況確認と条件整備がなされたため、「学校教育法施行規則の一部を改正する省令（平成18年文部科学省令第22号）」が、2006年3月31日に公布され翌日の4月1日に施行され、通級による指導の対象に、学習障害者と注意欠陥多動性障害者が加えられた。また、これまで情緒障害に含まれていた自閉症が、通級の対象として、別に明記された（表2-5）。

表2-5　通級による指導を受けている児童生徒数（2006）

言語障害		自閉症		情緒障害		弱視		難聴	
小	中	小	中	小	中	小	中	小	中
29,527	186	3,562	350	2,365	533	128	10	1,495	282
学習障害		注意欠陥多動性障害		肢体不自由		病弱・身体虚弱		総計	
小	中	小	中	小	中	小	中	小	中
1,195	156	1,471	160	5	1	16	6	39,764	1,684

出典：文部科学省初等中等教育局特別支援教育課「特別支援教育資料（平成18年度）」2007年
http://www.mext.go.jp/a_menu/shotou/tokubetu/material/013/001.pdf

（2）特別支援教育の目的・教育課程・指導の場

■障害児者に対する教育は、学校教育法の第8章「特別支援教育」に規定されている。特別支援学校の目的は、視覚障害者、聴覚障害者、知的障害者、肢体不自由者または病弱者（身体虚弱者を含む）に対して、幼稚園、小学校、中学校または高等学校に準ずる教育を施すとともに、障害による学習上又は生活上の困難を克服し自立を図るために、必要な知識技能を授けることとされている。つまり、特別支援教育は、対象児の障害による様々な教育的ニーズに対応しながら、その子の「自立」と「自己実現」を図るという教育の本

■ Since various situations had now been investigated and various conditions had been adjusted, the "Ordinance on Partial Revision of the Regulations to Implement the School Education Law" (Ministry of Education, Culture, Sports, Science and Technology, Ordinance number 22) was issued on March 31, 2006, and became effective on the following day. This ordinance included students with LD and ADHD among the type of students with disabilities for whom Special Needs Support in Resource Rooms is considered appropriate. It also made it specifically clear that students with autism, which had formerly been included in the category of emotional disturbances, could also be taught in the resource room (Table 2-5).

Table 2-5 Number of students using Special Support Service in Resource Rooms, 2006

Speech/Language Disorder		Autism		Emotional Disturbance		Visual Impairment		Hearing Impairment	
Elementary	Lower Secondary	Elementary	Lower Secondary	Elementary	Lower Secondary	Elementary	Lower Secondary	Elementary	Lower Secondary
29,527	186	3,562	350	2,365	533	128	10	1,495	282
Learning Disability		Attention Deficit Hyperactivity Disorder		Physical/ Motor Disability		Health Impairment		Total	
Elementary	Lower Secondary	Elementary	Lower Secondary	Elementary	Lower Secondary	Elementary	Lower Secondary	Elementary	Lower Secondary
1,195	156	1,471	160	5	1	16	6	39,764	1,684

Source: Ministry of Education, Culture, Sports, Science and Technology, Office of Primary and Secondary Education, Special Needs Division: "Special needs education materials for 2006 academic year", 2007
http://www.mext.go.jp/a_menu/shotou/tokubetu/material/013/001.pdf

(2) Special Needs Education: Aims, Curriculum and Placement

■ The education for children with disabilities is described in Chapter 8 "Special Needs Education" of the School Education Law. The aim of Special Needs schools is to provide education aligned with the education provided at regular kindergarten, elementary, middle and high schools for children with visual, auditory, intellectual or physical/motor disabilities, or children with health impairments. In addition, children in Special Needs School are to receive instruction to develop knowledge, skills, habits and attitudes, so that they can

質的目的の実現を図る営みであるといえる。この目的の実現のために、特別支援教育における教育内容の組織化は、通常の学校の「各教科」「道徳」「特別活動」「総合的な学習の時間」に、障害による学習上又は生活上の困難を主体的に改善・克服するために必要な知識，技能，態度及び習慣を養い、もって心身の調和的発達の基盤を培うことが目標の「自立活動」という独自の指導領域を加えた5領域で行われている。なお、知的障害教育においては、「通常の教科」以前の内容と以後の内容とを含む独自の教科設定がなされている。また、特別支援教育では、幼児児童生徒の障害の状態等に応じて弾力的な教育課程が編成できるようになっていることが特徴である。

■特別支援教育の提供の場は、大きくは特別支援学校と通常学校の2つである。特別支援学校においては、療養中の児童生徒のために、特別支援学級を病院や施設内に設けること（院内学級）や、教員を派遣して指導すること（訪問教育）が認められている。通常学校においては、児童生徒のニーズに応じて、特別な指導が、特別支援学級と「通級による指導」で行われるほか、通常学級においても、在籍する障害のある子どもの実態に応じて、指導内容や指導方法を工夫することとされている。また、通常学校における特別支援教育に関しては、2002年の学校教育法施行規則の一部改正により、特別支援学校での教育が適当なものであっても、市町村教育委員会が通常学校で適切な教育を受けられると判断した場合には、通常学校に就学させることができる「認定就学者」の規定が設けられた。さらに、2007年度からは小・中学校において障害のある児童生徒に対し、食事、排泄、教室の移動補助等学校におけ

fully develop their capabilities and cope with "difficulties in their school and home lives" caused by their disabilities. In other words, the objective of Special Needs Education is to fulfill what is considered to be the fundamental objective of education itself: to facilitate "independence", "social participation" and "self-realization" of each child by responding to their special educational needs. To meet this objective, the curriculum of Special Needs Education consists of five areas. Four of them are consistent with the curriculum in regular schools, which are "Academic Subjects", "Moral Education", "Special Activities" and "Period for Integrated Study". A fifth area, "Jiritsu-Katsudo", is added in the Special Needs Education curriculum (Fig. 2). "Jiritsu-Katsudo" provides each child with the particular knowledge, skills, attitude, behavior and practices they need to acquire in order to develop mentally and physically, so that they can cope with difficulties they face in school and everyday life. For children with intellectual disabilities, the specific content of subjects may cover basic materials that are usually learned by children before they study regular academic subjects to meet their needs. Also, the content may cover practical materials that are usually required for their daily and future lives. In Special Needs Education, the curriculum can be flexibly adapted to respond to each child's specific needs.

■ There are two main places where Special Needs Education is carried out: in Special Needs Schools and in regular schools. As for Special Needs Schools, special classes can be set up in hospitals or other institutions for children undergoing treatment, and teachers can also be sent out to teach these children. In regular schools, special instruction is carried out in Special Needs Classes and through "Special Needs Support in Resource Rooms", depending on what support a student needs. In addition, in regular classes the content and teaching methods are to be adapted and accommodated to meet their needs. Furthermore, regarding the Special Needs Education in regular schools, the 2002 revision of the regulations to implement the School Education Law stated that even if a child has a severe disability that meets the standards of enrollment in Special Needs School, if a local education committee decides that suitable education can

る日常生活動作の介助を行ったり、発達障害の児童生徒に対し学習活動上のサポートを行ったりする「特別支援教育支援員」の活用を進めるための国による地方財政措置も始められるようになった。特別支援教育提供の場としての通常学校の役割は大きなものとなっている（図2-8）。特別支援学校と通常学校の指導の場のうち、特別な指導の場について若干の説明を加えることにする。

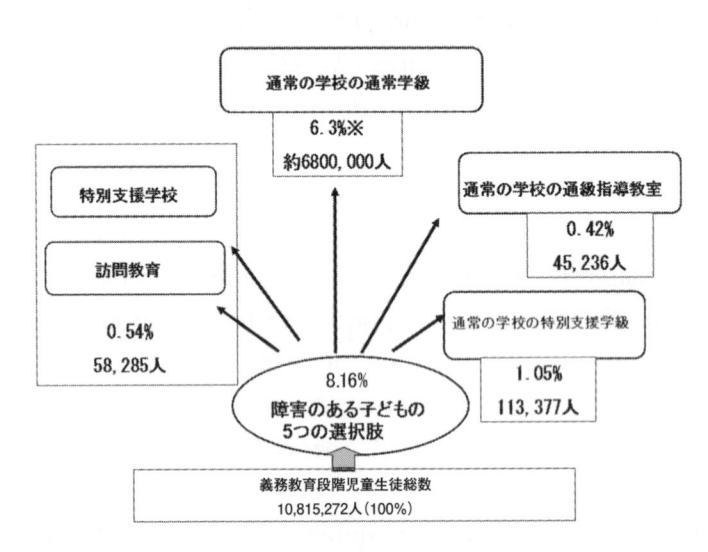

図2-8　障害のある子どもの教育の場・5つの選択肢とその人数

註：※印は「通常の学級に在籍する特別な教育的支援を必要とする児童生徒の全国実態調査」の結果による。
出典：文部科学省特別支援教育課（2008）http://www.mext.go.jp/a_menu/shotou/tokubetu/material/020/001.htm 及び中田（2007）をもとに筆者が作成。

■①**特別支援学校**：特別支援学校は、5つの特別支援教育領域（視覚障害者、聴覚障害者、知的障害者、肢体不自由者、病弱者）の障害の一つ、または二つ以上をあわせもつ児童生徒の教育をになう学校とされている。特別支援学校には、通常の幼・小・中・高のそれぞれの学校教育に対応する学部として、幼稚部・小学部・中学部・高等部が置かれる。特別な場合には、幼・小・中・

be provided in a regular school, then that child can attend regular school as an "Approved Entrant." Moreover, since 2007, the Japanese government has begun to provide funds for the local government to employ "Special Needs Education Support Staff", whose role is to support students with disabilities at elementary and middle schools by providing assistance in day-to-day situations, such as eating lunch, using the toilet facilities and moving between classrooms. Regular schools now have an unprecedented role as a place to provide Special Needs Education (Figure 2-8). Following is a brief explanation of places where special instructions are provided.

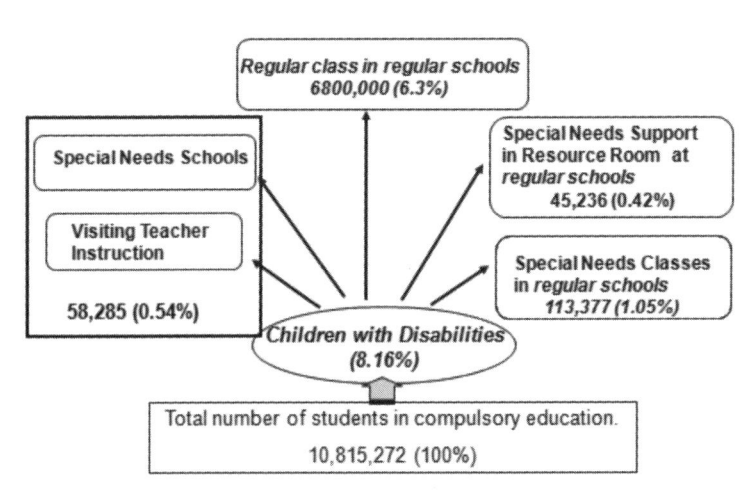

```
                    ┌──────────────────────────┐
                    │ Regular class in regular schools │
                    │      6800,000 (6.3%)      │
                    └──────────────────────────┘
                                 ↑
┌──────────────────────┐                    ┌──────────────────────┐
│ Special Needs Schools │                    │ Special Needs Support │
│                      │                    │ in Resource Room at   │
├──────────────────────┤                    │ regular schools       │
│ Visiting Teacher     │                    │    45,236 (0.42%)     │
│ Instruction          │                    └──────────────────────┘
│                      │                    ┌──────────────────────┐
│  58,285 (0.54%)      │                    │ Special Needs Classes │
└──────────────────────┘                    │ in regular schools    │
                                            │   113,377 (1.05%)     │
                                            └──────────────────────┘
                    ┌──────────────────────────┐
                    │  Children with Disabilities │
                    │        (8.16%)            │
                    └──────────────────────────┘
                                 ↓
                    ┌──────────────────────────────────────────┐
                    │ Total number of students in compulsory education. │
                    │            10,815,272 (100%)              │
                    └──────────────────────────────────────────┘
```

Figure 2-8 Where special needs education takes place – five scenarios, with the numbers of pupils currently involved in each

Source: Based on material from the Ministry of Education, Culture, Sports, Science and Technology, Office of Primary and Secondary Education, Special Needs Section (2008)
http://www.mext.go.jp/a_menu/shotou/tokubetu/material/020/001.htm and Nakata (2007)

■① Special Needs Schools

Special Needs Schools are schools for children who have one or more of the following five disabilities: visual, auditory, intellectual, or physical/motor disabilities, or health impairments. A Special Needs School consists of four divisions, i.e. kindergarten, primary, middle school and high school divisions,

高のうち一つの学部のみの特別支援学校も認められている（表2-6）。

表 2-6　特別支援学校在学者数及び教職員数（2007）

学校数	幼児児童生徒数					教職員数（本務者）		
	計	幼稚部	小学部	中学部	高等部	教員数	幼児児童生徒数/教員数	職員数
1,013	108,173	1,653	33,411	24,874	48,235	66,807	1.62	15,357

出典：文部科学省初等中等教育局特別支援教育課「特別支援教育資料（平成19年度）」2008年
http://www.mext.go.jp/a_menu/shotou/tokubetu/material/020/001.htm をもとに作成

■特別支援学校の制度化は、児童生徒の障害の重複化への適切な対応のための制度の弾力化であり、各特別支援学校が、どの教育領域に対応し、どのような学部を置く学校となるかは、地域の実情等にあわせて、設置者（多くは都道府県）により判断される。また、特別支援学校は、その在籍児童生徒の教育指導に加えて、小中学校等に在籍する障害児童生徒等の教育について助言援助に努めなければならないことが、学校教育法に明文化された。特別支援学校は、これまで以上に、その教育上の高い専門性を生かしながら、地域の特別支援教育の中核的な役割を担っていくことが期待されている。特別支援学校が担うべき地域の特別支援教育センターとしての具体的役割としては、ⅰ) 小・中学校等の教員への支援機能、ⅱ) 特別支援教育等に関する相談・情報提供機能、ⅲ) 障害のある幼児児童生徒への指導・支援機能、ⅳ) 福祉、医療、労働などの関係機関等との連絡・調整機能、ⅴ) 小・中学校等の教員に対する研修協力機能、ⅵ) 障害のある幼児児童生徒への施設設備等の提供機能、といったものがあげられている（中央教育審議会，2005）。

corresponding to schools in the regular education system. However, in special cases, a Special Needs School can establish only one division of kindergarten, elementary, middle school and high school divisions (Table 2-6).

Table 2-6 Number of students and teachers in Special Needs Schools (2007)

No of Schools	No of enrolled children					No of Teacher and Staff		
	Total	Kindergarten Section	Primary Section	Middle School Section	High School Section	No of Teachers	No of Enrolled Children/No of Teacher	No of Staff
1,013	108,173	1,653	33,411	24,874	48,235	66,807	1.62	15,357

Source:Ministry of Education, Culture, Sports, Science and Technology, Office of Primary and Secondary Education, Special Needs Division:
"Special needs education materials for 2007 academic year", 2008
http://www.mext.go.jp/a_menu/shotou/tokubetu/material/020/001.htm

■ The new system of Special Needs Education is given flexibility within the system to accommodate the increased number of children with multiple disabilities. Thus, the founding bodies (in most cases educational authorities in each prefecture) are to decide, depending on the circumstances in the areas where the schools are established, which types of education are needed and which departments should be placed in each Special Needs School. The partially amended School Education Law also states clearly that Special Needs Schools must play a role not only in providing education for students enrolled in them, but also in giving advice and supporting teachers and students in regular schools where students with disabilities attend. Special Needs Schools are expected to use their expertise to become the center of the community's Special Needs Education. The specific roles of the Special Needs School as a center for Special Needs Education should involve the following functions: i) To provide support for regular school teachers, ii) to give consultation and provide information about Special Needs Education, iii) to provide instruction and support for children of all ages who have disabilities, iv) to communicate and make arrangements with welfare service, medical, labor and other related institutions, v) to cooperate in training and fostering expertise in regular school teachers, vi) to provide facilities

■②**訪問教育**：訪問教育は、障害が重度または重複しているため、学校への通学（寄宿舎を含む）が困難で、日常生活において常時介護や医療を必要とし、学校生活が困難な児童・生徒を対象に、病院や施設に学級を開設したり、病院・施設や自宅等に特別支援学校の教員が訪問したりして、必要な指導を行う指導形態。週3回程度、1回2時間程度の指導が行われている。

■③**特別支援学級**：学校教育法の改正で、「小学校、中学校、高等学校、中等教育学校及び幼稚園においては、次項各号のいずれかに該当する児童、生徒及び幼児その他教育上特別の支援を必要とする児童、生徒及び幼児に対し、文部科学大臣の定めるところにより、障害による学習上又は生活上の困難を克服するための教育を行うものとする。」という文言が加えられ、通常学校における特別支援教育が義務づけられた。しかしながら、規定では、特別支援学級は、各学校に「置くことができる」学級であり、置かなければならないものではない。対象は、知的障害者、肢体不自由者、身体虚弱者、弱視者、難聴者、その他障害のあるもので特別支援学級において教育を行うことが適当なものとされている。

■④**通級による指導**：通級による指導は、小・中学校の通常学級に在籍している軽度の障害のある児童生徒が、ほとんどの授業を通常の学級で受けながら、障害の状態等に応じた特別の指導を特別な場（通級指導教室）で受ける指導形態である。通級の対象は、言語障害者、自閉症者、情緒障害者、学習障害者、注意欠陥多動性障害者、弱視者、難聴者、その他、とされている。

　なお、「通常の学級での学習におおむね参加でき、一部特別な指導を必要とする程度のもの」が通級による指導の対象であるので、全般的に発達の遅れのある知的障害者は、その制度化以来、対象外とされている。

for children of all ages who have disabilities.

■② Visiting Teacher Instruction

Some children have severe disabilities or multiple disabilities that require constant care or medical treatment in their daily lives, which could result in having difficulties to attend schools. For such students, classes can be held in a hospital or other institution, or a teacher from Special Needs School can visit either the student's house or the institution where they are receiving treatment to give them instruction. Usually Visiting Teacher Instruction consists of three visits per week, with each visit lasting about two hours.

■③ Special Needs Classes

The partially amended School Education Law states that all regular schools must provide students of all ages who require special educational support with "the education they need in order to cope with the difficulties they face in school and in daily lives that result from having disabilities", and all regular schools are bound by law to provide Special Needs Education. However, the law stipulates that this Special Needs Class is a class that schools are "able to place", which means that regular schools are not necessarily required to establish Special Needs Classes. Such classes are intended for students with intellectual disabilities, physical/motor disabilities, health impairments, low vision, children who are hard-of-hearing or students with other disabilities for whom education in Special Needs Class is considered appropriate.

■④ Special Needs Support in Resource Rooms (Tsu-kyu Class)

The students with mild disabilities enrolled in regular class are educated in a regular class for almost the entire day, but also given special instructions relevant to their disabilities in a separate classroom (referred to herein as a "Resource Room"). Students with speech/language disorders, autism, emotional disturbances, LD, and ADHD should be given support in a Resource Room.

Since Special Needs Support in Resource Rooms aims to support students who have special needs, but are able to participate mostly in regular class activities,

(3) 特別支援教育における卒業生の進路状況

■ 2007年3月の特別支援学校（盲・聾・養護学校）及び特別支援学級（特殊学級）卒業生の進路状況を表2-7に示す。中学部・中学校卒業生の90%以上は後期中等教育に進学している。特別支援学校高等部の卒業生では、施設・医療機関への入所・入院が56.1%と最も多く、ついで就職の約22.7%となっている。特別支援学校の教員は、福祉・医療・労働の各機関と連携し、卒業生の移行を確実に支援していくことが求められている。

students with intellectual disabilities, who have significant limitations both in intellectual functioning and in adaptive behavior, do not receive support in these Resource Rooms. This implies that students with intellectual disabilities are mostly educated in Special Needs Class instead of regular classes.

(3) Places for Graduates from Special Needs Education

■ The places that students from Special Needs Schools (Schools for the Deaf, Schools for the Blind, and Schools for the Children with Intellectual Disabilities, Physical/Motor Disabilities, and Health Impairments) and Special Needs Classes have gone after graduation are shown in Table 2-7. The figures show that 90% of graduates from middle school sections of Special Needs Schools and regular middle schools go on to further education. Most graduates (56.1%) from high school sections of Special Needs Schools go into hospitals, care homes or other such institutions, and about 22.7% are employed. Staff members at Special Needs Schools are expected to keep in close contact with welfare and medical services, and employers, and to do their utmost to support graduates as they make the transition from school.

表 2-7　特別支援学校・特別支援学級の卒業生の進路状況（2006）

中学部（中学校特殊学級）卒業者の進路状況

区分	卒業者	進学者	教育訓練機関等	就職者	施設・医療機関	その他
盲・聾・養護学校計（人）	7,333	7,093	40	6	107	87
％		96.7	0.5	0.1	1.5	1.2
中学校特殊学級計（人）	10,136	9,155	322	195	464	
％		90.3	3.2	1.9	4.6	

高等部卒業者の進路状況

区分	卒業者	進学者（人）	教育訓練機関等	就職者	施設・医療機関	その他
盲・聾・養護学校計（人）	13,853	542	532	3,148	7,769	1,862
％		3.9	3.8	22.7	56.1	13.4

出典：http://www.mext.go.jp/a_menu/shotou/tokubetu/013.htm

（注）
1　注意欠陥多動性障害（ADHD）とは、年齢あるいは発達に不釣り合いな注意力、及び／又は衝動性、多動性を特徴とする行動の障害で、社会的な活動や学業の機能に支障をきたすものである。また、7歳以前に現れ、その状態が継続し、中枢神経系に何らかの要因による機能不全があると推定される。
2　高機能自閉症とは、3歳位までに現れ、①他人との社会的関係の形成の困難さ、②言葉の発達の遅れ、③興味や関心が狭く特定のものにこだわることを特徴とする行動の障害である自閉症のうち、知的発達の遅れを伴わないものをいう。また、中枢神経系に何らかの要因による機能不全があると推定される。

Table 2-7 Places for Graduates from the School and the Class for Special Need Children, 2006

Career Students of Graduates from Middle School Section (Middle Section Class)						
Item	Graduates	Higher School Entrants	Education Training Institution, etc.	Employees	Facility, Hospital	Others
Total of Schools for Blind, Deaf, Intellectual and Physical Disability	7,333	7,093	40	6	107	87
%		96.7	0.5	0.1	1.5	1.2
Special Class at Middle School	10,136	9,155	322	195	464	
%		90.3	3.2	1.9	4.6	

Career Situation of Graduates from Higher School Section						
Item	Graduates	Higher School Entrants	Education Training Institution, etc.	Employees	Facility, Hospital	Others
Total of Schools for Blind, Deaf, Intellectual and Physical Disability)	13,853	542	532	3,148	7,769	1,862
%		3.9	3.8	22.7	56.1	13.4

Resource: http://www.mext.go.jp/a_menu/shotou/tokubetu/013.htm

(Endnotes)

1 Attention Deficit Hyperactivity Disorder (ADHD) is mainly distinguished by condition where child's attention span is not consistent with their chronological age or development, and/or they exhibit signs of impulsive behavior or an inability to settle down. This feature makes it hard for children to study or to actively participate in society. This disorder usually appears before the age of seven. It is supposed that it is caused by dysfunction of the central nervous system.

2 High functioning autism (HFA) usually appears before the age of three. This is one of the autistic spectrum disorders and its distinctions are: ① Difficulties in forming relationships with others, ② delays in language development, and ③ significant, highly-focused restriction of interests and activities. However, intellectual development is not impaired. It is supposed that it is caused by dysfunction of the central nervous system.

【引用・参考文献】

中央教育審議会『特別支援教育を推進するための制度の在り方について（答申）』, 2005.

中央教育審議会初等中等教育分科会教職員給与の在り方に関するワーキンググループ『（第16回）議事録・配付資料　答申案』, 2007.

(http://www.mext.go.jp/b_menu/shingi/chukyo/chukyo3/siryo/031/07022717.htm)

学習障害及びこれに類似する学習上の困難を有する児童生徒の指導方法に関する調査研究協力者会議『学習障害児に対する指導について（報告）』, 1999.

文部科学省『小・中学校におけるLD（学習障害）ADHD（注意欠陥／多動性障害）高機能自閉症の児童生徒への教育支援体制の整備のためのガイドライン（試案）』, 東洋館出版社, 2004.

文部科学省『平成19年度特別支援教育体制整備状況調査結果について』, 2008.

(http://www.mext.go.jp/b_menu/houdou/20/03/08032605.htm)

文部科学省初等中等教育局特別支援課『平成18年度特別支援教育資料』, 2007.

文部科学省初等中等教育局特別支援課『平成18年度特別支援教育資料』, 2008.

中田英雄『JICA南米地域障害児教育研修配布資料』, 2007.

21世紀の特殊教育の在り方に関する調査研究協力者会議『21世紀の特殊教育の在り方について（最終報告）』, 2001.

特別支援教育の在り方に関する調査研究協力者会議『今後の特別支援教育の在り方について（最終報告）』, 2003.

特殊教育に関する研究調査会『軽度心身障害児に対する学校教育の在り方(報告)』, 1978.

通級学級に関する調査研究協力者会議『通級による指導に関する充実方策について（審議のまとめ）』, 1992.

II. The Outline of Educational System

References:
Central Council for Education: "A system to promote special needs education (report), 2005.
Committee to research regular class special needs teaching: "Ways to enhance special needs teaching in regular classes (summary of deliberations)," 1992
Committee to research special education in the 21st century: "Special education in the 21st century (final report)," 2001
Committee to research the state of special needs education: "The Future Direction for Special Needs Education (final report)," 2003
Ministry of Education, Culture, Sports, Science and Technology: "Guidelines for setting up a support system for elementary and middle school pupils with learning difficulties (LD), ADHD or high functioning autism (provisional plan)." Toyokan Publishing, 2004
Ministry of Education, Culture, Sports, Science and Technology Office of Primary and Secondary Education, Special Needs Division: "Special needs education materials for 2006 academic year", 2007
Ministry of Education, Culture, Sports, Science and Technology Office of Primary and Secondary Education, Special Needs Division: "Special needs education materials for 2007 academic year", 2008
Ministry of Education, Culture, Sports, Science and Technology: "Report on the results of a survey on mainstream schools' preparedness for special needs education," 2008
(http://www.mext.go.jp/b_menu/houdou/20/03/08032605.htm)
Nakata, Hideo "Handouts for JICA South American area special needs education study session," 2007
Research group Conference to specifically study how to teach children with LD and similar disabilities: "Teaching children with learning difficulties (report)," 1999
Special education research group: "The school education of children with less severe physical or mental disabilities (report)," 1978

126　第Ⅱ章　教育の概要

Working Group of the Central Council for Education looking into the pay structure of teachers in primary and secondary education "Draft report on the 16th meeting with distributed materials" 2007
(http://www.mext.go.jp/b_menu/shingi/chukyo/chukyo3/siryo/031/07022717.htm)

4. 社会教育制度

(1) 社会教育の定義と範囲

■わが国における「社会教育」は、諸外国では成人教育、学校以外の青少年教育、あるいはコミュニティ教育など、一般的にはノンフォーマル教育とされる活動を指している。教育基本法第12条では、「社会教育」を「個人の要望や社会の要請にこたえ、社会において行われる教育」と定めており、さらに「社会教育」は国及び地方公共団体によって奨励されなければならないとされている。また、社会教育法第2条では、「この法律で『社会教育』とは、学校教育法に基づき、学校の教育課程として行われる教育活動を除き、主として青少年及び成人に対して行われる組織的教育活動（体育及びレクリエーションの活動を含む）をいう」と定義されている。この第2条の定義はノンフォーマル教育の定義とほぼ同一である。しかし、社会教育法は「社会教育に関する国および地方公共団体の任務を明らかにすることを目的」としており、この法律に規定されている社会教育は「狭義の社会教育」と考えられ、ノンフォーマル教育のなかでも、教育を主たる目的とした活動で、国や地方公共団体からの公共的支援を受けているのが特徴である。

■他方、すべての社会教育活動が社会教育行政の対象となるわけではないとも考えられている。1971年の社会教育審議会答申「急激な社会構造の変化に対処する社会教育のあり方について」では、「今後の社会教育は変化の激しい社会における社会教育への期待にこたえるため、国民の生活のあらゆる機会と場所において行なわれる各種の学習を教育的に高める活動を総称するものとして広くとらえる必要がある」としたうえで、「社会教育行政とは国と地方公共団体が社会教育を促進・援助するものである」とし、社会教育と社会教育行政とは密接に関連するが同一の概念ではないことが確認された。すなわち、社会教育における国と地方公共団体の役割は国民の社会教育活動

4. Social Education System

(1) The Definition and Scope of Social Education

■ Japanese "social education" is generally referred in foreign countries as non-formal education activities, such as education for adults, education of outside of school for young people, and community education. In Article 12 of the Fundamental Education Law, social education is defined as "the education conducted in society to meet demand from individuals and society", and "social education" should be promoted by the government and local public agencies. Moreover, in Article 2 of the Social Education Law, it is defined as "organized educational activity mainly for young people and adults outside the usual educational activities as prescribed by the school curriculum (includes athletic and recreational activities)". This definition in Article 2 is same with that of non-formal education. But the ofjective of the Social Education Law is to clarify the mission of national government and local public agencies for social education. The social education defined in the Social Education Law is considered as narrowly-defined social education, and characterized as an activity of which main objective is education and it receives public assistance by the national government and local public agencies.

■ On the other hand, it is regarded that not all social education activities are the objectives of social education administration. The report of the Social Education Council in 1971 "How social education should respond to the radical change of social structure" provides that "In order to respond to the expectation for social education in a greatly changing society, social education in the future must be regarded as a wide activity that improves all kinds of learning in the citizens' life" and says that "social education administration means that the nation and the local government promote and help social education". It is said that although social education and social education administration are closely related, they are

を援助・促進するものであり、その一部を担当するに過ぎず、社会教育行政の対象とはならない社会教育活動が幅広く存在することになる。

■したがって、教育の範疇には収まらないが社会教育と類似した活動も多く存在する。たとえば、社会教育と社会福祉とはその境界が明確ではない。児童が図書館で絵本を借りる場合と児童館備え付けの絵本を借りる場合、児童の行為としては同じであるが、前者は社会教育施設の利用であり、後者は福祉施設の利用となる。また公民館の老人講座に出席する場合は社会教育活動への参加であるが、老人福祉センターの主催する講習会の出席はそうではない。公民館で行われる健康講座と保健所主催の健康セミナーとの関係も同様である。また、労働省所管の高等技能専門校は、学校ではなく社会教育施設でもないが、重要な職業教育機関である。さらに、ピアノや書道、茶道などのおけいこごとや、新聞社やデパートなどの運営するカルチャー・センターなどの民間社会教育関連事業や、企業内教育など、民間セクターが組織する教育活動もある。このような教育活動を含めて社会教育を考えるのが「広義の社会教育」である。日本の社会教育の定義と範囲は、文部科学省と都道府県・市町村の教育委員会が管轄する、学校教育外の教育活動という「狭義の社会教育」と、学校教育以外の国民のあらゆる学習活動を含めて社会教育を考える「広義の社会教育」という2つの考え方が存在する。

■2006年に制定された新しい教育基本法の第3条では、「国民一人一人が、自己の人格を磨き、豊かな人生を送ることができるよう、その生涯にわたって、あらゆる機会に、あらゆる場所において学習することができ、その成果

not the same concept. Namely, in social education, national and local governments support and promote social education activities and play a limited role concerning these activities. There are a lot of activities which are outside the responsibility of the social education administration.

■ Therefore, there are many activities resembling social education activities but are not in the category of education. For example, the difference between social education and social welfare is not clear. A child's action is the same, when he borrows a picture book from a library, or from a children's community hall. The former is making use of a social education institution while the latter, a welfare institution. When a person attends a lecture for the aged in a public hall, he takes part in a social education activity. When he attends a lecture in a welfare center for the aged, his activity is not considered as a social education activity. The relationship between a health lecture in a public hall and health seminar organized by public health center is the same. Vocational training institutions of the Ministry of Health, Labour and Welfare is neither a school nor a social education institution, but it has an important role for vocational training. Moreover, there are education activities organized by public sectors which are enrichment lessons like piano, calligraphy, and tea ceremony; private social education business by newspaper companies and department stores; workers' training in companies. The social education including such education activities is "broad social education". There are two ways of thinking regarding the definition and range of social education in Japan. One is "narrowly-defined social education" which is the educational activities excluding school education controlled by the Ministry of Education, Culture, Sports, Science and Technology, and the metropolitan, prefectural and municipal board of education. The other is "broad social education" which includes all the educational activities of the citizens except school education.

■ In Article 3 of the Basic Act on Education which was newly regulated in 2006 "principle of lifelong learning" is shown which says "We must realize a society that individual citizens can learn any time and anywhere in their entire life, and

を適切に生かすことのできる社会の実現が図られなければならない」という「生涯学習の理念」が示されている。生涯学習社会において、社会教育は中心的役割を果たすものであり、狭義の社会教育にとどまらず、文教行政以外の行政機関や関係団体主催の教育活動、民間企業や市民団体が行う学習活動、そして家庭教育や個人学習などのインフォーマルな学習などのさまざまな学習活動を相互に関連させ、コミュニティを基盤として機能的に統合した学習機会のシステムの構築が課題とされてきている。また、ボランティア活動のような社会活動のなかで、学習成果をいかに活用していくかも課題とされている。さらに、社会教育と学校教育との相互関係に関しては、社会教育と学校教育とがその機能をお互いに補い合う学社連携、これをさらに発展させ、社会教育と学校教育とがその活動の一部を共有し、部分的に一体化する学社融合が取り組まれている。

（2）社会教育活動と社会教育施設

■以上のように、社会教育を幅広くとらえるならば、社会教育活動はさまざまな場所で多様な形態で実施されるものであるが、中心的な社会教育の場は、やはり狭義の社会教育である文教行政所管の社会教育施設と社会教育活動であり、主として以下のものがある。

①公民館

　原則として市町村が設置し、一定の地域の住民のために、実際生活に即する教育、学術及び文化に関する各種の事業を行い、住民の教養の向上、健康の増進、情操の純化を図り、生活文化の進行、社会福祉の増進に寄与することを目的としている施設である。この目的を達成するために、青年学級の実施、定期講座の開設、討論会・講習会・講演会等の実施、図書・資料等の利用、体育・レクリエーション等に関する集会の開催、各種団体・機関等の連絡、住民への施設の開放などの事業を行う。（社会教育法第20条）

make use of their achievement properly to be able to improve his/her personality and enjoy rich lives." Social Education plays a key role in a life-long learning society. So the issue is to establish a functionally integrated learning system by making community as a base by connecting not only the narrowly-defined social education, but also informal learning activities such as educational activities under administration other than educational administration and organizations concerned, learning activities of private companies and citizens' groups, family education and individual studies. How to make use of learning outcome in social activities such as volunteer activities is also an issue. Moreover, with regard to mutual relationship between social education and school education, followings are addressed: school-community collaboration in which social education and school education supplement their function each other; and school-community fusion in which school-community collaboration is enhanced more and a part of their activities of social education and school education are shared and partially integrated.

(2) Activities and Institutions of Social Education

■ As stated above, when the range of social education is considered so wide, it can be found at anytime, anywhere and in any style. Main social education activities, however, are social education facilities and social education activities which are narrowly-defined social education organized by the Ministry of Education, Culture, Sports, Science and Technology, and municipal education boards in the following locations:

① Citizen's Public Hall

The hall is usually established by city, town or village, and provides many projects concerning education for practical life, learning, and culture. By doing this, it tries to improve the culture and health of its residents, to nurture their aesthetics, to promote life culture, and to contribute for the promotion of social welfare. In order to achieve these purposes, the following activities are done: operating youth class, regular lectures, debate, course and lecture meeting, use

②図書館

　社会教育施設としての図書館については、図書館法にその設置運営に関する事項が定められている。図書館には、地方公共団体の設置する公立図書館と特定の法人が設立した私立図書館があり、私立図書館に対しては都道府県の教育委員会は必要な援助を行うが、その活動に対しての干渉や補助金の交付は行わないこととされている。図書館は、図書や資料の収集、整理、閲覧、貸出などの公開を行うばかりでなく、読書会、研究会、鑑賞会などを主催する。（図書館法）

③博物館

　博物館とは、図書館以外で、資料の収集・保管・展示をし、調査・研究を行い、それらを公開する施設を指し、美術館、動物園、植物園、水族館等も博物館に含まれる。博物館法にはその設置運営に関する事項が定めれられ、国公立博物館と私立博物館がある。（博物館法）

④青年の家

　団体宿泊訓練を通じて健全な青年の育成を図るための宿泊型のものと、日常生活圏で学習・スポーツ・文化活動を行い、仲間との交流を深めることを目的とする非宿泊型のものがある。それは国立（すべて宿泊型）と公立のものに分かれる。そのほか、中心的施設として国立オリンピック記念青少年総合センターがある。

⑤少年自然の家

　少年を自然に親しませ、団体宿泊訓練を通じて健全な少年の育成を図るための機関であり、国立と公立のものがある。

⑥児童文化センター

　都道府県あるいは市町村が設置する機関で、少年が文化財に接し、文化・科学に関する学習の機会を提供するものである。

⑦女性教育施設

　女性の特性を配慮した成人を対象とする施設を指し、女性教育活動の拠点となることを目的としている。

⑧社会体育施設

　社会体育施設としては、国や地方公共団体が設置している公共スポーツ施

of books and materials, sports and recreation meetings as well as contacting with other organizations, and leaving the institutes open to residents, etc. The citizen's public hall is the most general institution concerning social education. (Article 20 of the Social Education Law)

② Library

The establishment and management of the library as a social education institution is prescribed in the Library Law. Among the libraries, there are public libraries established by local governments and private libraries established by specified corporations. The prefectural board of education gives the latter the necessary help, but does not interfere in its activities or give subsidies. The library does not only lend out books and materials, but also organizes meetings for reading, studying and appreciation, etc. (Library Act)

③ Museum

Museum means the institute which collects, keeps and exhibits materials, as well as investigates and studies them, and open them to the public. It also includes galleries, zoos, botanical gardens, and aquariums, etc. The Museum Law prescribes for its establishment and management. There are public and private museums. (Museum Act)

④ House for Youth

There are two kinds of houses for youth. One is the lodging type which tries to cultivate healthy youth throughout the duration of the group stay. The other is the non-lodging type which aims at promoting friendship by doing studies, sports and cultural activities together. There are national houses (all lodging type) and public ones established by prefectures and municipalities. The National General Center of Youth, in commemoration of the 1964 Tokyo Olympic, is the leading institution of youth education.

⑤ Children's Nature House

The aim of these facilities is to make children appreciate and enjoy nature and bring up sound-minded children throughout the training of the group stay. There are both national and public houses.

設、会社等が従業員の福利厚生のために設置している職場スポーツ施設、民間の非営利団体の設置する施設、商業スポーツ施設がある。
⑨視聴覚センター
　学校や他の社会教育施設が単独では保有できない、視聴覚資料、教材、教具を集中的に管理し、学校と社会教育施設の共同利用に供する施設である。パソコンの研修講座等も行っている。
⑩学校開放
　学校の施設を社会教育活動のために開放するとともに、学校が主体となって社会教育講座を開設する。
⑪社会通信教育
　学校教育以外の通信教育であり、文部省に認定を受けたものについては郵便料金の軽減や、優秀者に対する文部大臣表彰などの奨励策がとられている。
⑫社会教育関係団体
　「法人であると否とを問わず、公の支配に属しない団体で社会教育に関する事業を行うことを主たる目的とするもの」(社会教育法(第10条))。代表的なものとして、PTA、子ども会、ボーイスカウト、ガールスカウト、体育協会などがある。

⑥ Cultural Center for Children

This is an organization established by prefectures, or cities, towns and villages, and gives children opportunities to appreciate culture and science observing cultural assets.

⑦ Educational Institution for Women

This is an institute only for women, and its aim is to play a role as a satellite center of activities to educate women.

⑧ Social Physical Institution

Among the physical institutions, there are national and public sport institutions, sport institutions established by companies for the recreation of those employees, institutions by private non- profit organizations, and sport institutions for business.

⑨ Audio-visual Center

This is the institute that intensively manages audio-visual materials and teaching aids which schools and social education institutes cannot keep by themselves. It is commonly used by schools and social education institutes. This institute facilitate training course for a personal computer also.

⑩ Opening Schools for the Community

This means opening schools for the social education activities and the schools provide educational lectures for the public.

⑪ Social Correspondence Education

This is a correspondence education outside of school education. As for the one which is authorized by the Ministry of Education, Culture, Sports, Science and Technology, postage fees are reduced, and the Minister of Education gives awards to excellent learners.

⑫ Social Educational Organization

This is defined as "Whether the organization is corporate body or not, who are not under the control of public authority and whose main purpose is to engage in the activities related to social education." (Article 10 of the Social Education Law). PTA, children's association, Boy Scouts, Girl Scouts, athletic association are the

（3）社会教育関係職員

■社会教育活動の範囲が多岐にわたるように、社会教育に関係する職員にもさまざまな種類があり、教育指導に直接従事する職員のほかに、管理系の職員、事務系の職員も含まれる。社会教育行政職員や、社会教育施設の職員には、①教育委員会や施設等で社会教育を行うものに専門的技術的な助言と指導を与える社会教育主事（社会教育主事補）、②公民館、図書館、博物館などの社会教育施設の各館長、③公民館の事業の実施にあたる公民館主事、④図書館の専門的事務に従事する図書館の司書（司書補）、⑤博物館資料の収集、保管、展示及び調査研究、その他これと関連する事業についての専門的事項をつかさどる学芸員（学芸員補）、などがある。またこのほかに、青年学級主事、青年学級講師や青少年教育施設、社会体育施設、婦人教育施設の専門の職員がいる。さらに、社会教育指導員、社会体育指導員、社会教育委員などの非常勤の職もある。

■このほか、学校以外の教育という点に着目すれば、高等技能専門校（職業訓練校）の教員や農業改良普及員、民間のカルチャーセンターやスポーツ・クラブの講師や指導員、職員も社会教育に関連する職務に従事していると考えられる。

■これらの職員のうち、公的な資格制度が確立しているのは社会教育主事（補）、司書（補）、学芸員（補）に限られる。それぞれ大学で必要な科目の単位を取得することにより、あるいは講習の受講や認定試験の合格によってその資格を取得することができる。ただし、これらの資格は学校の教員資格と異なり、公務員等として採用されその職について初めて有効となる任用資格であるととともに、経験年数と講習の受講によって、これに関連した職務やこれに準ずる職務に従事している者が、これらの資格を取得することは比較

example of social educational organizations.

(3) Social Education Staff

■ Because social education includes a variety of activities, there are various types of social education staffs. It includes not only teaching staff but also administrative and clerical staff. Social education staffs are: ① supervisor for social education (assistant supervisor for social education) who gives professional and technical advice and guidance to social education workers, and learners; ② director of social education institutions such as citizens' public hall, library, museum, etc.; ③ supervisor of citizens' public halls who implements activities; ④ librarian (assistant librarian) who engages in professional work of library; and ⑤ organizational staff of museum (assistant technical staff of museum) who engages in the research collection, custody and display of documents, and other professional duties related with the activities of the museum. Moreover, there are supervisors and lecturers of youth class, and technical staffs of youth education institutions, social physical institutions, and educational institutions for women. We also have instructors of social education and social physical education, and the members of social education committees who work as part-time staff.

■ Furthermore, teachers in vocational training institutions or agricultural extension workers, who are engaged in educational activities outside school, as defined in the Fundamental Education Law, are also considered social education staff. Lecturers of 'culture centers' and trainers in sports clubs are social education staff, too.

■ Among the social education staff mentioned above, only the supervisor for social education (assistant supervisor for social education), librarian (assistant librarian), and organizational staff of museum (assistant technical staff of museum) have an official qualification. Each qualification is recognized by taking the course in university or college, participating in training programs, or passing the examination. Different from the school teacher's certificate, however, these qualifications become in effect when they are employed as public servants

的容易である。社会教育関係職員は、資格を必要とする職が限られていること、その資格もそれに準じる職に従事することによって取得が可能であること、職務自体が一般事務職と重複する部分が多いことなどに示されるように、社会教育関係職員の教育専門職としての地位が確立されているとは言いがたい。この背景には、社会教育活動が多岐にわたるため、それぞれの活動についての指導者の資格制度を整備することが困難なこと、そして社会教育活動の主体は学習者であって指導者及び職員は学習者に指導助言を行うものであるとする社会教育の特性があるといえよう。

(4) 職業生活と社会教育

■従来、日本の企業の雇用形態の特徴は、終身雇用制と年功序列制であるといわれてきた。定年まで一つの企業に勤務し、学歴と勤続年数に応じて昇進・昇給することにより、従業員の会社への帰属意識が強固になり、労使関係が安定するという利点があった。しかしながら、1990年代半ば以降の長期にわたる日本経済の不振により、多くの企業で中高年層の高い給与コストの負担を軽減し、管理職ポストを削減することを余儀なくされている。その結果、終身雇用と年功序列の原則は崩壊し、中高年層の出向、勧奨退職、多角経営化に応じた配置転換などが広く実施されてきている。

■従来は会社内部での集合研修や職種別の研修が一般的であったが、従業員自身による自己の能力の啓発を促す方法が企業内教育・研修に求められている。例えば、小集団を組織して、日常的な業務に関する創意工夫を討議し提案していくQCサークルなどは、従業員の自発性を喚起するばかりでなく、経費節減・合理化にも役立つとされる。他方、企業からの派遣により、大学や大学院において最新の技術や知識を学習し、さらに高い学歴を取得する機

in either a city, town or village. In contrast, officials or employees working in related jobs can easily get these qualifications by way of their work experiences and participation in training programs. The social education staffs have not been established as educational profession. Because their works which need qualifications are limited, the qualifications can be obtained by engaging in semi works, and many educational works are duplicated with administrative works. The other reasons are: as social education has a variety of activities, it is difficult to prepare subjectively specific qualifications of the staffs for each activity; and as all the activities of social education should be made by participants and clients, the stuff usually give them only guidance and advice.

(4) Work Life and Social Education

■ It has been said that the characteristics of the employment system in Japanese firms are lifetime employment and seniority promotion. On the one hand, as an employee works for one firm until retirement age and is promoted according to school career and years of working experience, the employee is able to keep a stable life. The employer, on the other hand, feels that the employee has a strong sense of belonging and employer-employee relation is secured. Long-term Japanese economic slump since the middle of 1990s, however, has required firms to cut down personnel expenses of senior employees and reduce managerial positions. The system of lifetime employment and seniority promotion was broken down and many firms are enforcing middle-aged employees to transfer to affiliated smaller firms, to suggest redundancy, or to transfer to newly organized sections.

■ Group training and training for certain jobs were common in the past. However, some methods to develop ability of employees themselves have been required in company in-service education and training. For example, in quality control circles, employees organize small groups and discuss the improvement of daily work and suggest ideas that are useful to cut down expenses and rationalize management. On the other hand, linkage between industry and

会を提供するリフレッシュ教育プログラムや、夜間大学院の開設など、職業に関する教育・学習の分野での産業界と高等教育機関との連携が加速化されてきている。

■このような、産業構造と雇用状態の変化に応じて、職業技術の革新に対応した従業員の能力開発と、能力・資格に応じた昇進や配置転換の導入により、企業経営の効率化を実現することが求められる。さらに、転職や退職後の生活へのスムースな移行を目的として、人生設計プログラムを導入する企業もある。とくに40歳代以上の従業員を対象に、配置転換や退職後・転職後の人生設計を準備させるため、再就職準備コースの開設や再就職準備のための教育休暇の制度化、高等技能専門校（職業訓練校）の受講奨励、公的資格取得の援助、職種転換教育、生きがい講座・体力づくり講座・年金と財産形成の講座等の開設などが実施されている。従業員自身もこのような状勢を自覚し、資格取得や転職のための学習や、個々の企業活動にこだわらない人間関係のネット・ワークを広げる、職場や職域を越えた私的なサークル活動などに参加する事例がみられる。

移動図書館　A Travelling Library

university has been accelerated in "refresh education program" and evening courses of graduate schools which give employees educational leave or other measures to acquire new skills and knowledge on the job and to get a higher career of education.

■ Corresponding to rapid changes in the industrial structure and conditions of employment, it is required to realize the efficiency of business management by developing employees' abilities to respond to innovation of vocational skills and introducing promotion and transfer systems based on merit and qualification. Moreover, some firms adopt life plan programs to provide smooth transitions during job transfers and after retirement. Such programs are to enable particularly 40 year-old or older personnel to prepare for life after transfer or retirement, and includes following courses: a preparation course for reemployment, an educational vacation to prepare for re-employment, encouragement for study in higher vocational training institutions, assistance for taking official qualifications, job transfer education, courses on life values, courses for healthy life, courses for pension and property, etc. Employees themselves see this change in employment conditions and some private small learning groups have been organized beyond their working places by themselves in order to study for obtaining qualifications and changing jobs and extend the human relation network.

第Ⅲ章

教育行財政・経営の現状と課題

The Conditions and Issues of Educational Administration, Finance and Management

教育委員会の会議　Board of Education Meeting

1. 日本の政治機構

■日本の教育行財政を理解するためには、まず全般的な日本の政治機構の特色を知らなければならない。図3-1に示したように、日本の政治機構は①立法機関（国会＝国の最高機関、衆議院と参議院とからなる）、②行政機関（内閣）、③司法機関（裁判所＝最高裁判所、高等裁判所、地方裁判所、家庭裁判所、簡易裁判所）の3つの機関から構成されており、それらは互いにチェックしあうようになっている（国家権力の分立システム）。教育に関して簡単に述べると、教育に関する法律案や予算案は①国会で制定され、その決定に基づいて、②内閣および文部科学省が教育事務を執行する。また教育をめぐるトラブルが生じた際には、それを解決するために③裁判所で裁判が行われる。

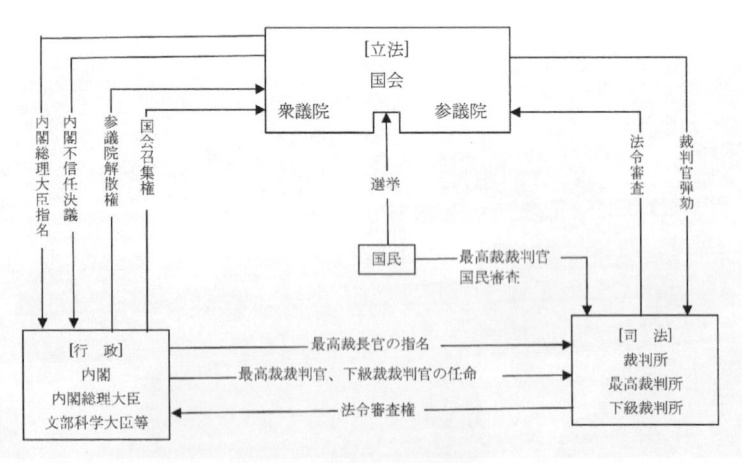

図3-1　日本の政治機構

1. Political Structure in Japan

■ In order to understand educational administration and finance in Japan it is necessary to understand the general characteristics of the Japanese political system. As illustrated in Figure 3-1, the Japanese political structure consists of the following: ① the Legislature (National Diet = The supreme national authority comprised of Lower and Upper Houses), ② the Administration (Cabinet), and ③ the Judiciary (Court = supreme court, high court, local court, family court and summary court). These branches of the government are organized to check one another (separate system of national power). As for the educational organization, the legal procedures are conducted in the following steps: ① the National Diet passes the legal and budget bills; ② on the basis of those decisions, the Cabinet and the Ministry of Education, Culture, Sports, Science and Technology execute the educational policies; and ③ when problems arise, cases are brought into courts.

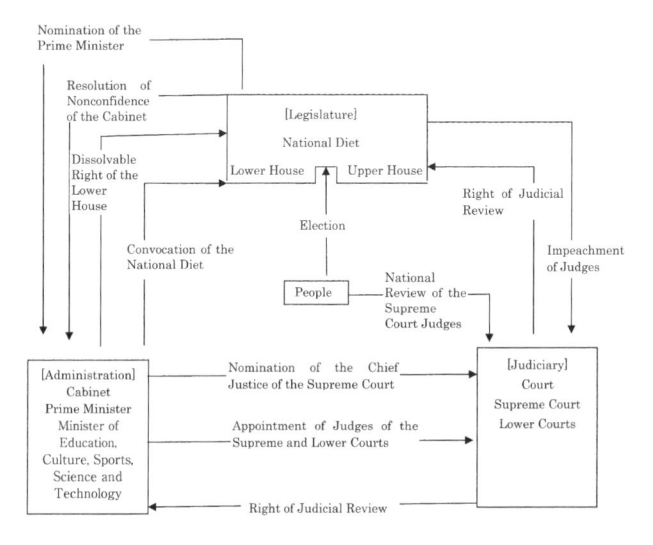

Figure 3-1 Political Structure in Japan

2. 教育行政の基本的原理

■日本の教育行政の特色を示す基本的原理について述べておこう。

①法律主義
　教育の重要な事柄は法律で定められるという原理である。第2次世界大戦前、教育の重要事項は勅令（天皇の命令）で定められ、議会・国民の影響力は 排除されていた。戦後の教育改革において、民主主義理念（教育における主権は国民にある）の確認により、教育の重要事項は国民の代表者で構成される議会で法律によって定められることになった。教育基本法第16条には「教育は、不当な支配に服することなく、この法律及び他の法律の定めるところにより行われるべき」と規定され、教育行政はこの自覚に立って行われるべきだとされる。

②民主行政主義
　民主主義の原理に基づき行政が行われる。戦前は、官僚行政主義により官僚の考えによって教育行政が行われた。戦後は民意が反映するように教育行政は、国民全体に対し直接に責任を負って行われるようになった。代議制の原理にそって人権尊重、教育機会均等を目指すのも、この民主行政主義の表れである。

③教育の自主性尊重主義
　教育は、元来、家庭や民間機関（寺院、教会、塾など）で自主的に行われてきたものであり、また高度の精神的活動を伴うが故にその自主性が尊重されなければならない。教育は基本的に自由に行われるべきものであり、自由主義国では教育の自由が認められてきた。欧米諸国では、教育の自由は、本来、学校設置の自由を意味したが、今日では親の学校選択の自由、あるいは学校における教育活動の自由（一定の制限を伴う）を含むものと考えられている。

2. Fundamental Principles of Educational Administration

■ In this section, the fundamental principles characterizing Japanese educational administration are reviewed.

① The Principle of Legalism

This principle states that important affairs concerning education should be decided by the law. Before World War II, educational affairs were decided by the Imperial Ordinance (order of His Majesty) and the influence of the parliament and the citizens were excluded. The postwar reforms in education, however, confirmed democratic ideals (educational sovereignty lies with the citizens) and that important educational affairs should be decided by law at the parliament. Article 16 of the Basic Act on Education stipulates that education shall not be subject to improper control and shall be carried out in accordance with this and other acts. Therefore, educational administration should be conducted realizing this article.

② The Principle of Democratic Administration

This principle states that education should be administered in line with democracy. Before World War II, the bureaucrats governed educational administration. After the war, education is carried out to reflect the public opinion, and is directly responsible to the people as a whole. This principle is manifested in its aims to respect human rights and provide equal educational opportunities.

③ The Principle of Respect for Independency of Education

Education was carried out in family or private institutions such as a temple, a church, a private cram school and is also concerned with high spiritual activities. Therefore the independency of education should be respected. And education has been fundamentally practiced freely. In many countries respecting freedom of education has been recognized. In Europe and American countries the freedom of education meant the freedom to establish school freely in the past, but nowadays

日本でも教育の自由は認められ、私立学校の設立、大学の自治、指導行政などが実施されている。また、教員を専門職従事者とみなし、彼らの教育における自主性も尊重されている。このように基本的に教育の自由を認めつつ、教育の自主性を尊重して教育行政は行われる。

④条件整備主義

　教育行政は教育の目的を遂行するに必要な種々の条件の整備確立を目標とするという原理である。教育行政機関が教育を統制的に管理監督するのではなく、教育活動や教育運営に指導・助言を与えることを意味している。それはまた前述の教育の自主性を尊重しようという考えの表れでもあり、指導行政とも言われる。かつて、この教育行政の条件整備主義をめぐって、教育行政は教育のどの範囲まで関与できるかが大きな論争点になっていた。現在ではカリキュラムなど教育の内的事項においても、ある程度まで（たとえば、学習指導要領＝カリキュラムの基準を定めること）、教育行政の条件整備の対象になると考えられている。

⑤中立主義

　教育行政は不当な支配に服することなく、政治的、宗教的に中立の立場で行われなければならない。教育基本法第14条第2項は教育の政治的中立については、「法律に定める学校は、特定の政党を支持し、またはこれに反対するための政治教育その他の政治活動をしてはならない」と規定した。また、教育基本法第15条の第2項は、「国及び地方公共団体が設置する学校は、特定の宗教のための宗教教育その他の宗教的活動をしてはならない」と宗教的中立について規定している。

many people consider that it has created the freedom of selecting schools by parents or the freedom of educational activities in school (though having certain limits). In Japan the freedom of education is admitted and it is found in the characteristics such as establishment of private schools, autonomy of university and the administration based on guidance and advice. Moreover, as teachers are regarded to be professional workers, they may enjoy some independency of education in school. The educational administration is implemented providing fundamental educational freedom and respecting independency of education in Japan.

④ The Principle of Providing and Maintenance of Educational Conditions

This principle states that educational administration should aim for the providing and maintenance of the various conditions required in the pursuit of the aims of education. That is, administrative agencies of education are not allowed to control education, but are limited to give guidance and advice on educational activities and management. This is also based on the idea of respect for the independence of education mentioned above. It is called the administration based on guidance and advice. In the past, concerning this principle, there was much controversy about the range of educational administration's involvement. At present, internal affairs in education are, to some extent, qualified to be the target of conditional adjustment in educational administrations (e.g. setting the criterion for the curriculum, that is, the Course of Study).

⑤ Neutralism

Education shall not be subject to improper control and shall be politically and religiously neutral. In relation to this, the second part of Article 14 stipulates that the schools prescribed by law shall refrain from political education or other political activities for or against any specific political party. And the second part of Article 15 prescribes that the schools established by the national and local governments shall refrain from religious education or other activities for a specific religion.

⑥地方分権主義

　教育は地方公共団体（都道府県、市町村）の固有事務とされ、地方自治の考えに基づいて（憲法第92条）、教育の管理運営を行うという原理である。第2次世界大戦前においては、教育の目的は国家に従順に奉仕する国民を育成することであった。これに対し、戦後、憲法に国民の教育を受ける権利が保障され、この権利を保障していくために、国民の生活の本拠である地方公共団体が第一義的な教育行政の主体とされたのである。

職員会議　Regular Teachers' Meeting

⑥ The Principle of Decentralization

This principle states that education should be managed on the basis of local autonomy (Article 92 of the Constitution of Japan) since education is a function of the local government (prefectures, cities, towns, and villages). Before World War II, the goal of education was to foster people who can obediently serve the nation. On the contrary, after the war, the right to education was ensured in the Constitution of Japan. To secure this right, the local government, which is close to the public's day-to-day living, became the main body responsible for educational administration.

3. 国レベルの教育行政

■日本の国レベルの教育行政の組織・権限については、教育行政の法律主義に基づき、「教育基本法」「文部科学省設置法」などで規定されている。国レベルの教育行政機関としては、内閣・内閣総理大臣、文部科学省・文部科学大臣があげられる。

（1）内閣・内閣総理大臣

■日本国の最高行政機関は内閣である（憲法第65条）。教育に関する国の最高行政権も内閣に属する。内閣は、内閣総理大臣とその他の国務大臣（文民でなければならない）によって構成される。

■内閣の教育行政に関する権限には以下のものがある。
①教育に関する法律案・教育予算案を閣議で決定すること。
②憲法・法律の実施に必要な教育に関する政令を制定すること。
③重要な教育施策について閣議決定すること。
④教育に関する条約を締結すること。

■内閣総理大臣は内閣の首長であり、閣議を主宰する。教育行政上の権限としては、①閣議決定した教育法案・予算案を国会に提出すること、②文部科学大臣の任免と指揮監督があげられる。

3. Educational Administration at the National Level

■ The organization and authority of the national administration in education are stipulated, based upon the principle of legalism, in the Basic Act on Education, the Law of the Establishment of the Ministry of Education, Culture, Sports, Science and Technology, etc. The national administrative agencies of education include the Cabinet/Prime Minister and the Ministry/ Minister of Education, Culture, Sports, Science and Technology.

(1) Cabinet and Prime Minister
■ The Cabinet is the supreme executive agency in Japan (Article 65 of the Constitution of Japan). The power to administer education also belongs to the Cabinet. The Cabinet consists of the Prime Minister and other ministers of state (they must be civilians).
■ Regarding educational administration, the Cabinet has the following authorities:
① Deciding the legal and budget bills concerning education at the Cabinet meeting.
② Enacting government ordinances required by the Constitution and other laws.
③ Deciding important educational policies at the Cabinet meeting.
④ Concluding treaties on education.
■ The Prime Minister is the head of the Cabinet and presides over the Cabinet meeting. The authority in educational administration provided for the Prime Minister includes the following:
① submission of the legal and budget bills agreed at the Cabinet meeting to the National Diet; and ② appointment/dismissal and supervision of the Minister of Education Culture, Sports, Science and Technology.

(2) 文部科学省・文部科学大臣

■国レベルの実際の教育行政は、内閣の統括の下に、文部科学大臣を長とする文部科学省によって行われる。文部科学省は、2001年1月6日から旧文部省と科学技術省が統合されて再編され、外局として文化庁がある。

■文部科学省は、学校教育、社会教育、学術・スポーツ・文化・科学技術の振興と普及を図るとともに、それらあらゆる面の指導・助言などを主な任務としている。

■文部科学省の組織は、図3-2に示したように、文部科学省本省と文化庁に分かれている。文部科学省の権限は、「文部科学省設置法」「学校教育法」「地方教育行政の組織及び運営に関する法律」などに規定されているが、行政上の根本原則として法律に規定がない限り、「監督」を行わないとされる。言い換えれば、日本の文部科学省は専門的な助言・援助を中心に、教育の条件整備を行う機関としての性格をもつということである。

■文部科学省の権限の内容を行政の対象領域ごとに分類してまとめておく。
①教育行政全般
教育・学術・スポーツ・文化・科学技術等の振興
②学校教育に関すること
初等中等教育の振興に関する企画・立案・援助・助言、初等中等教育の基準の設定、教科書の検定、義務教育諸学校(私立学校も含む)の教科書の無償給付、大学及び高等専門学校の運営に関する援助・助言など

III. The Conditions and Issues of Educational Administration, Finance and Management   157

(2) **Ministry and Minister of Education, Culture, Sports, Science and Technology**

■ The national administration in education is managed by the Ministry of Education, Culture, Sports, Science and Technology (Monbukagakusho) headed by the Minister under the control of the Cabinet. The Ministry of Education, Culture, Sports, Science and Technology unified the Ministry of Education, Culture and the Bureau of Science and Technology in January of 2001. Besides, this there is an Agency of Cultural Affairs as an external agency.

■ The main duties of the Ministry of Education, Culture, Sports and Technology is to promote and disseminate school education, social education, academic study, sports, culture, science and technology as well as to supervise and give advice.

■ As illustrated in Figure 3-2, the Ministry is divided into the Ministry itself and the Agency for Cultural Affairs. The authority of the Ministry is stipulated in the Law of the Establishment of the Ministry of Education, Culture, Sports, Science and Technology, the School Education Law, the Law concerning the Organization and Operation of Local Educational Administration, etc. However, the Ministry does not 'supervise', as an administrative principle, unless there is a law granting such authority. In other words, the Ministry is the government agency responsible for the establishment and adjustment of educational conditions while providing professional advice and support at its core.

■ The authority content of the Ministry is classified into the following administrative domains:

① Educational administration as a whole:
Inquires and planning concerning the promotion of education, culture, sports, science and Technology, etc., publication of their technical documents.

② School education:
To plan, support, and advise for promotion of primary and secondary education. To set the standard of primary and secondary education and curriculum (the Course of Study), etc., authorization of textbooks, free textbook distribution to compulsory education schools (including private schools), guidance and advice concerning the management of universities and technical colleges; etc.

③地方教育行政に関すること
地方教育行政に関する企画・立案、地方教育行政組織・運営に関する指導・助言・勧告など
④国際交流・国際協力に関すること
帰国児童生徒・外国人児童生徒の教育・指導、外国人留学生の受け入れ、海外への留学生派遣、ユネスコ活動の振興など
⑤内部組織編成に関すること

■文部科学大臣は文部科学省の長であり、国の教育行政事務の全体をまとめる役割をもつ。文部科学大臣は、法律あるいは政令を施行するために省令を出すことができ、また、文部科学省の事務について告示・訓令・通達を出すことができる。その他、大学等の設置認可、地方公共団体の教育に関し、必要な指導・助言・援助、調査を行うことができる。

教科書（無償）を受け取る新入生　New Students Receiving Free Textbooks

③ Local educational administration:
Planning concerning local educational administration, guidance, advice and recommendations concerning the organization and management of local educational administration, etc.
④ International educational administration:
International exchange, international cooperation, education for returnee children, education for children from abroad
⑤ Organization of the internal subdivisions

■ The Minister, as a head of the Ministry, integrates the national affairs in educational administration. The Minister is provided with the power to present the Ministerial ordinance for enforcing Cabinet ordinances and to present the public announcement, instruction and notification concerning Ministerial affairs to the concerned agencies. In addition the Minister is able to give advice, support and survey on the approval of establishment of universities, and the education which local public organization manage.

160　第Ⅲ章　教育行財政・経営の現状と課題

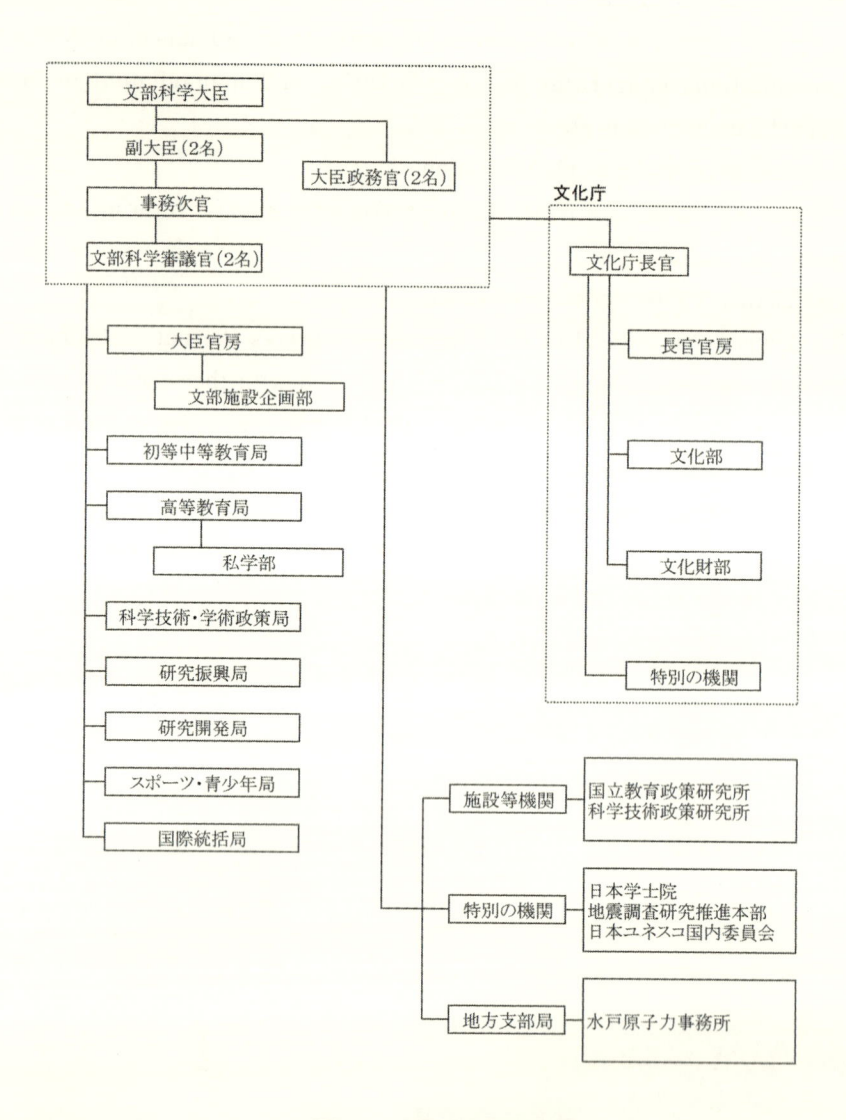

```
┌─────────────────────────────────────┐
│  文部科学大臣                        │
│    │                                │
│  副大臣(2名)    大臣政務官(2名)      │         文化庁
│    │                                │   ┌─────────────────────┐
│  事務次官                           │   │  文化庁長官          │
│    │                                │   │    │                │
│  文部科学審議官(2名)                │   │  長官官房            │
└─────────────────────────────────────┘   │    │                │
   │                                      │  文化部              │
   ├─ 大臣官房                            │    │                │
   │    └─ 文部施設企画部                 │  文化財部            │
   ├─ 初等中等教育局                      │    │                │
   ├─ 高等教育局                          │  特別の機関          │
   │    └─ 私学部                         └─────────────────────┘
   ├─ 科学技術・学術政策局
   ├─ 研究振興局
   ├─ 研究開発局
   ├─ スポーツ・青少年局
   └─ 国際統括局

   施設等機関 ─── 国立教育政策研究所
                  科学技術政策研究所

   特別の機関 ─── 日本学士院
                  地震調査研究推進本部
                  日本ユネスコ国内委員会

   地方支部局 ─── 水戸原子力事務所
```

図3-2　文部科学省の組織

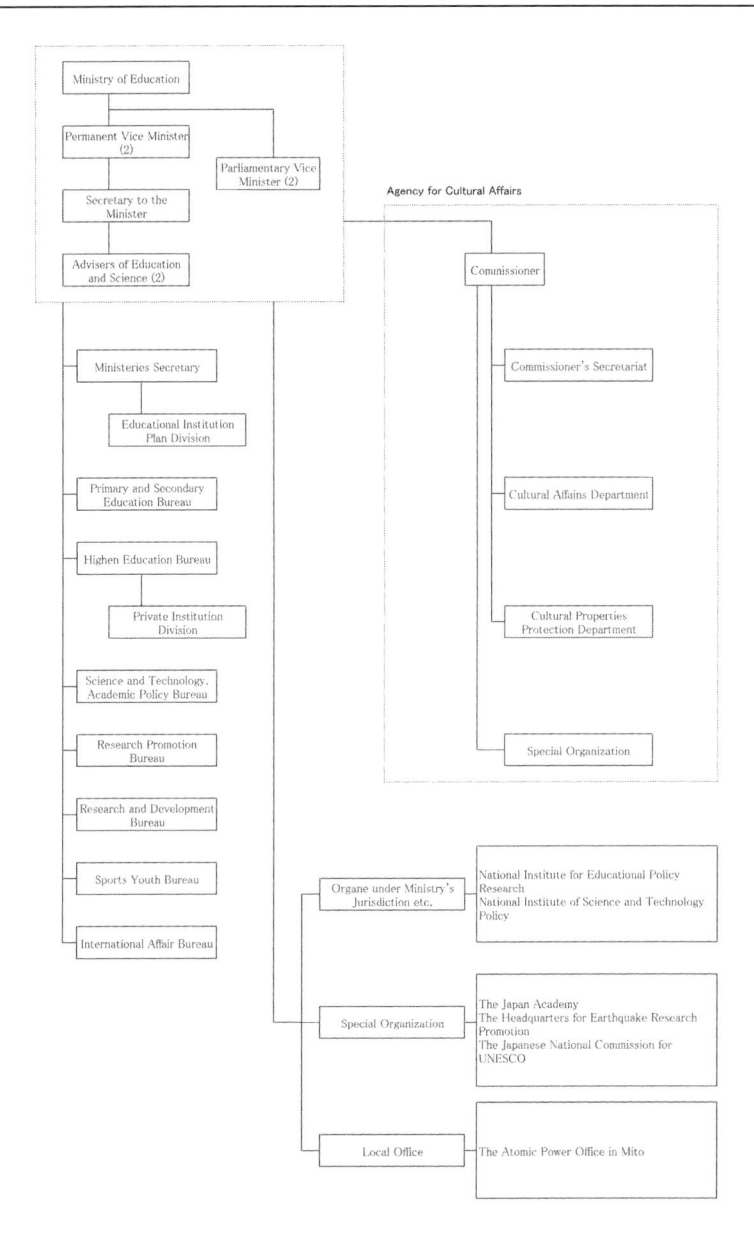

III. The Conditions and Issues of Educational Administration, Finance and Management 161

Figure 3-2 Organization of the Ministry of Education, Culture, Sports, Science and Technology

(3) 教育関係審議会等

■文部科学省には、科学技術・学術審議会や中央教育審議会などが置かれ、地方公共団体にも法律や条例に基づいて各種審議会が置かれている。特に、文部科学省の再編に伴って、教育課程審議会、教育職員養成審議会、大学審議会、生涯学習審議会等が中央教育審議会に統合された。中央教育審議会は、日本の教育・学術・文化に関する重要施策を扱い、日本の教育政策決定過程に大きな役割を果たしている。中央教育審議会の委員の数は、30人以内とされているが、必要に応じて臨時委員および専門委員を置くことができる。

■中央教育審議会答申でも、特に、今日の日本の教育のあり方に影響を与えた答申としては、例えば、「21世紀を展望した我が国の教育の在り方について（第一次、第二次答申）」(1996年、1997年)、「今後の地方教育行政の在り方について」(1998年)、「新しい時代にふさわしい教育基本法と教育振興計画の在り方について」(2003年)、「新しい時代の義務教育を創造する」(2005年)などがある。

■このうち、「今後の地方教育行政の在り方について」(1998年9月)においては、市町村における地域に根差した教育行政の主体的かつ積極的な展開、教育事務所の役割の見直し、市町村教育委員会の事務処理の広域化等が提言され、1999年7月の地方分権一括法の制定などにより、地方分権の視点に立った教育行政改革が進みつつある。

■中央教育審議会のほかに、日本の教育行政に大きな影響力を与えている審議会として、内閣総理大臣の諮問機関としての審議会がある。たとえば、四次にわたる答申を行い、今日の教育改革の直接のきっかけになった臨時教育審議会 (1984年〜1987年)、「教育を変える17の提案」を報告した教育改革国民会議 (2000年設置)、2006年10月の閣議決定により設定された「教育再

(3) Various Councils for Education

■ The Ministry of Education, Culture, Sports, Science and Technology constitutes the Science and Technology and Academic Council, the Central Education Council and so on. Also the local public bodies constitute the various Councils based on law and ordinance. Especially, when the Ministry of Education, Culture, Sports, Science and Technology was reorganized, the Central Education Council unified the Curriculum Council, the School Personnel Council, the University Council, the Life-long Learning Council and so on. It deals with important policies concerning education, science and culture and plays a crucial role in the establishment of Japanese educational policies. It is stipulated that the number of members of the Central Education Council is less than 30 people.
If necessary, the temporary members and professional members could be nominated to the Council.

■ Among the reports of the Central Education Council, the most influential reports on Japanese education are "Japanese Education for the 21st century" (1996,1997), "Local Education Administration in the Future" (1998), 'The New Fundamental Law of Education and the Education Promotion Plan Suitable to the New Age" (2003), and 'To Create Compulsory Education for the New Age' (2005).

■ "Local Education Administration in the Future" proposed that local educational administration deep-rooted in the local community should be developed independently and actively, roles of the education office are reviewed and the office work at municipal boards of education should be extended. Since the Package Law of Decentralization was established in July 1999, the Education Administration tends to be reformed in the light of decentralization.

■ Besides the Central Education Council, there are the Councils which strongly influence the Educational Administration in Japan as the Consultation Organs of the Prime Minister. For example, the National Task Force for Educational Reform submitted its reports to the Cabinet four times, and provided the first supply of present-day educational reforms (1984 ~ 1987), "The National Meeting

生会議」などがある。

■臨時教育審議会答申で提言された主要な具体的教育改革の方策は以下のような点である。
①生涯教育体系の提唱と推進
②個性化教育の重視
③学習指導要領・大学設置基準などの基準や学校設置等の認可の大綱化・簡素化
④教育の地方分権化の促進・教育委員会の活性化
⑤塾など多様な民間教育産業への対応の検討と民間活力の導入
⑥教育・研究、文化・スポーツへの重点的・効率的資金配分と教育費の官民分担と協力体制の再構築

for Education Reform" reported '17 Proposals about Reforming Education' (established in 2000), and "The Meeting for Education Regeneration" was established in October, 2006.

■ The main concrete plans of educational reform proposed by the National Task Force for Educational Reform reports are as follows:

① To propose and promote the life-long education system

② To emphasize education by respecting individual characteristics

③ To simplify standards such as the Course of Study, the regulations for the establishment of university and the school founding authorization.

④ To decentralize education and to activate the board of education.

⑤ To examine the relationship with diverse private educational enterprise such as a juku (a private cram school), and to introduce private vitality to education.

⑥ To heavily and efficiently allocate the fund to fields of education and research, culture and sports, and to reconstruct the system of allotment and cooperation between private and public sectors on educational expenditures.

4. 地方レベルの教育行政

(1) 地方教育行政の基本的性格
■第2次世界大戦前においては、教育は国の事務とされ、地方教育行政は、文部大臣・内務大臣の統制の下で、道府県知事が執行していた。教育の内容・方法等の内的事項はすべて国レベルで決定し、それを地方レベルで忠実に実行するようになっていた。すなわち、戦前日本の地方教育行政は、①中央集権化、②一般行政への従属、③官僚による統制を特徴としていたといえる。

■これに対し、戦後は、地方教育行政に対する考え方が逆転した。地方自治の原則（憲法第92条）に基づき、教育は地方の固有の事務とされ（地方分権化）、教育管理は、教育の自主性を尊重するために、一般行政から独立した教育行政機関としての教育委員会によって行われることになった（一般行政からの独立）。また、教育委員会の委員は、住民の意見を教育行政に反映する代表として、住民の選挙によって選出されることになった（民主的行政）。なお、1956年の地方教育行政の再編によって、現在、教育委員は地方公共団体の長が任命することになっている。

■また、教育の自主性を尊重するという考え方から、「専門的リーダーシップ」も地方教育行政の重要な原理となっている。

(2) 地方教育行政機関
■地方レベルの教育行政は、都道府県レベルと市町村レベルに分けられる。都道府県レベルでは知事と都道府県教育委員会が、市町村レベルでは市町村

4. Educational Administration at the Local Levels

(1) Fundamental Characteristics of Local Educational Administration

■ Before World War II, education was a national function and local educational administration was carried out by the prefectural governors under the control of the Minister of Education and the Minister of Home Affairs. All details such as educational contents and methods were determined at the national level and faithfully carried out at the local level. The Japanese local educational administration in prewar days, in short, was characterized by ① centralization, ② dependence on the general public administration and ③ bureaucratic control.

■ On the other hand, after World War II, the concept of local educational administration was drastically changed. Based upon the Principle of Local Autonomy (Article 92 of the Japanese Constitution), education became a local function (decentralization). To insure the independent decision making concerning education, the supervision of education was conducted by the board of education, independent from the general administration (independence from the general public administration). The members of the board were elected by the people (democratic administration) as representatives reflecting the public opinion on the educational administration. Since the reorganization of the local educational administration in 1956, however, the members have been appointed by the head of the local government.

■ Furthermore, due to the importance of the independent decision making concerning education, 'professional leadership' has become an important principle for the local educational administration.

(2) The Organization of the Local Educational Administration

■ The local level educational administration can be divided into the prefectural level and the municipal level. At the prefectural level, the governor and

長と市町村教育委員会が主な教育行政機関であるが、それぞれのレベルの議会も教育行政に関係している。図3-3は、地方レベルの教育行政機関の関係を示したものである。

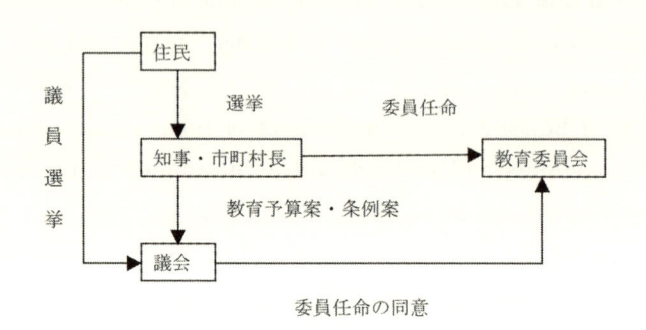

図3-3　都道府県・市町村レベルの教育行政機関

■また、表3-1は、教育委員会数を示したものである。

表3-1　教育委員会数

	都道府県	市	特別区	町	村
1998年	47	670	23	1,968	564
1999年	47	671	23	1,967	563
2001年	47	670	23	1,965	561
2003年	47	677	23	1,934	547
2005年	47	740	23	1,293	332
2007年	47	782	23	825	195

出典：文部科学省『教育行政調査』2008年

①議会
議会は、住民の選挙によって選出された代表によって構成される地方公共団体・都道府県・市町村の立法機関・意思決定機関である。教育に関しては、条例の制定、予算の決定、学校の授業料・入学金の徴収に関する議決、教育委員の任命における同意などの権限を持つ。

III. The Conditions and Issues of Educational Administration, Finance and Management

the prefectural board of education are the main institutions of educational administration while at the municipal level, they are the mayor and the municipal board of education. At each level, the local assemblies are involved in the educational administration. Figure 3-3 shows the relations among the institutions of the educational administration at the local level.

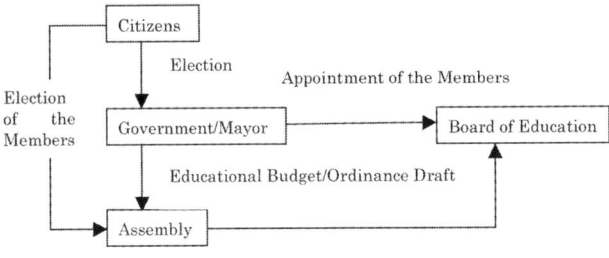

```
                    ┌──── Citizens ────┐
                    │         │        │
                    │      Election    Appointment of the Members
       Election     ▼                         
       of   the  Government/Mayor ──────────▶ Board of Education
       Members                                      ▲
          │         Educational Budget/Ordinance Draft
          │            │
          └──────▶ Assembly ──────────────────────────┘
                          Assent to the Appointment
```

Figure 3-3 The Institutions of the Educational Administration at Prefectural/Municipal Levels

■ Table 3-1 shows the number of boards of education.

Table 3-1 The Number of Boards of Education

	Prefecture	City	Special Ward	Town	Village
1998	47	670	23	1,968	564
1999	47	671	23	1,967	563
2001	47	670	23	1,965	561
2003	47	677	23	1,934	547
2005	47	740	23	1,293	332
2007	47	782	23	825	195

Resource: Ministry of Education, Culture, Sports, Science and Technology "Inquiry on Educational Administration", 2008

① Assembly

The assembly, which is composed of the elected members, is a legislative and decision-making institution of the local government (prefecture/municipality). With regards to education, it has the authority to pass ordinances, decide the budget, decide on tuition and entrance fees, and approve the appointment of the members of the board of education.

②都道府県知事・市町村長
都道府県知事・市町村長は、その地方公共団体の首長として、地方公共団体を全体的にとりまとめる地位にある。知事・市町村長の教育行政上の権限は以下の通りである。
(a) 大学（都道府県立・市町村立）の管理
(b) 私立学校の設置・廃止等の認可、私立学校に対する助成等
(c) 教育委員会委員の任免
(d) 教育に関する予算案・条例案の議会への提出、それら予算の執行
(e) 教育財産の取得・処分予算の執行
(f) 生涯教育・学習に関する管理
③教育委員会
教育委員会の性格を列挙すると以下の通りである。
(a) 教育委員会は合議制の行政委員会である。すなわち、複数のメンバーで組織され、その構成員の全会一致または多数決によって意思決定を行う委員会である。
(b) 教育委員会は一般行政から独立した機関である。教育の自主性を尊重する原理に基づき、議会や知事・市町村長に対して相対的ではあるが独立性を有する。
(c) 教育委員会は無党派性の行政機関である。教育の政治的中立性を確保するために、教育委員の半数以上が同一政党に所属してはならないとされている。また、委員は積極的な政治活動を行うことを禁止されている。

■以下、項を改めて、詳しく教育委員会の組織・権限などについて述べよう。

(3) 教育委員会の組織

■図3-4に示したように、教育委員会には2つの部分――教育委員によって構成されている議決機関と執行担当の教育長（その下には事務局がある）――からなる。
■議決機関としての教育委員会は5人の委員で構成されるが、小規模町村では条例で3人にすることもできる。委員は、その地方公共団体の首長の被選

② Governors/ Mayors

Governors and mayors, as heads of their local governments, are in the position to integrate in their totality. Their educational administrative functions are as follows:

(a) Supervision of universities and colleges (prefectural/municipal)
(b) Approving of the establishment and abolition of private schools; subsidies to private schools
(c) Appointment and dismissal of the members of the board of education
(d) Submission of the education budget and ordinance drafts to the assembly
(e) Management of acquisition / disposal of educational property
(f) Supervision of life-long education and learning

③ The Board of Education

The characteristics of the board of education are as follows:

(a) It is an administrative board with the council system. That is, it is comprised of a plural members who make the decision unanimously or by majority rule.

(b) It is an institution independent of the general public administration. Based on the principle of autonomy in education, it possesses a certain amount of independence from the assembly and the governor/mayor.

(c) It is a nonpartisan institution. To guarantee political neutrality in education, it is required that more than half of the members should not belong to the same political party. The members are also prohibited from conducting intensive political activities.

■ The next section gives a detailed description of its organization and authority.

(3) The Organization of the Board of Education

■ As shown in Figure 3-4, the board of education consists of two parts: the decision - making body composed of the members, and the superintendent in charge of policy implementation (also the secretariat exists under the superintendent).

■ The board of education as a decision-making body is comprised of five members, but according to the bylaws, three persons can comprise the board in

挙権をもつもので、人格が高潔で教育に関して識見をもつ者のうちから、地方公共団体の長が議会の同意を得て任命する。教育委員の任期は4年で、再任されることができる。

■教育委員のうちから互選によって教育委員長が選ばれる（任期は1年、再選可能）。委員長は委員会を召集し、ある議事について可否同数のときは、採決する権限を持つ。

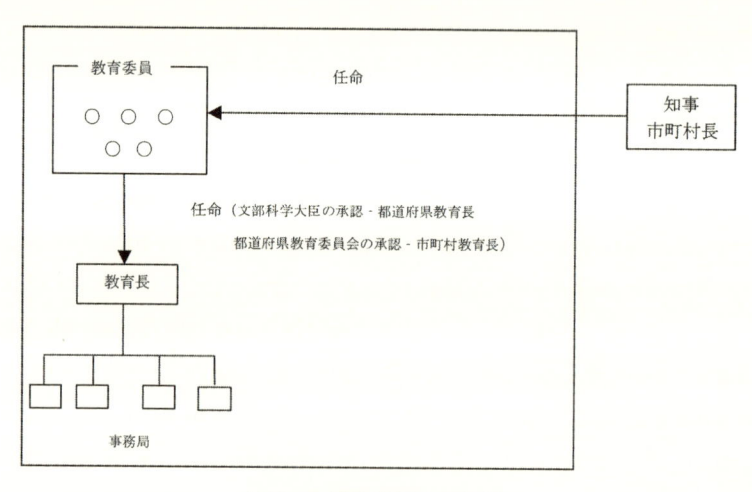

```
┌─────────────────────────────────────────────────┐
│  ┌─────────┐                                    │
│  │ 教育委員 │      任命                          │
│  │ ○ ○ ○ │◄─────────────────┐  ┌─────────┐    │
│  │  ○ ○   │                   │  │ 知事     │   │
│  └────┬────┘                   └──│ 市町村長 │   │
│       │                            └─────────┘   │
│       │任命（文部科学大臣の承認・都道府県教育長） │
│       │    （都道府県教育委員会の承認・市町村教育長）│
│       ▼                                          │
│  ┌─────┐                                         │
│  │教育長│                                        │
│  └──┬──┘                                         │
│     │                                            │
│  ┌──┼──┬──┬──┐                                   │
│  │  │  │  │  │                                   │
│  └──┴──┴──┴──┘                                   │
│   事務局                                         │
└─────────────────────────────────────────────────┘
```

図3-4　教育委員会の組織

■執行担当の教育長は、教育委員会によって任命される（任期は定められていない）。
■教育長の職務の性格を列挙すると次の通りである。
① 教育委員会の専門的助言者
　教育長は教育委員会の全ての会議に出席し、議事について専門家の立場から助言する。教育委員は住民の教育要求をくみとる代表だが、教育行政については「素人」である。その素人たちの会議で教育長が「専門家」として助言をする。ここには、「素人支配」と「専門的リーダーシップ」を統合する

small towns and villages. The members of the board are appointed by the head of the local government with the assent of the assembly. The members should have reached the age eligible to be elected, be noble minded, and have a good positive view toward education. The term of office is four years and they can be reappointed.

■ The chairperson of the board is elected by mutual vote among its members. (The term is one year and he can be reappointed). He/she has the authority to convene the meeting and to break ties regarding decision-making.

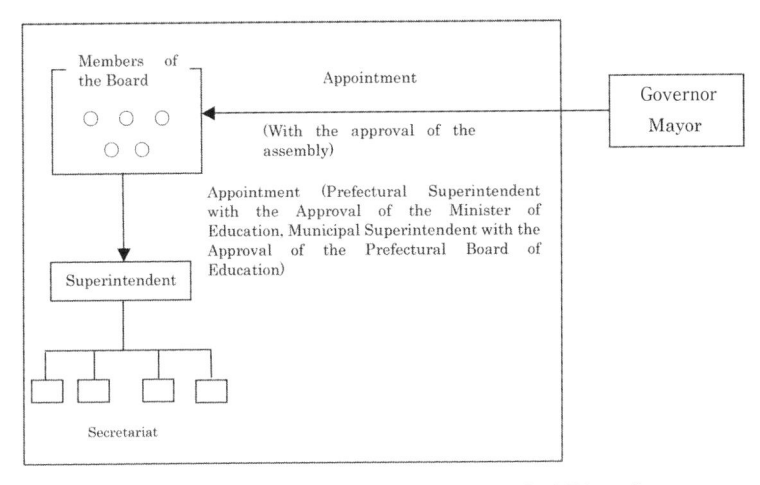

```
┌─────────────────────────────────────────────────────────────────┐
│   Members of                                                    │
│   the Board         Appointment                                 │
│                                           ┌──────────┐          │
│    ○  ○  ○ ◄──────                       │ Governor │          │
│      ○  ○         (With the approval of the│  Mayor   │          │
│        │           assembly)              └──────────┘          │
│        │                                                        │
│        │          Appointment (Prefectural Superintendent       │
│        │          with the Approval of the Minister of          │
│        ▼          Education, Municipal Superintendent with the  │
│  ┌──────────────┐ Approval of the Prefectural Board of          │
│  │Superintendent│ Education)                                    │
│  └──────────────┘                                               │
│        │                                                        │
│   ┌────┼────┐                                                   │
│   □    □    □                                                   │
│      Secretariat                                                │
└─────────────────────────────────────────────────────────────────┘
```

Figure 3-4　The Organization of the Board of Education

■ The superintendent is appointed by the board (The term of office is not stipulated).

■ The duties of the superintendent are as follows:

① Professional advisor to the board of education

The superintendent should attend all the board meetings and advise the board from the specialist's point of view. The board members are representing people's demand on education, but are laymen of the educational administration. In such meetings, the superintendent acts as a specialist and advises them. In this way,

ことによって地方教育行政を行うという考え方がみられる。
②教育委員会事務局の長
　教育長は教育委員会の権限に属するすべての事務をつかさどり、所属職員を指揮監督する。
③教育委員会の代行者
　教育委員会の権限に属する事務の一部を委任されて、代行する。

（4）教育委員会の職務
■教育委員会の職務権限は、地方教育行政の組織及び運営に関する法律の第23条に規定されている。主なものを挙げれば次のとおりである。
①学校その他の教育機関の設立・管理・および廃止
②教職員の任免やその他の人事
③学校の組織編成、教育課程、学習指導、生徒指導に関すること
④教科書やその他の教材の取り扱い
⑤校舎、その他の施設、設備の整備
⑥教育関係職員の研修
⑦環境衛生、学校給食の管理
⑧社会教育、スポーツに関すること
⑨文化財保護
⑩教育に係る調査、統計に関すること
ただし、大学や私立学校に関すること、教育財産の取得・処分に関しては、地方公共団体の長の職務権限となっている。

■都道府県・市町村の教育委員会は、自らの権限に関する事務について「教育委員会規則」を制定し、より詳細にその職務内容を規定することができる。

the concept of educational administration as the integration of 'layman control' and 'professional leadership' is reflected.

② Head of the board's secretariat

The superintendent attends to the duties of the secretariat, and supervises the staff.

③ Agent of the board of education

The superintendent is commissioned to carry out a part of the functions under the authority of the board.

(4) The Duties of the Board of Education

■ The duties of the board of education are stipulated in Article 23 of the Law concerning the Organization and Operation of Local Educational Administration. The main duties of the board of education are listed below.

① To establish, manage and abolish schools and other educational institutions

② To appoint and dismiss the teachers and other educational workers and make a personal administration

③ To manage school organization, curriculum, student learning, and student guidance

④ To provide textbooks and other teaching materials

⑤ To maintain school buildings, facilities and equipment

⑥ To provide in-service training of teachers and other staff concerned

⑦ To control the environment, hygiene and to manage the school lunch program

⑧ To administer and promote social education and sports

⑨ To promote the preservation of cultural properties

⑩ To make a survey of education and statistics

However, the power concerning university provided by the local government, private school and acquisition/disposal of educational property belongs to the Governor or Mayors, as explained previously.

■ Both prefectural and municipal boards of education may establish 'Regulations of the Board of Education' defining their own authority and prescribing their job

通常は所管の学校の管理運営等に関する学校管理規則を規定する。

(5) 教育委員会の教育指導行政
■教育委員会の機能としての指導・助言・援助は、教育委員会の活動のいろいろな場合にみられる。その中でも、指導主事制度は学校に対する指導・助言・援助の制度として特に重要なものである。指導主事は各教育委員会に置かれ、学校の教育課程、学習指導、教科書その他の教材の取扱い、研修など学校教育の専門的事項の指導、助言を担当する。その職務は、非常に実践的である。すなわち、学校訪問による指導・助言や種々の研修会・研究発表会などに参加して指導・助言を行うことも多い。

■このような指導主事の活動は、教育委員会と学校との情報伝達のパイプ役を担うことにもなっている。指導主事は教育委員会の教育指導方針や教育委員会作成のガイドブックの内容を学校に伝達し、逆に学校からの様々な要望は指導主事を通して教育委員会へ伝えられるからである。
■指導主事の職務は学校での教育実践に対する豊かな経験、知識および専門的力量が必要である。従って、指導主事は校長、副校長、熟練教員から任用されることが多い。
■指導主事は学校に対する専門的指導・助言を行う教育職員だが、教育委員会には社会教育に対する専門的指導・助言を行う「社会教育主事」も置かれている。

specifications in more detail. It also makes typical school management regulations concerned with school administration.

(5) Educational Guidance of the Board of Education

■ Guidance, advice and assistance as a function of school boards are provided in various situations of its activities. The system of supervisors is particularly significant as a function of guidance, advice and assistance. Supervisors belong to a board of education, and take charge of guidance or advice on school educational expertise such as instructions of curriculum or learning, uses of textbooks or other materials, and in-service training of teachers for student guidance. Their work is quite practical. They often give advice when visiting schools or when participating in research study meetings.

■ Supervisors form a link of communication between a board of education and a school. Supervisors deliver to the schools the course of instruction and contents of a guidebook made by the board. Also, they report back requests of the schools to the board.

■ Supervisors should be well experienced and knowledgeable in teaching. They are, herefore, appointed from among principals, vice-principals, or teachers with rich experience.

■ Some supervisors give expert guidance or advice on school education, while 'supervisors for social education' in the same board of education provide expert guidance or advice on social education.

5. 中央と地方教育行政の関係

(1) 中央と地方との関係
■第2次世界大戦後の地方分権制の下では、原則として、国の教育行政機関と地方の教育行政機関との間に上下の関係はない。しかし、今日の教育問題をめぐる様々な要求に対応し、それらを解決していくためには、中央と地方の教育行政機関が相互に連携して教育行政事務を行わなければならなくなってきている。教育行政における中央と地方の連携が要請されているのである。

■教育行政における中央と地方の関係は、具体的には、文部科学大臣と地方の教育委員会（都道府県教育委員会と市町村教育委員会）あるいは文部科学大臣と地方公共団体の長（都道府県知事と市町村長）との関係である。

■地方公共団体の長および教育委員会に対する文部科学大臣の権限のうち主要なものを列挙すると以下の通りである。
① 指導・助言
　文部科学大臣は、都道府県または市町村の教育が適正に行われるために必要な指導・助言を行う。
② 国庫補助の交付
　文部科学大臣は、地方公共団体の長から提出される教育関係の国庫補助の申請に基づき、それを交付する。
③ 調査・資料・報告の要求
　文部科学大臣は、地方の教育情報を収集するために、調査を行わせたり、必要な資料・報告の提出を求めたりすることができる。

III. The Conditions and Issues of Educational Administration, Finance and Management 179

5. Relationship between the Central and Local Institutions of Educational Administration

(1) Relationship between the Central and Local Institutions

■ Under decentralization in postwar years, there is no vertical connection between the central and local institutions of educational administration. The two levels of institutions, however, need to build a closer cooperation with each other in order to deal with today's educational problems. In other words, the educational administration is needed to develop a cooperation between the central and local institutions.

■ The relationship between the central and local institutions means the following relationships in reality; the Minister of Education , Culture, Sports, Science and Technology and the local board of education in both prefectures and municipalities; or the Minister of Education , Culture, Sports, Science and Technology and the heads of local governments (governors and mayors).

■ Here is a list of the major authorities given to the Minister of Education concerning the relationship with the heads of local governments and school boards.

① To give guidance and advice

The Minister of Education, Culture, Sports, Science and Technology provides necessary guidance and advice so that a local educational institution can carry out its task properly.

② To issue government subsidies

The Minister of Education, Culture, Sports, Science and Technology issues the government subsidy applied for by a head of local government.

③ To request survey, data, and reports

The Minister of Education, Culture, Sports, Science and Technology may ask a local institution to carry out a survey in order to collect educational information

④基準の設定

文部科学大臣は、学校設置基準や教育課程の基準などの学校教育に関する基準を設定する。地方教育行政機関はこれらの基準に従い行政事務を行わなければならない。

⑤是正要求

文部科学大臣は、地方の教育行政機関の行う教育事務が法令に違反しているかまたは怠りがあると認めるとき、あるいは教育の目的達成のために適正を欠いていると認めるときは、その違反や怠りの改善を求める措置をとることができる。

⑥機関委任事務の指揮監督

国から地方公共団体の長や教育委員会に委任された事務、たとえば都道府県教育委員会の教員免許授与に関する事務や市町村教育委員会の就学事務などについては、文部科学大臣の指揮監督を受ける。

(2) 都道府県教育委員会と市町村教育委員会との関係

■都道府県と市町村の関係は、国と地方公共団体の関係と同様に、上下の関係ではない。都道府県は市町村を包括する広域の地方公共団体として、都道府県内の、統一的な処理を必要とする事務、市町村が行うには不適当と認められる事務を行う。その目的は、地方行政事務の円滑な遂行を図るためである。

■地方分権化の流れの中で、文部科学省から都道府県教育委員会、そして都道府県教育委員会から市町村教育委員会への関与は縮減が図られてきた。しかし、教育基本法改正や中央教育審議会答申を受けて、教育委員会の責任の明確化や教育委員会の組織・運営の充実が図られた。その結果、地方教育行政の組織及び運営に関する法律の改正が行われ、教育委員会への保護者の選

and to submit significant data and reports.

④ To establish the standard

The Minister of Education, Culture, Sports, Science and Technology sets up the criteria for school education such as the standard of the school establishment and the curriculum. Local institutions of educational administration must conform to these criteria and perform their administrative tasks.

⑤ To request proper measures for correction and improvement

The Minister of Education, Culture, Sports, Science and Technology may request local institutions to take proper measures in cases such as the diversion from the legal specifications or the lack of proper actions to achieve the prescribed educational goals.

⑥ To supervise and direct delegated tasks

The Minister of Education, Culture, Sports, Science and Technology provides either a head of local government or a school board with supervision and direction for the functions delegated by national government; for example, to issue teaching certificates, and to enroll students in school.

(2) Relationship between the Prefectural and Municipal Boards of Education

■ There is no vertical relationship between the prefecture and municipality, as well as between the national and local governments. The prefectures are regarded as extensive local governments integrating municipalities. The prefectures are responsible for tasks of integration, connection and coordination of the municipalities as well as tasks beyond the municipal capacity. The purpose of the prefectural board is to carry out the local administrative functions smoothly.

■ Influenced by the trend of decentralization, the interventions of the Ministry of Education, Culture, Sports, Science and Technology in the Prefectural Boards of Education, and those of the Prefectural Boards of Education to the Municipal Boards of Education tend to be reduced. But influenced by the revision of the Fundamental Law of Education, the reports of the Central Education Council, it is

任の義務化（同法第 4 条）や、教育委員会の活動状況の自己点検評価及び議会への公表の義務化（同法第 27 条）などが規定された。

国旗　National Flag

Ⅲ. The Conditions and Issues of Educational Administration, Finance and Management 183

aimed to make clear the responsibility of the board of education and to improve the system and management of the board of education. As a result, the Law concerning Local Educational administration and Operation was revised and the board of education was regulated to have a duty composing of students parents as members of the Board (the Article 4 of the Law). Then the board of education has to evaluate its activities by itself and provide the results of the evaluation to inform the assembly (the Article 27 of the Law).

校章　School Logo

6. 学校経営

(1) 学校の校務分掌

■学校は国・地方公共団体・学校法人によって設置され（教育基本法第6条、学校教育法第2条）、教育委員会等の行政機関が管理するのである。しかしながら、教育行政機関による学校管理は、大枠だけであって、各学校には学校経営の自主性が認められている。つまり、各学校は教育目標を効果的に達成するために、独自の学校経営組織をもっている。その組織の特に重要な機能は、意思決定とそれに基づいた実施である。

■学校内部の意思決定の機関は校長、教頭を中心に、彼らからの諮問に応じて意思決定に参加する職員会議である。また、その意思決定に基づいて実施にあたる組織として、校務分掌組織がある。図3-5は一般的な校務分掌の組織図である。校長・教頭をトップに総務・教務等の各部が置かれ、さらにその下に各係をおく組織になっているものが多い。学校の規模にかかわらず、校務分掌は変わらないので、少子化によって小規模化しつつある多くの学校では、一人の教職員がいくつもの係を兼務することになる。

6. School Management

(1) Allotment of School Management Duties in School

■ The school is established by the national government, a local government or an educational corporation (the Basic Act on Education, Art.6, the School Education Law, Art.2) and is managed by the board of education. Such an educational administrative body, however, only sets the framework for school administration. Each school is autonomous to some degree in school management; it can set up its own system of school management in order to efficiently achieve an educational goal. The most important elements of this system are the decision-making function and the implementation afterward.

■ The decision-making function in school involves teachers' meetings where they provide advice and suggestions and make decisions according to requests of a principal and a vice-principal. The executive function in school involves the allotment of school management duties where they put decisions into practice. A general allotment of school management is shown in Figure 3-5. In the hierarchy, a principal, (a vice principal) and a deputy vice-principal take charge of the top management. Under them some other teachers manage departments such as general affairs and instruction. Under this structure teachers are in charge of several sections in each department. When the number of sections is greater than the number of teachers, one teacher may have to hold concurrently plural posts.

図3-5 校務分掌図

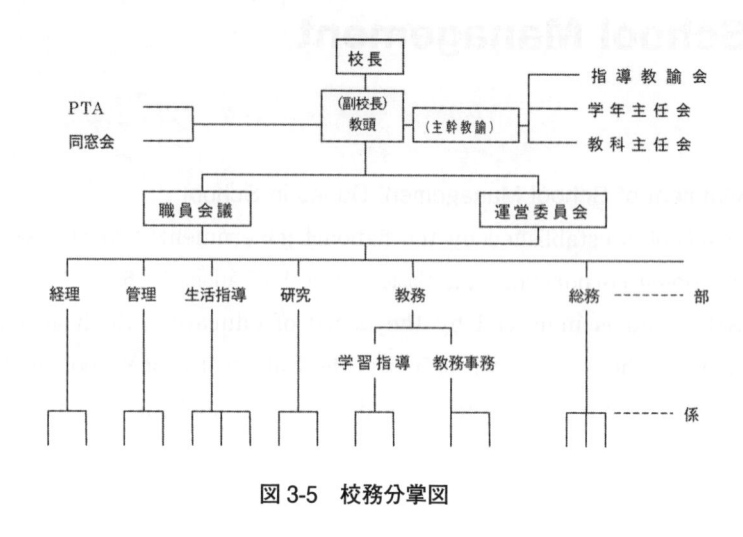

（2）校長・教頭・主任・職員会議

■校長は学校経営全般についての責任をもつ。校長の職務権限は「校務をつかさどり、所属職員を監督する」（学校教育法第37条4項）と規定されている。ここでいう「校務」とは、学校の運営に必要な全ての仕事、例えば、教育の内容に関する仕事、教職員の人事管理、児童・生徒の管理、学校の施設・設備の管理等を指している。

■教頭（副校長）は、校長の補佐役である。校長を援助し、校長に事故がある時は、その職を代理する（学校教育法第37条6項、8項）。

■学校には、校長の監督のもとで分担された校務について、教職員間の連絡調整および関係教職員に対する指導・助言を行う各種の主任が置かれている。主任は、いわば学校のチーム・リーダーの役割を期待されている。
■学校における組織運営体制や指導体制の確立を図るため、幼稚園、小・中学校等に、副校長、主幹教諭、指導教諭という職を置くことができるとされた（学校教育法第37条2項）。現在、全国の小・中学校において、教頭に代わっ

III. The Conditions and Issues of Educational Administration, Finance and Management 187

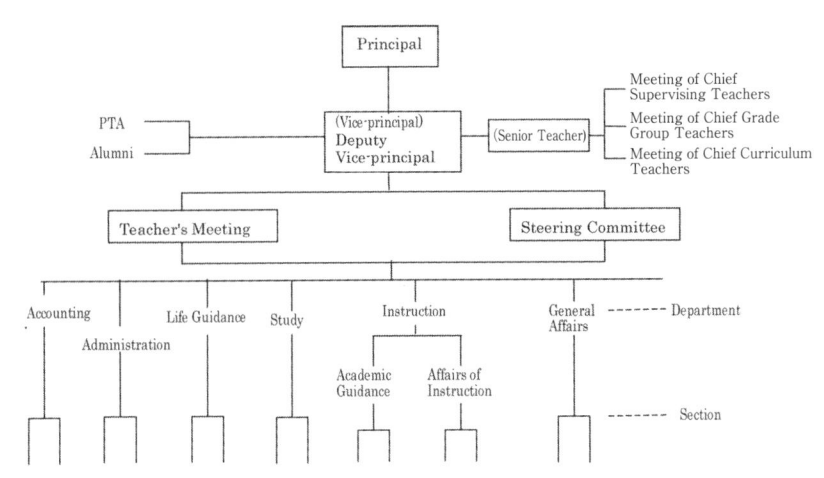

Figure 3-5 Diagram of Allotment of Educational Management Duties

(2) Principal, Vice-principal, Deputy Vice-Principal, Chief Teacher, and Teachers' Meeting

■ A principal is responsible for general management of a school. His or her duties and authorities are specified in the School Education Law, Art. 37-4 as "a principal takes charge of school affairs and supervises the staff." School affairs mean all duties needed for school management; for example, management of educational contents, school personnel, students, school facilities and equipment, and so forth.

■ A deputy vice principal (A vice-principal) is the assistant to the principal. He or she stands by the principal and performs the principal's duty if the former is incapacitated (the School Education Law, Art. 37-6 and 8).

■ Head teachers, under the principal's supervision, contact and coordinate among the staff, and provide teachers with guidance and advice. Head teachers are expected to play a team leader's role in school.

■ In order to establish the operation system of organization and instruction system of the schools, each school can set up the positions of vice-principal, senior teacher, and chief supervising teacher in kindergartens, primary, and

て副校長が、主任に代わって多くの主幹教諭が誕生している。

■校長は、リーダーシップを発揮して、自らの教育的信念に基づいた自律的・主体的な学校経営を行うべきとされる。しかし、その一方で学校管理機関である教育委員会と連携し、他方で教職員の意見も積極的にくみあげることが必要である。教職員の意見をくみあげるしくみとして、学校には、校長の諮問機関として職員会議が置かれている（学校教育法施行規則第 48 条）。また、ある程度以上の規模の学校では、校長を助けて校務の計画・運営を行う運営委員会が置かれている。経営におけるライン（命令系統）とスタッフ（助言系統）のバランスが求められている。

（3）年齢主義義務教育
■学校では、児童生徒が年齢とともに学年を進級する。そのため、原級留置や退学する児童生徒はほとんどみられず、児童生徒たちは毎年同じペースで一学年ずつ進級する。出席状況や学業が進級にふさわしくないと校長が判断したときのみ、原級留置となる。英才児童・生徒に対する飛び級制度は一部大学において認められているが基本的に採られていない。

（4）個性重視・学力問題
■従来、全国の学校や学級活動においては、集団主義に基づく一斉授業や集団特別教育活動などが行われてきた。しかし、1980 年代以降の教育改革の中で個性重視が強調され、とくに中学校や高等学校では、選択科目の重視、能力別・適性別クラス編成など、柔軟で多様なクラス編成がなされるようになってきた。集団主義から個性重視主義への転換が図られようとしてきている。ただ、いわゆる「学力低下」批判によって 1980 年代以降の「ゆとり」

lower secondary schools (Paragraph 2, Article 37 of the School Education Act). Currently, there are many vice-principals in place of deputy vice principals and senior teachers in place of chief teachers in primary and lower secondary schools nationwide.

■ A principal manages a school independently on the basis of his or her beliefs in education. Also, he or she needs to cooperate with the board of education, and listens to the requests and comments of the school teachers and personnel. Teachers usually request and comment in a teachers' meeting which has no legal authority, but takes part as an advisory board for the principal. Article 48 of the Ordinance for Enforcement of the School Education Act. Moreover, in some large schools, a steering committee is set up where the staff assists the principal in planning and managing school affairs. A balance between line (the chain of command) and staff (the chain of advice) is required.

(3) Compulsory Education according to Age

■ In schools, students are promoted automatically to the next grade according to age. Because of this system there are very few repeaters or drop-outs. Almost all children in school are promoted to the next grade every year. A few of them may repeat the same grade if the school principal thinks that they are not worthy of promotion because of poor attendance and unsatisfactory academic performance. At the same time, there is no system of skipping grades for gifted children.

(4) Emphasis on Individuality and Issues concerning Scholastic Ability

■ Traditionally, the school and class activities in Japan comprised whole class teaching and group special educational activities based on groupism. However, in the educational revolution after the 1980s, individuality was emphasized. In particular, in lower and upper secondary schools, more flexible and diversified class compositions which place more emphasis on elective subjects, group by ability, or group by adequacy have been made recently. School education aims

重視の教育から「学力」重視の教育に重点が移ってきており、全国学力調査結果の開示などによる学校間や地方自治体間の競争が懸念されている。

（5）教師の多忙化

■教職員の多忙感が問題になっており、その点、職員の疲労回復を図り、学校における教育活動を活性化させることも管理職にとって急務の事項である。地域ボランティアだけでなく、保護者や地域住民が気軽に入って来ることができるオープンな学校が目指されているなかで、教職員はその応対などに追われ、法律で認められている休憩でさえ取りにくくなっている。残業時間を減らして教員が授業を中心に児童生徒と関わる時間や職能開発に費やす時間を確保できる体制づくりの大切さが問題となっている。

（6）学校と家庭・地域の協力

■学校は、教科教育ばかりでなく、本来家庭が行っていた各種の機能を遂行している。例えば、給食指導、学校安全教育、学校掃除、健康診断、性教育などである。言い換えれば、学校は家庭の仕事の一部を分担しているわけである。そのため、教員は大変忙しく、通常、午前8時から午後5時まで働くが、多くの教員は5時以降も明日の準備に追われている。

■児童・生徒の保護者は、ＰＴＡ、授業参観、学校行事への参加、あるいは学校評議員などを通して学校教育に協力している。教育基本法13条にも「学校、家庭及び地域住民等の相互の連携・協力」が規定され、今後、学校支援ボランティアとして、保護者が学校教育に関わる機会も増えていくことが予想される。

to transform from groupism to the principle of placing emphasis on individuality. Still, due to the criticism of the decline of scholastic ability, the focus has been shifted from "more relaxed education" continued since the 1980s, to education placing emphasis on scholastic ability. The negative aspects of competition among schools and municipal governments by the disclosure of the results of the national achievement examinations are a future concern.

(5) Teachers Became Busier

■ Teachers and school staff have a busy schedule and that is a problem now. Relieving their fatigue and revitalizing teaching activities in the school is imperative for managerial posts. While pursuing an open school where not only the community volunteers, but also guardians and local residents can visit casually, teachers have been preoccupied to respond to it, and it is difficult to have a statutory break. It is vital to establish a system for the teachers to reduce overtime and secure time to spend with students mainly in the classes and develop their occupational abilities.

(6) Cooperation between School and Home

■ Aside from subject instructions, the school has various functions which originally belong to the family, such as the lunch program, safety program, school cleanliness program, medical check-up, and sex education. In other words, the school performs a partial function of the family. That is why the Japanese teachers are usually busy. They work from 8:00 a.m. to 5:00 p.m.. Some of them stay in the school even after 5:00 p.m. preparing for the next day.

■ Parents are encouraged to cooperate in school management through participation in PTA, class visits, and school events, and by becoming school councilors. Article 13 of the Basic Act on Education emphasizes "partnership and cooperation of schools, families, local residents, and other relevant persons." There will be greater opportunities for guardians to be involved in school education as volunteers in the future.

(7) 参加から参画へ

■中教審答申「今後の地方教育行政の在り方」(1998年9月)以降の教育改革は、これまで上からの法的な統制や指示などで制約されがちだった個々の学校の教育活動に対して、そうした制約を可能な限り取り除くことで、個々の学校の教育活動を起点とし、それを支援する教育体制をつくりあげようとしていることに特徴がある。特に、学校評議員制度が2000年から導入されて、これまでどちらか一方からの架け橋的なつながりしかできなかった学校と保護者、地域とのつながりは、責任のある連携となりつつある。

学校評議員制度は、学校外の有識者等の参加を得て、校長が行う学校運営に関し幅広い意見を聞き、必要な助言を求めるものである。地域の実情に応じて学校評議員を置くことができる。

■そして、学校評議員制度や学校における自己評価は、これまで閉鎖的だった学校教育に風穴をあける機会になりつつある。特に、学校評価に関わって、次のように規定され、自己評価だけでなく、いわゆる他者評価(学校関係者評価など)も求められるようになった。

「小学校は、当該小学校の教育活動その他の学校運営の状況について、自ら評価を行い、その結果を公表するものとする。」(学校教育法施行規則第66条①)

「小学校は、前条第1項による評価の結果を踏まえた当該小学校の児童の保護者その他の当該小学校の関係者(当該小学校の職員を除く。)による評価を行い、その結果を公表するように努めるものとする。」(学校教育法施行規則第67条)。

■保護者を含む地域住民の学校教育への参加の程度は、その地域の教育委員会や学校の対応に委ねられるという制度的な限界はあるものの、学校には情報を開示するためにそれなりの努力が求められるようになった。そして、教

(7) More Active Participation

■ Since the Central Council for Education reported, "The role of local educational administration in the future" in September 1998, educational reform was characterized by the following: By removing constraints of legal control and instructions from the central government, which tended to restrict educational activities of individual schools, the educational system which makes the educational activities of individual schools a base and makes a local government a supporter is aimed to be established. In particular, since the school councilor system was introduced in 2000, the relationship which used to be one way from either one of the school, guardians, and local community has begun to be a responsible partnership. The school council or system aims to have out-of-school intellectuals participate, listen to wide-ranging opinions about the principal's school operation, and receive necessary advice from them. A school council can be set up according to the local status.

■ Further, the school councilor system and self evaluation in schools are starting to be opportunities for a possible new approach to school education which had been closed until recently. Above all, not only self evaluation but also evaluations by others (persons who are associated with the school) are required in school evaluation now. With respect to these evaluations, there exist the following definitions: "Primary schools shall conduct self-evaluation with regard to their educational activities and status of school operation and announce the results officially." (Paragraph 1, Article 66 of the Ordinance for Enforcement of the School Education Act) and "Primary schools shall be evaluated by the guardians of the students, concerned parties (excluding the school personnel) based on the results of evaluation defined in Paragraph 1 of the preceding clause and make effort to announce the results officially." (Article 67 of the Ordinance for Enforcement of the School Education Act).

■ Although how much local residents and guardians participate in the school education owes to the local board of education and schools, the schools are required to make efforts to disclose information in some degree. In addition, the

育委員会は、首長部局と連携して教職員研修の充実など学校に対して支援をしたり、関係諸機関で子育て支援をしたりすることで学校に対しても地域住民に対しても責任ある教育体制を構築し、足腰の強い教育委員会になることを求められるようになってきた。

■今日、「設置者管理主義」と「設置者負担主義」を原則としながらも、地域の住民、保護者等が学校運営に参画する学校運営協議会を2005年から設置できるようになり（いわゆるコミュニティスクール、地教行法第47条の5）、公立学校の管理運営について、家庭、地域と学校が責任と権限を共有するガバナンス改革が進められている。学校運営協議会は、保護者や地域住民が一定の権限と責任を持って運営に直接参加する協議組織であり、地域運営学校に置かれる。同校は2005年度から設立が認められた。

boards of education are asked to establish a responsible educational system for the schools and local residents and to be a robust organization by supporting the schools in enriching teacher training programs, and providing child-raising support with relative institutions by collaborating with the bureaus of mayors.

■ Since 2005, by a revision of the Act Concerning Organization and Operation of Local Educational Administration, the school management board in which local residents and guardians can involve themselves in school operations was allowed to be established, while maintaining the basic principles that a school establisher should manage it and bear the cost. With regard to the management and operation of public schools, governance reform is underway for the family, local community, and the school which commonly have a responsibility and authority. The school operation council is an organization in which guardians and local residents directly participate in its operations with some degree of authority and responsibility. The council is set up in a locally operated school or a community school, which has been approved to be established since the fiscal 2005 year.

7. 教育財政

(1) 財政責任と財政格差
■日本では、学校経営の負担は「設置者負担主義」がとられている。これは、国・地方公共団体・学校法人がそれぞれの設置する学校の経費を自己負担するという原則である（学校教育法5条）。しかし、実際には、①地方自治体の財政力の貧困さから国と地方の財政格差（垂直的格差）、②産業構造の地域的不均衡による地方自治体間の財政格差（水平的格差）、③公立学校と私立学校間の財政格差などが生じ、それらの財政格差の是正をめざす多くの学校経費負担の特例が設けられている。例えば、垂直的財政格差の是正のためには、地方自治体に対する国庫負担金・補助金制度が設けられており、水平的財政格差の是正のためには、地方交付税制度が設けられている。また公立学校と私立学校間の格差に対しては、私学助成制度が拡充されてきている。

■したがって、設置者負担の原則が法的に規定されていながら、実際には、国・地方公共団体・学校法人・学習者（私費）がそれぞれの財政能力に応じて分担しあう形になっている。表3-2は、公立小中学校の主な教育費の負担区分を示したものである。

7. Educational Finance

(1) School Finance Responsibility and Financial Differences

■ In Japan, based on "the principle of sponsorship by founders", national government, a local government or educational corporation bears the expense of its own schools (the School Education Law, Art.5). In reality, however, there are a lot of exceptions to adjust financial gaps: ① a so-called vertical difference between national and local, in which public finance of local government is not adequate; ② a horizontal difference among local governments, because of local disparity in industry; and ③ difference between public and private schools. In order to solve these differences, exceptions are made for; the system of national subsidies to local governments in the vertical difference, and the system of local allocation tax grants in the horizontal difference, and the system of financial aid to private schools for the difference between public and private schools.

■ The school expenditure, in principle, lies in the hand of the school founders. In reality, however, it is shared by national government, local governments, educational corporations and students, according to their financial conditions. Table 3-2 shows the sharing of the main educational expenditure in public primary and lower secondary schools.

表 3-2　主な教育費の負担区分（公立小中学校）

教育費の種類	負担区分		
	国	都道府県	市町村
教科書費	1		
県費負担教職員の給与	1／3	2／3	
施設費			
・新増築	1／2		1／2
・危険建物費	1／3		2／3
災害復旧 （＊離島・沖縄県への国の補助率は上記の割合より高い）	2／3		1／3
学校建物の維持・修繕費			1

出典：公立学校施設法令研究会編『公立学校施設整備事務ハンドブック』等

（2）国の教育費

■図3-6は2007年度の国（文部科学省）の教育予算の構成を示したものである。国の歳出に占める教育予算の割合は、13.6％である。義務教育義務教育国庫負担金は毎年大きくなっている。義務教育国庫負担金（31.6％）、国立大学法人運営費交付金（22.8％）、私学助成（8.6％）を合わせて約60％を占めた。近年、行政改革と関連して予算の削減がきわめて重要事項となり、教育費に対する国庫負担の削減や教科書無償制度の再検討が改革の主要課題とされている。生涯学習の推進、学術の発展、私学助成など社会変化に対応する教育政策が実施されてきたが、国の教育予算は増加しなかった。

III. The Conditions and Issues of Educational Administration, Finance and Management 199

Table 3-2 Sharing of the Main Educational Expenditure (Public Primary and Lower Secondary Schools)

教育費の種類	Expenditure Sharing		
	National	Prefectural	Municipal
Textbooks	1		
Teachers Salary	1/3	2/3	
Facilities			
・Building & Expansion	1/2		1/2
・Hazardous Building	1/3		2/3
・Disaster Restoration (* Rate of National Subsidies to remote island's & Okinawa are higher than above)	2/3		1/3
Buildings Maintenance			1

Resource: The Society for the Study of Public School Facilities and Regulations (Edited),
"A Handbook for the Management of Facilities Arrangement of Public Schools"

(2) Educational Expenditure of the National Government

■ Figure 3-6 shows the educational budget of the nation (the Ministry of Education, Culture, Sports, Science and Technology) in 2007. The ratio of the educational budget to the whole national budget was 13.6%. The National Treasury Share of Compulsory Education Expenditure tends to be large every year. Subsidies to the National Treasury Share of Compulsory Education (31.6 %), national university bodies (22.8%) and private schools (8.6%) were about 60%. Recently slashing of the budget has become a very important task linked with administrative reform, therefore slashing the national subsidies to education and reexamination on the free distribution system of textbooks, etc., have been discussed as main issues of the reform. Therefore, the national education budget, has not increased recently even though the educational policies to meet the social changes, such as the promotion of lifelong learning, the development of academic study and aid to private schools have been carried out.

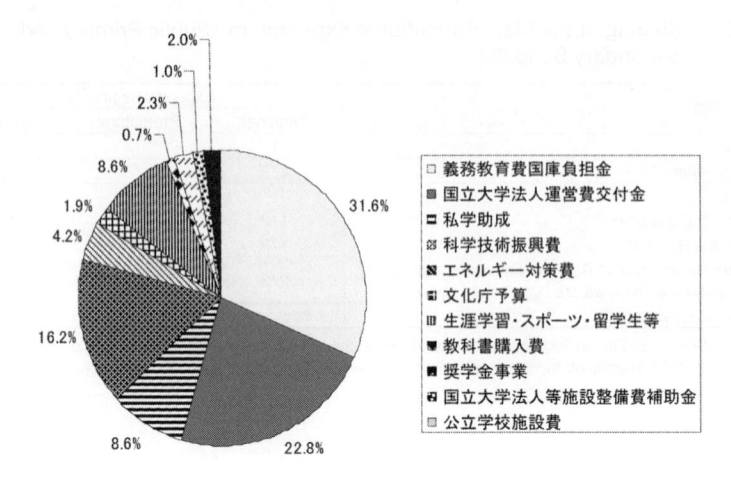

図3-6 国の教育予算（2007年度、総額5兆2,705億円）
出典：文部科学省ホームページ、2009年

凡例：
- 義務教育費国庫負担金 31.6%
- 国立大学法人運営費交付金 22.8%
- 私学助成 16.2%
- 科学技術振興費 8.6%
- エネルギー対策費 4.2%
- 文化庁予算 1.9%
- 生涯学習・スポーツ・留学生等 8.6%
- 教科書購入費 0.7%
- 奨学金事業 2.3%
- 国立大学法人等施設整備費補助金 1.0%
- 公立学校施設費 2.0%

（3）地方公共団体の教育費

■都道府県の教育費は、都道府県立の教育施設の経費、市町村立小中学校・定時制高校教員の給与・手当（国1/3、都道府県2/3）、市町村への教育費補助などを含む。一方、市町村の教育費は、市町村立小中学校の経費（教員給与は除く）、その他、市町村立教育施設の経費などを含む。表3-3（1）は最近5年間の地方教育費総額の推移を示したものである。また、表3-3（2）は、2007年度の地方教育費の教育分野別構成比を示したものである。

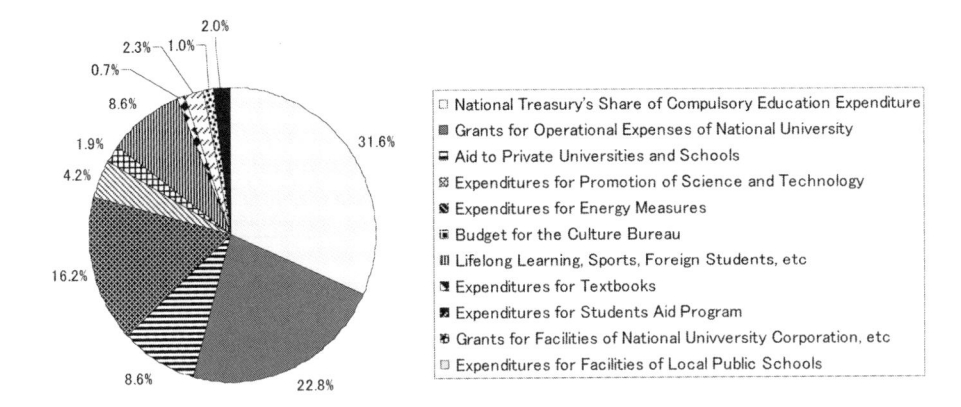

Figure 3-6　Educational Budget of the National Government (5,270.5 billion yen, 2007)
Resource: Home Pages of the Ministry of Education, Culture, Sports, Science and Technology, 2009

Legend:
- National Treasury's Share of Compulsory Education Expenditure
- Grants for Operational Expenses of National University
- Aid to Private Universities and Schools
- Expenditures for Promotion of Science and Technology
- Expenditures for Energy Measures
- Budget for the Culture Bureau
- Lifelong Learning, Sports, Foreign Students, etc
- Expenditures for Textbooks
- Expenditures for Students Aid Program
- Grants for Facilities of National Univversity Corporation, etc
- Expenditures for Facilities of Local Public Schools

Values: 31.6%, 22.8%, 8.6%, 16.2%, 4.2%, 1.9%, 8.6%, 0.7%, 2.3%, 1.0%, 2.0%

(3) Educational Expenditure of the Local Government

■ Prefectural governments are responsible for the expenditure of prefectural educational facilities, for salaries and allowances of teachers in municipal compulsory schools and part-time upper secondary schools (although a third of them are contributed by the national government), and for financial aid to municipalities. Municipal governments, on the other hand, are responsible for the expenditure of municipal compulsory schools (except salaries of teachers) and apart from expenditure of the other municipal institutions. Table 3-3 (1) shows the transition of the total educational expenditure of the local governments during the five-year period. In addition, Table 3-3 (2) shows the ratio of each field of education compared to the total educational expenditure of the local governments in the 2007 fiscal year.

表3-3 (1) 地方教育費総額の推移
(2) 地方教育費分野別構成比（2007年度）

(1)

年度	地方教育費総額（億円）	対前年度伸び率（%）
2003	176,320	−2.8
2004	172,614	−2.1
2005	169,947	−1.5
2006	166,655	−1.9
2007	165,584	−0.6

(2)

教育分野	構成比（%）
地方教育費総額	100.0
A 学校教育費	83.4
小学校	37.8
中学校	20.8
特別支援学校	5.3
高等学校	17.7
その他	1.8
B 社会教育費	10.9
C 教育行政費	5.7

出典：文部科学省『地方教育費調査』2007年

（4）父母負担教育費

■授業料は国公立義務教育学校（公立小中学校）では無償で、教科書費は国公私立小中学校とも無償である。しかし、教科書以外の図書費、学用品、交通費、ＰＴＡ会費等の学校教育費と学校給食費は父母が負担しなければならない。また、家庭教育費（塾、ピアノ・そろばん・習字等のおけいこごとに通う費用等）は全て父母が負担しなければならない。物価の高騰、進学熱の高まりなどを反映して、年々、父母の負担する教育費は増加してきている。

（5）児童生徒一人あたりの学校教育費

■表3-4は、2007年度の学校種類別児童生徒一人あたりの学校教育費を示したものである。盲・聾・養護学校（現在の特別支援学校）には、小学校の約9.4

Table 3-3 (1) Transition of Local Educational Expenditure
(2) Ratio of Local Education Expenditure according to Areas (School Year, 2007)

(1)

Year	Total Local Educational Expenditure (100 million yen)	annual growth rate (%)
2003	176,320	-2.8
2004	172,614	-2.1
2005	169,947	-1.5
2006	166,655	-1.9
2007	165,584	-0.6

(2)

Area of Education	Ratio (%)
Total Local Educational Expenditure	100.0
A School Educational Expenditure	83.4
Primary School	37.8
Lower Secondary School	20.8
Special Needs School	5.3
Upper Secondary Schools (Full-time)	17.7
Others	1.8
BSocial Education Expenditure	10.9
CEducational Administration Expenditure	5.7

Resource: Ministry of Education, Culture, Sports, Science and Technology, "A Survey of Local Government Expenditures on Education" 2007

(4) Educational Expenditure Shared by Parents

■ Tuition fees are free in public compulsory schools (public primary and lower secondary schools) and expenditures for textbooks are free in both public and private compulsory schools. However, expenditures such as those for books except school textbooks and other school necessities, transportation, PTA dues, and school lunch are paid for by the parents. Furthermore, parents must bear all of the home educational expenditure (e.g. expenses of private lessons at juku, and lessons in piano, abacus, calligraphy, and so on). Because of the rise in prices and the high enthusiasm for education, educational expenditure shared by parents is increasing every year.

(5) Educational Expenditure per Student

■ Table 3-4 shows the educational expenditure per student by types of school in 2007. It should be pointed out that about 9.4 times as much expenditure as that

倍の経費をかけている点が注目に値する。

表3-4　学校種類別、児童生徒一人あたり学校教育費（2007年度）

学校種類	在学者1人当り教育費（円）	指数
幼稚園	718,379	81
小学校	892,064	100
中学校	1,036,342	116
特別支援学校	8,390,908	941
高等学校（全日制）	1,191,140	134
（定時制）	1,792,959	201
（通信制）	256,648	29
中等教育学校	1,918,827	215
専修学校	1,474,415	165
各種学校	725,468	81
高等専門学校	1,875,353	210

出典：文部科学省『地方教育費調査』2007年

（6）就学奨励・援助

■経済的理由により就学困難な児童生徒に対する就学奨励・援助の制度は次の3つに分かれる。
①厚生労働省による教育扶助（教科書・学用品等）－「生活保護法」第13条で規定
②文部科学省、都道府県・市町村教育委員会による就学奨励（学用品・通学費・修学旅行費・学校給食費等）－「就学奨励法」「学校給食法」等多くの法律で規定
③障害児を対象とする就学援助（教科書費・寄宿舎費・通学、帰省、付添いに要する交通費等）－「発達障害者支援法」等で規定

of primary school is allocated to schools for the blind, schools for the deaf, and special schools (School for special Needs Children).

Table 3-4 Educational Expenditure per Student by Types of School (School Year, 2007)

Type of School	Expenditure per Student (yen)	Index
Kindergarten	718,379	81
Primary School	892,064	100
Lower Secondary School	1,036,342	116
School for Special Needs Children	8,390,908	941
Upper Secondary School (Full-time)	1,191,140	134
(Part-time)	1,792,959	201
(Correspondence)	256,648	29
Secondary School	1,918,827	215
Specialized Training College	1,474,415	165
Miscellaneous School	725,468	81
Technical College	1,875,353	210

Resource: Ministry of Education, Culture, Sports, Science and Technology, "A Survey of Local Government Expenditures on Education" 2007

(6) Student Aid Programs

■ The aid programs for students who have difficulty in receiving education for economic reasons are categorized into the following three;
① Support by the Ministry of Health, Labor and Welfare (such as supply of textbooks, and school necessities), as prescribed by Article 13 of the Welfare Law.
② Educational aid program by the Ministry of Education, Culture, Sports, Science and Technology, prefectural and municipal boards of education (such as supply of school necessities, transportation expenses, expenditure for school excursions, school lunch fee, and so on), as prescribed by laws such as the School Enrollment Promotion Law and the School Lunch Program Law.
③ Educational aid for handicapped children (such as providing for textbooks, dormitory expenses, transportation expenses of students and attendants, as well as transportation expenses for home visits), as prescribed by the School Enrollment Promotion Law for Handicapped Children.

■上記①②の就学奨励制度は義務教育の分野だけに適用される。高等学校・高等専門学校・大学等の学生に対しては、「日本学生支援機構」による奨学金貸与をはじめ多くの民間財団・地方公共団体等の奨学金制度がある。日本学生支援機構は、2004年に設立され日本育英会の事業を引き継いだ。ただし、高校生に対する奨学金は、主に地方公共団体が提供している。

（7）私立学校への助成

■1960年代以降、高等学校・大学への進学者数の増大の中で、私立学校経営の悪化が生じ、教育条件の低下・授業料等の公私間格差が大きな問題となった。このため、私立学校の教育条件の向上と学生・生徒の就学上の経済的負担の軽減をはかることを目的に、私立学校に対する国庫助成が拡充されてきた。1970年に私立学校の経常費へ助成を行う「日本私学振興財団」が創設され、1975年には「私立学校振興助成法」が制定された。「日本私学振興財団」を通じて交付される助成金は総経常費の1/2を限度としている。

■2007年度、私立大学等の経常費補助として、前年度より1％増の3,280億5,000万円が計上された。経常経費補助以外にも、私立大学等の学術研究の振興を図り、高等教育の高度化に対応するために、研究装置補助（106億3,000万円）、研究設備補助（73億3,000万円）も計上された。一方、私立高等学校等の経常費補助として、前年度と同額の1,038億5,000万円円が計上され、その他、情報教育施設整備費なども助成された。

■私立学校への助成をめぐっては数多くの問題が議論されてきた。その最も根源的な問題は、私立学校への公費助成が日本国憲法第89条「公の財産の

■ The aid programs mentioned in ① and ② are applicable to the students of compulsory education. Students of upper secondary schools, technical colleges, colleges and universities are able to receive scholarships from the Japan Student Service Organization, many private foundations, and local governments. The Japan Student Service Organization was established in 2004 and succeeded the works of the Japan Scholarship Foundation. The scholarships for the students of upper secondary school are provided mainly by local governments.

(7) Aid to Private Schools

■ Since the 1960's, as the number of students who go to upper secondary school or college increases, the management of private schools has experienced difficulties, and problems such as the deterioration of educational conditions and the gap between public and private schools, like tuition fees, have arisen. As a result, government aids to private schools have been expanded to improve educational conditions and to reduce individual burden in education. In 1970, the Foundation for the Promotion of Japanese Private Schools was established to share the running expenses of private schools, and in 1975, the Private School Promotion Aid Law was enacted. The aids to private schools, granted by the Foundation for the Promotion of Japanese Private Schools, are limited to one half of the sum of the actual running expenses.

■ 328,050 million yen (1 % increase from the previous year) was appropriated for the aid to the running expenses of private universities in the 2007 fiscal year. In addition, in order to promote scientific studies in the private universities and to meet the upgrade of higher education, the aid for research apparatus (10,630 million yen) and for research equipment (7,330 million yen), was appropriated. Furthermore aid for the running expenses of private upper secondary schools, 103,850 million yen (the same amount with the previous year) was appropriated, as well as aid to facilities for data processing education.

■ Many problems concerning the aid to private schools have been discussed. The basic problem is whether or not the governmental aid to private schools

支出利用の制限」の規定に違反しないのかという論点である。また、私立学校への公費助成が国の規制の強化につながり、私立学校の自主性や、独自性を歪めるのではないかという問題点もしばしば指摘されてきた。

校長室で開かれている学校評議員会　School Council Meeting Carried Out in a Principal's Room

violates Article 89 of the Constitution which restricts the use of public money or other property. Furthermore, the other problem which has been pointed out is that the aid to private schools might lead to stricter control by the government, and consequently the independence and originality of private schools might be restricted.

8. 教育行財政・経営の課題

■現在、日本は大きな教育改革に着手してきているが、その中で、教育行財政・経営の改革も重要な課題となっている。教育行財政・経営の様々な側面について数多くの意見・考えが提示され、教育改革の過度期にあるといえるが、ここでは現在の教育行財政・経営改革の動向と課題について、主なポイントを示す。

(1) 教育計画に基づく教育行財政
■教育基本法が改正され（2006年12月）、その理念を具現化するために教育振興基本計画に基づいて様々な教育改革が行われようとしている。すなわち、限られた教育資源をより有効に活用し、質の高い教育事業を行うことが要請されている。ここに、体系的な教育目標を策定することが重要課題となる。1960年代以降の高度経済成長下の日本においては、教育計画の目標は経済成長の担い手（マンパワー）を養成することにあった。しかし、その教育計画の実施によって、多くの教育問題が生じた。今後は、マンパワー計画の反省をもとに、教育の人間化をめざした教育計画が策定される必要がある。言い換えれば、憲法に定められた国民の教育を受ける権利の保障の実現をめざした教育計画の策定とその執行が日本の教育行財政の重要課題である。

(2) 教育の国際化に対応する教育行財政
■現在、教育の領域における国際交流や国際協力がますます活発になり、教育の国際化と呼ばれる状況が生じてきている。教育の国際化に対応できる国際人としての日本人育成が教育の重要課題となり、すでに日本各地でそのための実践も行われるようになってきている。小学校では、これまでも「総合

8. The Issues in Educational Administration, Finance and Management

■ In the educational reforms that the Japanese government has carried out to the present, the reform of educational administration, finance and management has become an important issue. While many people have stated their opinions on various aspects of educational administration, finance and management in the transitional phase of educational reform, the main points of the discussion are shown in the following.

(1) Educational Administration and Finance Based on Educational Planning
■ The Fundamental Law of Education was revised in December 2006 and various educational reforms have been attempted based on the basic promotion plan for education in order to shape its principle. It is required to effectively harness limited educational resources and launch high-quality educational projects. Therefore, systematic educational planning has become necessary. When the plan is made, the most important thing to keep in mind is what the goals should be. Since the 1960's, when Japan enjoyed a high economic growth, the goal of education has been to train manpower for economic growth. Nevertheless, implementation of that goal caused many educational problems. A plan should aim for a more human education. In other words, the important task in Japan's educational administration and finance is to make and carry out the program aiming to guarantee the right of the people to receive an education.

(2) Educational Administration and Finance for Internationalization of Education
■ Recently, international exchange and cooperation in education have been actively promoted. It has also become an important task to educate Japanese as internationally-minded persons and such attempts have already been carried out in some parts of Japan. In the future, preparing educational conditions to

的な学習の時間」において「国際化への対応」として英語活動が取り入れられてきたが、2011年4月から全国すべての小学校高学年において「外国語活動」が実施される。さらに、帰国児童生徒・外国人児童生徒や増加する留学生の受け入れ体制を整備することも緊急の課題となっている。今後は、このような教育の国際化の中で、日本の教育行財政が自らの組織変革を行うと同時に、日本の国際化をめざした教育の条件整備を行うことが重要な課題である。

（3）教育行財政における規制の緩和
■現代福祉国家においては必然的に国民生活のすみずみにまで行政が関与する。教育行財政についてもそれは同様である。現代日本において、中央教育行政の役割が強化され、国の教育財政負担も増大させられてきた。「国→都道府県教育委員会→市町村教育委員会→学校」という一連の統制の機構が確立してきたのである。このような状態を打開するために、教育行政の地方分権化の意義の再確認、こまごまとした規則の撤廃による教育の自由化が重要な課題となっている。

①地方分権化と財源移譲
■現在、政府の地方分権改革推進会議において、義務教育に関する国と地方の経費負担のあり方の見直しが提言され、義務教育費国庫負担金の一般財源化を視野に入れた義務教育費国庫負担制度の見直しが進められている。その結果、義務教育費国庫負担金の国庫負担率は2分の1から3分の1になり、また、負担金総額の使途を地方裁量とし、都道府県が給与・教職員の配置を自主的に決定する「総額裁量制」が導入された。

internationalize Japan will be an important issue. In primary schools, English activities have been carried out in the period for integrated studies to respond to internationalization, and foreign language activities will be implemented compulsory at a higher grade of all primary schools from April 2011. In addition, the establishment of the system to receive returnee students and students with foreign nationalities residing in Japan, provision of suitable instructions to them, and the establishment of a system to receive increasing international students are imminent issues to be tackled. Hereafter, amid ongoing internationalization of education, while the Japanese administrative and financial authorities reform the organizations themselves, a critical issue is to develop the condition of education aiming to internationalize Japan simultaneously.

(3) Deregulation of the Control in Educational Administration and Finance

■ In a modern welfare state, the government is necessarily involved in every aspect of the national well-being. This is also the same with education. In Japan today, as the role of the central educational administration has been strengthened, the national share in educational finance has increased. Also, the hierarchical system of control has been established from national government to prefectural board of education, to municipal board of education and further down to the schools. To reform such a situation, it is important to decentralize educational administration and liberalize education by abolishing many trivial regulations.

① Decentralization and devolution of financial resources

■ In the Decentralization Promotion Committee of the government, reconsideration of the apportionment of expenses of compulsory education between the national government and local government is proposed, and the system of the government financial contribution toward the management of compulsory education has been reviewed with the aim to incorporate the government financial contribution into the general budget. As a result, the government share of the contribution reduced from 1/2 to 1/3, and a

②構造改革特区
■また、政府の総合規制改革会議においても、構造改革特区において、「公設民営方式」を解禁するように提言し、地方公共団体が特別なニーズがあると認める場合に、株式会社並びに不登校児童生徒等の教育を行うNPO法人で一定の実績を有するものが学校を設立できるようになった。

③参画と責任
■しかし、教育基本法の改正をきっかけに、教育委員に保護者を必ず含む（地方教育行政の組織及び運営に関する法律第4条）など地方分権化や地域住民の意向の反映がいっそう進んだ半面、教育委員会の法令違反やいじめなど緊急事態に対して、文部科学省が是正や指示ができるようになるなど教育行政の責任も明確にされるようになってきた（同法49条、50条）。

④幼保一元化
■価値観が多様化し、変化が急激な現代社会において、子どもをめぐる課題が山積している中で、縦割り行政の課題も指摘されている。児童虐待、経済格差による子どもの貧困などの問題に関わって、教育行政の中心を担う文部科学省と福祉行政の中心を担う厚生労働省の連携も進み始めた。その点、「就学前の子どもに関する教育、保育等の総合的な提供の推進に関する法律」（2006年6月公布）によって発足した認定こども園制度は従来から懸案としてあった幼保一元化の具現化として注目されている。

"discretionally budget system" was introduced. By this, the local governments are able to use the budget freely within the total amount of contribution, and the prefectural governments are able to autonomously decide the salaries and allocation of teachers and school staff.

② Designated special zone for structural reform

■ In addition, lifting the ban of "public-establishment, private-operation system" in designated special zones for structural reform was proposed in the Council for Regulatory Reform of the government. As a result, stock companies and NPOs that provide education to truant students are allowed to establish schools if they have certain experiences in the case where local public authorities acknowledge there is a special need for that.

③ Involvement and responsibility

■ Triggered by the revision of the Basic Act on Education, power has been decentralized and local residents' opinions have been more reflected as exemplified by Article 4 of the Act Concerning Organization and Operation of Regional Educational Administration regulated to include a guardian in the educational board members. On the other hand, the responsibilities of educational administrations are clarified in Article 49 and 50 of the same Act as exemplified by Ministry of Education, Culture, Sports, Science and Technology can rectify and give instructions in case of emergency issues such as law violation by the board of education and bullying.

④ Unification of kindergartens and day care centers

■ In modern society, with diversified values and rapid changes, problems concerning the vertically-segmented administrative system are pointed out in the face of mounting issues regarding children. The Ministry of Education, Culture, Sports, Science and Technology, which plays a central role of educational administration, and the Ministry of Health, Labor, and Welfare, which plays a central role of welfare administration, have started collaborating to tackle the issues of child abuse and poverty of children due to economic disparity. The system of "certified institutions for early childhood education and care" was

(4) 教育行政・経営参加システムの創造

■国レベルで教育行政を行う主要な官庁は文部科学省である。2001年1月の中央省庁の改編により（旧）文部省と科学技術庁は、文部科学省に発展的に改組された。それに伴い、学識経験者や教育実践者が関与して、教育課程、教育職員養成、大学、生涯学習など様々な教育政策決定に関わる提言をしていたそれぞれの審議会が中央教育審議会に統合された。「新しい時代にふさわしい教育基本法と教育振興基本計画の在り方について」（2003年3月）、「今後の教員養成・免許制度の在り方について」（2006年7月）などの中教審答申に基づいて、教育基本法が改正され、また、教職大学院が創設された。教員免許更新制も2009年4月から導入されることとなったが、政権が代わってその行方が不透明になっている。

■過去、2大政党制をとる国においては、政権が変わると教育制度が変わることもあったが、今後、国民が教育行政に積極的に関わって、子どもの学習権を保障するためによりよい制度が検討されていく必要性が指摘されている。

launched by the Act on Advancement of Comprehensive Service Related to Education, Child Care, etc. of Pre-school Children, issued in June 2006. This has been drawing much attention as an example of the realization of the unification of kindergartens and day care centers, which had been a concern for some time.

(4) Establishment of the Participation System in Educational Administration and Management

■ The Ministry of Education, Culture, Sports, Science and Technology is the main authority that conducts educational administration at the national level. As a result of the central government reform, the Ministry of Education, Science and Culture was developmentally reorganized to the Ministry of Education, Culture, Sports, Science and Technology by integrating with the Science and Technology Agency. In consequence, each council, in which academic experts and educators were involved and made proposals related to various educational policy decisions, including issues of curriculum, fostering teachers and school staff, colleges/universities, and lifelong learning, was integrated into the Central Council for Education. The Fundamental Law of Education was revised and graduate schools of teacher education were established based on the reports of the Central Council for Education such as "The Fundamental Law of Education and the Basic Promotion Plan for Education Suitable for the New Era" (March 2003) and "The Future Form of teacher training and the Teacher Certification System" (July 2006). Hereinafter, the issue of teacher certificate renewal plan which was introduced in April of 2009 remains unclear because the governments have changed.

■ Due to the regime change, however, the prospect is unclear. In the past, there were cases in which the education system was changed when the regime was changed in the counties having a two-party system. It is pointed out that the national public must be positively involved in educational administration and a better system has to be discussed to guarantee children's right of learning in the future.

■地方レベルでは、教育の住民自治の観点から様々な教育行政参加のシステムが検討されねばならない。このために、例えば、教育に関する各種の情報の公開を推進すること、教育委員の公選制の再検討、教育に関する公聴会・諮問委員会等の拡充などが重要になる。すでに、指導要録の開示、高校入試・教員採用試験結果の開示などが進んできているが、現在のように、地方教育費が国庫補助に大きく依存している状態では教育の住民自治の実現は難しい。教育行政の構造の変換が求められている。

■学校経営のレベルでは、教師・親・生徒が参加できるシステムの確立が重要であろう（Ⅲ－6参照）。今日、学校評議員制度、学校運営協議会制度の導入、そして、学校評価や学校支援地域本部事業などを通じて、学校経営におけるガバナンス改革が進んでいる。日本において、まさに「社会総がかりの教育改革」が求められている。

■ At the local level, various systems enabling us to participate in educational administration must be planned from the viewpoint of the people's self-governance of education. For this purpose, it is important to disseminate public information about education, to reconsider the possibility of an elective board of education, and to expand the opportunity for public hearings and consultative committee concerning education. Now, since local educational expenditure largely depends on national subsidies, it is difficult to realize the people's self-governance of education. Therefore, the educational finance system has to be reformed.

■ With regard to school management, the establishment of a system of open school management in which teachers, guardians, and students can participate is important (refer to III-6). Today, through the school council system, the school management board system, school evaluation, and the school support regional program, a governance reform of school management has been advancing. In Japan, the all-out mobilization of the society for school reform is highly essential.

教員研修　Teachers' In-Service Training

第Ⅳ章

教員制度の現状と課題

The Conditions and Issues of Teachers

教員室　Teachers' Room

1. 日本の教職員の特徴

(1) 教職観

■教職という仕事をどのようなものとしてとらえるかについて、従来、「聖職者」観あるいは「全体の奉仕者」観と「教育労働者」観が対立してきた。ILO・ユネスコの「教員の地位に関する勧告」(1966年) 以来、「教育専門職」観が登場し、次第にわが国でもこの見方が強調されるようになった。しかし、専門職の内容や専門職性を確立する具体的方策についてはまだ意見の一致をみるにいたっていない。

(2) 日本の教職員の種類と職務内容

■日本の教職員は、職務内容により多くの職種に分かれている。表4-1は小・中・高校の主要な職種（校長、副校長、教頭、教諭等）と法令（学校教育法・同法施行規則）に示された職務内容を表したものである。

表4-1 小・中・高の教職員の主要職種と職務内容

職種	小	中	高	職務
校長	◎	◎	◎	校務をつかさどり、所属職員を監督する
副校長	△	△	△	校長を助け、命を受けて校務をつかさどる
教頭	○	○	◎	校長を助け、校務を整理し、必要に応じて児童・生徒の教育をつかさどる
主幹教諭	△	△	△	校長（副校長）・教頭を助け、命を受けて校務の一部を整理し、児童・生徒の教育をつかさどる
指導教諭	△	△	△	児童・生徒の教育をつかさどり、教諭その他の職員に対して、教育指導の改善・充実のために必要な指導・助言を行う
教諭	◎	◎	◎	児童・生徒の教育をつかさどる
教務主任	○	○	○	校長の監督を受け、教務に関する事項の連絡調整、指導、助言。指導教諭又は教諭をもって充てる。

1. Characteristics of Japanese Teachers and Staff

(1) Views on the Teaching Occupation

■ Two views on the teaching occupation have been in rivalry; 'sacred worker' or 'public servant for all' on the one hand, and 'teaching laborer' on the other. Since "The Recommendation Concerning the Status of Teachers" (1966) by ILO and UNESCO, the view of the 'teaching as a profession' gradually came to be emphasized in our country. However, there is no agreement on the content of the profession and the concrete policy of establishing professionalism.

(2) The Variety and Job Specifications of Japanese Teachers and Other School Personnel

■ Teachers and other school personnel in Japan are classified according to their job specifications. Table 4-1 illustrates the major types of school staff (principal, vice-principal, deputy vice-principal, teacher, etc.) in primary and secondary schools and their job specifications given by the School Education Law as well as its Enforcement Regulations.

Table 4-1 Major Types of School Staff and Their Job Specifications in Primary and Secondary Schools

Types of School Staff	Primary	Lower Secondary	Upper Secondary	Job Specification
Principal	◎	◎	◎	Take charge of school affairs and directs the personnel.
Vice-principal	△	△	△	Helps the principal, and takes charge of school affairs under direction of the principal.
Deputy Vice-principal	○	○	◎	Helps the principal, arrange school affairs, and educate students if necessary
Senior teacher	△	△	△	Helps the principal (vice-principal) and the deputy vice-principal, organizes some school affairs, and takes charge of students' education under the direction of the principal.

職	小	中	高	職務
学年主任	○	○	○	校長の監督を受け、学年の教育活動の連絡調整、指導、助言。指導教諭又は教諭をもって充てる。
進路指導主事	—	○	○	校長の監督を受け、生徒の職業選択の指導その他の進路の指導に関する事項をつかさどり、教職員間の連絡調整、指導・助言に当たる。指導教諭又は教諭をもって充てる。
生徒指導主事	—	○	○	校長の監督を受け、生徒指導に関する事項をつかさどり、連絡調整、指導・助言に当たる。指導教諭又は教諭をもって充てる。
養護教諭	◎	◎	△	児童・生徒の養護をつかさどる
栄養教諭	△	△	△	児童・生徒の栄養の指導・管理をつかさどる
事務職員	◎	◎	◎	事務に従事する
学校用務員	△	△	△	学校の環境の整備その他の用務に従事する

◎＝必置職
○＝特別の事情があるときは（当分の間）置かないことができる職
△＝置くことができる職

（3）日本の教職員の特徴

■日本の教職員に関する基本的な統計を示して、その全体的な特徴を説明する。

　まず、教員数（本務）を表 4-2 に示した。この表で教員には校長・学長が含まれる。女子教員の割合は、幼稚園・小学校・中学校・高等学校・大学と学校段階が上がるにつれて、その割合が低くなる。短期大学では、学生の約 90％ が女子であることや家政・人文・教育等を専攻する学生数が多いことなどが関係して、約 49％ が女子教員である。また、女子教員の割合は、小・中・高等学校とも、徐々にではあるが年々その割合が高くなる傾向にある。表 4-2 に、国・公・私立の教員配置の割合を示した。義務教育学校である小・中学校は市町村立、特殊教育学校は都道府県立が多いため、教員も同

IV. The Conditions and Issues of Teachers 225

Chief supervising teacher	△	△	△	Takes charge of students' education, and provides instruction and advice to teachers and other school personnel.
Teacher	◎	◎	◎	Takes charge of student education.
Chief curriculum teacher	○	○	○	Appoints lead support teacher or teacher as the head teacher of school affairs. Advanced skill teacher or teacher takes this work.
Chief grade group teacher	○	○	○	Communicates, guides, and advises on the educational activities of each grade under the supervision of the principal. Advanced skill teacher or teacher takes this work.
Chief career guidance teacher	—	○	○	Takes charge of career choice guidance and other courses, coordinates communication among teachers, and provides instruction and advice to teachers under the super vision of the principal
Chief guidance and counseling teacher	—	○	○	Takes charge of affairs involving student guidance and counseling, coordinates communication between teachers and guardians, and provides instruction and advice under the supervision of the principal. Advanced skill teacher or teacher takes this work.
Nurse-teacher	◎	◎	△	Takes charge of student nurse.
Food and nutrition teacher	△	△	△	Takes charge of the instruction and management of student's nutrition.
Clerk	◎	◎	◎	Engages in school clerical work.
School Janitor	△	△	△	Maintains the school environment and other task.

◎ = mandatory school staff
○ = optional school staff which would not be set in a special case
△ = optional school staff

(3) Characteristics of Japanese Teachers

■ The general characteristics of Japanese teachers will be illustrated by using fundamental statistics concerning them.

First, Table 4-2 below shows the number of teachers (full-time). The teachers in this table include the principals and presidents. The number of female teachers decreases as the grades go up from kindergarten, to primary school, to lower and upper secondary school, and to university. In junior college, 49% of the teachers are female partly because 90 % of the students are female, and partly because many students major in home economics, humanities, and education. Furthermore, the percentage distribution of teachers in national, local, and private schools is illustrated in Table 4-2. Most of the teachers in compulsory

様にそのほとんどが公立学校に勤務している。しかし、幼稚園・短期大学・大学は私立学校が多く（私立学校数の割合：幼稚園 60.7%、短期大学 92.6%、大学 77.0%）、教員の割合も同様に私立が高い（2008年5月現在）。

表 4-2　本務教員数、女子教員の割合、国公私立別教員割合, 2008年5月

	本務教員数（計）	女子教員の割合（%）	教員の割合（%）		
			国立	公立	私立
幼稚園	111,223	93.5	0.3	22.2	77.5
小学校	419,309	62.8	0.4	98.6	1.0
中学校	249,509	48.9	0.7	93.6	5.7
高等学校	241,226	28.5	0.2	75.3	24.5
中等教育学校	1,369	31.6	10.2	51.6	38.2
特別支援学校	68,677	58.7	2.2	97.4	0.4
高等専門学校	4,432	6.2	88.9	7.4	3.7
短期大学	10,521	48.9	1.7	7.6	92.4
大学	169,914	18.9	35.9	7.1	57.0
大学院 **	98,573	12.5	53.1	7.6	39.3
専修学校	41,602	50.9	0.3	6.8	92.9
各種学校	9,873	39.6	0	0.6	99.4
計・平均	1,327,655	48.4			

出典：文部科学省『学校基本調査、平成20年度』および『平成21年度版　文部科学統計要覧』より作成。

■表4-3は、初等教育段階における教員の年齢構成の国際比較、表4-4は、2008年度の教員採用試験受験者数および採用者数における新規学卒者数、新規学卒者率を示したものである。日本の教員の平均年齢は他の国と比べて、40〜49歳の年齢層が厚く、最近、若干、新規学卒者の教員採用試験の合格率が上がってはいるものの、児童・生徒数の減少に伴って、採用率が劇的に増加することは考えられない。しばらくは、逆ピラミッド型の年齢構成の教

primary and lower secondary and special schools serve at the local public schools since the former tends to be municipal and the latter prefectural. However, the percentage distribution of the teachers in kindergartens, junior colleges, and universities is high in the private sector because many of these types of schools are private in May of 2008 (the percentage of private schools: kindergarten 60.7%, junior college 92.6%, university 77.0%).

Table 4-2 Number of Teachers (full-time) and Percentage Distribution of Female Teachers (As of May, 2008)

	Number of teachers (full-time)	Percentage distribution of female teachers (%)	Percentage distribution of teachers by establishing body (%)		
			National	Local public	Private
kindergarten	111,223	93.5	0.3	22.2	77.5
Primary School	419,309	62.8	0.4	98.6	1.0
Lower secondary School	249,509	48.9	0.7	93.6	5.7
Upper Secondary School	241,226	28.5	0.2	75.3	24.5
Secondary School	1,369	31.6	10.2	51.6	38.2
Special Needs school	68,677	58.7	2.2	97.4	0.4
Technical College	4,432	6.2	88.9	7.4	3.7
Junior College	10,521	48.9	1.7	7.6	92.4
University	169,914	18.9	35.9	7.1	57.0
Graduate School**	98,573	12.5	53.1	7.6	39.3
Specialized Training College	41,602	50.9	0.3	6.8	92.9
Miscellaneous School	9,873	39.6	0	0.6	99.4
Total	1,327,655	48.4			

Resource: Ministry of Education, Culture, Sports, Science and Technology, "School Basic Survey 2008", and "Brief of Statistics in Education and Science of May, 2009"

■ Table 4-3 below shows the international comparative of the age composition of teachers in primary schools, table 4-4 shows the number of examinees for recruit and the number of new graduates who were accepted teachers and its percentage. The average ages of Japanese teachers are between 40 to 49 years. Though recently the percentage of new teachers who pass the tests for teacher adoption is a little increasing, the percentage is not expected to increase

員集団として学校組織が続くことが予想される。

表 4-3 教員の年齢構成の国際比較（初等教育）2006 年度

	30 歳未満	30～39 歳	40～49 歳	50～59 歳	60 歳以上
日本	10.1	26.4	40.8	22.3	0.4
アメリカ	18.4	24.0	25.2	28.3	4.1
イギリス	23.4	25.3	21.8	28.4	1.1
韓国	24.5	31.6	23.7	18.9	1.3
フランス	16.8	32.9	29.5	20.4	0.4
OECD 平均	15.9	26.4	29.0	25.3	3.5

出典：文部科学省編『データからみる日本の教育 2008』（2009 年 6 月）78 ページ所収のデータより作成
国公私立学校教員の年齢層別教員の割合である。

表 4-4 教員採用試験受験者、採用者における新規学卒者（率）2008 年度

区分	受験者		採用者		採用率 (%)
	新規学卒者	新規学卒者率（%）	新規学卒者	新規学卒者率（%）	
小学校	(12,851) 13,202	(25.9) 26.7	(3,447) 3,776	(32.8) 33.4	(26.8) 28.6
中学校	(16,976) 16,118	(30.1) 29.2	(1,345) 1,501	(23.6) 25.2	(7.9) 9.3
高等学校	(8,954) 7,862	(26.8) 25.2	(417) 502	(17.9) 17.6	(4.7) 6.4
特別支援学校	(1,124) 1,099	(18.8) 16.6	(273) 387	(19.8) 20.5	(24.3) 35.2
養護教諭	(2,275) 2,376	(29.3) 29.5	(194) 212	(24.7) 25.9	(8.5) 8.9
栄養教諭	(123) 137	(64.1) 52.9	(4) 15	(13.8) 34.1	(3.3) 10.9
計	(42,303) 40,794	(27.6) 27.1	(5,680) 6,393	(27.4) 27.9	(13.4) 15.7

注：1.（ ）内は、前年度の数値である。
2. 採用率（%）＝採用者数／受験者数。
3. 大阪府は受験者の学歴等を把握していないため、大阪府の受験者数・採用者数を除いた人数を基に計算している。
出典：「平成 20 年度公立学校教員採用選考試験の実施状況について」（文部科学省ウェブサイトより）

■表 4-5 は、公立小・中・高等学校の学歴別本務教員の比率を示したものである。小学校から高等学校まですべての学校で 90％以上の教員が高等教育

IV. The Conditions and Issues of Teachers   229

dramatically because the student number is decreasing. For a while the elder teachers will compose more than younger teachers in the teachers group.

Table 4-3 the comparative of the age composition of teachers in primary schools in 2006

	Under 30	30-39	40-49	50-59	Over 60
Japan	10.1	26.4	40.8	22.3	0.4
USA	18.4	24.0	25.2	28.3	4.1
UK	23.4	25.3	21.8	28.4	1.1
Korea	24.5	31.6	23.7	18.9	1.3
France	16.8	32.9	29.5	20.4	0.4
Average of OECD	15.9	26.4	29.0	25.3	3.5

Resource: The Ministry of Education, Culture, Sports, Science and Technology, Japan, "Japanese Education Based on the Data 2008" June, 2009, p.78

Table 4-4 the number of examinees for recruit and the number of new graduates who were accepted teachers and its percentage in 2008.

Section	Examinees		Recruited teachers		Average of newly recruited teachers (%)
	New graduates	Average of new graduates (%)	New graduates	Average of new graduates	
Primary School	(12,851) 13,202	(25.9) 26.7	(3,447) 3,776	(32.8) 33.4	(26.8) 28.6
Lower School	(16,976) 16,118	(30.1) 29.2	(1,345) 1,501	(23.6) 25.2	(7.9) 9.3
Upper Secondary School	(8,954) 7,862	(26.8) 25.2	(417) 502	(17.9) 17.6	(4.7) 6.4
School for special educational needs	(1,124) 1,099	(18.8) 16.6	(273) 387	(19.8) 20.5	(24.3) 35.2
School nurse	(2,275) 2,376	(29.3) 29.5	(194) 212	(24.7) 25.9	(8.5) 8.9
Diet and nutrition teacher	(123) 137	(64.1) 52.9	(4) 15	(13.8) 34.1	(3.3) 10.9
Total	(42,303) 40,794	(27.6) 27.1	(5,680) 6,393	(27.4) 27.9	(13.4) 15.7

1. The number of inside of ( ) indicates that of last year.
2. The average of newly recruited teachers (%) = the number of recruited teachers and the number of examinees
3. The numbers of examinees and recruited teachers of the Osaka prefecture are excluded from the figures in the above table due to the fact that Osaka prefecture does not obtain the educational backgrounds of the examinees.
Resource: Website of the Ministry of Education Culture, Sports, Science and Technology, "Implementation status of recruitment examination for public schools in 2008"

■ Table 4-5 below shows the percentage distribution of teachers (full-time) at primary school, lower secondary school, and upper secondary school by

機関（大学・短期大学）を卒業している。また、教員の高学歴化が進行している。

表 4-5　本務教員の学歴構成（%）

区分		計	大学院	大学	短期大学	その他
小学校	1998 年度	100	1.5	81.6	16.4	0.5
	2001 年度	100	2.0	82.5	15.2	0.4
	2004 年度	100	2.6	83.1	13.7	0.5
	2007 年度	100	3.0	84.1	12.5	0.4
中学校	1998 年度	100	3.2	88.5	8.0	0.3
	2001 年度	100	4.1	88.3	7.4	0.2
	2004 年度	100	4.5	88.8	6.4	0.3
	2007 年度	100	5.8	88.0	6.0	0.3
高等学校	1998 年度	100	3.1	88.5	8.0	0.3
	2001 年度	100	10.8	87.0	1.5	0.6
	2004 年度	100	11.1	86.7	1.5	0.8
	2007 年度	100	12.3	85.5	1.5	0.7

出典：文部科学省『平成 19 年度学校教員統計調査』

educational attainment. More than 90 % of the teachers from primary school to upper secondary school have graduated from institutions of higher education (university or junior college). This proves the trend for teachers to attain higher degrees.

Table4-5　Percentage Distribution of Teachers (Full-Time) by Educational Attainment

Section		Total	Graduate School	4-year University	Junior College	Others
Primary School	1998	100	1.5	81.6	16.4	0.5
	2001	100	2.0	82.5	15.2	0.4
	2004	100	2.6	83.1	13.7	0.5
	2007	100	3.0	84.1	12.5	0.4
Lower Secondary School	1998	100	3.2	88.5	8.0	0.3
	2001	100	4.1	88.3	7.4	0.2
	2004	100	4.5	88.8	6.4	0.3
	2007	100	5.8	88.0	6.0	0.3
Upper Secondary School	1998	100	3.1	88.5	8.0	0.3
	2001	100	10.8	87.0	1.5	0.6
	2004	100	11.1	86.7	1.5	0.8
	2007	100	12.3	85.5	1.5	0.7

Resource: Ministry of Education, Culture, Sports, Science and Technology,
"A Survey of School Teacher Statistics in 2007"

2. 教員養成・採用・研修

(1) 教員養成・免許制度

■各国の公教育制度における主要な問題の1つは、良質の意欲に富む教員を、いかなる機関・課程において養成するかということである。東京に師範学校が設置された1872（明治5）年に、わが国の教員養成がスタートするが、以来、戦後教育改革が行われるまで、師範学校による小学校の教員養成、高等師範学校（1886年設立）による師範学校および中等学校の教員養成というパターンが続けられた。

■1949年、現行大学制度の発足とともに成立した現在の教員養成制度は、教育職員免許法の規定する教員免許制度と密接に関連している。両制度を貫く基本原則として、第1に、大学における教員養成の原則があげられる。従来の師範学校による教員養成制度は廃止され、各都道府県の必ず1つの国立大学に教員養成系の学部等が設けられた。第2の重要な原則として、開放制の原則がある。文部科学大臣により教員養成のための課程認定を受ければ、上述の教員養成大学・学部に限らず、広く一般の大学（大学院・短期大学）においても教員養成ができるのである。2008年4月で、教員養成を行っている大学は575校（79.5%）、短期大学は280校（71.8%）、大学院は416校（70.5%）となっていた。これと関連して、2009年9月に発足した民主党を中核とする新政権は、教員の質向上の観点から教員養成制度を大学院2年間を含む6年制にすることを提案し注目されている。

2. Pre-Service Training, Adoption and In-Service Training of Teachers

(1) Teacher Training and Certificate System

■ One of the major problems in any country's public educational system has been what institution or curriculum is necessary to train excellent and highly-motivated teachers. In Japan, teacher training started in 1872 (Meiji 5) when the first normal school was established in Tokyo. Since then until the educational reform after World War II, normal schools had been in charge of the training of primary school teachers while higher normal schools (established in 1886) were responsible for the training of normal school and secondary school teachers.

■ The present teacher training system, which was established in 1949 simultaneously with the present university system, is closely related to the teacher certification system as stipulated in the Educational Personnel Certification Law. The first fundamental principle running through these two systems is the principle of teacher training in colleges and universities. The teacher training system by normal schools was abolished, and one or more teacher training course (s) were established in national university faculty in each prefecture. The second important principle is the principle of open system. Teacher training can be also performed in general colleges and universities (faculties, graduate schools, and junior colleges), as well as at the teacher training universities and faculties mentioned above, if their teacher training curricula are authorized by the Minister of Education, Culture, Sports, Science and Technology. As of April 2008, the number of colleges and universities that provide teacher training curricula was 575 (79.5%), that of junior colleges was 280 (71.8%), and that of graduate schools was 416 (70.5%). In a related move, the new administration headed by the Democratic Party of Japan, which came to power in September 2009, suggested to extend the teacher training system to 6 years, including 2 years of graduate school, in the hopes of improving the quality of

■なお、2008年、新たな専門職大学院として教職大学院の制度が導入された。初年度には、国立・私立の19大学に研究科が開設され、学士課程の修了生に加え、都道府県教育委員会等から派遣される現職教員を学生として受け入れ、理論と実践を融合させた実践的なカリキュラムのもと、新しい時代に対応した教員養成が進められている。それらの大学・大学院では、学部段階の教職課程を合わせた6年一貫の教員養成システムも模索されている。

■教科や教職などに関する専門科目の単位を取得して大学を卒業した者は、教員としての資格を有すると認められ、都道府県教育委員会から免許状が授与される。免許状は普通免許状、特別免許状、臨時免許状の3種類に分かれる。

■教員になるための最も一般的な方法は、高等教育機関において普通免許状を取得することである。普通免許状は教諭の免許状、養護教諭の免許状、栄養教諭の免許状の3種に分かれている。小学校、中学校、高等学校および幼稚園の教諭の免許状は、学校の種類ごとに授与されるが、それぞれ修士の学位を有することを基礎資格とする「専修」、学士の学位を有することを基礎資格とする「一種」、短期大学士の学位を有することを基礎資格とする「二種」の各免許状に分かれている（高等学校は専修と一種のみ）。特別支援学校の教諭の資格を得るには、小学校・中学校・高等学校または幼稚園の教諭の普通免許状を有したうえで、特別支援教育に関する科目の単位を取得しなければならない。また、中学校と高等学校の教諭の免許状は教科別に授与される（表4-6参照）。

teachers. This plan has drawn a great deal of attention.

■ Meanwhile, graduate schools for the education of teachers have been introduced as new professional graduate schools in 2008. In the initial year, a graduate school of teacher education was established in 19 national and private colleges and universities. Those schools accept in-service teachers dispatched from the prefectural board of education in addition to students with a four-year bachelor's degree, providing education programs that are suited to the needs of the new era with practical curricula integrating both theory and practice. These colleges, universities, and graduate schools are trying to establish a six-year consistent education system that unifies teacher training courses at the under graduate and graduate levels.

■ The students who complete the specialized courses related to teaching subjects and pedagogy are then qualified as teachers and receive their teaching certificate from the prefectural board of education. There are three classifications of certificates: regular, special, and temporary.

■ The most common way to become a teacher is to acquire the regular teacher certificate by completing the teacher training curricula at a higher education institution. There are three divisions of regular certificate classification: regular schoolteacher, nurse teacher, and teacher for food and nutrition. The certificate is given according to the division of educational stage, i.e., kindergarten, primary, lower secondary and upper secondary school, and also the type of it is classified into three, from what sort of higher education the student graduated and what kind of credits he/she obtained. That is, the advanced certificate for students who graduate from the graduate school with a master degree, who graduate from the undergraduate course with bachelor (the first class certificate), and who complete junior college (the second class certificate). The certificate for special needs school teachers is the requirement to graduate from an institution, to obtain a regular certificate and in addition they have to get the necessary credits of subjects concerning special needs education. The certificates for lower and upper secondary school teachers are also divided according to teaching subject

表 4-6　免許教科の種類

中学校	国語、社会、数学、理科、音楽、美術、保健体育、保健、技術、家庭、職業、職業指導、職業実習、外国語、宗教
高等学校	国語、地理歴史、公民、数学、理科、音楽、美術、工芸、書道、保健体育、保健、看護、看護実習、家庭、家庭実習、情報、情報実習、農業、農業実習、工業、工業実習、商業、商業実習、水産、水産実習、福祉、福祉実習、商船、商船実習、職業指導、外国語、宗教

(「教育職員免許法」4 条 5 項より)

■大学等において取得すべき専門教育科目の最低単位数は法令で定められている。例えば、小学校教諭一種免許状を例にとると、「教科に関する科目」を 8 単位以上、「教職に関する科目」を 41 単位以上、「教科または教職に関する科目」を 10 単位以上修得することが必要である。このうち、「教科に関する科目」については、国語（書写を含む）、社会、算数、理科、生活、音楽、図画工作、家庭、体育の各教科の指導法について、それぞれ 2 単位以上を修得することを要する。一方、「教職に関する科目」の 41 単位は、「教職の意義等に関する科目」2 単位、「教育の基礎理論に関する科目」6 単位、「教育課程および指導法に関する科目」22 単位、「生徒指導、教育相談および進路指導等に関する科目」4 単位、「教育実習」5 単位、「教職実践演習」2 単位から編成されている。

このほかに、日本国憲法、体育、外国語コミュニケーション、情報機器の操作（各 2 単位）の修得が必要である。また、小学校および中学校の教員免許状取得希望者は、社会福祉施設や特殊教育学校などで、7 日間以上、高齢者や障害者に対する介護、介助、交流等の体験を行うことが義務づけられている（小学校及び中学校の教諭の普通免許状授与に係る教育職員免許法の特例等に関する法律）。

■教育実習は、数週間大学を離れて、現職の教員の指導のもと、授業を観察したり、実際の教育・指導を経験したりすることによって、教育能力や技術

(See Table 4-6).

Table 4-6　Types of Certificate by Teaching Subjects

Lower Secondary School	Japanese, Social Studies, Mathematics, Science, Music, Fine Arts, Health and Physical Education, Health, Industrial Arts, Home Economics, Vocational Subject, Vocational Guidance, Vocational Practice, Foreign Language, Religious Education
Upper Secondary School	Japanese, Geometry and History, Civics, Mathematics, Science, Music, Fine Arts, Arts & Crafts, Calligraphy, Health and Physical Education, Health, Nursing, Nursing practice, Home Economics, Home-Economics Practice, Agriculture, Agricultural Practice, Industry, Industrial Practice, Business, Bushiness Practice, Fisheries, Fishery Practice, Mercantile Marine, Mercantile Marine Practice, Vocational Guidance, Foreign Language, Religious Education

(Educational Personnel Certification Law, Article 4-5)

■ The minimum numbers of credits to be earned at a college/university or a junior college are defined in the laws and regulations. For example, students who intend to obtain the first class certificate of primary school teacher must complete more than 8 credits of teaching subjects and more than 41 credits of professional subjects more than 10 credits of teaching subjects or pedagogy. The 41 credits of pedagogy comprise of 2 credits from subjects on the significance of teaching; 6 credits from subjects on the basic theory of education; 22 credits from subjects on curriculum and teaching methods; 4 credits from subjects on guidance, educational counseling, and career counseling; 5 credits from teaching practice; and 2 credits from practical teaching job exercises.

In addition, it is required that each student earns each 2 credit from courses on the Constitution of Japan, physical education, foreign language communication, operation of information technology devices. It is also obligatory for students who wish to acquire a teaching certificate for primary or lower-secondary school to experience caring for and interacting with the elderly and the disabled for a period of more than 7 days (Act on Special Provisions concerning the Education Personnel Certification Act in Relation to Granting Regular License to Teachers of Primary Schools and Lower Secondary Schools).

■ Teaching practice is required to enhance the educational capability and techniques through observing and conducting actual teaching and guidance

を高めることを目的として義務づけられている。教員養成大学・学部に所属する学生は、主に附属学校で実習を行うが、定員の関係で一般の学校（協力学校）に割り振られる場合もある。教員養成系以外の附属学校をもたない大学の場合、主に学生の出身校が受け入れている。なお、教育実習の単位のうち1単位は事前および事後の指導にあてられる。

■なお、以下に挙げるような条件のひとつに該当する者には普通免許状は授与されない。教員の欠格条項は一般の公務員よりも厳しい資格要件が付されている（「教育職員免許法」5条）。
・18歳未満の者
・高等学校を卒業しない者
・禁固以上の刑に処せられた者
・免許状取り上げの処分を受け、当該処分の日から3年を経過しない者、など。

■以上、説明してきたように、わが国の教員養成・免許制度においては、大学での教員養成を基軸としながらも、幅広い人材を教員として活用するための諸制度が整備されている。なお、その他の学校（大学、短期大学、大学院、高等専門学校）の教員に関しては、大学設置基準その他の法令が独自の資格体系を規定している。

（2）教員採用制度
■大学・短期大学の2007年3月卒業者のうち、教員免許状を取得した者は、小学校教諭17,198人、中学校教諭51,912人、高等学校教諭73,458人であった。同年4月の校種ごとの採用者数は順に11,588人、6,170人、2,563人となっており、免許状取得者がすべて教員として採用されるわけではない。校種ごとの競争率（受験者数／採用者数）は、それぞれ4.6倍、9.8倍、14.2倍となっており、依然として狭き門となっているが、都道府県・政令指定都市によってバラツキが大きい。免許状の取得から採用まで数年を要するケースも多く、

under the guidance of an experienced teacher. Most students at teacher training universities (faculties) conduct their teaching practice at schools attached to the institutions, but some students are assigned to local schools because of the limited capacity. Students at non-teacher-training universities without an attached school are accepted by the schools they graduated from. One credit of teaching practice is for the guidance before and after the practice.

■ Prospective teachers who are unable to satisfy teaching code requirements cannot become teachers. These employment guidelines are stricter for teachers than for general public officials (Educational Personnel Certification Law, Article 5). Prospective teachers can not qualify for the following reasons:
· Those under 18 years of age
· Those without an upper secondary school diploma
· Those who have been imprisoned
· Those who were punished by certificate confiscation within the last two years, etc.

■ As mentioned above, in the teacher training and certificate systems in Japan, systems for the recruitment of human resources in a variety of fields were established in order to supplement the teacher training at universities. Teachers of the other schools (universities, junior colleges, graduate schools, and technical colleges) are prescribed by the regulations like the Standards for the Establishment of Universities, and other regulations.

(2) Teacher Adoption System

■ Among the college, university, and junior college graduates of March 2007, the number of students who acquired a primary school teaching certificate was 17,198, that of lower secondary school was 51,912, and that of upper secondary school was 73,458. The number of recruited teachers in April of the same year was 11,588 for primary school, 6170 for lower secondary school, and 2,563 for upper secondary school. Not all of those that acquired teaching certificates were recruited to be teachers. The rate of competition is 4.6 times to be a primary

教職への道を断念し、民間企業等への就職を選ぶ者も少なくない。

■教員の新規採用は、教員としての適格性を都道府県（指定都市を含む）教育委員会の教育長が判断する教員採用選考試験によって行われる。選考方法としては、筆記試験や面接に加えて、実技試験、体力テスト、適性検査などが取り入れられており、教員としてふさわしい資質・能力を多面的に評価できるよう工夫されている。

■近年は、人物を重視した採用選考を進めるため、面接試験の改善に取り組む都道府県が多い。たとえば、一次・二次試験の両方で面接試験を実施したり、個人面接だけでなく集団面接を行ったり、模擬授業や場面指導を導入したりする場合が増えている。また、受験年齢の上限を緩和したり、優れた技能や実績を持つ者を採用するための社会人特別選考、スポーツ・芸術特別選考などの制度を設け、該当者には一部試験の免除を行っている教育委員会もある。障害のある受験者が不利にならないような配慮を行う都道府県も拡がっている。

■教員に限らず公務員の採用は、すべて条件付き採用とされている。条件付き採用の期間は、一般の公務員の場合6ヶ月であるが、教員の場合は1年間である。その間、良好な成績で勤務した場合に正式採用となるが、新任教員の場合、初任者研修を受けることが義務づけられている。
■初任者研修は採用後1年間行われ、実践的指導力、使命感を養うとともに、幅広い知見を修得することを目的としている。研修の形態は、大きく校内研

school teacher, 9.8 times to be a lower secondary school teacher, and 14.2 times to be a upper secondary school teacher. As you can see, it is still highly competitive to be a teacher, but the level of competition varies widely according to prefectures and ordinance-designated cities. There are many cases where it takes several years to become a teacher after acquiring a teaching certificate; consequently, there are some cases potential teachers giving up and seeking employment elsewhere.

■ In teacher selection, the superintendents of the boards of education in prefectures and ordinance-designated cities judge the eligibility of a teacher via examinations. These examinations include a practical exam, a physical strength test, and an aptitude test as well as a written examination and interview. In this way, the qualifications and abilities that are necessary for teachers are evaluated from various perspectives.

■ In recent years, many of the prefectural and city governments have been trying to improve the interview process in order to attach greater importance to the personalities of possible recruits. For instance, there are cases where interviews are given in both of the first and second stage examinations; individual interviews and group interviews are performed, and trial lessons and simulated guidance are requested. Moreover, some boards of education ease the maximum age limit for examinees or exempt a part of the examinations by introducing special screening for working people who have a strong skill, practical accomplishment, or excel in sports or arts. Furthermore, more prefectural and city governments make sure that examinees with disabilities are not at a disadvantage.

■ All public officials including teachers are adopted for an initial probationary period. The probationary period is six months for general public officials, but it is one year for teachers. Those who perform well during this period are formally employed, and new teachers are obligated to receive initial training.

■ Initial training is obligatory and it continues for a year after adoption and is intended to develop practical ability in guidance and a sense of teacher'

修（週 10 時間以上、年間 300 時間以上）と校外研修（年間 25 日以上）とに分かれる。校内研修は、同じ学校の教頭や教諭等が校内指導教員として置かれ、教科指導、生徒指導、学級経営等に関する指導を行っている。校外研修には、教育センター等での講義・演習、企業・福祉施設等での体験、社会奉仕体験や自然体験に関わる研修、青少年教育施設等での宿泊研修などが含まれる。

（3）教員研修制度

■初任者研修を経て、正式に採用された教員は、職責を遂行するために必要な知識・技能・教養を向上させるため、絶えず研究と修養（研修）に努める必要があり、その機会が与えられなければならない。研修の積み上げにより、上級・異種の免許状を取得することもできる。

■教員研修の形態は多様だが、大別すると、①自己研修、校内研修、各種団体等による研修、②教育行政機関による研修、③大学で行われる研修に分けられる。

■自己研修は教師自身の自発性に基づいて、読書などによる勉学、講演会・講習会・勉強会への参加などを通じて行われる。校内研修は、勤務校の共通の関心を持つ教師集団によって、研究授業、発表会、講習会などの形で行われる。また、全国ないし地方における各種研究団体や研究サークルなどに所属し、それらの主催による研修の機会もある。

■教育行政機関において実施される研修としては、文部科学省による中央研修、都道府県ないし市町村の教育委員会による研修などがある。このうち、都道府県教育委員会による研修としては、先に述べた初任者研修、5年・10年・20年経験者研修など、経験年数に応じた研修、生徒指導主事研修、新任教務主任研修、副校長・教頭研修など、教員としての職能に応じた研修が

s mission, as well as to broaden the knowledge. The training is divided into: in-school training (more than 10 hours per week and 300 hours a year) and training out of school (25 days a year). In-school training includes guidance that is given by the vice-principal and teachers of the same school. And training in teaching subjects, student guidance, and school management are provided. Examples of out-of-school training are: lectures and drills at educational centers, on-site training at private companies and welfare facilities, experience with social services and training related to nature experiences, and overnight training at youth educational facilities.

(3) In-Service Training for Teachers

■ Officially adopted teachers after finishing initial training are required to study continually so as to improve their knowledge and ability to teach. Therefore, teachers must be provided with the opportunity to do so. They can acquire higher or additional teaching certificates upon completion of in-service training.

■ The in-service training for teachers varies in form, but is generally divided into three areas: ① self-training, school-based training, and training by various organizations; ② training offered by the authorities of educational administration; and ③ training at universities.

■ Self-training is conducted through reading and studying based on each teacher' own initiative. School-based training involves model lessons, model meetings, and lectures with colleagues sharing a common interest. Moreover, there are opportunities for training through various national or local research organizations and groups.

■ Training offered by the educational administration includes workshops offered by the Ministry of Education, Culture, Sports, Science and Technology and the prefectural and local boards of education. The training offered by the prefectural boards of education includes training for newly recruited teachers, training designed for teachers with 5, 10, and 20 years of experience, training

含まれる。また、都道府県や政令指定都市などに設立されている教員研修センターは、これらの研修に中心的な役割を果たしている。

これらの中で、初任者研修と10年経験者研修が法律で義務づけられている法定研修にあたる。2003年に導入された10年経験者研修は、在職10年を迎える教員が各自の能力、適性等に応じた研修を受けることにより、教科指導、生徒指導等に関する指導力の向上を図ることを目的とする。

■大学での現職教育は、内地留学や外国への留学など、長期にわたるものが多い。具体的には、大学・大学院・大学の専攻科等に正規の学生として入学したり、研究生や聴講生などとして大学等の授業を聴講したりする。上級ないし異種の免許状の取得には、ここでの単位取得が欠かせない。

現職教員の大学院での研修機会を確保するために、新構想の教員養成大学・大学院も大きな役割を果たしている(1978年設立の上越教育大学ならびに兵庫教育大学、1981年設立の鳴門教育大学)。これらの大学では、学校づくりにおいて中核的な役割を果たすことのできる中堅教員を養成するための教職大学院も設置された(2008年)。

■以上、日本における教員の養成・採用・研修について、その概略を述べてきた。これらについては、教師の継続的な職能成長を重視する立場から、養成教育と現職教育とを有機的に結びつけ、体系的な教師教育制度として再構築する必要性も指摘されている。

commensurate with functions such as training for leading support teachers, newly appointed heads of school affairs, vice principals, and pro vice- principals. The teacher training centers that have been established in each prefecture and ordinance-designated city play a central role in the aforementioned training.

Among the types of trainings mentioned above, initial training and training for teachers with 10 years of experience are statute-based. An objective of the training for teachers with 10 years of experienced is for them to improve their teaching and student guidance abilities by receiving training commensurate with their abilities and aptitudes. This training was introduced in 2003.

■ Training at universities includes both long-term domestic and international training. For example, teachers enter a university or a graduate school as a regular student as well as being a student researcher or auditor. One of the aims of receiving such a program is to acquire the credits necessary for a higher or different certificate.

Recently, a new framework for teacher training has been introduced at some newly-established teacher training universities and graduate schools to ensure education opportunities for teachers. They are Joetsu University of Education and Hyogo University of Education established in 1978 and Naruto University of Education established in 1981. In these colleges and universities, graduate schools of teacher education were established in 2008 with the hope to nurture mid-level teachers who will play a central role in improving school systems.

■ As for the training, adoption, and in-service training of teachers, it is widely recognized that it is necessary to establish systematic teacher training. Pre-service and in-service training must be correlated with the teacher's professional development as the main goal.

3. 教員人事

(1) 教員の法的身分と服務義務

■日本の教員の法的身分は次の3つに区分される。つまり、①国立学校教員＝国家公務員（国立学校の校長、教員等は、2004年4月1日から、国家公務員の身分から国立大学行政法人または独立行政法人国立高等専門学校等の役員または職員となったが基本的には公務に従事する職員とみなされる）、②公立学校教員＝地方公務員（都道府県公務員あるいは市町村公務員）、③私立学校教員＝民間労働者である。また、国・公立学校教員は一般の公務員とは異なり、教育という特殊な職務を担当するという観点から、両者は「教育公務員」として位置づけられる。

■このような教員の法的身分の違い、特に教育公務員と私立学校教員の間の違いは、教員管理に関するさまざまな側面の違いとなってあらわれる。例えば、労働基本権（団結権、団体交渉権、争議権）について、教育公務員には団結権のみ保障されるのに対し、私立学校教員には3つの権利がすべて保障される。また、労働条件・給与等について、教育公務員の場合、法律・条例等で定められるが、私立学校教員の場合、就業規則・労働協約（使用者と組合の交渉によって締結される）で定められる。

■次に、教員の服務義務について簡単に説明しよう。教育公務員（＝国・公立学校教員）は、全体の奉仕者であって（憲法第15条）、自己の使命を自覚し、

3. Personnel Affairs of Teachers

(1) Legal Position and Service Regulations of Teachers

■ The legal position of teachers in Japan can be classified into three types: ① teachers in national schools (they are national employees). Although the positions of principals and teachers of national schools have changed from national government employees to executives or employees of independent administrative corporations, they are still considered to be officials who serve in public offices. ② teachers in local schools (they are prefectural or municipal employees), and ③ teachers in private schools (they are non-public employees). As the legal position of teachers is somewhat different from that of regular public employees in the light of the specific duties that the teachers have, both teachers in national and public schools are regarded as educational public employees.

■ The difference in teaching personnel management results from the difference in the legal position of teachers. Let us look at the difference in the case of educational public service personnel and teachers in private schools. In terms of fundamental rights of workers, including the right to organize, the right of collective bargaining, and the right of labor dispute, for example, the right to organize is the only one guaranteed to the educational public service personnel. However, all the fundamental rights of workers mentioned above are guaranteed to the teachers in private schools. Moreover, difference in working conditions and salary between educational public employees and private school teachers exists. Working conditions and salary are determined by law, in the case of educational public employees. In the case of private school teachers, in contrast, they are determined, depending on working regulations and labor agreements established by the employers and the representatives of employees.

■ The duties of teachers will be explained in this section. Educational public service personnel, teachers in national and public schools, are servants of

その職責の遂行に努めなければならない（教育基本法第9条）。この原則に基づいて、地方公務員法・国家公務員法等で、以下の具体的な義務項目が定められている。
・法令等および上司の職務命令に従う義務
・職務に専念する義務
・信用失墜行為の禁止
・職務上知り得た秘密を守る義務
・政治的行為の制限
・争議行為の禁止
・営利企業等への従事制限

■一方、私立学校教員の義務については、公務員法の適用を受けず、使用者（学校法人）の作成する就業規則に定められる。教育公務員も私立学校教員も、定められた義務に違反した場合には、当然のことながら処分（けん責、停職、免職等）を受ける。

(2) 教員任用のしくみ
■ある人を採用・昇任・降任・転任のいずれかの方法で、ある職につけることを任用という。教員の場合、その法的身分のちがいによって任命権者も異なり、任用のしくみは非常に複雑である。まず、私立学校教員と教育公務員では、前者の場合、各学校法人ごとに独自の基準・しくみがあるのに対し、後者の任用については、教育公務員特例法で規定されている。また、教育公務員だけをみても、特に市町村立の小・中学校教員の任用のしくみは、同じ市町村立の幼稚園・高等学校の教員とは全く異なり、より複雑である。しかしながら、すべての教育公務員の任用（採用・昇任）については、共通の方法が採用されている。それは、一般の公務員の任用の方法（競争試験）とは

the whole community (the Constitution of Japan, Art.15). As such, they shall be conscious of their mission and shall endeavor to perform their duties (the Basic Act on Education, Art. 9). On the basis of the principle just mentioned, the educational public employees should obey the following duties as stated in the Local Public Service Law and National Public Service Law:

- The duties of obeying not only laws and ordinances but also official order by superior officers
- The duties of devoting oneself to one's given works
- The prohibition of acts of losing reliance
- The duties of maintaining secrecy obtained during one's works
- The limitations on political activities
- The prohibition of labor dispute
- The limitations on engaging in a profit-making enterprise

■ The Public Service Law mentioned above is not applicable to teachers in private schools. Thus, the duties they have to follow are stated in the working regulations that their employers (educational corporations) stipulated. Both educational public service personnel and private educational employees are punished when they violate the duties they have to obey. The kinds of punishment are reprimand, suspension, dismissal, and so on.

(2) Teacher Appointment System

■ To give a person a position by means of new adoption, degradation, promotion, or transfer is called an appointment. Since teachers occupy different legal positions, as seen in the previous section, they have different appointing authorities. Thus, the teacher appointment system is very intricate. For example, there is a difference between the teacher appointment system of private educational employees and public educational employees. In the case of the former, each educational institution has its own standard and system of teacher appointment. In the case of the latter, however, the standard and system are stated in laws and ordinances. Even among educational public employees differences

異なる方法（選考）である。選考は試験による競争試験とは異なり、学力・経験・人物・身体等を一定の基準と手続きによって審査し、職務遂行能力の有無を判断する方法である。教員の任用に選考が用いられる理由は、教員になるには教員免許状の取得が前提条件とされており、また教育の職務は人格的要素が重要であることから、競争試験の方法は適切ではないと考えられるからである。

■さて、ここでは教員の最大多数を占める市町村立小・中学校教員の任用のしくみをみてみると、次の２点に注意する必要がある。第１に、市町村立小・中学校教員は市町村公務員の身分をもつが、その任命権は都道府県教育委員会にあることである。第２に、市町村立小・中学校教員の選考権は都道府県教育長にあることである（ただし、政令指定都市の教育委員会は任命権を有する）。

（3）勤務評定・教員評価

■勤務評定とは、教員の人事管理の適正化のために、教員の職務遂行の実績や教員としての能力・適性等を評価し、記録することである。歴史的には、1950年代の後半に、文部省の方針の下に都道府県教育委員会によって実施されたが、その過程では、日本教職員組合による強い反対運動が展開された。現在、教育公務員にも私立学校教員にも勤務評定は実施されている。例えば、市町村立小・中学校の場合、校長の評定は市町村教育委員会の教育長が行い、他の教員の評定はその学校の校長が行う。

exist. The teacher appointment system in primary and lower secondary school is quite different from that of kindergarten and upper secondary school even in the same municipality. Hence, it can be said that the system of teacher appointment is complicated. In the system of new adoption and promotion, however, there is something in common. In the adoption and promotion of educational employees, the selection system is different from that of general public servants for whom competitive examination is done. It is the way to judge achievement, experience, personality, and physical strength are judged in the light of the given standards and procedure, and hence it is emphasized whether or not a person is capable of performing his duties. Competitive examination is not appropriate for the system of teacher appointment because of the following reasons; first, the acquisition of a teacher's certificate is a prerequisite for becoming a teacher and second, a person's character plays very important role in education.

■ Now, let us call attention to the system of teacher appointment in municipal primary and lower secondary schools. There are two distinct characteristics. First, teachers of municipal primary and lower secondary schools are considered municipal public servants, although the prefectural board of education has the appointment authority. Second, the superintendent of the prefectural board has selection authority on the new adoption and the transfer of municipal teachers. (However, the boards of education in ordinance-designated cities have appointing power.)

(3) Efficiency Rating of Teachers

■ For adequate personnel management, teachers are evaluated. This means evaluating and keeping a record of the teacher's achievements, ability and aptitude as a teacher. Historically, the rating of teachers started in the late 1950s by the prefectural boards of education under the policy of the Ministry of Education, Science, Sports and Culture. However, strong opposition campaigns were raised by the Japan Teacher's Union. At present, both public and private educational employees are evaluated. In the municipal schools, for example, the superintendent in the municipal board of education evaluates the principals,

■最近になって、信頼される学校づくりの視点から、いわゆる「指導力不足教員」と認められた教員に対して、研修等必要な措置が講じられてもなお指導を適切に行うことができないと認められた場合にはその教員を「免職」し、引き続いて他の職に採用することができることとされた（「地方教育行政の組織及び運営に関する法律」一部改正、2001年）。

　また、2000年度に東京都において、被評価者の自己申告制、業績評価（学習指導・生活・進路指導、学校運営・特別活動等）、被評価者（教諭等）と評価者（校長等）との面談等を特色とする新しい教員評価制度（東京都では「教職員人事考課制度」と呼ばれている）が導入され、その後、全国的に実施されている。新しい教員評価制度は、(1) 学校の目標・経営方針に対応した業績評価を含むこと、(2) 教員一人ひとりの人材育成・能力開発、自己啓発を図ることがめざされていることという点に特色がある。組織としての学校についての評価である「学校評価」と教員評価とは、いわば「車の両輪」であり、日本の学校の教育活動の充実と向上を図るうえで重要な役割を果たすことが期待されている。

（4）勤務条件

①給与と手当

■公立学校教員の給与は、都道府県が定める条例に基づく俸給表によっている。それらは公立大学教員、高等学校教員、幼稚園・小学校・中学校教員、高等専門学校教員の4種類に分けられる。各俸給表は等級に分かれ、各等級に号俸段階が定められており、等級・号俸ごとに位置づけられるが、その後は主に経験年数によって昇給する。つまり、俸給表は日本的な年功序列的性格が表れている。また、表4-7に教員の平均給与月額（2004年9月）を示した。

while the principals evaluate teachers.

■ In recent years, in order to maintain to make quality of school education reliable, the Law concerning Organization and Operation of Local Educational Administration was partially revised in 2001 to allow the dismissal of teachers while continuing to employ the same person in a different position if he/she is judged to possess insufficient ability to properly teach students after necessary measures, such as training programs or workshops, have been taken.

The Tokyo Metropolitan Government introduced a new teacher evaluation system called the "Teacher job performance evaluation system," which was subsequently launched nationwide. The characteristics of the evaluation system are self reporting, performance evaluation (class teaching, life and career consultation, school operation, activities, and so forth), and interviews between teachers and an evaluator (e.g., the principal of the school). This new evaluation system is also characterized by the following: (1) a performance evaluation that takes the objectives and management policy of the school into account, and (2) a desire to nurture human resources, ability development, and the self-enlightenment of each teacher. A school evaluation, which is an evaluation of the organization and a teacher evaluation, which is an evaluation of personnel, are "two wheels of the same cart," so to speak. These two evaluations are expected to play a vital role in enriching and improving the educational activities of schools in Japan.

(4) Working Conditions

① Salary and Allowance

■ The amount of salary paid to teachers in public schools follows the salary chart based on the ordinance of prefectural governments. The salary scale of teachers are classified into four types according to the school: teachers in university, teachers in upper secondary school, teachers in kindergarten, primary and lower secondary school, and teachers in technical college. Each scale is sub classified into grades, and further into steps. Monthly salary of teachers depends on their grade type and step type. The grade and step to which he/she

表 4-7　平均給料月額（学校別、2004 年 9 月の俸給）

	幼稚園	小学校	中学校	高等学校
2004 年度	227.2 (34.7)	379.4 (44.1)	375.6 (42.9)	386.5 (44.3)
国立	345.8	356.4	361.7	396.6
公立	323.6	379.7	375.5	387.0
私立	200.3	357.0	378.8	385.0

単位：千円　＊（　）内は平均年齢

■教員給与はかつて民間の労働者と比較すると低い水準にあったが、さまざまな改善策が試みられてきた。まず、1966 年の ILO・UNESCO による「教員の地位に関する勧告」に基づき教職は専門職であると考えられるようになり、同勧告を受け入れた 1972 年以降、教員の給与は一般公務員のそれより高く支払われることになった。給与が高い代わり超過勤務手当は支払われなくなった。

また、1974 年 2 月に「学校教育の水準の維持向上のための義務教育諸学校の教育職員の人材確保に関する特別措置法」が制定された。この法律の制定を受けて、1974 年 3 月には俸給は平均 9 ％アップされ、1975 年には「義務教育等教員特別手当」が支給されるようになった。しかし、2004 年 4 月より都道府県の条例によって教員給与額が定められるようになった頃から教員の給与は画一的ではなくなった。

■教員俸給表は人事院（都道府県レベルでは人事委員会）の勧告に基づき、物価高に応じるように毎年改訂されるのが原則である。しかし、公的財政事情の悪化に伴い、勧告通りに実施されないこともある。

is assigned depends on his/her educational attainment and qualification status. Afterwards, years of experience as a teacher will also affect the salary. It can be said, therefore, that the salary scale system is characterized by seniority. Table 4-7 shows the average monthly salary of teachers as of September 2004.

Table 4-7 Average Monthly Salary of Teachers by School Types (in 1,000yen), Sep. 2004

	Kindergarten	Primary School	Lower Secondary School	Upper Secondary School
2004	227.2 (34.7)	379.4 (44.1)	375.6 (42.9)	386.5 (44.3)
National	345.8	356.4	361.7	396.6
Local Public	323.6	379.7	375.5	387.0
Private	200.3	357.0	378.8	385.0

* ( ) is the average age

■ Because the salaries of teachers were low when compared with those of workers in the private sector, various kinds of remedies have been taken. First of all, a teacher began to be considered as a professional based on the "Recommendation concerning the Status of Teachers" announced by ILO · UNESCO, and the government accepted this recommendation. Since 1972, the salaries of teachers were raised to be higher than those of general civil servants. Overtime compensation is not paid in lieu of this high salary. One of them is to enact a special law ensuring that compulsory education schools have capable education personnel by raising their teachers' salary. This law, enacted in Feb. 1974, aims to maintain and improve the level of school education. As a result, an average 9% salary raise was put into effect in 1974. In the following year, special allowance for compulsory school teachers began to be offered. Since April 2004, however, the prefectural governments could fix the salaries of teachers by their ordinance. As a result, the salaries of teachers are no longer uniform.

■ Depending on the recommendations of the National Personnel Authority (like the Local Personnel Committee in a prefecture), the salary scale of teachers is supposed to be revised every year in order to meet the rising cost of living.

■教員には各種の手当が支給される。いくつか例をあげると、管理職（校長・教頭等）手当、扶養手当、住居手当、通勤手当、へき地手当、寒冷地手当、そしてボーナスなどがある。このうちボーナスは、年2回（6月・12月）全教員に支給され、総額は月給の約3か月分にあたる。

②勤務時間
■労働基準法により、労働者の勤労時間は1日8時間、1週40時間以内を原則とするが、公立学校教員の場合、勤務時間は各都道府県の条例または人事委員会規則で定められる。現在、公立学校では学校週5日制を実施し、土曜および日曜を「勤務を要しない日」としている。

■教員には時間外勤務を命じないことが原則とされるが、生徒の実習や学校行事等の場合は一定の条件付きで時間外勤務が命ぜられる。

③ 福利厚生
■教育公務員のために、保健・レクリエーション・住宅等に関する各種の厚生事業が行われている。例えば、各種の健康診断、病院・保健所等の利用、スポーツ・レクリエーション施設の利用、住宅手当などである。これらの事業の多くは、「共済組合」の事業として行われているが、国・地方公共団体が援助を行っている。この他の共済組合の事業としては、給付金の支給がある。これは各教員が月給の中から一定の割合で共済費を出し、教員とその家族が病気・けが・災害に見舞われた場合、あるいは結婚・出産の場合などに給付金が支給されるものである（短期給付）。また、退職年金・生涯年金等の長期給付も行われる。

Occasionally, though, the salary scale is not revised because of government financial difficulties.

■ A variety of allowances are provided to teachers. Examples are: administration allowance (to principals and deputy vice principals), family allowance, housing allowance, traffic allowance, remote area allowance, cold region allowance, and bonus. Among these allowances, the bonus is paid twice a year (June and December) to all of the teachers, and the total amount is approximately equivalent to the amount of salary for three months.

② Working Hours

■ In principle, according to the Labor Standard Law, working hours are 8 hours a day and 40 hours a week. In the case of public school teachers, however, working hours are fixed by the Prefectural Ordinances, or Regulations of Local Personnel Committee. At present the five-day week (40 working hours a week) is carried out in public schools. The teachers are not required to work on Saturdays and Sundays.

■ As a general rule, overtime work is not allowed for teachers. However, they might be ordered to work overtime with certain conditions during practice training for students and school events.

③ Welfare Benefits

■ A variety of welfare programs relating to health, recreation, and housing, are provided for educational public service personnel. They include physical check-up, making use of hospitals and facilities for sports and recreation, and providing housing. Most of these welfare projects are a part of the undertakings of mutual aid association, and are supported by both the national government and the local governments. In addition to the undertakings of mutual aid association mentioned above, supply of allowance may be included. This is the system in which teachers pay some amount at a certain rate from their salary every month and receive an allowance when they and their family encounter the situations such as sickness, injuries, disaster, marriage or child birth. Also, the long term benefits of retirement annuity and life annuity is handled by a mutual aid association.

4. 教員団体

（1）教員団体の概念
■教員団体とは、教員を構成員とする団体と定義される。それは一般に、教員の経済的・社会的地位の向上を中心課題とする教職員組合と、専門職としての教員の資質向上を中心課題とする教員職能団体とに分けられる。しかし現実には、1つの教員団体が両方の性格を併せ持つことが多い。

（2）教職員組合
■日本国憲法第28条は、労働者に労働基本権としての団結権、団体交渉権、団体行動権（争議権）を保障しているが、国公立学校の教員は全体の奉仕者として、公共の利益に奉仕する公務員であることから、一般の雇用関係とは異なる規律に服することが求められる。すなわち、国公立学校の教員には労働組合法が適用されず、国家公務員法、地方公務員法の適用を受け、労働基本権が制限される。とりわけ、争議行為は禁止されている。また私立学校の教員については、労働組合法が適用されるが、「全体の奉仕者」（教育基本法第6条第2項）の見地から、就業規則等によって、公務員の場合に準ずる規定が置かれることが多い。以上の事情により、わが国の教職員組合は法律の上では労働組合ではなく、職員団体とされる。

■文部科学省の調査によると、2008年10月1日現在、教職員組合（教職員団体）の組織率は44.1％であり、1976年以降33年連続の低下となった。新採用教職員の教職員団体加入率も27.5％と低い（前年比では1.2％の増加）。

4. Teachers' Organization

(1) The Concept of Teachers' Organization

■ Teachers' organization is defined as an organization composed of teachers. Teachers' organizations, conceptually speaking, can be divided into two groups: teachers' unions and teachers' professional organizations. The former aims to raise teachers' economic and social status. The latter endeavors to improve their abilities and qualifications in the teaching profession. In reality, however, a given organization often has the characteristics of the two groups just mentioned.

(2) Teachers' Union

■ The Constitution of Japan, Article 28, ensures the fundamental rights of workers: the right to organize, the right of collective bargaining, and the right of labor dispute. As the teachers of national and public schools are public servants who are expected to serve the public interest, they are required to follow the rules which are different from general employment. In other words, the Labor Union Act is not applicable to them. The fundamental rights of public educational employees covered by the National Public Service Law or Local Public Service Law are limited. Particularly, labor disputes are forbidden. The Labor Union Act is applicable to teachers in private schools. They are required to follow similar regulations related to working conditions of those for public servants, because they are also serve the whole community. Judging from the legal grounds mentioned above, a teachers' union in Japan is not a labor union but a professional organization.

■ According to the investigations by the Ministry of Education, Culture, Sports, Science and Technology, the participation in teachers' organizations is 44.1% on October 1, 2008. The participation rate has been decreasing for 33 consecutive years since 1976. The decline in the participation rate seems to be associated

■現在の主な教職員組合としては、日本教職員組合（日教組）、全日本教職員組合（全教）、日本高等学校教職員組合（日高教）、全日本教職員連盟（全日教連）、全国教育管理職員団体協議会（全管協）などがある。
■日教組は28.1％の教員が加入する、わが国最大の教職員組合である。第2次世界大戦後の教職員組合運動を組織する形で、1947年6月に結成された。日高教とともに、日本労働組合総連合会（連合）に加盟している。

■組織的には、都道府県の教職員組合（都道府県教組）を単位団体とする全国連合体という性格を持つ。年度ごとの運動方針は、連合体組織の代表者が集まって開く定期大会・臨時大会において決定され、それに基づいて各都道府県教組の日常活動が展開される。
■日教組の活動は、大きく2つに分かれる。ひとつは、教育政策に対する運動である。その要求は多様であり、経済闘争ばかりでなく、専門職の立場から教育政策に反対を表明する教育闘争の性格をもつ場合もある。過去には、座り込み、授業打ち切り、半日ないし1日のストライキなどの戦術もとられ、多くの参加教職員の懲戒処分を招くこともあった。
■もうひとつの活動は、教育研究活動である。その中心は教育研究集会（教研集会）であり、毎年開催都市を変えて行われている。その報告書である『日本の教育』は毎年刊行され、現場教師による研修の機会としても大きな意義を持つ。

（3）教員職能団体

■教員職能団体は、労働組合に類する活動を行っている教職員組合とは異なり、教員の業務の質を高め、自らを専門職として向上させることを目的としている。

■わが国独自の教員職能団体として、教育会と呼ばれる団体がある。それは

with the low participation rate of newly-appointed teachers (27.5%, in 2008).
■ The main teachers' unions are: Japan Teachers' Union, Japan Upper Secondary School Teachers' Union, All Japan Teachers' Federation, and Japan Administrators' Educational Organization.
■ The Japan Teachers' Union (JTU), whose organizational rate is approximately 28.1%, is the biggest teachers' union in Japan. JTU was organized in June of 1947 and influenced by the movement of the Teachers Union, after World War II. In Japan, the JTU became a member of the Japan Labor Union.
■ Organizationally speaking, JTU consists of sub-unions in each prefecture. Every year the direction of the movement is decided by representatives from each union in the annual meeting, and/or special sessions. The union in each prefecture makes activities following the decisions made in the sessions.
■ One of the major goals of the JTU is for educational policy reform. Its demands are various; some are financial while others are, from a professional point of view, educational opposition to certain educational policies. The strategies the union members adopt are: sit-in demonstration, work stoppage, and half or one day strikes.
■ Another activity of the JTU is to conduct educational research. JTU holds an annual research meeting, the Education Research Assembly, every year in different cities. The main theme of the assembly reflects current campaign directions, and themes with a strong political tendency was adopted in the past. These annual meetings have been reported yearly as a publication of "Education in Japan", and the meetings offer a significant opportunity for teachers to study.

(3) Teachers' Professional Organization

■ A teachers' professional organization is different from a teacher's union because it does not engage in activities that a labor union does. Teachers' professional organization aims to improve the quality of the duties teachers perform, and to train teachers as professionals.
■ The Education Association (Kyouiku kai) is an example of a teachers'

一般に、教師たちが自発的に結成する自己教育の機関とされる。地方の教育会としては、長野県の信濃教育会が有力であり、また全国組織の教科別、問題領域別の団体もある。

■校長会、教頭会も職能団体の例であり、教師の現職教育や自主的研究活動、独自の教育改革案の策定、教育政策過程への参画など、多面的に活動している。全国組織の具体例として、全国高等学校長協会、全日本中学校長会、全国連合小学校長会、全国公立学校教頭会などをあげることができる。

■今日、教育活動の多様化・複雑化に伴って、専門職としての教員の資質向上が求められている。教員の自主的な現職教育、研究活動の母体として、教員職能団体にはきわめて大きな期待が寄せられている。

professional organization in Japan. The Education Association is an institution for self-education, organized voluntarily by teachers themselves. Among local educational associations, the Shinano Educational Association in Nagano prefecture is the leading one. Also, there are nationwide organizations specializing in particular subjects or issues.

■ Principals' associations and deputy vice-principals' associations are also good examples of teachers' professional associations. They manage in-service training, conduct voluntary research, give suggestions on educational reform, and participate in the process of formulating educational policies. The nationwide associations are the National Association of Upper Secondary School Principals, the All Japan Lower Secondary School Principals' Association, the National Association of Primary School Principals, and the National Association of Public School Deputy Vice-Principals.

■ Teachers are required to improve their qualifications as professionals because of the diversity and the complexity in activities of education. Therefore, teachers' professional organizations are expected to play a very important role as the basis for their independent in-service training and study.

外国人教員研修留学生研究発表会　Foreign Teachers' Final Report Presentation

第V章

国際教育の展開

Development of International Education

外国人留学生のスキー実習　Foreign Students' Skiing Experience

1. 教育の国際交流・協力の拡大

■今日では、交通・通信の急速な発達に伴って国家間の人的、物的、および情報の交流が著しく増大して各方面の国際交流が活発になってきた。世界は地球共同体として認識されるようにさえなってきている。教育分野においても、学生、生徒、教員、研究者等の人材や、教材、教育・学術情報など多方面の交流が盛んになっている。一方では、先進諸国間および発展途上諸国相互の教育協力、ならびに先進諸国の発展途上国に対する教育援助・協力も増大している。

（1）外国人留学生の増大

■近年、わが国へ留学する外国人学生が増えている。文部科学省発行の「わが国の留学生制度の概要」（2008年）によると2007年度において合計118,498人であった（図5-1参照）。そのうち109,495人（92.4％）はアジア系留学生であった。次いで欧州3,547人（3.0％）、北米2,612人（1.8％）中南米1,024人（0.9％）となっていた。国別では、中国が最も多く71,277人（60％）、韓国17,274人（15％）、台湾4,686人（4％）、ベトナム2,582人（2％）、マレーシア2,146人（2％）、タイ2,090人（2％）、アメリカ合衆国1,805人（2％）、などが多かった（図5-2参照）。

■日本の文部科学省奨学金によって留学する国費留学生は2007年度に10,020人、外国政府派遣留学生は2,181人で、主な派遣政府は中国、マレーシア、インドネシア、タイであった。一方、私費留学生は108,478人で最も多かった（図5-1参照）。レベル別では、学部レベルが59,510人で大学院レベル31,592人を上回っていたが、大学院レベルの留学生の増加が著しい。また、専修学校留学生が22,399人と増加した。学部レベルでは、文科系学生が理科系学生より多いが、大学院レベルになると理科系学生の方が文科系学生よ

1. Expansion of International Relations and Cooperation in Education

■ With today's rapid development of communication and transportation, the transfer of people, and information among nations has increased correspondingly. As a result, the world may be considered as one global community. In the field of education, these have taken the form of exchanges of teaching materials and educational information, as well as personnel exchanges of students, teachers and researchers. Likewise, educational cooperation among developed countries, and among developing countries has become stronger. Educational aid and cooperation to developing countries by developed nations has also increased.

(1) Increase of Foreign Students

■ According to "The Outline of the Acceptance System of Foreign Students in Japan" published by the Ministry of Education, Culture, Sports, Science and Technology in 2007, recently, the number of foreign students coming to Japan has increased, totalling 118,498 in 2007 (See Figure 5-1). Among them 109,495 (92.4%) were Asians. There were 3,547 (3.0%) Europeans, North American 2,612 (1.8%), Central and South Americans 1,024 (0.9%). By nationality students from China numbered the most at 71,277 (60%) : followed by the Koreans at 17,274 (15%) ; Taiwanese at 4,686 (4%) ; Vietnamese at 2,582 (2%) ; Malaysians at 2,146 (2%) ; Thais at 2,090 (2%) ; and Americans at 1,805 (2%) (See Figure 5-2).

■ Among these, 10,020 obtained scholarships from the Ministry of Education, Culture, Sports, Science and Technology of Japan and 2,181 were given financial aid from their governments. Main foreign governments which sent their own students to Japan included China, Malaysia, Indonesian and Thailand. On the other hand, students covering their own expenses numbered 108,478 (See Figure 5-1). The number of students at the undergraduate level reached 59,510, while the number of graduate students totalled 31,592. The number of students at the

り多くなっている。

■国費留学生制度は多様化され、一般留学生制度の他に、高等専門学校および専修学校留学生制度（1983年度）、外国人教員研修留学生制度（1980年度）、日本語・日本文化留学生制度（1980年度）、1997年度からヤング・リーダーズ・プログラム留学生制度等が加えられた。普通、高等専門学校制度、専修学校留学生制度は2年間、外国人教員研修留学生制度は1.5年間、日本語・日本文化留学生制度は1年間である。

■近年の新しい動向として注目されるのは、国立大学における外国人留学生のための英語による特別コース（大学院）の設立である。1981年に東京大学大学院に日本工業事情（1.5年制）が出来たのを皮切りに、1984年に埼玉大学大学院に政策科学研究科（修士課程2年制）、その後、京都大学、東北大学、名古屋大学、島根大学、東京大学などの大学院の工学・理学・農学研究科において5人〜30人程度の留学生受け入れを行っている。

また、1995年度から、1年以内の短期留学制度も開始された。これは、主に大学間交流協定に基づき、母国の大学に在籍しつつ、日本の大学で専門分野の学習、語学の習得、異文化体験などを行わせるものである。2006年5月で短期留学生数は7,423人でその86%は学部レベルであった。

graduate level has been increasing in the last few years. And the number of students at "special training schools" (Senshu Gakko) also has rapidly increased to 22,399. At the undergraduate level, students specializing in human and social sciences outnumbered those majoring in the natural sciences. The case with the graduate level is the opposite, that is, more students major in the natural sciences than those in the human and social sciences.

■ The types of foreign students have also diversified. Since 1983 in addition to the regular students there are those who are studying at "Higher Technical Schools" (Koto Senmon Gakko) and "Special Training Schools" (Senshu Gakko), and from 1980 there have been students participating in the In-service Training Program for Overseas Teachers, in the Japanese Language and Japanese Culture Program and from 1997 Young Leader Program. The period of study or training is usually two years for the Higher Technical Schools and Special Training Schools, one and a half years for the In-service Teacher Training Program, and one year for the Language and Culture Program.

■ It is new remarkable trend for some national universities to have established special courses for graduate school for foreign students in recent years where all the lectures are given in English. In 1981 the graduate school of Tokyo University established a special eighteen month English course called "Japanese Industrial Situation". It was followed by the Policy and Management Study Course for Masters Degree for two years in Saitama University in 1984. After that the special courses of technology, natural science, and agriculture have been established by the graduate schools of Kyoto University, Tohoku University, Nagoya University, Shimane University, Tokyo University and so on. Those courses accept usually 5 to 30 students respectively.

Since 1995, a one year short term study course within for foreign students has been introduced. It provides major studies, learning of Japanese language, and experiences of different cultures in Japanese universities based on the treaty of exchange program between Japanese universities and foreign universities while the students are registered in their foreign universities. In May of 2006, the

（2）外国人留学生政策の課題

■1984年7月に文部省は「21世紀への留学生政策」と題する提言を発表し、21世紀までに留学生を10倍にする構想を示した。それは、日本の教育の国際化にとってきわめて有意義な事業であるが、その構想は、2003年度に留学生数が109,508人に及び達成された。それでも、今なお次のような解決すべき課題が横たわっている。

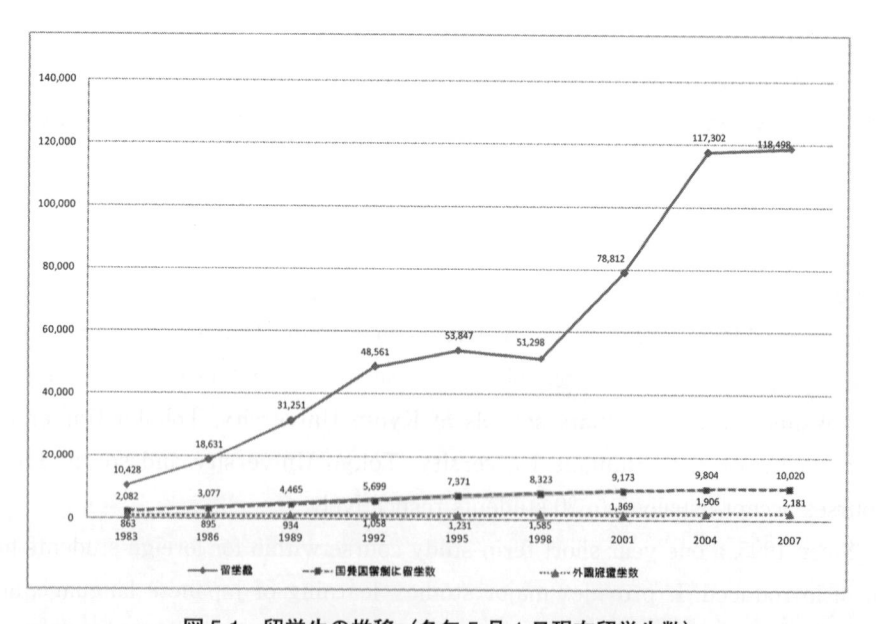

図5-1　留学生の推移（各年5月1日現在留学生数）
出典：文部科学省高等教育局学生支援課『我が国の留学生制度の概要』2008年、9頁

V. Development of International Education   271

number of the students enrolled in the course was 7,423 and 86% of them were under-graduate students.

(2) The Issues of the Policy on Acceptance of Foreign Students

■ In July of 1984 the Ministry of Education, Science, Sports and Culture announced the "Policy on Acceptance of Foreign Students towards the 21st Century" in which it described an idea to increase the number of foreign students by ten times by the beginning of the 21st Century. This was a very significant policy for the internationalization of Japanese education. In 2003, the number of foreign students reached 109,508 accomplishing the idea. However, there are still some important unresolved issues that must be solved in order to achieve the goal.

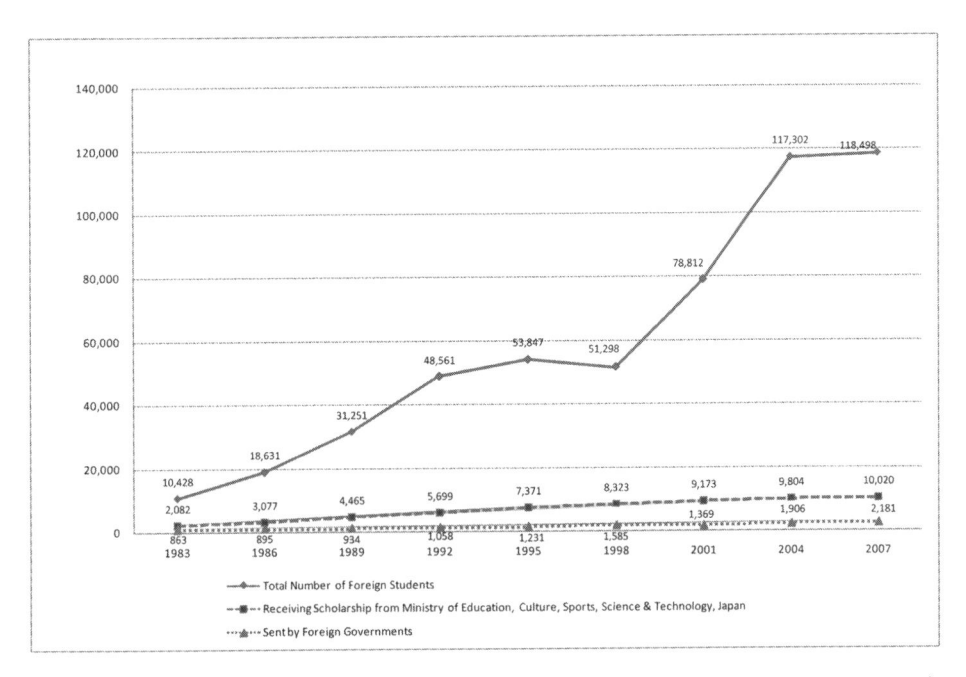

Figure 5-1   Increase of the Number of Foreign Students (As of 1st of May for each year)
Resource : Student Services Division, Higher Education Bureau, Ministry of Education, Culture, Sports, Science and Technology, in Japan, "The Outline of the Student Exchange System in Japan", 2008 p.9

①大学の主体性確立
■従来、留学生対策は文部省による国費留学生受け入れが主導となって行われ大学は留学生の受け入れ方針、教育、研究指導などにおいて受け身的であった。今後は、大学や受け入れ教育機関が主体的かつ計画的に留学生を受け入れ、彼らの教育指導に積極的に取組んでいく必要があろう。

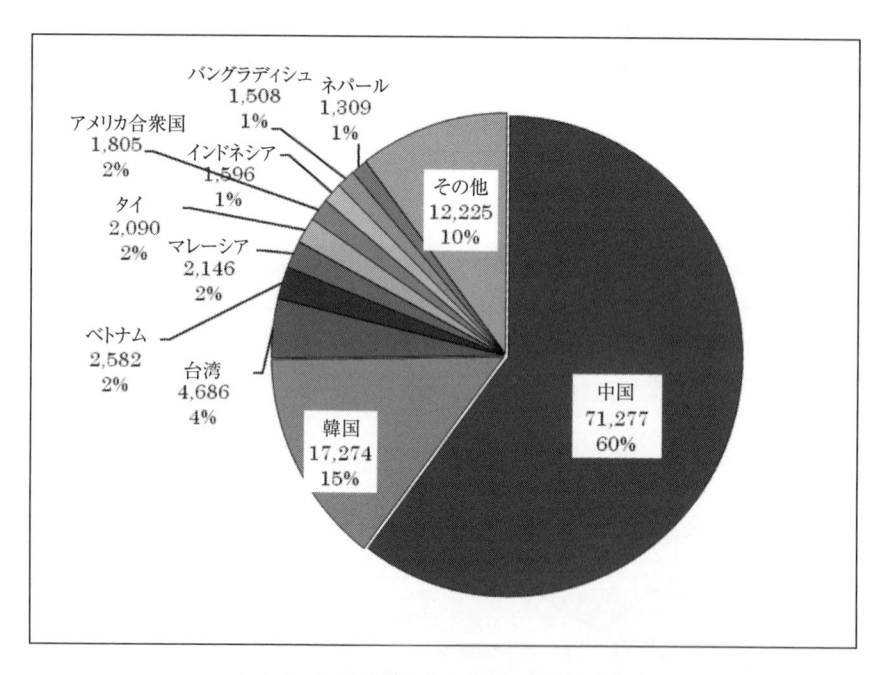

図 5-2　国別留学生数と割合（2007年度）
出典：文部科学省高等教育局学生支援課『我が国の留学生制度の概要』2008年、10頁

②私費留学生に対する援助
■日本留学にあたり、経費のうえからも、宿舎や設備などの厚生面、教育研究面でも困難を感じているのは、私費留学生である。近年の円高状況は私費留学生の生活を経済的に一層困難にしている。国、地方公共団体、民間によ

Ⅴ. Development of International Education 273

① The Establishment of Relative Interdependence of the Universities in Accepting Foreign Students
■ Even though the policy in accepting foreign students was initiated by the Ministry of Education, Science, Sports and Culture, the universities have been rather passive in accepting and educating foreign students. From now on, however, the universities and institutions concerned should take on a more active role in accepting and educating them, for example by the establishment of policy, plans and programs.

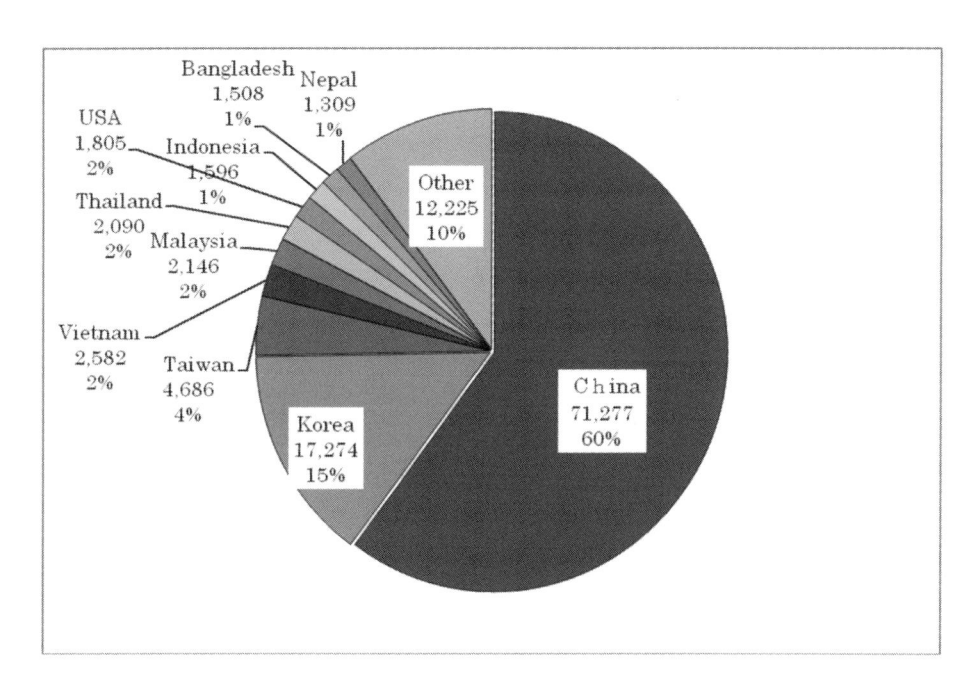

Figure 5-2 The Number and Ratio of Foreign Students by Country (2007)
Resource : The same as that of Figure 5-1, 2008 p.10

② Assistance to Foreign Students with Their Own Fund
■ It is the foreign students studying with their own funds who encounter difficulties for various expenditures, such as, for daily commodities, tuition fees, housing facilities, and study. The economic situation with a high yen value at

る奨学金、授業料減免措置、医療費補助等が増えているものの抜本的な対策を考えないと留学生受け入れ状況は改善されない。また、私費留学生の学力向上と学力判定を容易にする目的で、1995年からタイとマレーシアにおいて「私費外国人留学生統一試験」が実施されている。科目は、文科系が、数学、世界史、英語、理科系は、数学、理科、英語である。

③ 日本語教育の拡充
■来日する留学生のほとんどは、来日後に日本語の学習を始める。国費留学生の場合、学部レベルの留学生は東京外国語大学附属日本語学校、大学院レベルの留学生は大阪外国語大学留学生科、名古屋大学総合言語センター、北海道大学言語文化部などで学習したが、1984年度以降、東北大学、筑波大学、東京大学、京都大学、広島大学、九州大学などに留学生センターが設置され、大学院レベルの日本語教育を行うことになった。私費留学生は、国際学友会や私立大学の日本語教育機関、その他の民間の日本語学校で日本語を習っている。2007年度に383日本語教育機関、そこに学ぶ学生数は31,663人であった。

■本来は、来日前から日本語能力を身に付けておき、来日後は日本語の補習を行う程度にすることが望ましいが容易なことではない。それでも、1984年に日本国際教育協会が国際交流基金と協力して「外国人日本語能力試験」を実施した。外国でもその試験を受けられるようになってきた。

present makes their living conditions more difficult. Though the support of Scholarship, Medical and School Fees by the nation, local public bodies, and private enterprise has been increasing, the situation of accepting foreign students will not be improved without an appropriate policy for them. And in order to improve learning and the assessment of learning of the students paying their own way, "A General Examination for Foreign Students" has been carried out in Thailand and Malaysia by the Association of International Education, Japan (AIEJ) since 1995. The subjects of examination for students studying the humanities is Mathematics, World History, and English. On the other hand, the subjects of examination for students studying the natural sciences is Mathematics, Sciences, and English.

③ The Expansion of Japanese Language Education

■ Most foreign students start to learn primary level Japanese after they come to Japan. The students supported by the Japanese Government Scholarship learn Japanese in institutions such as Tokyo University of Foreign Studies (for undergraduate students); Osaka University of Foreign Studies, the Language Center of Nagoya University, and the Language and Culture Department of Hokkaido University. Since 1984, Educational Centers for Foreign Students were established in the University of Tohoku, University of Tsukuba, Tokyo University, Kyoto University, Hiroshima University and Kyushu University. These centers provide Japanese language education to graduate students. Students with their own funds learn Japanese in the Kokusai Gakuyukai (the International Students Institute), the Japanese language institutions of private universities or other private Japanese language schools. The number of Japanese language institutions was 383 and the number of students was 31,663 in 2007.

■ It is an ideal, however, that foreign students acquire some knowledge of Japanese language before coming to Japan, and thereafter receive only supplementary lessons in Japanese during their stay in Japan. But this ideal has yet to be realized. In 1984 the Association of International Education, Japan (AIEJ) started to implement the Japanese Language Proficiency Test for Foreign

■そのほか、日本語教員の養成、日本語教育法の確立、日本語テキスト・教材の開発など問題は山積している。

④教育内容・方法の適正化
■発展途上国からの留学生にとって教育研究の指導を受けるうえで問題なのは、教育研究の内容や方法が必ずしも彼らの要求と合致していないことである。せっかくの高度の科学的知識や技術を身に付けても、帰国後有用とはならず、先進国へ仕事を求めて頭脳流出してしまう問題もしばしば起きる。教育内容・方法の適正化が図られなければならない。

⑤ 学位取得の困難性打破
■2006年度の留学生の学位取得状況を見ると、標準修業年限での修士学位は平均で84.1%、文科系82.4%、理科系86.6%と高いが、博士号は平均で49.8%、文科系がわずか24.2%、理科系は66.4%であった。博士課程の文科系の取得率がきわめて低い状況にある。(文部科学省高等教育局学生支援課、「我が国の留学生制度の概要」2008年度参照」)

■現行の学位規則は、「研究者として自立して研究活動を行い得る能力水準を有する者に博士の学位を授与する」と定められている。この趣旨が生かされるように特に文科系博士課程をもつ各大学が主体性をもって学位授与を行うべきであろう。

Students in cooperation with the Japan Foundation. The test is now available in many foreign countries.

■ Furthermore, there are yet many problems to be solved such as: the training of Japanese language teachers; the improvement of methods in teaching Japanese; and the development of Japanese textbooks and materials.

④ Improvement of Teaching Contents and Methods Appropriate for Foreign Students

■ When foreign students from developing countries receive education in Japan, they are confronted with the problems that learning content and methods do not necessarily meet and coincide with their needs. It happens so often that even though they study highly advanced scientific knowledge and technology in Japan, what they have learned does not seem to be useful after going back to their countries. Also, some students do not return to their countries and instead look for jobs in developed countries which results in the so-called "brain drain." To solve these problems, it is necessary to improve course content and teaching methods in institutions dealing with foreign students.

⑤ Overcoming the Difficulty of Obtaining Degrees in Universities

■ The situation of the foreign students obtaining degrees from Japanese universities was as follows in the beginning of 2006 ; Master of Arts 82.4% , Master of Science 86.6 % , (the average 84.1 %). Doctor of Arts 24.2 % , Doctor of Science 66.4% , (the average 49.8%). The percentage of students, obtaining Doctor of Arts degrees is very low. (Resource: Student Services Division, Higher Education Bureau, Ministry of Education, Culture, Sports, Science and Technology, "The Outline of the Acceptance System of Foreign Students in Japan" 2008)

■ The present regulations prescribe that doctoral degrees be awarded to persons who have the ability to conduct any original research as independent researchers. Therefore, each university needs to provide more doctoral degrees to qualified individuals, particularly those of Human and Social Sciences as prescribed by the regulations.

⑥ Information and Guidance to Candidate Students before Coming to Japan for

⑥留学前の情報、ガイダンスと留学後のアフターケア
■本国において日本留学を志している者は、日本国や日本の大学のさまざまな事情について知りたいと思っている。現在、各国にある日本大使館日本広報文化センターが大学や奨学金などの情報を提供しているが、いまだ不十分である。各大学のカリキュラム、スタッフ、研究状況ということになると、説明書も説明してくれる人も一層少ない。1989年以来、アジア諸国に、日本のいくつかの大学における留学生担当官が出かけて行って「留学生フェア」を開催し、大学案内説明会を行うようになった。それは日本の文部科学省と各国の日本大使館が後援している。また、2004年に日本学生支援機構に留学生情報センターが設立され、日本留学希望者に対する留学情報の提供や留学相談の業務を行っている。

■留学後に帰国した者に対するアフターケアのサービスも重要である。最近は、留学生が帰国後3年経過すると、日本の大学を再訪する機会が与えられる。2008年～2009年で年に約60人が対象となっている。また、日本学生支援機構では、帰国留学生に対してメール・マガジンを送ったり、海外に指導教員を派遣して彼らに研修指導サービスも行ったりしている。しかし、その恩典に浴している元留学生はまだ限られている。特に帰国留学生達は、日本の大学の新しい変化に関する情報、ならびに大学再訪の要望が強いので、その面のアフターケア拡充に配慮しなければならないであろう。

Study, and Care Services after Going Back to Their Countries
■ Candidate students in foreign countries who are going to study in Japan want to get much information on Japan and Japanese universities and colleges. At present the Japan Information Service of the Japan Embassy in each country provides such information including scholarships. But they are still far from being adequate, concerning the curricula, academic staff, and research situations in the universities and colleges. There are very few pamphlets and advisers who can explain them. Since 1989 in some Asian countries the Information Fairs of Japanese universities for foreign people have been held under the sponsorship of the Ministry of Education, Culture, Sports, Science and Technology, Japan and the Japan Embassy. At that time the university officers concerned with foreign student affairs provide information and guidance on their universities to them. The Information Center for International Education in the Japan Student Service Organization established in 2004 offers the students who want to come to Japan for study the information on study in Japan and consultation regarding Japanese educational institutions and procedures for study in Japan.
■ It is also important to extend a variety of following services to the foreign students after they returned back to their countries. Recently the former students in foreign countries are given chances to revisit Japanese universities after three years since returning home. The number was about sixty per year during 2008 and 2009. The Japanese Student Service Organization is sending mail magazines to the former students. It also makes assistance service of study guidance to them by sending supervising teacher to their countries. But the former students who are able to receive such assistance are still limited in number. Since the former students strongly desire information on the change of Japanese universities and colleges and to visit the institutions once again, it is desirable to make these follow-up services more available to them.

(3) 教育行政官、技術専門家、青年等の交流と教育協力

■近年、アジア・アフリカ諸国の教育行政官をわが国に招き、約1ヶ月にわたり教育事情を視察調査させている。また発展途上国に対し技術専門家や教員の短期研修の受け入れにより教育協力を行っている。特に工業教育、農業教育、教育工学などの分野である。同時に、わが国からアジア、中近東、南アメリカ、アフリカなどの発展途上国へ技術専門家を派遣して技術教育協力も行っている。理数科教育、農業教育や教育工学の分野に多い。

近年、東南アジアのタイ、マレーシア、シンガポール等の中進国は、より開発の遅れたラオス、カンボジアやアフリカ諸国に対し学校設立、施設設備の提供、教員研修などの協力を行っている。そうした協力は南南教育協力と呼ばれるが、それらの協力にJICAも関与して専門家派遣や資金援助を実施している。

■また、総理府では、1974年以来「東南アジア青年の船」、1988年以来「世界青年の船」を企画して、アジア、アメリカ、オセアニア、ヨーロッパ諸国等と日本の勤労青年の交流を図っている。各県においても、主として中国、韓国、アセアン諸国、アメリカ合衆国へ「友好青年の船」や「親善青年の翼」等を募り、短期の旅行等を通して親善友好の輪を広めようとしている。それらは、各種のスポーツ交流を含めた、青年の国際的交流の場を提供している。

(3) International Exchange of Educational Administrators, Technical Experts, Youths and Educational Cooperation

■ Recently, educational administrators from Asian and African countries have been invited for one month stays to observe and study Japanese education. Technical experts and school teachers from developing countries are also accepted for short training, particularly in the fields of science and mathematics education, industrial education, agricultural education and educational technology. Likewise, Japanese technical experts are sent to developing countries in Asia, the Middle East, Latin America and Africa. They are mainly experts in science and mathematics education, agricultural education and educational technology.

Recently, mid-developed South-east Asian countries such as Thailand, Malaysia and Singapore are supporting school building, facilities and equipment supply and in-service training of teachers to less developing Laos, Cambodia and African countries. This support is called the "South-South Education Cooperation", JICA (Japan International Cooperation Agency) also assists such cooperation in sending educational experts or providing funds to those mid-developed countries.

■ The Office of the Prime Minister promotes the active exchange of working youths between Japan and Asian, American, Oceania, European countries through the so-called "Ship for South-East Asian Youth (since 1974) or for the World Youth (since 1988)" program. Some prefectures also promote friendly relations between Japan and other countries including China, Korea, the ASEAN countries and the U.S.A. by encouraging their youths to participate on a short term basis in programs similar to the Ship for Youth or Flight for Youth. These programs, which also include sports events, are good opportunities for international communication among the youths of different countries.

2. 学校教育の国際化

■教育の国際交流・協力の拡大は、必然的に学校教育の国際化を促すことになる。それは、学校制度、教育内容の両面からみることができよう。学校制度面では、海外児童生徒、帰国児童生徒、外国人児童生徒の教育の確立、教師の国際化、学校制度の国際化などの課題がある。教育内容面では、国際教育ということばで表現されるような、国際理解の教育、平和教育、人権教育、開発教育などの促進が課題となっている。

（1）海外児童生徒・帰国児童生徒・外国人児童生徒の教育

■日本の経済や文化をはじめとする国際諸活動が活発化するにつれ、外国で勤務する親と同行して学齢期間を海外で過ごす子ども達が増えてきた。文部科学省の統計によれば、その数は、2008年度で61,252人に達している。そのうち約31.6%は全日制日本人学校、41.1%は現地校、残りの27.3%は補習授業校と現地校等に通っていると推定される（図5-3参照）。彼ら海外児童生徒は、いずれは帰国児童生徒として帰ってくる。その際は帰国児童生徒の教育が問題となる。

■2008年度における海外児童生徒の教育の場合、北米地域（計21,045人）では、日本人学校就学者が2.3%、補習授業校と現地校等55.9%、現地校とその他41.0%で補習授業校及び現地校の就学者が多いのに対し、アジア地域（計23,827人）では、その比率がそれぞれ61.3%、4.1%、34.6%と日本人学校就学者が極めて多くなり、両地域は著しい対照を示している。ヨーロッパ地域（計11,234人）では、それは、それぞれ27.6%、27.8%、44.6%で、現地校とその

2. Internationalization of School Education

■ International exchange and cooperation in education necessarily promotes the internationalization of school education as a whole. To realize the "Internationalization" scheme, two factors have to be taken into consideration: the school system and teaching content. The former includes such aspects as the establishment of educational facilities for Japanese children abroad, those coming back from foreign countries, and foreign children, and the internationalization of teachers and the school system. The latter is mainly concerned with international education such as the promotion of education for international understanding, education for peace, education for human rights and development education.

(1) Education for Children Staying in and Coming Back from Foreign Countries and Foreign Children

■ As Japan expands international activities in the fields of economy, culture and so on, the number of school age children staying with parents in foreign countries increases. According to the data of the Ministry of Education, Culture, Sports, Science and Technology, there was approximately 61,252 of these children in 2008. Among them, attendees numbered about 31.6 % in full-time schools for Japanese, 41.1% in local schools in these countries, and 27.3% in supplementary education schools (See Figure 5-3). After their return to Japan, problems on how to educate them arise.

■ In North America (21,045 students), about 2.3% of the Japanese children go to full-time schools for Japanese while 55.9% attend supplementary education schools and local schools and 41.0 % go to local local and other schools in 2008. The breakdown for Asia (23,827 students) is 61.3%, 4.1%, and 34.6% respectively. The two regions showed a marked contrast in the percentage of the children attending schools for Japanese and supplementary education schools or local

他の割合が高くなっている。

■海外児童生徒が増加するにしたがい、日本国内の受験競争を持ち込むような海外児童生徒教育も行われるようになってきた。その結果、現地の社会や文化に無関心あるいは偏見を持つ子ども達が育ちつつある。従って、海外児童生徒の教育では、現地社会に開かれた日本人学校の確立が大きな課題である。最近では、授業で現地語を教えたり、現地の学校と交流したりする日本人学校も増えている。また、帰国児童生徒の教育では、帰国児童生徒のわが国教育への適応のみならず、身に付けた国際感覚をいかに伸長させるかが重要な問題となっている。

■近年、外国人留学生・研修生のみならず外国人労働者として来日する者も増えてきた。同時に彼らに同伴してくる学齢段階の子どもも増加している。一時滞在の外国人児童生徒は、従来、大都市にある国際学校や外国人専用学校に通学する者が多かったが、最近では、地方の公立小・中学校に就学する者も目立つようになってきた。文部科学省統計によれば、2008年度に日本の公立小・中・高等学校等に就学した外国人児童生徒で日本語教育を必要とした者は総数28,575人であった。小学生で19,504人、中学生で7,576人に達した。彼らを母語別にみると、ポルトガル語が11,386人（39.8%）と最も多く、次いで中国語5,831人（20.4%）、スペイン語3,634人（12.7%）であった（図5-4参照）。外国人児童生徒を受け入れた学校では、彼らに対する日本語教育、適応教育、および、彼らと日本人児童生徒を含めた国際教育の確立が課題となっている。特に、彼らの母語や文化に対しても考慮することが重要である。

schools. In the breakdown for Europe (11,234 students), the percentage is at 27.6%, 27.8%, and 44.6% respectively, while the percentage of local schools and the others was higher than the other two groups.

■ As the number of Japanese children living overseas increase, their education has been influenced by upper secondary school and college entrance examinations in Japan. As a result, some children tend to show little interest in, or have prejudice against, their local community and culture. Thus, for the education of overseas children, the main task is to establish Japanese schools which are also receptive to the local communities. Recently, Japanese schools that teach local languages and have the opportunity of exchange with local schools, increasingly continue. On the other hand, regarding education for the returning children, it is necessary to develop their cosmopolitan outlooks acquired from foreign countries as well as to seek ways of adapting them to domestic education in Japan.

■ In recent years foreign workers as well as foreign students and researchers have been coming to Japan in increasing numbers. At the same time their school-age children have also accompanied them to Japan. Until now foreign students have gone to international schools and schools for foreigners in larger cities. Recently foreign students have increasingly gone to local public primary schools and lower secondary schools. According to statistics surveyed by the Ministry of Education, Culture, Sports, Science and Technology, the number of foreign students, entering primary schools, lower secondary schools, or upper secondary school in 2008 who needed Japanese language education was 28,575 in total, 19,504 for primary school and 7,576 at lower secondary school. By native language, Portuguese numbered the most at 11,386 (39.8%) ; followed by Chinese at 5,831 (20.4%) and Spanish at 3,634 (12.7%) (See Figure 5-4). In the schools accepting foreign students there are issues of Japanese language education, education to make them adapt to the schools, and the establishment of international education suitable to these students and Japanese students. In particular, it is important to give consideration to their native language and culture in the school education.

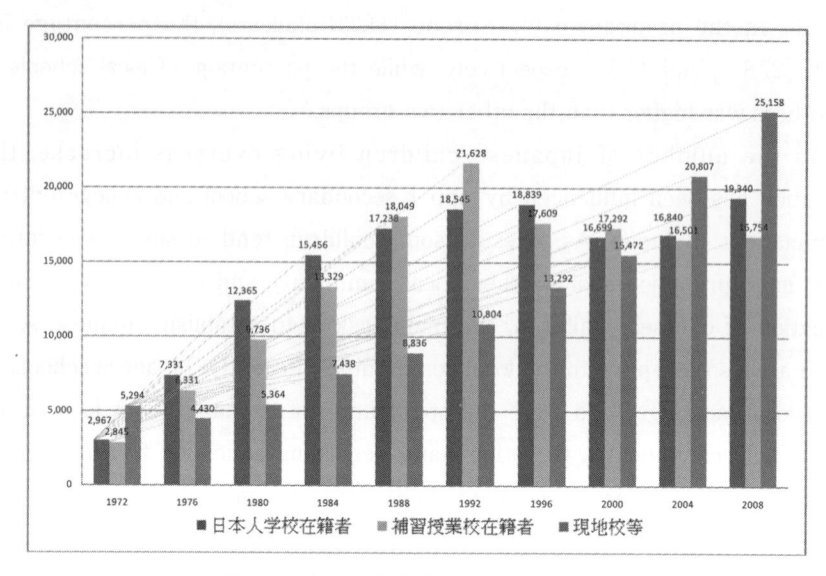

図 5-3　海外児童生徒の就学形態別推移
出典：外務省調査、「管内在留邦人子女数調査」2008 年

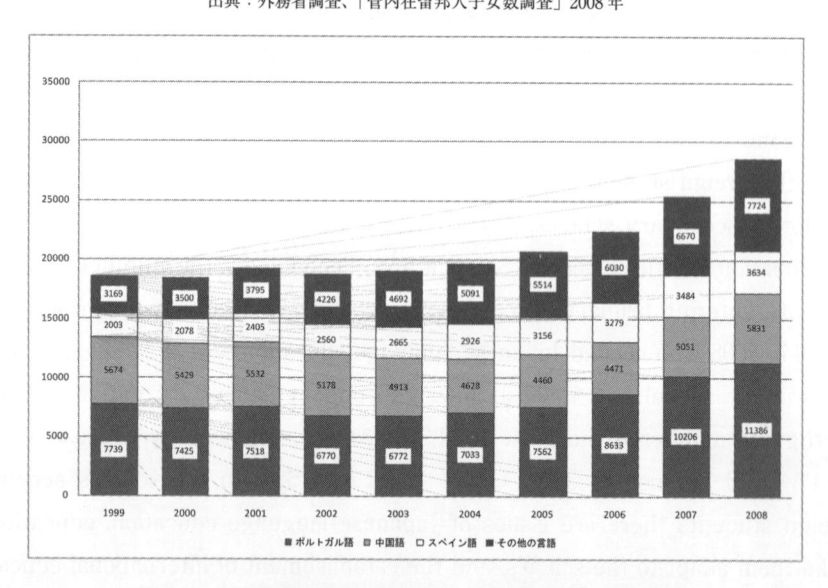

図 5-4　日本語指導が必要な外国人児童生徒数（母語別）
出典：文部科学省ホームページ、「日本語指導が必要な外国人児童生徒の受入れ状況等に関する調査」について、2008 年

V. Development of International Education

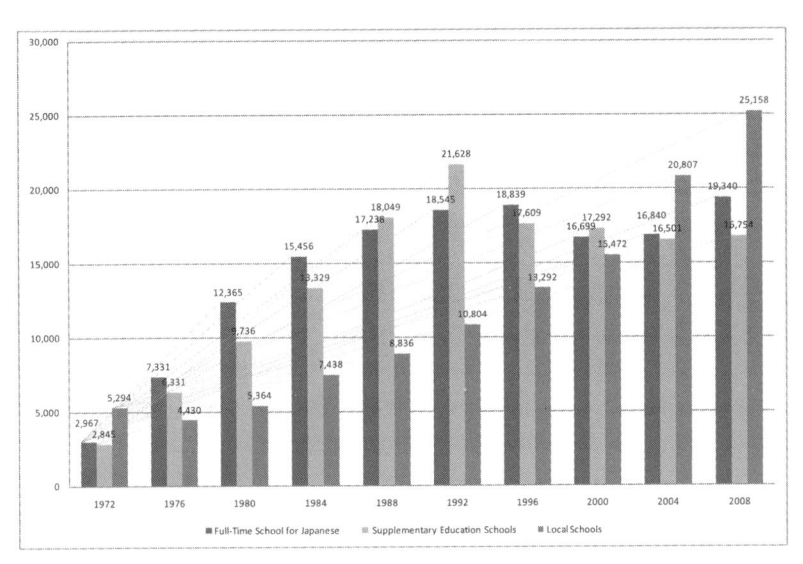

Figure 5-3 Increasing Number of the Japanese Children Staying and Studying Abroad
Resource : Ministry of Foreign Affairs, Japan, "A Statistical Survey of Japanese Overseas Children", 2008

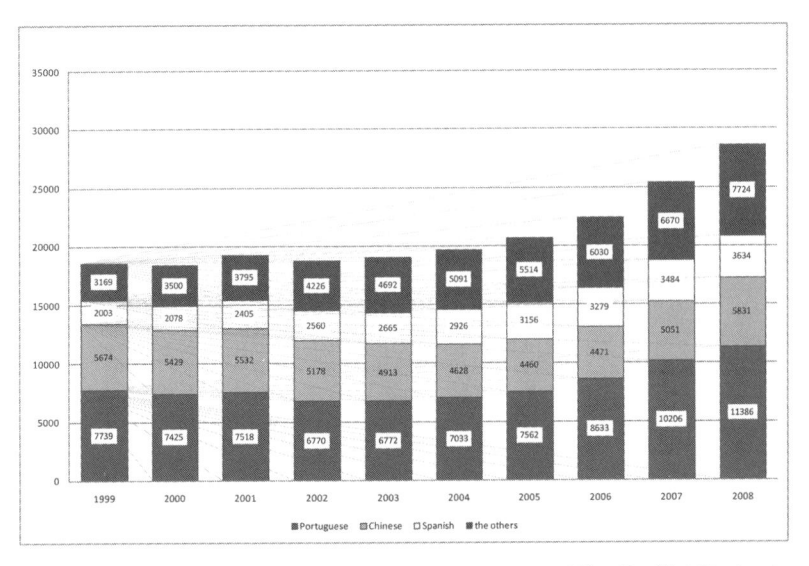

Figure 5-4 The Number of Foreign Pupils and Students Who Do Not Understand Japanese by Mother Tongue
Resource: Home Page of Ministry of Education, Culture, Sports, Science and Technology, Japan, "A Survey of the Acceptance of Foreign Students in Japanese Schools Who Need Japanese Language Teaching", 2008

（2）教師の国際化

■教師の国際交流も盛んになってきた。日本人教師のうち初等・中等学校教員については、1959年に発足した教員海外派遣研修制度があり、1973年以降毎年5,000人の教員が短期間（2〜6ヶ月）派遣されている。そのうち英語教育コース（2ヶ月と6ヶ月）は、アメリカ、イギリス、オーストラリア、カナダ、国際理解教育コース（3ヶ月）は、アメリカまたはオーストラリアに派遣される。大学教員や研究機関の研究員は、文部科学省、日本学術振興会、国際交流基金等の海外派遣制度を利用する。

■外国人教師の受け入れは、主として大学に多く、2007年度で国公立および私立の大学を含めて約5,700人であった。1980年10月からは、外国の教師を対象とする1年半の国費研修留学生制度が発足し、2008年度においては筑波大学や広島大学など53の国立大学で約155人の外国人教員研修留学生、主に初等中等現職教員が受け入れられている。その対象国は、主にアセアン諸国、韓国、中国、中南米諸国、アフリカ諸国など発展途上国64ヶ国におよんでいる。

■大学における外国人教師の任用に関しては、私立大学においては以前から認められてきたが、国公立大学では正規のスタッフになることは不可能であった。それが、1982年9月に「国立または公立の大学における外国人教員の任用等に関する特別措置法案」が可決され、外国人教師も国公立大学において教授や助教授のスタッフになれるようになった。しかし、実際はまだその人数は限られている。

（3）学校制度の国際化

■わが国では、高等学校の入学者は「外国において学校教育における9年の課程を修了した者」（学校教育法施行規則63条、大学入学者は「12年の課程修了者」（同規則69条）と規定されている。外国には多様な学校制度があり、このよ

(2) Internationalization of Teachers

■ Teacher exchange programs have been implemented recently. In 1959, a program was established to send Japanese primary and secondary school teachers to foreign countries for a short period of 2-6 months. Since 1973, a total of about 5,000 teachers have been sent abroad on a yearly basis. In the English Education Courses (2 months course and 6 months course), teachers are dispatched to the United States, England, Australia, or Canada. In the International Understanding Education Course (3 months course) teachers are dispatched to the United States or Australia. University academic staff and the researchers of institutes utilize the program for further study in foreign countries through the Ministry of Education, Culture, Sports, Science and Technology, the Japan Society for the Promotion of Science, the Japan Foundation, and so on.

■ Foreign teachers are accepted mainly by universities and colleges. They numbered about 5,700 in 2007. The In-Service Training Program for Overseas Teachers, which are for a one and a half year period was set up in October 1980. In 2008, fifty three national universities including the University of Tsukuba and Hiroshima University accepted 155 overseas teachers as trainees. They came mainly from 64 developing countries in ASEAN, Korea, China, Latin America and Africa.

■ Foreigners had not been allowed to obtain employment as regular academic staff in the national and public universities, although this was allowed in the private universities. In September 1982, a Bill to correct the unfair treatment was adopted and it has enabled foreigners to be employed as regular staff like professors or associate professors in the universities. However, their number is still very small.

(3) Internationalization of the School System

■ According to the present school law in Japan, the prerequisites for admission to upper secondary school and university are the completion of a nine and twelve year course in foreign countries respectively (Articles 63 and 69 of the Enforcement

■大学教育の履修に関しては、1972年の法律改正により学生が留学先の外国の大学で履修した単位も、国内の大学の卒業に必要な単位として認められるようになった。各国の大学へ入学するための共通資格を付与する国際バカロレアは、欧米では普及しているが、アジア諸国ではいまだあまり普及していない。アジア地域においてその資格を認めている国は、わが国の外に香港、フィリピン、マレーシア、シンガポールなどである。最近、アジア諸国の教育環境に合致した共通の試験問題を作成するために国際会議を通じて検討が行われている。しかし、わが国において、国際バカロレアを入学資格として認めている大学は数校にしか過ぎない。

（4）国際学校
①インターナショナル・スクール、民族学校
■初等・中等教育レベルにおいて多様な国籍・民族の幼児・児童・生徒を対象に教育を行う学校を指す。学校教育法第1条に定められている「学校」は少なく、第134条規定の各種学校が多い。インターナショナル・スクールには、特定の国籍・民族を対象とする学校と複数の国籍・民族の幼児・児童・生徒を受け入れ特定の国に依存しないカリキュラムにより教育を提供する学校がある。前者には、韓国学校、朝鮮学校、中華学校、アメリカン・スクール、ドイツ学校、フランス学院、インドネシア学校などがあり、民族学校とも呼ばれる。後者の学校には、WASC（アメリカ西部学区大学協会）やCIS（イギリス・インターナショナル評議会）などの国際評価団体の認可を受けた学校（約40校）や国際バカロレア資格参加校（15校）が含まれる。また、日本の大学入学資格が認められる学校（2003年に23校）も増えている。

　インターナショナル・スクールには各種学校が多いため私立学校のような政府補助を受けることができない点に問題がみられる。

Regulations for School Education Law). The regulations can hardly cope with some existing cases because of a variety of school systems in foreign countries.

■ The revision of the regulation made in 1972 concerning credit exchange provided that credits obtained from overseas universities be valid for conferring degrees in universities in Japan. The International Baccalaureate, which provides for admission to overseas universities, is not as common in Asian countries as it is in European and American countries. In Asia, it is adopted only by Japan, Hongkong, the Philippines, Malaysia and Singapore. A plan to prepare common examinations in Asia is now under discussion in international seminars. However, in Japan, only a few universities recognize the International Baccalaureate as a qualification for admission.

(4) International School
① International School and Ethnic School

■ Schools which teach pupils and students of diverse nationalities and ethnic groups in the primary and secondary education stage are called an international school or ethnic school. Few of them are "a school" which is defined in Article 1 of the School Education Law and most of them are a miscellaneous school which is defined in Article 134 of the same Law. There are two types of international schools. One accepts pupils and students of specific nationality or ethnic group, and the other accepts those of any nationalities and ethnic groups, providing education which does not depend on one specific country. Former schools include Korean, Chinese, American, German, French, Indonesian and others. They are also called ethnic schools. The latter includes about 40 schools accredited by international accreditation organizations such as WASC (Western Association of School and College, U.S.A.) or CIS (Council of International Schools, England) and about 15 schools which received an international baccalaureate qualification. Moreover, schools which are granted to be qualified for admission to Japanese universities have been increased (23 schools as of 2003).

A problem is that many of the international schools are categorized as a

②国際高校

■東京都教育庁に1983年7月に設置された高等学校教育改善推進本部は、新しいタイプの高等学校の1つとして国際高校の設立を計画し、1989年度に国際学科のみを持つ公立高校として発足した。国際高校は、帰国児童生徒や外国人留学者などの増加と学校の国際化に対する高まる要請を考慮し、日本人、帰国児童生徒、外国人青少年を一緒に生活させて教育しようとするものである。当初は、237人の生徒（帰国生徒31人、外国人生徒15人）が入学した。2008年4月には、生徒総数は、720人（1学年240人、帰国生徒40人、在京外国人25人）となっていた。

■そのねらいは、共同体験の中から民族間の人権尊重、異民族間の友好、異文化理解などを学びつつ国際性を身に付けて世界の平和と福祉に貢献していく人材養成におかれている。教育においては、国際理解教育、外国語教育に力を入れるとともに、世界連帯意識の育成、豊かな人間性の育成、個性の尊重、日本の文化・伝統の理解、および他の国民・民族との共生の姿勢を心掛けている。専門教科として、国際理解科、外国語科、情報・表現科、課題研究などが置かれている。国際理解科には、文化理解（日本文化、比較文化、伝統芸能、外国文学）と社会理解（国際関係、社会生活、地域研究、福祉）がある。外国語科では、英語以外に、ドイツ語、フランス語、スペイン語、ロシア語、中国語、朝鮮語なども学べることになっている。

miscellaneous school and cannot receive a government subsidy while private schools do.

② International Upper Secondary School

■ A committee to promote the improvement of upper secondary school education was set up by the Tokyo Board of Education in July 1983. It established an international upper secondary school in 1989 which had only an international department. This new type of school is designed to educate together ordinary Japanese students, Japanese students returning from abroad, and foreign students in order to meet the growing demand for school internationalization and the increasing number of student returnees. In the beginning 273 students entered the School. Among them there were 31 Japanese students returning from abroad and 15 foreign students. In April of 2008 the total number of the students reached 720 including 40 Japanese students returning from abroad and 25 foreign students living in Tokyo.

■ It aims to train students who can contribute to world peace and welfare through cultural understanding, friendly relations among different people and respect for human rights through common experience. The school focuses on teaching international understanding and foreign languages. It is promoting students' consciousness of interrelationship among world people, richness of humanity, respect for students' individuality, understanding of Japanese culture and tradition, and the way of living together with other national people and ethnic people. Through major subjects, students can learn international understanding, foreign language, information processing, way of expression, study of assignment and so on. The subject of international understanding is divided into cultural understanding and social understanding. The cultural understanding includes Japanese culture, comparative culture, traditional arts, and foreign literature. The social understanding contains international relations, social life, area studies, and welfare. In the subject of foreign languages German, French, Spanish, Russian, Chinese, and Korean are taught as well as English.

③国際大学

■わが国の既設の国公私立大学において国際化がなかなか進展しないことに対する反省、しかも、国際化する社会に対応できる人材育成に対する要請の高まりに応えようと、1982年に新しく私立の国際大学が新潟県に設立された。この新大学は、国際社会に活躍できる高度な専門的知識を持った職業人の育成と発展途上国の人材養成に寄与する目的で設立された2年制の大学院大学である。卒業すれば国際学修士号を授与する。1982年に国際関係学研究科、1988年には国際経営学研究科が開設された。1983年4月の開学当初、新入学生数は56人であったが、2008年5月には289人となった。国際関係研究科には、国際関係学プログラム、国際平和学プログラム、国際開発学プログラム、国際経営学研究科には国際経営学プログラムとE-ビジネスプログラムがある。2009年11月の正規学生数は272人で、国際関係学研究科147人、国際経営学研究科125人であった。そのうち外国人留学生は約9割の254人であった。留学生は約40ヶ国から来学している。主にインドネシア、インド、ベトナム、中国、ミャンマー、モンゴル、タイ、キルギスなどである。

■その他、大学院附属研究所として、日米関係研究所、中東研究所、アジア発展研究所、国際経営研究所が設置されている。

■同大学の特色としては、第1に、国際性を持つ研究者と専門的職業人の養成をめざすこと。第2に、大学の国際化として、外国人教授の採用、外国人留学生の受け入れ、教授用語に英語と日本語使用、海外の研究・教育機関との交流促進、全寮制による内外の学生や教員との日常的交流を図ること。第3に、国際関係研究と地域研究との学際的統合を図り、国際研究を深化すること。第4に、社会に開かれた大学として、実社会（企業、官公庁など）で職

③ International University
■ Taking into account the fact that the universities in Japan have hardly been internationalized, a private international university was founded in Niigata in 1982 to meet the rising demand for people who can keep pace with the internationalized world. This two-year graduate school is designed to train experts and professionals who have advanced academic knowledge and who can contribute to the development of developing countries. The graduates who are granted a degree on Master of International Affairs, are expected to play an active role in the international society. The university was opened in April 1983 and accepted 56 freshmen. In May 2008, the number has reached 289. Various schools have been established and include the Graduate School of International Relations in 1982 and the Graduate School of International Management in 1988, with the former School having had an International Relation Program, International Peace Studies Program, International Development Program, and the latter had an International Management Program and E-Business Program. In November 2009 the number of regular students was 272 in total, , with 147 in International Relations and 125 in International Management. Among all the students, 245, or about 90%, was from overseas countries. The foreign students have come from about 40 countries. They are mainly from Indonesia, India, Vietnam, China, Myanmar, Mongolia, Thailand and Kyrgyz.

■ In addition the Institutes attached to the Graduate Schools have been established. They are the Center for Japan - U.S. Relations, the Institute of Middle Eastern Studies, the Institute of Asian Development, and the Institute of International Management.

■ It has several characteristics and functions: ① the training of researchers and professionals with a cosmopolitan outlook, ② for the purpose of internationalization of the university, the following steps were undertaken: (a) adoption of foreign researchers as regular staff, (b) acceptance of foreign students, (c) use of Japanese and English as the media of instruction, (d) promotion of exchange programs with overseas institutes and educational institutions, (e) improvement

業に従事している者も受け入れる。第5は、卒業生は国際的業務に従事し、国際機関の専門職員、企業、官公庁の国際問題担当者、国際ジャーナリスト、大学・研究機関の研究者などになること。

■こうした国際大学においては、日本人学生に対し、日本人としての教養、専門領域における専門知識、外国における経験なども深めさせることが大きな課題であろう。一方、近年、私立大学の中に国際大学と称する大学が増え、2008年には東京国際大学、大阪国際大学、吉備国際大学、九州国際大学など26大学に及んでいた。また、国公私立大学において国際学部、国際文化学部、国際関係学部などを設置する大学も増加している。

(5) 国際教育の確立
■国際化に対する教育内容として国際教育の確立が課題となってきた。国際教育の中身としては、国際理解の教育、平和教育、人権教育、異文化理解の教育、開発教育、環境教育などがあげられる。

①ユネスコ憲章と平和教育
■1947年に国際連合によって採択されたユネスコ憲章は、その前文で「戦争は人の心の中で生まれるものであるから、人の心の中に平和の砦を築かなければならない。相互の風習と生活を知らないことは、人類の歴史を通じて世界の諸人民の間に疑惑と不信をおこした共通の原因であり、この疑惑と不信のために、諸人民の不一致があまりにもしばしば戦争となった。」と宣言した。諸国民間における相互の偏見、不信、憎悪を取り除き平和の砦を築く

of communication between students and teachers through common dormitory life, ③ development of international study by promoting interdisciplinary studies on international relations and area studies, ④ acceptance of working students as a way of opening the university to society, ⑤ training students to become skillful professionals and researchers of international affairs to work in international agencies, enterprises, government, journalistic society, universities, institutes and so on.

■ With this kind of international university, it is indispensable for Japanese students to deepen their understanding of their own culture aside from their major field of study, as well as to broaden their experience in and about foreign countries. On the other hand the private universities named International University have increased in recent years. In 2008 there were 26 such private universities such as Tokyo International University, Osaka International University, Kibi International University, Kyushu International University and so on. In national, public, and private universities some universities have set up an International Department, International Culture Department, and International Relations Department.

(5) Establishment of International Education
■ The educational contents corresponding to internationalization are becoming important in the establishment of international education. International education refers to education for; international understanding, peace, human rights, understanding different cultures, development, and the environment.
① The UNESCO Charter and Education for Peace
■ The UNESCO Charter adopted by the United Nations in 1947 states in its preamble that: "Since wars begin in the minds of men, it is in the minds of men that the defences of peace must be constructed. Ignorance of each other's ways and lives has been a common cause, throughout the history of mankind, of that suspicion and mistrust between the peoples of the world through which their differences have all too often broken into war." In order to get rid of prejudice,

ために、ユネスコが提唱する国際理解の教育、平和教育を推進することは、すべての国における国民教育の課題となっている。

② 人権教育と国際理解の教育
■他国民を理解し国際協力を促進するためには、その精神的基盤として人権尊重の態度が形成されなければならない。これが、世界人権宣言の理念を受けて1974年の第18回ユネスコ総会が採択した「国際理解、国際協力、および国際平和のための教育、並びに人権および基本的自由についての教育に関する勧告」の主旨であった。国際理解教育は、人権尊重の精神を基盤としつつ、他国、他民族、他文化への理解と世界平和、世界連帯意識の育成を図るものであり、人権に関する教育を含むのが普通である。

③ 異文化理解の教育
■島国でほとんど単一民族、単一言語の下で生活する日本人にとっては、異なる民族の風習、生活様式や考え方、感じ方、価値観を理解することは容易ではない。まして彼らと一緒に生活し共存していくことになると一層不慣れである。また、他国の文化を見る場合に、文化を序列化して考えたり、自国の文化を他民族や他社会の人々に強制したりすることもあった。他の文化の良さを理解できないと自己の文化を絶対視して、ついには自民族中心主義（エスノセントリズム）に陥ることになりかねない。人々は、とかく自分の属している文化を客観視し得ないからである。世界にある多様な文化を研究し、異質な文化の特質を認識することにより、かえって自国の文化の理解を深めることになる。他国や他民族の文化を知るようになると、自国文化を相対的に認識し客観視できるようになってくる。言いかえれば、文化には唯一絶対のものはないという文化相対主義の認識が生まれる。従って、自国の文化を理解し異質な文化を持つ人々と共存を図っていくためにも、異文化に遭遇しそれを理解することは、きわめて大切なことである。こうした意味から国際教育の基礎には、異文化理解の教育がなければならないであろう。

distrust and hatred among different people, and in order to establish a pillar of peace, every country should recognize the necessity for the promotion of international understanding and education for peace in each educational system.

② Education for Human Rights and International Understanding

■ In order to understand other people and to promote international cooperation, the respect for human rights should be formed as the spiritual basis in education. This is a recommendation made in the UNESCO general meeting in 1974. The meeting, following the concept of World Declaration of Human Rights, made a recommendation concerning Education for International Understanding, Cooperation and Peace, and Education Relating to Human Rights and Fundamental Freedom. Education for International Understanding makes understanding between different nations, ethnic groups and cultures possible and consequently leads to world peace and solidarity based on the spirit of esteem for human rights. Thus, it includes education for human rights.

③ Education for Understanding Different Cultures

■ It is not easy for Japanese to understand the customs, life style, way of thinking and value systems of other races because the Japanese are mainly composed of one race with a single language throughout the island nation. Therefore, the Japanese are not accustomed to living together with people of various races. Japanese tend to rank all cultures, including their own, from superior to inferior and in some cases expect foreigners to follow Japanese culture. Unless one is able to understand the good aspects of other cultures, one is likely to regard his own culture as the best, eventually leading to ethnocentrism. This is because people are unable to see their own culture objectively. If one studies various types of cultures and recognizes their characteristics, one understands his own culture more deeply. When one knows other nations and different cultures, he regards his own culture relatively with an objective view. In other words, one can realize cultural relativism, or that there is no one absolute culture. Henceforth, it is necessary for everyone to be introduced to different cultures and understand them so as to have comprehension of his

④開発教育と持続可能な開発のための教育
■1960年代から先進国と発展途上国の経済的、社会的格差が大きくなるに従って、南北問題の解決が重要な課題となった。それに伴い先進国では、開発教育が注目されてきた。開発教育は、人々がそれぞれの地域社会、国、および世界全体の開発に参加できるように適切な態度を養うことを目的としている。特に、先進国と発展途上国双方の人権、尊厳、自立、社会正義の確立を考慮しつつ、発展途上国の低開発の原因への理解を深めその克服を図ろうとするものである。取組の立場には、主に人道主義、相互利益主義、文化摩擦回避主義がある。しかし日本では開発教育に対する関心はまだ薄い。

■アジア、アフリカ、ラテン・アメリカの発展途上国では、2000年代から持続可能な開発のための教育という考え方が広まった。その内容には、人口教育、保健教育、識字教育、技能・技術教育、農・漁村教育、婦人教育などが含まれる。

⑤環境教育
■わが国では、1960年代の高度経済成長に伴い産業公害が問題にされるようになった。大気や水質などの環境汚染は、人々の生命・健康を脅かした。1980年代以降、地球の温暖化、酸性雨の増加、熱帯雨林の減少、野生生物の減少など、地球的規模の環境破壊が進み、国際的な重要な問題となっている。

■学校教育・社会教育においても公害から生活環境を守り、人々の健康を維

own culture, and to be able to live harmoniously with people from other cultures. In this context, international education should be based on education related to the understanding of different cultures.

④ Development Education / Education for Sustainable Development

■ Economic and social disparity between developed and developing countries has been increasing since the 1960's. As a result, the north-south relationship has become a major world problem. Meanwhile, developed countries have paid particular attention to "development education". The purpose of development education is to form an appropriate attitude which makes people participate in the development of their community, their nation and the world. In particular, development education is an attempt to let students understand the causes of low level of development in the developing countries and to think of how to overcome these problems. However, the ultimate purpose is the establishment of human rights, esteem, independence and social justice in both developed and developing countries. In development education, three main principles operate: humanism, reciprocity, and avoidance of cultural friction. In Japan, however, people have yet to cultivate interest in development education.

■ In the developing countries of Asia, Africa and Latin America, the concept of "Education for Sustainable Development" has been spreading since the 2000's. It includes the following fields: population education, health education, literacy education, skill and technical education, rural education, education for women and so on.

⑤ Environmental Education

■ In Japan industrial pollution occurred as a result of high economic development in the 1960s. The air and water pollution endangered the life and health of many people. Since the 1980's, global environmental destruction, such as an increase of average temperature of the earth, increase of acid rain, decrease of the forests in the tropical zones, decrease of wild animals and so on has occurred. This kind of destruction has become a serious international issue.

■ In school education and social education, environment education is emphasized

持するために環境教育が重視されつつある。特に、人間と自然との調和、環境・資源についての正しい認識、国際理解と国際協力の重要性を教えることがその基本である。また、環境教育では、グローバルな視野でものを考え、身近な問題に対して行動を取ることが教えられる。地球的環境破壊について理解を深めると同時に、日常の生活と結びついたゴミ処理、水・空気汚染、騒音、消費スタイル等に関心を持ち、問題に対し適切な態度、行動が取れるように生徒を指導することも大切である。

in order to protect people's environment from pollution and to maintain people's health. The main purpose of environmental education is to teach the importance of harmony between humans and nature, proper understanding of the natural environment and resources, and international understanding and cooperation. Through environmental education students should be taught to think from a global perspective and to take action for tackling environmental problems which occur in daily life. In this field, the students will develop their interest in the disposal of solid waste, pollution of air and water, noise, and consuming style, and learn how to develop a proper attitude and action towards daily environmental problems, as well as to further understanding issues related to global environmental destruction.

3. 国際教育行政の発展

(1) 国際教育行政
■近年、教育の国際化の高まりに対応して国際機関が各国の教育に関与するケースも増えている。例えば、国際連合機関の専門組織であるユネスコ、IBE、ILO など、また、地域共同機関としては、ヨーロッパを中心とする OECD や東南アジア諸国の文部大臣機構である SEAMEO などである。これらの機関は、各国共通の教育問題を取り上げて討議し、共通の目標を達成するために各国に対し適切な教育政策や教育計画の確立を勧告して教育行政活動を展開している。さらに、国際機関は立法機能を有し、定められた権限内で条約や勧告を制定してその目的・任務を遂行する上で役立っている。このように国際機関が行う教育行政は、国際教育行政と呼ばれている。国際教育行政の進展により、わが国の教育もますます国際機関の影響を受けつつある。

(2) 国際教育行政の基本原理
■国際教育行政は次の5つの原理に沿って行われている。

①国際主義
■国内の教育行政は国家主権にもとづいて行われるが、国際教育行政は国家主権が絶対的なものではなく、国家が協同で国際社会を形成しその国際社会が取り決める条約や勧告などの拘束を受けることによって成立するという国

3. The Development of International Educational Administration

(1) International Educational Administration
■ Recently, influenced by the internationalization of education, international organizations have taken more interest in education in many countries. They are professional organizations of the United Nations like UNESCO (United Nations Educational Scientific and Cultural Organization), IBE (International Bureau of Education), and ILO (International Labor Organization), and as regional organizations, OECD (Organization for Economic Cooperation and Development) in developed countries and SEAMEO (South-East Asian Ministers of Education Organization) in developing countries. These organizations discuss the common educational problems in many countries and plan activities for educational administration and recommend suitable educational policies and plans to member countries in order to fulfil common goals. Since international organizations have the advantage of having broad jurisdiction, they can set up treaties or recommendations within their powers that are useful in attaining their goals and functions. This kind of educational administration established by the international organizations is called international educational administration. With the development of international educational administration, education in Japan is increasingly influenced by international educational organizations.

(2) The Basic Principles of International Educational Administration
■ International Educational Administration is carried out based on the following five principles:
① Internationalism
■ Domestic educational administration is carried out by each country based on its national sovereignty. On the other hand, international educational administration is based on internationalism. It is assumed that national

際主義に基づくのである。国際主義を基盤におく国際協同社会において、各方面の国際交流ばかりでなく国際行政も可能となるのである。国際主義による国際行政が教育分野において成立すると考えられるもう一つの理由は、教育自体の持つ普遍人類的性格および国際主義的性格によっている。

②法律主義
■国内行政と同様に、国際行政においても法律主義が一大原理となっている。国際教育行政は教育に関する条約や勧告の実施という形で行われ、法の支配の原則が生かされている。

③内政不干渉主義
■ユネスコは、同憲章第1条第3項において「この機関は、加盟国の国内管轄権に本質的に属する事項に干渉することを禁止される」と規定した。これは、各国が行う教育上の内政事項に関して国際機関は不干渉・不介入の原則を守ることを意味する。しかし、国際教育行政は教育の普遍的、国際的性格に基づいて行われているのであるから、教育行政の国内管轄権は国際機関の干渉・介入を一切許さないというほど厳格かつ広範なものではない。

④分権主義
■国内行政において権力の分散を図るために分権主義を採用している国が多くみられる。国際行政においても、行政作用を地域毎に処理する地域主義がみられるが、これは分権主義の現れと言ってよい。ユネスコ本部と各地域のユネスコ地域事務所、および各国のユネスコ国内委員会の関係は、一種の分権主義に基づくものといえよう。

⑤人権尊重主義
■世界人権宣言は、その前文において「加盟国は、人権および基本的自由の

sovereignty is not absolute and that a nation should be restrained by treaties or recommendations made by the international community. In the international arena, which is supposed to respect internationalism, international communication in various fields as well as international administration is feasible. Another reason why international administrations has been conceived in the field of education is that education itself has a universal, humanistic and international character.

② Legalism

■ In international administration as well as in domestic administration, legalism is one of the main principles. International educational administration is carried out by implementing treaties and recommendations on education, in which the principle based on the Rule by Law is observed.

③ The Principle of Non-Intervention

■ Paragraph 3 of Article 1 of the UNESCO Charter states that "this organization is prohibited from intervening in the affairs which essentially belong to the domestic jurisdiction of the member state." This means that international organizations would observe the principle of non-intervention in the domestic affairs of each nation. However, since international educational administration is carried out in conformity with the universal and international character of education, the domestic jurisdiction over educational administration is not so rigid and extensive as to prohibit any intervention by the international organizations.

④ The Principle of Decentralization

■ Many nations have adopted the principle of decentralization with the aim of delegating powers in domestic administration. Even in international administration, regionalism is observed; thus, administrative work is done in each region. This can be regarded as one manifestation of decentralization. It can be said that the relation of the UNESCO headquarters to the UNESCO regional offices and to the domestic board in each nation is based on the principle of decentralization.

⑤ The Principle of Respect for Human Rights

■ The Declaration of Human Rights in its preamble states: "Since every member

世界的な尊重および遵守の促進を国際連合と協力して達成することを誓約したので…この宣言を布告する」と規定した。そして同第26条において、すべての国民は教育を受ける権利を有することを規定した。このような基本的人権の尊重ということは人類普遍の原理であり、国際教育行政においても一大原理となっている。

(3) 国際機関の教育・学術・文化協力活動
■わが国において行われている国際連合やユネスコによる主な教育・学術・文化の国際協力活動をみてみれば次のようなものがある。

①開発のためのアジア地域教育革新事業計画（APEID）
■アジア地域の教育協力を一層強化し革新的な協力活動を展開するために、1974年からユネスコの支援を受けて実施された。APEIDプロジェクトと活動は、アジアの参加17カ国によって協同で企画開発され、各国に置かれた協同センターにおいて実施されている。日本は、主に教育工学の分野で協力を行っているが、外にカリキュラム開発、道徳教育・勤労体験学習の振興などに重点が置かれている。日本で行われる研修事業には、国立教育政策研究所が積極的に協力している。2005年以降、持続可能な開発のための教育（ESD）の展開や教授学習過程の革新を重視し、特に教員による情報コミュニケーション技術（ICT）、視聴覚教育技術（AV）の向上を目指し国際的なワークショップも開催している。

②ユネスコ学術文化協力
■国際的な文化協力のために1971年に設立されたユネスコ・アジア文化センター（ACCU）は、日本文学の代表作品の翻訳、アジア諸国音楽教材、アジア諸国民の共通読物（民話、テキスト）、アジア太平洋識字NFEデータベース、環境に関するパッケージ教材、防災教材、アジア・カレンダー、ならび

state pledged to attain both respect for human rights and fundamental freedom and their observation in cooperation with the United Nations.... We proclaim this declaration. "

Moreover, Article 26 provides that every person has the right to education. Such respect for fundamental human rights as mentioned above is a universal principle. It is also one of the main principles in international administration.

(3) Cooperative Activities of International Organization in Education, Science and Culture

■ The main activities of international cooperation in education, science and culture performed by UNESCO and other international organizations in Japan are as follows:

① Asian Program of Educational Innovation for Development (APEID)

■ APEID with the assistance of UNESCO has been functioning since 1974 in order to further strengthen the educational cooperation in Asia and to develop cooperative activities with innovative programs. The projects and activities of the APEID are planned and developed in collaboration with 17 Asian member states, and they operate at the cooperative center of each nation. Japan cooperates with it mainly in the field of educational technology. Besides this, it puts emphasis on the development of curriculum, moral education and work-oriented education. The National Institute for Educational Research extends much assistance to the training activities held in Japan. Since 2005, emphasis on Education for Sustainable Development (ESD), renovation of teaching and learning processes, and international workshops are held to aim for improvement of Information and Communication Technology (ICT) and Audiovisual technologies (AV).

② Scientific and Cultural Cooperation of UNESCO

■ The Asian Cultural Center for UNESCO (ACCU) was established in 1971 for international cultural cooperation. It has undertaken several projects: the translation of masterpieces of Japanese literature, the production of teaching materials of Asian music, common readings for Asian people (such as folk tales

に子ども用 VTR などを作成しその普及に努めている。

③国連大学
■1972 年の第 27 回国連総会は国連大学の創設を決定し、次いで翌年の第 28 回国連総会において国連大学憲章が可決された。国連大学の研究領域としては、発展途上国の課題である飢餓、経済社会開発、天然資源の管理が主な対象となっている。ただし、学生は受入れていない。日本は、この国連大学に対し本部事務局の提供のみならず、大学基金の拠出などにより進んで国連大学の確立に協力してきた。

④東南アジア文部大臣機構（SEAMEO）地域センター（Regional Center）
■SEAMEO のメンバー国が共同で各種の教育分野における研究開発と研修（セミナー、ワークショップを含む）を行う国際地域センターを設立運営している。その活動にメンバー国の教員・教育行政官・教育研究者等が参加する。主な地域センターとして、教育技術革新センター（INNOTECH、フィリピン）、理数科教育センター（RECSAM、マレーシア）、高等教育開発センター（RIHED、タイ）、言語センター（RELC、シンガポール）などがある。これらのセンターは、1970 年前後に創設され、その後規模、研究開発・研修内容を拡大している。

and textbooks), Asia Pacific Literacy/Non-formal Education (NFE) database, package materials for environmental education, materials for disaster-prevention education, Asian calendar and VTR for children, and their diffusion to Asian countries.

③ University of the United Nations

■ In the 27th General Assembly of the United Nations the Assembly decided to establish the University of the United Nations in 1972 and the 28th General Assembly adopted the University Charter in the next year. The main study fields of the University are starvation, economic and social development and control of natural resources, which are becoming important issues in developing countries. While the University does not accept students, Japan has actively extended cooperation by establishing the headquarters in Tokyo and by extending support for the University funding.

④ The Southeast Asian Ministers of Education Organization (SEAMEO) Regional Center

■ Member countries of SEAMEO have collectively established and operated international regional centers where R&D and training courses including seminars and workshops in various educational fields are conducted. Teachers, administrative officials and educational researchers join in the activities of the regional centers. The main regional centers are as follows: Regional Center for Educational Innovation and Technology (INNOTECH, Philippines) ; Regional Center for Education in Science and Mathematics (RECSAM, Malaysia) ; Regional Center for Higher Education and Development (RIHED, Thailand) ; Regional Language Center (RELC, Singapore). These centers were founded around 1970 and have been enhancing their scale and contents of R&D and training.

4. 教育の国際化・グローバル化の課題

■日本の教育が直面している国際化を実現していくための主な課題にどんなものがあるだろうか。次の六点を指摘しておきたい。

（1）地球社会の認識―異質との共存・共生―
■国際関係の緊密化は、国々の物的交流、情報交流から進んで人的交流、文化交流を促している。このような国際交流が盛んな世界においては各国の相互依存が強くなり、各国民は、ボーダーレスの地球社会といわれるような運命共同体の中に置かれているという認識が必要になってきていると思われる。また、この地球社会にはさまざまな異なる文化を持った民族が生存しており、彼らの交流が盛んになれば、異質な文化を有する人々が平和に共存・共生し協力し合って行くことが求められる。地球社会を考える際には、この異質との共存・共生ということの重要性を認識する必要がある。

■こうした認識があれば教育を国際化し、世界各国との教育交流や教育協力を促進していかなければならない必然性も理解できるであろう。

（2）教育・学術における国際主義原理の確認
■現在、国際教育行政は国際主義原理に基づき行われている。教育の国際化にあたっては、国際教育行政ばかりでなく教育一般についても国際主義原理を基本としなければならない。国際主義原理は、偏狭な国家主義に陥ることなく、国際連帯、国際協調を重んずるものである。この観点に立てば、学校

4. Main Issues Concerning the Internationalization and Globalization of Education in Japan

■ What are the main issues to realize the internationalization of education in Japan at present ? The following six issues can be pointed out:

(1) The Realization of a Global Community - Coexistence and the Living-together of Different Peoples

■ A closer international relationship existing nowadays among nations has promoted not only an exchange of materials and information but also of persons and culture. In an age of such an extensive international exchange, it seems that the interdependence between nations becomes more solid and that it has become necessary for people of all nations to realize that they are placed in a community bound together by common fate. That community is called a global community. Various ethnic peoples with different culture are living in this global community. If they encounter and communicate with each other more than they did in the past, they must learn to live together peacefully and cooperate with each other. When we consider the global community, we have to recognize the importance of living - together peacefully, even though the human race consists of different ethnic peoples.

■ Such realization would make them understand the necessity of internationalizing education and promoting educational interchange and cooperation between nations.

(2) A Confirmation of the Principle of Internationalism in the Fields of Education and Science

■ International educational administration today is carried out in accordance with the principle of internationalism. With regards to internationalizing education, it involves not only international educational administration but also, that education in general should be based on the principle of internationalism as

や大学を国際的に開放することは当然なことである。

(3) 国際教育の確立

■ユネスコは、1974年の第17回総会において、「国際理解、国際協力、および国際平和のための教育並びに人権および基本的自由についての教育に関する勧告」を出した。その中で、ここにいう国際理解、国際協力、および国際平和のための教育、人権、基本的自由に関する教育を総称して国際教育と呼んだ。この国際教育の確立が教育国際化の最も大きな課題になると考えられる。

■なかでも、国際理解の教育の一部と考えられる異文化理解の教育を進めることが重要である。内容的には、これまであまり考慮されてこなかった東アジアや東南アジアなどの近隣諸国、ならびに中近東、中南米、アフリカ諸国など発展途上国の社会、文化を理解する教育が重視される必要があろう。

■そのためには、①学校教育の内容にそれらの国々の社会、文化をより多く取り上げる、②大学や学校において、それらの国々の文献や資料を整備し、地域研究や比較教育・文化を盛んにすること、③外国語教育の中にそれらの国々の母国語を含めて教えていくこと、④日本の人々とそれらの国々の人々との交流、共同体験を増進すること、⑤留学生や研修生を招くばかりでなく日本人の学生や教職員がそれらの国々へ出かけていって海外経験を拡大すること、などが考えられる。

well. The principle of Internationalism is to put emphasis on international relation and cooperation resisting narrow nationalism. In light of internationalism, it is natural to open schools and universities to the international community.

(3) The Establishment of International Education

■ At its 17th general assembly in 1974, UNESCO presented its recommendation concerning Education for International Understanding, Cooperation, and Peace and Education Relating to Human Rights and Fundamental Freedom. In the recommendation, international education is defined as education for international understanding, international cooperation and international peace as well as human rights and fundamental freedom. It seems that the establishment of international education will become the most crucial problem for the internationalization of education.

■ Above all, it is important to promote education for understanding different cultures which is considered part of education for international understanding. Specifically, it will be necessary to emphasize education for understanding the socio-cultural structures of neighboring countries in East Asia and Southeast Asia, and the developing countries in the Middle East, Latin America and Africa which so far have not yet received much attention in Japan.

■ To achieve these goals the following methods should be implemented: ① incorporate the society and culture of these countries into the teaching content of school education, ② provide universities and schools with reference books and materials about these countries and expand area studies and comparative education and culture in the institutions, ③ teach the native language of these countries as part of foreign language education, ④ promote better communication between the Japanese people and the people from those countries through joint exchanges with them, and ⑤ send Japanese students and teachers to these countries, as well as invite foreign students and trainees to Japan, in order to enhance their experience abroad.

（4）地球市民教育の展開

■国際教育は国民の存在を前提にした教育である。国民が外国の国民を理解し、彼等と相互に協力し平和な世界を築くことを目標にしている。地球社会においては、それと同時に運命共同体の一員として共通の認識や協力精神を育てる地球市民教育を行っていくこともきわめて重要であろう。人々はとかくエスノセントリズム（自民族中心主義）に陥りがちであるが、基本的に重層的なアイデンティティを有しているのである。すなわち、国民アイデンティティとともに民族アイデンティティ、さらに地域住民のアイデンティティを有している。これからの教育は、これらのアイデンティティに加えて地球市民のアイデンティティを持ってグローバルな問題に対処しうる市民を育成していかねばならないであろう。

（5）日本語・日本事情に関する教育の拡充

①外国人に対する日本語教育

■日本へ留学する学生はもとより、それ以外の外国人でも日本の社会、文化、日本語に興味を持つ人々に対しても、適切な日本語教育を行っていくことが必要である。それには、日本語教育機関の拡充、日本語教員の養成、日本語テキストや教材の開発などを行っていかなければならない。

■外国人のための日本語教育は、日本で行うばかりでなく、外国において行うことも大切である。世界各国における、日本語教育は増加傾向にあるが、中国とマレーシアでは日本へ留学する学生のために日本語予備教育をそれぞれ1979年と1983年から行っている。また、韓国、中国、マレーシアやインドネシア、タイの中等学校では、日本語を第2外国語として教えるところもある。オーストラリアでは、小学校から日本語を教えることが可能になっている。

(4) Development of Education for Global Citizens

■ International Education is supposed to be provided to national people. Its aims are such that national people promote understanding of the people of foreign countries, to cooperate with foreign people, and to establish a peaceful world. In a global community it will be very important that education for global education is provided for the community members to have a common recognition and cooperative spirit as a member of the borderless community with a common fate. National people are inclined to become ethnocentric. However, they have multi-layer identities which are usually composed of not only national identity but also ethnic identity and local identity. From now, in addition to those identities, all people are expected to have an identity of being a global citizen and to try to solve global problems in collaboration with each other. This is a main purpose of education for global citizens.

(5) The Expansion of Japanese Language Education for Foreigners and the Diffusion of Education about Japan

① The Expansion of Japanese Language Education for Foreigners

■ It is necessary to provide an appropriate Japanese language education not only to foreign students studying in Japan but also to other foreigners who are interested in the Japanese society, culture, and language. For that purpose, expansion of the institutions of Japanese language education, training of Japanese language teachers, and development of the textbooks and teaching materials for Japanese language should be carried out.

■ It is also important that Japanese language education for foreigners should be provided in foreign countries as well as in Japan. In many countries of the world Japanese language education is now on the rise. In China and Malaysia, a preparatory and basic education of Japanese language has been provided to those students who were going to study in Japan since 1979 and 1983 respectively. Some secondary schools in Malaysia, Indonesia and Thailand teach Japanese as the second foreign language. In Australia it is possible to teach Japanese in the

②日本事情に関する教育
■「国際人養成とは、真の日本人を育成することだ」とも言われている。外国人と交われば交わるほどナショナル・アイデンティティが問われ、日本人として必要な幅広い教養を身に付けることが要請される。日本の文化、歴史に関する知識ばかりでなく、日本人的な態度、興味、たしなみなどを身に付けることが望ましいであろう。

■外国人に対する日本事情の教育も、日本理解を促す上で不可欠である。しかし実際には何をどのように教えるのがよいかについて共通理解がなく、定まったテキストや教育方法もあまり開発されていない。

（6）日本の教育経験の世界への発信
■日本の歴史、文化に関する知識の習得、勤勉や時間厳守などの日本人的態度の育成は大切であるが、それとともに日本の文化的特質や教育の歴史的発展の有用な経験を世界に発信していく重要性を認識しその適切な方法を工夫することもこれからの課題であろう。日本は近代化を達成するために欧米諸国の社会制度や科学技術をモデルとしてそれらの知識技術を受容することに力点を置いてきた。経済的、社会的、教育的に発展した日本は、今後、伝統文化や発展経験の中から特質・長所を世界に発信していくことにも留意する必要があろう。日本の教育近代化の過程を振り返ると、近代学校の普及、女子教育の確立、へき地教育の振興、特別支援教育の整備、理数科教育の発展など、多くの開発途上国にとって有益な経験が豊富にみられる。それらを開発途上国の関係者と協働しつつ適切に発信していく方法を探求し実践することが重要である。

primary schools.

② The Diffusion of Education about Japan

■ It is said that rearing a Japanese who can be effective in the international community is equivalent to rearing a Japanese who can really understand Japan. The more the Japanese associate with foreigners, the more they might be called upon to consider their national identity and to acquire a deeper sense of culture as a Japanese. It is therefore desirable that the Japanese not only acquire knowledge of their own culture and history but also of the attitude, hobbies, and way of life appropriate to Japanese.

■ Educating foreigners about things on Japan is also indispensable for enhancing their understanding of Japan. In fact, however, there has been no common understanding on how and what to teach about Japan, and textbooks and teaching methods have not yet been fully developed.

(6) Share Japanese Educational Experiences with the World

■ It is important to acquire knowledge on Japanese history and culture and nurture attitude as Japanese, like diligence and punctuality. At the same time, we need to acknowledge the importance of sharing the cultural nature of Japan and the valuable experiences of historical development of education in the country. Contriving ways toward these ends are challenges for the future. Japan has concentrated efforts on adopting the knowledge and technologies of Western developed countries by observing and deriving from their social system and scientific technologies to accomplish modernization. Japan, as an economically, socially, and educationally developed country, should pay attention to sharing the nature and richness of its traditional culture and development experiences with the world. The modernization of the Japanese education system can provide many useful lessons to many developing countries with regard to the establishment of modern schools, promotion of female education, promotion of education in remote areas, enhancement of special needs education, and development of science and mathematics education. It is vital to look for

（7） 教育行政の国際化

■上に述べた課題を実現していくためには、教育行政の協力が必要である。その教育行政自体も国際化する必要に迫られている。特に、次のような点に対する配慮が必要になってきている。

■第1は、国際機関が行っている国際教育行政を有効に推進していくことである。それには、国内教育行政と国際教育行政を切り離すのではなく一体化していくことが重要である。

■第2は、国際的な教育・学術の交流、協力が増えれば、国際関係の仕事を特定の部局にまかせるということでは済まなくなり、多くの部局の協力体制の確立が要求されよう。

■第3は、国際教育の確立や外国人に対する日本語・日本事情教育の拡充、日本の教育経験の世界への発信のためには、国際的な情報が正確迅速に整備提供される必要がある。国際教育情報センター、国際教科書センターなどの整備が急がれる。

■第4は、国際化に必要な財政措置に対する配慮である。外国人留学生の受け入れや外国人との交流の増大を図るにしても、予算の裏付けがなければ実現できない。しかも、その財政措置は、大学、カレッジや社会教育機関など教育現場の自主性、自立性を尊重した適切なものでなければならない。

and implement a method to effectively share experiences with the developing countries in collaboration with the relevant people in these countries.

(7) The Internationalization of Educational Administration

■ In order to realize the issues mentioned above, the cooperation of educational administration is indispensable. Educational administration itself needs to be internationalized. It is especially necessary to consider the following points.

■ First of all, it is necessary to promote effectively the international educational administration carried out by international organizations in Japan. For this purpose, we should not separate domestic educational administration from international educational administration, but instead unify them.

■ Secondly, the increase of international exchange and cooperation of education and science will make it impossible to leave the work of international relations in charge of a particular department. It will require that a cooperative system among various departments be established.

■ Thirdly, in order to establish international education, to expand the education of Japanese language and Japanese affairs for foreigners, and to share Japanese educational experience with the world, international information should be ready for use and can be offered accurately and promptly. For these services an information educational center and an international textbook center should be expanded as soon as possible.

■ Fourthly, financial measures should be taken into consideration for internationalization. Even if we plan to increase the intake of foreign students and exchanges with foreign people, it cannot be realized without financial support. Moreover, the financial measures should be appropriately taken so as to respect the institutional independence of universities and colleges.

第Ⅵ章

教育内容・方法の概要

Outline of Curriculum and Teaching Method

学習指導要領
The Course of Study for Primary and Lower Secondary Schools Revised in 2008

1. 教育課程

■日本の学校では、生徒に教える教育内容を計画的に編成したものを「教育課程」と呼んでいる。教育課程は、「カリキュラム（curriculum）」という英語で表現されることも多い。「カリキュラム」という言葉は、今日では、学校における教育内容計画を表すことばとして、広く普及し、定着している。
■どのような教育課程を編成し、実施し、さらにどのように評価・改善するかという問題は、学校経営上の要（かなめ）となる重要な課題である。教育課程は、いわば学校教育の全体的なデザインであり、学校の教育目標を達成するうえで、重要な役割を果たしている。

■教育課程は、文部科学大臣が教育課程の基準として公示する「学習指導要領」と教育委員会が定める事項に基づいて、それぞれの学校において編成され、実施される。教育課程の編成と実施について最終的な責任を負うものは校長であるが、実際の編成の作業はすべての教員の協力によって行われる。

■現行の学習指導要領によれば、各学校の教育課程の編成は次のような4つの原則によって行われる。
　①各学校は、適切な教育課程を編成しなければならない。
　②各学校における教育課程の編成は、法令および学習指導要領に示すところに従わなければならない。
　③地域や学校の実態を考慮しなければならない。
　④生徒の心身の発達段階や特性等を考慮しなければならない。
　各学校はこのような原則に基づいて教育課程を編成するが、②の原則からは教育課程における全国的な共通性が、③の原則からは地域や学校による特色、独自性が導き出されることになる。

1. Curriculum

■ In Japanese schools, "kyoiku-katei" is referred to as educational content planning. "Kyoiku-katei" is often expressed in English as "curriculum". The word "curriculum" is currently used in a broad and well established context in Japan meaning the plan of educational contents in school.

■ The type of curriculum to be drawn up and implemented, in addition to knowing how to evaluate and improve it are the most important tasks and are the key of school management. The curriculum is also said to be the holistic design of school education and plays an important role in achieving the educational goal of schools.

■ Curriculum is drawn up and implemented in each school based on the Course of Study which is published by the Ministry of Education, Culture, Sports, Science and Technology (MEXT) and items prescribed by the board of education of each municipal government. Although the principal is ultimately responsible for development and implementation of curriculum, they are actually designed by teachers.

■ According to the present Course of Study, curriculum is drawn up based on the following four principles:

① Each school should plan the appropriate curricula.

② Drawing up of curriculum in each school should follow both the regulations and the Course of Study.

③ The actual conditions in the community and the school should be taken into consideration.

④ The developmental stages and characteristics of student's mind and body should be taken into consideration.

Each school draws up its curriculum on the basis of these principles. From principle ② the national characteristics of curriculum are identified, and from

326　第Ⅵ章　教育内容・方法の概要

授業参観　Parental Class Observation

principle ③ the unique characteristics and identity of community and school are derived.

IT 教育　IT Education

2. 学習指導要領

■学校教育における教科の種類、それぞれの教科に充てられる1年間の標準的な授業時数については、学校教育法施行規則によって定められている。
■小学校の教科等の種類と標準授業時数は表6-1に示す通りである。

表6-1　小学校の年間標準授業時数

区分		第1学年	第2学年	第3学年	第4学年	第5学年	第6学年
各教科の授業時間	国語	306	315	245	245	175	175
	社会			70	90	100	105
	算数	136	175	175	175	175	175
	理科			90	105	105	105
	生活	102	105				
	音楽	68	70	60	60	50	50
	図画工作	68	70	60	60	50	50
	家庭					60	55
	体育	102	105	105	105	90	90
道徳の授業時間		34	35	35	35	35	35
外国語活動の授業時数						35	35
総合的な学習の時間の授業時数				70	70	70	70
特別活動の授業時数		34	35	35	35	35	35
総授業時数		850	910	945	980	980	980

■小学校の教育課程は、この表にみられる通り、国語、社会、算数、理科、生活、音楽、図画工作、家庭、体育の各教科、道徳、外国語活動、総合的な学習の時間並びに特別活動によって編成される。なお、私立の小学校では、宗教を加え、それをもって道徳に代えることができる。また、必要がある場合には、一部の各教科について、これらを合わせて授業を行うことができる。小学校の授業時数の1単位時間は、45分である。

2. Course of Study

■ The variety of subjects and the standard class hours in a year are prescribed by the Enforcement Regulations for the School Education Law.
■ The variety of subjects and the standard hours of class sessions in primary schools are as Table 6-1:

Table 6-1 Standard Number of Yearly School Hours in Primary Schools

Subjects etc.		1st	2nd	3rd	4th	5th	6th
School ahours of Each Subject	Japanese Language	306	315	245	245	175	175
	Social Studies			70	90	100	105
	Arithmatics	136	175	175	175	175	175
	Science			90	105	105	105
	Life Environment Studies	102	105				
	Music	68	70	60	60	50	50
	Drawing and Handicraft	68	70	60	60	50	50
	Homemaking					60	55
	Physical Education	102	105	105	105	90	90
School Hours of Moral Education		34	35	35	35	35	35
School Hours of Foreign Language Activities						35	35
School Hours of Period for Integrated Study				70	70	70	70
School Hours of Special Activies		34	35	35	35	35	35
Total School Hours		850	910	945	980	980	980

■ As illustrated above, the curriculum in primary school consists of Japanese language, social studies, arithmetic, science, life environment studies, music, drawing and handcraft, homemaking, physical education, moral education, foreign languages, period for integrated study, and special activities. In private primary schools, class sessions on religion can be added instead of moral education. Moreover, part of the subjects can be taught together at the same time if necessary. One class period is 45 minutes in primary schools.

■中学校の教科等の種類と標準授業時数は表6-2に示す通りである。

表6-2　中学校の年間標準授業時数

区　　分		第1学年	第2学年	第3学年
各教科の授業時間	国　語	140	140	105
	社　会	105	105	140
	数　学	140	105	140
	理　科	105	140	140
	音　楽	45	35	35
	美　術	45	35	35
	保健体育	105	105	105
	技術・家庭	70	70	35
	外国語	140	140	140
道徳の授業時間		35	35	35
総合的な学習の時間の授業時数		50	70	70
特別活動の授業時数		35	35	35
総授業時数		1015	1015	1015

■中学校の教育課程は、この表にみられる通り、国語、社会、数学、理科、音楽、美術、保健体育、技術・家庭および外国語の各教科、道徳、総合的な学習の時間並びに特別活動によって編成される。なお、それぞれの学校においては、選択教科を開設し、生徒に履修させることができる。選択教科は上記の各教科の他、特に必要な教科とする。なお、中学校の授業時数の1単位時間は、50分である。

■高等学校の教育課程は、教科・科目、総合的な学習の時間および特別活動によって編成される。その内、特別活動は、ホーム・ルーム活動、生徒会活動および学校行事から構成される。高等学校の各学科に共通する教科・科目の種類と標準単位数は、次の表6-3に示す通りである。

VI. Outline of Curriculum and Teaching Method

■ The variety of subjects and the standard hours of class sessions in lower secondary schools are as Table 6-2:

Table 6-2 Standard Number of Yearly School Hours in Lower Secondary Schools

Subjects etc.		1st	2nd	3rd
School hours of each Subject	Japanese Language	140	140	105
	Social Studies	105	105	140
	Mathematics	140	105	140
	Science	105	140	140
	Music	45	35	35
	Fine Arts	45	35	35
	Health and Sports	105	105	105
	Industrial Arts and Homemaking	70	70	35
	Foreign Language	140	140	140
School Hours of Moral Education		35	35	35
School Hours of Period for Integrated Study		50	70	70
School Hours of Extracurricular Activities		35	35	35
Total School Hours		1015	1015	1015

■ As illustrated above, the curriculum in lower secondary schools consists of Japanese language, social studies, mathematics, science, music, fine arts, health and physical education, industrial arts and home economics and foreign languages, moral education, period for integrated study, and special activities. Each school is allowed to set up elective subjects for the students. Elective subjects are particularly necessary subjects in addition to the above-mentioned subjects. One class period is 50 minutes in lower secondary schools.

■ The curriculum in upper secondary schools consists of the subjects, extracurricular activities and period for integrated study. The extracurricular activities consist of homeroom activities, students' council activities and school events. Subject areas, subjects and standard numbers of credits for general education in upper secondary schools are shown in the table 6-3 :

表6-3　高等学校の各学科に共通する教科・科目の標準単位数

教科等	科目	標準単位数	教科等	科目	標準単位数
国語	国語総合	4	保健体育	体育	7～8
	国語表現	3		保健	2
	現代文A	2	芸術	音楽Ⅰ	2
	現代文B	4		音楽Ⅱ	2
	古典A	2		音楽Ⅲ	2
	古典B	4		美術Ⅰ	2
地理歴史	世界史A	2		美術Ⅱ	2
	世界史B	4		美術Ⅲ	2
	日本史A	2		工芸Ⅰ	2
	日本史B	4		工芸Ⅱ	2
	地理A	2		工芸Ⅲ	2
	地理B	4		書道Ⅰ	2
公民	現代社会	2		書道Ⅱ	2
	公民倫理	2		書道Ⅲ	2
	政治・経済	2	外国語	コミュニケーション基礎英語	2
数学	数学Ⅰ	3		コミュニケーション英語Ⅰ	3
	数学Ⅱ	4			
	数学Ⅲ	5		コミュニケーション英語Ⅱ	4
	数学A	2			
	数学B	2		コミュニケーション英語Ⅲ	4
	数学活用	2			
理科	科学と人間生活	2		英語表現Ⅰ	2
	物理基礎	2		英語表現Ⅱ	4
	物理	4		英語会話	2
	化学基礎	2	家庭	家庭基礎	2
	化学	4		家庭総合	4
	生物基礎	2		生活デザイン	4
	生物	4	情報	社会と情報	2
	地学基礎	2		情報の科学	2
	地学	4	総合的な学習の時間		3～6
	理科課題研究	1			

■それぞれの教科や領域の目標、内容および指導計画の作成と内容の取扱いについては、学習指導要領によって示されている。学習指導要領は、先にも

Ⅵ. Outline of Curriculum and Teaching Method 333

Table 6-3 Standard Number of Credits for General Education Subjects in Upper Secondary Schools

Subject Area	Subject	Standard Unit	Subject Area	subject	Standard unit
Japanese Language	Japanese language	4	Health & Phsical Education	Physical Education	7～8
	Japanese Expression	3		Health	2
	Modern Japanese A	2	Arts	Music Ⅰ	2
	Modern Japanese B	4		Music Ⅱ	2
	Calssics A	2		Music Ⅲ	2
	Calssics B	4		Fine Arts Ⅰ	2
Geography and History	World History A	2		Fine Arts Ⅱ	2
	World History B	4		Fine Arts Ⅲ	2
	Japanese History A	2		Handicraft Ⅰ	2
	Japanese History B	4		Handicraft Ⅱ	2
	Geography A	2		Handicraft Ⅲ	2
	Geography B	4		Calligraphy Ⅰ	2
Civics	Contemporary Society	2		Calligraphy Ⅱ	2
	Civics and Ethics	2		Calligraphy Ⅲ	2
	Politics & Economy	2	Foreign Languages	Communication Basic English	2
Mathematics	Mathematics Ⅰ	3
	Mathematics Ⅱ	4		Communication English Ⅰ	3
	Mathematics Ⅲ	5
	Mathematics A	2		Communication English Ⅱ	4
	Mathematics B	2
	Appliction of Mathematics	2		Communication English Ⅲ	4
Science	Science and Human Life	2
	Basic Physics	2		English Expression Ⅰ	2
	Physics	4		English Expression Ⅱ	4
	Basic Chemistry	2		English Conversation	2
	Chemistry	4	Homemaking	Basic Home Economics	2
	Basic Biology	2		General Home Economics	4
	Biology	4		Living Design	4
	Basic Earth Science	2	Information	Society and Information	2
	Earth Science	4		Science of Information	2
	Study of Science Problems	1	Period for Integrated Study		3～6

■ The Course of Study defines the goal, contents of each subject, domain and measures of drawing up and dealing of the teaching plan. The Course of

ふれたように、文部科学大臣が定める教育課程の国家的な基準であり、法的な拘束力をもっており、日本の学校の教育課程の内実を決める上で、重要な役割を果たしている。なお、地方の教育員会も、地方の教育事情を考慮して必要があると判断される場合には基準や規則を定めることができる。

■現在、次に挙げるような5種類のものが「文部科学省告示」として出されている。
　①幼稚園教育要領
　②小学校学習指導要領
　③中学校学習指導要領
　④高等学校学習指導要領
　⑤特別支援学校学習指導要領

■学習指導要領には、国家の教育内容に関する方針や国民の教育内容に対する期待が反映されており、その改訂については国民の大きな関心と期待が寄せられてきた。明治以後、「教則大綱」、「教授要目」の名称で出されていた教育内容の国家的な基準が「学習指導要領」として初めて出されたのが1947年のことであるが、それ以後、現在に至るまで、学習指導要領は、小学校の場合を例にとると、1951年、1958年、1968年、1977年、1989年、1998年というように、ほぼ10年の間隔を置いて改訂が重ねられてきた。

■ごく大まかな言い方をすれば、1951年の改訂ではアメリカ教育の影響を受けた経験主義の思想が強くあらわれていた。民主主義社会の建設に貢献する学校教育の構築がめざされていた。1958年、1968年での改訂では、経済の高度成長を背景にして、基礎学力の充実、科学技術教育の振興、道徳教育の強化がめざされていた。1977年以後の改訂では、人間中心の教育がめざされ、ゆとりのある教育環境の中で個性的な人間の形成を図ることが課題とされてきた。日本の教育改革は、学力重視の教育とゆとりのある人間中心の教育との間で振り子のように揺れ動いてきたとみることができる。2008年

Study is, as mentioned above, based on a national curriculum criterion which is prescribed by the Minister of Education, Culture, Sports, Science and Technology. It has a binding legal force, and plays an important role in determining the contents of the curriculum in Japanese schools. In addition, the local board of education can lay down its own standards or rules, if necessary, considering local educational circumstances.

■ At present, the following five courses of study are announced and enforced as the Ordinance of the Ministry of Education, Culture, Sports, Science and Technology:
① The Course of Study for Kindergarten Education
② The Course of Study for Primary Schools
③ The Course of Study for Lower Secondary Schools
④ The Course of Study for Upper Secondary Schools
⑤ The Course of Study for Special-Needs Schools

■ What is reflected in each Course of Study are the principles and expectations of the nation and the people toward educational contents. The people have been strongly interested in and anticipating the revised editions. The national standard of educational contents, which had been announced as "Guidelines for Education" (Kyoshoku Taiko) and "Syllabus" (Kyoju Yomoku) since the Meiji era, was announced as "The Course of Study" for the first time in 1947. Since then, the editions of Course of Study for primary school," for example, had been revised about every ten years: in 1951, 1958, 1968, 1977, 1989, and 1998.

■ Generally speaking, the 1951 revision reflected empiricism under the influence of American educational philosophy. It aimed to establish school education which contributes to construction of democratic society. The 1958 and 1968 revised editions, on the other hand, emphasized improvement of basic scholastic achievement, promotion of science and technology education, and enforcement of moral education. The revised editions in 1977 or later put emphasis on a human-centered education, aiming to build individual character in a more relaxed educational environment. The Japanese education reforms have been oscillated

3月の改訂では、学力向上ということが中心的な課題になっている。

between education emphasizing scholastic ability and a more relaxed human-centered emphasis. The revised edition of March 2008 focuses on improvement of scholastic ability.

3. 教科書

■教科書は、学校における教科の指導の際の「主たる教材」としてその使用が法律の上で義務づけられており、授業の展開および生徒の学力形成にきわめて重要な役割を果たしている。それ故、教科書の編集、検定、採択、授業における使用の仕方などについて慎重な配慮が払われ、工夫と改善が重ねられてきている。

■制度的には、教科書は、文部科学大臣の検定を経たもの、または文部科学省が著作を有するものに限られている。検定は、民間で著作された教科書の内容を国（文部科学大臣）が調査し、内容が教育基本法、学校教育法等の趣旨に合致し、学習指導要領に示されていることと一致し、公教育における教科用図書として適切であるかどうかを検定するものである。

■文部科学大臣による検定に合格した教科書の中から教育委員会の手によって所管する学校の教科書が採択される。いったん採択された教科書は、4年間同じものを採択することになっている。小学校、中学校の教科書は無償で生徒に支給されている。

■教科書以外の図書や資料で教科の指導のために教材として使われているものは、副読本とか補助教材と呼ばれている。教科書は主要な教材であるが、それを補うために多様な補助教材が教師の手によって作成され、授業場面での生徒の学習を豊かにするために活用されている。補助教材には、地図、ワークブック、ドリルブック、問題集、参考図書、視聴覚教材、パソコン教材など、実に多様なものが含まれている。

3. Textbook

■ Teachers are obligated to use textbooks by law as 'the main materials' for subject-instruction in schools, and significantly assist teachers for teaching procedure and students for scholastic achievement. Thus, textbooks have been given thoughtful considerations in their compilation, examination, selection and usage method in classes and have been revised and improved many times.

■ In the educational system, only textbooks authorized by the Ministry of Education, Culture, Sports, Science and Technology or of which copyright is owned by the Ministry can be used. During the textbook-authorization, the government (the Ministry of Education, Culture, Sports, Science and Technology) investigates the contents of each textbook published by private organizations to determine whether its contents are consistent with the spirit of both the Basic Act on Education and the School Education Law, whether its contents conform with the Course of Study, and whether it is an appropriate textbook for public education.

■ From among those which passed the textbook-authorization the Ministry of Education, Culture, Sports, Science and Technology, the board of education may select textbooks for the schools in its jurisdiction. Selected textbooks can be used for four years. The students in primary and lower secondary schools are given free textbooks.

■ Books and materials for subject-instructions, other than set textbooks are called supplementary readings and materials. The textbooks are the main materials but various supplements have been created by teachers themselves so as to support the main materials and textbooks and are utilized in order to enrich students' learning. Supplementary aids may include various materials like maps, workbooks, drill books, exercise books, reference books, audio-visual materials, personal computer teaching aids, and so forth.

4. 学校暦・時間割

■1年間にわたる学校行事の計画のことを学校暦と呼んでいる。表6-4に挙げたものはある公立小学校の学校暦の例である。儀式としては、始業式や入学式・卒業式が組み込まれており、行事としては遠足や運動会・学芸会・学習発表会などが組み込まれている。児童会活動やPTAの活動に関したものも含まれている。学校暦をみれば、1年間における学校の主な出来事の展開を知ることができる。多様な行事が開催されているところに日本の学校教育の特色がある。

表6-4 小学校の学校暦の事例

月	学期、休み	学校行事
4月	春休み	
	1学期	始業式、入学式、身体検査
5月		遠足、修学旅行
6月		父兄参観日
7月		大そうじ
8月	夏休み	臨海学校、林間学校
9月	2学期	始業式 夏休み作品展示会
10月		運動会
11月		学習発表会
12月		父兄参観日 避難訓練 大そうじ、終業式
1月	冬休み	
	3学期	始業式
2月		マラソン大会 父兄参観日
3月	春休み	大そうじ、終業式 卒業式

■時間割（日課表）は、学校の教育課程として編成されている種々の教育活

4. School Calendar and Timetable

■ School calendar means the one-year plan and sequence of school events throughout the year. An example of a public primary school calendar is shown in Table 6-4. It includes the opening, entrance and graduation ceremonies, some events like school excursions, athletic meeting, school art festival, learning presentation and so forth. It also includes several activities of the student council and PTA. The variety of events that are held is a characteristic of Japanese school education.

Table 6-4 An Example of a School Calendar in Primary School

Month	Term, Vacation	School Event, etc.
April	Spring Vacation	
	First Trimester	Opnening Ceremony, Entrance Ceremony Health Examination
May		Home Visit by Teachers
June		School Excursion, School Trip
July		School Visit by Parents, General Cleaning
August	Summer Vacation	Seaside School, Camping School
September	Second trimester	Opening Ceremony Exhibition of Home Work During Vacation
October		Athletic Meeeting (Undokai)
November		Presentation of Students Works at Open House
December		School Visit by Parents Fire Drill General Cleaning, End of Term Ceremony
January	Winter Vacation	
	Third Trimester	Opening ceremony
February		Marathon-race School Visit by Parents
March	Spring Vacation	General Cleaning, End of Term Ceremony Graduation Ceremony

■ The school timetable (daily task table) is a list which shows the alloted time of

動を週単位で時間配当したものである。月曜日から金曜日までの間に、どの教科等をいつ、何回学習させるかということが明らかにされている。

表6-5 小学校の日課表（時間割）の事例

	校時	月	火	水	木	金
8:30 ～ 8:40 8:40 ～ 8:50		朝読書 朝の会	朝読書 朝の会	朝読書 朝の会	朝読書 朝の会	朝読書 朝の会
8:50 ～ 9:35	1					
9:35 ～ 9:40		5分間休憩				
9:40 ～ 10:25	2					
10:25 ～ 10:50		25分間休憩				
10:50 ～ 11:35	3					
11:35 ～ 11:40		5分間休憩				
11:40 ～ 12:25	4					
12:25 ～ 1:00		昼　食				
1:00 ～ 1:25		昼休み（25分間休憩）				
1:25 ～ 1:40		掃　除		1:30 ～ 2:15		掃　除
1:40 ～ 1:45		5分間休憩		5校時		5分間休憩
1:45 ～ 1:55		チャレンジタイム				チャレンジタイム
1:55 ～ 2:40	5			2:15 ～ 2:30		
2:40 ～ 2:55		終わりの会		終わりの会		終わりの会
3:00 ～ 3:45	6	3:00 ～ 4:00 クラブ活動 部会		2:45 完全下校		
		注：部活終了は3:45				
4:30（3〜10月）						
4:15（11〜2月）						

■小学校における時間割は、年間35週（第1学年は34週）、授業の1単位時間45分として、先に「学習指導要領」の項目のところで示しておいた標準授業時数を満たすことができるように編成されている。中学校における時間割の編成も小学校と同じ原則で行われるが、授業の1単位時間は50分になっ

several activities in each week which comprise the school curriculum. It makes clear what subjects are studied in each week and how many times and on what day of the week.

Table 6-5 An Example of a Timetable in Primary School

	period	Monday	Tuesday	Wednesday	Thursday	Friday
8:30 ～ 8:40		Morning Reading	Morning Reading	Morning Reading	Morning Reading	Morning Reading
8:40 ～ 8:50		Students' Meeting	Students' Meeting	Students' Meeting	Students' Meeting	Students' Meeting
8:50 ～ 9:35	1					
9:35 ～ 9:40		Recess for 5 Minutes				
9:40 ～ 10:25	2					
10:25 ～ 10:50		Recess for 25 Minutes				
10:50 ～ 11:35	3					
11:35 ～ 11:40		Recess for 5 Minutes				
11:40 ～ 12:25	4					
12:25 ～ 1:00		Lunch				
1:00 ～ 1:25		Recess				
1:25 ～ 1:40		Cleaning		1:30 ～ 2:15 5th Period	Cleaning	
1:40 ～ 1:45		Recess for 5 Minutes			Recess for 5 Minutes	
1:45 ～ 1:55		Challenging Time			Challenging Time	
1:55 ～ 2:40	5			2:15 ～ 2:30		
2:40 ～ 2:55		Meeting		Meeting	Meeting	
3:00 ～ 3:45	6	3:00 ～ 4:00 Club Activities Meeting		2:45 Going Back to Home		
4:30 (Mar. ～ Oct.) 4:15 (Nov. ～ Feb.)						

■ The primary school year consists of 35 weeks (34 weeks for the first grade) and each class period is 45 minutes. This timetable is planned to satisfy the standard number of class hours as shown in the paragraph "Course of Study". A lower secondary school year is made up in the same way as a primary school but one

ている。
■日本の学校における時間割は、固定的で画一化の傾向が強い。しかし、最近では、朝の時間や帰りの時間の活用、授業の1単位時間を短縮して、余った時間を寄せ集めて第6時限目の授業を設けること、モジューラー・スケジューリングのようなさまざまな工夫が試みられている。

class period is 50 minutes.

■ The school timetables of Japanese schools show a strong tendency of being unchanged and standardized. Recently, however, innovative ideas are being tested such as utilizing a little time in the morning and before leaving school, shortening a class hour to make extra time to set up 6th period, and modular scheduling.

5. 授業

■日本の社会では、学校における教師の仕事の特色を言い表す表現として、「教師は授業で勝負する」ということが言われる。「勝負する」とは、勝ち負けを競うことであるが、ここでは、「教師は教師としての自分の値打ちは授業で決まると考えている」というぐらいの意味である。教師は教師としての仕事の中で授業を一番大切にしており、よい授業を行うために全力を尽くしている。このことは日本の学校教育の伝統として、広く日本の学校全体に根付いている。

■授業は、ごく大まかに言って、①教師の教授活動、②児童生徒の学習活動、③教材という3つの要素から構成される。教師は授業に先立って教材を準備し、授業の場面で児童生徒に提供する。児童生徒は教材に取り組む（学習）が、その過程で教師は必要な指導を行う（教授）。つまり、教材を仲立ち・媒介にして、教えることと学ぶことが一体化される過程、これが授業である。授業は教授・学習の過程である。

■授業では教授と学習とが相互に作用しあって45分（小学校）あるいは50分（中学校と高等学校）の時間的な流れをつくる。これが1単位時間の授業である。授業は、ふつう、導入・展開・まとめという3つのステップで構成される。実際の授業に先立ち教師によって作成される計画のことを「指導案」もしくは「学習指導計画」と呼んでいる。指導案や学習指導計画を作成することは教師の大変重要な仕事になっている。

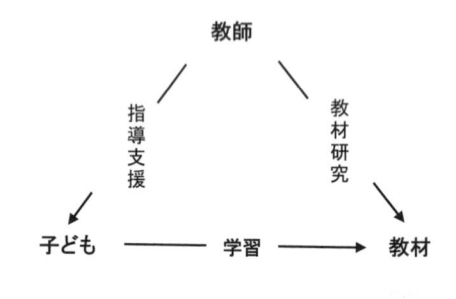

■小学校の授業は、学級担任の教師がすべての教科、道徳、外国語活動、総合的な学習の時間および特別活動の時間を担当する。これを「学級担任制」

5. Class Hour

■ In Japanese society, there is an expression "Teachers compete on their teaching" to show uniqueness of their job at school. "To compete on" is to determine a winner or loser. In this case, however, this simply means "teachers consider their value as a teacher being determined by their teaching". Teachers think teaching is more important than any task of their job and do their best to conduct good lessons. This mentality has taken root throughout the Japanese schools widely as a tradition of the Japanese school education.

■ The classes, broadly, consist of three elements, which are ① Teaching activities of teachers, ② Learning activities of students, and ③ learning materials. A teacher prepares learning materials for the class and provides them to students. Students work on the learning materials (study), and a teacher provides necessary instruction (teach). In other words, a process of teaching and learning are integrated through learning materials as a bridge or medium: this is what class is meant to be. A class is a process of teaching and learning.

■ Teaching and learning interact with one another in a class to make a time flow of 45 minutes (in primary schools) or 50 minutes (in lower and upper secondary schools). This is one class hour unit. Generally speaking, a class is composed of three steps: introduction, development, and summary. A plan made by a teacher prior to an actual class is called "teaching plan" or "plan for guidance of study". Making such a plan is a very important task for teachers.

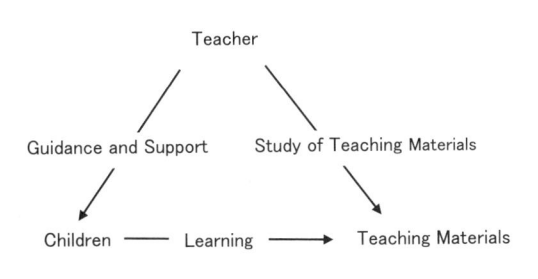

```
                    Teacher
                   /       \
                  /         \
        Guidance and Support   Study of Teaching Materials
                /               \
               /                 \
          Children —— Learning ——→ Teaching Materials
```

■ In primary schools, a classroom teacher is in charge of every subject, moral education, foreign language activity, period for comprehensive study, and special

と呼んでいる。ただし、音楽、図画工作、体育など専門的な技術の指導が求められる教科については、それぞれの教科の教員免許状を持っている教師が授業を担当しているケースが多い。これを「専科制」あるいは「小学校教科担任制」と呼んでいる。最近では、小・中教育の連携・接続を図るという観点および専門性を高めるという観点から、小学校高学年の理科、算数、国語などの教科についても、専科制・教科担任制が実施されているケースが増えている。

中学校の教科の授業および高等学校の教科・科目の授業は、それぞれの教科に関する教員免許状を持つ教員が授業を担当している。小学校の場合とは異なり、教科教育の専門家が授業を担当している。これを「教科担任制」と呼んでいる。

■日本の学校の授業は、伝統的に、一斉授業・一斉指導の傾向が強い。一斉授業・一斉指導とは、多くの児童生徒を対象にして同一の時間に同一の内容を同一の方法で指導する指導の形態のことを指している。この方法は効率的、経済的であり、明治以後の日本における学校教育の普及に役立ったが、その一方で、多人数・画一的・教師中心・伝達中心などの問題状況を生起させることになった。そのため、1987年の臨時教育審議会答申によって「教育改革の視点」として「個性重視の原則」が打ち出され、それ以後、「個に応じた指導」を強力に進めるためのさまざまな授業改善の取り組みが展開されてきた。少人数指導、ティーム・ティーチング、習熟の程度に応じた指導、補充的学習、発展的学習、少人数学級編成を可能にする学級編成基準の弾力化などがそれである。「個性重視の原則」に基づく「個に応じた指導」の充実をどのように図るのかということが授業改善の重要な課題となっている。

activities. This system is called "class-based teacher assignments". In many cases recently however, the subjects require special technical instruction such as music, drawing and handcraft and physical education and are taught by teachers who have a teacher's license in each subject. This is called "Senkasei" or "subject-based teacher assignment in primary schools". In recent years from the perspective of seeking coordination and connection between primary schools and lower secondary schools as well as to improve expertise of subjects, Senkasei or subject-based teacher assignment in primary schools are often implemented in the subjects of science, arithmetic, and Japanese language for fifth and sixth grades of primary school.

Subjects in lower and upper secondary schools are taught by a teacher who has a teacher's license of the subject. Unlike the case of primary schools, experts of each subject are in charge of the subject. This is called "subject-based teacher assignment".

■ Japanese classes traditionally have a strong tendency of mass teaching or mass instruction. Mass teaching or mass instruction means a style of instruction in which a teacher teaches a large group of students the same subject simultaneously with the same method. This effective and economical way has helped to disseminate Japanese school education after the Meiji era. This, however, caused problematic situations such as too many students in a class, uniform teaching, teacher-centered teaching, and one-way transmission teaching. To solve these problems, the "principle of putting emphasis on individuality" was announced by the National Task Force for on Educational Reform in 1987 as a viewpoint of educational reform. Since then, various efforts to improve classes have been made in order to vigorously push forward individualized instruction. For example, small group lessons, team teaching, ability-grouping, supplementary study, evolutionary learning, and introduction of more flexible class composition standards provide smaller group class composition. How to enhance lessons according to individual needs and special abilities, based on the principle of putting emphasis on individuality is an important issue to improve classes.

■日本の学校の授業は、歴史的にみると、教師中心で、知識を伝達することを重視するスタイルが長く続いてきた。この種の授業が多人数授業・一斉授業と相まって、日本の授業の伝統的なスタイルをつくりあげてきた。それは既成の知識を効率的に伝達し、普及させることに一定の役割を果たした。

■しかし、21世紀の「知識基盤社会」に求められる「自ら学び自ら考える」能力の育成をはぐくむためには、画一的で知識の伝達・注入型の授業を個性を重視し、主体的な学びを重視する探求型の授業へと変える必要がある。そうした考え方に基づいて、1989年の学習指導要領の改訂や1991年の「指導要録」の改訂では、関心・意欲・態度、思考・判断、表現などを重視する「観点別評価」が導入された。これは、当時、「新しい学力観」と呼ばれた。2002年4月から実施された「総合的な学習の時間」は、「新しい学力観」に基づいて「自ら学び自ら考える」機能的な学力をはぐくむことを意図したものであり、探求的で課題解決型の授業を実施するために創設されたものであった。

■この頃から、従来から使われてきた授業における教師の「指導」という言葉と並んで「支援」という言葉が広く使われるようになるのもそうした流れの中でのことであり、「支援」という言葉には、授業の主人公は児童生徒一人ひとりであることを意識し、自立した学びを促すことが大切であるという考え方がこめられている。

■2008年の学習指導要領の改訂では、学習意欲の向上や学習習慣の確立を図るとともに、教科の知識や技能を活用する学習活動を充実させることができる授業のあり方を探求する必要があることが強調された。しかし、その一方で、児童生徒の自主性を尊重する余り、教師が「指導」を躊躇（ちゅうちょ）する状況があったのではないかという疑問が投げかけられた。基礎学力の充実と向上を図るという観点から、教科の基礎的・基本的な知識・技能を確実に習得させることの必要性が改めて強調された。

■ Historically, Japanese school classes have long been teacher-centered with emphasis on transmitting knowledge. These kinds of class, coupled with mass class teaching and whole-class teaching, have been the established traditional style of Japanese classes. This style of teaching performed a certain function in order to transmit and diffuse existing knowledge effectively.

■ However, in order to accelerate development of ability to learn and think for oneself which are required in the knowledge-based society of the 21st century, it is necessary to change the uniform and knowledge-transmission style lessons, to inquisitive lessons which value individuality and independent-minded learning. In response to this need, the 1989 version of the Course of Study and the 1991 version of the cumulative guidance record included "criterion-referenced assessment" which values interest, willingness, attitude, cogitation, judgment, and expression. This was called "the new direction of scholastic ability" at that time. The "period for comprehensive study" started from April 2002, and was set up with the intention to cultivate functional scholastic abilities to learn and think on their own initiative based on the new direction of scholastic ability, and to implement inquisitive and problem-based classes.

■ Since this time, the word "support" has started to be used widely along with the conventionally used word "teaching" in a class by a teacher. This was due to the fact that previously mentioned trends, whereby the word "support" reflects the idea that the central character of a class is an individual student encouraged by the importance of independent learning.

■ The 2008 revised version of Course of Study highlights that there is a necessity to seek how classes should be conducted in order to enhance learning activities utilizing knowledge and techniques of subjects as well as encouraging willingness to learn and develop a study habit. On the other hand, however, it was questioned as to whether teachers may have hesitated instructing their students because they respected independency of the students too much. Necessity to allow students ensure the acquisition of basic knowledge and skills of the subjects was again emphasized from an aspect to enrich and improve

■このように、授業のあり方については、伝統的な一斉指導や指導法のよいところを効果的に活かすとともに、21世紀に求められる新しいタイプの授業を創造することが課題となっている。授業の改善と創造はいつの時代にも求められている古くて新しい課題である。

授業の準備　Lesson Preparation

students' basic scholastic ability.

■ As explained above, it is a major task to tackle in order to create new types of lessons required in the 21st century, while effectively harnessing the traditional whole class teaching method and its merit. Improvement and creation of classes have been timeless challenges.

6. 教育評価

■日本の学校では、小学校、中学校、高等学校等の別なく、さまざまな教育評価が行われている。主なものを挙げると次のようになる。
　①学校評価：学校の教育活動の成果や経営の実態を自己点検・自己評価する。
　②教員評価：教員の教育活動の成果や資質・能力の向上を評価する。
　③カリキュラム評価：教育課程や年間指導計画について評価する。
　④授業評価：実際の授業を観察して、研究、評価する。
　⑤生徒指導評価：児童生徒の実態や生徒指導の成果について評価する。
　⑥学習状況・学力評価：児童生徒の学習状況や学力について評価する。
　これらの教育評価は、当然、相互に関連している。それぞれの学校の教育や経営の実態の点検を行い、改善を図る上で教育評価は欠かすことができない重要な役割を果たしている。

■教育評価は、学校や教師が児童生徒に指導を通して身に付けさせることを意図した知識や技能、その他の能力（教育目標）が実際にどの程度達成されているか（学力達成状況）を客観的なデータに基づいて判断し、その結果に基づいて、カリキュラムや指導のあり方を検討し、改善を図ることを内容としている。典型的には、カリキュラム評価に見られるように、計画（プラン）→実施（ドゥ）→点検（チェック）→改善（アクション）のサイクルで展開される。今日では、指導の成果を評価し、その結果を直ちに指導の改善のためにフィードバックする「指導と評価の一体化」を図るという観点からの評価が大切であると言われている。

6. Educational Evaluation

■ In Japanese schools, various educational evaluations are carried out at all school levels : primary schools, lower secondary schools and upper secondary schools. The educational evaluations are mainly as follows:
① School evaluation: a self-inspection and self-evaluation of achievement of a school and actual situation of management
② Teacher evaluation: an evaluation of achievement in educational activities, qualification and ability of teachers
③ Curriculum evaluation: an evaluation of the curriculum and annual teaching plans
④ Class evaluation: a study and evaluation of actual observed classes
⑤ Student Guidance evaluation: an evaluation of the actual life situation of students and achievement of student guidance
⑥ Evaluation of learning situation and scholastic ability: an evaluation of students' learning situation and scholastic ability

Needless to say, the above mentioned educational evaluations are interrelated. Educational evaluations play an inevitable role of inspecting the situation of school education and management and to improving upon them.

■ The contents of educational evaluation include: judging status of achievement of study or extent to which educational goals (knowledge, skills, and other abilities, which schools or teachers intended to allow students to gain) were achieved on the basis of objective data; discussing how the curriculum and instruction should be and improving them based on the judgment results. Typically the evaluation is conducted in a PDCA (Plan-Do-Check-Action) cycle. Today, it is said that evaluation from an aspect of integration of instruction and evaluation is important. This integration means that the achievement of instructions is evaluated and its result is fed back to the teachers to improve their instructions.

■児童生徒一人ひとりの学力などの評価を行う上で重要な役割を果たしているのが、「小学校児童指導要録」「中学校生徒指導要録」「高等学校生徒指導要録」などである。「指導要録」は、学校教育法施行規則によって、学校に備えなければならない公的な表簿であり、校長がこれを作成しなければならないこと、また、「学籍に関する記録」は20年間保存しなければならないこと、「指導に関する記録」は5年間保存しなければならないことが定められている。

　進学に際して高等学校や大学等に送付される「調査書」・「内申書」は「指導要録」に基づいて記載される。また、学期末や学年末に保護者に渡される「通信簿」・「通知簿」では児童生徒の教科等の成績が評価し、表示されるが、「指導要録」での評価・評定と密接な関係をもっている。

■「指導要録」における児童生徒の学力評価は、教科ごとの「観点別評価」、教科ごとの「評定」、「総合的な学習の時間」の「記録」、「特別活動」に関する「特別活動の記録」、「道徳」に関する「行動の記録」、「総合所見及び指導上参考となる諸事項」から成っている。このうち、「観点別評価」は教科によって若干の違いはあるが、関心・意欲・態度、思考・判断、技能・表現、知識・技能から成っている。ここには、学力形成における向上目標や「自ら学び自ら考える」機能的な学力を重視する評価の考え方が反映されている。教科の「評定」については、小学校では3、2、1の3段階の表示、中学校と高等学校では5、4、3、2、1の5段階の表示が行われることになっている。また、「観点別評価」では、A,B,Cの3段階の表示が行われることになっている。いずれも、「目標に準拠した評価」・「絶対評価」であり、「個人内」評価であることを基本としている。ただし、「教科」の「評定」については、高等学校や大学の入学試験のために使われることもあり、「相対評価」を考慮しなくてはならないという事情がある。

■ An important role when evaluating scholastic abilities of individual students includes the Cumulative Guidance Record of Primary School, Cumulative Guidance Record of Lower Secondary School, and Cumulative Guidance Record of Upper Secondary School. The Cumulative Guidance Record is a public record which is regulated by the Ordinance for Enforcement of the School Education Act to be prepared in school. This ordinance also regulates that the Cumulative Guidance Record should be made by the principal, the "academic records" should be kept for 20 years, and the "guidance records" should be kept for 5 years.

The student record, which is submitted to upper secondary school or college when the student goes on to higher education, is filled in based on the Cumulative Guidance Record. Students' academic performance is graded in a report card and it is given to their custodian at the end of school term and school year. This evaluation closely relates to an evaluation and grade in the Cumulative Guidance Record.

■ Evaluation of scholastic ability of students in the Cumulative Guidance Record includes criterion-referenced assessment of each subject, grade of each subject, record of period for integrated study, record of special activities, record of attitude with regard to moral education, and "overall observation and issues can be a reference in guidance". Among these, criterion-referenced assessment includes assessments of interests/willingness/attitude, thought/judgment, skill/expression, and knowledge/skill. This reflects the means of evaluation emphasizing on an aim to improve scholastic ability in ability formation and functional scholastic ability of learning and thinking for themselves. The grading of subjects should be a three-grade evaluation of 3, 2 or 1 in primary schools, and a five-grade evaluation of 5, 4, 3, 2 or 1 in lower and upper secondary schools. In a criterion-referenced assessment, it is a three-grade evaluation of A, B or C. They are all basically absolute evaluations and intra-individual evaluations. However, when these evaluations results are used as judgment sources for enrollment in upper secondary schools or colleges, teachers have to take into account relative evaluation.

■日本の学校における教育評価は、大きく、「相対評価」・「集団内評価」から「絶対評価」・「個人内評価」へと変わってきた。そこには評価観や教育観の変化が反映している。すなわち、教育における比較・競争重視から個性・よさや伸び・共生の重視への変化ということが基調になっている。このことの意義は大きいと言わなければならない。

■1970年代にアメリカのB.ブルームに代表される行動主義心理学をベースにした教育評価論が導入され、日本の教育界に大きなインパクトを与えた。目標分析、観点別評価、診断的評価・形成的評価・総括的評価、完全習得学習（マスタリー・ラーニング）・学力保障などの重要な考え方と手法が導入され、評価のあり方を大きく変えることになった。

■2002年4月から「総合的な学習の時間」が実施された。それに伴って、児童生徒が学習の過程で自らの学習を振り返り、評価し、軌道修正していくためのデータを提供することができる「ポートフォリオ評価」の方法が導入されたことの意義は大きい。ポートフォリオとは、もともと書類等の紙挟み、綴じ込みケースのことを言うが、学習の過程で児童生徒が作成し、利用した創作物や資料などを収集しておき、それに基づいた自己点検、自己評価を行いつつ、探求的な学習を進めていくのがポートフォリオ学習の特徴である。児童生徒自身の手になる評価活動を基盤とした総合的な学習を進める上で大きな役割を果たすことになった。

■日本の学校で実施されている全国的あるいは国際的な学力テストには以下のようなものがある。いずれも国による教育施策の立案や教育委員会による施策、さらにそれぞれの学校における教育評価に基づく指導の改善の取り組みに大いに活用されている。

　・経済協力開発機構（OECD）による生徒の学習到達度調査（PISA）
　・国際教育到達度評価学会（IEA）による国際数学・理科教育動向調査（TIMSS）

■ Evaluation of Japanese schools has been significantly changed from relative evaluation/intra-group evaluation to absolute evaluation/intra-individual evaluation. Changes of mind-set in evaluation and the education system are reflected in this change. In other words, education has basically changed from pro-comparison and pro-competition to putting emphasis on individuality, positive changes for the improvement of individual students, better understanding of coexistence among a variety of student. This change has great significance.

■ A theory of educational evaluation based on behaviorist psychology acccording to B. Bloom, et al in the USA was introduced in the 1970's and had significant impact on Japanese educational system. An important ways of thinking and methods such as analysis of goals; criterion-referenced assessment; diagnostic evaluation; formative evaluation; summative evaluation; mastery learning; competency-based education; were introduced and drastically changed the evaluation methods.

■ The Period for integrated study started from April 2002. Concurrently with this, Portfolio Assessment was introduced and was of great significance because Portfolio Assessment provides data for students to review what they learned in the process of study, assess it and make adjustments. Portfolio originally means a document file or case. Portfolio study is characterized by students collecting materials and data they used in their studies, conducting self-inspection and self-assessment based on what they collected, and proceed inquisitive studies. Portfolio Assessment plays a major role for students to pursue comprehensive studies based on assessment by students themselves.

■ The following are examples of nation-wide or international achievement tests implemented in Japanese schools. These are largely utilized for drawing up the national education platform and board of education platform, and improving instruction based on educational assessment by each school.

· Program for International Student Assessment (PISA) by the Organization for Economic Co-operation and Development (OECD),

· The Trends in International Mathematics and Science Studies (TIMESS) by

・文部科学省による小・中学校教育課程実施状況調査。「全国学力テスト」と呼ばれている。

教科書と補助教材　Textbook and Supplementary Materials

the International Association for the Evaluation of Educational Achievement (IEA).
- "National Achievement Test" or The Survey of Curriculum Implementation of Primary and Lower Secondary Schools conducted by the Ministry of Education, Culture, Sports, Science, and Technology.

パソコンルーム　Computer Room

第Ⅶ章

教科教育等の特色

The Characteristics of Courses

音楽発表会　Students Chorus Performance in a Public Hall

1. 国語

(1) 国語科とは何か

■国語科は 1900 年に小学校の教科として誕生した。その後、100 年以上にわたって、教科の名称として「国語」は存続している。現在では国語という言葉は、国の言語あるいは、日本語という意味で使用されている。

現在、小学校入学時の子どもたちは、言語を獲得している。その言語は、母語あるいは第一言語と呼ばれ、日本語であることが多い。国語科教育は、第一言語が日本語であることを前提としている。

日本でも、国際化に伴い、また、その後に続くグローバル化の中で、第一言語が日本語ではない学習者を教室に迎える状況が見られるようになった。このような状況に対応するカリキュラムの開発も行われている。

■国語科教育は、学校以外の場面での言語習得を考慮して行われる必要がある。また、学校を卒業してから、身につけていく言の力の基盤となることも考慮しなければならない。国語科以外の教科学習においても、言葉の力は必要である一方で、国語科以外の教科学習の中でも言葉の力はついていく。このような広がりの中で国語科教育は構築されなければならない。

現代的な課題としては、2003 年、2006 年の OECD による国際学力調査である PISA 調査によって、日本の読解リテラシーの低下が指摘されている。この指摘は、近年の国語科教育にも少なからず影響を与えている。

(2) 国語科の基本的特質

■国語科の内容として、領域的広がりを把握し、考察した湊吉正の論によりながら、みていこう。湊は言語文化、言語生活、言語体系を以下のように図

1. Japanese Language

(1) What is kokugo (Japanese Language)?

■ A subject, kokugo (Japanese Language), was established for primary schools in 1900. Since then, kokugo has been used as a subject name for over 100 years. Currently, the term kokugo refers to the language of a nation or Japanese language.

These days, children in Japan have acquired a language before entering primary school. This language is called a native language or the first language, and is usually Japanese. Education of kokugo is provided, assuming that the first language is Japanese.

However, with growing globalization, students whose first language is not Japanese sometimes enter school in Japan. To respond to such a situation, specific curriculums are being developed.

■ Education of kokugo should be provided, considering that a language has been acquired out of schools. It should also be considered that the education of kokugo will become a base of language skills developed after graduating from schools. Language skills are necessary for learning other subjects, and are improved when learning other subjects. Education of kokugo should be established considering these situations.

Currently, decline in Japanese literacy, or reading and understanding skills in Japanese, is pointed out by a survey of PISA, an international research on academic levels. This result has considerably affected recent education in kokugo more than a little.

(2) The Basic Characteristics of Japanese Language

■ It is possible to view the contents of Japanese Language based on the logic of Yoshimasa Minato, who identified and examined the extent of the domain

示している。

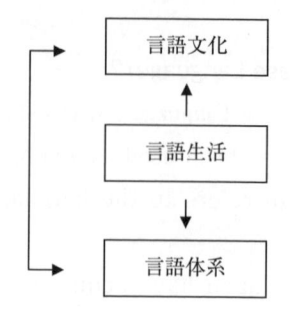

```
    ┌──→ 言語文化
    │      ↑
    │    言語生活
    │      ↓
    └──  言語体系
```

図7-1　言語生活・言語体系・言語文化間の相互関係
出典：野地・中西・安西・湊編『新編　中学校・高等学校国語科教育法』桜楓社、1984年より引用

　湊は、それぞれの概念をつぎのように述べている。
　言語生活の実際的な場面は、言語活動の主体による「話す」「聞く」「書く」「読む」「内的言語活動」の言語活動の基本的形態に現実的な場がともなうことによって得られる。
　言語体系を構成するものには、まず、形式性と慣習性をもつ音声・文字・文法・語彙・談話文章・文体などの諸言語形式の諸単位とそれらの複合的・重層的な選択・統合の規約の総体であり、さらに、それらをめぐる使用・歴史・位相等に関する知識の総体である。
　言語文化には、さまざまな文学・非文学の言語作品において、さらに語りの様式のような言語活動様式などにおいて、文化価値を担っているものが属するとみられる。
　■このように、湊はそれぞれの概念を説明している。これを、具体的な場面をあてはめて考えてみたい。
　言語生活はすべての人々が等しく送っているものであるが、一方で、その質的側面においては多くの多様性が含まれている。自然な言語習得のみにた

of Japanese Language. Minato illustrated a language culture, language life and language system as shown in the following diagram.

```
    ┌──▶ ┌─────────────────┐
    │    │ Language Culture│
    │    └─────────────────┘
    │            ▲
    │            │
    │    ┌─────────────────┐
    │    │ Language Life   │
    │    └─────────────────┘
    │            │
    │            ▼
    │    ┌─────────────────┐
    └──▶ │ Language System │
         └─────────────────┘
```

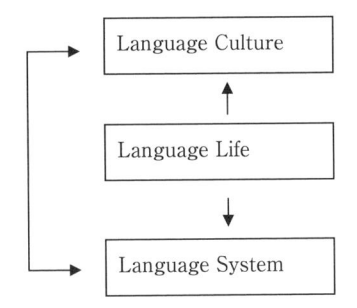

Figure 7-1 The Relationship between Language culture,
Language Life and Language System
Resouce : Nogi, Nakanishi, Anzai, and Minato (Ed.)
"A New Edition : Teaching Method of Japanese Language in Lower School", Ofusya, 1984

Minato explains each concept as follows:

The actual cases of language life are found through the basic form of language activities of the person such as 'speaking', 'listening', 'writing', and 'reading' and internal language activities, in conjunction with real situations. The language system consists of, first, the total units of language forms such as sound, letters and characters, grammar, vocabulary, discourse, and style, as well as, the rules of complex, stratified selection and combination of the units. Furthermore, it includes the total knowledge concerned with use, history, aspects, etc. about forms. Language culture includes the value of culture in the literary works of a variety of literature or non-literature, and furthermore, in the style of language activities such as the style of narration.

■ The following will consider each of the above concepts specifically.

All people equally lead a Language Life, but a Language Life can be significantly different in quality, depending on the person. It is a challenge for public school education in Japanese Language to nurture children who can lead

よる言語生活だけではなく、公教育においてどのような言語生活をおくる子どもたちを育てるかが、国語科において問題とされるのである。これは社会の状況、とりわけ、メディアの状況と関連している。

言語体系には、学習指導要領に対応するものとして、言語事項があった。これらは、自然な言語の習得をいわば、メタ認知していくことを含んでおり、教科として十分に指導されるべき内容である。

言語文化においては、これまで、言語作品が重要視されていた。より具体的には、国民的文学作品や作家、および書き手の言語表現作品を受容することであった。2008年の学習指導要領改定に伴い、それまでの言語事項にかわって〔伝統的な言語文化と国語の特質に関する事項〕が加えられた。具体的には、故事成語、ことわざなどが含まれている。

言語生活から言語体系へ、言語生活から言語文化へと関連づけていくことが目指されるのだが、それらは結果的には言語生活の向上へと導かれていくと考えられる。

(3) 国語科の目標および内容

■学習指導要領では国語科の目標は次のようにあげられている。

国語を適切に表現し正確に理解する能力を育成し、伝え合う力を高めるとともに、思考力や想像力及び言語感覚を養い、国語に対する関心を深め国語を尊重する態度を育てる。

「伝え合う力」は平成10年告示の学習指導要領からみられるようになった文言であり、コミュニケーション能力が重視されている。

■小学校国語科の内容

小学校国語科の各学年における総授業時数は第1学年306時間、第2学年315時間、第3学年245時間、第4学年245時間、第5学年175時間、第6学年175時間とされている。全学年を通じて、各教科の中で最も多い授業時間数が配当されている。(授業時間は45分)

a quality Language Life, rather than just relying on children's natural language acquisition. This issue relates to social conditions, particularly media conditions.

The Language System corresponds to the Language Item in the previous Course of Study. The Language Item includes metacognition of natural language acquisition, which should be fully instructed in the subject.

Regarding the Language Culture, importance has been placed on language works. Specifically, national literature, writers and pieces of works expressed in a language have been appreciated. Under the revised Course of Study in 2008, the "Item concerning traditional language culture and Japanese language characteristics" were added in replacement of the Language Item. Specifically, the new item includes old sayings and proverbs.

The aim is to relate Language Life with the Language System and Language Culture, which will result in improvement in Language Life.

(3) Objectives and Contents of Japanese Language

■ According to the Course of Study, the objectives of Japanese Language are as follows:

To develop one's ability to express one's thoughts properly and understand others' thoughts precisely in Japanese; to improve communicative ability; to develop ability to think and imagine; to improve a sense of language; to deepen interest in Japanese language and nurture the attitude to respect Japanese language.

"Communication ability" is a term that has been used in the Course of Study since 1998, which places the importance of communication ability.

■ Contents of Japanese Language Education for Primary School

The first grade of primary school has 306 class hours of the Japanese Language per year, the second grade has 315, the third grade has 245, the fourth grade has 245, the fifth grade has 175 and the sixth grade has 175. A large number of class hours are allotted for the Japanese Language for all grades (One

指導内容の領域は、第1学年～第6学年を通して、「A　話すこと・聞くこと」「B　書くこと」「C　読むこと」〔伝統的な言語文化と国語の特質に関する事項〕3領域1事項である。これまでの言語事項に対応する内容と今回の改訂で新たに設けられた伝統的な言語文化がある。

■それぞれの領域には、指導事項とともに言語活動の例が挙げられており、具体的な指導がわかりやすく示されている。たとえば、高学年（第5学年、第6学年をさす）の「A　話すこと・聞くこと」では次のような言語活動が挙げられている。これらの言語活動の例は1998年告示の学習指導要領から挙げられていたが、2008年告示の学習指導要領はより詳しく具体的に述べられている。

　ア　資料を提示しながら説明や報告をしたり、それらを聞いて助言や提案をしたりすること。
　イ　調べたことやまとめたことについて、討論などをすること。
　ウ　事物や人物を推薦したり、それを聞いたりすること。

また、〔伝統的な言語文化と国語の特質に関する事項〕では、同じ高学年において、次のような内容が挙げられている。

　ア　伝統的な言語文化に関する事項
　　(a)　親しみやすい古文や漢文、近代以降の文語調の文章について、内容の大体を知り、音読すること。
　　(b)　古典について解説した文章を読み、昔の人のものの見方や感じ方を知ること。

このような内容はこれまで小学校国語科では扱われなかった内容で、平成20年告示の学習指導要領で初めてあげられた内容である。

class hour is 45 minutes.).

The teaching contents of all grades are divided into three domains, "A.-Speaking and Listening," "B.-Writing," and "C.-Reading," and one item, the "Item concerning traditional language culture and Japanese language characteristics." The teaching contents include the contents corresponding to the "Language Item" in the previous Course of Study and the "traditional language culture" newly added in the latest revision.

■ For each domain, instructions and the examples of language activities are provided to help understand specific instruction methods. For example, regarding the domain, "A. Speaking and Listening," for the fifth and sixth grade students, the following examples of language activities are shown. Although such examples were already shown in the Course of Study in 1998, examples with more detailed information are shown in the Course of Study in 2008.

    a. To explain/report with presentation materials, and receive advice or ideas from the audience.

    b. To discuss a research on study topics.

    c. To recommend materials/persons to others, and listening to an other person's recommendation.

Regarding the "Item concerning traditional language culture and Japanese language characteristics" for the fifth and sixth grade students, the following examples of language activities are shown.

    a. Items concerning traditional language culture

        (a) To learn the outline of easy-to-approach classic Japanese and Chinese literature and modern literature in written language; and to read them aloud.

        (b) To read interpretation of classic literature and learn views and perspectives of people in old times.

These examples shown above have been adopted for the first time in the revised Course of Study in 2008 in Japanese Language classes of primary schools.

■中学校国語科の内容

　中学校国語科の各学年における総授業時数は第1学年140、第2学年140、第3学年105とされている。(授業時間は50分)

　指導内容の領域は「A　話すこと・聞くこと」「B　書くこと」「C　読むこと」〔伝統的な言語文化と国語の特質に関する事項〕の3領域1事項である。これまでの言語事項に対応する内容と今回の改訂で新たに設けられた伝統的な言語文化がある。

■それぞれの領域には、指導事項とともに言語活動の例があげられており、具体的な指導がわかりやすく示されている。たとえば、第3学年の「A　話すこと・聞くこと」では次のような言語活動があげられている。これらの言語活動の例は1998年告示の学習指導要領からあげられていたが、2008年告示の学習指導要領ではより詳しく具体的に述べられている。

　ア　社会生活の中から話題を決め、自分の経験や知識を整理して考えをまとめ、語句や文を効果的に使い、資料などを活用して説得力のある話をすること。
　イ　場の状況や相手の様子に応じて話すとともに敬語を適切に使うこと。
　ウ　聞き取った内容や表現の仕方を評価して、自分のものの見方や考え方を深めたり、表現に生かしたりすること。
　エ　話し合いが効果的に展開するように進行の仕方を工夫し、課題の解決に向けて互いの考えを生かし合うこと。

　このような言語活動例からも現在の国語科が「伝え合う力」を重視していることがわかる。

■高等学校国語科の内容

　高等学校の国語には、国語総合、国語表現、現代文A、現代文B、古典A、

■ Contents of Japanese Language Education for Lower Secondary Schools

The first grade of lower secondary school has 140 class hours of the Japanese Language per year, the second grade has 140 and the third grade has 105 (One class hour is 50 minutes.).

The teaching contents are divided into three domains, "A.-Speaking and Listening," "B.-Writing," and "C.-Reading," and one item, the "Item concerning traditional language culture and Japanese language characteristics." The teaching contents include the contents corresponding to the "Language Item" in the previous Course of Study and the "traditional language culture" newly added in the latest revision.

■ For each domain, instructions and the examples of language activities are provided to help understand specific instruction methods. For example, regarding the domain, "A. Speaking and Listening," for the third grade students, the following examples of language activities are shown. Although such examples were already shown in the Course of Study in 1998, examples with more detailed information are shown in the Course of Study in 2008.

a. To select a topic from their social life, organize one's thoughts based on one's experiences and knowledge and make a persuasive speech, using phrases, sentences and materials effectively.

b. To make a speech considering the response of the audience and using appropriate honorifics.

c. To evaluate other people's speech including their expressions, deepen one's views and perspectives, and incorporate outstanding parts into one's expressions.

d. To devise methods to effectively proceed discussions, and listen to each other's opinions well, to solve problems.

As shown in these examples, the current Japanese Language places importance on communication ability.

■ Contents of Japanese Language Education for Upper Secondary Schools

In the Japanese Language Education for upper secondary schools there are

古典Bの科目がある。このうち、国語総合が必修である。

　指導内容の領域は「A　話すこと・聞くこと」「B　書くこと」「C　読むこと」〔伝統的な言語文化と国語の特質に関する事項〕3領域1事項である。これまでの言語事項に対応する内容と今回の改訂で新たに設けられた伝統的な言語文化がある。

■それぞれの領域には、指導事項とともに言語活動の例があげられており、具体的な指導がわかりやすく示されている。言語活動は、前回までの学習指導要領には見られなかったが、2009年の改訂から新たに設けられた。以下、国語総合の言語活動を見ておく。

　A　話すこと・聞くこと
（中略）
　ア　状況に応じた話題を選んでスピーチしたり、資料に基づいて説明したりすること。
　イ　調査したことなどをまとめて報告や発表をしたり、内容や表現の仕方を吟味しながらそれらを聞いたりすること。
　ウ　反論を想定して発言したり疑問点を質問したりしながら、課題に応じた話合いや討論などを行うこと。
（中略）
　ア　情景や心情の描写を取り入れて、詩歌をつくったり、随筆などを書いたりすること。
　イ　出典を明示して文章や図表などを引用し、説明や意見などを書くこと。
　ウ　相手や目的に応じた語句を用い、手紙や通知などを書くこと。
（中略）
　ア　文章を読んで脚本にしたり、古典を現代の物語に書き換えたりすること。
　イ　文字、音声、画像などのメディアによって、表現された情報を、課題

the subjects of General Japanese, Japanese Expression, Modern Sentence A, Modern Sentence B, Classic A and Classic B. Among those General Japanese is compulsory.

The teaching contents are divided into three domains, "A. Speaking and Listening," "B. Writing," and "C. Reading," and one item, the "Item concerning traditional language culture and Japanese language characteristics." The teaching contents include the contents corresponding to the "Language Item" in the previous Course of Study and the "traditional language culture" newly added in the latest revision.

■ For each domain, instructions and the examples of language activities are provided to help understand specific instruction methods. The language activities was not found in the former Course of Studies but set up in that of 2009. Let see the details of the language activities in a general Japanese language.

A Speaking and Listening

(an omission of explanation)

a. To make speakers selecting topics in correspondence to situation, and explain based on materials.

b. To make report of investigation and present the results, and listen the presentation examining the content and the method of expression.

c. To make exchange opinions of the problems and make debate while speaking out thinking of objections and asking questions.

(an omission of explanation)

a. To make poems and songs and write essays considering fine scenes and one's feeling.

b. To write explanation and opinions citing sentences, figures and tables shown the resources.

c. To write letters and notices using phrases in response to companions and objects.

(an omission of explanation)

a. To make dramas reading sentences, and rewrite classics changing into

に応じて読み取り、取捨選択してまとめること。
　ウ　現代の社会生活で必要とされている実用的な文章を読んで内容を理解し、自分の考えをもって話し合うこと。
　エ　様々な文章を読み比べ、内容や表現の仕方について、感想を述べたり批評する文章を書いたりすること。
（後略）
　以上のような言語事項が追加された。
小学校、中学校の2008年告示の学習指導要領と高等学校の2009年度告示の学習指導要領に即して、国語科の内容をみてきた。
　学習指導要領はほぼ10年おきに改訂されてきた。先にあげた目標やあるいは内容においても、時代状況に応じて、手直しをされる一方で、中核は変更されることはないと考えられる。

■最後に、内容に関して重要と考えられる点をあげる。
　①話す、書く、聞く、読むなどの言語活動は、これまで、2領域（話す、書くをまとめて表現領域、聞く、読むをまとめて理解領域）とされたこともあったが、どれも欠かすことのできないものである。この4つの言語活動を相互に関連させる指導方法の開発。
　②読むことに関しては、国語科の主要な領域として、これまでも研究されてきたが、今後、読み方─資料の扱い方や読書指導、レファレンスの利用、ネットの利用も含めて、引き続き研究がされること。
　③読む材料に関しても、時代の要請にこたえ、新しい材料を求める一方で、すぐれた言語文化財としての古典作品を文学のみならず、思想に関わるものも含めて、教材化していくこと。
　④PISA調査問題で求められた読解リテラシーでは、読むと同時に書く力も必要とされている。文章表現である書くことに関して読むと書くの関連をより具体的に意識化して指導すること。
　⑤談話や討論の指導を充実させていくこと。談話や討論を通じて新しい価値の創造に結び付けていくための指導方法の開発。

modern stories.

b. To select and arrange the information expressed by media using letters, sounds and pictures considering the kind of issues.

c. To understand the contents reading useful sentences necessary for modern social life and talk with friends having own ideas.

d. To read various sentences and compare the contents and the way of expression, and give one's impression or write down the critical sentences.

(an omission of other items)

These are the overview of the Japanese Language under to the Course of Study for lower secondary school in 2008 and the Course of Study for upper secondary school in 2009.

The Course of Study has been revised about every 10 years. Although objectives and contents are revised according to the needs of the times, the core part has not changed and will not change.

■ Lastly, the following are regarded as the important points of the Japanese Language subject.

① Although language activities of speaking, writing, listening and reading were sometimes classified into two (an expression domain consisting of speaking and writing, and an understanding domain consisting of listening and reading), all these activities are essential. It is important to develop instruction methods to interrelate these four language activities.

② Reading has been studied as a major domain of the Japanese Language. The study of reading should be continued, including how to use materials, reading guidance, and use of references and the Internet.

③ New reading materials should be sought for responding to the needs of the times, while classic works, including literature and thought-related materials, should also be used for course materials as excellent language cultural assets.

④ According to the results of a PISA survey, Japanese students are behind in reading literacy. Reading literacy requires not only reading but also

⑥メディア・リテラシーに関しても、指導が行われているが、メディアを読むという面だけが重視されている。機器の改善によって、だれもがメディアの作り手となることが可能となった状況をふまえた作り手となる指導方法の開発。

writing ability. Instruction of writing should be provided in a specific form considering the relations between reading and writing extensively.

⑤ It is important to improve the guidance on conversations and discussions. Instruction methods to create new values through conversations and discussions should be developed.

⑥ Although guidance on media literacy is provided, more importance has been placed on reading of media. It is important to develop instruction methods of guiding media creation, based on the fact that anyone can create media due of technologies.

2. 社会科

■社会科は、学校教育法施行規則によって、小学校の教育課程および中学校の教育課程を構成する教科の1つとして設けられている。

■小学校における社会科の年間の標準授業時数は、表7-1に示すように、第3学年では70時間、第4学年では90時間、第5学年では100時間、第6学年では105時間である。また、中学校では、第1学年では105時間、第2学年では105時間、第3学年では140時間である。

表7-1　小学校および中学校における社会科の授業時数

小学校における社会科の授業時数		中学校における社会科の授業時数	
第3学年	70	第1学年	105
第4学年	90	第2学年	105
第5学年	100	第3学年	140
第6学年	105		

出典:「学校教育法施行規則」別表第一および別表第二による

■高等学校には、社会科という教科は設けられていない。しかし、地理歴史科および公民科という2つの教科は、小学校および中学校の社会科と、次に挙げるような2つの点で、密接な関連をもっている。(1)高等学校がスタートした1948年4月から1989年3月の高等学校学習指導要領の改訂に至る41年間、高等学校には小、中学校と同様に社会科という教科が設けられていた。1989年3月の改訂によって、従来の社会科が地理歴史科と公民科とに再編成され、現在に至っている。なお、この点については、後述する社会科の変遷過程を参照していただきたい。(2)小、中学校の社会科の目標と内容および高等学校の地理歴史科と公民科の目標と内容には共通するところが多い。

2. Social Studies

■ Social Studies is stipulated as a subject of the curriculum for primary and lower secondary school in the School Education Enforcement Regulation.

■ As seen in Table 7-1, the standard class hours of Social Studies in primary school is 70 at third grade, 90 at fourth grade, 100 at fifth grade, and 105 at sixth grade. In lower secondary school 105 hours are allocated in first and second year and 140 hours in third year.

Table 7-1 Class Hours of Social Studies in Primary School and a Lower Secondary School

Class Hours of Social Studies at Primary School		Class Hours of Social Studies at Lower Secondary School	
The 3rd grade	70	The 1st Year	105
The 4th grade	90	The 2nd Year	105
The 5th grade	100	The 3rd Year	140
The 6th grade	105		

(Resource: The School Education Enforcement Regulation, Special Table 1, 2)

■ Social Studies has not been established as a subject in upper secondary school. The two subjects of "Geography and History" and "Civics" have a close relation with the subject of Social Studies at a lower secondary school and an upper secondary school.

(1) In upper secondary school Social Studies which was similar to that of primary school and lower secondary school had been established and maintainted for 41 years since April 1948, which in when upper secondary school started until March in 1989. In March 1989 the upper secondary schools' Course of Study was revised. Through the revision, Social Studies was reorganized as subjects of "Geography and History" and "Civics" in March of 1989. For this point, you may view the transition process of Social Studies described in the following paragraphs.

■社会科の目標については、学習指導要領によって、次のように示されている。
　小学校の社会科の目標：社会生活についての理解を図り、我が国の国土と歴史に対する理解と愛情を育て、国際社会に生きる平和で民主的な国家・社会の形成者として必要な公民的資質の基礎を養う。
　中学校の社会科の目標：広い視野に立って、社会に対する関心を高め、諸資料に基づいて多面的・多角的に考察し、我が国の国土と歴史に対する理解と愛情を深め、公民としての基礎的教養を培い、国際社会に生きる平和で民主的な国家・社会の形成者として必要な公民的資質を養う。
　こうした記述にあらわれているように、社会科は、社会生活や社会に関する理解や認識を深めるとともに、国際社会に生きる国家・社会の形成者として必要な公民的資質の基礎を養うこと目標としている。

■小学校の社会科の内容は、第3学年および第4学年では、主として地域や都道府県に関する事柄が取り上げられる。第5学年では、主として我が国の地理と産業が取り上げられる。第6学年では、主として我が国の歴史や世界の中での日本の役割が取り上げられる。中学校の社会科の内容は、分野ごとに、〔地理的分野〕、〔歴史的分野〕、〔公民的分野〕に分けて、取り上げられている。
■社会科は、先に指摘したように、高等学校の地理歴史科および公民科と密接な関連をもっている。その他、小学校の生活科、小、中、高校の総合的な学習の時間や特別活動、さらに小、中学校の道徳の時間などとも関連するところが多い。

■明治以後の日本の学校では歴史（国史）、地理、修身などの教科が教えられていたが、1947（昭和22）年に戦後教育改革の一環として「社会科」という新しい教科が誕生することになった。初期の社会科はアメリカのソーシャル・スタディーズ（social studies）の影響を強く受けており、生活や社

(2) The objectives and contents of Social Studies in primary school and lower secondary school and "Geography and History" and "Civics" in upper secondary school have many common characteristics.

■ The objectives of Social Studies are shown in the Course of Study.

The objective of Social Studies at primary school: to make students understand about life in society, deepen understanding of and love for the Japanese country and history and raise the foundation of quality as citizens who are members of a peaceful and democratic country and society.

The objective of Social Studies at lower secondary school: to make students have an interest in society, deepen their understanding and love for the Japanese country and history, and cultivate a civic foundation as citizens and raise the quality as people to compose a peaceful and democratic country and society.

As mentioned above, Social Studies has objectives to deepen students' understanding and knowledge about society and to form the foundation of a civic quality as citizens who compose the country and society.

■ The content of Social Studies at primary school: the students in the third and fourth grade learn mainly about communities and prefectures. In the fifth grade, they focus on geography and industry of the country. In the sixth grade, they learn about history of the country and Japanese role in the world.

The content of Social Studies at lower secondary school is divided into the realm of [Geography], [History] and [Civics].

■ As was mentioned in the proceeding paragraph, Social Studies has a close relation with Geography and History and Civics at upper secondary school. In addition, it is closely related to Life Study at primary school, Period of Integrated Study, and Special Activities at primary, lower secondary and an upper secondary schools, and Morals at primary and lower secondary schools.

■ After the Meiji period, Japanese schools had taught History, Geography and Morals (Syusin) but in 1947, a new subject of Social Studies was introduced as a part of educational reform after WW II.

Since the beginning Social Studies was influenced by the Social studies of

会の問題を学習者自身が主体的に解決する問題解決学習を中心にして進められた。社会科に対しては、戦後の民主主義をになう市民の育成に中心的な役割を果たすことが期待されていた。

■社会科は、1947年9月、連合軍の占領下でスタートしてから、現在まで9回改訂され、現在では、社会科は、小学3年生から中学3年生までの7年間に学ばれる教科になっている。ただし、先にも指摘したように、高等学校の地理歴史科と公民科は、その目標や内容のうえで、社会科と密接に関連する教科である。

■戦後の社会科の変遷は次の5段階に分けられるが、各時期の教科構造を当時における学習指導要領の内容に応じてわかりやすく図示（図7-2）し、その特色を概観してみると次の通りである。

(1) 教科構造の変遷

図7-2　社会科の教科構造の変遷（384～396頁）

第1段階：

① 1947（昭和22）年版学習指導要領

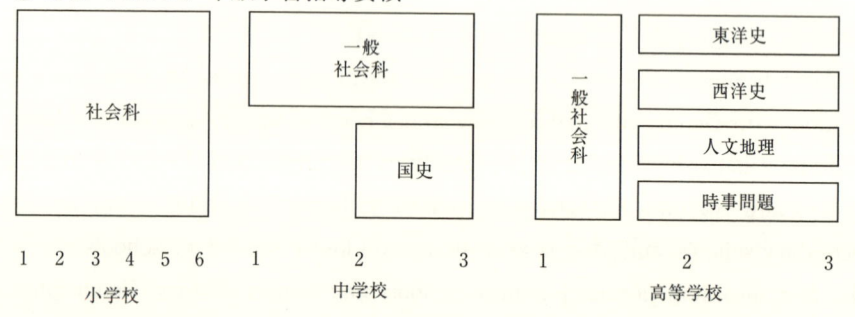

Ⅶ. The Characteristics of Courses 385

America, whereby its content was mainly a problem solving study in which students learned how to solve problems in their life and society. Social Studies had been expected to play an important role for training citizens to form a democratic society after the war.

■ The course which is referred to as Social Studies, and which begins in the third grade of primary school continues for seven years, or until the third grade of lower secondary school (lower secondary school). This was established in September 1947 under the Allied Occupation and revised nine times since then. The Geography and History Subjects and Civics Subjects of Upper Secondary School shown in Figure 7-2 are closely related to Social Studies in terms of the objectives.

■ The transition of social studies after WWII is able to be divided into five stages. Figure 7-2 below logically illustrates the structure and characteristics of Social Studies in each stage corresponding to the Course of Study concerned.

(1) Transition of Course Structure

Figure 7-2 Transition of the Course Structure in Social Studies (pp.385-397)

The First Phase:
① The Course of Study in 1947

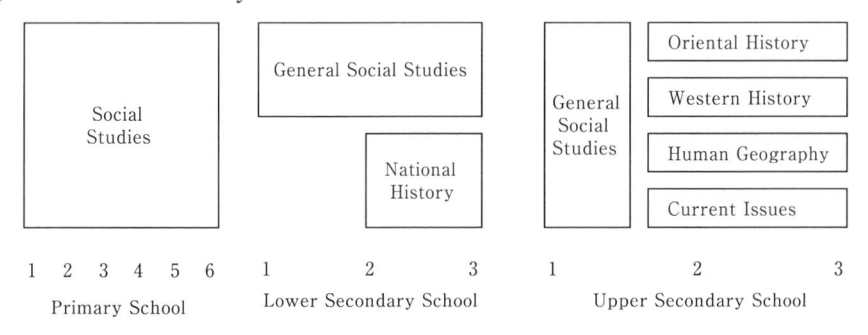

Social Studies	General Social Studies	General Social Studies	Oriental History
			Western History
	National History		Human Geography
			Current Issues
1 2 3 4 5 6	1 2 3	1	2 3
Primary School	Lower Secondary School	Upper Secondary School	

② 1951（昭和26）年版学習指導要領

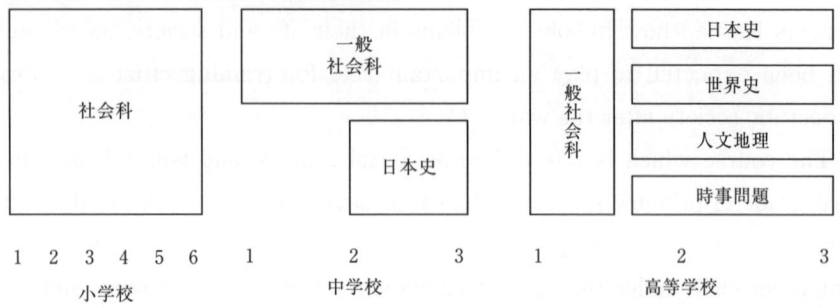

小学校	中学校	高等学校
社会科（1〜6）	一般社会科（1・2・3）／日本史（2）	一般社会科（1・2・3）／日本史・世界史・人文地理・時事問題

■第1段階というのは、一般に「初期社会科」と呼ばれているものである。「初期社会科」の提供された時期は、日本が民主主義の実現を目指し、平和的・民主的な国家建設に真剣に取り組んでいた時期である。またその大半は、連合軍の占領政策の強い影響を受けた。

　1947年版、1951年版学習指導要領では、小・中・高一貫の10年構想が示された。そして、経験主義のコア・カリキュラムが実施され、「一般社会科」を中心とする、問題解決をめざす総合的な単元学習が確立された。また、「一般社会科」とは別に「国史」（1947年版）もしくは「日本史」（1951年版）が位置づけられた。

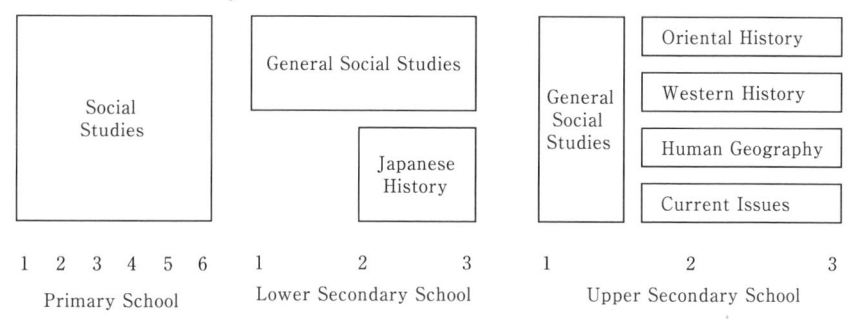

② The Course of Study in 1951

Social Studies	General Social Studies		General Social Studies	Oriental History
				Western History
		Japanese History		Human Geography
				Current Issues

1 2 3 4 5 6   1   2   3   1   2   3
Primary School   Lower Secondary School   Upper Secondary School

■ The social study at the first stage is generally called "Social Studies in the Early Period". The period when the first stage of Social Studies was offered, was characterized by the nation's struggle in the construction of a peaceful and cultural state to realize democracy. Almost all the periods were characterized by the occupation policies of the allies.

The Courses Study in 1947 and 1951 had the following features.

(a) A ten-year plan for primary, lower secondary, upper secondary schools was considered.

(b) Core curriculam based on empiricism was carried out. And with "general social studies" as the main focus, comprehensive unit-study aiming at problem solving was implemented. Apart from "General Social Studies", "History of the Nation" (1947) or "History of Japan" (1951) was set.

第 2 段階：
③ 1955（昭和 30）年版学習指導要領

社会科	社会科			社会
	地理的分野	歴史的分野	政・経・社会的分野 *	日本史 / 世界史 / 人文地理

1 2 3 4 5 6　　1　　2　　3　　1　　2　　3
　小学校　　　　　中学校　　　　　高等学校

＊「政・経・社会的分野」＝ 政治・経済・社会的分野

④ 1958（昭和 33）年版（小・中）、1960（昭和 35）年版（高）学習指導要領

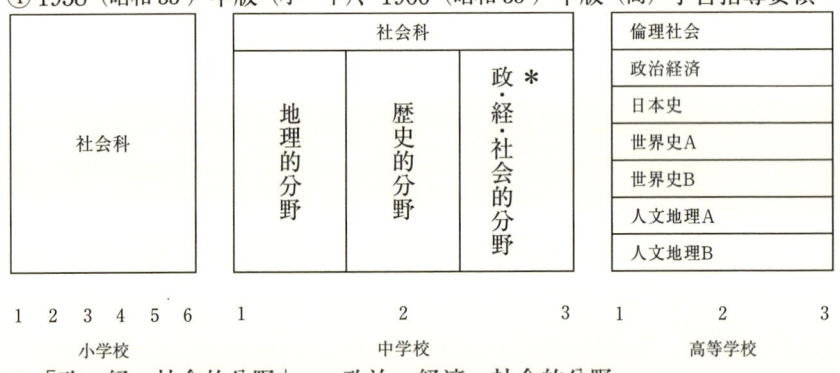

社会科　　　　社会科　　　　　　　倫理社会 / 政治経済 / 日本史 / 世界史A / 世界史B / 人文地理A / 人文地理B

　　　　　　地理的分野　歴史的分野　政・経・社会的分野 *

1 2 3 4 5 6　　1　　2　　3　　1　　2　　3
　小学校　　　　　中学校　　　　　高等学校

＊「政・経・社会的分野」＝ 政治・経済・社会的分野

高校の世界史Bと地理Bは、それぞれ世界史Aと地理Bを深化、充実するもの。

The Second Phase:
③ The Course of Study in 1955

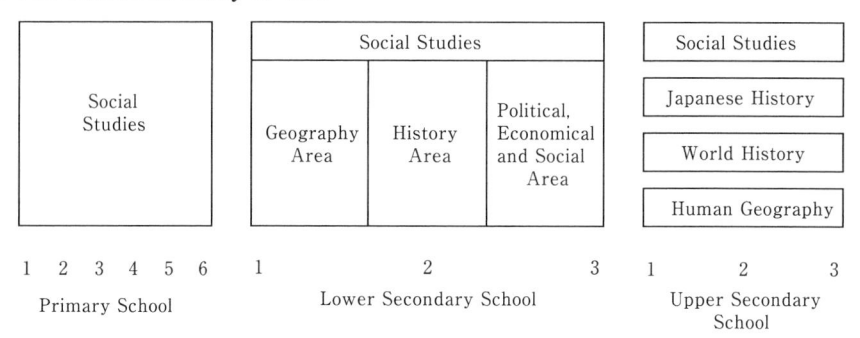

Social Studies	Social Studies			Social Studies
	Geography Area	History Area	Political, Economical and Social Area	Japanese History
				World History
				Human Geography

1 2 3 4 5 6   1   2   3   1   2   3
Primary School   Lower Secondary School   Upper Secondary
                                                   School

④ The Course of Study in 1958 (Primary and Lower Secondary School) and 1960 (Upper Secondary School)

Social Studies	Social Studies			Ethics and Sociology
	Geography Area	History Area	Political, Economical and Social Area	Politics and Economics
				Japanese History
				World History A
				World History B
				Human Geography A
				Human Geography B

1 2 3 4 5 6   1   2   3   1   2   3
Primary School   Lower Secondary School   Upper Secondary School

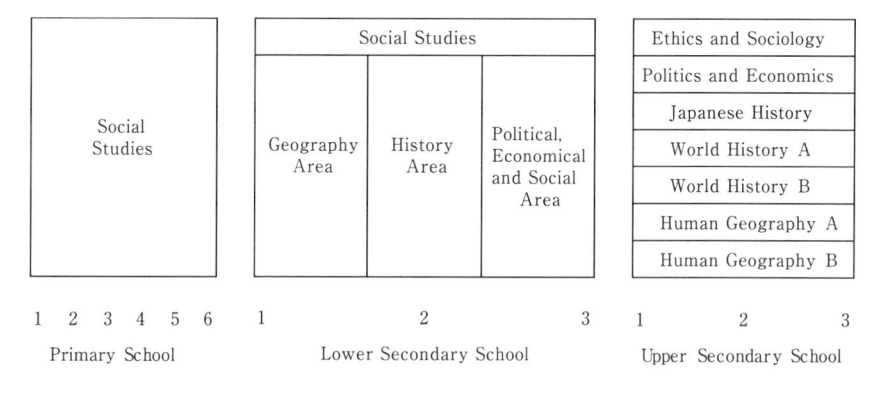

World History B and Geography B in Upper Secondary School expand upon the contents of those A subjects.

⑤ 1968（昭和43）年版（小）、1969（昭和44）年版（中）、 1970（昭和45）年版（高）学習指導要領

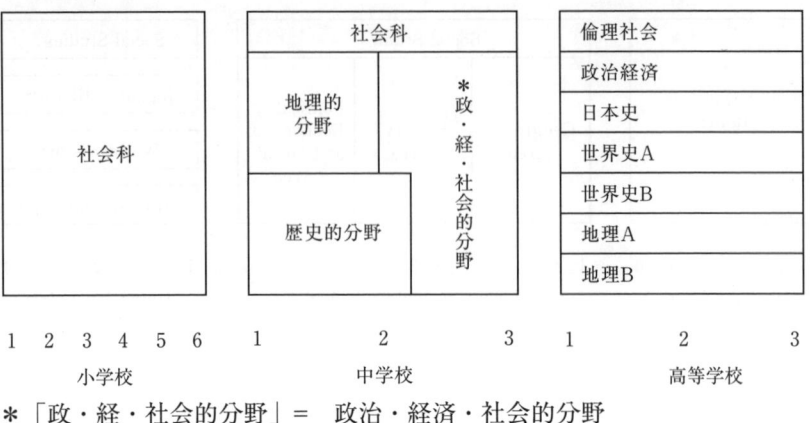

小学校	中学校	高等学校
社会科	社会科 　地理的分野 　歴史的分野 　＊政・経・社会的分野	倫理社会 政治経済 日本史 世界史A 世界史B 地理A 地理B
1 2 3 4 5 6	1　2　3	1　2　3

＊「政・経・社会的分野」＝　政治・経済・社会的分野
高校の地理Aは系統地理、地理Bは世界地誌を中心とするもの。

■第2段階は、朝鮮戦争の特需景気によって日本の経済再建のめどがつき、国連加盟もできて、日本の国際社会への復帰が実現した。そして1964年のオリンピック東京大会の成功に象徴されるように、高度経済成長が世界瞠目のうちに進んだ時期である。しかしこの時期の末期の1970年12月には、国会でいわゆる公害が問題にされ、翌年環境庁が発足した。また、1974年から始まった世界的経済不況の結果、手放しの経済成長期は終わりをみることになる。だが、この時期を特徴づけるのは、何といっても、経済と科学技術のめざましい発展ということであり、社会科教育もそれに同調していたと言うことができる。さしずめ『高度成長期社会科』と呼ぶことができよう。

　第2段階の1955年版、1958年版、1969年版学習指導要領では、中学校と高等学校との関連を重視しながらも中学校3年間の分離構想が示された。また、地理・歴史・政治経済社会（公民）の3分野に分け、基礎学力の充実をめざす系統学習に重点が置かれた。

⑤ The Course of Study in 1968 (Primary School), 1969 (Lower Secondary School) and 1970 (Upper Secondary School)

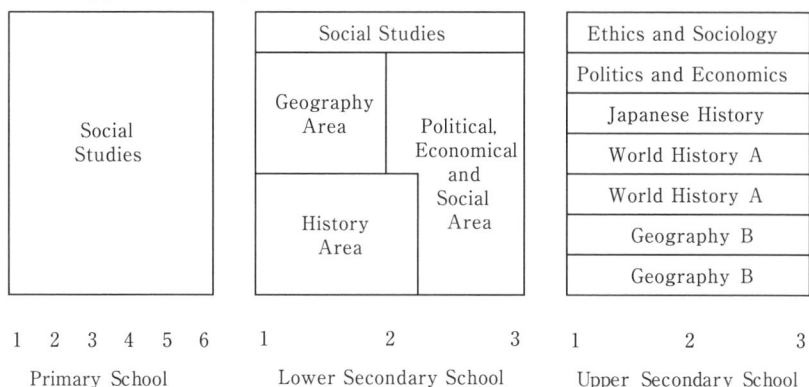

Social Studies	Social Studies			Ethics and Sociology
				Politics and Economics
	Geography Area	Political, Economical and Social Area		Japanese History
				World History A
				World History A
	History Area			Geography B
				Geography B

1 2 3 4 5 6	1　　　2　　　3	1　　　2　　　3
Primary School	Lower Secondary School	Upper Secondary School

Geography A and B in Upper Secondary School deal mainly with systematic geography and world geography respectively.

■ The Second Phase : The period when the second stage of Social Studies was offered, was characterized by the Korean war. The war gave Japan an opportunity to reconstruct her economy. At the same time, Japan succeeded in re-entering the international community with her membership to the United Nations. It was also the time when the world watched with astonishment Japan's continuous economic growth, and reconfirmed it by the success of the Tokyo Olympic Games in 1964. At the end of the period, however, the nation's uncontrolled economic growth alarmed the National Diet, and on December 1970 during its session, it discussed environmental pollution problems and established the Ministry of Environment in the following year. Japan's high economic growth period came to an end as a result of the world wide economic dilemma beginning 1974. This period, however, was characterized by remarkable development of economy and scientific technology. Social studies education keeping in line with the trend, has thus come to be called, "Social Studies in the High Economic Growth Period".

In the Courses of Study in 1955, 1958, and 1969 the significance of the

第3段階：

⑥ 1977（昭和52）年版（小・中）、1978（昭和53）年版（高）学習指導要領

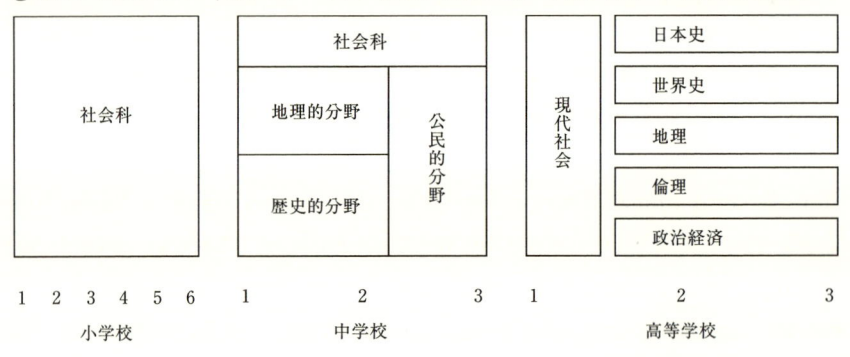

小学校	中学校	高等学校
社会科	社会科（地理的分野／歴史的分野／公民的分野）	現代社会／日本史／世界史／地理／倫理／政治経済
1 2 3 4 5 6	1 2 3	1 2 3

■第3段階の社会科は、高度経済成長のひずみを修正する意図が加味されて成立した。人間尊重の立場を強調していることが端的にそれを示しているが、もう一つの特色として、初期社会科との共通性もいくつか見られたのである。

　1977年版学習指導要領では、小・中・高一貫の10年構想への一部回帰がみられた。また、地理、歴史、公民の3分野制は受け継ぐが、内容精選をめざし、総合性が再び強調された。

relationship between lower and upper secondary schools was emphasized. Additionally, it was thought that the three years of lower secondary school should be separated from upper secondary school. As such social studies of lower secondary school was divided into geography, history, and civics, with the emphasized contents of politics, economy and social issues. At this time a systematic learning method was implemented which emphasized the development of basic knowledge.

The Third Phase:
⑥ The Course of Study in 1977 (Primary and Lower Secondary School) and 1978 (Upper Secondary School)

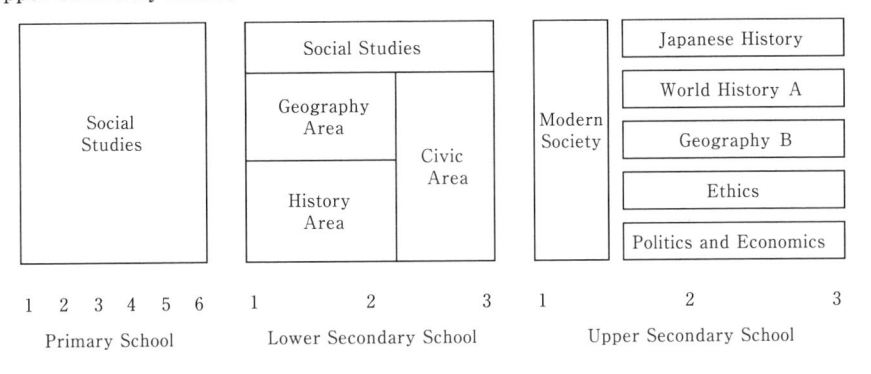

Social Studies	Social Studies		Modern Society	Japanese History
	Geography Area	Civic Area		World History A
				Geography B
	History Area			Ethics
				Politics and Economics

1 2 3 4 5 6	1 2 3	1 2 3
Primary School	Lower Secondary School	Upper Secondary School

■ The Third Phase: The Social Studies courses in the third stage had an additional objective, to suggest solutions to the problems caused by the high economic growth. This was clearly illustrated by the fact that courses emphasized respect for human beings. Another feature was that they had several common characteristics with the social studies courses in the early period.

In the Course of Study in 1977, the third period of revision was a partial return to the ten-year plan covering primary, lower secondary, and upper secondary schools. The three-area system of geography, history, and civics continued, but greater emphasis was directed toward the synthetic approach with content being carefully selected.

第4段階：
⑦ 1989（平成元）年版学習指導要領（生活科・地理歴史科・公民科を含む）

生活科	社会科	社会科		地理歴史科	公民科
		地理的分野	公民的分野	世界史A、世界史B	現代社会
				日本史A、日本史B	倫理
		歴史的分野	選択社会		政治・経済
				地理A、地理B	

1 2　3 4 5 6　　　1　2　3　　　1　2　3　　1　2　3
小学校　　　　　　中学校　　　　高等学校　　　高等学校

⑧ 1998（平成10）年版（小、中）1999（平成11）年版（高校）

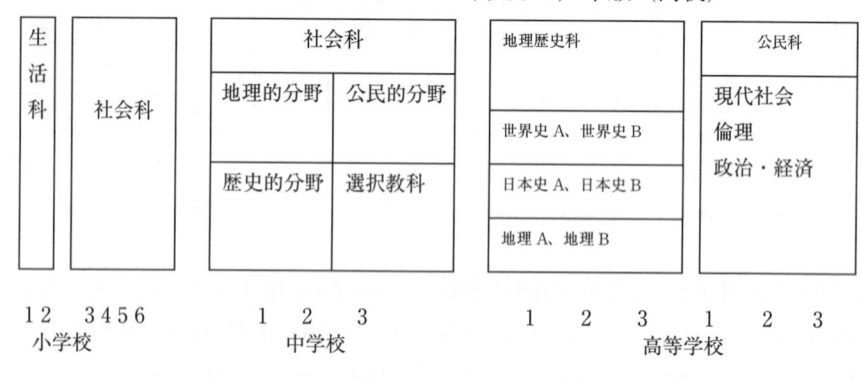

生活科	社会科	社会科		地理歴史科	公民科
		地理的分野	公民的分野	世界史A、世界史B	現代社会
				日本史A、日本史B	倫理
		歴史的分野	選択教科	地理A、地理B	政治・経済

1 2　3 4 5 6　　　1　2　3　　　1　2　3　　1　2　3
小学校　　　　　　中学校　　　　高等学校　　　高等学校

■第4段階の1989年版、1998年版学習指導要領では、小学校低学年から社会科が消え、生活科になり、中学校では、地理、歴史、公民の3分野は受け継ぐが、第3学年生に選択教科「社会」が設置された。高校の社会科は、専門的・系統的な学習重視の観点から廃止され、地歴社会科と公民科の2教科

The Fourth Phase:
⑦ The Course of Study in 1989

	Social Studies			Geography and History Subjects	Japanese History A
					Japanese History B
					World History A
Life Environ -ment Studies	Social Studies	Geography Area	Civic Area		World History B
					Geography A
					Geography B
		History Area	Optional Course	Civics Subjects	Contemporary Society
					Ethics
					Politics and Economy

1 2 3 4 5 6	1 2 3	1 2 3
Primary School	Lower Secondary School	Upper Secondary School

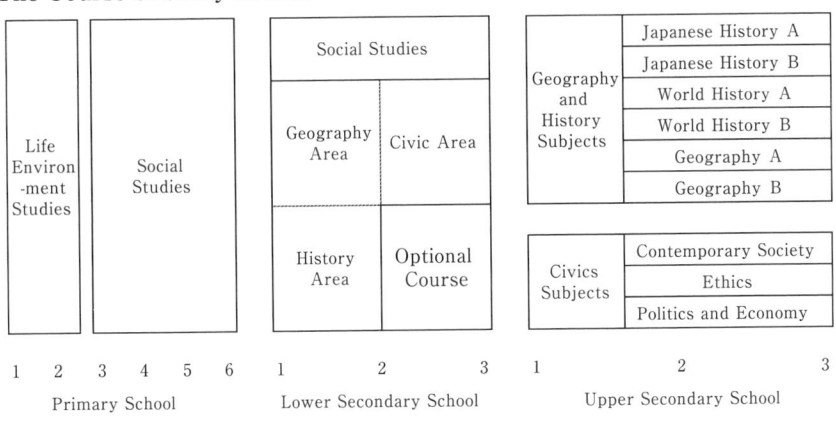

⑧ The Course of Study in 1998 (Primary and Lower Secondary School) and 1999 (Upper Secondary School)

	Social Studies			Geography and History Subjects	Japanese History A
					Japanese History B
					World History A
Life Environ -ment Studies	Social Studies	Geography Area	Civic Area		World History B
					Geography A
					Geography B
		History Area	Optional Course	Civics Subjects	Contemporary Society
					Ethics
					Politics and Economy

1 2 3 4 5 6	1 2 3	1 2 3
Primary School	Lower Secondary School	Upper Secondary School

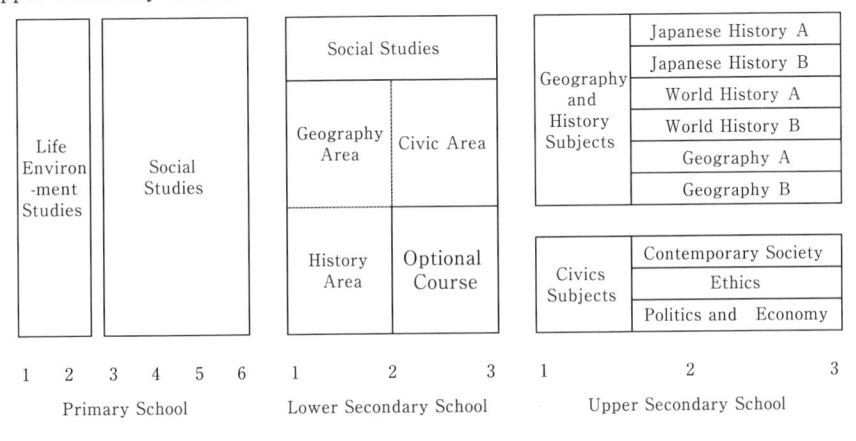

■ The Fourth Phase: In the Course of Study in 1989 and 1998 social studies was omitted from the curriculum of the lower grades of primary school and it was replaced by life environment studies. In lower secondary school, three fields of geography, history, and civics remained in the curriculum but social studies

に再編された。小・中・高校一貫の社会科の構造はなくなった。この教科再編は、教科のあり方についての一つの考え方であった。この時期は、学習の個別化や興味関心に応じる教育が重視され、学習選択が行われ、全体として社会科の系統性が弱められた。その背景として、産業構造の変化、国際化や情報化の進展に対応しようとしたことが挙げられる。特に、高校では、国際化への進展に伴い歴史・地理学習を重視し、世界史を必修化したのである。

第5段階：

⑨ 2008（平成20）年版（小、中）、2009（平成21）年版（高校）

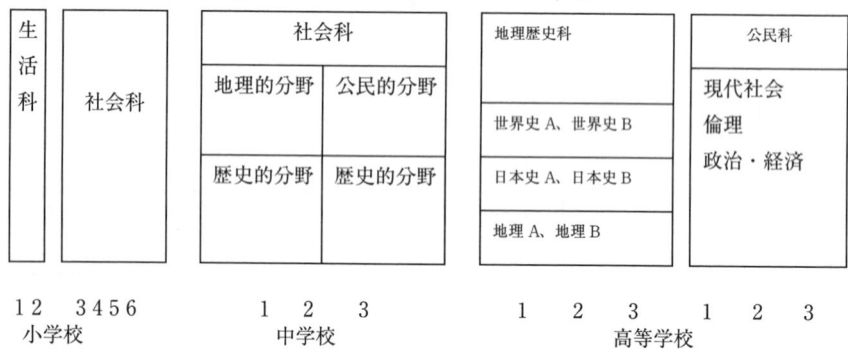

生活科	社会科	社会科		地理歴史科	公民科
		地理的分野	公民的分野	世界史A、世界史B	現代社会
					倫理
		歴史的分野	歴史的分野	日本史A、日本史B	政治・経済
				地理A、地理B	

1 2　3 4 5 6　　　1　2　3　　　　1　2　3　1　2　3
小学校　　　　　　中学校　　　　　　高等学校

■第5段階の2008年、2009年版社会科は、現在の社会科（図⑨）である。基本的な構造は前のものを継承しているが、学力重視の方向から、各分野の時間数が増え、特に歴史分野は中学校第3学年でも学習されることになった。

was set up in the third grade as an elective subject. In upper secondary school, social studies was transformed to two subjects: geography/history and civics in view of emphasizing specialized and systematic learning. The structure of consistent education of social studies in primary, lower secondary and upper secondary schools disappeared. This reorganization of subjects was one of the ideas how subjects should be structured. At that time, individualization and education responding to interests of the students were emphasized, subjects were selected, and the systematic form of social studies was undermined. As a background of this reform, there was a necessity to correspond to the change of industrial structure and the development of internationalization and information society. Particularly, in upper secondary school geography/history was emphasized and world history was made a required subject in correspondance to internationalization trends.

The Fifth Phase:
⑨ The Course of Study in 2008 (Primary and Lower Secondary School) and 2009 (Upper Secondary School)

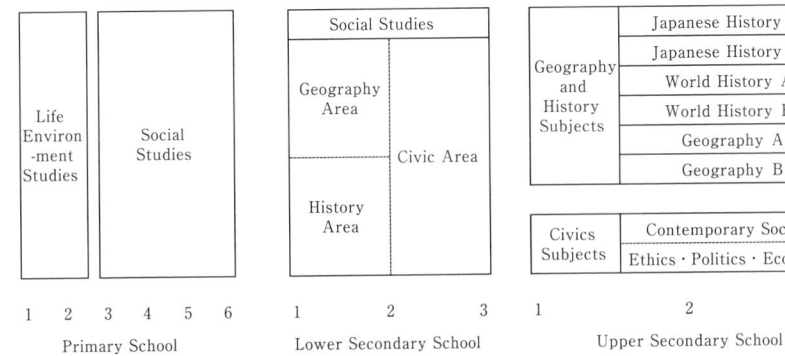

Primary School	Lower Secondary School	Upper Secondary School
Life Environ-ment Studies / Social Studies (1 2 3 4 5 6)	Social Studies: Geography Area, Civic Area, History Area (1 2 3)	Geography and History Subjects: Japanese History A, Japanese History B, World History A, World History B, Geography A, Geography B; Civics Subjects: Contemporary Society, Ethics · Politics · Economy (1 2 3)

■ Figure ⑨ shows the current form of social studies. In social studies the Course of Study in 2008 and 2009 indicates that the basic structure succeeds previous forms of social studies. However, the class hours of each field are increased to

それに伴い、興味関心の充実から生まれた選択教科がなくなり、教科指導の充実の方向が鮮明となっている。高校の必修は従来通りとなったが、日本史の必修を求める動きがみられた。また、教育基本法の改正に伴い、我が国の国土や歴史、伝統や文化に対する愛情をはぐくみ、日本人としての自覚をもって国際社会に生きるとともに、規律や規範を尊重する教育の重視や、公共的な事柄への社会参加などの充実が図られた。

(2) 現行社会科の特色
■最後に現行社会科の特色と課題について述べる。
新しく改訂された学習指導要領では、大きな変化があったわけではないが、中学校における選択教科「社会」の廃止によって、各分野の時間数が増えている。また、歴史的分野が中学校の3年生にも位置づけられて、各分野の基礎・基本の内容の習得、活用、探究の学習の充実が図られたのが目立った特徴である。
■小学校、中学校、高等学校の学習指導要領の改訂が、今回教育基本法の改正を受けて行われたこともあり、社会科では「公共の精神」「社会参画」などの方向の充実が基本的には共通して図られている。さらに、地理では地誌学習の充実、歴史では近現代史の充実、公民では法教育の充実などが図られるとともに、宗教・文化の学習なども求められることになった。合わせて、環境教育の充実もみられ「持続可能な社会」の理解が求められている。

■高校の世界史必修については継続されたが、日本史の必修化などの動きも見られた。これらの教育課程の問題は、我が国の政治の変動とも関係して、今後の検討課題となっている。

focus on improving scholastic ability and particularly, history, is also studied in the 3rd grade of lower secondary school. As a result, elective subjects aimed to enhance interest of students are omitted and a clear tendency to enrich course instruction appears. Compulsory subjects of upper secondary school remain the same but there was a move to require to make Japanese history a compulsory subject. Moreover, education to value discipline and norms as well as love for Japanese country, history, tradition and culture was taken seriously and social participation to public events was promoted in accordance with the revision of the Fundamental Law of Education.

(2) Characteristics of Current Social Studies

■ There was no major change in the newly revised Course of Study. However, as a result of the abolishment of social studies as an elective course, class hours of each field have increased. In addition, the following are distinguishing characteristics: The field of history is set up in the 3rd grade of lower secondary school; learning and application of basic contents of each area and inquisitive study are aimed to be enhanced.

■ Presently the revisions of Course of Study of primary, lower secondary, and upper secondary schools are followed by the revision of Fundamental Law of Education. Due to this, "public-mindedness" and "social participation" in social studies are promoted commonly in the revisions. Furthermore, the additional topography study in the geography subject, modern history study in the history subject, and law education in the civics subject are promoted and studies of religion and culture are required. Moreover, environmental education is promoted for students to understand "sustainable society".

■ World History remains a compulsory subject in upper secondary school but there was an indication to include a requirement of Japanese history into compulsory subjects. Such issues of curriculum are related to fluctuation of Japanese politics and the agendas to be examined in the future.

3. 算数・数学

(1) 算数・数学科の基本的特質
■日本では小学校で教えるのは算数、中等学校以上では数学と呼ばれている。

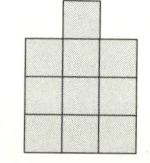

■算数・数学科は、思考力やコミュニケーション能力を育成する教科であり、固有な数学的な見方や考え方を育てる教科である。
　ア）算数・数学科でなければ獲得し得ない見方・考え方
　　例：右の図で単位正方形はいくつあるか？ 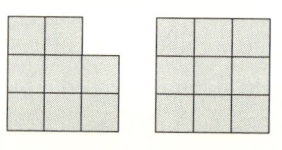
　　方法1：最初から、最後まで順に数える
　　方法2：左が8、後は9、10。
　　　　　8＋9＋10
　　方法3：真ん中が9。1個右から左へ動かせば、かけざんで9×3。
　　方法1〜3の相違は、対象を異なる見方や考え方で表象して推論したことの証である。
　　方法1は小学校1年生の最初のころ、方法2は小学校1年生の終りのころ、方法3は小学校2年生の終りのころに期待される反応である。算数・数学では計算も教えるが、同時にそこで必要な見方や考え方を教えていくことが大切である。
　イ）算数・数学科に固有な表現方法
　　表現：数、式、表、グラフ、時刻（10進法、60進法、12進法、24進法）、関数
　　体系を記す表現様式：公理、定義、命題、定理、補題、仮定、結論、証明
　ウ）算数・数学科であればこそより育成しやすい思考力・判断力・論証力判断と一般性、Why：正しいか、正しくないか。いつでも言えるか。理由を述べなさい。
　　反例と弁証法、背理法：もし、貴方の言っていることが正しいとすれば、‥‥

3. Artithmetic and Mathematics

(1) Basic Features of Mathematics

■ In Japan, the subject name 'Arithmetic' means 'mathematics for primary school' and Mathematics is used in secondary schools.

■ Arithmetic and Mathematics are subjects that develop abilities to think and communicate, as well as mathematical views, thinking and ideas, which cannot be achieved through other subjects.

a) Views, thinking and ideas, which cannot be achieved through other subjects.

ex.: How many unit squares are there in the right figures?

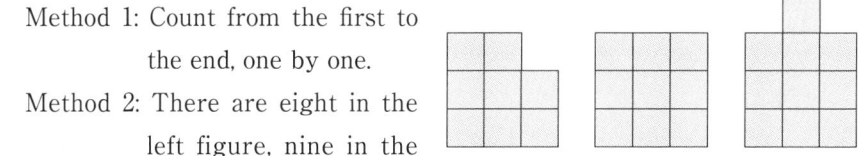

Method 1: Count from the first to the end, one by one.

Method 2: There are eight in the left figure, nine in the middle and ten in the right. Thus, calculate $8 + 9 + 10$.

Method 3: There are nine in the middle figure. If one moves from right to left, calculate 9×3.

Three types of methods to count represent different views and ideas. Method 1 is an expected response of the earlier stage of the first-grade primary children, Method 2, the later stage of the first-grade primary children, and Method 3, the last stage of the second-grade primary children. Although calculation is taught in Arithmetic and Mathematics, it is important to teach mathematical views, thinking and ideas necessary for calculation.

b) Specific representations of Arithmetic and Mathematics

Representations: numbers, expressions, tables, graph, time (decimal system, sexagesimal system, duodecimal system, base-24 system), functions.

System: axiom, definition, proposition, theorem, lemma, hypothesis, conclusion, proof

貴方が正しいと思っている前提と矛盾しませんか？

(2) 算数・数学教育の目標
■①日本では中島健三の主張を基盤に、なぜ算数・数学を教えるかは、大きく次の4点で指摘される。
ア）実用：使うから教える必要がある。
イ）教養：即使わなくても教養として必要だから教える必要がある。
ウ）人間形成：教養としてだけではなく思考力や論理性など人間形成に必要だから教える。
エ）活動：将来はともかくも今、人として生きる喜びを味わうために教える。

■②米国数学教師協会（NCTM）では、算数・数学教育課程の基準として、以下の内容スタンダード5件とプロセススタンダード5件を同等に大切なものとして提示している。
内容スタンダード：数と計算、代数、幾何、測定、資料の整理と確率
プロセススタンダード：問題解決、推論と証明、コミュニケーション、つながり、表現

■③OECD、PISAでは、数学的リテラシーを次のように定義する。「数学が世界で果たす役割を見つけ、理解し、現在及び将来の個人の生活、職業生活、友人や親族との社会生活、建設的で関心を持った思慮深い市民としての生活において確実な数学的根拠に基づき判断を行い、数学に携わる能力」。そして、教科学力としてではなく人間として期待されるコンピテンシーという考

c) Ability to think, judge and argue that can be developed effectively particularly through the study of Arithmetic and Mathematics ;

Judgment and Generality, Why: Whether true or not; Whether it is always true; Give reasons.

Counterexample and Dialectics (Reductio ad absurdum) : If your speculation is true, this contradicts the premise that you have accepted something as true, doesn't it?

(2) Objectives of Mathematics Education

■ ① Based on Kenzo Nakajima, the following four reasons are pointed out for Mathematics Education in Japan:
a) Practical: Need to teach because people need to use it
b) Educational: Need to teach to enrich one's education, although mathematics may not be necessary immediately
c) Human development: Need to teach because mathematics is necessary not only for special subject but also for one's character formation including thinking ability and logical thinking for better life.
d) Activities: The need to teach how to live and enjoy life, at least in their class
■ ② The US National Council of Teachers of Mathematics (NCTM) sets the following five content standards and five process standards as equally important standards of mathematics curriculums.
Content standards: Number and operations, Algebra, Geometry, Measurement, Data analysis and probability
Process standards: Problem solving, Reasoning and proof, Communication, Connections, Representation
■ ③ OECD PISA define mathematical literacy as follows: Mathematical literacy is an individual's capacity to identify and understand the role that mathematics plays in the world, to make well-founded judgements and to use and engage with mathematics in ways that meet the needs of that individual's life as a constructive, concerned and reflective citizen. OECD PISA also classifies the

え方のもとで測定対象とするプロセスを以下のように分類した。「思考と推論、論証（Argumentation）、コミュニケーション、モデル化、問題設定と解決、記号表現・式表現・専門語表現・計算の利用、手段と道具の利用」

■④日本の教育課程における算数・数学科の目標の変遷と実現

1) 日本の算数・数学科教育課程は、算術、幾何、代数というような分科型から融合型への転換に第2次世界大戦以前及び大戦中に成功している。その時期にすでに数学化を主張し、数学的な見方や考え方の育成を求めている。小学校の算術科を今日の数学科の意味での算数科に名称を改めたのは1941年のことである。

2) 今日の教育課程の目標記述の基盤は、戦後の占領下に作られたという指摘が一部にあるが、戦前からの考え方を具体化したと考えることもできる。ただし、用語上の相違もある。数学的な価値は「よさ」や「美しさ」という言葉で、数学的な活動は「見方」や「考え方」という言葉で強調されてきた。

3) 日本の教育課程の改定は、海外動向に依存しているという主張がある。日本の教育課程が米国に影響を与えることもあり相互に影響を与えあったことは確かであるとしても、国の教育は常に内部的な改善努力があればこそ実現しうるものである。それぞれの国の発展はそれぞれの国で自律的に推進されている。

4) 特に近年、「自ら学び自ら考える」子どもを育てる立場から、見方や考え方、よさ（学ぶ価値）の学習、学び方の学習、数学の生み出し方の学習、活用の仕方の学習などが重視されている。目標に対する評価の観点では、関心・意欲・態度、見方や考え方、表現・処理、知識・理解が設定されている。

processes measured under the concept of competency expected to have as a human rather than academic ability, as follows: Mathematical Thinking; Mathematical Argumentation; Communication; Modeling; Problem posing and solving; Representation; Symbolism and Formalism ; and Aids and Tools.

■ ④ History of objectives and results of Japan's curricula in Sansu (Arithmetic) and Sugaku (Mathematics)

1) Japan's curricula in Sansu (Arithmetic; elementary school mathematics) and Sugaku (Mathematics) succeeded in shifting from sectionalized mathematical subjects such as Sanjutsu (Arithmetic), Geometry and Algebra to integrated mathematics before and during the Second World War. In those days, mathematization was already focused on and development of mathematical views, thinking and ideas were regarded as necessary. The subject 'Sanjutsu' of primary school was renamed to 'Sansu', whose meaning is closer to 'Sugaku' (mathematics), in 1941.

2) Although some people say the base of the current Japanese curriculum objectives was established while Japan was under the occupation of the US, it is also reasonable to consider that the concept before World War II gave a concrete form to the current Japanese curriculum objectives. There are some differences in the terms used in the concept between before and after the WW II. Mathematical values were emphasized using the terms, yosa (worth of learning) and utsukushisa (beauty), and Mathematical activities are emphasized using the terms mikata (views) and kangaekata (thinking and ideas).

3) Some people say that Japanese curriculum is revised according to the trends in overseas curricula. Both Japanese and overseas curricula can be agents, indeed there are evidences that Japanes curricula influenced US and other countries, but the national education can be properly provided only when internal efforts to improve are made. The development of each country's education has been rather promoted autonomously, which was proven by each country's development.

4) Particularly in recent years, under the policy to nurture children who can

5）日本の弛まない改善努力によって日本の算数・数学の到達度は世界有数である。他方で、学力低下は、戦後2度、出現した。最初の学力低下は終戦直後の混乱期である。特に占領軍は、日本の教育課程は難しすぎる、生活を中心に再編成すべきという関心からその内容を1年遅延させた。戦中・戦後の混乱期のデータをいかに比較すれば妥当か、またそこで求められた学力は同じであるかが論争となった。続く学力低下は、週5日制に対応するために1998年改訂の教育課程によって授業時数が2割削減され、教育内容が3割削減されたことによって発生したと指摘されている。中学校数学は世界有数に少ない授業時数である週3時間を余儀なくされ、その結果、PISA調査（2000、2003、2006）によって顕著な学力低下実態が明らかになった。この経験は、日本の場合には教育課程が、数学の達成度の大きな要因であることを示している。

(3) 日本の教育課程における目標と内容

①小学校算数科の場合

ア）算数科の目標

■学校教育法では、小学校教育の目標を「生涯にわたり学習する基盤が培われるよう、基礎的な知識及び技能を習得させるとともに、これらを活用して課題を解決するために必要な思考力、判断力、表現力その他の能力をはぐく

learn and think for themselves, importance has been placed on views and perspectives, learning yosa (worth of learning), learning how to learn, learning how to lead to an answer, and learning how to effectively use; and evaluation for the objectives have been made regarding interest, willingness, attitude, mathematical views, thinking and ideas, representations and operations, and knowledge and understanding.

5) Due to continuing efforts for improvement, Japanese students' achievement on mathematics is at the top level in the world. Meanwhile, the decline in achievement was identified twice after World War II; the first time was during the chaotic period immediately after the war. US occupation forces shifted the curriculum one year later, considering that the Japanese curriculum was so difficult that it was better to reconstruct the curriculum and place more importance on daily life. Many people argued about whether the comparison of data during and after World War II was feasible, when Japan was in confusion, is reasonable, and whether the data of the academic ability collected can be comparable. Next, the decline in academic ability occurred in 1999, when the number of class hours was reduced by 20% and thus the curriculum was also reduced by 30 % in response to the transition to the 5-day school week. The class hours of mathematics in lower secondary school was forced to reduce to three hours a week, which was at the lowest in the world, and later decline in academic ability has become evident according to PISA surveys in 2000, 2003 and 2006. Those experiences tell us that the mathematics curriculum is one of the basics of high achievement in the case of Japan.

(3) Objectives and Contents of Japan's Curriculum
① Arithmetic in Primary School
a) Objectives of Arithmetic
■ The School Education Law states that the objectives of arithmetic in primary school is "to help students acquire basic knowledge and skills to develop the base of lifelong learning; develop students' ability to think, judge, express etc.

み、主体的に学習に取り組む態度を養うことに、特に意を用いなければならない。」と定めている。その目標のもとで、2008年改訂の小学校学習指導要領では、小学校算数科の目標を「算数的活動を通して、数量や図形についての基礎的・基本的な知識及び技能を身に付け、日常の事象について見通しをもち筋道を立てて考え、表現する能力を育てるとともに、算数的活動の楽しさや数理的な処理のよさに気付き、進んで生活や学習に活用しようとする態度を育てる」と記している。

イ）．算数科の授業時間と領域

算数科	第1学年	第2学年	第3学年	第4学年	第5学年	第6学年
1989 改訂	136	175	175	175	175	175
1998 改訂	114	155	150	150	150	150
2008 改訂	136	175	175	175	175	175

■学力低下が指摘され、授業時数が復活した。算数科は、数と計算、量と測定、図形、数量関係の4領域からなる。日本では戦前から、図形、数量関係を明瞭に扱っている。

ウ）．算数科教育課程の系統性
■日本の算数科の教育課程の系統は世界有数に優れた系統であると日本の数学教育研究者は自負している。例えば、日本では、引き算は足し算であり、かけ算は足し算であり、割り算はかけ算であり引き算であることは、小学校の先生方にとって、当然のこととされている。教育課程の系統性を重視する算数固有の立場が「既習を生かす」「素地指導で学んだことを生かす」「後の学習で使えるように今教える」というような表現に凝集されている。以下にそのわかりにくい教育理論を特にかけ算の系統性に注目して、日本の教育課程の特質がわかるように記す。

required to solve problems using the acquired knowledge and skills; and develop attitude to voluntarily work on learning." Based on these objectives, the Course of Study in primary school revised in 2008 states that the objectives of arithmetic in primary school is ; "Through mathematical activities, to help pupils acquire basic and fundamental knowledge and skills regarding numbers, quantities and geometrical figures, to foster their ability to think and express with good perspectives and logically on matters of everyday life, to help pupils find pleasure in mathematical activities and appreciate the value of mathematical approaches, and to foster an attitude to willingly make use of mathematics in their daily lives as well as in their learning."

b) Class hours and areas

Arithmetic	Grade 1	Grade 2	Grade 3	Grade 4	Grade 5	Grade 6
Revision in 1989	136	175	175	175	175	175
Revision in 1998	114	155	150	150	150	150
Revision in 2008	136	175	175	175	175	175

■ To address the decline in academic abilities, the number of class hours was increased to the previous level. Arithmetic consists of four areas: Numbers and operation, Quantity and Measurement, Figures, and Numbers and Relations. Japan has taught Figures, and Numbers and Relations since before World War II.

c) Sequence of Arithmetic curriculum

■ Japan's mathematics education researchers believe that Japan's arithmetic curriculum sequence is one of the best in the world. For example, in Japan, subtraction is regarded as addition, multiplication is regarded as addition, and division is regarded as multiplication and subtraction, which are the norm for Japanese primary school teachers. The curriculum sequence, which is shared among schools, is typically expressed in phrases such that "effectively use what has been learned," "effectively use what has been learned in the basic class," and "teach so that what has been learned can be used in the class later", as well as expressions specific to sequential Arithmetic curriculum. The following

■1年：日本では、かけ算を導入する前の学年で、かけ算の場面をとりあげている。

例1．数え方：に、し、ろの、やの、とお。ご、じゅう、じゅうご、にじゅう、

例2．机と消しゴム：机のよこは、消しゴムで10個分

例3．2＋2＋2＋‥

2年：日本では、かけ算は、「いくつぶん（例2）」と「累加（例3）」で定義される。「倍」は、後々、比例的推論と小数倍、分数倍を導入する素地として、テープ図で導入される。日本では、かけ算九九は必ず覚えさせるが、覚えたら九九表に隠された様々なパターンを発見するために活用される。日本では、2×3＝（〇〇）＋（〇〇）＋（〇〇）と3×2＝（〇〇〇）＋（〇〇〇）は、同時に文章題において区別する。2×3＝3×2はアレイ図によって個数が同じ、値が同じであることは扱うが、問題場面としては違うことを学ぶ。

3年：日本では、割り算の文章題は、2×X＝6の解を求める文章題を包含除（2こずつX回配る）と呼び、X×3＝6の解を求める文章題を等分除（3等分、X個を3回配る）と呼ぶ。前者では、割り算は引き算でもある。

3年、4年：テープ図を比例数直線で表し、倍という言葉使いに慣れる。

4年：正方形、長方形の面積の学習で、単位正方形の個数がかけ算で求められることを学ぶ。

5年：三角形、四角形、円の面積を求める方法を既習を生かして探し出す。その際、長方形の面積公式を、三角形、四角形、円の場合へ漸次、拡張する。

5年：小数のかけ算、割り算に比例数直線を活用する。その際、倍という言葉で説明する。

is the explanation of Japan's education theory which is difficult to understand for non-Japanese people. The description is provided, using the examples of the systematic characteristics of multiplication, to show the characteristics of Japan's education curriculum.

■ Grade 1: In Japan, students learn multiplication-related materials before they learn multiplication.

Ex. 1: count by double: ni (2), shi (4), ro (6), yano (8), toh (10); count by five; goh (5), ju (10), jugo (15), niju (20)

Ex. 2: measuring Desk by Eraser: The width of a desk is the length of ten erasers.

Ex. 3: 2 + 2 + 2 + ⋯

Grade 2: In Japan, multiplication is defined as "equal to how many a unit of a number (Ex. 2)" or "repeated addition (Ex. 3)." Multiplication is introduced using a tape image, to establish a base of introducing proportional reasoning, decimal multiplication and fractional multiplication. In Japan, memorizing kuku, multiplication from 1 by 1 to 9 by 9, is obligatory, and kuku is effectively used to detect various patterns hidden in the table of kuku. In Japanese "two times these" in English express "3 x 2" . In Japan, "2 x 3 = (**) + (**) + (**)" and "3 x 2 = (***) + (***)" are regarded as different in word problems. "2 x 3 = 3 x 2" is taught that the answers are same using an array, but that "2 x 3" is different from "3 x 2" in word problems.

Grade 3: In Japan, word problems of division are divided into two: measurement division, word problems to obtain a solution for 2 x X = 6 (distribute two things X times), and partitive division, word problems to obtain a solution for X x 3 = 6 (equally divide into three; distribute X things three times). In the former case, division is also regarded as subtraction.

Grades 3 and 4: A tape image is used to express a proportional number line in order to be familiar with the term, multiply.

Grade 4: When teaching

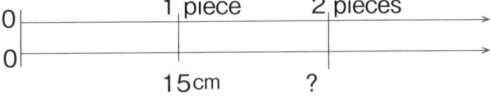

6年：分数のかけ算、割り算に比例数直線を活用する。その際、倍という言葉で説明する。

■日本の『小学校学習指導要領解説：算数編』では、乗法は比例数直線による定義が正式な定義である。2年生で倍を取り上げて以降、テープ図と比例数直線が、算数の表現「倍」を表すために繰り返し用いられる。比例数直線で乗法除法を解説する際の解説の仕方は、デカルトが幾何学（1634）のなかで表した乗法・除法の考え方と同じである。このデカルトの乗法定義は、正負の数でも成り立つが、デカルト自身は負の数を認めなかった。日本では比例数直線を使うのは小学校までであり、中学校で学ぶ正の数・負の数・中点連結定理、平行線と比の定理との関係は曖昧である。
　以上のような考え方は、世界の数学教育界では比較的新しい考え方であるが、日本では戦前から1960年代にまでにかけて成立した考え方である。

②中学校数学科の場合
ア）中学校数学科の目標
■「数学的活動を通して、数量や図形などに関する基礎的な概念や原理・法則の理解を深め、数学的な表現や処理の仕方を習得し、事象を数理的に考察し表現する能力を高めるとともに、数学的活動の楽しさや数学のよさを実感

square and rectangular areas, students relearn that the number of unit squares which can be obtained by multiplication.

Grade 5: Students seek how to obtain the areas of a triangle, rectangle and circle, based on the knowledge already acquired. At the same time, students apply the formula of obtaining rectangular areas to the ways of obtaining the areas of triangles, rectangles and circles.

Grade 5: Students use proportional number lines for decimal multiplication and division. To explain this operation, the term, multiplication, is used.

Grade 6: Students use proportional number lines for fractional multiplication and division. To explain this operation, the term, multiplication, is used.

■ In the description of Japan's curriculum, multiplication is formally defined with a number of units with the idea of proportionality. After multiplication is first taught to Grade 2 students, a tape image and a proportional number line are repeatedly used to express mathematical "multiplication." Explanation of multiplication and division using a proportional number line is the same as the concept of multiplication and division explained in the geometry by Descartes (1634). The definition of multiplication by Descartes can be used for both positive and negative numbers, but Descartes did not use negative numbers. In Japan, proportional number lines are used only for primary school students. Relations among positive and negative numbers, midpoint theorem, and parallel lines and proportion theorem, which are taught to lower secondary school students, are vague.

These concepts are relatively new in the mathematics education in the world, but were established in Japan during a period befor WW II period to the 1960s.

② Mathematics in Lower Secondary School
a) Objectives of Mathematics in Lower Secondary School
■ "Through mathematical activities, to help students deepen their understanding of basic concepts, principles and rules concerning numbers, quantities and diagrams; acquire the methods of mathematical expression and treatment;

し、それらを活用して考えたり判断したりしようとする態度を育てる。」

イ）中学校数学科の授業時数と内容
■1999年改訂の教育課程では、1年生、2年生、3年生がそれぞれ週3時間であったが、学力低下の批判を受けて2008年より1年生4時間、2年生3時間、3年生4時間に修正された。数と式、図形、関数、資料の活用の4領域からなる。

ウ）中学校数学の内容と系統
■中学校3年間で、数と式・関数では、平方根、2次方程式の初歩、2次関数の初歩まで、図形では相似と円まで学ぶ。日本の中学校数学の顕著な特徴は、米国の高校数学で言う代数や幾何を中学校で学ぶことである。中学校の学校制度そのものは戦後の設立であるが、この高い水準は、日本の戦前の旧制中学校の教育課程に起源するもので、東アジアに共通している。

③高等学校数学科の場合
ア）高等学校数学科の目標
■数学的活動を通して、数学における基本的な概念や原理・法則の体系的な理解を深め、事象を数学的に考察し表現する能力を高め、創造性の基礎を培うとともに、数学のよさを認識し、それらを積極的に活用して数学的論拠に基づいて判断する態度を育てる。

イ）高等学校数学科の授業時数と内容

enhance their ability to think and express in a mathematical way; and appreciate the mathematical way of viewing and thinking, and thereby develop attitudes willing to applying mathematical methods to thinking and judging."

b) Class Hours and Curriculum in Lower Secondary School

■ The number of class hours was originally three hours a week according to the revised curriculum in 1999, but the number was increased to four hours a week for grade 1, three hours a week for grade 2 and four hours a week for grade 3 in 2008, in response to the decline in academic abilities. The curriculum consists of four areas: Numbers and Expressions, Figure, Functions and Making use of do.

c) Sequence of Mathematics Curriculum in Lower Secondary School

■ In Lower Secondary school, students learn square root, rudimentary second-degree equation and rudimentary quadric in the area of Number and Expressions, and Function classes; and learn Homology and circle in the Diagram class. A distinctive feature of Japan's mathematics education in lower secondary school is that algebra and geometry that US upper secondary school students learn are introduced at lower secondary school level. The schooling system of lower secondary school was reestablished after World War II, but this higher education standard originated in the education curriculum for lower secondary school before the war, and is common to schools in East Asia as well.

③ Mathematics in Upper Secondary School

a) Objectives of Mathematics in Upper Secondary School

■ Through mathematical activities, this enables students deepen their systematic understanding of the basic concepts, principles and rules of mathematics; enhance their ability to mathematically consider and describe events; and cultivate basic creativity as well as to help students appreciate mathematics and develop their attitude to judge based on mathematical theory, actively using mathematical skills.

b) Number of Yearly Class Hours and Contents of Mathematics in Upper Secondary Schools

■高等学校数学科では、数学Ⅰ（3単位）が必修である。選択科目には、数学Ⅱ（4単位）、数学Ⅲ（5単位）、数学Ａ（2単位）、数学Ｂ（2単位）、数学活用（2単位）がある。数学的活動の指導を一層重視して数学Ⅰ、数学Ａには「課題学習」が設けられている。数学活用では、数学的な見方や考え方のよさやデータの分析を学ぶことに一層配慮している。

■日本では、小学校、中学校、高等学校で、各学校毎に校長が自校の教育課程を定めることができる。義務教育段階の小学校・中学校では、全国、ほぼ一律の教育課程が実施されている。入試を経て入学する高等学校では、生徒の学力に応じたよりよい教育課程を工夫するため、上記の科目名と、実際の履修内容が一致しない場合がある。

ウ）高等学校の内容と系統
■数学Ⅰでは、数と式、図形と計量、二次関数、データの分析、そして「これら4つの内容領域又はそれらを相互に関連付けた内容に関連した課題を設け、それらの解決を通して数学のよさを認識できるようにする」課題学習が求められている。数学Ⅱでは、場合の数と確率、整数の性質、図形の性質に対する課題学習が求められている。

(4) 世界で注目される日本の「問題解決の指導」

①授業研究による指導法の開発
■日本では指導内容が共有されるため、指導法も共有しやすい。教育目標を実現するための授業研究が恒常的に行われ、「問題解決の指導」も開発されてきた。

■ Mathematics I (3 credits) is a required course. Elective courses are Mathematics II (4 credits), Mathematics III (5 credits), Mathematics A (2 credits), Mathematics B (2 credits) and Mathematical Application (2 credits). To further enhance the instruction of mathematical activities, task-based learning is prepared for Mathematics I and Mathematics A. Mathematical Application particularly focuses on the appreciation of mathematical viewing and thinking as well as learning of data analysis.

■ In Japan, principals in primary schools, and lower and upper secondary schools can decide the curricula of their own schools. In reality, most primary and lower secondary schools, where compulsory education is conducted, take the same curricula. In upper secondary schools, where entrance examination is conducted, actual curriculum contents are sometimes different from those defined by the above subjects in order to provide students with better education according to the students' ability.

c) Curriculum Sequence of Mathematics in Upper Secondary Schools

■ In Mathematics I, it is required to teach numbers and algebraic expressions, geometrical figures and measurement, quadratic functions and data analysis; "provide tasks relating to these four areas or interrelating tasks of these four areas; and help students appreciate mathematics through the solution of these tasks." In Mathematics II, it is also required to provide task-based learning concerning combinatorics and probability, nature of integer, and nature of figures.

(4) Japan's "Problem Solving Approach" Attracting Public Attention across the World

① Developing teaching approaches through lesson study

■ Since teaching contents are fixed by the national curriculum standards, it is easier to share teaching approaches. Lesson study has been conducted to achieve the objectives of education, and "Problem Solving Approach" has also been developed.

②自ら学び自ら考える子どもを育てる「問題解決の指導」

■日本では、「自ら学び自ら考える子どもを育てる」ために、学習指導案では「○○を通して××を育てる／できるようにする」というように、2つの目標を記す。そのうち一つは前述の数学的な見方や考え方などの高次目標であり、将来の学習で役立つ学び方や今後の学習の素地を築くものである。例えば、「等積変形と合同図形の考えを利用して、三平方の定理の証明ができるようにする」「三平方の定理の証明を理解することを通して、等積変形と合同図形の考え方の使い方を知る」では、指導内容も指導展開もまるで異なる。

③「問題解決の指導」を実現するための教材研究

■問題を解く行為は、問題、解法、解答という3つの変数に分類される。ア）普通、問題が決まれば、解答は一つでも、解法は多様にある（解法がオープン）。イ）問題の条件が多すぎるか、不足すれば（オープンエンドの問題）、解答は一つに定まらない（解答がオープン）。ウ）問題そのものを変数にすれば、問題も一つに定まらない（問題がオープン）。

　いずれにしても、問題、解法、解答を可変的にみることは教材研究の基本である。「$a^2 + b^2 = c^2$ であることを証明せよ」と言えば、証明法は多様にある。それぞれの証明法を発見するには、それぞれに必要なアイデアがあり、そのアイデアを事前に知らなければ本時で生徒はその証明を構想することはできない。「$a^2 + b^2 = c^2$ である a，b，c を求めよ」と言えば、解答は無数にある。自然数に限定すれば、ピタゴラス数と呼ばれる。特定のピタゴラス数の場合、面積図（タイル張り）による説明のきっかけになる。そして何をどう取り上げるかで指導目標もかわってくる。

■教材研究では、対象とする子どもたちが学んでいること、そして後の学習

② "Problem Solving Approach" to develop children to learn and think for themselves
■ To develop children to learn and think for themselves, the lesson plan in Japan states two objectives in one sentence, that is, "to develop xx ability or to lead students to be able to do xx, through **." One of them is a high-level objective such as mathematical views thinking and ideas stated above, which can develop the study method useful in the future study and establish the base of future study. For example, "to instruct students to be able to prove the Pythagorean theorem, using the concepts of equivalent transformation and congruous figures" and "to teach students the use of concepts of equivalent transformation and congruous figures, through understanding of the proof of the Pythagorean theorem" are completely different in terms of instruction contents and instruction development.
③ Subject matter research to conduct "Problem Solving Approach"
■ Problem solving activity has the following variables: problem, method of solving and answer. a) Once a problem is determined, a variety of solution methods usually exist, even though there is only one answer (solutions are open). b) If there are too many or too few conditions on the problem (open-ended problem), there is more than one answer (answers are open). c) If a problem itself is a variable, there is more than one problem (problems are open).

In any case, it is a fundamental of subject matter research to regard problems, solution methods and answers as variables. For the question, "Prove $a^2 + b^2 = c^2$," there are various proof methods, and specific ideas, already known, are necessary to find each of the proof methods. If students do not know the ideas, they cannot develop the proof. For the question, "Find a, b and c such that $a^2 + b^2 = c^2$," there are infinite answers. If the answer is limited to natural numbers, the answer is called Pythagorean numbers. When the answer is a specific Pythagorean number, the solution can lead to an explanation of area diagrams (tiles). Instruction objectives will vary depending on how to put forward particular ideas.
■ In the subject matter research, instruction objectives and proposals (issues in

で子どもたちが準備しておかないと困ることという学習の系統の中で、本時の指導目標と提示課題（本時の問題）を吟味していく。

④「問題解決の指導」の焦点：子どもの問題意識に基づく教訓の多様性

■問題に対する多様な解答が得られれば、様々な解法、その前提知識と本時の学習内容、そこで求められる考え方などが議論し得る。その議論から本時の学習内容がまとめられる。

参考文献
・Isoda, M (2010). English translation of 'The Guide of the Course of Theory for Elementary School Mathematics/Junior High School Mathematics' CRICED, University of Tsukuba.
http://math-info.criced.tsukuba.ac.jp
http://e-archives.criced.tsukuba.ac.jp
・Isoda, M., Stephens, M., Ohara, Y., and Miyakawa, T.,, (2007). Japanese Lesson Study in Mathematics: Its Impact, Diversity and Potential for Educational Improvement. Singapore: World Scientific.
・JICA (2004). The History of Japan's Educational Development. (in English, Spanish and French)
http://www.jica.go.jp/english/resources/publications/study/topical/educational/index.html

a class) will be examined, considering the curriculum sequence that focuses on what children already learned, achieved and what children have to prepare for the later-stage class.

④ Focus of the "Problem Solving Approach" : A variety of lessons learned based on Problematic reasoning.

■ If a variety of problems can be obtained for a question, discussions can be made for a variety of solutions, related pre-knowledge and lessons in the class, and logic to find these solution methods. Through the discussion, children achieve the objectives of the class.

References :
・Isoda, M (2010). English translation of "The Guide of the Course of Theory for Elementary School Mathematics/Junior High School Mathematics" CRICED, University of Tsukuba.
http://math-info.criced.tsukuba.ac.jp
http://e-archives.criced.tsukuba.ac.jp
・Isoda, M., Stephens, M., Ohara, Y., and Miyakawa, T.,, (2007). Japanese Lesson Study in Mathematics: Its Impact, Diversity and Potential for Educational Improvement. Singapore: World Scientific.
・JICA (2004). The History of Japan's Educational Development. (in English, Spanish and French)
http://www.jica.go.jp/english/resources/publications/study/topical/educational/index.html

4. 理科

(1) 理科教育の歴史

■わが国の近代的な教育制度が成立した1872年の「学制」において、自然科学に関する内容は学校教育に取り上げられた。しかしそこでは理科という教科は存在せず、窮理学、化学、博物学という分科理科的な科目から構成されていた。これらの科目はその後何回かの変遷を経た後、1886年の「小学校令」の公布により、自然科学に関する教科の教育は「理科」という教科名のもと統一された。「理科」では、生活との関連が強調され、児童が日常生活の中で出会う天然物および自然現象に関する内容、機械や器具や生活との関連において学習する内容が中心となった。その後、1900年、1907年、1911年、1919年の改訂によって、理科の内容や履修開始時期に部分的な変更が加えられたが、その基本的性格は1941年の「国民学校令」の施行まで変わることはなかった。

■1941年の「国民学校令」の公布により、理科は算数と統合され「理数科」となり、理科は理数科理科としてその一部に位置づけられた。また、小学校1年生から3年生を対象に自然の観察(教科名「自然の観察」)を主とする低学年理科が開始されたが、これはわが国の理科教育史上特筆すべきことである。

■戦後の学習指導要領の特質の変遷をまとめると以下のようになる。
① 1947年版学習指導要領(生活理科)
　・児童生徒中心カリキュラム
　・生活経験の重視
　・問題解決学習
② 1951、1952年版学習指導要領(生活理科)
　・生活単元から教材単元へ

4. Science

(1) History of Science Education

■ Natural science first appeared in Japan's school education in 1872 under the School Ordinance, a law on the educational system of modern Japan. At first, Natural Science was not taught as a single subject called Science, but taught as separate subjects such as Physics, Chemistry and Natural History. After several changes in the constitution, natural science subjects were integrated into a single subject called Science, or Rika in Japanese, after the promulgation of Primary School Ordinance was established in 1886. The subject of science focused on relations to daily lives, such as natural objects and phenomena that children can find, and machines and tools that children use around their lives. The basic feature of the science subject had not changed until 1941, when the National School Ordinance was enacted, although the contents and class length of the science classes were partially changed in 1900, 1907, 1911 and 1919.

■ After the promulgation of the National School Ordinance in 1941, science and mathematics were integrated as a Science-Math Course. School Science was designated as part of the Science-Math Course. Furthermore, Science in the lower grades: first to third grade of the primary school, began to deal mainly with the observation of nature (The exact name is; Observation of Nature). This was a remarkable event in the history of science education in Japan.

■ The Characteristics of the Course of Study after World War II changed as follows;

① The Course of Study in 1947 (Science for Daily Life)
 : Child - Centered Curriculum
 : Emphasis on Daily Life Experience
 : Problem Solving Method

② The Course of Study in 1951 and 1952 (Science for Daily Life)

- ・問題解決学習の徹底
- ・児童生徒中心カリキュラムの強調

③ 1958、1959、1960 年版学習指導要領（系統理科）
- ・系統学習の強調
    - 小学校：学習の順序性、指導の系統性
    - 中学校：分野別内容の系統
    - 高等学校：分科科学の体系的系統

④ 1968、1969、1970 年版学習指導要領（探究理科）
- ・探究学習の強調
- ・基本的科学概念より構造化された教育内容の精選
- ・科学の方法の重視

⑤ 1977、1978 年版学習指導要領
- ・学習者の側に立つ教育
- ・内容の総合化
- ・体験的学習の強化

⑥ 1989 年版学習指導要領
- ・観察・実験の一層の重視
- ・科学技術の進歩、情報化社会への対応；日常生活との関連
- ・特に中等教育段階での生徒の実態に対応した多様化

⑦ 1998、1999 年版学習指導要領
- ・学習内容と授業時間数の大幅な削減
- ・個に応じた指導の充実：中学校の選択科目の増加、高等学校の必修科目の減少
- ・高等学校に新設科目：理科基礎、理科総合 A、理科総合 B

⑧ 2008、2009 年版学習指導要領
- ・1998、1999 年に比べて授業時間数の増加
- ・探究的な学習活動の充実、観察・実験や自然体験、科学的な体験の充実
- ・「エネルギー」「粒子」「生命」「地球」を科学の基本的な見方や概念の柱とする系統性

: From Daily Life Experience Units into Teaching Materials Units
: Throughout the Problem Solving Method Around the Country
: Emphasis on Child-Centered Curriculum
③ The Course of Study in 1958, 1959 and 1960 (Systematic Science)
: Emphasis on Systematic Learning
Primary School: Order for Learning, System for Instruction
Lower Secondary School: Systematic Instruction for Content of Each Field
Upper Secondary School: Systematic Instruction for Each Science Field
④ The Course of Study in 1968, 1969 and 1970 (Inquiry Science)
: Emphasis on Learning through Inquiry
: Selecting for Teaching Contents Based on Scientific Basic Concept of Structure
: Emphasis on Scientific Method
⑤ The Course of Study in 1977 and 1978
: Teaching from Learner's Standpoint
: Integration of Teaching Content
: Reinforcement of Experience-Based Learning
⑥ The Course of Study in 1989
: More Emphasis on Observations and Experiment Work
: Correspondence to the Advance of Science and Technology, and Information-oriented Society; Relation with Daily Life.
: Diversification Corresponding to Actual Situation of Students at Secondary School
⑦ The Course of Study in 1998 and 1999
: Drastic Reduction of Teaching Contents and Class Hours
: Improvements of Instruction for Individual Students; Increase of Elective Subjects in Lower Secondary School, Decrease of Compulsory Subjects in Upper Secondary School
: New Sciense Subjects: Basic Science, Integrated Science A, Integrated Science B

■第2次世界大戦後の1946年頃から10年間あまり、アメリカの進歩主義教育のもとに、児童や生徒を中心とする生活理科が推進された。この生活理科の特色は、子どもの興味、関心などをよりどころにし、生活における問題を子どもが解決していく学習を中心としていた。内容構成においては「単元」制が取り入れられ、それに基づいて教材の選定、配列が行われた。後に、この生活単元学習による理科は、児童生徒の基礎学力低下という問題を招き、「はいまわる理科」として批判されるようになる。そのため、1958年、1959年、1960年の学習指導要領改訂では、系統理科と称される科学の系統性に基づいた内容構成に代わった。そこでは、家庭科的、保健衛生的内容や、交通機関、応用科学、生物の保護や利用などに関する内容は大幅に削減された。

■1969年と1970年の中等学校理科の学習指導要領の改訂は、1950年代後半より米国で展開された科学教育のカリキュラム改革運動の影響を全面的に受けた。現代自然科学と学校における自然科学教育のギャップを埋めること、科学における人材を育成すること、科学の基本概念の学習を目指して、内容の構造化と探究の過程を重視することなどが目標とされた。それゆえ、探究理科と称された。1977年と1978年の学習指導要領の改訂では、公害や環境の保全という諸問題・諸課題が取り上げられ、ゆたかな生活とは何かが追及された。小学校理科においても楽しい理科、直接体験の重視、問題解決の育成などを目指した内容の精選が行われた。

⑧ The Course of Study in 2008 and 2009
: Increased Class Hours Compared with Those in 1998 and 1999
: Enhancement of Inquisitive Study Activities, Enhancement of Observation, Experiment, Experiences in Nature, and Scientific Experiences
: Organized Science Curriculum Framework Consisted of "Energy", "Particle", "Life", and "Earth" as Teaching Contents

■ After World War II, from 1946 to the early 1950's, the idea of Child-Centered Science for Daily Life based on the American Progressive Education was promoted. Science for Daily Life was characterized by the child's learning through solving daily life problems which were of interest for him/her. In the content construction, the concept of "Unit Learning" was introduced and was made the basis for the selection and arrangement of teaching materials. Afterwards, this was criticized as the cause in the decline of basic achievement of children, and was called "Crawling Science" "(Haimawaru-Rika"). As a result, a change was brought forth; content construction of science was based on a system of science called "Systematic Science" in the 1958, 1959 and 1960 revision. A large number of content material was deleted, including Homemaking, Health and Hygiene, Transportation, Applied Science, Protection and Utilization of Living Things, and so on.

■ The revision of the Science Course of Study at secondary school in 1969 and 1970 was strongly influenced by New Science Curriculum Movement in the US from the late-1950's. These revisions were aimed at obtaining the following objectives: to fill the gap between modern natural science as up to date and school science, to nurture students who will become employed in the field of science, and to learn the basic scientific concepts. This revised Course of Study in school science emphasized structuring of teaching content and inquiry process. Thus, these revised school sciences were called "Science Through Inquiry". In the revision of these courses of study in 1977 and 1978, they introduced problems and issues on pollution and environment conservation as teaching contents and

■1989年には、小学校、中学校、高等学校の学習指導要領がそろって改訂された。この改訂では、従来の知識・技能を重視する学力から、関心・意欲・態度の重視と個性の重視が謳われた。理科の内容では、今後予想される高度科学技術社会、高度情報化社会、国際化の時代に対応するため、多様な生徒の実態に対応するため、現実社会との関連を図り、従来以上に観察・実験を重視して、科学的な観点から問題解決能力が活用できる人材の育成をめざした内容改訂がなされている。これらの指導に当たっては、コンピュータ等の活用への配慮も含めた。

■小学校の第1学年より第6学年までを通して理科が教えられることになったのは、第2次世界大戦中の1941年の国民学校令により制度的に実現したいわゆる「低学年理科」である「自然の観察」（第1学年より第3学年の理科）の制定による。それ以来小学校理科は単独の教科として、第1学年より第6学年まで教えられてきた。しかし1989年に改訂され1992年実施の学習指導要領では、小学校では第1学年より第2学年までは理科という教科が廃止された。これに伴い、理科という教科は小学校3学年より始まるという日本の理科教育史上、例を見ない事態に立ち入ったのである。

■1998年には、小学校、中学校、1999年に高等学校の指導要領が改訂された。改訂においては、学校完全週5日制の実施、「総合的な学習の時間」の導入、高等学校の情報科の新設に伴い、小学校、中学校理科で内容が大きく削減され、高等学校理科の学習内容に移行された。学習指導要領においては、体験的・問題解決的な学習活動の重視を謳うが、理科の時間数が減ったため必修科目である理科の教科内では扱えず、選択科目や総合的な学習の時間の扱いとなり、理科の体験的・問題解決的な学習活動は必ずしも十分に行うことが

pursued what makes up a well-off society. In primary school science, selection of teaching contents was done with the aim of the following: to make science enjoyable, in regards to direct experience and the nurturing problem solving ability.

■ In 1989, the Courses of Study for primary school and lower and upper secondary schools were revised together. The revision was made to shift the focus from knowledge- and skills-oriented study to students' interest-, motivation- and attitude-oriented study. The Course of Study in science was revised to respond to the expected advancing science and technology society, advancing information society and globalization; to teach science focusing on relations with real world; to place more importance on observation and experiments; and to develop human resources who can solve problems based on scientific points of view. Making use of computers in the science class was also considered.

■ Science began to be taught to all-grade primary school students (from the first grade to the sixth grade) after the subject, observation of nature, was introduced as a science subject for lower-grade primary students (from the first grade to the third grade) under the National School Act, established in 1941. Since then, science had been taught to the first-grade through to sixth-grade primary students as a single subject of science until 1992, when the subject of science for the first-grade and second-grade primary school students was abolished under the Course of Study revision in 1989 and enforced in 1992. Since 1992, science has been taught to the third-grade or older primary school students, which has been the first experience in science education history in Japan.

■ In 1998, the Courses of Study for primary school and lower secondary school were revised, and in 1999, the one for upper secondary school was revised. These revisions were made in response to the introduction of the five-day school week system, Period for Integrated Study, and the Information Technology school course for upper secondary school. Due to these revisions, class hours and contents of science for primary and lower secondary schools were significantly reduced. These reduced contents were shifted to upper secondary school.

できなくなった。

■2008年には、小学校、中学校、2009年に高等学校の指導要領が改訂された。改訂では「総合的な学習の時間」の削減に伴い、理科の授業時間数が比較的増加した。科学的な思考力・表現力を育成する探究的な学習活動の充実や、科学的な知識や概念の定着と科学的な見方や考え方を育成する観察・実験や自然体験、科学的な体験の充実が謳われた。理科の学習内容は、「エネルギー」「粒子」「生命」「地球」が科学の基本的な見方や概念を柱とする系統性として示され、高等学校では、「科学と人間生活」基礎を付した科目の履修2科目もしくは基礎を付した科目を3科目必履修とし、学習領域が増えることとなった。

(2) 理科の性格・目標
■現行の理科は小学校3学年より始まり、中学校及び高等学校で教えられている。各学校段階での理科の目標は学習指導要領において以下のように記述されている（小中は2008年3月、高校は2009年3月）。

・小学校「自然に親しみ、見通しをもって観察、実験などを行い、問題解決の能力と自然を愛する心情を育てるとともに、自然の事物・現象についての実感を伴った理解を図り、科学的な見方や考え方を養う。」
・中学校「自然の事物・現象に進んでかかわり、目的意識をもって観察、実験などを行い、科学的に探究する能力の基礎と態度を育てるとともに自然の事物・現象についての理解を深め、科学的な見方や考え方を養う。」
・高等学校「自然の事物・現象に対する関心や探究心を高め、目的意識をもって観察、実験などを行い、科学的に探究する能力と態度を育てるとともに

Though the Course of Study emphasized the teaching activities focused on experience and problem solving, it was not enough to do these activities and also to teach compulsory science contents of because of reduction in class hours of science. Therefore, these science activities and contents were inevitable to deal with elective subjects or Period for Integrated Study.

■ In 2008, the Courses of Study for primary school and lower secondary school were revised, and in 2009, the one for upper secondary school was revised. Related to the decrease of class hours of the Period for Integrated Study, the class hours of science was comparatively increased. The following are advocated in the revised Course of Study: Enhancement of inquiry learning activities to nurture scientific thinking skills and expressiveness; acquisition of scientific knowledge and notion; enhancement of observation, experiments, experiences in nature, and scientific experiences to foster scientific views and thinking skills. The contents of science study have been systematized by making "Energy", "Particle", "Life", and "the Earth" the pillars of basic perspective and notion of science.

(2) Characteristics and Objectives of School Science in Japan

■ Science is currently taught to students from third-grade primary school to upper secondary school. The Course of Study, determined the objectives of science for primary, lower secondary and upper secondary schools as follows:
(March 2008 version for primary and lower secondary schools, March 2009 version for upper secondary schools)

· Primary school: To commune with nature; conduct observation and experiments after making prediction or hypothesis; develop problem-solving ability and love for nature; deepen understanding for natural things and phenomena; and nurture scientific views and thinking.

· Lower secondary school: Willing to be concerned about natural things and phenomena; conduct observation and experiments with a sense of purpose;

自然の事物・現象についての理解を深め、科学的な自然観を育成する。」

■これらの目標表現からわかるように、日本の学校理科の性格は各学校段階で異なっている。小学校では、自然への直接経験を重視し、自然界の規則・法則を探る問題解決を強調する。また、小学校において、自然を愛する心情を育てることも目標とされていることも特徴的である。一方、中学校と高等学校では、科学の探究能力の習得・育成、科学概念の獲得、科学的な思考様式の獲得が重視される。

（3）理科の教科目名、時間時数および内容構成上の特色、2008年

表7-2　小学校、中学校、高等学校の理科の教科目名

学校段階	教科目名
小学校 （3学年～6学年）	理科
中学校理科 （1学年～3学年）	理科　第一分野（物理・化学領域） 　　　　第二分野（生物・地学領域）
高等学校理科 （1学年～3学年）	科学と人間生活 物理基礎、化学基礎 生物基礎、地学基礎 物理、化学、生物、地学、理科課題研究　「科学と人間生活」を含む2科目　又は　基礎を付した科目を3科目　必履修

develop scientific inquiry ability and attitude; deepen understanding for natural things and phenomena; and nurture scientific views and thinking
• Upper secondary school: To develop interest and inquiring minds for natural things and phenomena; conduct observation and experiments with a sense of purpose; develop scientific inquiry ability and attitude; deepen understanding for natural things and phenomena; and nurture scientific views on nature.

■ As shown by objectives, features of school science are different depending on the school level. While lower and upper secondary schools place importance on acquisition and development of scientific inquiry ability and attitude, scientific concepts and thinking skills, primary school places importance on direct contact with nature and emphasizes abilities to explore rules or laws of nature for problem solving. Primary school also places importance on the development of love for nature.

(3) Names, Class Hours and Constitutional Features of Current Science Subjects in 2008

Table 7-2 Names of Science Subjects in Primary, Lower Secondary and Upper Secondary Schools

School	Subject name	
Primary school (3rd to 6th grade)	Science (Rika)	
Lower secondary school (1st to 3rd grade)	First Field (Physics, Chemistry) Second Field (Biology, Earth/Space)	
Upper secondary school (1st to 3rd grade)	Science and Human Life Basic Physics, Basic Chemistry Basic Biology, Basic Earth/Space Physics, Chemistry, Biology Earth/Space, Study of Scientific Research	Select Science and Human Life and other Two Subjects or Three Basic Subjects

表 7-3 小学校・中学校の理科の標準授業時数
小学校の 1 単位時間は 45 分、中学校の 1 単位時間は 50 分

小学校	第 3 学年	第 4 学年	第 5 学年	第 6 学年
	90	105	105	105
中学校	第 1 学年	第 2 学年	第 3 学年	
	105	140	140	

表 7-4 高等学校理科の教科目の単位数

教科目名	単位数
科学と人間生活、物理基礎、化学基礎、理科基礎、生物基礎、地学基礎	2
物理、化学、生物、地学	4
理科課題研究	1

■現行の理科の教科目名、小学校および中学校の授業時数、高等学校の単位数をまとめると表 7-2 〜 7-4 のようになる。(文部科学省、2008a, 2008b, 2009)。

■小学校理科における各学年の内容構成については、「エネルギー」「粒子」を科学の基本概念とする「A 物質・エネルギー」、「生命」「地球」を科学の基本概念とする「B 生命・地球」、の 2 領域から構成されている。児童が見通しを持って観察、実験などを行うことによって主体的な問題解決の活動を行うことが出来るように構成され、ものづくりなどの科学的な体験や身近な自然を対象とした自然体験の充実、環境学習という観点からの学習の充実も図られている。

■中学校理科は、物理と化学の内容が第 1 分野と称され、生物と地学の内容が第 2 分野と称されている。現行の学習指導要領は、科学的な見方や考え方、総合的なものの見方を育成すること、科学的な思考力、表現力の育成を図ること、科学を学ぶ意義や有用性を実感させ、科学への関心を高めること、科

Table 7-3 Class Hours of Science in Primary and Lower Secondary Schools

The class period of primary school is 45 minutes, and that of lower secondary school is 50 minutes.

Primary school	3rd grade	4th grade	5th grade	6th grade
	90	105	105	105

Lower secondary school (Compulsory subjects)	1st grade	2nd grade	3rd grade
	105	140	140

Table 7-4 Number of Credits for Science in Upper Secondary School

Subject name	No. of credits
Science and Human Life Basic Physics, Basic Chemistry, Basic Science Basic Biology, Basic Earth/Space	2
Physics, Chemistry, Biology, Earth/Space	4
Study of Scientific Research	1

■ Table 7-2 through 7-4 show the names of science subjects in primary, lower secondary and upper secondary schools, class hours of science in primary and lower secondary schools, and number of credits for science in upper secondary school. (Ministry of Education, Culture, Sports, Science and Technology, 2008a, 2008b, 2009).

■ Science for each grade of primary school consists of two areas: A. Materials and Energy based on "energy" and "particle" as scientific basic concept. B. Life and Earth based on "life" and "earth" as scientific basic concept. The subject of science is constructed so that students can conduct independent problem-solving activities through observation and experiments prospects. The subject is also constructed focusing on enhancing scientific experiences like manufacturing, experiences in immediate nature, and environment study.

■ In science for lower secondary school, physics and chemistry areas are called the First Field, and biology and geosciences areas are called the Second Field. The current Course of Study is revised to nurture scientific perspectives and notions, comprehensive views, scientific thought and expressiveness, and raise

学的な体験、自然体験の充実を図ることを基本的な考え方として改訂されている。

■高等学校理科は、「科学と人間生活」が新設された。「科学と人間生活」は、自然に対する理解や科学技術の発展がこれまで私たちの日常生活や社会にいかに影響を与え、どのような役割を果たしてきたかについて、身近な事物・現象に関する観察、実験などを中心にして学び、科学的な見方や考え方を養い、科学に対する興味・関心を高めていくという点に特色をもつ科目である。純粋な科学の性格を重視した「物理」「化学」「生物」「地学」は、「物理基礎」と「物理」のように2科目とし、基礎を付した科目を先に履修することとしている。基礎を付した科目は、より基本的な内容で構成し、観察、実験などを行い、基本的な概念や探究方法を学習する科目である。これまで学問領域に対応する科目において扱われていた課題研究は、先端科学や学際的領域も扱えるよう「理科課題研究」という新しい科目とした。「理科課題研究」は、生徒自らが科学に関する課題を設定し、探究活動などで用いた探究の方法を活用して個人又はグループで研究を行わせ、科学的に探究する能力と態度を育てるとともに、論理的な思考力や判断力、表現力を養うことを意図した科目である。

（4）日本の理科教育の特徴

■①日本の理科教育の特徴として、観察、実験の重視が挙げられる。各学校段階の目標において「観察、実験などを行い」という表現が含まれており、また教科書にも学習内容に即した観察、実験活動が掲載されている。また、施設と設備面での充実にも力が入れられている。1953年の理科教育振興法の公布により、学校の設置者に対し、理科教育に必要な施設や設備の経費の2分の1が国から援助され、残りの2分の1が地方の都道府県および市町村が負担するようになっている。対象となる実験機械や器具、標本、模型などの項目は学習指導要領の改訂のたびに改定されて充実が図られ、現在、ほと

students' interest in science by letting them realize significance and effectiveness of learning science, and enhance scientific experiences and experiences in nature. The Course of Study was revised based on these ideas.

■ In science for upper secondary school, Science and Human Life was newly added. Science and Human Life is characterized by the following points: Learning how understanding of nature and development of science technologies affect our daily lives and society and what kind of role they played by observing familiar objects and phenomena and conduct experiments; nurturing scientific perspectives and notions; and raising interest in science as a result. Pure sciences such as physics, chemistry, biology, geosciences are divided into two subjects, eg. basic physics and physics. Students should take the basic subject first. Basic subjects are composed of more basic contents. Students conduct observation and experiments and learn basic notions and methods of inquiry in the basic subjects. Subjective studies which had been learned in the subject of academic fields changed to become a new subject, Study of Scientific Research for teachers to teach advanced science and interdisciplinary fields. The objectives of Study of Scientific Research are enabling students to set research themes related to science by themselves, or in groups using inquiry method with inquiry actives, and nurture ability and attitude to research scientifically as well as fostering logical thinking, abilities to judge and express.

(4) Features of Science Education in Japan

■ ① The main feature of Japan's science education is its focus on observation and experiments. The objectives of all school levels have an expression, "doing observation and experiments," and textbooks often encourage observation and experiments according to the Course of Study. Another feature of science education in Japan is its focus on improvement of facilities and equipment. According to the promulgation of the Science Education Promotion Act in 1953, half the cost for facilities and equipment necessary for science education is born by the national government, and the other half by local prefectural and municipal

んどの小、中、高、および盲、聾、養護学校に普及している。

②学習指導要領により、日本国内の理科で教える内容が統一されている。この結果、いかなる環境に児童や生徒が置かれていても、一定水準の理科教育は保障され、全国的に標準的な理科教育が可能となっている。

③理科授業に活用可能な教材が豊富に作られており、インターネットでも利用することで利用可能である。それらの教材には、映像の他に、アニメーション、図などがある。教材には、準備に手間がかかる実験、時間がかかる現象の観察、安全性の面から生徒に実験をさせない方がよい実験、科学的概念の動画での説明などがあり教育効果は高い。インターネット経由で利用できる教材の例として、科学技術振興機構による「理科ネットワーク (http://www.rikanet.jst.go.jp/)」や、「サイエンスチャンネル (http://sc-smn.jst.go.jp/)」がある。その他にも、様々な理科教科書会社、理科教材会社、都道府県教育センター、なども教材コンテンツを作成しており、授業への利用が可能となっている。このように多様な教材が作られている背景には、先に述べたように教育内容が日本国内で統一されており国内で統一して活用できる教材が開発可能なことに加え、国が公的資金で科学技術振興として開発を推進したこと挙げられる。しかし、実際に学校で活用されるか否かは、教室でこれらの教材を利用しやすい環境が整っているか、教師が十分に活用できるスキルがついているかに左右され、利用の程度は学校及び教師により差がある。

④文部科学省主導による理科教育振興がいくつかの方策により図られている。2002年度より科学技術・理科、数学教育を重点的に行う高等学校を「スーパーサイエンスハイスクール」として指定している。また、科学技術振興機構は、理科教員研修、小学校への理科支援員配置、学校等と大学・科学館等の連携促進などを行っている。

VII. The Characteristics of Courses 439

governments. The kinds of experimental machines and instruments, specimens and models that can receive financial support have been reviewed to improve education, every time the Course of Study was revised. Currently, most primary, lower secondary and upper secondary schools, and schools for disabled children have enough facilities and equipment, by receiving financial support.

② The Course of Study guarantees the contents of science, which should be commonly taught in Japan. Thus, wherever students live in Japan, they can always receive the standard level science education. It is possible for students to accept one kind of standard science education everywhere in the country.

③ A variety of teaching materials, which can be also obtained through the Internet, are prepared for science classes. Such materials are provided in the forms of movies, animation and images. They are highly effective in education because actual experiments and observation are often under various constraints: Experiments are troublesome for preparation, observation of phenomenon is time consuming, and students had better not to conduct experiments in some cases for safety reasons. Also, the explanation of scientific notions using movies is educationally effective. The Internet sites that provide teaching materials include the Science Network (http://www.rikanet.jst.go.jp/), and the Science Channel (http://sc-smn.jst.go.jp/)(organized by the Japan Science and Technology Agency.) Science textbook companies, science teaching material companies and prefectural governments' education centers also develop teaching material contents which are usable in classes at schools. In this way, various teaching materials are developed, which is possible because, as stated above, all schools in Japan provide common educational contents to students, it is possible to develop common teaching materials, and the government has financially supported the development of educational materials to promote science and technology. Whether or not these materials are effectively used in schools, however, depends on the school's environment and teachers' skills to use these materials. The Degree of those contents differs in each school or with each teacher.

④ Science education has been promoted using various approaches, under the

（5）日本の理科教育の問題
①小学校理科に関する問題
■小学校の1・2年生では理科が教科として教えられることがない。このため、小学校3学年以降に学ぶ理科とそれ以前の教育との接続が図れず、幼児から小学校低学年も含めた発達段階にあわせ、どのように子どもに科学的な考え方を養うのかに関しての実践と研究が乏しい。このことは、日本の理科教育者が、小学校低学年より教科として理科を教える世界の科学教育界と情報交換を困難にさせている。

　小学校は、教員が全教科を教えることが多い。小学校教員養成においては、一般に理科の科目が少ないため、小学校教員に理科を教える十分な知識技能が乏しい場合がある。子どもの頃からの理科好きを育てるため、小学校教員の理科指導に関する支援が必要とされている。

②中等教育段階での選択科目に関する問題
■高等学校では、必修科目は最低単位が4ないし6と少なく、多くの生徒に最低限必要となる共通の基礎的内容を身につけさせることを困難にする。また、大学受験に必要な科目のみに偏った履修は、幅広い理科の素養を身につけた研究者や技術者の育成という観点からも問題がある。最低限必要となる共通の基礎的内容をどのように身につけさせるかが問題である。

leadership of the Ministry of Education, Culture, Sports, Science and Technology. Since FY2002, upper secondary schools that specifically put emphasis on science technology, science and mathematics have been designated as Super Science High Schools. In addition, the Japan Science and Technology Agency (http://www.jst.go.jp/) has been conducting training of teachers, allocating assistant science teachers to primary schools, promoting collaboration between schools, colleges, and science museums.

(5) Problems of Japan's Science education
① Problems of science classes in primary school
■ Currently, science is not taught as a subject to the 1st and 2nd grade students of primary school. Therefore, there is minimal theoretical research and practice on how to develop scientific views of pre-school and lower-grade primary school students and how to provide a smooth connection to the science class for the 3rd grade primary school students. It is a problem for Japanese science educators who have difficulties in exchanging information on these issues, while most schools in the world provide science classes to the lower grade primary school students and progressively older students.

In primary schools the teachers usually teach all the subjects. As there are few science subjects in the teacher training college, some of them lack the knowledge and skills to suitably teach those subjects. In order to raise children being fond of science it is required to support the science teaching of primary school teachers.

② Elective subjects in secondary education
■ In upper secondary school, the minimum credit of compulsory subjects is only 4 or 6. This makes it difficult to provide students with common basic science knowledge which many students need. Moreover, some students may select only subjects required for university entrance examinations, which may lead to difficulty in fostering researchers and technologists who have a wide range of scientific basic knowledge. Enabling students to acquire the minimum common

③児童生徒の理科嫌いに関する問題
■国際教育到達度評価学会（IEA）の TIMSS 2003 の調査において、中学校2年生の理科の得点は6位とトップクラスであるのに対し、理科の勉強が楽しいとの回答は 59％であり他国に比べ非常に低い。理科の成績はよくても理科を楽しくない、嫌いという生徒が他国に比べて多いことが問題である。別の調査では、中学生の他教科との比較においては、好きという意見の多い順に、社会科 46.2％、理科 44.9％、英語 41.4％、国語 38％、数学 35.7％であり（小倉 2001）、他教科に比べ低くないとの結果もある。

④国際調査から指摘される問題
■PISA2006 の結果において、思考力・判断力・表現力等を問う読解力や記述式問題、知識・技能を活用する問題に課題が指摘されていることから、学習指導要領では思考力・判断力・表現力等の育成が強調された。それに対応し理科では、理科の観察・実験レポートの作成を行う学習活動が示された。また、PISA2006 の結果では理科の指導法に関して、「対話を重視した理科の授業」や「モデルの使用や応用を重視した理科の授業」などの教授学習活動が活発でない問題も指摘されている。

⑤授業時間数が少ない問題
■2008 年の学習指導要領改訂により表 7-5、表 7-6 に見る通り小学校および中学校における理科の授業時間数は、以前よりはある程度増加した。それでも 1980 − 1991 年間の時間数に戻った程度で 1971 − 1979 年間の時間数には及ばない。授業時間数が相対的に少ないことは問題であり、今後その増加が課題となっている。

basic science knowledge is an important issue.

③ Children who do not like science

■ According to research on science in TIMSS 2003 by the International Association for the Evaluation of Educational Achievement (IEA), the average score of the 2nd grade of lower secondary school students in Japan was ranked 6th in the world, which was at the top level. In contrast, the ratio of who like studying science was 59%, which was significantly lower than that of other countries. It is a problem that many Japanese students do not like science even though they have better academic scores in science compared with students in other countries. Meanwhile, another survey shows that 46.2% lower secondary school students in Japan like social studies (shakai), 44.9% like science (Rika), 41.4% like English, 38% like Japanese language (kokugo), and 35.7% like mathematics (Ogura, 2001).

④ Results of international assessment

■ According to the assessment result of PISA 2006, Japanese students were weak in reading comprehension and answering written questions, which aim to evaluate abilities of thinking, decision making and expressing, and application of knowledge and skills. Due to this, nurturing of abilities of thinking, decision making and expressing was emphasized in the Course of Study. With regard to science in the Course of Study, learning activities to write reports on observation and experiment were listed. PISA2006 assessment also pointed out that schools were not active in teaching/learning activities such as "discussion, using models and emphasizing application".

⑤ Few class hours

■ As seen in Table 7-5 and 7-6, the class hours of science after 2010 have increased, influenced by the revision of the Course of Study in 2008. However, the class hours after 2011 become similar to those during 1980-1991 but still fewer than those during 1971-1979. It is a problem that the class hours are few and it is an important issue to increase the class hours in the future.

表7-5 小学校理科の年間授業時数の変遷
（1単位時間：45分、割合の計算は、1970年代を100とした）

	1学年	2学年	3学年	4学年	5学年	6学年	合計	割合
1971-1979	68	70	105	105	140	140	628	100
1980-1991	68	70	105	105	105	105	558	89
1992-2001	0	0	105	105	105	105	420	67
2002-2010	0	0	70	90	95	95	350	56
2011-	0	0	90	105	105	105	405	64

表7-6 中学校理科（必修科目）の年間授業時数の変遷
（1単位時間：50分、割合の計算は、1970年代を100とした）

	1学年	2学年	3学年	合計	割合
1972-1979	140	140	140	420	100
1980-1991	105	105	140	350	83
1992-2001	105	105	105-140	315-350	75-83
2002-2011	105	105	80	290	69
2012-	105	140	140	385	92

出典　文部省、文部科学省『小学校学習指導要領』（1971年～2008年）
　文部省、文部科学省『中学校学習指導要領』（1972年～2008年）
（引用文献）
文部科学省『小学校学習指導要領』2008年a
文部科学省『中学校学習指導要領』2008年b
文部科学省『高等学校学習指導要領』2009年
2001、小倉　康、『理科学習の重要性に関する中学生の意識の実態』、国立教育政策研究所

Table 7-5 Change in annual class hours of Science in primary schools
(The class period of primary school is 45 minutes. The ratios of class hours are calculated with the class-hour ratio of 100 representing the 1970s.)

	1st Grade	2nd Grade	3rd Grade	4th Grade	5th Grade	6th Grade	Summary	Ratio
1971 - 1979	68	70	105	105	140	140	628	100
1980 - 1991	68	70	105	105	105	105	558	89
1992 - 2001	0	0	105	105	105	105	420	67
2002 - 2010	0	0	70	90	95	95	350	56
2011 -	0	0	90	105	105	105	405	64

Table 7-6 Change in annual class hours of Science in lower secondary schools
(The class period of primary school is 50 minutes.
The ratios of class hours are calculated with the class-hour ratio of 100 representing the 1970s.)

	1st Grade	2nd Grade	3rd Grade	Summary	Ratio
1972 - 1979	140	140	140	420	100
1980 - 1991	105	105	140	350	83
1992 - 2001	105	105	105 - 140	315 - 350	75 - 83
2002 - 2011	105	105	80	290	69
2012 -	105	140	140	385	92

(References)
· Ministry of Education, and Ministry of Education, Culture, Sports, Science and Technology, "Course of Study of Primary Schools" (1971 - 2008)
· Ministry of Education, and Ministry of Education, Culture, Sports, Science and Technology, "Course of Study of Lower Secondary Schools" (1972 - 2008)
· Ministry of Education, Culture, Sports, Science and Technology, "Course of Study of Primary School", 2008a,
· Ministry of Education, Culture, Sports, Science and Technology, "Course of Study of Lower Secondary School" 2008b,
· Ministry of Education, Culture, Sports, Science and Technology, "Course of Study of Upper Secondary School" 2009
· Yasushi Ogura, "Field survey on lower secondary school students' awareness of importance on science", National Institute for Educational Policy Research, 2001

5. 生活

■「生活」は小学校第1学年と第2学年に設けられている教科であり、「生活科」とも呼ばれている。授業時数は第1学年が1年間に102時間、第2学年が105時間であり、1週当たり3時間の時間配当になっている。

■生活科の目標は、具体的な活動や体験を通して、自分と身近な人々、社会及び自然とのかかわりに関心をもち、自分自身や自分の生活について考えさせるとともに、その過程において生活上必要な習慣や技能を身に付けさせ、自立への基礎を養うことに置かれている。

■生活科の授業で取り上げられている学習活動の内容は、(1) 学校と生活、(2) 家庭と生活、(3) 地域と生活、(4) 公共物や公共施設の利用、(5) 季節の変化と生活、(6) 自然や物を使った遊び、(7) 動植物の飼育・栽培、(8) 身近な人々や地域との交流、(9) 自分の成長などである。いずれも、児童の生活の内容や身近にあるものであり、それらを対象あるいは場として、体験的に学ばせるところに、教育活動としての生活科の特色がある。

■生活科の目標とされている「自立への基礎」とは、具体的に言うと、(1) 学校という集団生活の場に初めて入った児童が集団や社会の一員として集団生活ができるようになること、(2) 自分でできることは自分でするようになること、(3) 自分の思いや考えを適切な方法で表現できるようになること、(4) 自分のよさや可能性に気付き、自信や意欲をもって自分自身のあり方を一層強化することができるという精神的自立へと向かうことなどを指している。

■生活科は1989年の小学校学習指導要領の改訂によって創設され、1992年4月からすべての小学校で実施された。生活科の創設に伴って従前から小学校低学年に設けられていた社会科と理科は廃止された。そのため、創設の当

5. Life Environment Studies

■ Life Environment Studies is a subject for the first and second grades of primary school. The first grade of primary school has 102 class hours per year and the second grade has 105 class hours. Both grades have three class hours per week.

■ The purposes of Life Environment Studies is to raise interest in the relations with oneself and people around oneself, society and nature through specific activities and experiences; to look back on oneself and one's lifestyle; and to learn customs and skills required in life to achieve self-sustainability.

■ The learning contents of Life Environment Studies include (1) school and lifestyle, (2) home and lifestyle, (3) community and lifestyle, (4) use of public objects and facilities, (5) seasonal change and lifestyle, (6) play using natural and artificial objects, (7) looking after animals and plants, (8) communications with people around oneself and people in one's community, (9) development of oneself. All these items are closely related to students' lives. Learning of or in the lives of students through experiences is the educational feature of Life Environment Studies.

■ Self-sustainability, a purpose of Life Environment Studies, means that students, who first experience a group life in school, become able to (1) harmonize with others in a group or society, (2) take care of themselves, (3) express their thoughts and feelings using appropriate means, (4) achieve emotional autonomy through the notice of their own strong points and possibilities, and building of confidence and motivation.

■ The subject of Life Environment Studies was established in 1989 according to the revised Corse of Study for Primary School, and has been taught in all primary schools since April 1992. After the establishment of the subject of Life

初から、生活科と社会科あるいは理科との関係のあり方が問題点として指摘されていた。第３学年から実施される教科の学習（社会科と理科）への円滑な接続を可能にする指導のあり方を明らかにすることが課題となっている。また、幼児教育から小学校教育への円滑な接続を図るという観点から生活科の指導のあり方を探求することも課題となっている。

■生活科は、小学校低学年児童の発達的特色である思考と活動の未分化性に対応した教育活動として重要な役割を果たしており、その充実を図るために大きな努力が払われている。

休み時間　Free Time Play

Ⅶ. The Characteristics of Courses 449

Environment Studies, the social and science subjects established for lower grades of primary school was abolished. Thus, the relations between Life Environment Studies, and social and science subjects have been a controversial issue since the establishment of the subject of Life Environment Studies. It is necessary to clarify a smooth transition from Life Environment Studies for the first and second grades to social and science subjects starting to be taught to the third grade. It is also important to consider how to instruct Life Environment Studies to achieve smooth transition from pre-school to primary school.

■ The subject of Life Environment Studies plays an important role in dealing with the developmental characteristics, that is, unseparated thoughts and actions, of lower-grade primary school students. Significant efforts have been made to enhance the Life Environment Studies class.

子どもを見守る先生　Supervised Play

6. 芸術

■学校教育における芸術教育は、小学校では音楽科、図画工作科の2教科、中学校では音楽科、美術科の2教科、高等学校では、教科「芸術」として音楽科、美術科、工芸、書道が設けられている。なお、高等学校では、上掲の教科・科目の他に、「主として専門学科において開設される各教科・科目」として音楽科、美術科の2教科が設けられている。

■高等学校学習指導要領に示されている教科「芸術」の目標は、「芸術の幅広い活動を通して、生涯にわたり芸術を愛好する心情を育てるとともに、感性を高め、芸術の諸能力を伸ばし、芸術文化について理解を深め、豊かな情操を養う。」とされる。すなわち、芸術教育は、人生を豊かにするとともに、日本や世界の芸術文化を理解し、尊重する態度や芸術的な感性と情操をそなえた豊かな人間を形成することを目指して行われている。

■標準授業時数は、次のとおりである。
　小学校の音楽と図画工作は、第1学年：68時間、第2学年：70時間、第3学年：60時間、第4学年：60時間、第5学年：50時間、第6学年：50時間となっている。中学校の音楽と美術についてはそれぞれ、第1学年：45時間、第2学年：35時間、第3学年35時間となっている。高等学校の「芸術」については、「音楽Ⅰ」（2単位）、「美術Ⅰ」（2単位）、「工芸Ⅰ」（2単位）、「書道Ⅰ」（2単位）のうちから1科目（2単位）をすべての生徒に必ず履修させること（「必履修」と呼ぶ）になっている。

（1）音楽
■日本の学校における音楽科教育は、小学校と中学校では必修教科として、すべての子どもが学ぶものとして位置づけられている。また、高等学校では、芸術教科の中から一つ履修する選択必修教科として位置づけられている。内

6. Arts

■ In Arts Education at school there are two subjects, music and drawing / handicraft in primary school. Also, two subjects, music and fine arts in lower secondary school, and arts subjects, music, fine arts, industrial arts and calligraphy are in upper secondary school. In specialized course of upper secondary school students can learn a music subject and a fine arts subject as special subjects in addition to the subjects mentioned above.

■ The purpose of the arts subjects described in the Course of Study at upper secondary school is to nurture the students' feeling for loving art in their whole life, cultivate their sensitivity, develop their various abilities of arts, deepen their understanding of art and culture, and develop their high sentiments. In other words the arts education aims at enabling a student's life to be rich and forming nice people who understand and respect art and culture in Japan and the world and have artistic sensitivities and keen sentiments.

■ The standard school hours are as follows:

Those of music and drawing/handicraft in primary school are 68 hours in 1st grade, 70 hours in 2nd grade, 60 hours in 3rd grade, 60 hours in 4th grade, 50 hours in 5th grade, and 50 hours in 6th grade. Those of music and fine arts in lower secondary school are 45 hours in 1st year, 35 hours in 2nd year, and 35 hours in 3rd year. Regarding the Arts provided in upper secondary school, all the students have to select one subject from "Music I" (two units), "Fine Arts I" (two units), "Industrial Arts I" (two units) and "Calligraphy I" (two units).

(1) Music

■ Because music education is considered important for all children, "General Music" is a mandatory subject in Japanese primary and lower secondary schools. In upper secondary schools, music is an elective arts class. Chorus, band, and

容は、歌唱、器楽、創作、鑑賞の諸領域にわたるものとなっており、一つの演奏領域(合唱やオーケストラなど)に集中する形ではない。ブラスバンド、オーケストラなどは、課外活動のクラブとして行われることが多い。

■学習指導要領は、各学校段階、学年段階の目標や内容のスタンダードを示し、特に小学校や中学校では「共通教材」という学年毎の必修歌唱教材まで細かく規定しようとしているのが特徴的である。しかし、教科の特性として、学校毎に実践されるカリキュラムには幅があり、また学校行事の一環としての合唱祭や文化祭などとの連携の仕方によっても、実施内容は学校によって違ってくる。

① 小学校の音楽

■小学校の音楽は、歴史的には1872年の学制公布時から、「唱歌」という名称で設置されていた。しかし、当初は適切な教材と教育人材が得られないということから、現在の東京芸術大学の前身である音楽取調掛(おんがくとりしらべかかり)をつくり、米国の音楽教育法にも学びながら、東西二様の音楽を折衷して新しい音楽を作り、また音楽教師を育てて全国の学校で音楽教育を実施しようとした。しかしこうした経緯から、かえって日本の音楽の伝統を教育内容として取り入れることができず、結果として西洋音楽への著しい偏りが生じた。また、唱歌の歌詞を通して徳性を涵養しようとする教育が行われた。

■第二次世界大戦後は、戦前の唱歌教育の反省から、音楽科教育の目的は「美的情操の教育」と捉えられるようになった。さらに、音楽を愛好する心情を育てることや、音楽に対する感性を育てることも目標として加えられた。

orchestra are also extracurricular activities in public schools.

■ The Course of Study establishes the objectives and content of music instruction, even stipulating some songs as the "common materials" for each grade, of primary shcool and lower secondary school. These are called the "Common Song Teaching Materials."

Nonetheless, each school enjoys a certain degree of flexibility in music instruction. Provided the content conforms to Course of Study requirements, each school can develop a program that meets the needs of its students and accommodates their musical abilities and interests through the chorus and cultural festival as school events.

① Music in Primary Schools

■ The tradition of music in primary schools dates to the Education System Order of 1872. However, due to a lack of teachers and songs appropriate for school teaching, a new institute for music education first had to be founded. Namely, the Ongaku Torishirabe Gakari, a former institute of Tokyo Arts University, aimed at establishing an eclectic new music that comprised elements of both Eastern and Western music to develop repertoires of songs for use as teaching materials. Learning from school music education in the USA, its goal was to establish a music education curriculum and to train music teachers to promote music education. However, it failed to make use of Japanese musical traditions, and a bias toward Western music resulted. Moreover, music education was aimed at the moral development of students through the song lyrics chosen.

■ After World War II, the basic aim of music education was reconsidered to be that of cultivating aesthetic sentiments, based on reflection on pre-war educational history. Currently, music education goals also include the development of a love of music and increased appreciation of music, so that

■多くの場合授業で中心となるのは、クラスでの集合的表現を可能にする歌唱であり、合唱表現を工夫し、クラス全体で響きを楽しみながら歌うことがめざされる。さらに器楽による副旋律やリズムの工夫を行ったり、小グループでアンサンブル表現をつくりあげて互いに聴き会う活動をとおして、子どもたち自らの表現活動を作り上げる授業も行われる。

■しかし音楽科教育の授業時間数は減少の傾向にある。戦後すぐの学習指導要領では小学校高学年で週に2～3時間あった標準授業時数が、今日では1.5時間にまで減らされていることは、現場の指導における困難の主因となっている。

■器楽は、低学年ではリズム打楽器のほかハーモニカ、鍵盤ハーモニカが用いられ、中学年からはソプラノリコーダー（縦笛）が用いられる。最終的には子どもたちはその学年で歌う曲程度の旋律がリコーダーで演奏できる力がつくことがめざされる。

■日本の伝統音楽は、戦後の学習指導要領においても、はじめは取り上げられていなかったが、近年になってその重要性が意識されるようになってきた。また、世界の民族音楽も取り上げられる。「総合的な学習の時間」において、多文化共生教育ともリンクしながら展開させる事例も増えている。

■また、既成の表現様式にとらわれず「つくって表現する」活動は、1989年の学習指導要領から取り入れられ、徐々に広まってきた。身の周りの音に耳を澄ませたり、口笛や手拍子、足拍子など身体の音で表現したり、身近な音素材を選んで即興的に表現したり、図形楽譜としてより自由な視覚的表現を用いたりして、構成的活動が行われる。

■2008年の学習指導要領の改訂により、「共通事項」が示され、「音色、リズム、速度、旋律、強弱、音の重なりや和声の響き、音階や調、拍の流れやフレーズなどの音楽を特徴付けている要素」を聴き取ることと、「反復、問いと答え、変化（音楽の縦と横の関係）などの音楽の仕組み」を聴き取ることによって、「そ

students realize that music education is a lifelong endeavor.

■ Singing is the main focus of music education repertoires, allowing students to enjoy collective expressive activities. Various chorus repertoires enable students to enjoy harmony and the singing of their fellows. Students also have the opportunity to play instruments in small ensemble groups and to devise rhythmic instrumental accompaniments. By listening to one another's performances, students nurture their own musical expression.

■ Recently, however, the standard time for music education has tended to be reduced to 1.5 hours a week in the upper grades of primary schools though there were 2~3 hours in The Course of Study after WWⅡ, and teaching music has become more difficult.

■ First graders are introduced to simple instruments, such as rhythm instruments or keyboard harmonica, and third graders learn to play the soprano recorder. Eventually, many students become skilled at playing selected songs on the recorder.

■ The importance of Japanese traditional music is increasingly emphasized in educational materials, as is world ethnic music. Because the nature of music transcends language, music education offers opportunities to develop children's understanding of the diversity of cultures as part of an integrated framework of multicultural education.

■ Increasingly, "creative music making" has become a recommended learning activity according to the Course of Study revised in 1989. It encourages children to listen to sounds around them and to experience and express sound using household objects or their bodies as instruments, for example by whistling, hand clapping, or foot tapping. Children enjoy this activity, as they can see their imaginations take shape in musical form.

■ In 2008, "common items for each activity" were introduced in both the primary and secondary music education course of study. It includes timbre, rhythm, tempo, melody, dynamics, vertical relationships of pitches or harmony, beat and phrase, which are the elements that characterize music. Musical

れらの働きが生み出すよさや面白さ、美しさを感じとるということ」が、演奏や鑑賞における教育課題として意識されるようになった。

② 中学校・高等学校における音楽科教育
■中学校の授業時数は、1年生では 1.3 時間、2・3年生では週1時間となった。高等学校では、芸術科目として美術や工芸、書道、音楽から一つを選択することになっていて、2単位が必履修となっている。

■中学校段階では、器楽にアルトリコーダーを用いる他、1998 年の学習指導要領以来、全員が必ず一つ以上の和楽器を経験することが必須となった。各学校ごとに和太鼓や箏や三味線などから選んで、生徒が演奏をとおして伝統音楽を理解するように工夫している。また 2008 年からは、伝統的な歌唱の指導も重視されるようになった。
■音楽教育の目標の一つとして、2008 年からは、音楽文化についての理解を深めることが含まれるようになった。また、音や音楽と社会生活のかかわりも、教育内容に含まれるようになった。音環境への関心を深める他、音楽に関する知的財産権などについての理解をもち、著作物等を尊重する態度を育てることも、音楽科における教育課題となっている。
■音楽関係のクラブ活動も盛んで、それらの活動とも関連させた特色のある授業を行い成果を上げている学校もある。合唱祭など、学校行事におけるクラス単位の演奏も、音楽科の授業を基盤として行われている。2部合唱から混声4部合唱まで様々な形態が可能であり、また器楽合奏も含めると各学校によって実践の様相は大きく異なるが、仲間と共に演奏表現を作り上げる経験を持つことは、思春期の生徒の学校生活において他に代え難い意義をもつ。

structures, such as repetition, call and response, and changes in vertical and horizontal tonal relationships and texture, are also expected to be learned.

② Music Education in the Lower and Upper Secondary Schools

■ In the first year of lower secondary school, students receive about 1.3 class hours of music instruction per week. In the second and third years, this is reduced to only 1 hour a week. In upper secondary school, music is provided as an elective subject. Students must choose one course from among fine arts, craft production, calligraphy or music and must earn two credits of art education.

■ Among musical instruments, the alto recorder is introduced in lower secondary school. The 1998 revision of the course of study required all lower secondary students to experience a traditional Japanese instrument, e.g., traditional drums or string instruments such as the koto or shamisen. Traditional singing was also introduced in 2008.

■ In 2008, an understanding of musical culture was added as a goal of music education. The relationship between music and society, understanding of and interest in sound environments, understanding of intellectual property issues in music and forming attitude to respect books and materials related to music are also being added to music curricula.

■ Some schools also provide extracurricular music classes in conjunction with after-school club activities. In addition, music instruction is conducted in conjunction with certain school events, such as chorus festivals and instrumental ensembles. Although the quality of musical activities varies from school to school, e.g., from two-part choruses to mixed four-part choruses or elaborate instrumental ensembles, students gain significant experience in performing with their peers through these activities. They develop meaningful relationships with one another, and their accomplishments add significance to their school life.

＜資料：小・中学校の歌唱共通教材＞

小学校の歌唱共通教材

〔第1学年〕

　「うみ」　　　　　　　　（文部省唱歌）　林　柳波作詞　　井上武士作曲

　「かたつむり」　　　　　（文部省唱歌）

　「日のまる」　　　　　　（文部省唱歌）　高野辰之作詞　岡野貞一作曲

　「ひらいたひらいた」　　（わらべうた）

〔第2学年〕

　「かくれんぼ」　　　　　（文部省唱歌）　林　柳波作詞　　下総皖一作曲

　「春がきた」　　　　　　（文部省唱歌）　高野辰之作詞　岡野貞一作曲

　「虫のこえ」　　　　　　（文部省唱歌）

　「夕やけこやけ」　　　　中村雨紅作詞　　草川信作曲

〔第3学年〕

　「うさぎ」　　　　　　　（日本古謡）

　「茶つみ」　　　　　　　（文部省唱歌）

　「春の小川」　　　　　　（文部省唱歌）　高野辰之作詞　岡野貞一作曲

　「ふじ山」　　　　　　　（文部省唱歌）　巌谷小波作詞

〔第4学年〕

　「さくらさくら」　　　　（日本古謡）

　「とんび」　　　　　　　葛原しげる作詞　梁田貞作曲

　「まきばの朝」　　　　　（文部省唱歌）　船橋栄吉作曲

　「もみじ」　　　　　　　（文部省唱歌）　高野辰之作詞　岡野貞一作曲

〔第5学年〕

　「こいのぼり」　　　　　（文部省唱歌）

　「子もり歌」　　　　　　（日本古謡）

　「スキーの歌」　　　　　（文部省唱歌）　林　柳波作詞　　橋本国彦作曲

　「冬げしき」　　　　　　（文部省唱歌）

〔第6学年〕

　「越天楽今様（歌詞は第2節まで）」　　（日本古謡）

　「おぼろ月夜」　　　　　（文部省唱歌）　高野辰之作詞　岡野貞一作曲

<appendix: Common Singing Materials in Primary School and Lower Secondary School>
Common Singing Materials in Primary School
[Grade 1]
  Umi (A Sea), Monbushō-shōka (a song copyrighted by Ministry of Education) (melody by Takeshi Inoue, lyrics by Ryuha Hayashi)
  Katatsumuri (A Snail), Monbushō-shōka
  Hi no maru (Rising Sun), Monbushō-shōka (melody by Okano Teiichi, lyrics by Tatsuyuki Takano)
  Hiraita, Hiraita (bloomed-bloomed), Warabe-uta (Children's traditional play song)
[Grade 2]
  Kakurenbo (Hide-and-Seek), Monbushō-shōka (melody by Kanichi Shimofusa, lyrics by Ryuha Hayashi)
  Haru ga kita (Spring has come), Monbushō-shōka (melody by Okano Teiichi, lyrics by Tatsuyuki Takano)
  Mushi no Koe (Sound of insects), Monbushō-shōka
  Yuyake, Koyake (A sunset glow), (melody by Shin Kusakawa, lyrics by Kou Nakamura)
[Grade 3]
  Usagi (A rabbit), Traditional Japanese Song
  Chatsumi (Tea picker's song), Monbushō-shōka
  Haru no Ogawa (A brook in spring), Monbushō-shōka (melody by Teiichi Okano, lyrics by Tatsuyuki Takano)
  Fujisan (Mt. Fuji), Monbushō-shōka (lyrics by Sazanami Iwaya)
[Grade 4]
  Sakura Sakura (Cherry Blossoms), Traditional Japanese Song
  Tonbi (A Black Kite), (melody by Tadashi Yanada, lyrics by Shigeru Kuzuhara)
  Makiba no Asa (A Pasture Mornig), Monbushō-shōka (melody by Eikichi

「ふるさと」　　　　　（文部省唱歌）　高野辰之(たかのたつゆき)作詞　岡野貞一(おかのていいち)作曲
「われは海の子（歌詞は第3節まで）」　（文部省唱歌）

中学校の歌唱共通教材
　　（各学年ごとに1曲以上を含める）

「赤とんぼ」　　　三木露風(みきろふう)作詞　　山田耕筰(やまだこうさく)作曲
「荒城の月」　　　土井晩翠(どいばんすい)作詞　　滝廉太郎(たきれんたろう)作曲
「早春賦」　　　　吉丸一昌(よしまるかずまさ)作詞　　中田　章(なかだあきら)作曲
「夏の思い出」　　江間章子(えましょうこ)作詞　　中田喜直(なかだよしなお)作曲
「花」　　　　　　武島羽衣(たけしまはごろも)作詞　　滝廉太郎(たきれんたろう)作曲
「花の街」　　　　江間章子(えましょうこ)作詞　　團伊玖磨(だんいくま)作曲
「浜辺の歌」　　　林　古渓(はやしこけい)作詞　　成田為三(なりたためぞう)作曲

Funabashi)
Momiji (A Maple), Monbushō-shōka (melody by Tei ichi Okano, lyrics by Tatsuyuki Takano)
[Grade 5]
Koinobori (A Carp Streamer), Monbushō-shōka
Komoriuta (A Cradle Song), Traditional Japanese Song
Ski no Uta (A Skiing Song), Monbushō-shōka
 (melody by Kunihiko Hashimoto, lyrics by Ryuha Hayashi)
Fuyu-geshiki (A Winter Scene), Monbushō-shōka
[Grade 6]
Etenraku-Imayo (Etenraku-Imayo) (as far as the second verse of the lyrics), Traditional Japanese Song
Oborozukikyo (A Night with a Hazy Moon), Monbushō-shōka (melody by Teiichi Okano, lyrics by Tatsuyuki Takano)
Furusato (The Home Country), Monbushō-shōka (melody by Teiichi Okano, lyrics by Tatsuyuki Takano)
Ware wa Uminoko (Born by the Sea) (as far as the third verse of the lyrics), Monbushō-shōka

Common Singing Materials in lower secondary school
 Akatonbo (A Red Dragonfly), (melody by Kosaku Yamada, lyrics by Rofu Miki)
 Kojo no Tsuki (A Moon at a Ruined Castle), (melody by Rentaro Taki, lyrics by Bansui Doi)
 Soshunfu (An Early Spring), (melody by Akira Nakada, lyrics by Kazumasa Yoshimaru)
 Natsu no Omoide (Memory of the Summer), (melody by Yoshinao Nakada, lyrics by Shoko Ema)
 Hana (Blossoms), (melody by Rentaro Taki, lyrics by Hagoromo Takeshima)
 Hana no Machi (A Town of Flowers), (melody of Ikuma Dan, lyrics by Shoko

（2）図画工作・美術・工芸

■第2次世界大戦後の美術・工芸教育は表現と鑑賞を領域の二本柱とし、表現領域は絵画・彫塑・デザイン・工芸などの既存の文化財項目と造形遊び（材料や場をもとにした総合的造形活動）の項目から編成されている。鑑賞は表現活動を支え、表現学習と表裏一体の関係として位置づけられている。

■現行の美術・工芸教育は、幼稚園・小学校・中学校・高等学校の一貫教育としてカリキュラム編成や教科書作成がなされ、全国的に指導されている。

■教科の目標においては、小学校では「表現及び鑑賞の活動を通して、感性を働かせながら、造形的な創造活動の基礎を培う」こと、中学校では、「表現及び鑑賞の活動を通して、感性を豊かにし美術の基礎的な能力を伸ばす」こと、高等学校の「美術Ⅰ」では「美術の創造活動を通して、感性を高め、表現と鑑賞の能力をのばす」こととなっている。

■このように日本の美術・工芸教育は、表現と鑑賞の活動を通して造形的な創造活動の基礎を培うと同時に創造の喜びを味わわせ、美術を愛好する心情を育て、豊かな情操を養うことを教科のねらいとしている。また、特に「感性の育成」こそが「生きる力」の根幹であり、生活や社会と豊かに関わるコミュニケーション能力を培うことと位置づけている。そして幼児、児童、生徒の発達段階も充分に考慮した目標の一貫性も図られている。

■指導の時間数については、小学校第1学年及び第2学年で週2時間が補償されるほかは、第3学年～第6学年では週2時間の確保は難しく、中学校に

Ema)
Hamabe no Uta (A Seashore Song), (melody of Tamezo Narita, lyrics by Kokei Hayashi)

(2) Arts and Handicrafts, Fine Arts and Craft Production

■ Education of fine arts and craft production after World War II has focused on both expression and appreciation. In the area of expression, students are able to work in the areas of item of cultural asset, for example, painting, carving and modeling, designing, and industrial art activities, and item of molding play (comprehensive playing activity based on materials and places). Also, as part of their formative education, students learn to appreciate art through these activities.

■ The curriculum and textbooks for fine and technical arts are uniform throughout the country from kindergarten through primary and lower secondary schools, and up to upper secondary schools.

■ The objectives of arts education are as follows: the primary school level objective is to develop the basis of creative molding activity through expression and appreciation with sensitivity. In lower secondary schools the focus is to allow the students to have sensitivity and develop fundamental ability of art through expression and appreciation. In upper secondary schools, students are able to further develop their sensitivity and expressive and appreciative abilities through creative activities of fine arts.

■ Thus, fine and technical arts education in Japan aims to develop students formative creativity, to make them feel the joy of creative activities, to develop a positive attitude toward arts, and to enhance their aesthetic sensitivity, through various activities of expression and appreciation. And "developing sensitivity" is the basis of the "zest for living" and developing communication skills. Those objects are considered to be suitable for students' developmental stages and to have a character of consistency.

■ The hours of instruction for art are two hours per week for the first and second grade of primary schools. But it is difficult to secure two hours per week

おいては週1時間である。表現領域で指導の偏向をきたさないよう配慮されてはいるものの、小学校においては題材の精選や教材の工夫が強く求められ、中学校では内容の一部を重点的に扱うことも認められている。このことは高等学校での指導内容の取り扱いにも見受けられる。
■実習教科として材料・用具の準備、構想、技法、後片付け、安全指導の面から一学級の児童生徒数を減らす、工芸関係の教員養成や施設を充実させる、また、抜本的に授業時間数の増加を図ることなどが強く望まれる。

①小学校における図画工作
■学習指導要領の目標には「表現及び鑑賞の活動を通して、感性を働かせながら、つくりだす喜びを味わうようにするとともに、造形的な創造活動の基礎的な能力を培い、豊かな情操を養う」とあり、子どもが自ら感じ取り、思いや考えを心の中につくりだし、それを色や形につくりだす喜び味わうことに力点がおかれている。
■内容は大きく表現領域と鑑賞領域とからなり、表現領域は「造形遊び」と「表したいことを絵や立体、工作に表す活動」の二つの項目から構成されている。

■低学年（第1学年及び第2学年）では、材料経験を中心とした総合造形としての造形遊び、クレヨンやパスを使っての絵や紙版画、紙、土や粘土などの可塑材による立体表現、簡単な生活を楽しくするものや飾るもの、想像したものをつくる表現活動が行われる。

■中学年（第3学年及び第4学年）は、造形遊びが材料からだけでなく場所などの特徴からも発想してつくる活動として展開する。絵や立体に表わす活動では、観察と想像の両面から素描、水彩、版画による表現や、素材が木切れや板材など加工に抵抗のあるものにも広がり、多様になる。工作に表わす活動では、見通しをもって計画を立てて作ることが行われ、機構的な作品の製作のために工具類の基本的な扱い方が指導される。

for the third – sixth grade of primary school. There is one hour per week for secondary school. In primary school, teachers are required to select subjects and teaching materials. Teachers are allowed to focus on certain topics in lower secondary school. These apply to secondary school.

■ An effort is being undertaken to reduce the class size in order to improve preparing materials and tools, conception, skill, clarity and safety, to improve the teacher training programs and facilities related to technical arts, and to drastically increase the teaching hours.

① Arts and Handicrafts in Primary School

■ The aim of arts and handicrafts in primary schools is set forth in the Course of Study as follows, "through expression and appreciation students enjoy making works with sensitivity and developing basic ability of creative activity and rich aesthetic sensitivity". The point is that students feel, think, and express that as color and shape.

■ The contents consist of both expression and appreciation areas. The expression area consists of molding play and expressing what they want to express as picture, cube and handiwork.

■ In the first and second grades students are allowed to take part in molding play using art materials. They make drawings and paper prints with crayons and pastels. They also can make objects of solid expression from paper, soil, clay, simple objects to make their life pleasant, ornaments, and objects which they have imagined.

■ In the third and fourth grades students learn molding play and enrich it using art materials and getting ideas from playing places. In painting and plastic art, students learn a way of expression making sketches, water color printing and wood prints by way of both observation and imagination of an object. Arts materials include different ones such as pieces of board which is difficult to make in the stage process. In expression activities by plastic art, students are required to have plans for making works and are taught how to use tools to make systematic work.

■高学年（第5学年及び第6学年）になると、造形遊びは、材料とともに周囲の環境や現象にも働きながら、また働き返される連続性のなかで捉えて行われる。絵や立体、工作の表現も、これまでの学年で学習した知識や技法を有機的に関連付けて、より総合的に働かせ発展させる内容となっている。
■鑑賞は身近なものや自他の作品から、自然美、造形美を主体的に発見する喜びを味わうとともに、自分の思いを語り伝え合うことを通して感じとる力、思考する力を育成する。また、美術文化の継承と創造への関心を高め、我が国の美術や文化に関する指導の充実が図られる。

②中学校における美術
■指導要領に示された目標は、小学校とほぼ同じ内容であり、指導の一貫性がとられている。

■中学校における内容も、表現領域と鑑賞領域からなる。表現領域は心象表現（絵や彫刻）や機能表現（デザインや工芸）活動を通した「発想や構想」に関する項目と、表現の「技能」に関する項目とに分けて示され、柔軟な発想力と技能がよく関連して働くよう配慮されている。
■絵は、観察と想像の両面から素描、水彩、版画などの表現手段を用いて制作を行うことが多い。また彫刻では粘土や石膏を素材とする塑像と木や軟石などを扱った彫造の制作などが行われる。これらの制作を通して造形の要素や原理がもたらす性質や感情を理解し、主体的、個性的、効果的な造形表現ができるように指導される。デザインや工芸の学習では、色や形の構成練習、身近な環境を美しくデザインする学習、木や竹、金属、樹脂、焼成用粘土などを用いた用途性の高い作品が制作される。また、新たな表現の可能性を広げるために、漫画やアニメーションなどの表現形式、写真、ビデオ、コンピュータなどの映像メディアも積極的に活用されている。色や形や素材ばかりでなく光や運動なども含めたビジュアル・コミュニケーションを通して、生活、社会や自然と豊かに関わる態度をはぐくみ、生活を美しく豊かにする

■ In the fifth and sixth grades molding play is conducted as an activity which has interaction between a student and art materials, environment and a phenomenon. In painting and plastic art, students learn how to develop existing knowledge and skills activity comprehensively.
■ Students are taught how to appreciate natural and creative beauty in things around them and from their own works and other's works and how to develop ability of feeling and ability in thinking through communication. Through appreciation, students become interested in a succession and creation of art culture and learn art and culture from our country.

② Fine Arts in Lower Secondary Schools
■ Pursuant to the official Course of Study, the goal of art education in lower secondary schools is almost the same as it is in primary schools. This helps to maintain a consistency of teaching methods in art from primary to secondary education.
■ Content consists of a field of expression and a field of appreciation. A field of expression consists of "an idea and a conception" and "skill". Attention is paid to develop both of them.

■ Pictorial art is taught through sketches, water colors, and wood block prints, by way of both observation and imagination of an object. In the sculpture component, students use both plastic forms using clay or gypsum and wood carving or soft stones. The aim here is to provide students with understanding about nature and a feeling which comes from an element and a principle of molding, and to enable students to express independently, individualistically and effectively. In design and craft production, composition of color and figure, designing environment around us beautifully, making useful products made of wood, bamboo, metal, resin, and clay are conducted. Expression from such mediums as cartoon and animated cartoon and image media such as picture and video are used actively to widen possibility of expression. Through the study of

造形や美術の働きを実感させることをねらいとしている。

■鑑賞は自然美、造形美を対象に主体的に行い、よさや美しさを感じる喜びを味わい批評しあうことで、自分なりの意味や価値をつくりだしていくことをねらいとしている。また、日本の美術や文化に関する学習が重視され、文化遺産の保護や国際理解の役割も求められている。

③高等学校における美術・工芸
■高等学校の美術科および工芸科は「芸術」の中の一選択科目として位置づけられ、Ⅰについては選択した全ての生徒に履修されている。

■美術科目・工芸科目のⅠ、Ⅱ、Ⅲにはそれぞれ目標が示され、内容が次第に深化専門化されている。

■美術科目の内容は、絵画と彫刻、デザイン、映像メディア表現の三つの分野からなる表現領域と鑑賞領域で構成されている。工芸科目においては工芸制作とプロダクト制作からなる表現領域と鑑賞領域である。

■具体的には、絵画と彫刻は観察や想像による具象および抽象表現が、素描や水彩画、版画、油絵、日本画、漫画、イラストレーション、塑像、木彫、石彫、金属やガラス、合成樹脂などの形式と材料を表現意図に応じて単独あるいは複合的に活用できるように指導される。

■デザインでは、配色、構成、装飾、機能、環境を課題に生活におけるデザインの果たす役割について、主題の生成から、発想、構想、制作、活用、交流までを一連の計画の中で捉え、生活や社会、環境形成などに活用できるデザインの感性や知識、技能を身につけることに重点をおいている。

visual communication by not only color, figure, and material but also light and motion, students can acquire relationship to life, society and nature and realize the function of molding and art which make our life beautiful and rich.

■ Appreciation is conducted in natural beauty and molding beauty, and aims to make students create their own sense and value by feeling pleasure, feeling goodness and beauty and by making comments to each other. Fine art and culture in Japan are emphasized and protection of cultural heritage and international understanding are learned.

③ Fine Arts and Craft Production in Upper Secondary Schools

■ Fine arts and craft production in upper secondary schools are studied as an elective subject in the art field. All students who select art take Fine Arts and Craft Production Ⅰ.

■ The course for fine and technical art is divided into three components, Ⅰ, Ⅱ, and Ⅲ, and each has its goals and content designed to enrich the educational process.

■ In the course on fine arts, students are provided with instruction on painting and molding, design and image media expression. Each of them has an expression area and appreciation area. In industrial arts, students learn production industrial art and making products. Each of them has an expression area and appreciation area.

■ That is to say, sketch by observation and imagination is conducted in painting and molding. Representative expression and abstract expression are conducted by water color painting, wood printing, oil painting, Japanese painting, cartoon, illustration, clay figure, wood carving, stone carving, metal, glass and plastic. Students are instructed to use ways to express themselves with materials according to their intention.

■ In the design, it is emphasized that making a plan about the creation of the subject, conception, making, using and exchange about the role of designing in life, focusing on graphic design, composition, decoration, function and environment composition and that acquiring sensitivity, knowledge and skill of

■映像メディア表現は進展する情報社会に主体的、積極的に参加していくためのビジュアル・コミュニケーション能力育成をねらいとし、写真、ビデオ、コンピュータなどを使って基礎的な表現能力を養い高めることが行われる。
■工芸制作では、生徒が身近な生活体験の中で感じ取った必要性や夢や願望などをもとに発想し、構想し、主体的に創造的に制作できるように指導される。
■プロダクト制作は社会生活や身近な環境を心豊かにするための創造的な発想を身につけることをねらいとして、用途や機能、生産性を考えた製作の構想が重視され、マークやレタリング表示、実用品や装飾品の作成、家具や照明、住宅、公園などの模型製作が行われる。

■鑑賞は美術、工芸ともに造形美を感じ取りながら、生活や環境との関連、文化遺産や国際協調に対する深い理解を導く役割が担われる。

(3) 書道
■「書とは文字を素材としてこれを視覚化したものである」と定義づけられている。書を大別すると、(1) 芸術としての書、及び (2) 教科としての書写・書道教育に分類される。
　(1) は、書芸・書法・書芸術といわれ、日本においては戦後の近代的概念で「芸術」として扱われている。(2) は、小学校・中学校・高等学校での授業で学習する書写・書道教育である。

■書写・書道教育は、現行の小・中学校の学習指導要領では国語科で行われ、高等学校では普通教育の教科である芸術科に書道Ⅰ・書道Ⅱ・書道Ⅲの3つの科目が設けられており、その中で行われている。

■「書写」教育は、文字・語句・言葉・文章を正しく理解し、丁寧に文字を表現する学習である。書写教育では、小学校は日常生活や学習活動の目的に応じて文字を正しく丁寧に書くこと、さらに中学校では文字を正しく整え速

design useful for life, society, and creation of environment are carried out.

■ Image media expression aims to develop student's ability to participate in developing within an information-oriented society actively and student's basic expression ability using picture, video, and computer is developed.

■ In craft production, students get an idea from need, dreams and hopes which they feel in their life, and plan and make works actively and creatively.

■ In product making, students are required to get creative ideas enriching the environment around them, and plan for making, considering use, function, and productivity was emphasized and mark, lettering expression, making daily necessities and decorations, and making models of furniture, light, houses and parks is conducted.

■ Appreciation of fine art and industrial art contribute to the relationship with molding beauty, life and environment, and protection of cultural heritage and international cooperation.

(3) Calligraphy

■ Calligraphy is defined as "visualized art using characters as material" and is classified broadly into two categories; (1) Calligraphy as an art and (2) handwriting and calligraphy education as coursework.

The first is called "Syogei", penmanship, art of calligraphy and treated as an "art" in the sense of the modern post-war concept. The second is the handwriting and calligraphy education in primary school, lower secondary school and upper secondary school.

■ Handwriting and calligraphy education is conducted as a class in the Japanese course for primary school and lower secondary school. It is also provided in upper secondary school as "Shodo I", "Shodo II" and "Shodo III", the classes of art course for general academic subjects.

■ "Handwriting" education is the study to appreciate characters, sentences, words and phrases and to represent characters carefully. We set our goals to improve the skills to write correctly and politely for primary school students and

く書くことができるようにするとともに、社会生活に役立てる態度を育て、文字文化に親しむことを目標とする。

■高等学校の「書道」教育は、小・中学校の書写学習で培われた基礎・基本をさらに発展させる。書道の幅広い活動を通して、書を愛する心情を育てるとともに感性を高め、書を学習することにより、表現と鑑賞の基礎的能力を伸ばす。さらに、書の文化や伝統を理解、尊重する豊かな情操を養うことを目標とする。

■書写の指導のための年間授業時間数については、小学校第1学年から第6学年は各学年30単位時間程度、中学校第1学年及び第2学年では年間20単位時間程度、第3学年では年間10単位時間程度とし、高等学校の標準単位数は書道Ⅰ・書道Ⅱ・書道Ⅲ各2単位である。

■日本で使用される文字には、中国から伝承された漢字とそれを母体にした仮名がある。
　漢字には楷書(かいしょ)・行書(ぎょうしょ)・草書(そうしょ)・隷書(れいしょ)・篆書(てんしょ)の書体があり、仮名には単体と二字以上を続けて書く連綿(れんめん)がある。

■小学校の書写学習では、文字の形・大きさ・配列・配置などを正しく整えて書くことを学ぶ。中学校の書写学習では、速く書くことを考慮して第2学年から漢字の楷書と行書、さらにそれらに調和した仮名を学ぶ。第3学年では身の回りの多様な文字に関心を持ち、効果的に文字を書くことを学ぶ。

■高等学校の芸術科の「書道」学習では、中学校の書写学習との関連を考慮し、「漢字仮名交じりの書」・「漢字」・「仮名」の書の表現及び鑑賞を含め、

to write correctly and quickly for lower secondary school students, respectively. It also aims for the lower secondary school students to have an attitude useful to social life and to enjoy the letter culture.

■ "Calligraphy" education in upper secondary school is developed based on the fundamentals and basics acquired from handwriting education in primary school and lower secondary school. It is also aimed to foster a love of calligraphy as well as to heighten the sensitivity through a wide range of activities of calligraphy. Thereby, the fundamental capability of representation and appreciation of calligraphy is improved by studying calligraphy. Furthermore, it is aimed to cultivate the aesthetic sentiments; understanding and respecting the culture and tradition of calligraphy.

■ The number of calligraphy classes per year are: about 30 units in first-through sixth-grade of primary school about 20 units in first-grade and second-grade, about 10 units in third-grade of lower secondary school. Those units in upper secondary school are 2 units for each Shodo I, II, and III.

■ The characters used in Japanese are Chinese characters imported from China and kana characters derived from Chinese characters. Chinese characters have the scripts; standard script, semi-cursive script, cursive script, clerical script and seal script. Kana characters also have the scripts; standard script and RENMEN script, where each character is connected to the succeeding one.

■ Students in primary school study the correct figure, size, arrangement, and disposition for standard script of Chinese characters and Kana characters in "handwriting" class. Considering to write correctly and quickly in the "handwriting" class of lower secondary school, the students of second-grade study the standard script, semi-cursive script of Chinese characters and Kana characters, well-matched with those scripts and the students of third-grade learn to write characters effectively, having interests in various characters found around them.

■ "Calligraphy" class in the art course of upper secondary school further elaborates on the handwriting education in lower secondary school and aimed

総合的に書道に対する理解を深める。漢字の楷書・行書・草書・隷書・篆書、篆刻（てんこく）や刻字（こくじ）および平仮名・片仮名・変体仮名（へんたいがな）の全てを学習する。

■使用する用具は、鉛筆・ボールペン・フェルトペンなどの「硬筆」と、毛筆を用いる「毛筆」に分けて学習する。小学校第3学年以上から毛筆書写指導が行われ硬筆と毛筆を用いて学習するが、「書道」では毛筆を重点的に用いて学習する。

■漢字・仮名の書の技法を学習するために、中国・日本の名蹟・名筆の古典を基本として学ぶ「臨書（りんしょ）」方法が用いられる。これらの技法を効果的に表現できるように紙・筆・墨などにも注意を払い、文字を素材とした創造的な表現活動ができるように学ぶ。

■書道教育の目的は、文字を「書く」ことによって自ら表現・創作し、鑑賞することによって伝統的芸術文化に親しむことにある。

　現在、情報機器の発達・普及により、文字を書く機会が少なくなりつつある。日常生活における「書く」ことは、単に文字・文章を「書く」だけでなく、個性的な表現、自らの内面を文字、文章を通して「表現しよう」とする行為である。そこには自分なりに「美しく書こう」とすることが内在される。人の手で文字を「書く」ことは、お互いの人間関係を豊かにするものである。日本語を正しく美しく書くことは、日本の文化である日本語を大切にすることにつながる。

to deepen the understanding of calligraphy comprehensively, learning the expression and appreciation of the mixture of Chinese characters and Kana characters, Chinese characters and Kana characters. In "Calligraphy" class, students study all of the following scripts and characters; standard script, semi-cursive script, cursive script, clerical script, seal script, Hiragana, Katakana and obsolete Kana.

■ "Calligraphy" has two styles of writing; "Kohitsu" and "Mohitsu". Pencils, ballpoint pens, felt tipped pens, etc. are used for "Kohitsu". Brushes are used for "Mohitsu". Students in the third grade or higher study both "Mohitsu" and "Kohitsu". "Mohitsu" is studied intensively in "Calligraphy" class.

■ The "Rinsho" method is used to study calligraphy techniques of Chinese characters and Kana characters. "Rinsho" is the method of studying classic masterpieces of calligraphy as a basic element. Paying attention to paper, brushes, and ink sticks to be able to represent fruitfully, students learn how to conduct creative activities of expression making use of characters.

■ The purpose of calligraphy education is to express and create oneself by writing letters and to make the students enjoy traditional arts culture by appreciation of them.

Today, the chance for writing by hand has decreased due to the development and proliferation of information technology. "Writing" in daily life is not only to "write" characters, sentences, words and phrases, but also to "attempt to represent" the unique work or minds through the characters and sentences. Also, it includes "writing beautifully" in their own way. "Writing" by hand enriches human relations by making communication with each other. Writing Japanese correctly and beautifuly is closely relates to respecting Japanese language, which represents Japanese traditional culture.

7. 家庭科、技術・家庭科

(1) 家庭科教育と技術科教育の変遷
■現在、日本における家庭科教育と技術科教育は、一般普通教育として、小学校で「家庭科」、中学校で「技術・家庭科」、高等学校で「家庭科」（家庭基礎、家庭総合、生活デザイン）の名称で行われている。

■技術科教育は、現在の学校教育では、中学校「技術・家庭科」の技術教育の部分が、普通教育として制度化された唯一のものになっている。第2次世界大戦前には、「手工科」として1886年（明治19年）より始まり、明治30年代の実業教育重視の時代には、農業や商業といった実業諸教科とのかかわりが問題とされるなど、普通教育としての教科のあり方が常に問題とされてきた。

■一方、家庭科教育は、「家庭科」として、第2次世界大戦後、アメリカ教育使節団の勧告により、民主的な家庭の建設のために新たに誕生した教科である。戦前における家庭科教育は、「家事科」「裁縫科」として女子の教育の中心的役割をはたしてきた。そこでは、社会経済の発達段階からみて必然のことであったが、家庭作業主義の傾向があり、家庭生活を社会との関連を含めて総合的に検討することは少なかった。その歴史の上に、戦後は、①従来の家事・裁縫の踏襲ではない、②女子のみの教科でない、③単なる技能教科でない、という三否定の原則を理念として、家庭生活について総合的に学習する全く新しい教科としてスタートすることになったのである。
■とりわけ、小学校「家庭科」は、第5、6学年ではあったが、成立当初からの理念が生かされ、その後若干の内容の精選はあったが、大きな変化はなく今日まで続いている。
■しかし、中学校・高等学校の教育課程においては、急速な産業構造や生活の変化に対応して、教科の名称や教科の性格などに変化がみられる。

7. Homemaking, Industrial Arts and Homemaking, and Home Economics

(1) Changes of Home Economics Education and Industrial Arts Education

■ In Japan today, these subjects are taught as general education in the name of "Homemaking" at primary school", Industrial Arts and Homemaking" at lower secondary school, and "Home Economics" ("Basic Home Economics", "Comprehensive Home Economics", "Home Life Designs") at upper secondary school.

■ Industrial arts are only taught at the lower secondary level as part of "Industrial Arts and Homemaking". Before the end of the Second World War, the subject was called "Handicraft Education" in 1886 (Meiji 19). However, during the 1890's industrial education gained much attention. As a result, "Handicraft Education" faced difficulties in connection with "Industrial Education", which concerned agriculture and business education. There was also the problem of how to teach these subjects as general education.

■ After the War, the American Education Mission suggested that in order to develop democratic principles at the family level, home economics should be established as a subject. Prior to this, this subject was taught to female students as "Domestic Science" and "Sewing". This was necessary to promote social economic development, even though the subject was not comprehensively discussed. Historically, after the war, this subject started as a new subject to comprehensively study family life and to consider the three "nots", i.e. not continue domestic science and sewing, not have subjects only for girls, and not teach only techniques.

■ Initially, "Homemaking" has been taught at the fifth and six grade level in primary schools. Though some contents were improved, there has been little change in the content of instruction.

■ To keep pace with changes in industrial structure and life styles, the names and character of subjects were modified at the lower secondary and upper

■具体的に、学習指導要領の改訂における変遷の特徴をまとめると次のようになる。
① 1947年版学習指導要領
　〈小学校〉:「家庭科」
　〈中学校〉:「職業科」として「農業」「工業」「商業」「水産」「家庭」のうち1科目〜数科目を選択
　〈高等学校〉:「実業科」として「農業」「工業」「商業」「水産」「家庭」のうち1科目を選択
② 1951年版学習指導要領
　〈小学校〉:「家庭科」…「主として創造的表現活動を発達させる教科」に含まれる。
　〈中学校〉:「職業・家庭科」…'実生活に役立つ仕事'をする教科
　〈高等学校〉:普通教育としては、「家庭科」として独立(「一般家庭」「家族」「保育」「家庭経理」「食物」「被服」の自由選択制)。他に職業教育としては「家庭技芸科」(17科目の自由選択制)がおかれる。
③ 1958、1960年版学習指導要領
　〈小学校〉(1958年):「家庭科」
　〈中学校〉(1958年):「技術・家庭科」…男子向き(技術系列)、女子向き(家庭科系列)に分化
　〈高等学校〉(1960年):「家庭一般」…普通科に限り女子のみ必修
④ 1968、1969、1970年版学習指導要領
　〈小学校〉(1968年):「家庭科」
　〈中学校〉(1969年):「技術・家庭科」
　〈高等学校〉(1970年):「家庭一般」…職業科も含むすべての女子に4単位以上必修
⑤ 1977、1978年版学習指導要領
　〈小学校〉(1977年):「家庭科」
　〈中学校〉(1977年):「技術・家庭科」…相互乗り入れ方式(男子は家庭科系列から1領域、女子は技術系列から1領域を必修)

secondary schools.
■ The specific changes of characteristics in the Course of Study are as follows:
① The Course of Study in 1947
<Primary School> : 'Homemaking'
<Lower Secondary School> : as 'Vocational Education', to select one or a few of the following: 'Agriculture', Industry', Commerce', Fishery' and 'Homemaking'.
<Upper Secondary School> : as ' Industrial Education', to select one of the following: 'Agriculture', 'Industry', 'Commerce', 'Fishery' and 'Home Economics'.
② The Course of Study in 1951
<Primary School> : 'Homemaking,' included in the subject to develop the activity of creative expression.
<Lower Secondary School> : 'Vocational learning and Homemaking', the subject to practice jobs useful in daily life.
<Upper Secondary School> : 'Home Economics' became an independent subject in general education, and included the following electives: 'General Home Economics', 'Family', 'Nursing', 'Family Economics', 'Food', and 'Clothing'. 'Home Economics Arts' for vocational education was set up as a subject with seventeen electives.
③ The Course of Study in 1958 and 1960
<Primary School> (1958) : 'Homemaking'
<Lower Secondary School> (1958) : 'Industrial Arts and Homemaking', divided for boys (Industrial Arts scope and sequence), and for girls (Homemaking scope and sequence).
<Upper Secondary School> (1960) : 'General Home Economics', the only required subject for girls in the general course.
④ The Course of Study in 1968, 1969 and 1970
<Primary School> (1968) : 'Homemaking'
<Lower Secondary School> (1969) : 'Industrial Arts and Homemaking'

〈高等学校〉(1978年):「家庭一般」…女子のみ必修;実験・実習の強化
⑥ 1989年版学習指導要領
　〈小学校〉:「家庭科」
　〈中学校〉:「技術・家庭科」…男子向き、女子向きの廃止
　〈高等学校〉:「家庭一般」「生活技術」「生活一般」の中から1科目選択男
　　　　　　　女必修
⑦ 1998、1999年版学習指導要領
　〈小学校〉(1998年):「家庭科」
　〈中学校〉(1998年):「技術・家庭科」
　〈高等学校〉(1999年):「家庭基礎」「家庭総合」「生活技術」の中から1
　　　　　　　　　　　科目を選択必修
⑧ 2008年版学習指導要領
　〈小学校〉(2008年):「家庭科」
　〈中学校〉(2008年):「技術・家庭科」
　〈高等学校〉(2009年):「家庭基礎」「家庭総合」「生活デザイン」の中か
　　　　　　　　　　　ら1科目を選択履修

■まず、①②の時期は、戦後初期家庭科の誕生期であり、民主的な家庭の建設を担う教科としての家庭科に対する期待が大きかった時期である。それと同時に、ＣＩＥの指導のもとにわが国として独自の方向を歩もうとする模索

<Upper Secondary School> (1970) : 'General Home Economics', the required subject of more than four credits for all girls including the vocational course.
⑤ The Course of Study in 1977 and 1978
<Primary School> (1977) : 'Homemaking'
<Lower Secondary School> (1977) : 'Industrial Arts and Homemaking', to extend to each other (boys should select one area from Homemaking scope and sequence, and girls select one from Industrial Arts scope and sequence as the required subject).
<Upper Secondary School> (1978) : 'General Home Economics', the required subject for girls only, with emphasis on experiment and practice.
⑥ The Course of Study in 1989
<Primary School> : 'Homemaking'
<Lower Secondary School> : 'Industrial Arts and Homemaking', abolition of all girl all boy subjects,
<Upper Secondary School> : to select one from 'General Home Economics', 'Home Life Techniques' and 'General Life' as the required subject for both boys and girls.
⑦ The Course of Study in 1998 and 1999
<Primary School> (1998) : 'Homemaking'
<Lower Secondary School> (1998) : 'Industrial Arts and Homemaking'
<Upper secondary school> (1999) : to select one from "Basic Home Economics", "Comprehensive Home Economics" and "Home Life Techniques"
⑧ The Course of Study in 2008
<Primary School> (2008) : 'Homemaking'
<Lower Secondary School> (2008) : 'Industrial Arts and Homemaking'
<Upper secondary school> (2009) : to select one from 'Basic Home Economics', 'Comprehensive Home Economics' and 'Home Life designs'
■ During the first and second periods of revisions, home economics, as a subject, was established with an eye toward the development of the democratic families. It was also a time for Japan to develop its independence under

期でもあり、新教育の影響からの教科の構想期であった。当時、高等学校にアメリカから取り入れられた「ホームプロジェクト」(個人による活動)や「学校家庭クラブ」(生徒のグループによる活動)は、生活を見直し、課題解決に取り組む能力と実践的態度を養うことを目的とし、家庭科の学習にとって重要な意義をもつものとして現在にも継承されている。また、この時期の中等教育においては、科目選択制がとられ、制度上は男女に開かれたものであったことも特徴の1つであるが、実際には、男子は「農業」、女子は「家庭」を選択することが多く、中学校卒業後の就職者が半数以上である状況から、職業教育の側面と職業指導の性格も担ってきた。

■続く③④の時期は、科学技術教育の振興によって、中学校では、「技術・家庭科」が新設された。目標も、「生活に必要な基礎的技術」と変わり、男子は生産技術中心、女子は家庭生活技術中心に学習する扱いとなり、技術中心の教科とされた。進学率の向上とともに、職業指導の領域は、進路指導として学級会活動の中に組み込まれることになった。この時期に、家庭科教育では家庭科における技術と技能の議論が活発になるにつれ、単なる手技にとどまる技術論に対する懐疑から新たな動向を生むことになる。

■これは⑤の時期、人間中心の教育課程による改訂によって、具現化されることになる。そこでは、実践的態度の育成が目標とされ、教科の性格として、総合的性格や実践的性格が明らかにされた。

■⑥の時期は、21世紀へ向けて、「家庭を取り巻く環境や社会の変化に対応し、男女が協力して家庭生活を築いていくことや、生活に必要な知識や技術を習得させる観点に配慮し、その内容および履修のあり方について改善を図るとともに、実践的・体験的な学習がいっそう充実するように改善を図る」(教育課程審議会答申)ことから、小学校・中学校・高等学校男女共修の家庭科として全面的に改訂された。

guidance from CIE for a new type of education. In order to help the students solve real problems with practical attitudes the subject of home economics was implemented using the American model. In upper secondary schools students could, and currently still do, participate in such activities as "Home Project", and "School Family Clubs". In the secondary schools at that time the system of elective classes was implemented and all subjects were open to both boys and girls. However, in practice, the boys studied agriculture and the girls selected home economics as part of their vocational training, since over half of all students went to work after finishing lower secondary school.

■ During the third and fourth periods of revision, scientific technique education was implemented and "Industrial Arts and Homemaking" were established in lower secondary schools. The purpose was to focus more on "necessities of basic techniques for daily life" education, and boys learned manufacturing techniques while girls focused on techniques for home life. As the number of students going to upper secondary school increased, more emphasis was placed on vocational guidance and related class activities. Also, there was concern that the simple techniques which had been taught in home economics should be changed and improved.

■ With the fifth period of revision came a new approach in education to make it more human - centered. It became clear that a comprehensive and practical approach to this subject was necessary with the aim of developing practical attitudes.

■ With a vision for the 21st century, the sixth period of revision brought with it a realization that education must keep pace with environmental and societal changes affecting the family. Males and females should learn to establish family life helping each other, and acquire practical knowledge necessary for everyday life. At the same time, further improvement must be made not only to the content and the way to take courses but also on practical learning and experience (Report of the Commission on Education Curriculum). The subject of home economics was completely revised so that both boys and girls study some aspect

■⑦の時期は、小・中・高を通して男女がともに学ぶ教科として、学校教育の中で定着した。教科の特徴である実践的・体験的な学習活動を通して、生活に必要な知識や技能を習得し、生活をよりよくしようとする能力と実践的な態度を育てるとともに、男女が協力して家庭生活を築き、充実向上を図る能力と態度を育てることをねらいとして、学習が展開された。

■⑧は、2008年2009年版新学習指導要領では、実践的・体験的な活動を通して、家族と家庭の役割、生活に必要な衣、食、住、情報、産業等についての基礎的な理解と技能を養うとともに、それらを活用して課題を解決するために工夫し創造できる能力と実践的な態度の育成を一層重視する観点から改善が図られた。

(2) 新学習指導要領の小学校「家庭科」、中学校「技術・家庭科」、高等学校「家庭科」の特徴

■小学校「家庭科」・中学校「技術・家庭科」(2008年版) と高等学校「家庭科」(2009年版) の学習指導要領における目標は、以下の通りである。
①小学校(家庭)(2008年版)
　「衣食住などに関する実践的・体験的な活動を通して、日常生活に必要な基礎的・基本的な知識及び技能を身に付けるとともに、家庭生活を大切にする心情をはぐくみ、家族の一員として生活をよりよくしようとする実践的な態度を育てる。」
②中学校(技術・家庭)(2008年版)
　「生活に必要な基礎的・基本的な知識及び技術の習得を通して、生活と技術とのかかわりについて理解を深め、進んで生活を工夫し創造する能力と実践的な態度を育てる。」

of this subject at primary, lower secondary, and upper secondary schools.

■ During the seventh periods of revision, homemaking and industrial art education became entrenched in school education as subjects for students of both genders to learn throughout primary, lower secondary, and upper secondary schools. The objectives were to enable the two genders to mutually cooperate to establish family life and nurture abilities and attitudes to enrich and improve their lives as well as to acquire the knowledge and skills necessary for life, and nurture ability and a practical attitude to improving life through practical and hands-on learning activities, which is a characteristic of the subject.

■ The Course of Study of the eighth periods of revision (2008 and 2009) improve the following points: enable students to gain a basic understanding and skills related to family and the role of the family as well as food, clothing, housing, information, and industries required for life through practical and hands-on activities; nurturing abilities and practical 'can-do' attitude and being creative to solve problems by utilizing understanding and skills.

(2) Characteristics of "Homemaking" in primary school, "Industrial Arts and Homemaking" in lower secondary school and "Home Economics" in upper secondary school found in the new Course of Study

■ The purposes of "Homemaking" in primary school, "Industrial Arts and Homemaking" in lower secondary school (2008), and "Home Economics" in upper secondary school (2009) found in the new Course of Study are as follow:

① Primary Schools (Homemaking), 2008

To acquire the basic knowledge and skills which are necessary for daily life and to let students respect family life through practical and hands-on activities concerning clothing, food and housing, and to develop a positive attitude towards an improved family life as a member of the family.

② Lower Secondary Schools (Industrial Arts and Homemaking), 2008

Students will acquire knowledge and skills headed in life, to help them understand the relationship between family life and social life skills, and to

・(技術分野の目標)

「ものづくりなどの実践的・体験的な学習活動を通して、材料と加工、エネルギー変換、生物育成及び情報に関する基礎的・基本的な知識及び技術を習得するとともに、技術と社会や環境とのかかわりについて理解を深め、技術を適切に評価し活用する能力と態度を育てる。」

・(家庭分野の目標)

「衣食住などに関する実践的・体験的な学習活動を通して、生活の自立に必要な基礎的・基本的な知識及び技術を習得するとともに、家庭の機能についての理解を深め、これからの生活を展望して、課題をもって生活をよりよくしようとする能力と態度を育てる。」

③高等学校(家庭)(2009年版)

「人間の生涯にわたる発達と生活の営みを総合的にとらえ、家族・家庭の意義、家族・家庭と社会とのかかわりについて理解させるとともに、生活に必要な知識と技術を習得させ、男女が協力して主体的に家庭や地域の生活を創造する能力と実践的な態度を育てる。」

■以上のように、小学校では、「家庭生活を大切にする心情をはぐく」むとともに、生活を「工夫」することから「よりよく」するという目標が示された。

■中学校では、基礎的・基本的な知識・技能の習得とともに、「これからの生活を展望する」ことが目標にされた。

■高等学校の普通教育においては、上記の最終目標を達成するために、各科目の目標は下記のようになっている。

「家庭基礎」:「人の一生と家族・家庭及び福祉、衣食住、消費生活などに関する基礎的・基本的な知識と技術を習得させ、家庭や地域の生

develop an ability to devise and create a practical attitude.
(The objectives of the field of Industrial Arts)

Acquiring basic knowledge and skills related to materials, processing, energy transformation, growing living matter, and information through practical and hands-on learning activities such as manufacturing; deepening understanding of the relationship among technologies, society, and the environment; and nurturing abilities and attitude to evaluate technologies properly and harness them.
(The objectives of the field of Homemaking)

Acquiring basic knowledge and skills necessary for a self-sufficient life through practical and hands-on learning activities related to clothing, food, and housing; deepening understanding of family function; and nurturing abilities and attitude to improve life while remaining aware of their tasks by looking into life in the future.

③ Upper Secondary Schools (Home Economics), 2009

Apprehending the development and living activities of the human lifespan comprehensively; enabling students to understand the significance of family/home and relations between family/home and society as well as acquiring the knowledge and skills necessary for life; and nurturing abilities and a practical attitude whereby both sexes mutually cooperate to actively create lives in the family and community.

■ As mentioned above, the objective of homemaking in the course of study for primary schools was revised to include "nurturing mentality to value family life" and "improving life" from "using one's ingenuity for life".

■ The objectives of the revised Course of Study for lower secondary schools include to "look into life in the future" in addition to acquiring basic knowledge and skills in the revised course of study.

■ In upper secondary schools, in order to realize the above purposes, the purposes of each subject can be seen below:

Basic Home Economics: Enabling students to acquire basic knowledge and skills related to the human lifespan, family/home, welfare, clothing, food, housing,

活課題を主体的に解決するとともに、生活の充実向上を図る能力と実践的な態度を育てる。」

「家庭総合」:「人の一生と家族・家庭、子どもや高齢者とのかかわりと福祉、消費生活、衣食住などに関する知識と技術を総合的に習得させ、家庭や地域の生活課題を主体的に解決するとともに、生活の充実向上を図る能力と実践的な態度を育てる。」

「生活デザイン」:「人の一生と家族・家庭及び福祉、消費生活、衣食住などに関する知識と技術を体験的に習得させ、家庭や地域の生活課題を主体的に解決するとともに、生活の充実向上を図る能力と実践的な態度を育てる。」

■次に教科の履修時間・内容構成について示すと次のようになる。

表7-7 家庭科、技術・家庭科の年間標準授業時数

名称	小学校 家庭科		中学校 技術・家庭科			高等学校 家庭科
学年	5年	6年	1年	2年	3年	下記、3科目から1科目選択 ((　) 内は週あたり時数) ・家庭基礎 (2) ・家庭総合 (4) ・生活デザイン (4)
年間授業時数	60	55	70	70	35	
週あたり授業時数	1.7	1.6	2	2	1	

and consumer life; nurturing abilities and practical attitudes to try to enrich and improve life as well as actively solving problems in the family and community.

Comprehensive Home Economics: Enabling students to comprehensively acquire knowledge and skills concerning the relationship between the human lifespan and family, children, and the elderly, welfare, consumer life, clothing, food, and housing.

Home Life Designs: Enabling students to acquire knowledge and skills concerning the human lifespan, family/home, welfare, consumer life, clothing, food, and housing, and nurturing abilities and a practical attitude to try to enrich and improve life as well as solve problems in family and community life.

■ The Standard number of weekly school hours and contents are as follows:

Table 7-7 Standard Number of Weekly School Hours of Homemaking, Industrial Arts and Homemaking, and Home Economics

School	Primary		Lower secondary			Upper secondary
Subject	Homemaking		Industrial Arts & Homemaking			Home Economics
Grade	5	6	1	2	3	Choose one of the following subjects. ( ) = class hours per week: · Basic Home Economics (2) · Comprehensive Home Economics (4) · Home Life Designs (4)
Annual class hours	60	55	70	70	35	
Class hours per week	1.7	1.6	2	2	1	

表7-8　小学校「家庭科」の内容

学年	内　　容
第5・6学年	A　家庭生活と家族 (1) 自分の成長と家族 (2) 家庭生活と仕事 (3) 家族や近隣の人々とのかかわり B　日常の食事と調理の基礎 (1) 食事の役割 (2) 栄養を考えた食事 (3) 調理の基礎 C　快適な衣服と住まい (1) 衣服の着用と手入れ (2) 快適な住まい方 (3) 生活に役立つ物の製作 D　身近な消費生活と環境 (1) 物や金銭の使い方と買物 (2) 環境に配慮した生活の工夫

表7-9　中学校「技術・家庭科」の内容

学年	履修分野	
	技術分野	家庭分野
1〜3年	A　材料と加工に関する技術 (1) 生活や産業の中で利用されている技術 (2) 材料と加工法 (3) 材料と加工に関する技術を利用した製作品の設計・製作 B　エネルギー変換に関する技術 (1) エネルギー変換機器の仕組みと保守点検 (2) エネルギー変換に関する技術を利用した製作品の設計・製作 C　生物育成に関する技術 (1) 生物の生育環境と育成技術 (2) 生物育成に関する技術を利用した栽培又は飼育 D　情報に関する技術 (1) 情報通信ネットワークと情報モラル等	A　家族・家庭と子どもの成長 (1) 自分の成長と家族 (2) 家庭と家族関係 (3) 幼児の生活と家族 B　食生活と自立 (1) 中学生の食生活と栄養 (2) 日常食の献立と食品の選び方 (3) 日常食の調理と地域の食文化 C　衣生活・住生活と自立 (1) 衣服の選択と手入れ (2) 住居の機能と住まい方 (3) 衣生活、住生活などの生活の工夫 D　身近な消費生活と環境 (1) 家庭生活と消費 (2) 家庭生活と環境

Table 7-8 Contents of Homemaking of Primary Schools

Grade	Content
5 · 6	A. Family life and family (1) His/her Growth and family (2) Family life and work (3) Relationship with the family and neighbors B. Daily diet and basics of cooking (1) Role of diet (2) Nutritious diet (3) Basics of cooking C. Comfortable clothing and housing (1) Wearing and caring for clothes (2) Comfortable lifestyle (3) Making things useful to daily life D. Familiar consumer life and the environment (1) How to use belongings/money and shopping (2) Device for eco-friendly life

Table 7-9 Contents of Industrial Arts and Homemaking of Lower Secondary Schools

Grade	Field of Curricula	
	Field of Industrial Arts	Field of Homemaking
1 ∫ 3	A. Techniques related to materials and processing (1) Technologies harnessed in life and industry (2) Materials and processing method (3) Designing and production of the products harnessing technologies related to materials and processing B. Technologies related to energy transformation (1) Mechanism of energy transformers, maintenance and inspection (2) Designing and production of products harnessing technologies related to energy transforming C. Technologies related to growing living matter (1) Growing environment and technologies of living matter (2) Cultivation or farming utilizing technologies related to raising living matter D. Technologies related to information (1) Information communication network and information morals etc.	A. Family and child development (1) Development of oneself and family (2) Family and family relationship (3) Life of infant children and family B. Dietary habit and self-sufficiency (1) Dietary habit and nutrition of lower secondary school children (2) Daily menu and how to choose food (3) Daily cooking and local food culture C. Clothing/housing and self-sufficiency (1) How to choose and care for clothes (2) Function of houses and how to live (3) Devises for life with clothes and housing D. Familiar consumer life and the environment (1) Family life and consumption (2) Family life and the environment

表7-10　高等学校「家庭科」(「家庭基礎」「家庭総合」「生活デザイン」)の内容

科目 学年	家庭基礎	家庭総合	生活デザイン
1〜3年	(1) 人の一生と家族・家庭及び福祉 (2) 生活の自立及び消費と環境 (3) ホームプロジェクトと学校家庭クラブ活動	(1) 人の一生と家族・家庭 (2) 子どもや高齢者とのかかわりと福祉 (3) 生活における経済の計画と消費 (4) 生活の科学と環境 (5) 生涯の生活設計 (6) ホームプロジェクトと学校家庭クラブ活動	(1) 人の一生と家族・家庭及び福祉 (2) 消費や環境に配慮したライフスタイルの確立 (3) 食生活の設計と創造 (4) 衣生活の設計と創造 (5) 住生活の設計と創造 (6) ホームプロジェクトと学校家庭クラブ活動

■小学校では、これまでの8領域の構成から、4領域の内容に整理統合して、中学校の内容構成と枠組みを同じにし、小学校と中学校の関連をはかった内容が示された。また、食育の推進の観点から、「五大栄養素の働き」について、中学校から小学校へ内容が移行した。

■中学校では、これまでの技術分野2領域と家庭分野2領域の4領域の構成から、技術分野4領域、家庭分野4領域に再編され、内容が示された。また、「幼児とのふれあいとかかわり方の工夫」と「日常食や地域の食材を生かした調理」については、これまでの「選択」から「必修」となった。

■また、小学校と中学校において、内容の枠組みを同じにし、内容の体系化がはかられたことは、大きな特徴である。

■以上のように、現在、この教科は、男女ともに学ぶ普通教育として制度化されており、歴史的にも、社会的にも、その意義は大きい。少子高齢化社会や高度情報化社会等の社会の変化に対応し、家庭生活を中心とする人間の生活を充実・発展させる能力を持った人間の育成にかける期待も今後ますます大きい。また、その一方で、完全学校週五日制以降、教科全体の授業時数減により、この教科の独自性である実践的・体験的な学習の時間を充分確保で

Table 7-10 Contents of Home Economics (Basic Home Economics, Comprehensive Home Economics, and Home Life Designs) of Upper Secondary Schools

科目	Basic Home Economics	Comprehensive Home Economics	Home Life Designs
1〜3 Grade	(1) The human lifespan (2) Self-sufficient life, consumption, and the environment (3) Home projects and club activities in school and family	(1) The human lifespan and family/home (2) Relationship with children and the elderly, and welfare (3) Financial plan and consumption in life (4) Chemistry and the environment in life (5) Lifetime life planning (6) Home projects and club activities in school and family	(1) The human lifespan, family/home and welfare (2) Establishment of a lifestyle with awareness of consumption and the environment (3) Designing and creation of dietary habits (4) Designing and creation of life with clothes (5) Designing and creation of life with housing (6) Home projects and club activities in school and family

■ In the revised Course of Study for primary schools, the contents of homemaking were reorganized from 8 fields to 4 in order to conform with the content structure and framework of homemaking and industrial arts for lower secondary schools and allow them to be associated. Moreover, "the functions of the five nutrients" was adapted for teaching in primary schools from lower secondary schools to promote dietary education.

■ In the revised Course of Study for lower secondary schools, the contents of industrial arts and homemaking are reorganized from having 2 fields each to 4. Moreover, "Relationship with infant children and devising how to involve them" and "Cooking of daily menu and utilizing local foods" switches from an elective to a mandatory subject.

■ In addition, a major feature sees the contents frameworks of those of primary and lower secondary schools conform with each other and the contents systemized.

■ Currently, as prescribed above, homemaking and industrial arts are incorporated in the education system as regular subjects for both male and female students to learn and are of great significance historically and socially. There will also be ever-increasing expectations to foster persons capable of responding to the declining birth rate and the aging society and advanced information society, and those with the abilities to enrich and develop family-

きなくなってきている状況は、問題点として指摘できる。今後は、引き続き、男女がともに学ぶ教科として、十分な学習効果が上げられるよう、時間数の確保に努めるとともに、教育内容の面からは基礎的・基本的内容を充実することが求められている。また、小学校・中学校・高等学校のすべての学校段階を通して発展していくような内容構成上の工夫と、子どもたちひとりひとりにあった教育内容の一層の工夫が求められている。

家庭科室　Home Making Room

centered human life. On the other hand, the problem of lacking sufficient time for practical and hands-on learning, as the key feature of these subjects, has been highlighted due to reduced overall class hours following the introduction of the comprehensive five-day school week. Henceforth, as co-educational subjects, there is a need to ensure continual enrichment of the basic educational contents as well as seeking to secure class hours for sufficient learning effects. Furthermore, it is necessary to improve content composition for the students to develop throughout all levels of primary, lower secondary, and upper secondary schools, and improve the educational contents and make them relevant for individual students.

みんなでそうじ Cooperative Classroom Cleaning

8. 体育、保健体育

(1) 体育

■日本の体育・スポーツは、歴史的に学校体育を中心として発展してきており、「学校体育を除いたら日本の体育は成り立たない」と言われるほどその果たす役割は重要である。学校体育の領域は、下表に示されるように学校教育活動全般にわたって総合的に行われているが、その中心となるのは教科体育と運動部活動である。したがって、以下では小学校から高校までの教科体育の概要と運動部活動について概説する。

表7-11　学校体育の領域

教育課程内	教科	体育授業
	教科外 (特別活動)	クラブ活動（運動クラブ練習等） 学級活動（学級レクリエーション活動等） 生徒会活動（体育レクリエーション委員会の活動等） 学校行事（体育祭・校内競技会・野外活動等）
教育課程外	組織的に営まれる運動部活動 非組織的・個人的に行われる運動	

小学校

■小学校の教科体育の目標は、「心と体を一体としてとらえ、適切な運動の経験と健康・安全についての理解を通して、生涯にわたって運動に親しむ資質や能力の基礎を育てるとともに健康の保持増進と体力の向上を図り、楽しく明るい生活を営む態度を育てる」ことである。この目標は、健康増進、体力の向上を図ることを強調するとともに、運動を手段としてでなく、運動それ自体を目的としてとらえようとしていること、すなわち体を動かすことの喜び、楽しさを体得し、それを生涯を通じて実践する能力や態度の育成を目指すことを重視しようとしていることに特徴がある。さらに豊かな人間性の育成に向けて、心と体を一体としてとらえる視点を明確にしたこともまた特

8. Physical Education, Health and Physical Education

(1) Physical Education

■ In Japan physical education and sports, historically speaking, have been mainly organized and developed in school education, and school physical education is an integral part of it. Physical education at school has played a key role. As shown below, it covers the entire spectrum of school education activities. Most important parts of physical education at school are: physical education as a subject, and sports club activities. The following gives an outline of physical education and sports club activities in primary and secondary education.

Table 7-11 The Spectrum of Physical Education at School

Curriculum	Subjects	Physical Education
	Special Activities	Club Activities Class Activities Recreational Activities etc.) Students Councils (a Steering Committee of Physical Education or Recreation, etc.) School Events Athletic Meeting Sports Games, Outdoor Activities, etc.)
Extra-curricular		Systematically Organized Sports Club Activities Non-Systematically and Personally Conducted Exercises

Primary School

■ The objectives of physical education in primary school is thinking of our mind and body as one unit, to cultivate stature and ability to familiarize with appropriate exercises, and to help them keep and maintain a healthy condition and make it possible for them to lead a happy life through adequate kinetic experience and understanding about health and safety. The unique point of these objectives is that the students would be able to regard exercises not as a means for achieving something, but as the goal itself. In other words, it aims to cultivate an appropriate attitude towards a pleasant and happy life, making them aware of the joy and pleasure of physical exercises. In addition to cultivating good

徴である。
　次に教科体育の内容であるが、低学年は、それまでの基本の運動とゲームの2領域から、体つくり運動、器械・器具を使っての運動遊び、走・跳の運動遊び、水遊び、ゲーム、表現リズム遊びの6領域で示されている。また、中学年は低学年と同様に6領域であるが、体つくり運動、器械運動、走・跳の運動、浮く・泳ぐ運動、ゲーム、表現運動という領域名で示されている。さらに高学年では、体つくり運動、器械運動、陸上運動、水泳、ボール運動、表現運動という領域名である。

■年間授業時数は、一単位時間45分として1年が102時間、2年～4年が105時間、5年～6年が90単位時間である。

中学校
■中学校における教科目標は、「心と体を一体としてとらえ、運動や健康・安全についての理解と運動の合理的な実践を通して、生涯にわたって運動に親しむ資質や能力を育てるとともに健康の保持増進のための実践力の育成と体力の向上を図り、明るく豊かな生活を営む態度を育てる」ことである。
この目標の特徴は、小学校における目標と同様に、運動それ自体を目標としてとらえようとし、運動を生涯を通じて実践する能力や態度の育成を目指すことを重視するとともに、教科として豊かな人間性の育成に貢献しようとしている。

■教科内容は、中学校の場合、目標達成のための各種の運動とそれに関する知識により構成されている。運動領域は、体つくり運動、器械運動、陸上競技、水泳、球技、武道、およびダンスの7領域となっている。生涯にわたる豊かなスポーツライフを実現する視点から、多くの領域の学習を十分に体験させ

personality, it is characterized clearly that we should unify our mind and body.

Contents and activities of physical education in different grade levels include the following: in the first two grades students learn exercises to build the body, game exercise with apparatus, running and jumping games, playing with water games, and expressive and rhythm games. (Formerly, they were two activities: basic exercises and games) ; in the third and fourth grades, students are expected to accomplish six activities too, and they are named exercise to build the body, exercises with apparatus, running and jumping exercises, floating and swimming exercises, game, and expressive exercise . In the fifth and sixth grades, students are expected to accomplish six activities named exercises to develop the body, exercises with apparatus, track and field, swimming, ball games, and expressive exercise.

■ Annual class of Plysic Education are 102 at 1st grade, 105 at 2 ~ 4 grade, and 90 at 5 ~ 6 grade for 45 minutes for one class period.

Lower Secondary School

■ The objectives of physical education in lower secondary schools are to develop an endowment and ability and interest in sports positively through understanding of exercises, health and safety, and rational practice of exercises, thinking of our mind and body as one unit, so as to develop a faculty of practice to strive for saving and promoting health and improvement of physical strength, and to cultivate the attitude of having a sound life both mentally and physically. As in the primary schools, the exercises themselves are regarded as the objectives, as well as the cultivation of ability and positive attitude towards exercises for students' future life and to try to bring up students to be good humans through this subject.

■ The contents of physical education instruction at this level include various types of exercises and knowledge about these exercises to meet the above mentioned objectives. Physical exercises have seven fields of activities: exercise for building the body, sports for individuals (exercises with apparatus, athletic

たうえで、それらをもとに自らが更に探求したい運動を選択できるようにすることが重要とされている。このため、中学校1年・2年でこれまで選択必修であった武道とダンスを含めすべての領域を必修とし、3年から領域選択を開始する。また、武道の学習を通じて、我が国固有の伝統と文化に、より一層触れることができるようになっている。

■年間授業時数は、1単位時間50分として各学年とも105単位時間である。

高校
■高校における教科体育の目標は、「心と体を一体としてとらえ、健康・安全や運動についての理解と運動の合理的な実践を通して、生涯にわたって計画的に運動に親しむ資質や能力を育てるとともに、健康の保持増進のための実践力の育成と体力の向上を図り、明るく豊かで活力のある生活を営む態度を育てる」ことである。ここでも小・中学校と同様に生涯を通しての運動実践能力・態度の体得と、心身ともに健康な生活態度の育成が強調されている。

■教科体育の内容は、目標達成のための各種の運動とその理論的基礎となる体育理論により構成されている。運動領域については、運動の特性などを考慮しながら、生徒の能力・適性などについての効果的な指導ができるようにしている。とりわけ大幅な選択制の導入により、生涯体育の基礎作りをめざして、体つくり運動、器械運動、陸上競技、水泳、球技、武道、ダンスの7領域で構成されている。体育理論については「社会の変化とスポーツ」、「運動技能の構造と運動の学び方」「体ほぐしの意義と体力の高め方」の三点にまとめられている。

sports, swimming), ball games, martial arts (Budo), and dance. For realizing a good lifelong sports life, it is important that students have the opportunity to experience many kinds of activity, and they choose activities that they want to learn more. Consequently, all activities become compulsory including Budo and dance that used be optional in the first and second grades, and students can select the field on their own in the third grade. Then, through learning Budo, it is considered that students can experience Japanese tradition and culture.
■ One school hour is 50 minutes, and each grade has 105 yearly school hours for this subject.

Upper Secondary School
■ The objectives of physical education in upper secondary schools are to acquire advanced athletic techniques through rational practice of exercise, to appreciate exercise, to adjust health improvement of physical strength, to develop their attitude toward fairness, cooperation, and responsibility, and to develop their endowment and ability to continue physical training and sports throughout their lives. The same as in primary and lower secondary schools, the acquisition of ability and attitude for exercise and cultivation of attitude for healthy life in mind and body is emphasized.
■ The contents of physical education in the Course of Study consist of various types of exercises and knowledge about these exercises to meet the above objectives. In the field of physical exercise, emphasis is placed on the attempts to instruct the exercises efficiently and effectively, clarifying the characteristics of each exercise and considering students' ability and aptitude. Introducing optional exercises to a large extent is to formulate the base for lifelong physical education, and physical education in this level has seven areas: exercises for developing the body, exercises with apparatus, athletic sports, swimming, ball games, martial arts (Budo), and dance. The theory of physical education is composed of three parts: "changing of the society and sports" ", physiological characteristics and dynamic characteristics of exercises", and " the meaning of loosening up and

■年間授業時間は、高校では単位制をとっているので、1単位について1学年35単位時間（1単位時間は50分）の標準として3年間で7〜8単位取得するものとされている。
■以上が小学校から高校までの教科体育の概要であるが、いずれも健康増進、体力の向上を図るとともに、生涯を通じて運動に親しみ、運動生活を充実させていくための基礎づくりを重視したものと言えよう。

運動部活動
■教科課程外ではあるが、運動部活動は教科体育とともに体育指導上大きな役割・機能を果たす。これは、スポーツなどに興味と関心を持つ同好者が運動部を組織し、より高い水準の技能や記録に挑戦し、それを追求して自らを厳しく律し、その目的を果たそうとする中で喜びや楽しさを体験する活動である。

■運動部活動はその教育的意義も認められて、中学校で5〜8割ほど、高校で3〜5割ほどの生徒が所属している。しかしながら、現在ではさまざまな弊害や問題も指摘され、議論が交わされている。運動部活動は、教育課程外の財政的裏付けのない学校教育活動で、しかも若干の部活動手当などはあるにしても、勤務時間外における教員の自発的・自主的ないわば奉仕的勤務ともいうべきものに支えられているのが実状である。しかし、公教育の一環であるにもかかわらず、勝利主義志向による長時間練習による学業との両立問題、施設・設備の独占化、対外試合や遠征の増加、それに伴なう費用負担の問題や安全管理にかかわる責任問題などさまざまな問題が出現している。これらに対し、運動部活動が学校教育の一環であるという原点に立ち戻って活動の指導や管理運営を検討しなおし、改善していくべきであるという主張がなされている。しかし、現在のところ高校野球をはじめとしてエリート・スポーツマンの養成としての活動と、学校教育における人間形成としての活動

improvement of strength ."

■ According to the credit system, physical education at this level gives 7-8 credits in three grades, accounts for 35 school hours of lessons per school year (one school hour is 50 minutes as a standard) and is counted as one credit.

■ As the above-mentioned explanation is an outline of physical education from primary to upper secondary schools, in all levels, physical education aims to improve and strengthen one's health and body. At the same time, it aims to provide the foundation so that students can get accustomed to physical exercises all their life and enrich their life with sports.

Sports Club Activity

■ Sports Club activity plays a very important role in physical education in additiion to regular subjects, although it is outside the subject area. Students, who are interested in sports will organize sports clubs. They intend to acquire advanced skills, and try to smash records. Through sports club activities students can have pleasant experiences and at the same time they can learn to develop self-control and feel happy through those activities.

■ The importance of sports club activity in school education is clear, and 50 to 80% of lower secondary school students and 30 to 50 % of upper secondary school students are members of various sports clubs. At present, however, various kinds of problems have been pointed out and have been discussed. Sports club activity does not have financial support from school, and it depends upon teachers' voluntary services. Although sports clubs activity is a part of public education, teachers and students are so eager to gain victory, they are forced to practice for a long time, resulting in study of academic subjects being neglected. Club activities' priority for using school facilities, increasing number of tours for games with clubs of other schools, lack of financial base or support for these tours, and responsibility for safety control are the major problems. Regarding these problems, it is insisted that management and guidance of sports club activity should be changed from the point of view that it is a part of school

との間には、なお多くの問題がある。

（2）保健

■教科として保健が正式に教えられるようになったのは、第2次世界大戦後のことである。それ以前は、保健に関係する教育内容は、「養生」、「博物」、「生理」、「衛生」、「理科」あるいは「体操」などの教科の一部で扱われてきた。このように教科としての歴史が浅いということも手伝って、現在もなおかなり多くの問題点を抱えている。

■またわが国では保健教育を、その性格から学校保健活動の一翼を担うものとしても位置づけているため（図7-3参照）、一教科としての役割を複雑にしている。

■このように、保健教育を保健学習と保健指導とを含む総合的なものであると捉えられる場合が多いが、その中心は、体育あるいは保健体育の授業の中で行われる保健学習である。

education. But it is still difficult to keep a balance between fostering the sports elite, represented by upper secondary school baseball, and sports activity for human formation in school education.

(2) Health Education

■ It was only after World War II that health education was first taught as one of the subjects in school. Before that, matters related to health had been dealt with as part of such subjects as "regimens, natural history, physiology, hygiene, science education and physical education". As it has been only a short time since Health Education became a subject, there are many problems in Health Education.

■ Moreover, in Japan, health education takes the role of school health activities, (Figure7-3) making it a more complicated subject.

■ Though Health Education is often considered as having a joint feature that contains both health learning and health guidance, its principal function is health education which is carried out through the subject of Physical Education or Health and Physical Education.

■小学校から高校までの現況は、おおよそ次のようである。

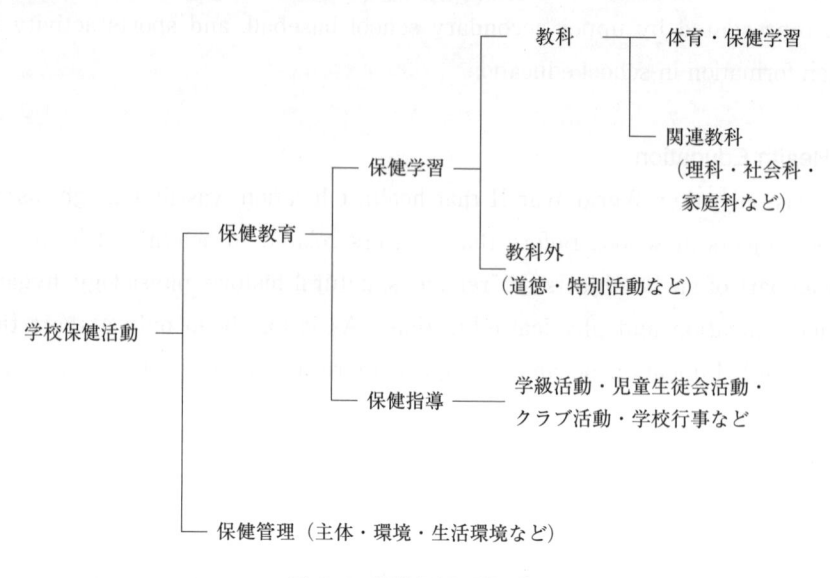

```
学校保健活動 ─┬─ 保健教育 ─┬─ 保健学習 ─┬─ 教科 ─┬─ 体育・保健学習
              │              │            │        └─ 関連教科
              │              │            │           （理科・社会科・
              │              │            │            家庭科など）
              │              │            └─ 教科外
              │              │               （道徳・特別活動など）
              │              └─ 保健指導 ── 学級活動・児童生徒会活動・
              │                             クラブ活動・学校行事など
              └─ 保健管理（主体・環境・生活環境など）
```

図7-3　学校保健活動の領域

小学校の保健教育
■小学校における保健教育は、3、4年の2学年間で8単位時間程度、5、6年の2学年間で16単位時間程度とされている。
■3、4年では「健康の大切さの認識と健康によい仕方の理解」および「体の発育・発達についての理解」が、5、6年では「けがの防止についての理解とけがなどの簡単な手当」および「心の発達及び不安、悩みへの対処の仕方についての理解」「病気の予防についての理解」がその内容になっている。

■ The current state of Health Education from primary to the upper secondary school is as follows:

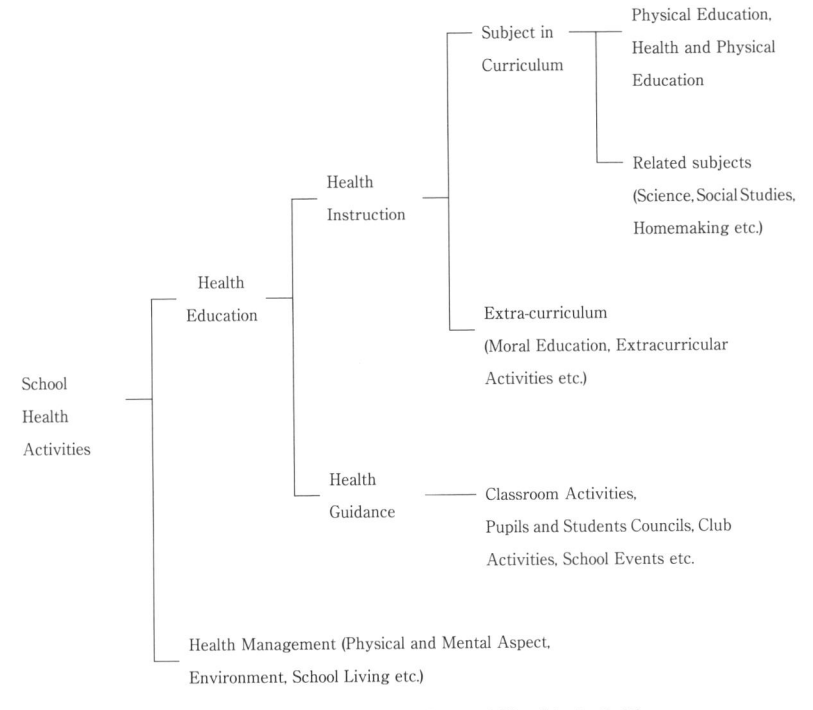

```
School
Health
Activities ┬─ Health      ┬─ Health       ┬─ Subject in    ┬─ Physical Education,
           │  Education   │  Instruction  │  Curriculum   │  Health and Physical
           │              │               │               │  Education
           │              │               │               │
           │              │               │               └─ Related subjects
           │              │               │                  (Science, Social Studies,
           │              │               │                  Homemaking etc.)
           │              │               │
           │              │               └─ Extra-curriculum
           │              │                  (Moral Education, Extracurricular
           │              │                  Activities etc.)
           │              │
           │              └─ Health       ┬─ Classroom Activities,
           │                 Guidance     │  Pupils and Students Councils, Club
           │                              │  Activities, School Events etc.
           │
           └─ Health Management (Physical and Mental Aspect,
              Environment, School Living etc.)
```

Figure 7-3 Structure of School Health Activities

Health Education in Primary School

■ Health education in primary school is about 8 yearly school hours in the third and fourth grades, and about 16 yearly school hours in the fifth and sixth grades.

■ The contents are "understanding the importance of a healthy daily life and the way to lead a healthy life", "understanding the development of the body", in the third and fourth grades, "understanding of prevention of injury and basic treatment", "understanding of emotions and the way to care for worries and anxieties", "understanding of prevention of disease", in the fifth and sixth grades.

中学校の保健教育
■中学校の保健教育は、「保健体育」の中の「保健分野」として位置づけられ、小学校および高校の保健教育との連続性を考慮して、1～3年を通して学習するように設定されている。保健分野の授業時数は、3学年間で、48単位時間程度を配当することと学習指導要領に示されている。

■学習内容としては、疫学的発想に基づいて（つまり主体・環境・病因にかかわって）、「心身の機能の発達と心の健康」、「健康と環境」、「傷害の防止」、及び「健康な生活と疾病の予防」の4領域が設けられている。

■これらは、現在および将来における健康生活を設計し、そしてそれを実施することができるような能力の獲得と態度の形成というねらいに基づいている。

高校の保健教育
■高校では「保健体育」の中の科目「保健」とされ、1・2年次に各35時間ずつ配当されている。授業の担当者は中学と同様である。

■目標としては、「個人および社会生活における健康・安全について理解を深めるようにし、生涯を通じて自らの健康を適切に管理し、改善していく資質や能力を育てる」ことが示されている。またそれを達成するための学習内容として、「現代社会と健康」、「生涯を通じる健康」、「社会生活と健康」が取り上げられている。
■以上のようにわが国の保健教育は、これまでアメリカ合衆国の影響を特に強く受けてきたものであるが、その形態、内容などについて、独自のものをめざす必要がある。

Health Education in Lower Secondary School

■ Health Education in the lower secondary school is included in the subject of Health and Physical Education, and it is supposed to be studied in each grade level as a continuation from primary school and to that which is to be learned in the upper secondary school. The time allotted for health education in about 48 hours which is described in the Course of Study.

■ As for the content of the subject, it is divided into four fields: 'development of physical and intellectual function and mental health', 'health and environment', 'protection against injury' and the 'healthy life and prevention of diseases' on the basis of epidemiological concepts (in relation to body, environment, and cause of diseases).

■ The purpose of those fields is to encourage students to plan a healthy life now and in the future, and to develop the ability and attitude to be able to realize the same.

Health Education in Upper Secondary School

■ In upper secondary schools, Health Education is included in the subject "Health and Physical Education", and 35 hours are allotted to the subject at the first and second grade levels. The subject teachers are almost the same as those in lower secondary school.

■ The contents of the course are: "contemporary society and health", "lifelong health" and "social life and health". The main objective states "to deepen students understanding of health and safety in the individual and social life, and to foster their endowment and abilities to manage and improve health properly in their whole life".

■ As has been earlier pointed out, health education in Japan has been strongly influenced by the American system, and it is necessary to come to show the originality of Japanese health education in the form and content of Health Education.

現代の課題

■各学齢期の保健学習は、児童生徒が発育・発達の著しい時期であることなどから、他のライフステージにおける健康に関する教育・学習では代替できない重要な意義と役割をもっている。このため児童生徒期においては、生涯を通じて心身ともに健康で安全な生活を送るための基礎を培うという観点から、学校において組織的・体系的な教育活動（健康教育）を行うことは極めて重要である。現在、肥満や生活習慣病の兆候、性の逸脱行動、いじめや不登校、薬物乱用、基本的生活習慣の乱れ、食生活の乱れ、睡眠時間の減少、運動不足、心の健康問題や人間関係の希薄化、ストレスの増大など児童生徒に対する健康問題は山積している。これらの課題に適切に対応するためには、健康的な生活行動を実践するという一次予防を重視することが必要である。

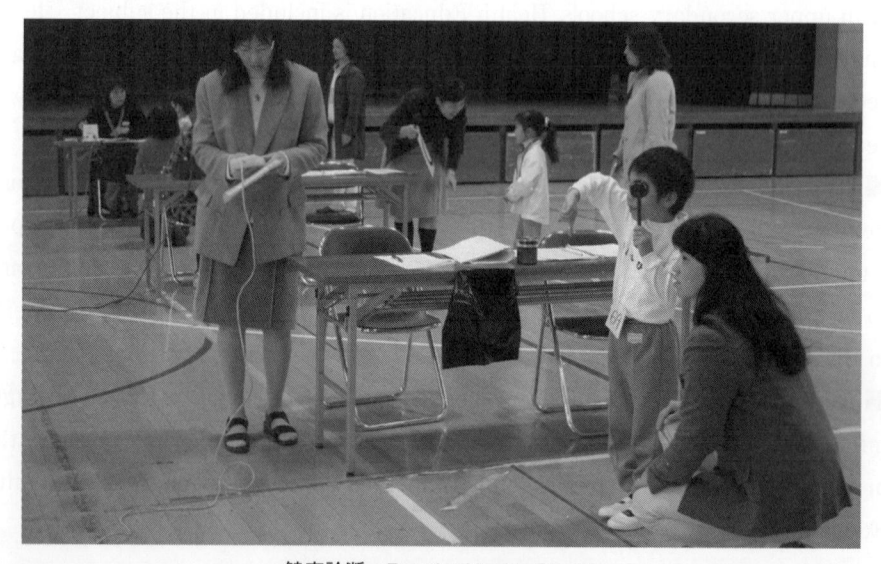

健康診断　Regular Health Check

Issues in a present time

■ As the health learning in each school stage cannot be replaced by the health learning in other life stages, it has an important significance and role. When students are educated in school, they gain a foundation of healthy and safe life in body and mind. Therefore, it is quite important to provide them with systematic health education in school. At present, students have many health problems such as growing fat, sickness based on breaking down of healthy life customs regarding food and sleep, immoral sexual behavior, bullying and truancy, taking too many drugs, poor eating habits, lack of sleep, lack of exercise, mental problems, weak human relations, increase of stress and so on. In order to suitably solve those problems, it is necessary to emphasize a basic prevention undertaking healthy behavior in daily life.

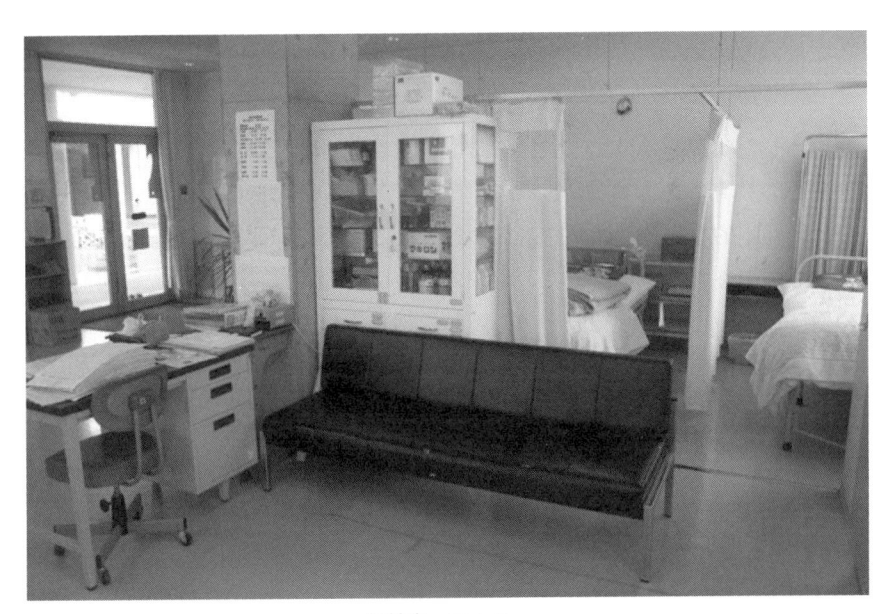

保健室　Sick Bay

9. 道徳教育

(1) 道徳をめぐる日本の現状

■「世界で最も安全な国の一つ」、これが日本に対する、従来のイメージといってよいだろう。たしかに、主要先進国の中では、いまでも犯罪の少ない国ではある。しかし、ここ数年、日本における犯罪が増加傾向にあることは否定できない。冒頭に示したイメージが、過去のものになる日も近いのかもしれない。こうした状況が、「日本の道徳の危機」を象徴的に示しているように思われる。

■このことは統計の上からも確認できる。たとえば、学校の三大病理といわれる、暴力行為、いじめ、不登校についてみてみると、暴力行為の低年齢化（たとえば小学校の校内暴力は 2002 年 1,253 件だったのが、2005 年には 2,018 件）、いじめの陰湿化・潜在化、不登校児童生徒数の増加傾向（少子化にもかかわらず 1994 年 77,449 名だったのが、2004 年には 123,358 名）が顕著である。

■こうした状況を受けて、ここ 10 年ほどにわたって、文部科学省（旧文部省）は「心の教育」をスローガンに、「道徳教育の強化」を推進してきた。そこでは、基本的な道徳的習慣を身につけさせるために、家庭の道徳的教育力の回復も強調されている。また、学校での道徳教育では、教員の資質向上のための「自己研鑽」や、校長を中心とした指導体制の整備・強化、自然体験活動や集団宿泊活動、職場体験活動などの体験型学習の積極的な導入、先人の生き方、伝統と文化、スポーツなど、児童生徒が感動を覚える魅力的な教材の活用、地域社会との連携などが叫ばれている。

9 Moral Education

(1) Present Situation Surrounding Japanese Moral

■ "One of the safest countries around the world", it would be a conventional image of Japan. It is true that Japan is still a low-crime country compared to the other major industrial countries. However, it can't be denied that the number of crimes in Japan has recently been on the rise. The image of Japan mentioned at the beginning may soon become an old one. Such situation seems to represent the "Crisis of Japanese morals".

■ It is also confirmed statistically. For example, in regards to violence, bullying and truancy which are called as three major causative factors at school, it is of particular note that violence has been committed by students of younger age (for instance, the number of school violence at elementary school was increased from 1,253 cases in 2002 to 2,018 cases in 2005), bullying has been getting more insidious and latescent, and the number of truant students has been increased (in spite of fewer children, it was increased from 77,449 in 1994 to 123,358 in 2004).

■ In response, over the last decade the Ministry of Education, Culture, Sports, Science and Technology (former Ministry of Education) has promoted to strengthen a moral education by setting "Education of Mind" as a slogan. To guide students to acquire a basic moral behavior, the ministry also emphasized to restore the influence of home life in moral educational process. Also, the following are required in the moral education at school: "brainstorming" to improve the quality of teachers; upgrading and strengthening the teaching system under principals; active introduction of experience-based studies such as activity in nature environment, lodging activity in a group and experience in a workplace; usage of attractive teaching materials by which students will be impressed such as life story of ancestors, tradition and culture, sports and so on. Cooperation with local community is also required.

■このような道徳教育強化の主張をみると、どちらかというと保守的伝統的道徳、いわゆる「慣習的道徳」の見直しという色彩が濃いように思われる。もちろん慣習的道徳が道徳の基盤であることは間違いない。しかし、経済情勢と強く結びついた社会構造の急激な変化や、いわゆる国際化、情報化の進展などの新たな状況に対応するためには、単に慣習的道徳を遵守するだけでは不十分であろう。そのためには、自らの力で適切な道徳的判断や行動ができる、道徳的反省力、言い換えれば能動的主体的な道徳を創造する力を育てることも重要である。2006年に改正された教育基本法の前文では、「豊かな人間性と創造性を備えた人間の育成」および「自主および自立の精神を養うこと」が重視されている。

■むろん、道徳教育を強化すれば犯罪の数が減少し学校の病理が解決するといった考えは、短絡的に過ぎるだろう。こうした現象の背景は複雑で、広く、深い。たとえばそうした背景として現今優勢な倫理的意識、それと結びついた社会の私事化、身近な共同体の弱体化などがあげられよう。

■「人に迷惑や危害さえ加えなければ、自分の行為は自分で決める。干渉されたくないし、干渉しない。社会全体として快適な状態が増進されればよい。」このような言葉で表現される、いわゆる「他者危害則」と「自己決定権」と「快楽主義的功利主義」が結合したところに今日もっとも一般的な倫理的意識があると言えよう。戦後の日本が目指してきた自由主義社会において、そうした倫理観が一定の妥当性をもってきたことは認められてよい。しかし、これが唯一視、絶対視されることは危険である。たとえば「自己決定権」の絶対化は、容易に自己の「排他的主権性」の主張となり、倫理そのものを裏切る他者への無関心、他者の排除に通じかねない。言い換えれば、今日の倫理的意識には「他者と共に」という意味での「公共」という面が薄弱である。

■ It is felt that the opinions to strengthen moral education give strong suggestion for a review of conservative and traditional moral so-called "customary moral". Needless to say, there is no doubt that the customary moral is a foundation of moral. However, it is insufficient only by complying with the customary moral in order to respond to a new situation such as a drastic change in social structure which is strongly linked to an economic condition and development of internationalization and informatization. To be sufficient, it is also important to foster a moral reflective consciousness which is to make a morally appropriate judgment and behavior by oneself, in another words, the ability to create active and proactive moral. The preceding sentence of the Basic Act on Education, which is revised in 2006, puts stress on "bring up people who are rich in humanity and creativity" and "a spirit of autonomy and of independency" as its educational aim.

■ Obviously, it is too simplistic to imagine that strengthening moral education would reduce the number of crime cases and solve the cause of the problems in schools. The background of those phenomena is complex, wide-ranged, and deep-rooted. A currently dominant sense of morality, lack of public spirit as its consequence, and weakened surrounding communities may be listed as examples of the background.

■ "I will do whatever I want to do unless it troubles other people or harms them. I do not want to be interfered with or interfere with others. I just want the situation of society as a whole to be improved." As expressed in this saying, a mind-set of a combination of so-called harm-to-others principle, the right of self-determination and hedonistic utilitarianism could be the most general sense of morality today. It could be admitted that such a sense of morality has shown a certain level of properness in the liberal society which postwar Japan pursued. However, it is risky to consider this sense of morality to be absolute. For instance, one would easily claim exclusive sovereignty by absolutizing the right of self-determination and may lead to being indifferent towards others who ignore ethic itself and invite ostracism of others. In other words, the current

■このような倫理的意識を是正することは容易ではない。それには政治や経済など多岐にわたる社会変革も必要だろう。だが、いわゆる「新自由主義（ネオ・リベラリズム）」に代わって親密圏としての共同体を見直し、その再構築を主張する「共同体主義（コミュニテリアニズム）」への関心の高まりや、「格差社会」の改善を目指すイデオロギーに囚われない草の根的な社会運動など新たな動きも出てきた。
■道徳教育が実効性をあげるためにも、「公共性」を回復しようとする社会全体の努力と道徳教育の連携が求められている。

（2）日本における道徳教育の変遷

■19世紀後半（明治）以降、日本では欧米をモデルとした近代化を進めるために政治が道徳教育をリードしてきた（教学主義）。しかし、20世紀後半、追いつき・追い越せ型の近代化が一応達成されることで、そうした政治と教育との関係モデルが通用しなくなった、あるいは方向性を見失う状況に陥った。アノミー状態におかれた日本の道徳教育、これが偽らざるその一面だろう。

■学校教育の開始（1872年）当初、道徳教育は必ずしも最重視されていたわけではない。むしろ、社会的な地位の流動化が期待される中でのいわゆる「立身出世」の道具としての知識、また進歩した西洋文明の移入に役立つ実用的知識が最重視された（実学重視）。

■ところが、1880年頃から、伝統的封建的道徳（儒教道徳）をベースとした道徳教育（修身）が、前面に出てくる。やがて、たとえば小学校において、「修身」は、少なくとも形式上、他のすべての教科をリードする教科として位置づけられた。
■このように、日本において、道徳教育が際だって重視されるようになった理由はいくつかあるが、それは何よりも、政府によって、道徳教育が近代化を推進するのに不可欠だと判断されたことによる。明治政府は、「富国強兵」

sense of morality lacks the sense of "public" or "coexistence."
■ It is not easy to remedy such a sense of morality. It requires wide-ranging social reforms including political and economic reforms. However, as an alternate to neo-liberalism, people have started showing interest in communitarianism, which reconsiders communities as an intimate sphere and claims the rebuilding of communities. In addition, nonideological, grass-rooted social movements that aim to reform the gap-widening society have been observed.
■ For a more effective moral education, efforts of society as a whole to regain publicness and moral education need to be collaborated.

(2) Transition of Moral Education in Japan

■ Since the letter half of the 19th century (Meiji), the Japanese government has taken the lead in moral education to promote modernization by referring to the Western culture (doctrine of teaching and learning). However, in the late 20th century, by almost achieving a catch-up-with-and-overtake type of modernization, such a relationship model between government and education had no longer been effective or got into a situation to lose the sense of direction. Japanese moral education in anomie, this is the one of its true aspects.
■ At the beginning of starting school education (in 1872), moral education was not exactly placed as a high priority. Instead, the top priority was knowledge as a tool for "social climbing" where social position was expected to be mobile or practical knowledge which is useful to import advanced Western civilization. (significant concern for practical learning)
■ However since around 1880, moral education (Shusin) based on traditional and feudalistic moral (Confucian moral) came to the fore. Later, for example at primary school, "Shusin" was put as a subject leading all the other subjects, at least in form.
■ As above, there are some reasons why moral education remarkably became an increased center of focus, but the primary reason was because the government determined that moral education was vital to proceed modernization. The

を国家目標としたが、そのためにはいわば遮二無二なって、国家に奉仕する国民の育成が必要だと考えられた。思想信条や「生き方」に関わる道徳教育こそ、そうした方向に相応しいと判断されたのである。

■こうした方向を決定づけたものとして、1890年に出された「教育勅語」があげられる。その第一の特徴は、天皇を「親」とし、国民（臣民）を「子」とする天皇中心主義にある。「万世一系」の天皇を価値体系の中心として、そこから個人道徳、社会道徳、国家道徳に至るまですべての道徳が引き出されている。

■1910年代半ばから1920年代前半にかけて、「教育勅語」を拠り所とする教育体制に、若干の変化が認められた。当時、欧米を中心にして、児童中心主義をスローガンにした新しい教育運動が起こっていたが、その波が、ようやく近代国家としての体裁を備えつつあった日本にまでやってきたのである（大正自由教育）。

■しかし、こうした変化は表面的なものに留まった。教育の改革が、教育勅語の体制そのものを揺るがすことはなかった。1930年代に入ると、経済的破綻に陥った日本は、これを打開するために、軍事力を背景にして、海外に植民地を求め、領土を拡大しようとする帝国主義的施策をとった。道徳教育は、こうした施策を推進する役割を担うことになる。

1930年代後半になると、全体主義的・国家主義的な道徳教育の基調は、軍国主義的道徳教育へと尖鋭化・極端化して行き、ついには、多くの子どもたちを犠牲にして、第2次世界大戦の敗戦という形で、悲劇的な結末を迎えることになる。

■1945年8月15日は、軍国主義的道徳教育が終わった日であるとともに、民主主義に相応しい仕方で、道徳教育の再建を目指す出発の日でもあった。二ヵ年ほどの空白期間があったものの、1947年9月に、修身、地理、歴史、公民からなる総合科目・統合科目「社会科」が設置され、「社会科」を中心にした道徳教育が再開された。「社会科」は、アメリカの"Social Studies"

government in Meiji era set "wealthy nation and strong army" as a national goal, and to achieve that, it was believed that desperately educating the public who would be willing to serve their country was necessary. It was determined that the moral education which was linked to thought and creed and a "way of life" was right for such direction.

■ What dictated such direction includes "Education Rescript" issued in 1890. The first characteristic is a doctrine of emperor-centered which assumes the emperor as a "parent" and citizens as "children". By setting the emperor as an "unbroken line" as a center of the value system, all morals such as individual moral, social moral and national moral was extracted from it.

■ From the middle of 1910 to the first half of 1920 the education system based on Education Rescript was changed to some extent. At that time, there was a new education movement led by western countries under the banner of child-centered education. The wave reached Japan, which had finally started to present itself as a modern state (Liberal education in the Taisho era).

■ However, such changes only occurred for superficial things. Evolution of Education didn't rock the system of Education Rescript. In the 1930s, Japan suffered from economic collapse, and to make a breakthrough, the government implemented imperialistic measures which was to try to expand territory by advancing overseas with military might, seeking areas to colonize. Later, moral education was soon taking a role to promote such measures.

In the late 1930s, the tone of totalitarian and nationalistic moral education was turning to radical and extreme, towards imperialistic moral education, and finally it came to the tragic end of sacrificing many children's lives and losing the second worldwide war.

■ August 15th in 1945 was not only the last day of the militaristic moral education centering on the imperial rescript on education but also a new beginning to rebuild the moral education with the suitable way for democracy. Even though there was about a 2-year blank period, in September 1947 "social studies" which was a comprehensive subject consisting of Shusin (moral education

を参考にしたものであり、子どもの生活体験を重んじ、方法原理としては「問題解決学習」が採用された。正しい社会認識を通して、民主主義社会が求める道徳的資質を育てること、これが道徳教育の第一のねらいとされた。

■しかし、「社会科」を中心とした道徳教育は、10年足らずで終わることになる。地理や歴史の学力低下という批判も中止の理由のひとつだが、道徳教育は社会科で事が足るのではなく、「全教育課程」を通じて力説しなければならない、とした「第二次米国教育使節団」の提言（1950年9月）の影響力が大きい。この提言を受けて、文部省でも、当面、教科としての道徳教育は設置せず、学校のあらゆる場面で道徳教育の振興に努めていく方針が明示された。これが、いわゆる「全面主義道徳教育」である。全面主義は、今日までわが国の道徳教育を支える基本的な理念となっている。

■だが、全面主義も、やがて、見直されることになる。見直しの理由として、指導が断片的・偶発的になりがちで、道徳教育全体の計画化が困難だとする声、青少年の問題行動の増加に対処するには全面主義だけでは生ぬるいといった声があった。しかし、それと共に、当時の政治的な情勢下（米ソの冷戦など）、教育によって国防意識・愛国心を育成するためには、教科としての道徳教育が必要だとする、政治家の声もあった。

■これらの声を受けて、1958年4月から、小、中学校で週1時間、特設「道徳の時間」が実施されることになった。道徳教育を計画的に推進していくための核ができたとして、これを歓迎する人も多かったが、政治的な背景に特に敏感な人たちからは、国家主義的な戦前の「修身」の復活だ、として強い反対もあった。政治的な情勢が一変した現在、政治的な理由から道徳の時間に反対する人は少ない。ただ、設置当初の躓きが、「道徳の時間」を推進する上で、マイナスに働いたことは否定できない。

conducted from Meiji era until 1945), geography, history and civics was established, then teaching the moral education as a subject was started again. The "social studies" referred to the "Social Studies" in the U.S., respected the life experience of children and adopted "learning problem resolution" as a principled method. The first purpose of the moral education was to develop moral qualities by understanding the society correctly which is required in a democratic society.

■ However the "social studies" was ended in less than 10 years. One of the reasons was a decline in scholastic standards in geography and history, but a bigger impact on ending it was from a recommendation made by "the second U.S. educational mission" in September 1950 which asserted that the moral education was not good enough if learnt only in a social studies and should put emphasis on it in all curriculums. In response to the recommendation, it was clearly specified by the Ministry of Education not to teach morals as a subject for some time to come but try to promote moral education in various situations at school. That is what is called "overall moral education". The overall moral education is the basic idea supporting Japanese moral education until today.

■ But before long the overall moral education was also reviewed. As the reasons of the review, there were opinions saying that it was difficult to make a plan for whole moral education as the lessons tended to be fragmentary and accidental, or it was too soft to deal with the increasing problematic behavior of young people. In the meantime, some politician said that a moral education as a subject was needed to develop a sense of national defense and patriotism by education under the political condition at that time (e.g., the cold war between the U.S. and Soviet)

■ In response to the opinions, primary and lower secondary schools started to have one "moral education class" per week from April 1958. Many welcomed it because it can be a core to promote a moral education systematically, but some people who were especially sensitive to the political context strongly opposed it as it was a regeneration of nationalistic "Shusin" before the war. Today after political condition was changed, only a few people oppose to the moral education class because of political reasons, however, it cannot be denied that the faltering

■ここまで見たように、日本の道徳教育の歴史は、必ずしも、平坦ではなかった。しかし、紆余曲折があったものの、現在、道徳教育は、何よりも基本的な人権を重んじる民主主義を大前提として、「全面主義」の理念と「道徳の時間」を車の両輪にして進められているとは言えるだろう。

■20年足らず前のバブル期に日本人全体のモラルが大きく変化した、と言われる。その変化とは、例えば、無節操な私欲の追求や拝金主義、刹那的な欲望充足や公共精神と背馳するプライバタイゼーションの進展などである。こうしたモラルの解体をかかえながら、市場原理至上主義の徹底により経済構造が激変し、「一億総中流社会」から「格差社会」へと社会の在り方がドラスティックに変貌した。それは貧困層の拡大を意味するものであり、結局モラルの低下を含め、社会の不安定化をもたらした。

普通の人が普通に暮らせる社会、弱者が泣き寝入りしなくてよい社会を実態として創らない限り、小手先で道徳教育をいくら工夫しても、社会における道徳の解体という現象に歯止めをかけるのには限界があろう。度重なる道徳教育の「改善」や「強化」が、必ずしも十分な実効性をあげて来なかったことが、このことを物語っているようにも思う。

■教育の憲法ともいわれた教育基本法が、2006年12月に改正された。改正教育基本法は従来のもの以上に道徳教育を意識したものとなっている（たとえば第2条「教育の目標」と学習指導要領「道徳」との関連）。とりわけ先に示した「他者と共に」ということが希薄な今日の一般的道徳的意識に鑑みて、「公共の精神」がとくに強調されている（前文と第2条）。「自主および自律の精神」と「公共の精神」とのバランスの上に立った「人格の完成」が求められているのである。

■だが、新自由主義経済原理によってもたらされた社会の分断化（例えば「格差社会」など）を、ある意味で糊塗するために、新保守主義的な道徳原理や道徳イデオロギーが持ち出されるなら（例えば「伝統」「慣習的道徳」をことさ

start hampered effort to promote the "moral education class".

■ As seen so fan, the histosy of moral education in Japan has been complecated. It can be said that after many changes the present moral education runs with the idea of "overall moral education" and a "moral education class" based on a democracy which respects a basic human rights more than anything.

■ It is said that whole Japanese moral was greatly changed during the bubble years 20 years ago. The changes are, for example, pursuing one's own interest unscrupulously, worshipping money, satisfying momentary desire and promoting privatization which is inconsistent with public spirit. While the moral was breaking down, the economic structure was rapidly changed because of intensive market fundamentalism, Japanese society was drastically changed from "all-Japanese-are-middle-class" to "income gap society". It means a increasing poverty and finally it destabilized the society including moral degeneration.

Unless we create a society in which ordinary people can have an ordinary life and the weak is helped, it would be difficult to stop the moral to be broken down even if devising the moral education with cheap tricks. It seems to confirm the above with the insufficient effects of "improvement" and "strengthening" of moral education.

■ The Basic Act on Education, which was even called "constitution of education," was amended in December 2006. This new version emphasized on moral education more than the previous versions. For instance, it can be seen in the connection between Article 2 "Objectives of Education" or the Act and "Moral Education" of the Course of Study. Above all, public-mindedness is particularly emphasized (in the preamble and Article 2), given the previously mentioned fact that current general sense of morality lacks the awareness of coexistence. Perfecting human character based on the premise of balancing "the spirit of independency and autonomy" and "public-mindedness" are essential.

■ If a new conservative moral principle and a moral ideology are brought up (i.e. an assertion stressing "tradition" and "customary moral" and etc) to connect the society broken by a new liberal economic principle (i.e. "income gap society" and

ら強調する主張など)、それに基づく道徳教育は、現状を肯定させ、本当に求められる社会の実現をかえって遠ざけることにもなりかねない。見方によれば、今進められようとしている道徳教育改革にもこうした傾向がないとは言い切れない。そうした懸念を払拭して、あるべき日本の道徳教育が追求されるべきであろう。

(3) 道徳教育の構造と展開

■具体的に道徳教育を直接規定しているのは、日本の学校教育全般にわたる指針である「学習指導要領」(法的拘束力を持つ)である。指導要領がはじめて出されたのは1947年3月のことであるが、道徳教育については特設「道徳の時間」が始まる1958年に改訂されたものが重要である。道徳教育の「目標」「内容」「指導計画作成」についての考え方など、それ以後の指導要領の基本的な枠組みがこのとき定まったと言ってよい。

■学習指導要領は、ほぼ10年ごとに改訂されている。現行の指導要領(2008年3月告示)は、5回目の改訂によるものである。従来と違って学習指導要領の冒頭に改正されたばかりの教育基本法の全文が収録されるなど、基本法との対応が強く意識されている。それは「総則」の道徳教育の項に「伝統と文化を継承し」とか「公共の精神を尊び」といった教育基本法の文言がそのまま繰り返されているところに、明確に認められる。

■特に注目されるのは、「道徳の時間」が「要」化された点、「集団宿泊活動」(小学校)や「職場体験活動」(中学校)など「公共の精神」や「社会の形成に参画する態度」を養うための「体験活動」が従来にもまして重視された点、「校長の方針」の下での「道徳教育推進教師」(新設)を中心とした指導体制を示した点などである。そこで、この指導要領に即して、日本の道徳教育が、何を目標に、どのような内容を、いかに教えようとしているのかをみてみよう。

etc.), the moral education based on it would affirm the current condition and could make it difficult to create the society which people really need. Depending on how one looks at it, such tendency could be seen in the current reform of moral education. Dispelling such grave concerns, and an appropriate moral education for Japan should be pursued.

(3) Structure and Development of Moral Education

■ What directly lay down moral education is the Course of Study (having a force of law) which is a guidance for overall school education in Japan. The Course of Study was first issued in March 1947, but the important one for moral education is the revised edition issued in 1958 by which "Moral Education Class" was specially set up. The fundamental framework of the Course of Study such as a way of thinking about "objectives", "contents" and "teaching plan" was determined by that edition.

■ The Course of Study has been revised every 10 years. The latest one (issued in March 2008) is the 5th revised edition. It is the first time that whole text of the Basic Act on Education which was just amended is written at the front of the Course of Study. It shows a consciousness of responding the Course of Study to the Basic Act on Education. It is clear by the fact that the same wordings, "pass on traditional and cultures for future generations" and "respect the public spirits" were added to the section of the moral education in "The General" in the Basic Act on Education are used.

■ Especially the followings are noticeable: the "moral education class" is changed to "necessary" education, "Experiential Activities" such as a "lodging activity in groups" (at elementary schools) and "experience in a workplace" (at lower secondary schools) to improve the "public sprits" and "attitude to participate a community assembly" are emphasized, the teaching system which is mainly carried out by a newly created "promoter of moral education" under the "policy of a principal" is determined. Now, along with the Course of Study, look at how the Japanese moral education is going to be provided with what kind of contents

(ア) 道徳教育の目標
■道徳教育の目標については、次のように述べられている。
「道徳教育は、教育基本法及び学校教育法に定められた教育の根本精神に基づき、人間尊重の精神と生命に対する畏敬の念を家庭、学校、その他社会における具体的な生活の中に生かし、豊かな心をもち、伝統と文化を継承し、発展させ、個性豊かな文化の創造を図るとともに、公共の精神を尊び、民主的な社会及び国家の発展に努め、進んで平和的な国際社会に貢献し未来を拓く主体性のある日本人を育成するため、その基盤としての道徳性を養うことを目標とする。」

■このように、指導要領では以下の4つの特性を持つ「主体性のある日本人」の育成と、その基盤としての道徳性を養うことが、目指されている。4つの特性とは、①「人間尊重の精神」と「生命に対する畏敬の念」をあらゆる具体的生活場面に生かすこと、②「伝統と文化」に基づいて「個性豊かな文化」の創造を図ること、③「公共の精神」を尊重しつつ「民主的な社会及び国家」の発展に努めること、④進んで「平和的な国際社会」に貢献できることである。

■急速に国際化、グローバル化が進展している中で、「主体性のある日本人」の育成という言葉が盛り込まれていることは特に重要である。国民性・民族性を基盤としない国際性は、観念的・抽象的なものにすぎない。他国の文化や伝統を深く理解し、心から尊敬するためには、まず、日本人としてのアイデンティティの確立が必要だ、と言うのである。「伝統と文化」の強調も、こうした文脈で理解される。
　ただし、このような教育目標が偏狭なナショナリズムにつながるのではないか、個人の自由を侵すのではないかと言った危惧の声も、少なからずある。

and objectives.
(a) Objectives of Moral Education
■ The objectives of Moral Education are as follows:
"Moral Education are, according to the basic sprit of education stated in the Basic Act on Education and the School Education Law, to foster the morality in children as the foundation, by which they can realize a spirit of respect for human dignity and reverence for life in a family, school, and community life, endeavor to develop a democratic society and state while having a rich spirit, inherit and develop traditions and cultures, pursuing creation cultures with great individuality, to foster independent Japanese citizens who are capable of contributing willingly to a peaceful society and opening the way to the future."

■ As above, in the Course of Study the goal of moral education is to cultivate independent morality, aiming to foster "independent Japanese" with the following four characteristics. First, he/she should be able to realize "respect for human dignity" and "reverence for life" in various life situations. Second, he/she should endeavor to create a "unique culture" based on "tradition and culture". Third, he/she should make an effort to develop a "democratic society and national" along with respecting "public spirit". Finally, he/she should be able to contribute to a peaceful international society.

■ In the rapid development of internationalization and globalization, it is especially notable that the sentence of developing an "independent Japanese" is written in. It implies that Internationality which is not based on nationality and ethnicity is ideological and abstract and, to deeply understand and respect the culture and traditions of other countries, it is needed to establish an identity as a Japanese first. Stressing on the "Tradition and Culture" is also in the same context.

On the other hand, there are also opinions such as setting such an educational goal could lead people to parochial nationalism and invade people's individual freedom.

（イ）道徳教育の内容
■道徳の指導内容については、小学校・中学校における道徳教育の全体構成及び相互の関連性と発展性とを明確にするという意図から、次の４つの視点に基づいて分類がなされている。
①主として自分自身に関すること
②主として他の人とのかかわりに関すること
③主として自然や崇高なものとのかかわりに関すること
④主として集団や社会とのかかわりに関すること

■具体的な内容項目としては、たとえば中学校では、次のようなものがあげられている。
①主として自分自身に関すること
・望ましい生活習慣を身に付け、心身の健康の増進を図り、節度を守り節制に心掛け調和のある生活をする。
・より高い目標を目指し、希望と勇気をもって着実にやり抜く強い意志をもつ。
・自律の精神を重んじ、自主的に考え、誠実に実行してその結果に責任をもつ。
②主として他の人とのかかわりに関すること
・礼儀の意義を理解し、時と場に応じた適切な言動をとる。
・温かい人間愛の精神を深め、他の人々に対し思いやりの心をもつ。
・それぞれの個性や立場を尊重し、いろいろなものの見方や考え方があることを理解して、寛容の心をもち謙虚に他に学ぶ。
③主として自然や崇高なものとのかかわりに関すること
・生命の尊さを理解し、かけがえのない自他の生命を尊重する。
・自然を愛護し、美しいものに感謝する豊かな心をもち、人間の力を超えたものに対する畏敬の念を深める。
・人間には弱さや醜さを克服する強さや気高さがあることを信じて、人間として生きることに喜びを見いだすように努める。
④主として集団や社会とのかかわりに関すること
・法やきまりの意義を理解し、遵守するとともに、自他の権利を重んじ義務

(b) Contents of Moral Education

■ The guidance content of moral education from the standpoints of clarifying the total structure of moral education, the mutual relationship of each element, and the possibility of their development in primary and lower secondary schools. Accordingly, they are classified into the following four viewpoints.

① Content focusing on oneself
② Content focusing on relationships with other individuals
③ Content focusing on nature and a supreme being
④ Content focusing on relationship with groups and society

■ For example, concrete details of the guidance content include the following in the case of lower secondary schools.

① Content focusing on oneself
· Guiding students to contract a lifestyle habit, try to enhance mental and physical health, and exercise moderation and live a harmonious life.
· Guiding students to seek higher goal with strong and constant will, hope and courage.
· Guiding students to make importance of the spirit of independence, think autonomously, and practice one's thought sincerely with taking responsibility for the result of one's act.

② Content focusing on relationships with the other individuals
· Guiding students to understand the meaning of courtesy and behave appropriately according to time and circumstance.
· Guiding students to love human deeply with warm heart and show sincerity for others.
· Guiding students to respect individual characteristics and positions, understand there are various ways of thinking and looking at things, and learn from others humbly with generous spirit.

③ Content focusing on nature and a supreme being
· Guiding students to understand the preciousness of life and respect one's life and the others' which cannot be substituted by anything.

を確実に果たして、社会の秩序と規律を高めるように努める。
・正義を重んじ、誰に対しても公正、公平にし、差別や偏見のない社会の実現に努める。
・日本人としての自覚をもって国を愛し、国家の発展に努めるとともに、優れた伝統の継承と新しい文化の創造に貢献する。
・世界の中の日本人としての自覚をもち、国際的視野に立って、世界の平和と人類の幸福に貢献する。

■これらの内容項目は、道徳の時間の指導内容であるだけでなく、家庭や地域社会と協力・連携して進められる学校での全教育活動を通じて実現されるべきものである。
■ここで道徳教育と宗教教育との関係について、一言述べておこう。政教分離の原則に立って、日本では公立学校で、道徳教育の一環として、特定の宗教を教えることは禁じられている。しかし、「人間の力を超えたものに対する畏敬の念」といった言葉は明らかに宗教的な意味を帯びている。また、「生命の尊さ」に宗教的価値を認めることもできよう。このような宗教的意味や価値が「自然」との関連で取り上げられていることが重要である。というのも、日本人は伝統的に「自然」の中に「永遠な生命」を感得する宗教的感性を大切にしてきたからである。
　しかし、政教分離を反故にし、偏向した天皇崇拝の国家神道を押しつけた、第二次世界大戦以前の道徳教育へのアレルギーもあり、道徳教育に宗教的価

- Guiding students to love nature, have a matured heart which can be moved by beauty, and reverence for the being beyond the human ability.
- Guiding students to believe that human-being has strength and nobility to overcome weakness and ugliness, and try to find a joy to live as a human being.

④ Content focusing on relationship with groups and society
- Encouraging students to understand the meaning of laws and rules, obey them, respect one's right and others', do one's duty certainly and try to strengthen discipline and order of the society.
- Encouraging students to value justice, be fair for anybody and try to create a society free from discrimination and prejudice.
- Encouraging students to love Japan with the awareness of nationality and endeavor for the sake of the development of the nation, the inheritance of the superior tradition, and creation of a new culture.
- Encouraging students to see themselves as "Japanese in the world" and endeavor for the sale of the realization of the peace in the world and happiness of all humankind from the international viewpoint.

■ These contents should not only be taught in the moral education class but also be achieved through all educational activity at schools which is coordinated with family and the local community.

■ Here I would like to say about the relationships between moral education and religious education. On the principle of separation of politics and religion, in Japan it is prohibited to teach specific religion as a part of moral education. However, it is obvious that the sentence of "reverence for the being beyond the human ability" has a religious meaning. Also, you could see a religious value in the expression of "preciousness of life". It is important that such a religious meaning and value is featured in connection with "nature". Because, Japanese has always been traditionally placing a greater importance on religious sensibility which is enable them to sense an "eternal life" in the "nature".

However, many advised to be careful about bringing the religious value in

値を持ち込むことに慎重な意見も多い。

　（ウ）全面主義と道徳の時間
■既に指摘したように、全面主義と道徳の時間は、道徳教育を推進するための両輪である。これについて、指導要領では、次のように記されている。
　「道徳教育の目標は、・・・・学校の教育活動全体を通じて、道徳的な心情、判断力、実践意欲と態度などの道徳性を養うこととする。
　道徳の時間においては、以上の道徳教育の目標に基づき、各教科、総合的な学習の時間及び特別活動における道徳教育と密接な関連を図りながら、計画的、発展的な指導によってこれを補充、深化、統合し、道徳的価値及びそれに基づいた人間としての生き方についての自覚を深め、道徳的実践力を育成するものとする。」

■「全面主義」の理念は、「学校の教育活動全体を通じて・・・道徳性を養う」という文言によく反映されている。
■教科学習は、人文科学的な教科、社会科学的な教科、自然科学的な教科、それに体育などの表現的教科から成っている。
■人文科学的な教科の代表として、国語科があげられるだろう。国語科教育は、言語体系を理解させその知識を生活の中に活かすこと、認識力や表現力などを開発・発達させることをねらいとしている。こうした理解力や能力それ自身が、道徳の実践には不可欠であるが、すぐれた文学作品に触れさせることなどを通して、人間としていかに生きるべきかについて深く考えさせる機会を与えることができる。
■社会科教育のねらいは、現実の社会生活についての基礎的な知識を与え、それらを現実の社会に応用して、様々な矛盾を発見し解決する能力（問題発

moral education because of an allergy to the moral education before the World War II which broke the separation of politics and religion and force people to believe the state sponsorship of Shintoism combined with biased emperor worships.

(c) Overall Moral Education and the Class

■ As mentioned above, the overall moral education and the class are "two wheels of one cart" to promote the moral education. It is written in the Course of Study as below:

"The objectives of moral education are······to develop the morality such as a moral mind, judgment, motivation and attitude to practice morally through the whole educational activity at schools."

In the class of moral education, based on the above objectives, instruction should be given so as to develop students' ability to practice morality by maintaining close relations with moral education conducted in the class of each subject, in the class for period for integrated study and in special activities, and supplementing, intensifying, and integrating this moral education through systematic and developmental instruction, by realizing moral values and the ways to live as a human being based on that values. "

■ The philosophy of "overall moral education" is clearly shown in the sentence of "to develop the morality······through the whole educational activity at schools."

■ Subject studies consist of humanity subjects, social-science subjects, natural-science subjects and expressive subjects such as physical education.

■ A typical subject of humanity would be a Japanese language. The Japanese language education aims at learning the language system and using the knowledge in daily life, and developing and enhancing recognition and expression. Such comprehensive faculty and the ability itself are essential to practice morality. It can also provide a chance to think about how we should live our life as a human-beings through studying excellent literary works.

■ The aim of social studies is to develop an ability to find various contradictions and solve them (ability to find problems and solve them) by providing a fundamental

見能力、問題解決能力）を育成することにある。平和で住みよい民主的な社会・国家を作り出すことは道徳教育の目標でもあるだけに、社会科の意義はきわめて大きい。

■数学（算数）科や理科から成る自然科学教育のねらいは、普遍妥当的な真理の探究と論理的な推論や判断能力を養成することにある。道徳教育にとって特に重要なのは、客観的で公正な判断力、筋道を立ててものごとを捉える論理的思考力であろう。

■表現的教科を代表する体育では、身体の健康と体力に関する知識や身体の正しい鍛錬方法の習得、競技の実践などを通じて秩序ある共同性を身に付けさせることなどに、教科の目標がある。かつて命令服従型の人間を育てるために体育が利用されたことがあったが、勝ち負けにこだわらない寛容さ、フェアーなルールの実践などは道徳教育にとっても有効である。

また、中学校で従来選択科目であった武道が必修化されたが、「伝統と文化の尊重」というねらいにおいて、道徳教育との関係がいっそう強くなった。

■「総合的な学習の時間」は、画一的であると言われがちな日本の学校教育の現状を改善するために導入されたものである。いわゆる教科学習に比較して、指導要領にその詳細な内容が定められてはいない。学校や教師の「創意工夫」が、強く求められている。そのねらいは、児童生徒が自主的に問題を選び取り、主体的に判断を下し、問題の解決と探求に主体的、創造的に取り組む資質や能力を涵養して、個々の児童生徒の人間として「生きる力」を育てることにある。こうした主体的な「生きる力」が、道徳教育とっても不可欠であることは論を待たない。また、総合的学習で実践される自然体験や、職業体験を含む社会体験、グループ学習や異年齢集団による学習などの多様な学習形態、地域の人々の協力なども、道徳性の育成に資するものと期待される。

■学級活動、クラブ活動、生徒会活動、学校行事などを内容とする特別活動の特徴は、これらが、児童・生徒の自主的実践を中心とする集団生活及び集団活動によって支えられているところにある。したがって、道徳教育との関

knowledge about actual social life. Social studies have great significance because a creating a peaceful democratic society/nation is also an aim of moral education.

■ The aim of natural-science studies which consist of mathematics (arithmetic) and science is to cultivate an ability of pursuing universal truth, logical reasoning and making decisions. The most important thing for moral education would be an objective fair judgment and logical thinking power to understand things reasonably.

■ For physical education of expressive subjects, the aim is to acquire an orderly cooperativity by gaining knowledge of physical health and strength, learning how to train the body, and playing sports. Originally physical education was used to develop people to obey orders, but the tolerance not to get hung on the outcome of games and practicing fair rules are also effective for moral education.

At lower secondary schools, martial arts class which used to be elective has changed to compulsory, under the aim of "respecting tradition and culture", enabling the relationships with moral education to become stronger.

■ The "period for integrated study" is introduced to improve the current condition of Japanese education at schools which tends to be called "uniformed". There is no detailed content in the Course of Studies compared to subject studies. Incorporating "originality and ingenuity" into education by schools and teachers is strongly needed. The aim is to cultivate the ability and quality of students to choose problems voluntarily, to make a decision independently, and to pursue and solve the problems independently and originally, then to foster each student's "zest for living" as a human being. Such an independent "zest for living" is also essential for moral education. Also, natural experiences done in comprehensive studies, social experiences including career experiences, various learning style such as group studies and multiage group studies, and cooperation with local community are expected to help the development of morality.

■ The characteristics of special activities such as classroom activities, student club activities, activities of students' council, school events, and so on are backed by group activities and group living independently done by children

連から見るならば、団結、連帯、援助、責任の尊さなどを体験させることで、自主・自立と共に協力の態度を育てるのに有効である。

■「道徳の時間」は、これを教科化すべきだという声が強い。しかし、教科とすることで、それ以外の場面での道徳教育がかえって後退するのではないかという懸念もあり、従来通り教科としては扱わないことになった。だが、道徳教育の「要」であることが明示され、「道徳の時間」は今まで以上に重視されている。

■「道徳の時間」の役割は、それが設置された当初から一貫して、他の場面での道徳教育と「密接な関連」を図りながら、これを計画的・発展的に「補充、深化、統合」することにある、とされてきた。

■それぞれ程度に差異はあるものの、他の場面での道徳教育は、各領域の学習や指導に伴う付随的、断片的な指導にとどまらざるをえない。「道徳の時間」は、学校での道徳教育全体に一定の見通しを持ちながら（計画性）、付随的、断片的指導では不十分な点を「補い」、道徳的な意識を主体的自覚へと「深め」、各場面でなされた道徳学習を児童生徒の内面において「一つにまとめあげる」ことをめざしている。

　「道徳の時間」が、最終的に求めているのは、「道徳的実践力」の育成である。そのためには、道徳的心情を豊かにし、道徳的判断力を高める必要がある。道徳的実践力は、そうした心情と知性とがバランスよく按配された道徳性に基づかなければならない。ただし、心情と知性のいずれに優位をおくかについては、理論上多様な議論がある。

■道徳教育のための優れた副教材や資料の作成が求められているが、2002年に文科省が全小学生・中学生に配布した「心のノート」は注目すべきものである。「教育活動全体を通じて行う道徳教育に資する冊子として活用を図る」とか、「心に響く多様な教材を開発」するために参考にすべきものと言われるように、「心のノート」はいわゆる教科書ではない。それは理念とし

and students. Therefore, to see it from the connection with moral education, it is effective for developing cooperative attitude with independence/self-motivation, by experiencing preciousness of union, alignment, support, responsibility and etc.

■ There is a strong call for making "moral education class" to a subject. However, by making it a subject, there are concerns that moral education may be provided less in other situation. As a result, moral education wasn't changed to a subject. But it is clearly indicated that moral education class is "necessary", and the "moral education class" is emphasized more than ever.

■ A role of "moral education class" has always been to supplement, intensify and integrate the moral education through systematic and developmental instruction by maintaining close relations with moral education conducted in other situations consistently from its start.

■ On one level or another, moral education conducted in other situations can get no further than incidental guidance accompanying the studies and guidance of each area. The "moral education class" aims first, to "supplement" the inadequate areas of moral education by incidental guidance, second, to "intensify" the moral consciousness into the independent self-awareness, and further, to "integrate" moral learning conducted in each situation into children's/students' inner-self, with a certain prospect of whole moral education at schools.

What the class of moral education needs in the end is to develop the "ability to practice morality". It is required to enrich students' moral sentiment and enhancing their ability to make moral judgment. The ability to practice morality must be based on morality which has well-balanced mind and knowledge, however, it is highly controversial which should be prioritized, mind or knowledge.

■ Worth nothing that it is now required to create good supplemental educational materials and documents for moral education, whereby a "note of the heart" was distributed to all students in elementary school and lower secondary school by the Ministry of Education, Culture, Sports, Science and Technology in 2002. As it is said to "use the note as a book which contributes to moral education conducted

ての全面主義と、「要」としての道徳の時間の両方に対応し、さらには保護者にも関心を持たせることで、家庭の道徳的教育力の回復も図ろうとするものである。

　ただし、「心のノート」については、戦前の国定教科書に準ずるものではないかとか、最新の臨床心理学の知見に基づくその巧みな構成が児童・生徒を一定の方向に誘導することにならないかといった声もある。

■小学校、中学校において、「道徳の時間」は、毎週1時間、年間総授業時間数35時間（小学校1年生は34時間）が標準と定められている。授業は、学級担任教師が行う。それだけに、教師の研鑽が、常に、強く、求められている。

■教科ではないが、「道徳の時間」についても、当然「評価」が求められる。評価には、一般に、診断的評価（授業前）や形成的評価（授業中）や総括的評価（授業後）などが挙げられるが、いずれにせよ指導要領では「数値」による評価は行わないことになっている。道徳教育では、数値化できない児童生徒の微妙な変化を教師が捉えるスキルやタクトが重要である。しかし、そこに客観性を担保した評価の難しさもある。

■こうしたなか、「道徳教育推進教師」（道徳教育を主に担当する教師）が設置されることになった。設置の趣旨は、道徳教育推進教師に、道徳教育の全体計画や道徳の時間の年間指導計画作成においてイニシアチブを与え、他の教師の関心を高め、文字通り全教師が一丸となって、協力して道徳教育を展開させる点にある。

　しかし、研修や資格認定体制など、道徳教育推進教師の質を確保する方策をどのように整えるのか、「校長の方針」を前提とするトップダウン体制の強化が、管理強化となって、かえって道徳教育に資する一般教師の自由な発想や活動を削ぐのではないか、といった課題や懸念も多い。

through a whole educational activity", and to refer to "develop various materials which get to the heart", the "note of the heart" is not a so-called textbook. It responds to both overall moral education as a philosophy and the class of moral education as a "keystone", moreover, by encouraging parents to have interests, it tries to regain the power of moral education at home.

However, in regards to the "note of the heart", there are some opinions stating that it seems to be based on a government-designated text book before WWII, and the skillful composition of aspects based on the latest findings of clinical psychology may lead children/students towards a particular direction.

■ The moral education class is required to be provided for one hour per week and for 35 hours per year in primary schools and lower secondary schools (34 hours per year for first year in primary schools). The lesson is conducted by homeroom teachers. Therefore, improving the quality of teachers is always required strongly.

■ Moral education is not a subject but still its class unsurprisingly needs an "assessment". Generally, the assessment includes a diagnostic assessment (before the lesson), a formative assessment (during the lesson), an overall assessment (after the lesson) and etc. The Course of Study instructs not to conduct numeric assessment. In the moral education, it is important for teachers to have skills and tact to detect subtle changes of students which cannot be quantified. But it is also difficult to conduct assessment securing objectivity.

■ Recently, it has been decided to create "promotion teachers for moral education" (teachers in charge of moral education). The purpose is to raise other teachers' awareness of moral education by giving an initiative in making a master-plan of moral education and annual plan of the class to the promotion teachers and develop moral education with all teachers' cooperation.

However, there are concerns and issues such as how to have enough measures to maintain the quality of promotion teachers for moral education which are training, the qualification system and etc., and strengthening the top down system on the premise of the "principal's policy" may cause tighter

■なお、高等学校では、道徳の時間は設けられておらず、「倫理社会」などの社会科系科目を通して、どちらかと言えば理論的な学習が行われている。

学級会　A Class Meeting

controls and a put damper on free thinking and activities of general teachers.

■ At upper secondary schools, there is no moral education class but logical study is carried out through social studies such as "Ethical socials".

自主的学習　Independent Learning

10. 外国語活動、外国語

（1）外国語教育の全体的な枠組
■日本の学校における外国語教育は、小学校では「外国語活動」、中学校では教科「外国語」、高等学校では教科「外国語」を通して行われている。このうち、小学校における「外国語活動」は、第5学年と第6学年に行われる。標準の授業時数は両学年ともに、それぞれ年間35時間、週当たり1授業時間（45分）である。

■小学校の「外国語活動」で取り上げられる外国語の種類については、小学校学習指導要領によって、「英語を取り扱うことを原則とする」ことが示されている。実際にも、英語以外の外国語が取り扱われるケースは、国際学校やミッション系の学校などの例外を除けば、ほとんどみられない。

■中学校における「外国語」は、必修教科の1つとして位置づけられている。高等学校における教科「外国語」は、普通科・専門学科・総合学科のいずれにも共通する「教科」として位置づけられている。「外国語」は、英語表現や英会話など7科目に分けられているが、「コミュニケーション英語Ⅰ」は全ての学科の生徒に必修科目となっている。
■英語教育を重視し、指導の充実を図るという観点から、①小学校・中学校・高等学校の英語の授業におけるALT（Assistant Language Teacher：外国語指導助手）やネイティブ・スピーカーの協力によるティーム・ティーチング、②中学校の英語の授業における少人数指導の実施（例えば、英語担当教員を特別に増やして配置することによって、2クラスの生徒を3クラスに分けて授業を行う）、③スーパー・イングリッシュ・ランゲージ・ハイスクール（ＳＥＬＨｉ）の指定、④英語教員の海外派遣研修、英語担当教員の資質の向上等、さまざまな取り組みが、国、自治体、学校のそれぞれにおいて力強く展開されている。

10. Foreign Language Activities and Foreign Language

(1) A Framework of Foreign Language Education

■ The foreign language education in Japanese school is carried out as "Foreign Language Activities" in a primary school, and as a teaching subject of foreign language in a lower secondary school and an upper secondary school. The "Foreign Language Activities" in a primary school are conducted in the fifth and six grade. And the standard class hours are one hour (45 minutes) per week and 35 hours in a year.

■ As for the kind of language being taught as "Foreign Language Activities", the Course of Study in a primary school describes that English is learned as a rule.

There are seldom found the schools in which teach other languages than English except international shools and missionary schools.

■ The subject of foreign language becomes in a lower secondary school. And it is a common subject in general course, special course and integrated course of the upper secondary school. Though the foreign language subject is divided into seven subjects, such as English Expression and English Conversation, "Communication English I" is compulsory to every student of all the courses.

■ Attaching importance to English education and trying to improve English teaching, various plans and methods are going to be implemented by national government, local governments and schools. Main plans and methods which have been tried are as follows:

① To practice team teaching of English in cooperation with Assistant Language Teachers (ALT) and native English speakers.

② To teach English in a small size class of a lower secondary school. It is also considerable to increase English teachers and make the class size smaller.

③ To establish Super English Language High Schools.

（2）英語教育の始期

■日本の学校教育における英語教育の始期は従来から中学校第1学年に置かれており、小学校段階における英語教育は実施されてこなかった。しかし、1998年12月に告示され、2002年4月から全面実施された小学校学習指導要領によって、新しい学習活動の領域として「総合的な学習の時間」が創設され、その中で行われる国際理解教育の一環として外国語会話活動を行うことが可能になった。小学校における外国語活動の主な目的は、外国語および外国の生活や文化に親しむことである。本来この活動では、外国語として様々な言語が扱われることが可能であるが、実際のところ、開始当初から英語活動を行う学校が圧倒的多数を占めていた。この英語活動の実施は各学校にゆだねられるため、実施回数や内容が異なるなど学校間のばらつきが見受けられるようになった。

■この混沌とした状況から脱するため、2008年3月の小学校学習指導要領の改訂によって小学校に「外国語活動」が新しく設けられ、2011年4月から全ての小学校で実施されることになった。「外国語活動」は第5・6学年の児童を対象にして、週に1時間（年間35時間）実施される。この「外国語活動」においては「英語を取り扱うことを原則とする」ことが小学校学習指導要領に示されている。「英語活動」は、国語や算数などの教科とは異なる。教科書はなく、代わりに副読本が使用される。また、教師は、各児童の到達度を評価しない。学級担任が主に英語活動の担当者であるが、日本人英語担当教員や英語ネイティブ・スピーカーが授業に加わる場合もある。

④ To send positively English teachers abroad for training and improve their quality.

(2) The Period to Begin English Teaching

■ In Japan English had been introduced as an academic subject from the first grade of lower secondary schools, and English had not been introduced in public primary schools. However, in the Course of Study, which was announced in December 1998 and was completely implemented from April 2002, the Period for Integrated Study was set up. During the period, it became possible to do foreign language conversation activities as a part of Education for International Understanding. The main objective of the foreign language conversation activities in primary schools is for pupils to become familiar with foreign languages and the daily lives and cultures related to these languages. With these activities it is possible for each school to deal with various languages; however, from the program's beginning the majority of primary schools conducted English activities. Since the execution of the English activities was entrusted to each school, some differences, such as its execution frequency and content came to be seen among the schools.

■ Because of this chaotic situation, in the revision of the Course of Study in March 2008 (the new version of the Course of Study), "Foreign Language Activities" was newly introduced. From April 2011 "Foreign Language Activities" will be completely implemented in all public primary schools in Japan. The "Foreign Language Activities" will be for the fifth and sixth grade students of primary school, and it will be executed for one hour a week (for 35 unit hours a year). In terms of the "Foreign Language Activities" the new version of the Course of Study indicates that "in principal English should be selected for foreign language activities." This "English Activities" is different from other academic subjects such as Japanese Language, Arithmetic and so on. Textbooks are not used, but supplementary materials are available instead. Furthermore, teachers do not evaluate each student's progress. Homeroom teachers are mainly in charge

■「英語活動」における目標は、「外国語を通じて、言語や文化について体験的に理解を深め、積極的にコミュニケーションを図ろうとする態度の育成を図り、外国語の音声や基本的な表現に慣れ親しませながら、コミュニケーション能力の素地を養うこと」である。具体的な活動には、主にあいさつや自己紹介など音声コミュニケーション活動が含まれる。このような活動は、中学校よりも小学校段階にふさわしいと考えられている。アルファベットや単語を書く活動は限定的であり、音声コミュニケーション活動の補助程度である。

■小学校教育に「英語活動」が導入された理由としては、今日、英語が世界の国際語として重要視されるようになったことが挙げられる。例えば、経済界は日本人の英語運用能力の向上を強く期待している。また、小学校からの英語教育を開始する国が増加している事実もある。日本の小学校における「英語活動」は、これからの国際化社会を生きる子どもたちに、国際的な視野をもった外国語コミュニケーション能力を身に付けさせるものであると考えられている。

■日本の小学校における「英語活動」の主な課題には、まず、教員養成と現職教員研修を充実させることがある。学級担任が活動の中心である以上、英語力の向上は必須である。次に、中学校英語教育とスムーズな連携を構築していくことがある。将来的には、小学校・中学校の一貫した英語カリキュラムが必要となるであろう。最後に、「英語活動」の成果を見きわめることがある。「英語活動」の実行を客観的に評価し、改善していくことが求められる。

of the activity, and Japanese teachers of English and native English speakers occasionally join the classes.

■ The overall objective in the "English Activities" is "To form the foundation of pupils' communication abilities through foreign languages while developing the understanding of languages and cultures through various experiences, fostering a positive attitude toward communication, and familiarizing pupils with the sounds and basic expressions of foreign languages." Spoken communication, such as greetings and self introductions, is mainly included as a main component of the activity. It is thought that such activities are more suitable for the primary school stage than lower secondary school. Activities such as writing the alphabet and basic words are limited and are supplementary for the spoken communication activities.

■ The reason why the "English Activities" was introduced into public primary school education is that English is now emphasized as an international language for people all over the world. For instance, the Japanese economic world is strongly counting on Japanese people to improve their English communication skills. Moreover, it is a fact that the number of countries that are introducing English education from the primary school stage is increasing. In Japan, it is also considered that the "English Activities" at the primary schools is essential for pupils who will live in the future of a globalized society, and it will help them acquire foreign language communication skills with an international perspective.

■ There are several issues with respect to the "English Activities" at the primary schools. First, the initial teacher preparation and in-service teacher training should be enhanced. Because the homeroom teachers are at the center of the activity, the improvement of their English skills is indispensable. Second, a smooth connection between primary and lower secondary school English education should be constructed. An English syllabus which connects primary and lower secondary schools will be necessary in the future. Finally, the results of the "English Activities" in the primary schools should be ascertained. The implementation of the "English Activities" should be objectively evaluated, and

（3）英語教育の目的

■外国語としての英語教育の目的には、教養主義的なものと実用主義的なものがある。教養主義的目的とは、外国語を教えることによって教養を身に付けさせるというものであり、実用主義的目的とは、外国語を教えることによって外国語が実際の場面で使用できるようになるというものである。近年、国際政治や国際経済の場において、英語が重要なコミュニケーションの道具になっている。それにより、英語は、国際語として広く認知されるようになった。このような状況から、現在、日本の英語教育においては、実用主義的目的が重視されている。中学校と高等学校の英語教育の目標は学習指導要領に示されている。その目標は、指導要領が改訂されるたびに、より実践的な技能の習得を重視するようになってきている。

■2008年3月に告示された新しい中学校学習指導要領によれば、中学校における外国語の目標は、「外国語を通じて、言語や文化に対する理解を深め、積極的にコミュニケーションを図ろうとする態度の育成を図り、聞くこと、話すこと、読むこと、書くことなどのコミュニケーション能力の基礎を養う。」ことである。また、2009年3月に告示された新しい高等学校学習指導要領によれば、高等学校における外国語の目標は、「外国語を通じて、言語や文化に対する理解を深め、積極的にコミュニケーションを図ろうとする態度の育成を図り、情報や考えなどを的確に理解したり適切に伝えたりするコミュニケーション能力を養う。」ことに置かれている。

■中学校と高等学校の目標においては、どちらも「積極的にコミュニケーションを図ろうとする態度の育成を図る」ことが共通している。その上で、中学校ではコミュニケーションの基礎的能力の養成に力点が置かれている。高等学校では、「情報や考えなどの的確な理解」と「適切に伝達」という発展的なコミュニケーション能力の養成に重点が置かれているといえよう。

should then be improved.

(3) **Objectives of English Teaching**

■ The aims of teaching English as a foreign language at school include culturalism and pragmatism. In brief, culturalism insists on teaching a foreign language to enable students to cultivate themselves, while pragmatism insists on teaching a foreign language so that students can use it in actual situations. English has recently become an important tool for communication in international politics and the international economy. As a result, English has been widely recognized as an international language. Based on this situation, the pragmatism is currently emphasized in English teaching of Japan. The objectives of English teaching are indicated in the Course of Study. With each revision of The Course of Study, the objectives have been emphasizing students' acquisition of more practical skills.

■ In the new version of the Course of Study for lower secondary school, which was announced in March 2008, the overall objective of foreign language education is "to develop students' communication abilities such as listening, speaking, reading and writing, deepening their understanding of language and culture and fostering a positive attitude toward communication through foreign languages." In the new version of the Course of Study for upper secondary school, which was announced in March 2009, the overall objective of foreign language education is "to develop students' communication abilities in which information and thoughts are adequately understood and are appropriately conveyed, deepening their understanding of language and culture and fostering a positive attitude toward communication through foreign languages."

■ The objectives that the lower and upper secondary schools have in common are "deepening their understanding of language and culture fostering a positive attitude toward communication through foreign languages." Based on this point, the development of basic communication skills is focused in lower secondary school. And in upper secondary school, the development of progressive communications skills is emphasized for adequate understanding and appropriate

（4）英語の授業時数

■1998年12月告示の学習指導要領（改定前指導要領）では、中学校の英語の標準授業時数は各学年、年間105時間、週3時間である。高等学校の英語の授業時数は、科目ごとに単位数で規定されている。高等学校における単位は、1単位時間を50分とし、35単位時間の授業を1単位として計算される。改定前学習指導要領では、各科目の、標準単位数は「英語Ⅰ」が3単位、「英語Ⅱ」が4単位、「リーディング」、「ライティング」が各4単位、「オーラルコミュニケーションⅠ」が2単位、「オーラルコミュニケーションⅡ」が4単位である。

■しかし、日本の英語教育において、コミュニケーション能力の育成が重視されるようになるとともに、英語授業時数の増加を求める要望が多く出されるようになった。この状況を踏まえ、文部科学省は、新しい学習指導要領において英語の授業時数を増加させることとした。中学校では各学年週4時間となる。高等学校では、これまでの英語科目が再編され、各科目の標準単位数は「コミュニケーション英語基礎」が2単位、「コミュニケーション英語Ⅰ」が3単位、「コミュニケーション英語Ⅱ」が4単位、「コミュニケーション英語Ⅲ」が4単位、「英語表現Ⅰ」が2単位、「英語表現Ⅱ」が4単位、「英語会話」が2単位となっている。

（5）英語の教科書

■日本の英語教科書は、中学校、高等学校ともに学習指導要領に示された目標や内容を基に、民間出版社によって編纂される。その後、文部科学省による検定を受け合格しなければならない。

communication of information and thoughts in upper secondary school.

(4) Class Hours of English

■ In the Course of Study, which was announced in December 1998 (the previous version of the Course of Study), the standard number of English classes for each grade in lower secondary school was prescribed as 105 hours a year, or, three hours a week. The standard number of English classes for upper secondary school was prescribed separately for each English subject area, and each subject was prescribed a number of credits. One credit means 35 unit hours (one unit hour is 50 minutes). In the previous version of the Course of Study, "English I" was assigned 3 credits; "English II," "Reading," and "Writing" were each assigned 4 credits; "Oral Communication I" was assigned 2 credits, and "Oral Communication II" was assigned 4 credits.

■ However, when the development of the communication ability began to be emphasized more in Japanese English education, there was a lot of demand that the number of English classes be increased. Based on this situation, the Ministry of Education, Culture, Sports, Science and Technology decided that the number of English classes would be increased in the new version of the Course of Study. The number of English classes given in lower secondary school is prescribed as 140 hours a year, that is, four hours a week. With regard to upper secondary school, English subjects are renewed. "Communication English Basic" is assigned 2 credits. "Communication English I" is assigned 3 credits. "Communication English II" is assigned 4 credits. "Communication English III" is assigned 4 credits." "English Expression I" is assigned 2 credits. "English Expression II" is assigned 4 credits. "English Conversation" is assigned 2 credits. "

(5) Textbooks of English

■ In Japan, English textbooks for both lower and upper secondary school are compiled by private publishers, based on the objectives and content shown in the Course of Study. Afterwards, each textbook has to be authorized by the Ministry of Education, Culture, Sports, Science and Technology.

■中学校の英語教科書は、「聞く、読む、書く、話す」という4技能を向上させるために編集されている。教材は、言語の使用場面や機能と文法事項を組み合わせて、体系的に配列されている。新しい学習指導要領における言語の使用場面例は以下の通りである。
〔言語の使用場面の例〕
a. 特有の表現がよく使われる場面
・あいさつ・自己紹介・電話での応答・買物・道案内・旅行・食事 など
b. 生徒の身近な暮らしにかかわる場面
・家庭での生活・学校での学習や活動・地域の行事 など
〔言語の働きの例〕
a. コミュニケーションを円滑にする
・呼び掛ける・相づちをうつ・聞き直す・繰り返す など
b. 気持ちを伝える
・礼を言う・苦情を言う・褒める・謝る など
c. 情報を伝える
・説明する・報告する・発表する・描写する など
d. 考えや意図を伝える
・申し出る・約束する・意見を言う・賛成する・反対する・承諾する・断る など
e. 相手の行動を促す
・質問する・依頼する・招待する など

■新しい学習指導要領に示されている以下の文法事項が中学校教科書に含まれる。
A. 文：
a. 単文、重文及び複文
b. 肯定及び否定の平叙文
c. 肯定及び否定の命令文
d. 疑問文のうち、動詞で始まるもの、助動詞（can、do、may など）で始まるもの、

■ The English textbooks for lower secondary school are edited so that students develop four skills: listening, reading, writing, and speaking. Teaching materials include language-use situations or functions of language and grammar. They are systematically arranged. In the new version of the Course of Study, the language-use situations and functions of language are indicated as follows:

[Examples of Language-use Situations]

a. Situations where fixed expressions are often used:
・Greetings ・Self-introductions ・Talking on the phone ・Shopping
・Asking and giving directions ・Traveling ・Having meals etc.

b. Situations that are likely to occur in students' lives:
・Home life ・Learning and activities at school ・Local events etc.

[Examples of Functions of Language]

a. Facilitating communication:
・Addressing ・Giving nods ・Asking for repetition ・Repeating etc.

b. Expressing emotions:
・Expressing gratitude ・Complaining ・Praising ・Apologizing etc.

c. Transmitting information:
・Explaining ・Reporting ・Presenting ・Describing etc.

d. Expressing opinions and intentions:
・Offering ・Promising ・Giving opinions ・Agreeing ・Disagreeing ・Accepting ・Refusing etc.

e. Encouraging others to act:
・Asking questions ・Requesting ・Inviting etc.

■ The English textbooks for lower secondary school include the following grammatical items indicated in the new version of the Course of Study.

Grammatical items

A. Sentences
  a. Simple, compound and complex sentences
  b. Affirmative and negative declarative sentences
  c. Affirmative and negative imperative sentences

or を含むもの及び疑問詞（how、what、when、where、which、who、whose、why）で始まるもの

B. 文構造：

a. ［主語＋動詞］

b. ［主語＋動詞＋補語］のうち、

(a)　　主語＋be 動詞＋ $\begin{bmatrix} 名詞 \\ 代名詞 \\ 形容詞 \end{bmatrix}$

(b)　　主語＋be 動詞以外の動詞＋ $\begin{bmatrix} 名詞 \\ 形容詞 \end{bmatrix}$

c. ［主語＋動詞＋目的語］のうち、

(a)　　主語＋動詞＋ $\begin{bmatrix} 名詞 \\ 代名詞 \\ 動名詞 \\ to不定詞 \\ how（など）to不定詞 \\ thatで始まる節 \end{bmatrix}$

(b)　主語＋動詞＋what などで始まる節

d. ［主語＋動詞＋間接目的語＋直接目的語］のうち、

(a)　　主語＋動詞＋間接目的語＋ $\begin{bmatrix} 名詞 \\ 代名詞 \end{bmatrix}$

(b)　主語＋動詞＋間接目的語 how（など）to 不定詞

e. ［主語＋動詞＋目的語＋補語］のうち、

d. Interrogative sentences that begin with a verb or an auxiliary verb (such as "can," "do," "may," etc.), that contain "or" and that begin with an interrogative (such as "how," "what," "when," "where," "which," "who," "whose" and "why")

B. Sentence structures
  a. [Subject + Verb]
  b. [Subject + Verb + Complement]

  (a) Subject + be + $\begin{bmatrix} \text{noun} \\ \text{pronoun} \\ \text{adjective} \end{bmatrix}$

  (b) Subject + non-be + $\begin{bmatrix} \text{noun} \\ \text{adjective} \end{bmatrix}$

  c. [Subject + Verb + Object]

  (a) Subject + verb + $\begin{bmatrix} \text{noun} \\ \text{pronoun} \\ \text{gerund} \\ \text{to-infinitive} \\ \text{how (etc.) + to-infinitive} \\ \text{clause beginning with that} \end{bmatrix}$

  (b) Subject + verb + clause beginning with what etc.

  d. [Subject + Verb + Indirect Object + Direct Object]

  (a) Subject + verb + indirect object + $\begin{bmatrix} \text{noun} \\ \text{pronoun} \end{bmatrix}$

  (b) Subject + verb + indirect object + how (etc.) + to-infinitive

  e. [Subject + Verb + Object + Complement]

  (a) Subject + verb + object + $\begin{bmatrix} \text{noun} \\ \text{adjective} \end{bmatrix}$

(a) 主語＋動詞＋目的語＋ $\begin{bmatrix} 名詞 \\ 形容詞 \end{bmatrix}$

f. その他
（a）There ＋ be 動詞〜
（b）It ＋ be 動詞＋〜（＋ for 〜）＋ to 不定詞
（c）主語＋ tell、want など＋目的語＋ to 不定詞
C. 代名詞
a. 人称、指示、疑問、数量を表すもの
b. 関係代名詞のうち、主格の that、which、who 及び目的格の that、which の制限的用法
D. 動詞の時制など
　現在形、過去形、現在進行形、過去進行形、現在完了形及び助動詞などを用いた未来表現
E. 形容詞及び副詞の比較変化
F. to 不定詞
G. 動名詞
H. 現在分詞及び過去分詞の形容詞としての用法
I. 受け身

■語彙に関して、中学校英語教科書には、約 1,200 語、in front of、a lot of、get up、look for などの連語、excuse me、I see、I'm sorry、thank you、you're welcome、for example などの慣用表現が含まれる。

■高等学校では、科目ごとに教科書が発行される。各科目の教科書に含まれる内容は、基本的に中学校での学習内容を発展させたものになっている。「コミュニケーション英語基礎」、「コミュニケーション英語Ⅰ」、「コミュニケーション英語Ⅱ」、「コミュニケーション英語Ⅲ」のコミュニケーション英語科目に関しては、4技能の統合的かつ総合的な育成を図るための内容が含まれる。「英語表現Ⅰ」と「英語表現Ⅱ」には、生徒の論理的表現力を向上させ

f. Other sentence structures
   (a) There + be + ~
   (b) It + be + ~ (+ for ~) + to-infinitive
   (c) Subject + tell, want, etc. + object + to-infinitive
C. Pronouns
   a. Personal, demonstrative, interrogative and quantitative pronouns
   b. Restrictive use of the relative pronouns "that," "which" and "who" used in the nominative case, and "that" and "which" used in the objective case
D. Verb tenses, etc.
   Present, past, present progressive, past progressive, present perfect and future formed with, for example, auxiliary verbs
E. Comparative forms of adjectives and adverbs
F. to-infinitives
G. Gerunds
H. Adjectival use of present and past participles
I. Passive voice

■ In terms of vocabulary, the English textbooks for lower secondary school include about 1,200 words and phrases such as "in front of," "a lot of," "get up," "look for," etc, and idiomatic expressions such as "excuse me," "I see," "I'm sorry," "thank you," "you're welcome," "for example," etc.

■ In terms of upper secondary school, the textbooks are published in each subject. The content of the textbook in each subject is basically an expansion of what is learnt in lower secondary school. In the subjects of English communication : "Communication, English Basic" "Communication English I," "Communication English II," and "Communication English III," the content attempts to integrate an overall promotion of the four skills. In "English

るための内容が含まれる。「英語会話」には、会話する能力を高めるための内容が含まれる。

■新しい学習指導要領に示されている、高等学校英語科目に共通する言語の使用場面や言語の機能は以下の通りである。各科目においては、このような言語の使用場面や言語の機能の中で、目標を達成するのにふさわしいものを適宜取り上げ、組み合わせて活用される。

［言語の使用場面の例］
a 特有の表現がよく使われる場面
・買物・旅行・食事 ・電話での応答・手紙や電子メールのやりとり など
b 生徒の身近な暮らしや社会での暮らしにかかわる場面
・家庭での生活・学校での学習や活動・地域での活動・職場での活動 など
c 多様な手段を通じて情報などを得る場面
・本、新聞、雑誌などを読むこと・テレビや映画などを観ること
・情報通信ネットワークを活用し情報を得ること など

［言語の働きの例］
a コミュニケーションを円滑にする
・相づちを打つ・聞き直す・繰り返す・言い換える・話題を発展させる・話題を変える など
b 気持ちを伝える
・褒める・謝る・感謝する・望む・驚く・心配する など
c 情報を伝える
・説明する・報告する・描写する・理由を述べる・要約する・訂正する など
d 考えや意図を伝える
・申し出る・賛成する・反対する・主張する・推論する・仮定する など
e 相手の行動を促す
・依頼する・誘う・許可する・助言する・命令する・注意を引く など

Expression I" and "English Expression II," the content includes improving students' ability for logical expression. In "English Conversation," the content includes developing students' conversation ability.

■ In the new version of the Course of Study, the language-use situations and functions of language which are common in the English subjects are indicated below. In each subject, the language-use situations and functions of language that are suitable for reaching the objective are appropriately selected, combined, and used.

[Examples of Language-use Situations]

a. Situations where fixed expressions are often used:
・Shopping ・Traveling ・Having meals ・Talking on the phone
・Sending and receiving electric mail and letters etc.

b. Situations that are likely to occur in students' lives:
・Home life ・Learning and activities at school ・Local events ・Places of work etc.

c. Situations where information is gathered through various methods.
・Reading books, newspaper, and magazines ・Watching TV and movies
・Getting information by using telecommunications network

[Examples of Functions of Language]

a. Facilitating communication:
・Giving nods ・Asking for repetition ・Repeating ・Paraphrasing ・Expanding the topic ・Changing the topic etc.

b. Expressing emotions:
・Praising ・Apologizing ・Expressing gratitude ・Complaining ・Hoping
・Being surprised ・Worrying etc.

c. Transmitting information:
・Explaining ・Reporting ・Describing ・Giving reasons ・Summarizing
・Correcting etc.

d. Conveying thoughts and intensions:
・Offering ・Agreeing ・Disagreeing ・Claiming ・Inferring ・Supposing etc.

■高等学校の教科書に含まれる文法事項は、中学校での学習事項が基となる。新しい学習指導要領には、文法事項は、コミュニケーションを支えるために、言語活動と関連付けて取り扱うことが示されている。なお、以下の文法事項については、「コミュニケーション英語Ⅰ」の中に必ず含まれる。
（ア）不定詞の用法
（イ）関係代名詞の用法
（ウ）関係副詞の用法
（エ）助動詞の用法
（オ）代名詞のうち、itが名詞用法の句及び節を指すもの
（カ）動詞の時制など
（キ）仮定法
（ク）分詞構文

■高等学校における語彙については、科目ごとに扱いが異なる。各科目の教科書に含まれる語彙は以下の通りである。
a 「コミュニケーション英語Ⅰ」にあっては、中学校で学習した語に400語程度の新語を加えた語
b 「コミュニケーション英語Ⅱ」にあっては、「コミュニケーション英語Ⅰ」に示す語に700語程度の新語を加えた語
c 「コミュニケーション英語Ⅲ」にあっては、「コミュニケーション英語Ⅱ」に示す語に700語程度の新語を加えた語
d 「コミュニケーション英語基礎」、「英語表現Ⅰ」、「英語表現Ⅱ」及び「英語会話」にあっては、生徒の学習負担を踏まえた適切な語

■中学校、高等学校の英語教科書に含まれる題材には、英語圏を中心とするさまざまな国の人々および日本人の日常生活、風俗習慣、物語、地理、歴史、伝統文化や自然科学などに関するものが含まれる。このような題材の取り扱

e. Encouraging others to act:
・Requesting ・Inviting ・Permitting ・Advising ・Ordering ・Attracting one's attention etc.

■ Grammatical items included in English textbooks for upper secondary school are based on those dealt in lower secondary school. The new version of the Course of Study points out that the grammatical items should be dealt with language activities in order to support communication. The following grammatical items must be included in "Communication English I."
(a) Infinitives
(b) Relative pronouns
(c) Relative adverbs
(d) Auxiliary verbs
(e) Pronoun " it " which stands for the following noun phrase or noun clause
(f) Tense forms etc.
(g) The subjunctive mood
(h) Participial construction

■ In terms of upper secondary school, vocabulary is dealt with differently in each subject. Vocabulary dealt in each subject is as follows:
a. In "Communication English I" the words dealt with in lower secondary school and about 400 new words are included.
b. In "Communication English II" the words dealt with in "Communication English I" and about 700 new words are included.
c. In "Communication English III" the words dealt with in "Communication English II" and about 700 new words are included.
d. In "Communication English Basic," "English Expression I," "English Expression II," and "English Conversation," appropriate words are selected in accordance with students' learning difficulties.

■ In the materials included in the English textbooks for both lower and upper secondary school, a variety of topics should be chosen from daily life, manners and customs, stories, geography, history, traditional cultures, and natural science,

いについては、生徒の発達段階及び興味・関心に即するべきであるとされている。

外国語補助教員(ALT)による授業　Class Teaching by Assistant Language Teacher

etc. of people from various countries, particularly those who use English, as well as from Japan. They should correspond with the students' maturity level and be relevant to their interests and concerns.

外国語補助教員（ALT）による授業　Class Teaching by Assistant Language Teacher

11. 総合的な学習の時間

■「総合的な学習の時間」は、1996年の第15期中央教育審議会答申「21世紀を展望した我が国の教育の在り方について　第一次答申」において、新設される方向性が示された。
　この答申の中では、子どもたちを取り巻く社会環境を概観して、彼らの「生きる力」の低下が指摘されているが、そうした力の伸長の必要性から、既存の複数の教科に関わる国際理解教育・情報教育・環境教育といった、教科横断的・総合的な指導の推進が主張された。

■さらに、同答申では、「その具体的な扱いについては、子どもたちの発達段階や学校段階、学校や地域の実態等に応じて、各学校の判断により、その創意工夫を生かして展開される必要がある。」として、実施の形態・時期など取り扱いについては、各地域・学校の裁量権を大幅に認め、各学校の特色を生かした学習内容の展開が求められた。

■この答申を受けて1997年の教育課程審議会において、文部大臣より「自ら学び、自ら考える力などをはぐくみ、創造性を育てる」教育内容のあり方についての諮問があり、1998年の同審議会答申において、「総合的な学習の時間」が規定され、同年の学習指導要領の改訂において既存の教科・道徳の時間（小学校・中学校）・特別活動に加えた第4の領域として新設された。ただし、「小学校については、低学年において総合的な性格をもつ教科である生活科が設定されていることや生活科を中核とした他教科との合科的な指導が進められていることなどを考慮して、第3学年以上に設定」されることになった。

11. Period for Integrated Study

■ The 15th session of the Central Council for Education published its first report entitled "The Model for Japanese Education from the Perspective of the 21st Century" in 1996 and laid out the direction for newly creating the "period for integrated study" in the report.

The report first reviewed the social environment surrounding children and pointed to the decline in "zest for living" in children and thus the need for cultivating it. Then, it stressed the increasing need for cross-curriculum studies that relate to all the existing subjects, such as international understanding, information and environment and accordingly the need for promotion of cross-synthetic and comprehensive teaching.

■ Furthermore, the report asserted that each local community and school should have more discretionary powers in determining the form and timing of implementation of the period so that the content could reflect the characteristics of each school, by stating "each school should be able to show ingenuity in determining the specific handling of the period, taking into account children's developmental and educational stages and the reality of the local community and school."

■ In light of the report, in 1997, the curriculum council was instructed by the Minister of Education to consider educational content that helps children to "develop ability to learn and think independently and foster creativity." Then, the report of 1998 published by the council stipulated the "period for integrated study". Finally, in the 1998 revised version of Course of Study, the period was newly created as the fourth field in addition to the existing subjects, moral education (in primary and lower secondary school) and special activities. However, it was decided that the period for integrated study would be "introduced from the third grade of elementary school, since in the lower grades, the life environment

■なお、1998年の学習指導要領においては、小学校では「総合的な学習の時間」は、第3・第4学年で年間105時間、第5・第6学年で年間110時間、中学校では、第1学年は年間70～100時間、第2学年では年間70～105時間、第3学年では70～130時間と、かなりの授業時数を配分しており、高校においても卒業までに105～210時間が実施されている。

■「総合的な学習の時間」の指導のねらいは、以下のような3つのことに置かれている。
　①自ら課題を見付け、自ら学び、自ら考え、主体的に判断し、よりよく問題を解決する資質や能力を育てる。
　②学び方やものの考え方を身に付け、問題の解決や探求活動に主体的、創造的に取り組む態度を育て、自己の生き方を考えることができるようにする。
　③各教科、道徳及び特別活動で身に付けた知識や技能を相互に関連付け、学習や生活において活かし、それらが総合的に働くようにする。

■「総合的な学習の時間」に実際に行われている学習活動は大きく次のような3つの種類に分類することができる。
　①国際理解学習、情報学習、環境学習、福祉・健康学習など、横断的・総合的なテーマ学習
　②さまざまな遊びやものづくり、季節や行事に関連した活動等、児童生徒の興味や関心に基づいて行われる活動
　③地域体験学習、地域行事に参加する活動、職場体験活動、ボランティア活動など、地域や学校の特色に応じた課題に取り組む活動

■「総合的な学習の時間」における学習活動の特色は、自然体験、ボランティ

studies, which is an integrated subject, has already been established and cross-curriculum teaching has already been promoted putting the life environment studies at its core."

■ The Course of Study 1998 version allocates a considerable amount of school hours to the "period for integrated study" with 105 school hours annually for the third and fourth graders and 110 school hours for the fifth and sixth graders at elementary school, and 70~100 school hours annually for the first graders, 70~105 school hours for the second graders and 70~130 school hours for the third graders at lower secondary school. The period has been allocated 105~210 school hours at upper secondary school as well.

■ The aims of the period for integrated study are as follows:
  ① Develop abilities to identify problems, and learn, think, judge and effectively solve the problems for oneself.
  ② Learn how to study and think, develop one's attitude to solve problems, and explore creative ideas for oneself, and thereby think about one's way of life.
  ③ Relate student's knowledge and skills obtained in each subject, moral education and special activities with each other through the "period for integrated study" and apply such knowledge and skills in their learning and living comprehensively.

■ Actual learning contents of the period for integrated study can be classified into the following three areas:
  ① Study under cross-sectional and comprehensive themes, such as international understanding, information technology, environmental issues, welfare and health issues.
  ② Activities based on students' interest and attention, including games, craft arts and activities relating to seasons and events.
  ③ Learning through activities relating to the region and school, such as experiences of work, and joining events and volunteer activities in the community.

■ The period for integrated study often involves learning through experiences

ア活動などの社会体験、観察・実験、見学や調査、発表や討論、ものづくりや生産活動など、体験活動を通して行われることに求められる。また、多くが問題解決的な学習であること、グループ学習や異年齢集団による学習であること、地域の人々の協力を得て行われることなど、教科の学習には見られない特色がある。

■「総合的な学習の時間」は大きな成果を上げている。「総合的な学習の時間」は児童生徒にとって楽しい、充実した学習の場である。「知識基盤社会」に求められる自ら学び、自ら考える主体的な能力を育てる上で効果を発揮している。環境問題や福祉問題、地域の課題やキャリア教育など重要な社会的課題に対する主体的な取り組みを促す上でも大きな役割を果たしている。「総合的な学習の時間」が導入され、日本の学校教育は大きく変わることになった。

■しかしながら、「総合的な学習の時間」において多様な内容を扱うことは、教員に対して各領域の趣旨に対する理解をもとにした学習目標の設定といった、新しい課題を生み出すこととなった。また、児童生徒の主体的関心を軸に展開しなければならないために、教員にとっては、それらの関心に対応できるような高度な指導力が必要となってくる。
　また児童生徒がこの「総合的な学習の時間」において学んだ内容を、総合的に生かすことができるようになるかについては導入期においては検証が難しい問題であった。
■「総合的な学習の時間」が導入された後、2003年の中央教育審議会答申「初等教育における当面の教育課程及び指導の充実・改善方策について」において「総合的な学習の時間」についての検証が行われ、次のような批判を受けた。
　①目標や内容が不明確なままである。
　②めざすべき力が身に付いたかの検証が不十分である。
　③教科との関連に充分に配慮されず、生徒の主体性や興味関心にもっぱらゆだねて、教師による適切な指導が行われていない。

such as activities in nature, volunteer and other social activities, observation, experiments, field trip, investigation, presentation, discussion, craft arts and production activities. This study also has features such as learning from problem solving processes, learning in a group consisting of different age groups, and learning in cooperation with people in one's community. Other subjects do not have such features.

■ The period for integrated study has shown great effects. Students have enjoyed the study very much. The study has shown effects in terms of developing one's ability to learn and think for oneself, which is required in this knowledge-base society. The study plays an important role in encouraging students to work on important social issues for themselves, such as environmental issues, welfare issues, regional issues and career education. After the period for integrated study was introduced, Japanese school education has greatly changed.

■ However, handling a diversity of contents in the "period for integrated study" created new challenges for teachers such as setting the objectives based on their understanding of the differences in purposes of each field. Also, the lesson is supposed to revolve around students' spontaneous interests, which can be dealt with by only highly competent teachers.

Moreover, in the introductory period, it was difficult to verify that students were able to comprehensively utilize the content they learnt in the "period for integrated study".

■ After the implementation of the "period for integrated study", the Central Council for Education evaluated the period in its report entitled "Immediate Policies to Enhance and Improve the Curriculum and Instruction in Primary and Secondary Education" in 2003, and criticized the period based on the following reasons.

① Objectives and content remain unclear.
② Examinations on whether children have acquired targeted abilities have not fully been conducted.

■また2007年の中央教育審議会教育課程部会では、2002年以降の「総合的な学習の時間」の実施を肯定的にとらえつつも、導入当初の課題を下記のように指摘している。
　①学校間の成果の差が大きく、また学校間において重複の取組が見られる。
　②総合的な学習の時間において、その拡大解釈的な教育活動を行う事例がみられる。
■そこでこれらの課題の解決のために、2008年の学習指導要領の改訂においては、「確かな学力を確立するために必要な時間の確保」という名目のもと、「総合的な学習の時間」の授業時数が、小学校においては各学年とも年間70時間に、中学校においても第1学年は年間50時間、第2・第3学年は年間70時間に削減され、高校についても3-6単位とするが特に必要がある場合には2単位とすることができるとされた。

■新設されてからのさまざまな反省をふまえて、改訂の具体的事項として次の諸点が示された。
　①日常生活における課題を発見し解決しようとするなど、実社会や実生活とのかかわりを重視し、総合的活動、探究的活動により、育てたい力を学習方法、自分自身、他者や社会とのかかわりなどの視点から明確にする。
　②身につける能力を規定し、達成状況を適切に評価する。
　③小学校は、地域の人々の暮らし、国際理解、伝統や文化、情報が日常生活や社会に与える影響などに関する学習を充実させる。中学校は、職業や自己の将来、自己の生き方を考えるなどの学習を充実させる。
　④地域の人との意見交換など他者と協同して課題を解決する学習、分析し、まとめ、表現する問題解決や探求的活動を重視する。中学校修了段階で

③ Relevance with other subjects are not fully taken into account and focus is so much on students' initiatives and interests that teachers do not give them proper instructions.

■ Also in 2007, while making a positive assessment of the implementation of the "period for integrated study", the curriculum committee of the Central Council for Education pointed out the following problems concerning the "period for integrated study" in the introductory period.

① The outcomes differ greatly between schools and some activities are overlapping between elementary schools and secondary schools.

② In some cases, the period for integrated study is used for learning activities in which the concept of the period is stretched too far.

■ In order to solve these problems, the revised Course of Study of 2008 reduced the number of school hours allocated to the "period for integrated study" to 70 hours annually for all graders at elementary school and to 50 hours for the first graders and 70 hours for the second and third graders at lower secondary school, for the reason that "the time necessary for consolidating solid academic capabilities should be secured." In the case of upper secondary school 3-6 were allocated for the period but if necessary 2 units could be applied.

■ Meanwhile, based on various reflections since the implementation of the period, the guideline articulated the following points as specific matters for revision.

① Emphasize relationships with the real world and real life by, for example, trying to discover problems in everyday life and solve them. Also, clarify the perspectives from which children's abilities should be developed, such as learning methods, thinking of children by themselves and interaction with others and society.

② Specify children's abilities to be developed and properly evaluate the level of achievement.

③ At primary school, enhance learning activities regarding local people's

論文をまとめることに配慮する。
　⑤事例収集、コーディネーターの育成、地域の教育力の活用などを進める。
　⑥教育委員会の指導を受け、各学校は組織的に取り組み、その状況を点検・評価する。

■また、「総合的な学習の時間」を学習指導要領の総則から独立させ、各学校の教育課程においてその位置づけを明確にした。さらに、「総合的な学習の時間」の一層の充実を目指して、体験活動と言語活動を重視し、内容的にもより踏み込んだ改訂がなされた。

■ところで、この「総合的な学習の時間」については、導入のほぼ同時期に高等教育および教育社会学の研究者等から提起された学力低下論との関係で論じられることが多かった。これらの議論の多くは、2000年のPISA調査結果にみられたように日本の「学力」は「低下」傾向にあり、その要因は「ゆとり教育」にあるとするものであるが、これを「総合的な学習の時間」と結びつける見方も今なお多く存在する。
　しかしながらPISA型学力調査において、日本の子ども達のもつ学力的課題は「思考力・判断力・表現力等を問う記述式問題、知識・技能を活用する問題に課題」があるとされているが、これはまさに「総合的学習の時間」に

lives, international understanding, tradition and culture, and the influence of information on everyday life and society. At lower secondary school, promote learning activities that make students think about occupations, their future and their own way of life.

④ Put emphasis on activities that require students to solve problems in cooperation with others, such as learning from each other and exchanging opinions with local people, and problem-solving and inquiry activities that require students to analyze, organize and express something. It is also considered that students should be able to complete their dissertation before graduating from a lower secondary school.

⑤ Collect case examples, cultivate coordinators, and utilize local educational power.

⑥ Each school should receive instructions from the board of education, conduct activities systematically and evaluate the situation.

■ Also, the revised Course of Study has a chapter for the "period for integrated study" independently from the general provisions, clarifying its place in the curriculum of each school. Furthermore, the Course of Study gives more specific instruction on the content, noting that hands-on learning activities and language activities are vital to enhance the "period for integrated study". Therefore it can be said that this revision aims to further enrich the "period for integrated study."

■ The "period for integrated study" has often been discussed in relation to the declining academic standards theory raised by higher education researchers and educational sociologists around the same time as the implementation of the period. Many of them argued that Japan's "academic achievement" indicated by PISA results of 2000 showed a declining tendency and this was attributed to "education with room to grow". The view that links "declining academic achievement" to the "period for integrated study" still remains persistent.

However, the PISA style survey on academic performance indicates that Japanese children have "problems in solving descriptive questions that test their

よってこそ克服を目指すべき課題であり、総合的学習に対する前述の批判は直接的には当たらないといえる。

ただ、「総合的な学習の時間」については、改訂後も地域・学校や教員などにより、学習内容が大きく変わることも予想され、その目標が定着し、その著しい効果が出るのはまだ先のことであるとも言える。しかし、日本には戦前より経験主義的教育による優れた実践も数多く存在しており、これらの経験を踏まえ、更なる充実が今後期待できよう。

地域の人の協力による自然観察活動
Nature Appreciation Experience Carried Out by Community Members

cogitation, judgment and expressiveness", which should precisely be overcome through the "period for integrated study", and therefore this argument does not seem valid.

On the other hand, the content of the "period for integrated study" varies greatly depending on the community, school and teacher, even after the revision of the Course of Study, and it will still be a long time before the objectives take root and any significant effect is seen. Nevertheless, Japanese people have produced a number of excellent practices arising from empirical education since prewar periods, and hopefully, the "period for integrated study" will be further enhanced on the basis of those achievements.

12. 特別活動

(1) 特別活動の意味
■特別活動の主な活動

　特別活動とは日本の小学校、中学校、高等学校の教育課程を構成する要素の1つであり、児童生徒の学校生活の維持と充実のために大切な役割を果たしてきた領域である。具体的には、学級やホームルームでの活動や、学年・学校全体での活動などがあり、特別活動が児童生徒の将来の生き方あり方に与える影響は大きい。

　このように、人々に長期間にわたって影響を与える学校生活の中で、自主的・実践的な活動を意図的、計画的に実施する領域が特別活動である。学校生活の中で無意図的にも進められることがある人間形成を、特別活動を通して教師は意図的に実施している。

　集団活動を通して民主的な社会の形成者を養成する特別活動には、小学校、中学校の学級で実施される活動や高等学校のホームルームで実施される活動がある。また、全校的規模で行われる小学校の児童会活動、中学校、高等学校の生徒会活動がある。さらに、学校生活に変化を与える学校行事がある。小学校ではこれらに加えて同好の児童が集まるクラブ活動がある。中学校、高等学校では部活動が実施されているが、現行では部活動は課外活動であり、教育課程内の領域としての特別活動には含まれていない。しかし、部活動もクラブ活動と同様に教育効果のある活動である。

■「人格の完成」に寄与する特別活動

　教育基本法では、教育の目的を「人格の完成」としているが、人格は個人

12. Extracurricular Activities

(1) The Meaning of Extracurricular Activities

■ Main Activity of Extracurricular Activities

We can remember events from the age of primary school, lower secondary school, upper secondary school with nostalgia today. This is because events of those days have various influences on a human beings formation. Through upbringing of a social nature, for example, or upbringing of personal adaptation ability, the influence that school life gives the present and the future ideal method concerning the way of life of students impacts them greatly.

Such activities of school life affect people in the long term. A domain for carrying out practical activity intentionally is extracurricular activities. Human development takes place indirectly in school life. Teachers carry out human development directly through extracurricular activities.

Extracurricular activities train people for democratic social formation through group activities. These extracurricular activities, are carried out in primary school classes and lower secondary schools and also in upper secondary school homerooms. There are child society activities of primary schools done on a whole school-wide basis. There are student council activities in lower secondary schools and upper secondary schools. Furthermore, there are school events to give school life variation. There are club activities that children with the same interest gather for, which also take place in primary schools. Club activities are carried out in lower secondary schools and upper secondary schools, but existing club activities besides primary schools are not included in extracurricular activities as a domain in a course of study. However, club activities in lower secondary schools and upper secondary schools are activities with educational effects, also.

■ Extracurricular Activities to Contribute to "Completion of Character"

In the Basic Act on Education, a purpose of education is "the completion of

の成長の過程で体験等を通して形成されていくものである。学校では集団活動を通じてこうした体験を積むことができるように計画を立てている。特別活動は、児童生徒の人格形成の機会を十分に提供することによって、教育の目的達成に寄与している。

特別活動の領域は集団活動を通した自主的、実践的な態度の育成が目標であるため、生徒指導との関連をはかり、生徒指導の機能を十分に生かすことができる。

(2) 特別活動の目標と指導原理
■特別活動の目標

特別活動の目標について、各学習指導要領では、学校段階別に、次のように明記している。

表 7-12　特別活動の目標、2008 年度

小学校学習指導要領（2008 年）	中学校学習指導要領（2008 年）	高等学校学習指導要領（2009 年）
望ましい集団活動を通して、	望ましい集団活動を通して、	望ましい集団活動を通して、
心身の調和のとれた発達と個性の伸長を図り、	心身の調和のとれた発達と個性の伸長を図り、	心身の調和のとれた発達と個性の伸長を図り、
集団の一員としてよりよい生活や人間関係を築こうとする自主的、実践的な態度を育てるとともに、	集団や社会の一員としてよりよい生活や人間関係を築こうとする自主的、実践的な態度を育てるとともに、	集団や社会の一員としてよりよい生活や人間関係を築こうとする自主的、実践的な態度を育てるとともに、
自己の生き方についての考えを深め、	人間としての生き方についての自覚を深め、	人間としての在り方生き方についての自覚を深め、
自己を生かす能力を養う。	自己を生かす能力を養う。	自己を生かす能力を養う。

特別活動は「望ましい集団活動」を通して「なすことによって学ぶ」という指導原理に基づいて行われる教育活動である。

■小学校の目標の特徴

小学校では、「心身の調和のとれた発達と個性の伸長」という個人的課題や、

character". We form character through experiences gained during a process of personal growth. We carry out this experience through group activities premeditatedly at school. Extracurricular activities contribute to achievement of purpose of education by offering ample opportunities for character formation.

Independence through group activity and upbringing of a practical manner are domain aims of extracurricular activities. Therefore extracurricular activities measure the connection with student guidance and can be a function of student guidance.

(2) The Aim and Guiding Principle of Extracurricular Activities
■ The Aim of Extracurricular Activities

Regarding the aim of extracurricular activities, I'll specify them according to the school stage by each course of study as follows.

Table 7-12 The Aim of Extracurricular Activities, 2008

Course of Study for Primary schools (2008)	Course of Study for Lower Secondary Schools (2008)	Course of Study for Upper Secondary Schools (2009)
It enables desirable group activity to take place.	It enables desirable group activity to take place.	It enables desirable group activity to take place.
Development which harmony of mind and body is able to take place, and extensions of individuality are aimed at.	Development which harmony of mind and body is able to take place, and extensions of individuality are aimed at.	Development which harmony of mind and body is able to take place, and extensions of individuality are aimed at.
The independent and practical attitude which tries to build a better life and better human relations as a collective member is raised.	The independent and practical attitude which tries to build a better life and better human relations as a collective member of a group or society is raised.	The independent and practical attitude which tries to build a better life and better human relations as a collective member of a group or society is raised.
The idea about one's way of life is deepened.	The consciousness about the way of life as a person is deepened.	The consciousness about the way of life as a person is deepened.
The capability to employ self efficiency is supported.	The capability to employ self efficiency is supported.	The capability to employ self efficiency is supported.

Extracurricular activities are carried out through "desirable group activity" and education activities are based on the guiding principle of "learning by doing".
■ Characteristics of the Aim of Primary Schools

An aim of primary schools is "the development and extension of personality

「集団の一員」という社会的関係が目標設定されており、この目標は中学校、高等学校でも一貫している基盤的なものである。

■中学校・高等学校の目標の特徴
　中学校では「社会の一員」としての意識や「人間としての生き方」への自覚が付加されている。高等学校では、中学校に加えて「人間としての在り方」への自覚が付加されている。

(3) 特別活動の系譜
■1951（昭和26）年まで
　戦前から「生活が人間を形成する」というペスタロッチ（Johann Heinrich Pestalozzi）の生活教育の影響が公教育に見受けられる。教科外の活動を重視し、協同作業によって「生活者」を形成していく思想である。その後、デューイ（John Dewey）がアメリカで新教育運動を展開し、学校で自治的活動を導入する。
　1947（昭和22）年に『学習指導要領一般編（試案）』が文部省によって示され、教科の1つとして「自由研究」（小学校4年から中学校3年まで）が登場する。「児童の活動をのばし、学習を深く進める」ために設置されたこの教科が、従来の教科外活動を教科として教育課程に位置づけた出発点である。
　1951（昭和26）年の　『学習指導要領一般編（試案）改訂版』によって、小学校で「教科以外の教育活動」、中学校と高等学校で「特別教育活動」が登場する。このことにより、教科外の教育活動が1つの領域として教育課程に位置づけられた。この領域については、児童会、委員会、児童集会、奉仕活動、学級会、クラブ活動、ホームルーム、生徒会、生徒集会などが例示されている。

gained with harmony of mind and body". Furthermore, the social relation named "a member of a group" is an aim, too. These aims are consistent in lower secondary schools and upper secondary schools.

■ Characteristics of the Aim of Lower Secondary Schools and Upper Secondary Schools

Consciousness as "a social member" and awareness to "way of life as a human being" have been added in lower secondary schools. In upper secondary schools, awareness to "an ideal method as a human being" is added as well as in lower secondary schools.

(3) The Genealogy of Extracurricular Activities

■ Until 1951 (Showa 26)

The supposed influence of education through living by Pestalozzi (Johann Heinrich Pestalozzi who claimed that "life forms a human being", was brought forward since before World War II for public education. Many kinds of extracurricular activities, are thought forming of "good personality" by using cooperative work. Dewey (John Dewey) developed a new education movement in the U.S.A. and introduced self-governing activities at school.

"The Course of Study" (a tentative plan) of 1947 (Showa 22) is published by the Ministry of Education, and "a free study" (from fourth graders to lower secondary school third graders) appears as one of the subjects. This subject, that was introduced as "increase activity of children, and to advance learning deeply" is the starting point that placed conventional subjects and outside activities in a Course of Study as a subject.

Based on "The Course of Study revised edition" (a tentative plan) of 1951 (Showa 26), we work on "education activities external to subjects" in primary schools, and "extracurricular education activities" in lower secondary schools and upper secondary schools. By this, education activities external to subjects was located in a Course of Study as one domain. In this domain, we work on child society, a committee, a child meeting, service, and there are class societies, club activities,

■それ以後ほぼ10年ごとの改訂
　1958（昭和33）年の『学習指導要領』で、小学校、中学校、高等学校で名称が統一され、「特別教育活動」が誕生した。なお、この時は学校行事が特別教育活動に含まれなかった。その後『学習指導要領』がほぼ10年ごとに改訂され、1968（昭和43）年から1970（昭和45）年に改訂された『学習指導要領』で、学校行事を含んだ「特別活動」が誕生し、改訂されつつ現在に継承されている。
　戦後は、明治期以降、教育課程外で実施されてきた修学旅行、運動会などの学校行事や、自治的活動などの教育的意義が十分に評価され、教育課程に明確に位置づけられ現在に至っている。このことは、集団活動を通した社会化が個人的な知識の習得とともに重視されてきた結果であろう。

（4）特別活動の内容と特性
■学校種別ごとの特別活動の内容
　小学校の特別活動の内容は、学級活動、児童会活動、クラブ活動、学校行事で構成される。
　中学校の特別活動の内容は、学級活動、生徒会活動、学校行事で構成される。小学校と比較して、児童会活動が生徒会活動に変わっている。小学校では学習者を児童と称し、中学校では生徒と称するための変更である。また、中学校では、クラブ活動が廃止されていることが特色である。これは、中学校では課外活動である放課後の部活動が充実しているためである。
　高等学校の特別活動の内容は、ホームルーム活動、生徒会活動、学校行事によって構成される。小学校と中学校の学級活動が高等学校ではホームルーム活動に変更されている。この理由は、高等学校では、学校における生徒の基礎的な生活集団として編成した集団をホームルームと呼んでいるためである。

homeroom, a student council, and student meetings.

■ The Revision about every 10 Years

In "the Course of Study" in 1958 (Showa 33), names were unified in primary schools, lower secondary schools, upper secondary schools, and "extracurricular education activities" was born. In addition, school events were not held then by extracurricular education activities. "The Course of Study" was revised afterwards about every 10 years. "The Course of Study" revised from 1968 (Showa 43) to 1970 (Showa 45), "extracurricular activities" included the creation of school events. And it has succeeded to the present while it is being revised.

The school events such as a school excursion and an athletic meeting or a self-governing activity have been carried out after the Meiji period outside of the Course of Study. Educational significance was adequately evaluated after WW II, and has been included to the Courses of Study at present. This proves that the socialization acquired through group activities has been emphasized together with the acquisition of personal knowledge.

(4) Contents and Characteristics of Extracurricular Activities

■ Contents of Extracurricular Activities for School Classification

The contents of extracurricular activities of primary schools are applied to class activities, child society activities, club activities and school events.

The contents of extracurricular activities for lower secondary schools consist of class activities, student council activities and school events. In comparison with primary schools, child society activities turn into student council activities. This happens because the student is called "Jido" in primary schools but "Seito" in lower secondary schools. In addition, in lower secondary schools, it is characteristic that club activities within school hours have been abolished. This is because the club activities provided after school are more active in lower secondary schools.

Contents of extracurricular activities of upper secondary schools consist of homeroom activities, student council activities and school events. Class activities

■特別活動の内容の比較
　特別活動の内容についての名称は、まとめると、学校種によって下記の違いがある。ただし、それぞれの内容の具体的な活動は小学校の特別活動を基盤として共通する部分が多い。

表 7-13　学校種ごとの特別活動の内容

小学校	中学校	高等学校
学級活動	学級活動	ホームルーム活動
児童会活動	生徒会活動	生徒会活動
クラブ活動		
学校行事	学校行事	学校行事

　上記内容の中で、小学校のクラブ活動以外は全学年が対象の活動である。小学校のクラブ活動のみ、学習指導要領では、「主として第4学年以上の同好の児童をもって組織する」と規定している。現在の特別活動の各内容は、独自に目標を持ちつつも、特別活動の目標を達成するために、それぞれの特質を生かしつつ、内容相互に関連を図って工夫して実施することが大切である。

(5) 学級活動とホームルーム活動
■小学校および中学校の学級活動
　小学校および中学校の学級活動は学級を単位として行われる。小学校の学級活動では、学級や学校の生活づくりと適応や健康安全が目指され、この活動は中学校でも共通である。

of primary schools and lower secondary schools are changed into homeroom activities in upper secondary schools. The reason is to call the group with which they organized as a fundamental life group of a student, in upper secondary school homerooms.

■ Comparison of Contents of Extracurricular Activities

I discovered that there are the following differences in names about contents of extracurricular activities by school classification. But there are many parts which are common as a base with extracurricular activities of primary school activity of contents.

Table 7-13 Contents of extracurricular activities for every school classification

Primary schools	Lower secondary schools	Upper secondary schools
Class activities	Class activities	Homeroom activities
Child society activities	Student council activities	Student council activities
Club activities		
School events	School events	School events

When club activities of primary schools are removed from the above contents, it is the activity of students for all school years. According to the Course of Study, we decide to "organize club activities of primary schools with children who are mainly in more than the fourth grade with the same interests". Contents of current extracurricular activities do not have an original aim. As for us, it is important that contents are mutual and a connection plan is devised and carried out while making use of each characteristic to achieve an aim of extracurricular activities.

(5) Class Activities and Homeroom Activities

■ Class Activities of Primary Schools and Lower Secondary Schools

In class, the production of a good life, school adaptation, including the health and safety aim are activities common to primary school classrooms and lower secondary schools.

小学校では、学級や学校の生活づくりのために、そこでの生活上の諸問題の解決、学級内の組織づくりや仕事の分担処理、学校における多様な集団の生活の向上が学級活動で目指されている。また、適応や健康安全のために、希望や目標をもって生きる態度の形成、基本的な生活習慣の形成、望ましい人間関係の形成、清掃などの当番活動等の役割と働くことの意義の理解、学校図書館の利用、心身ともに健康で安全な生活態度の形成、食育の観点を踏まえた学校給食と望ましい食習慣の形成についての指導がなされる。

　中学校では、小学校の活動を基盤としつつ、思春期の心身の成長に関する指導や学業と進路に関する指導が加わる。学業と進路に関する指導では、学ぶことと働くことの意義の理解、自主的な学習態度の形成と学校図書館の利用、進路適性の吟味と進路情報の活用、望ましい勤労観・職業観の形成、主体的な進路の選択と将来設計が指導される。

■高等学校のホームルーム活動

　高等学校では、生徒の学校での基礎的な生活集団をホームルームと呼ぶため、小学校および中学校の学級活動についても、高等学校ではホームルーム活動という。

　ホームルーム活動の内容については、小学校および中学校の学級活動を継承しており、次の3つの内容で構成される。

①ホームルームや学校の生活づくり
② 適応と成長及び健康安全
③ 学業と進路

　なお、②には、青年期の悩みや課題とその解決に関する内容や、生活態度や習慣の確立に関する内容などが含まれる。

At the primary school level, solutions of many problems in life in a class or school, assignment processing of the production of an organization in a class or work, and improvement in the life of various groups in a school are carried out by classroom activities. Moreover, the next instruction is made for adaptation or health and safety. Formation of the attitude to live with hope or a target, formation of a fundamental lifestyle, formation of desirable human relations, an understanding of the meaning of working with task roles, such as cleaning activity etc., and use of the school library. Additionally formation of a life attitude, healthy mind and body and safety, and advice on the school lunch are included, based on the viewpoint of food education, and desirable eating habits.

In lower secondary schools, instruction about growth of the adolescent mind and body and instruction about studies and courses are added, which are based on activities of primary schools. In the instruction about the meaning of learning and courses, many themes are selected as follows. An understanding of the meaning of learning and working, independent formation of study attitude and use of school library, examination of course aptitude, practical use of course information, formation of desirable labor view and work values, selection of an active course, and future design, are included.

■ Homeroom Activities of Upper Secondary Schools

In upper secondary schools, we call the fundamental life group in students schools, homeroom. Therefore we say homeroom activities are class activities of primary schools, lower secondary schools and high schools.

The contents of homeroom activities succeed class activities of primary schools and lower secondary schools and consist of the following contents.
① Improvement of life of homeroom and school.
② An ideal method and way of life as an individual and a social member, health and security.
③ Academic studies and career.

In also, ②, solutions to youth troubles and problems, life manners and establishment of customs are included.

(6) 児童会活動と生徒会活動
■活動の概要

　児童会活動と生徒会活動はともに児童生徒の自治的な活動である。児童会活動と生徒会活動は教師の適切な指導の下に、すべての学習者によって構成され、運営される教育活動であり、この活動を通して、学校での児童生徒の生活を児童生徒自らの手によって充実させていくことができる。

　小学校から高等学校まで、学校での生活の充実向上について共通した方針が一貫している。つまり児童会活動・生徒会活動の基本的な目的は生活の充実向上にある。中学校と高等学校では、生活の充実向上のための活動に加えて、生徒の諸活動についての連絡調整、ボランティア活動などがある。特にボランティア活動は、『学習指導要領』（平成10年12月・平成11年3月）で新規に加えられた活動である。

■活動の内容

　小学校から高等学校までの児童会活動と生徒会活動の内容等をまとめると、次のようになる。

(6) Child Society Activities and Student Council Activities

■ A summary of activities

Child society activities and student council activities are self-governing activities by students as a group. Child society activities and student council activities consist of persons of all learning with appropriate guidance of teachers, and it is an administered educational activity. Through these activities, we can let the life of students in schools be enriched by the students themselves.

From primary schools to upper secondary schools, we aim for consistent substantiality about improvement of life in schools. Base activities of child society activities and student council activities are, so to speak, basic for the improvement of life. In addition to the improvement in fullness of life in lower secondary schools and upper secondary schools, there are liaison and adjustments made regarding many student activities and volunteer activites, etc. In particular, volunteer activities have been newly added to the "Course of Study" (December, 1998 and March, 1999)

■ Contents of Activities

The following is a summary of contents of the activities from primary schools to upper secondary schools.

表 7-14　児童会活動と生徒会活動の内容等、2008 〜 2009 年度

	小学校 (2008 年)	中学校 (2008 年)	高等学校 (2009 年)
名称	児童会活動	生徒会活動	
構成員	全児童	全生徒	
活動	児童会の計画や運営	生徒会の計画や運営	
		異年齢集団による交流	
		生徒の諸活動についての連絡調整	
		学校行事への協力	
		ボランティア活動などの社会参加	ボランティア活動などの社会参画

(7) クラブ活動

■小学校クラブ活動

　現在、クラブ活動は小学校でのみ実施されている特別活動の内容であり、学習指導要領では次のように目標を示している。

> クラブ活動を通して、望ましい人間関係を形成し、個性の伸長を図り、集団の一員として協力してよりよいクラブづくりに参画しようとする自主的、実践的な態度を育てる。

　クラブ活動は、学校や地域の実態等に応じて多様であるが、例えば体育系クラブ、文化系クラブ、芸術系クラブに分けることができる。

Table 7-14 Contents of child society activities and student council activities, 2008 & 2009

	primary schools (2008)	lower secondary schools (2008)	upper secondary schools (2009)
name	child society activities	student council activities	
member	all children	all students	
activity	plan and management of child society	plan and management of a student council	plan and management of a student council
	exchange by different age groups	exchange by different age groups	exchange by different age groups
		adjustment about many activities of students	adjustment about many activities of students
	event cooperation	event cooperation	event cooperation
		social participation, such as volunteer activities	positive social participation, such as volunteer activities

(7) Club Activities
■ Club Activities of Primary Schools

More recently, club activities are the contents of extracurricular activities currently carried out only at the primary school level, and the teaching purposes prescribed in the Course of Study are as follows

> To let students have independent and practical attitude through club activities, having ideal human relations, trying to develop their inividuality, making them join in and develop their club activities in cooperation with friends as a member of a group.

Club activities are carried out in accordance with the school or various aspects of the local environment. They are various, and can be divided into physical education clubs, culture clubs and art clubs.

表 7-15　クラブ活動の例

区分	クラブの例
体育系クラブ	野球、ソフトボール、サッカー、バスケットボール、バレーボール、卓球、陸上競技、等
文化系クラブ	コンピュータ、理科実験、写真、新聞、読書、ボランティア、茶道、等
芸術系クラブ	合唱、合奏、絵画、音楽鑑賞、芸術鑑賞、等

■中学校および高等学校の部活動

　現在、中学校および高等学校ではクラブ活動は実施されていない。その代わり、小学校のクラブ活動での教育効果と同様のものが期待される教育課程外の教育活動としての部活動に、中学校では多くの生徒が参加している。課外の部活動は学習指導要領の総則において教育課程の実施等に当たって配慮すべき事項として「生徒の自主的、自発的な参加により行われる部活動については、スポーツや文化及び科学等に親しませ、学習意欲の向上や責任感、連帯感の涵養等に資するものであり、学校教育の一環として、教育課程との関連が図られるよう留意すること。」と指摘されている。

　高等学校の体育・スポーツ活動の振興を図る団体としては財団法人全国高等学校体育連盟 があり、全国高校総体をはじめとする全国の各種競技大会で高校生は部活動の成果を競い合っている。

(8) 学校行事
■学校行事の概要

　学校行事は、全校規模または学年規模で行う体験的な活動で、望ましい人間関係、集団への所属感や連帯感、公共の精神、自主的、実践的な態度の育成を目指して実施される。学校行事の内容は、①儀式的行事、②文化的行事、③健康安全・体育的行事、④遠足（小学校）・旅行（中学・高等学校）・集団宿泊的行事、⑤勤労生産・奉仕的行事の5つの内容で構成されている。学校段階、学習者の発達段階、学校の実態にもよるが、各内容では、具体的には次のような活動が実施されている。

Table 7-15 Examples of Club Activities

division	examples of a club
physical education club	baseball, softball, soccer, basketball, volleyball, table tennis, track-and-field events
culture club	computer, science experiment, photography, newspaper, reading, volunteering, tea ceremony
art club	chorus, ensemble, picture, music appreciation, art appreciation

■ Club Activities of Lower Secondary Schools and Upper Secondary Schools

More recently club activities in school hours are not carried out in lower secondary schools and upper secondary schools. Many students in lower secondary schools and upper secondary schools participate in club activities during out of school hours instead. Club activities during out of school hours are pointed out to be considered complementing the curriculum in the general provisions of Course of Study, "Club activities practiced independently and positively by the students should be familiar with sport, culture and science, and contribute to promoting learning will and stregthening their responsibility and cooperation which should be related to school curriculum as a part of school education."

There is a Japan upper secondary school physical education federation for promotion of physical education / sports activity in upper secondary schools. Upper secondary school students compete in their club teams in various national competition meets.

(8) School Events

■ A Summary of School Events

School events are experiences of activities performed in a school or a grade level and are held for aiming at desirable human relations, a feeling of affiliation to a group and a sense of solidarity, public soul, and training of an independent and practical attitude. Contents of school events consist of five events. There are ① ceremony events, ② cultural events, ③ health safety / physical education events, ④ excursions (primary schools) / trips (lower secondary schools / upper secondary schools) / group lodging events, and ⑤ work production / service

■儀式的行事
　入学式や卒業式、始業式、終業式などのような、学校生活に変化を与える活動が含まれる。
■文化的行事
　文化祭（学芸会）、音楽会（合唱祭）、作品発表会（展覧会）、映画や演劇鑑賞などのような、学習活動の成果を総合的に生かす活動が含まれている。

■健康安全・体育的行事
　健康診断、交通安全を含む安全指導、避難訓練や防災訓練、体育祭（運動会）などのような、心身の発達、健康の保持増進、安全な行動に関る活動が含まれる。

■遠足・集団宿泊的行事（小学校）と旅行・集団宿泊的行事（中学校・高等学校）
　遠足、修学旅行、集団宿泊、野外活動などのような、平素と異なる生活環境による活動が含まれる。

■勤労生産・奉仕的行事
　就業やボランティアにかかわる体験的な活動、上級学校や職場の訪問・見学、全校美化の行事、地域社会への協力などのような、職業観の形成、進路選択、社会奉仕に関する活動が含まれる。

events.

It moves from various school stages, regarding the development stage of persons learning, the reality of a school, but, in detail, the following activities are carried out.

■ Ceremony Events

Activities to indicate changes are included in school life such as an entrance ceremony, graduation ceremony, opening ceremony, and closing ceremony.

■ Cultural Events

Activities to indicate results of learning such as a school festival (a school arts festival), a concert (chorus festival), a work announcement society (an exhibition), a movie or drama are included.

■ Health Safety / Physical Education Events

This includes a medical examination, safe guidance including road safety, a fire drill and protection against disasters training, an athletic meet, an activity concerned with the development of mind and body, maintenance for improving health, and safe action is included.

■ Excursions / Group Lodging Events (primary schools) and Trip / Group Lodging Events (lower secondary schools / upper secondary schools)

Activities incorporating different living environments such as school excursions, group lodgings, and outdoor activities are included.

■ Work Production / Service Events

Experiences about working operations and volunteering, a visit to an upper grade school and a place of work, an event of whole school beautification, cooperation with a community, an activity relating to the formation of an outlook of an occupation, course choice and social service are included.

表 7-16　現行『学習指導要領解説特別活動編』における例示
（林尚示「これからの学校行事に関する一考察」、兵庫県総合教育センター『兵庫教育』第 55 巻 9 号、17 頁、2003 年 12 月を一部変更した。）

	小学校	中学校	高等学校
儀式的行事	入学式、卒業式、始業式、終業式、終了式、開校記念に関する儀式、新任式、離任式、朝会、など	入学式、卒業式、開校記念日における行事、始業式、終業式、立志式、など	入学式、卒業式、開校記念日における儀式、始業式、終業式、対面式、朝会、など
文化的行事	【発表】学芸会、学習発表会、作品展示会、音楽会、読書感想発表会、クラブ発表会、など 【鑑賞】音楽鑑賞会、演劇鑑賞会、など	文化祭（学芸会）、音楽会（合唱祭）、作品発表会（展覧会）、映画や演劇鑑賞、講演会、など	文化祭（学芸会）、音楽会（合唱祭）、弁論大会、各種の発表会（展覧会）、映画や演劇の鑑賞会、伝統芸能等の鑑賞、講演会、など
健康安全・体育的行事	【健康】健康診断、給食に関する意識を高める行事、など 【安全】避難訓練、交通安全、など 【体育的】運動会、球技大会、など	健康診断、交通安全指導、薬物乱用防止指導、避難訓練や防災訓練、健康・安全や学校給食に関する行事、運動会（体育祭）、競技会、球技会、など	健康診断、疾病予防、交通安全を含む安全指導、薬物乱用防止指導、避難訓練や防災訓練、健康・安全に関する行事、体育祭（運動会）、競技会、球技会、など
遠足・旅行・集団宿泊的行事	遠足、修学旅行、野外活動、集団宿泊、など	遠足、修学旅行、移動教室、集団宿泊、野外活動、など	遠足、修学旅行、移動教室、集団宿泊、野外活動、など
勤労生産・奉仕的行事	飼育栽培活動、校内美化活動、地域社会の清掃活動、公共施設の清掃活動、福祉施設との交流活動、など	全校美化の行事、各種の勤労体験や生産活動、上級学校や職場の訪問・見学、地域社会への協力やボランティア活動、など	就業体験（インターンシップ）、各種の生産活動、上級学校や職場の訪問・見学、全校美化の行事、地域社会への協力や学校内外のボランティア活動、など

注

1　財団法人全国高等学校体育連盟の競技には、陸上、体操・新体操、水泳（競泳）（飛込）（水球）、バスケットボール、バレーボール、卓球、ソフトテニス、ハンドボール、サッカー、ラグビー、バドミントン、ソフトボール、相撲、柔道、スキー、スケート、ボート、剣道、レスリング、弓道、テニス、登山、自転車競技、ボクシング、ホッケー、ウエイトリフティング、ヨット、フェンシング、空手道、アーチェリー、なぎなた、カヌーがある。http://www.zen-koutairen.com/f_regist.html、2005 年 11 月 29 日閲覧。

Ⅶ. The Characteristics of Courses

Table 7-16 Existing Table in "A Commentary of the Course of Study, Extracurricular Activities"
(Masami HAYASHI, "A Consideration about School Events in the Future", Hyogo General Education Center "Hyogo Education" Vol. 55-9, p.17 December, 2003)

	primary schools	lower secondary schools	upper secondary schools
ceremony events	an entrance ceremony, a graduation ceremony, opening ceremonies, closing ceremonies, a closing, a ceremony in memory of the opening of a school, a new appointment ceremony, a leaving office ceremony, a morning gathering	an entrance ceremony, a graduation ceremony, an event in the anniversary of the founding of a school, opening ceremonies, closing ceremonies, setting an aim in life ceremony	an entrance ceremony, a graduation ceremony, a ceremony on the anniversary of the founding of a school, opening ceremonies, closing ceremonies, a meeting ceremony, a morning gathering
cultural events	[announcement] a school arts festival, a learning announcement meeting, a work exhibition, a concert, a reading impression announcement meeting, a club announcement society [appreciation] music appreciation society, drama appreciation society	a school festival (a school arts festival), a concert (a chorus festival), a work announcement society (an exhibition), a movie and drama appreciation, a special lecture	a school festival (a school arts festival), a concert (a chorus festival), a various announcement society (an exhibition), a movie and drama appreciation, a special lecture
health safely / physical education events	[health] an event to make a medical examination and to raise awareness of health consciousness about lunch [security] a fire drill, a road safety [physical education] an athletic meet, a ball game meet	a medical examination, road safety guidance, a prevention of drug abuse guidance, a fire drill and protection against disasters training, health safety and school meal, an athletic meet, a competition, a ball game society	a medical examination, an illness prevention, a safe guidance including road safety, a prevention of drug abuse guidance, a fire drill and protection against disasters training, a health security, an athletic meet, a competition, a ball game society
excursion / trip / group lodging events	a school excursion, an outdoor activity, a group lodging	a school excursion, a movement classroom, a group lodging, an outdoor activity	a school excursion, a movement classroom, a group lodging, an outdoor activity
work production / service events	a breeding cultivation, campus beautification, cleaning of a community, cleaning of public accommodation, an interchange with a welfare institution	a whole school beautification, various work experiences and production, a visit to an upper school and place of work, cooperation with a community or volunteering	an experience about medical examination and volunteering, a visit to an upper school and place to work, a whole school beautification, cooperation with a community or society participation

Notes

1　There are competitive and additional sports activities under the Japan federation of upper secondary school physical education.

　Track and field events, exercises / rhythmic gymnastics, swimming (a swimming race) (platform and springboard diving) (water polo) basketball,

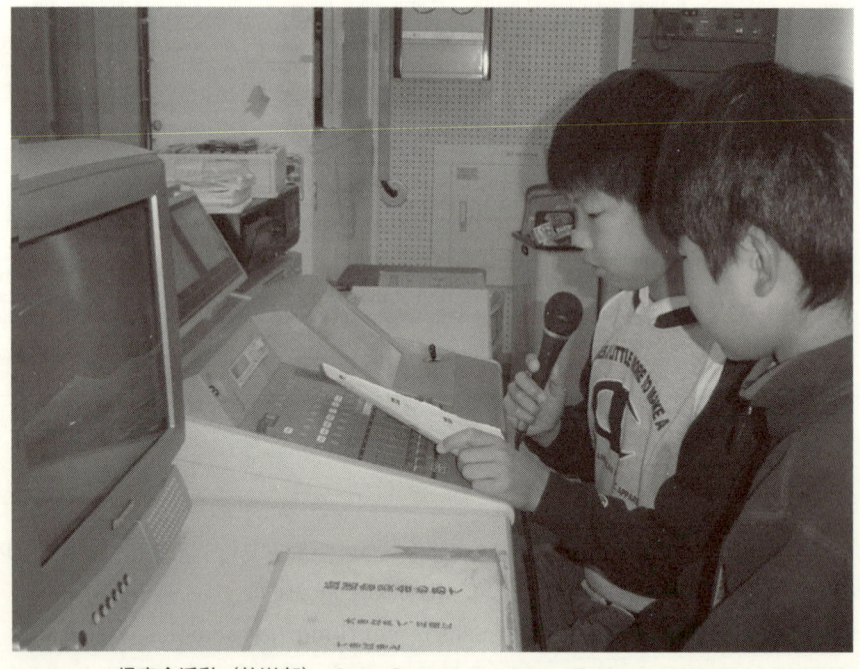

児童会活動（放送部）　Child Society Activities : Broadcast Activity

volleyball, table tennis, soft tennis, handball, soccer, rugby, badminton, softball, sumo, judo, skiing, skating, boating, kendo, wrestling, archery, tennis, mountain climbing, bicycle racing, boxing, hockey, weightlifting, yachting, karate, archery, Japanese halberd, and canoeing.

http://www.zen-koutairen.com/f_regist.html,
Examined on November 29, 2005.

児童会活動（新聞部） Child Society Activities : Newspaper Publishing Activity

13. 職業教育

(1) 職業教育の意味とその内容
■英語の「職業」ということばは、もともと、神より召された個人の使命という意味と、専門職に対する技能的、熟練的な仕事という意味をもっている。したがって、職業教育とは、キリスト教を基盤として成立する個人をまさにその人自身とならしめる仕事への適応のための教育を意味している。

■これに対して、わが国においては、職業に関する教育は、欧米的な近代化をめざした明治期から、第２次世界大戦後の高度経済成長期に至るまで、常に、国家・社会からの経済的要請と密接にかかわり、その強い影響を受けながら発展してきた。そのため、欧米における個人の職業的発達を目的とする職業教育とは著しく異なる「世のため人のため」の実業教育、産業教育という概念が成立した。それゆえ、わが国の文部行政の中で展開されてきたこの分野の教育は、実業教育・産業教育であり、欧米に起源をもつ職業教育という概念は実態として存在しないとも言えると指摘されることさえある。

■今日の学校教育において、職業教育という用語は、主として、中等教育段階における普通教育に対する用語として用いられている。それは、おおむね以下の４つの内容領域を含んでいる。
　①ある特定の職業分野に直接関連して、その基礎をなす自然科学と技術学の教育
　②ある特定の職業分野で必要な技能の教育

13. Vocational Education

(1) The Meaning and Content of Vocational Education

■ The English word "vocation" has two meanings. One means a "person's mission as commanded by God". The other means technical and skilled trades, which is also compared to the meaning of the word "profession". The term "vocational education" therefore also includes the Christian meaning, that is, education for adapting a person to the job which would help individual derelop his/her character.

■ On the other hand, education concerning vocation in Japan has had something to do with the economic needs of the nation and the society since the Meiji period when Europe and America were models of its modernization to the present period of high economic growth, which came after World War II. The concept of vocational education in Japan is, however, different from that of Europe and America where the aim was mainly to improve one's personal achievement through vocational education. In Japan, the notion of business education and industrial education which teaches mainly how students must work for the sake of others and for society is emphasized. Thus, it is even pointed out that in fact the vocational education suggested by the Ministry of Education, Culture, Sports, Science and Technology does not mean vocational education which originated from Europe and America, but that kind of business education and industrial education specific to Japan.

■ Nowadays, the term vocational education is used as a relative term to general education given at the secondary level. For instance, it consists of the following fields.

① Education in fundamental natural science and technology which is directly related to certain vocations.

② Education for skills acquisition necessary for certain vocations.

③職業に関連する社会的・経済的知識の教育
④職業に従事する者に必要な労働態度の教育

■実際の教育場面においては、これら4つの内容領域が、生徒の発達段階、学校の教育理念、地域の産業・経済の特質、国の教育政策などとの関連で具体化され、それぞれ特色のある職業教育が展開されている。

■現代の日本においては、社会人として実社会に出る人間のほとんどすべてに職業教育は要請されている。そのため、すべての学校教育の目標には、よりよい職業生活を送ることができるようになるための資質の形成ということが含まれている。したがって、普通教育と職業教育を教育制度のうえで複線的に分離して捉えることには、教育内容・方法の点から見ても大きな矛盾が生じてきている。本来、普通教育と職業教育は、人格陶冶の両面である。両者は、人間存在の1つの基本的な経験である「働く」ということを介して相互にかかわりあいながら、全人格的な人間の形成に寄与する。この場合、普通教育は、社会人としての人間の全面的発達をめざす教育であり、職業教育は、個人をまさにその人自身とならしめる仕事を通して、一人ひとりの卓越性の伸長を図る教育であると見ることができる。それゆえ、職業教育は、中等教育段階において、ある特定の職業分野に関連する知識や技能を習得するための教育と狭く考えるのではなく、生涯教育という観点から広く考えるべきである。すなわち、それは、全教育段階において行われ、また、学校教育および学校外教育を含めた、普通教育としての職業に関する教育、職業準備教育、専門教育の一部、現職教育を包括する概念である。言いかえれば、広義の職業教育は人間の社会的経験の一領域である「働く」ということにかかわる総合的な、しかも普遍性と卓越性を合わせ持った能力の育成を通して、学習者一人ひとりの個性的な自己実現を図る教育であると定義される。この意味で、「個人が人間の生き方の一部として職業や進路について学び、人生上の役割やその選択と職業的価値観とを関連づけることができるように計画された経験の全体である」というキャリア教育の考え方が参考となるであろう。

③ Education for social and economic knowledge which is related to a vocation.

④ Education for the development of appropriate attitude towards work necessary for a worker.

■ The practices above have been specified in relation to the developmental stage of students, the respective ideals and objectives of the school, the characteristics of the local industry and economy, and the general educational policy of the country.

■ At present, almost all members of Japanese society should have their own respective vocational education. It is therefore necessary that schools should aim at developing the capability of each individual to live a better life by engaging themselves in a vocation. The separate treatment of general education and vocational education in the educational system has caused a great number of contradictions in terms of the contents and methods of education. Originally, general education and vocational education both aim at character formation. Both of them contribute to the formation of the whole character related to each other through the concept of "work" which is man's basic experience for existence. In this case, general education aims at developing a man in his totality as a member of society, while vocational education aims at developing the potentials of the individual to the maximum through work which helps to build character. Thus, vocational education should not be viewed in its narrow sense which aims at the acquisition of knowledge and skills of a particular vocation at the secondary stage, but should be taken in its broad sense in terms of life-long education. It is a broad concept that covers many types of education including a vocational part of general education, a preparatory education for a vocation, a part of specialized vocational education and education for the incumbents. It is the type of education that takes place inside and outside of the school at all levels of education. In other words, vocational education in a broad sense is defined as one which aims at personal self-realization of the learner through a cultivation of the general, universal and excellent ability related to "work", which is a part of social

(2) 日本の職業教育機関

■以上の観点から見ると、現在の我が国において、広義の職業教育を行っている教育機関としては、主に次のようなものをあげることができる。

① 義務教育諸学校

　家庭科（小学校）、技術・家庭科（中学校）、特別活動、総合的な学習の時間などを中心とする、普通教育としての職業に関する教育を行う。

② 高等学校

　家庭科、特別活動、総合的な学習の時間などを中心とする普通教育としての職業に関する教育、および、農業、工業、商業、水産、家庭、看護、情報、福祉等の職業に関する各教科・科目を中心とする専門教育としての職業教育を行う。

③ 高等専門学校

　実践的な中堅技術者・中級技術者を養成することを目的として、主に工学・技術系の職業専門教育を行う。

④ 工学系、農学系等の短期大学

　それぞれの分野に関する職業専門教育を行う。

⑤ 専修学校および各種学校

　これらの学校のうちの多くの課程では、公的な職業資格（例えば、自動車整備士、電気工事士等）の取得を目的とする職業教育が行われる。

⑥ 文部科学省以外の官庁の管理する職業教育学校

　これには、海上保安大学校、航空大学校、水産大学校、防衛大学校等がある。

⑦ 公共職業訓練施設

　職業能力開発促進法に基づいて、厚生労働省の管轄下で行われる公共職業訓練施設には、雇用・能力開発機構が設置する職業能力開発短期大学校、職業能力開発促進センター、職業能力開発大学校、および都道府県または市町

experience. In this sense, vocational education in Japan might be furnished from the ideas of career education: "It is about a whole experience which is planned for individuals to learn vocation and career options as a part of the way of life, and to enable to relate to a roll in life and its choice to vocational value.

(2) Institutions of Vocational Education in Japan
■ From the viewpoint stated above, the current main institution of vocational education in Japan is as follows:
① Compulsory Education Schools

They provide education concerning vocations as a part of general education, mainly homemaking (in primary school), industrial and homemaking (in lower secondary school), special activities and period for integrated study etc.

② Upper Secondary Schools

It provides education concerning vocations as a part of general education, centeredon homemaking, special activities and period for integrated study, vocational education as a part of professional education which is based on vocational subjects such as agriculture, industry, commerce, fishery, home economics, nursing, information technology or welfare.

③ Technical Colleges

It provides mainly engineering and technical vocational education to foster practical middle-ranking and intermediate engineers

④ Junior Technical Colleges, Junior Agricultural Colleges etc.

They provide professional education in each field of study.

⑤ Specialized Training Colleges and Miscellaneous Schools

The greater part of the curricula of these schools consists of vocational education necessary to obtain vocational licenses for the public services such as car mechanics, electrical engineering, and others.

⑥ Other Vocational Schools

Many vocational training and academic schools are managed by government agencies other than the Ministry of Education, Culture, Sports, Science and

村立の職業訓練校と障害者職業能力開発校がある。ここでは、高等学校または中学校を卒業した未就職の人を対象とする養成訓練、すでに職に就いている人、または、以前に職に就いていた人を対象とする向上訓練、能力再開発訓練、指導者訓練が行われている。

⑧認定職業訓練

職業能力開発促進法に基づいて、事業主が単独あるいは共同で行う職業訓練のうち、都道府県知事によってそれぞれの教科や施設などが一定の基準を満たしていると認定されたもの。

⑨企業内教育

雇用関係を前提として、被雇用者に対して企業がその経費の主な部分を負担してなされる教育。その形態に応じて、職場内職業訓練、職場外職業訓練などに分けられる。

⑩その他

現在では、大学や大学院等における専門教育、現職者の継続教育の一部なども職業教育の一領域と考えられる。

Technology. These are the Maritime Safety Academy, the Civil Aviation College, the College of Fisheries, and the National Defense Academy.

⑦ Public Facilities for Vocational Training

According to Human Resources Development Promotions Act, the Health, Labor and Welfare Ministry manages many facilities for vocational training. These include national and municipal facilities. National facilities include Junior Vocation Training Colleges, Human Resources Development Promotion Centers, and Vocational Training Colleges established by the Employment and Human Resources Development Organization of Japan. Municipal facilities include Vocational Training Schools and the Vocational Training School for the disabled, all of which are established by the municipalities. of eadn prefectre Pre-professional training and in-service training are two main purposes of these facilities. There are courses for the training of graduates of secondary schools who have not been employed yet, as well as developmental courses for professionals or for the training of instructors who are or have been employed.

⑧ Approved Vocational Training

According to the Human Resources Development Promotions Act, some entrepreneurs may provide independent or joint vocational training facilities. When the subjects of the training courses and the facilities are standardized, the Prefectural Governors may recognize them as authorized facilities.

⑨ Company In-Service Training

Under the premise of employer-employee relations, companies help their employees get in-service training for their finances. These types of training systems are divided into on-the-job training, and off-the-job training.

⑩ Other Training Courses

Today, specialized education in the universities and graduate schools is thought of as vocational training education. A part of the in-service, continual training of workers is also thought of as one of the courses included in this type of vocational education.

（3）高等学校における職業教育の現状と課題

■学校教育法第50条には、高等学校の目的が「中学校における教育の基礎の上に、心身の発達及び進路に応じて、高度な普通教育及び専門教育を施すこと」と記されている。また、同法第51条には、高等学校の教育目標として、「社会において果たさなければならない使命の自覚に基づき、個性に応じて将来の進路を決定させ、一般的な教養を高め、専門的な知識、技術及び技能を習得させること」と記されている。これを受けて、高等学校学習指導要領（2009年版、以下同）には、「学校においては、地域や学校の実態等に応じて、就業やボランティアにかかわる体験的な学習の指導を適切に行うようにし、勤労の尊さや創造することの喜びを体得させ、望ましい勤労観、職業観の育成や社会奉仕の精神の涵養に資するものとする」（総則第１款の４）と記されている。

■現在、高等学校の学科は、高等学校設置基準によって、普通教育を主とする学科（普通科）、専門教育を主とする学科（専門学科）、普通教育及び専門教育を選択履修を旨として総合的に施す学科（総合学科）に分けられている。専門教育を主とする学科のうち、農業、工業、商業、水産、家庭、看護、情報、福祉に関する学科は、我が国の産業経済の発展を担う人材を育成するため、職業に関する専門教育を行うとされている。

■職業教育を主とする学科（職業科）の教育課程は、普通教育の教科・科目（最低必履修単位31単位）と職業に関する教科・科目（25単位以上履修）によって構成されている。職業に関する教科・科目としては、農業（農業経営を含む30科目）、工業（工業技術基礎を含む61科目）、商業（ビジネス基礎を含む20科目）、水産（漁業を含む22科目）、家庭（消費生活を含む20科目）、看護（基礎看護を含む13科目）、情報（情報産業と社会を含む13科目）、福祉（社会福祉基礎を含

(3) Present Situation and Problems of Vocational Education in Upper Secondary Schools

■ Article 50 of the School Education Law states that the purpose of upper secondary school is to provide "general course education and the specialized education in the upper secondary school should be given on the basis of the type of education given in the lower secondary school, according to the career options and the intellectual and physical development of the students." Moreover, article 51 of the law states that the educational goal of upper secondary school is to encourage their students to choose the future path which best suits their individual capabilities, improve their mind and acquire expertise, techniques and skills, based on the awareness of their mission in society." The Course of Study for Upper Secondary Schools (Edition in 2009) states that "schools should provide an appropriate instruction for hands-on learning such as experiencing jobs and volunteer activities according to the situation of the school and community, guide their students to learn the dignity of labor and joy in creation, and contribute to cultivate a good view of career and work and volunteer spirit". (Provision 1-4 in the General)

■ According to the Standard for the Establishment of Upper Secondary School, education in the upper secondary schools is currently divided into three courses: the general education course, the specialized education course, and the comprehensive education course. In the specialized education course, agriculture, industry, commerce, fishery, home economics, nursing, information technology and welfare are set up to give vocational education to develop human resources to improve our industrial economy.

■ A curriculum in the vocational education course consists of general academic subjects (the minimum number of required credits : 31 credits) and vocational subjects (25 or more credits required). For the vocational subjects, the following are provided: agriculture (30 subjects including a basis of agricultural management), industry (61 subjects including a basis of industrial techology), commerce (20 subjects including a basis of business), fishery (22 subjects including fishery), home economics

む9科目）が設定されている。職業科の教育課程を編成・実施するにあたっては、以下の点に配慮する必要がある。
・職業に関する各教科・科目については、実験・実習に配当する授業時数を十分確保する。（通常、生徒は30～40単位程度の職業科目を履修するが、その学習時間の約半分が実験・実習にあてられている。）
・職業に関する各教科・科目については、就業体験をもって実習に替えることができる。
・家庭、農業及び水産に関する各教科・科目の指導にあたっては、ホームプロジェクト並びに学校家庭クラブ及び学校農業クラブなどの活動を活用して、学習の効果を上げるように留意する。

■総合学科の教育課程は、普通教育の教科・科目（最低必履修単位31単位）に加え、「産業社会と人間」及び専門教育に関する各教科・科目を合わせて25単位以上設けることとされている。「産業社会と人間」は、産業社会や職業生活を通して人間の生き方や将来の進路に対する生徒の自覚を深めるために、就業体験等の体験的な学習や調査・研究などを通して、以下の事項について指導することが求められる。
・社会生活や職業生活に必要な基本的な基本的な能力や態度及び望ましい勤労観、職業観の育成。
・我が国の産業の発展とそれがもたらした社会の変化についての考察。
・自己の将来の生き方や進路についての考察及び各教科・科目の履修計画の作成。

■普通科においても9.0％の生徒が卒業後就職するという実情（2009年度学校基本調査より：なお職業科では約51％、総合学科では約29％）をふまえて、職業に関する教科・科目を開設し、履修することができるようになっている。高等学校学習指導要領では、「普通科においては、地域や学校の実態、生徒の特性、進路等を考慮し、必要に応じて、適切な職業に関する各教科・科目の履修の機会の確保について配慮するものとする」（総則第5款の4）と記され

(20 subjects including consumer goods life), nursing (13 subjects including basic nursing), information technology (13 subjects including information industry and society) and welfare (9 subjects including basic social welfare) To plan and offer the curriculum for the vocational education course, the following needs are considered :
· For the subjects of vocational education, secure enough credits of lessons for experiment and exercise. (Normally, students complete vocational subjects of about 30-40 credits, and about half of them are allocated to experiment and exercise.)
· An internship can be counted as a credit of practice for vocational subjects.
· For the subjects of home economics, fishery and agriculture, attempts to increase the effect of study through a home project and activities of home economics club as well as agriculture club etc.

■ The curriculum of comprehensive education course requiras a total of 25 or more credits totally for the subjects of "industrial society and human beings" and specialized education, in addition to general subjects (the minimum number of required credits : 31 credits). To raise students' awareness about their life and future path through studying industrial society and work life, the subject of "industrial society and human being" is required to teach the points listed below through experiential study, survey and research, such as internships.
· Developing a fundamental skill and attitude required in the social and work life and cultivating a good view of career and work.
· Considering the development of our industries and its consequences.
· Considering students, own future life and career, and plan ning what subjects to take.

■ Considering about 9.0% of the students in the general education course find employment after leaving school (about 51% in the vocational course, about 29% in the comprehensive course according to the School Basic Survey conducted in 2009), vocational subjects are arranged in the general education course so that they can study them. The Course of Study for Upper Secondary School states that in the general education course one should consider giving students opportunities to

ている。

■1948年に発足した新制高等学校全体の学校数、学科数、生徒数は、過去60年間で急激に増加し、1989年に生徒数のピークを迎えた（以後、減少に転じる）。その中で、普通科と職業科を比べてみると、普通科が大幅に増えているのに対して、職業科は昭和40年代以降減少を続けているという対照的な傾向が現れている。1960年から2009年までの職業科生徒数の推移をみると、1970年以降この39年間で60％以上も減少している。2009年度の学科別生徒数の割合は、普通科72.3％（2,414,344人）、専門学科22.7％（758,752人）（うち職業科19.7％（657,047人））、総合学科5.0％（165,765人）である。

■以上の結果、1970年から1980年までの10年間に普通科と職業科の間に決定的な差が生じていることがわかる。この時期は、日本の高度経済成長が頂点を迎えるとともに、その後急速に低成長時代に落ち込んでいった時期である。現在の高等学校職業科の教育がかかえている問題は、この時期の職業教育政策に大きな原因がある。

■1966年、中央教育審議会は、「後期中等教育の整備拡充について」という答申を行い、生徒の適性、能力と職種の専門的分化に対応した職業教育の教育内容の「多様化」政策を提唱した（能力と適性に応ずる多様化）。この政策は、基本的には、高度経済成長下で「すぐに役立つ」中堅労働力の確保をめざしたものであり、産業や技術の発展に対する明確な見通しをもっていなかった。そのため、結果的には、職業学科の細分化および普通科との序列的格差を招いた。これによって、職業科自体の魅力は大幅に損なわれ、「能力」別に振り分けられた学力の低い生徒が職業科に集中することとなった。これらの生徒は、自分の希望をあまり考慮されることなく、「普・商・工・農」の序列の下に振り分けられて進学する傾向が見られる。そのため、もともと進学動

VII. The Characteristics of Courses 613

learn subjects concerning the appropriate vocation, considering the situation of the school, the locality, characters and future paths of the students. (Provision 5-4 in the General)

■ The total number of upper secondary schools, courses and students under the new system established in 1948 has rapidly increased for the past 60 years, and peaked in 1989. A comparison of the general course with the vocational course, however, shows a tendency of the latter to have decreased since 1965 as the former increased. The number of students in the vocational course has shifted from 1960 to 2009 as follows, which has been decreased over 60% during the last 39 years from 1970. The ratios of the number of students per subject in 2009 are as follows: 72.3 % (2,414,344 students) taking the general education course, 22.7 % (758,752 students) taking the specialized course (including 19.7 % (657,047 students) in vocational course) and 5.0% (165,765 students) taking the comprehensive education course.

■ The above result shows a major change in enrollment in the general and vocational course for a period of 10 years from 1970 to 1980. That was the time when Japan reached its peak of economic growth, but suffered an immediate severe low economic blow soon after the peak. Many of the problems which the present vocational course in upper secondary schools faces are the result of the government's policy towards vocational education during this period.

■ In 1966, the Central Council for Education submitted a report on the adjustment and expansion of upper secondary education. The report proposed that course and contents of vocational education should be diversified so as to suit the students' ability and aptitude, and to cope with job specialization. Basically, the diversification policy aimed to secure useful laborers needed for high economic growth. The policy, however, lacked a definite vision for the development of industry and technology, and created further subdivision of the vocational course and difference in quality between the general course and the vocational course. As a result, the gap in the scholastic attainment of students in the vocational course and those in the general course widened. Students were divided into

機が弱いうえに、基礎学力が低く、「落ちこぼされる」傾向が強いことと併せて、学習意欲の減退から中途退学をしたり、あるいは、非行等の問題行動を起こしたりする割合が高くなっている。

■この「多様化」政策は、結果的に多くの批判を受け、また、それ自体のもつ矛盾が大きくなることによって、再検討を迫られることとなった。文部省は、1973年に理科教育および産業教育審議会の中に職業教育の改善に関する委員会を設けた。この委員会は、1976年5月に、「高等学校における職業教育の改善について」と題する報告を行い、職業科における基礎学力の重視、教育課程の弾力化、学科構成の改善、普通科における勤労体験学習の導入等を提言した。また、同審議会は、1985年2月に、「高等学校における今後の職業教育のあり方について」という答申を行った。これは、情報産業、バイオテクノロジー等の発展にみられる最近の産業構造、職業構造の変化や、高等学校教育の著しい普及に伴う生徒の能力・適性等の多様な実態に対応することのできる職業教育のあり方について検討し、職業学科の再編成、教育課程の多様化と弾力化、学科間の枠を超えた協力連携、普通科における職業教育の充実を骨子とする改善方策を提示した。

■1990年代以降、我が国は、高度情報化社会を迎え、IT化、国際化への対応を求められることとなった。さらに、少子高齢化社会の急速な進展と相まって、学校教育も、臨時教育審議会（1984-1987）が示した基本方針（個性重視の

ranks according to their scholastic attainment. And from this, a trend has formed wherein the students were grouped into four courses enumerated from highest to lowest rank, namely: general, commerce, industry and agriculture courses. Thus, vocational courses became unattractive. Motivation to study as well as the fundamental scholastic ability of the students in the lower rank was not adequate; hence, they tended to leave school halfway. For these reasons they caused more trouble than those in the general courses.

■ This diversification policy was very much criticized because the actual turnout of graduates was far from the ideal. Under heavy pressure, it was placed for review. In order to improve vocational education, the Ministry of Education, Culture, Science and in 1973, set up a Committee for the Improvement of Vocational Education in the Council of Science Education and Industry Education. This committee reported on "The Improvement of Vocational Education in Upper Secondary School" in May of 1976, and suggested the following: to lay emphasis on basic attainment in vocational courses, making the curriculum more flexible: to improve the formation of subjects and to introduce learning through an internship in the general courses. In February 1985, this committee also submitted the report on "What Vocational Education in Upper Secondary School Should Be". The report investigated on the change in recent industry and occupation structure, such as the development of Micro-Electronics, Information Industry, and Biotechnology. It also examined the revisions made on vocational education to adjust to the abilities and aptitudes of the students caused by a remarkable expansion of upper secondary school education. Based on the investigation, it proposed a guideline for improvement that focuses on the following matters: reorganization of vocational courses, diversity and flexibility of the curriculum, integration of courses beyond traditional courses, and emphasis on vocational education in the general courses.

■ Since the 1990's, we have been facing an advanced information society and required to cope with progress of IT and internationalization. Combined with the rapid aging of the population resulting from the decline in the birthrate, overall

原則、生涯学習体系への移行、国際化・情報化など社会の変化への対応）に基づいて、21世紀に向けた学校教育全般にわたる教育改革を行うこととなり、職業教育も新たな展開が求められることとなった。

■経済のグローバル化や国際競争の激化、規制緩和等に伴う産業構造の変化、技術革新・国際化・情報化等に伴う産業社会の高度化、就業形態の多様化などに見られる就業構造の変化等により、我が国の産業社会や企業の専門高校に対する期待や、専門高校の生徒に求める資質・能力は変化してきている。また、専門高校の生徒の意識の変化や進路の多様化が進んでいる中で、「大学全入時代」の到来等も相まって、これまで以上に明確な目的意識をもった進路選択が促進されるよう、適切な対応が求められている。こうしたなか中央教育審議会は、2008年1月に「幼稚園、小学校、中学校、高等学校及び特別支援学校の学習指導要領等の改善について」という答申を行った。そこでは、高等学校における職業教育の改善に関して、以下のような提言がなされている。（この答申に基づく高等学校学習指導要領の改訂は、2009年3月に公示された。）

（ⅰ）改善の基本方針
■専門高校における職業に関する各教科・科目 については、その課題や改正教育基本法等で示された職業にかかわる規定等を踏まえ、将来のスペシャリストの育成という観点から専門分野の基礎的・基本的な知識、技術及び技能を身に付けるための教育とともに、社会に生き、社会的責任を担う職業人としての規範意識や倫理観等を醸成し、豊かな人間性の涵養等にも配慮した教育を行うことが重要である。

また、産業構造の変化、科学技術の進歩等の情勢の変化に対応し、それぞ

school education has been decided to move forward with educational reform for the 21st century according to the basic policy announced by the National Task Force for Educational Reform (1984-1987) (e.g., principle of respect for the individual, transition to a lifelong learning system, response to the change of society such as internationalization and informatization). Along with that, vocational education was also required to take a new turn.

■ Economic globalization, intensifying international competition, change of industrial structure along with easing of regulations, upgrading industrial society along with technical innovation, internationalization and infomatization, and change of working structure because of diversified working style has taken place. Due to those facts, companies' expectation toward specialized schools and industrial society, and quality and skills for the specialized schools that ask students to have, are changing. Also, while diversifying students' future path and changing students' consciousness in specialized schools, along with the coming of "an era of all-enter-university", appropriate actions are required to guide students to make a career choice with clearer purpose. In January 2008, the Central Education Council reported about "Improvement of the Course of Study for kindergarten, elementary school, lower and upper secondary school". The report pointed out the issues of vocational education as follows and announced the improvement of vocational education at upper secondary school as below: (The revision of the Course of Study for Upper Secondary School based on the report was made in March 2009.)

(i) Outline of improvement

■ In regard to each vocational subject in specialized schools, based on the issues and policy for the vocation specified in the revised Basic Act on Education, it is important to provide an education to cultivate an enriched humanness and foster a sense of ethics and normative consciousness as a worker assuming social responsibilities, along with the education to acquire basic knowledge, technique and skills in a certain specialty from a standpoint of developing specialists in the future.

れの専門分野で真に必要とされる教育内容に精選するとともに、新たに求められる教育内容・方法を取り入れることが重要である。

さらに、専門高校における職業教育の充実のためには、小学校・中学校段階におけるキャリア教育や進路指導との接続、専門高校生に産業社会や大学等が求める能力・資質との関連、社会や大学等の専門高校生への積極的評価、次代を担う人材の育成という観点から、関係各界・各機関等との連携強化なども重要な視点である。このような基本的考え方の下、各教科について科目の構成及び内容の改善を図る。

（ⅱ）改善の具体的事項
■（教科横断的な事項）
　次の三つの視点を基本とし、各教科を通して横断的な改善を図る。

　第一は、将来のスペシャリストの育成に必要な専門性の基礎・基本を一層重視し、専門分野に関する基礎的・基本的な知識、技術及び技能の定着を図るとともに、ものづくりなどの体験的学習を通して実践力を育成する。

　さらに、資格取得や有用な各種検定、競技会への挑戦等、目標をもった意欲的な学習を通して、知識、技術及び技能の定着、実践力の深化を図るとともに、課題を探究し解決する力、自ら考え行動し、適応していく力、コミュニケーション能力、協調性、学ぶ意欲、働く意欲、チャレンジ精神などの積極性・創造性等を育成する。

　第二は、将来の地域産業を担う人材の育成という観点から、地域産業や地域社会との連携・交流を通じた実践的教育、外部人材を活用した授業等を充実させ、実践力、コミュニケーション能力、社会への適応能力等の育成を図るとともに、地域産業や地域社会に対する理解と貢献の意識を深めさせる。

　第三は、人間性豊かな職業人の育成という観点から、人と接し、自然やものとかかわり、命を守り育てるという職業教育の特長を生かし、職業人とし

It is also important to carefully select the educational content which is truly required in each specialty and adopt new method and content of education to respond to the changes of industrial structure and development of science technology.

Moreover, to enhance the vocational education in a specialized school, it is essential to connect it with career education and career guidance in primary and lower secondary schools, to have an association of ability and quality of specialized school students which are required by industrial sectors and universities, to make a positive evaluation of the students in society and university, and to strengthen the coopretion between the scooles and industry related arganizations in ouder to develop human resources who take responsibility for the on going society. Under such a fundamental idea, improvement of composition and content of each subject will be planned.

(ii) Concrete ideas for improvement

■ (cross-curricular points)

The plan is to have a cross-curricular improvement as below, based on the following three standpoints.

Firstly, one is to put more emphasis on the fundamentals which are required to develop a specialist in the future, to encourage students to acquire basic knowledge, skills and technique in specialized fields, and to develop the ability to use those skills and knowledge through experiential learning such as manufacturing

Also, ambitious study containing a concrete goal such as to get qualifications or useful certification and to enter a competition will help students to have knowledge, skills and technique and deepening the ability to use them. In addition to that, it will cultivate students' creativity and positive attitude such as challenge spirit, motivation for working and learning, cooperativeness, a capability to explore and solve issues, think and act according to one's own idea and comply with others.

Secondly, the develop ment of human resources for local industries in the

て必要な人間性を養うとともに、生命・自然・ものを大切にする心、規範意識、倫理観等を育成する。

　上記の他、生徒の意識の変化や進路の多様化等に対応するため、弾力的な教育課程を編成することに加えて、より実践的な職業教育や就業体験等を通じて、職業選択能力や人生設計能力を身に付けさせる教育が可能となるよう配慮することも必要である。

■今日のように、ITを中心とする科学技術の急速な発展や規制緩和の進展による産業社会の構造的変化、リストラ、ニート、フリーターの増大等による雇用環境の不安定化、個人の価値観とそれに伴うライフ・スタイルの多様化など社会の大幅な変革期においては、職業教育は特定の職業のための教育だけでなく、あらゆる職業に共通の実際的な知識・技術・価値観等を習得させることのできる、すべての人間の生涯教育の基礎的な教養として位置づけられることが必要である。教育基本法第2条（教育の目標）、学校教育法第21条（義務教育の目標）、同法第51条（高等学校教育の目標）における職業教育に関する規定をふまえ、各教育段階における職業教育は、そのような観点からその固有の意義が問い直されなければならない。とりわけ、高等学校職業科の教育は、物的・人的条件に恵まれていること、実験・実習が教育課程の中核となっていること等により、学習を生産や生活と結びつけるさまざまな教育内容、方法を工夫するための条件に恵まれている。このことは、生徒一人ひとりの個性的な自己実現の促進という点からみて、幅広い教育的可能性を有しているということができる。職業科における職業教育を改善するた

future, provide practical lessons through a cooperation and exchange with local industry and society, enhance the classes by using outside personnel, and to improve students' adaptability for society, communication skills and power of execution. Along with that, it is necessary to encourage students to understand the local industries and communities and deepen their consciousness of social contribution.

Thirdly, from the view of training workers to gain rich humanity it is conaidered to render the mind to respect life, nature, and related things, and to develop the mind, keeping rules and ethical views emphasizing vocational education which enables human interaction combined with nature.

Furthermore, it is required not only to create a flexible curriculum but also be careful for providing an education to develop abilities to choose one's job and plan one's life by experiencing more practical vocational education and internships in order to respond to the change of students' consciousness and diversified career options.

■ Nowadays, society itself is in the process of major change. It is evidenced by a change of structure in the field of industry due to a rapid development of science and technology focusing on information technology and a progress of easing of regulations, unstable employment circumstances because of restructuring and increase of NEET and part-timers, or diversity of one's value as well as one's lifestyle. The vocational education is no longer an education for certain occupations. Rather, it enables people who will engage in a variety of occupations to master practical knowledge, skills, or values that are common to those occupations. Based on the rules for vocational education mentioned in Article 2 of the Basic Act on Education (Educational goal), Article 21 of School Education Act (a goal of compulsory education) and Article 51 of that, the meaning of vocational education implemented at each school level must be reconsidered from such point of view. Especially, education in the vocational course in upper secondary school is benefited from physical and human resources and from the curriculum that usually centers on experiment and exercise. In other words, it

めには、生徒の基礎学力を保障することと、実験・実習および体験学習の充実によって魅力ある授業を実現することが不可欠である。それとともに、普通教育の偏重という現状を克服するためには、前述したような広い視野で職業教育を捉えたうえで、普通科と職業科、その他の職業教育機関、地域社会等との緊密な連携協力に基づいて、自己実現における「働く」ということの意味を、教育内容・方法との関連で改めて問い直すことが重要な課題となっている。

職場体験（本屋） Work Experience in a Bookstore

is benefited from good conditions to devise a variety of educational content and methods that connect student learning with production and everyday living. In upper secondary school, therefore, it is possible to provide students with a wide opportunity to enhance each student's self-realization. In order to revise vocational education in the vocational courses, it is imperative to maintain students' basic achievement and to conduct lessons that appeal to the students by providing enough activities concerning experiment and exercise. In addition, in order to overcome the current tendency of overemphasis on general education, it is important to look at vocational education from a wider perspective as described above. It is further important to ask the meaning of "work" in relation to students' self-realization, along with its relationship to educational content and methods, which is made possible through substantial support by general and vocational education courses, other institutions of vocational education, or by communities.

14. IT 教育

■情報化社会が進展する中、コンピュータやインターネット等、「IT」(Information Technology) と総称される情報通信技術の導入・活用が教育分野においても要請されている。そうした状況に対応した学校教育の内容、方法、環境、人的資源等の改善・充実に関する一連の施策は「教育の情報化」と呼ばれる。IT 教育とは、「教育の情報化」の中で展開される具体的な教育内容・方法の総称であり、大きく、IT に関する知識・技能等を学習内容とする教育と IT を学習方法として活用する教育がある。なお、情報通信技術の略は「ICT」(Information and Communication Technology) が世界的に定着しているが、日本では「IT」が同義で使用されている。最近は ICT に変更されつつある。

■すでに 1980 年代半ばに情報化に対応した教育の必要性は強調されていたが、IT が急速に発展した 1990 年代後半、あらためて「教育の情報化」として文部科学省の重要政策の1つに位置づけられるようになった。さらに、2001 年には、「2005 年までに世界最先端の IT 国家となる」ことを目標に「高度情報通信ネットワーク社会推進戦略本部 (IT 戦略本部)」が内閣に設置され、そこで策定された「e-Japan 戦略」(2001 年)、「IT 新改革戦略」(2006 年) においても「教育の情報化」が盛り込まれ、一層の推進が図られている。

■IT 教育の主な目標は次の3つである。
①情報活用能力の育成
②各教科等の目標を達成するための効果的な IT 活用
③IT 分野の最先端で活躍する高度な IT 人材の育成
このうち、初等中等教育段階での基本的な目標は上記①と②である。

14. IT Education

■ With the progress of information society, the education field has been encouraged to introduce and effectively use Information Technology (IT). A series of measures to meet such needs, including improvement and enhancement of learning contents, teaching methods, educational environment and human resources, are called "Informatization of Education", or "Digitization of Education". IT education, a general term for specific learning contents and teaching methods developed under the policy, can be roughly divided into two: education for acquiring IT knowledge and skills, and education driven by IT. Incidentally, the term ICT is more often used than IT around the world. In Japan, IT is used as the same meaning as ICT, but the number of people who use ICT is gradually increasing.

■ In the mid-1980s, the needs for the Informatization of Education were already emphasized. In the late 1990s, when IT rapidly developed, the Informatization of Education was positioned anew as a key policy of the Ministry of Education, Culture, Sports, Science and Technology. In 2001, the Strategic Headquarters for the Promotion of an Advanced Information and Telecommunications Network Society (IT Strategic Headquarters) was established within the Cabinet, aiming at developing Japan as the world's most advanced IT nation by 2005. The Strategic Headquarters created the e-Japan Strategy in 2001 and the New IT Reform Strategy in 2006. The Education for the Information Age was emphasized also in these strategies, which shows the promotion of IT education by the government.

■ The purposes of the IT education are as follows:
① Develop the information literacy
② Effectively use IT to achieve the targets of various school subjects
③ Develop excellent human resources in Information Technology
Of these purposes, basic ones, ① and ②, are for primary and lower secondary

■上記①の「情報活用能力」とは、次の3つから構成される。
1)　情報活用の実践力　課題や目的に応じて情報手段を適切に活用することを含めて、必要な情報を主体的に収集・判断・表現・処理・創造し、受け手の状況などを踏まえて発進・伝達できる能力
2)　情報の科学的な理解　情報活用の基礎となる情報手段の特性の理解と、情報を適切に扱ったり、自らの情報活用を評価・改善するための基礎的な理論や方法の理解
3)　情報社会に参画する態度　社会生活の中で情報や情報技術が果たしている役割や及ぼしている影響を理解し、情報モラルの必要性や情報に対する責任について考え、望ましい情報社会の創造に参画しようとする態度

■こうした情報活用能力の育成を目的とするのが情報教育である。小学校、中学校、高等学校の各段階に応じた体系的な情報教育の実施をめざし、1998年度告示、2002年度から施行された学習指導要領から本格的に開始された。次の表7-17に示す通り、情報教育は特定の教科においてではなく、すべての教科を通じて包括的に実施することが求められている。

schools.
■ Information literacy mentioned in ①, consists of the following three items:
1) Ability to practically use information
Ability to make use of IT tools according to issues and objectives; ability to collect, judge, express, process and create required information on one's own and to send and communicate the information considering the receivers' needs.
2) Ability to scientifically understand information
Ability to understand the characteristics of IT tools (basic knowledge to use information), and to understand basic theories and methods to appropriately handle information and evaluate/improve one's information use.
3) Attitude to participate in information society
Positive attitude to understand roles and influences of information and information technology in the society, to consider importance of information ethics and responsibility for sending information, and to create a desirable information society.
■ The information education is provided to develop the information literacy as explained above. Information education has been officially promoted after the Course of Study (announced in 1998) was introduced by the government in 2002 aiming at systematic information education according to the study level of primary, lower secondary and upper secondary schools. As is shown in the following table, information education needs to be implemented comprehensively in all subjects, rather than in a specific subject.

表 7-17　学習指導要領に示された情報教育に関する指導の要点、1998 年と 2008 年

	1998 年 12 月告示、2002 年 4 月実施の学習指導要領	2008 年 3 月告示、2011 年 4 月実施の学習指導要領
小学校	・総合的な学習の時間や各教科でコンピュータや情報通信ネットワークを活用する。	・各教科等の指導に当たっては、児童がコンピュータや情報通信ネットットワークなどの情報手段に慣れ親しみ、コンピュータで文字を入力するなどの基本的な操作や情報モラルを身に付け、適切に活用できるようにする。 ・「道徳」の時間では、情報モラルに関する指導に留意する。
中学校	・技術・家庭科の〔技術分野〕の内容として「情報とコンピュータ」が取り上げられ、学習される。 ・総合的な学習の時間や各教科でコンピュータや情報通信ネットワークを活用する。	・各教科等の指導に当たっては、生徒が情報モラルを身に付け、コンピュータや情報通信ネットワークなどの情報手段を適切かつ主体的、積極的に活用できるようにするための学習活動を充実する。 ・技術・家庭科の〔技術分野〕の内容として「情報に関する技術」が取り上げられ、著作権や発信した情報に関する責任を知り、情報に関する技術の適切な評価・活用について考える。 ・「道徳」の時間では、情報モラルに関する指導に留意する。
高等学校	・普通教育に関する教科として「情報」が設けられている。「情報」は「情報 A」「情報 B」「情報 C」の 3 科目から構成されており、それぞれ 2 単位である。1 科目が必履修である。 ・専門教育に関する教科として「情報」が設けられている。専門教科「情報」は 11 科目から構成されている。	・各学科に共通する教科として「情報」が設けられている。「情報」は「社会と情報」「情報の科学」という 2 科目（いずれも 2 単位）から構成されており、ずれか 1 科目が必履修とされている。 ・専門教科「情報」の科目構成を 13 科目に変更。
特別支援学校	・小、中、高校に準じるとともに、障害の状態等に応じてコンピュータ等の情報機器を活用する。	・小、中、高校に準じるとともに、障害の状態等に応じてコンピュータ等の情報機器を活用する。

■さらに、2008 年告示、2011 年施行の学習指導要領においては、「社会の変化への対応の観点から教科等を横断して改善すべき事項」として情報教育があげられ、情報に関する基礎的な知識・技能の個人差の解消、及び、情報モラルの指導の充実を柱に科目構成や目標・内容の見直しが図られた。例えば、中学校では、技術・家庭科における「情報とコンピュータ」が「情報に関する技術」に改称され、それまで学校選択項目であった「マルチメディアの活用」や「プログラムと計測・制御」に関する内容をすべての生徒に学習させることになった。また、高等学校の普通教育教科「情報」については、将来、

Table 7-17 Outline of the Information Education Described in the Course of Study, 1998 and 2008

	Course of Study announced in December 1998, introduced in April 2002	Course of Study announced in March 2008, introduced in April 2011
Primary school	-Make use of computers and information networks in the Periods for Integrated Study and other subjects	-In all subjects, enrich learning activities to enable pupils to become familiar with computers and information networks and to acquire basic skills such as keyboard operation and information ethics so as to make use of ICT properly - Take into consideration teaching of information ethics in Moral education
Lower secondary school	- "Information and Computer" is compulsory in the subject of Industrial Arts and Home Economics. - Make use of computers and information networks in the Periods for Integrated Study and other subjects	-In all subjects, enrich learning activities to enable students to acquire information ethics and to make use of computers and information networks properly, subjectively, and actively - "Information and Computer" in the subject of Industrial Arts and Home Economics is renamed to "Information Technology" and its contents are expanded. - Take into consideration teaching of information ethics in Moral education
Upper secondary school	- "Information Study" is newly established as a compulsory subject for the General Course (Students should choose one of the three sub-subjects; "Information Study A", "Information Study B" and "Information Study C" ; two credits are given for each sub-subject.). - "Information Study" consisting of 11 sub-subjects, is newly established for the Specialized Course.	- "Information Study" is improved (Students should choose one of the two sub-subjects; "Society and Information" and "Information Science" ; two credits are given for each sub-subject.). - "Information Study" is improved and 13 sub-subjects are newly established for the Specialized Course.
Special needs school	-Conform to guidelines for primary, lower secondary and upper secondary schools, and make use of information technologies such as computers to meet the needs of challenged children	-Conform to guidelines for primary, lower secondary and upper secondary schools, and make use of information technologies such as computers to meet the needs of challenged children

■ The latest Course of Study in 2008, which specifies that "Information education shall be provided in a cross-curricular manner to respond to social changes," reviewed the constitution, aims and contents of information-related subjects, based on the main pillars of the elimination of digital divides (difference in basic IT knowledge and skills among people) and the promotion of information ethics education. For example, the study of "Information and Computer" in the subject of Industrial Arts and Home Economics was renamed to "Information Technology," and elective studies, "Multi-media use" and "Programs and

いずれの進路を選択した場合でも必要となる情報活用能力を身につけさせるため、3科目構成から「社会と情報」、「情報の科学」の2科目構成になった。一方、情報モラルの指導については、インターネットを利用した人権侵害や違法行為等に子どもが被害者としてだけでなく、加害者としても巻き込まれるケースが多発する状況に鑑み、新しい学習指導要領全般を通して一層の充実が強調されている。例えば、小学校・中学校の「道徳」では、「道徳の内容との関連を踏まえ、情報モラルに関する指導に留意すること」と明記されている。

■初等中等教育段階におけるIT教育のもう一つの基本的な目標は、「各教科等の目標を達成する」ためにITを活用することである。IT活用は、「魅力ある授業」、「わかる授業」を実現する新しい方法論として位置づけられ、現行の学習指導要領において重視される「確かな学力」の向上や個に応じた指導に効果を発揮することが期待されている。そうした方針は、新しい学習指導要領にもそのまま継承されている。また、IT活用の効果も実証されつつあり、それらを踏まえて、各教科等の指導における具体的なIT活用のガイドラインの整備が文部科学省や関連諸機関によって進められている。今後、とくにIT活用の推進が図られる領域として、英語教育、ならびに、障害のある児童生徒や不登校児童生徒の学習支援が挙げられている。

■IT教育にとって、IT環境の整備、教員のIT指導力の向上、教育用コンテンツの充実・普及が不可欠である。このうち、IT環境と教員のIT指導力については、「e-Japan戦略」において2005年度までに、①すべての教室がインターネットに接続できる（校内LAN整備率100％）、②すべての公立小学校、中学校、高等学校等が高速インターネットに常時接続できる、③教育用PC1台あたり児童・生徒数5.4人、④概ねすべての公立学校教員が、ITを活用して指導ができるという目標が設定された。しかしながら、2006年3

measurement/control" became compulsory. The study of "Information," consisting of Information-A, B and C, for the students of the General Course of Upper Secondary School was reorganized into "Society and Information" and "Information Science," to provide students with IT skills useful for any study courses. Meanwhile, the study of information ethics has been further emphasized by the new Course of Study, considering frequent recent incidents that children were involved not only as victims of human-rights abuse and illegal acts on the Internet, but also as perpetrators. For example, the guidelines for the study of Moral for primary and lower secondary school students specify that "Information ethics education shall be provided, considering the relation with Moral education."

■ Another basic purpose of IT education in primary and lower secondary schools is to make use of IT to "achieve the targets of each subject." IT use, positioned as a new method to provide "attractive and easy-to-understand classes," is expected to improve academic ability and to instruct students according to each of their academic levels, which are major points of the current Course of Study. This policy is stipulated in the new Course of Study as well. Meanwhile, the effects of IT use have been proved in an increasing number of cases, based on which effective IT use guidelines for each subject have been developed by the Ministry of Education, Culture, Sports, Science and Technology and its related institutions. IT use is regarded as useful for English class as well as effective in supporting students who are physically/mentally challenged and who refuse to go to school.

■ To provide excellent IT education, it is essential to prepare an IT environment, improve teachers' IT instruction ability, and enhance and spread IT education contents. Regarding the IT environment and teachers' IT instruction ability, the following targets by FY2005 were established by the e-Japan Strategy: 1) The Internet is accessible from all classrooms (100 % LAN accessibility in school) ; 2) The Internet is always accessible at high speed from all public primary, lower secondary and upper secondary schools; 3) One PC is available for every 5.4

月時点で、①普通教室の LAN 整備率 50.6％、②高速インターネット（400kbps 以上）接続学校数はインターネット接続学校数の 89.1％、③教育用コンピュータ 1 台あたりの児童生徒数は 7.7 人、④コンピュータを使って指導できる教員の割合は 76.8％であり、目標が達成されたとは言い難い状況にある。2006 年度以降も引き続き両者の強化が課題となっている。例えば、2010 年度までにすべての小中高等学校などが超高速インターネット（30Mbps 以上）に常時接続できる、教育用 PC 1 台あたり児童・生徒数 3.6 人などの目標があらためて設定されている。また、教員の IT 指導力の評価基準の具体化・明確化が進められている。

■教育用コンテンツの充実・普及については、個別的なデジタル教材の開発に対して文部科学省等が予算的な支援を行うとともに、ネットワークによる共有・再利用が図られている。その中核的な役割を果たしているのが、国立教育政策研究所が開設している教育情報ナショナルセンター（NICER）(http://www.nicer.go.jp/) である。学校種・教科等ごとに、授業で使える画像や動画等の教育用コンテンツ、ならびに、IT を活用した授業実践事例、指導案等の教育支援情報が収集・登録され、それらを効率的に検索できるようになっている。2006 年度で 271,000 件の情報が登録されている。今後も、その役割が期待されており、一層の拡充が進められている。

students for educational use; and 4) Most teachers in public schools can instruct students using IT. However, as of March 2006, ① The rate of LAN installation for general classrooms was 50.6%; ② The rate of schools accessible to the High-Speed Internet (400 kbps or more) on the schools accessible to the Internet was 89.1%; ③ One PC was available for every 7.7 students for educational use; and ④ The rate of teachers who can instruct students using a computer was 76.8%. These results show the targets were hardly achieved. Improvement of both IT environment and teachers' IT ability remains an issue to be addressed in and after 2006. For example, the following targets by 2010 were established: ① All primary, lower secondary and upper secondary schools are always connected to the Super High-Speed Internet (30 Mbps or more); ② One PC is available for every 3.6 students for educational use. Meanwhile, the specific standards to assess teachers' IT instruction ability have been under development.

■ Regarding enhancement and spread of IT education contents, digital educational materials have been developed with financial support by MEXT, to be shared and reused on the Internet. The core institute that promotes such tasks is the National Information Center for Educational Resources (NICER) (http://www.nicer.go.jp/), established by the National Institute for Educational Policy Research. NICER collects educational contents (images and movies) as well as practical cases of class and instruction plans using IT for various types of schools and subjects, and makes them available on the Internet using an effective searching method. As of 2006, 271,000 pieces of information were available. NICER is expected to continue and further expand its tasks.

15. 生徒指導

(1) 生徒指導の意義と歴史
■生徒指導の意義

　生徒の学校生活は学力形成に寄与する教科等の学習指導と、人間形成に寄与する生徒指導によって構成されている。生徒指導の意義は『生徒指導の手引き』(文部省、1981年)によると、次の5つにまとめられる。①個別的、発達的な教育を基礎とする。②個性の伸張を図り、社会的な資質を高める。③具体的、実際的な活動として進められる。④すべての生徒を対象として実施される。⑤統合的な活動である。

　生徒指導をめぐる問題状況の背景としては、社会の変化に伴う子どもの生活環境の変化などが指摘されている。このような中で生徒指導をめぐる問題状況は多様化しているが、それは、「子ども達の成長を取り巻く環境や子ども達自身が抱えている課題が、複雑・多様化していることと関係している。」と指摘されている。

■生徒指導の歴史

　生徒指導の概念は、ドイツの教育学者ヘルバルト(Johann Friedrich Herbart)に遡ることができる。ヘルバルトは、教育方法として「管理」、「教授」とともに「訓練」を提唱し、道徳的品性の陶冶を教育の目標にしている。ヘルバルトの思想はラインらヘルバルト学派によって、教授と指導の2つにまとめられてドイツからアメリカに伝播する。

　アメリカでは1900年代以降、職業に就く生徒に職業への適性や職業の選択を支援する教育活動、つまり職業指導(vocational guidance)が盛んに行われるようになった。

　このアメリカのガイダンスの思想と実践は第二次世界大戦後に日本で新し

15. Student Guidance

(1) Significance and the History of Student Guidance

■ Significance of Student Guidance

School lives of students consist of teaching and student guidance. According to "the guide of student guidance", significance of student guidance is summarized in the following five points.

1) It is based on individual treatment, developing education.
2) It plans extension of personality and raises social nature.
3) It is conducted as actual, practical activity.
4) It is carried out for all students as an objective.
5) It is an integrated activity.

As a background of the problem situation involving student guidance, the change of children's life environment accompanying change of society etc. is pointed out. Thus, the problem situation involving student guidance is diversified. "The subject which the environment which surrounds growth of children, and problems the child is holding, are becoming complicated and diversified" is indicated.

■ The History of Student Guidance

A general idea of student guidance dates back to German scholar and pedagogic researcher Herbart (Johann Friedrich Herbart). He proposed "training" with "management" and "teaching" as an education method, and asserted the importance of the cultivation of moral character. The Thoughts of Herbart is summarized in instruction and guidance developed by W. Rein and others, and spread to the U.S.A. from Germany.

After the 1900's, vocational guidance became popular in the U.S.A.. It supported the students to find the vocational aptitude and select suitable jobs.

When a new Course of Study was developed after World War II in Japan,

い教育課程が展開される際に導入され、戦前からの生活綴方教育での生活指導の概念と融合して現在に至っている。[1]

（2）生徒指導に関連する主事
■生徒指導主事

　生徒指導主事や進路指導主事といった生徒指導に関する教員配置基準は、「学校教育法施行規則」によって規定されている。

　生徒指導主事は、中学校、高等学校、中等教育学校、特別支援学校の中等部および高等部に原則として置かれる。役割としては、「学校教育法施行規則」第52条第2項に次のことが定められている。

> ・生徒指導主事は、指導教諭又は教諭をもって、これに充てる。
> ・生徒指導主事は、校長の監督を受け、生徒指導に関する事項をつかさどり、当該事項について連絡調整及び指導、助言に当たる。

　実際の学校運営では、生徒指導主事を中核として生徒指導部が組織され、他の教員と連携して生徒指導を実施する場合が多い。

■進路指導主事

　教員配置基準については生徒指導主事とともに進路指導主事も同施行規則に規定されている。進路指導主事は、中学校、高等学校、中等教育学校、特別支援学校の中学部および高等部に置かれる。役割としては、『学校教育法施行規則』第52条第3項に次のことが定められている。

the thoughts and practices of this American guidance were introduced. This guidance mixed with a general idea of life guidance practiced through life composition education to stress the practical education experienced in community life was implemented before the war and has been practiced at present.[1]

(2) The Director Related to Student Guidance
■ Chief guidance and counseling teacher

A teacher placement standard about chief guidance and counseling teacher and chief career guidance teacher is prescribed by "the School Education Act Enforcement Regulations".

In principle chief guidance and counseling teachers are found in the lower secondary school and upper secondary school and the middle and higher section of special support schools. The second item of article 52 "School Education Act Enforcement Regulations" regulates following those characters.

1) Chief supervising teachers or teachers take charge of chief guidance and counseling teachers.
2) Chief guidance and counseling teacher is supervised by the principal and controls <u>the matters relating to student guidance</u>, and makes communication adjustment, guidance, and advice about the matters concerned.

In real school education, the student guidance section is organized as the core of chief guidance and counseling theacher. In many cases of student guidance a student counselor cooperates with other teachers.

■ Chief career guidance teacher

The teacher placement standard of chief career guidance teacher is prescribed in the same way as chief guidance and counseling theacher, too. In principle chief career guidance teachers are found in lower secondary schools and upper secondary schools, and the middle and higher section of special support schools. The third item of article 52 "School Education Act Enforcement Regulations"

> ・進路指導主事は、指導教諭又は教諭をもつて、これに充てる。
> ・校長の監督を受け、生徒の職業選択の指導その他の進路の指導に関する事項をつかさどり、当該事項について連絡調整及び指導、助言に当たる。

　実際の学校運営では、進路指導主事が他の教員と連携して組織的に進路指導を実施する場合が多い。

（3）生徒指導の内容
■学業指導
　学校教育での教師の指導は、学習指導と生徒指導によって構成されているため、教科の学習指導を充実させるためには、その基盤として「なぜ学ぶのか」といった学習そのものについての関心や意欲に関わる学業指導は不可欠である。学業指導としては、学習の意義、学習の方法などについての認識を深める活動が考えられる。

■進路指導・キャリア教育
　生徒の職業選択の指導や進路の指導に関する機会を設定し、就職や進学についての連絡調整を行うとともに、生徒に職業指導や進学指導などを実施する。また、生徒からの進路に関する相談について助言を行う。具体的な内容としては、職業調べや上級学校調べなどの活動が考えられる。また、近年、中学校における職場体験活動、高校における職業体験活動などが広く行われるようになってきている。さらに、小学校段階から勤労を重んじ、目標に向かって努力する態度の形成を図るなど、児童生徒が勤労観、職業観を身に付け、社会人・職業人として自立できるようにキャリア教育を推進している。

regulates the following two points.

> 1) Chief supervising teachers or teachers take charge of chief career guidance teachers.
> 2) Chief career guidance teacher is supervised by the principal and controls matters related to vocational guidance and other career guidance. And he/she makes communication adjustment, guidance, and advice about the matter concerned.

In real school education chief career guidance teacher cooperates with other teachers, and carries out career counseling systematically.

(3) Contents of Student Guidance

■ Educational Guidance (Studies guidance)

Guidance of a teacher in school education consists of subject guidance and student guidance. And in order to fulfill subject learning, educational guidance to be related with interest about learning itself, such as "why I learn" as the base will be indispensable. For educational guidance, there are activities to deepen recognition about significance of learning and the method of learning.

■ Career Guidance · Career Education

With career guidance, we enable the opportunities for occupational guidance by students. And we give information on employment and entrance into higher institutions. Furthermore, we carry out job guidance or entrance guidance into higher institutions for students. In addition, we give advice to students when they consult about careers. For detailed content of career guidance, activities such as occupation investigation and higher educational institution investigation are considered. Moreover, in recent years, the work experience activities in lower secondary schools, the occupation experience activities in upper secondary schools, etc. are being performed increasingly and more widely. Furthermore, teachers promote career education so that labor is respected and the attitude

■適応指導
　思春期の前後で児童生徒はさまざまな悩みを抱える。その児童生徒がそれぞれに抱える悩みなどの解決を図り、自己指導の力や態度を育て、主体的な在り方、生き方へと導く活動を行う。

■社会性指導
　学校や学級での集団生活には社会的適応能力が必要である。この能力は、児童生徒の将来においても一貫して必要なものであるため、学級や学校での生活集団への適応等を図る活動が実施される。
■その他
　健全な生活習慣の形成や災害対応などを行う健康安全指導や、長期休業前などに休暇の有効な活用方法などについて指導を行う余暇指導などがある。[2]

（4）集団を対象とした生徒指導
■集団指導
　児童生徒は学級や学校での生活集団の中で、一人では学べない集団での達成感、成就感、所属感、安心感そして自己の個性の理解など、多様なことを学ぶ。集団指導は、クラスでの教師の講話やグループ学習などを通して従来から実施されてきた。それに加えて、臨床心理学での集団へのアプローチの研究成果があるため、その成果の中で、生徒指導に導入可能なロールプレイングと構成的エンカウンターグループについて説明する。
■ロールプレイング
　ロールプレイング（役割演技）の手法は、モレノ（Moreno,J.L.）が創始した心理劇（Psychodrama）に始まる。生徒指導では、いじめや不登校について、具体的に考えさせる際に、役割を実際に即興で演じて、それぞれの者の立場を実感として理解させる学習の方法として活用される。例えば、不登校をテー

to try their best for accomplishment of a target is formed. It is also aimed that students may learn working views and work values and become independent as members of society or as workers.

■ Personal Adaptation Guidance

Students have various troubles in adolescence. The personal adaptation guidance aims at solutions of the students' troubles, raising his/her power and the attitude of self-instruction, and makes him/her perform activities which lead to independent learning and a way of life.

■ Social Nature Guidance

Social adaptation ability is necessary for school life and class activities. Because this ability is necessary in the future career of a student, school activities to plan adaptation to a life group in a class and a school are carried out.

■ Other

Health-safety guidance conducts the formation of healthy habits and teaches about how to react to natural disasters. In addition, leisure-time guidance (Sparetime guidance) deal with effective and practical uses of holidays.[2]

(4) Student Guidance for a Group

■ Group Guidance

A student learns the feeling of achievement in a group, feeling of accomplishment, feeling of position, feeling of relief and understanding of personality of self through group life in school. Group guidance has been carried out so far by means of a teacher's lecture or group learning in a class. In addition, a teacher explains role playing and encounter group which he/she can introduce to student guidance based on the results of group research in clinical psychology.

■ Role Playing

The technique of role playing (a role performance) began in psychological drama (Psychodrama) founded by Moreno, J.L,. When we let the students think about bullying and non-school attendance, we utilize this method. It really plays an impromptu role, and it is a method of learning to let them understand

マとしたロールプレイングの場合は、児童生徒が、登校できない者の役、担任教員の役、家庭の父母の役、登校できない者を心配するクラスメートの役、傍観者役などを演じる疑似体験により、知識としての理解だけではなく不登校について多面的に考える感覚を身に付けることができる。

■構成的エンカウンターグループ
　エンカウンター（encounter）とは、困難や妨害などに遭うという意味とともに、偶然出会う、邂逅（かいこう）するという意味のある言葉である。学校教育では、実践的研究を通して、他者との出会いや自己の内面との出会いを意図的に作るウォーミングアップ、エクササイズ、シェアリングを実施し、望ましい人間関係を育成するさまざまな取り組みが行われている。エクササイズの例としては、クラス作り、友人関係作りなどがあり、エクササイズを生徒指導で実施する場合に期待できる効果としては不登校傾向の減少などがある。

（5）個人を対象とした生徒指導
■児童生徒理解
　現在、数学や理科など教科の領域では、発展的な学習や補充的な学習を推進することを目的として、個に応じた指導に関する研究が進められている。生徒指導では、教科の指導と比較しても早期から、個別指導の名称で個に応じた指導が進められてきた。生徒指導の目的が個々の児童生徒の人間形成にあるため、個別指導を行う場合、適切な児童生徒理解にもとづく指導が必要不可欠である。適切な児童生徒理解のために、観察法、面接法、質問紙法、検査法、作文や日記、交友関係からの理解などの方法を活用するとよい。
　児童生徒の行動観察を行ったり、二者面談のような面接を実施したり、クラスでの質問紙調査の結果から児童生徒の内面を把握したり、作文や日記に表現される感情を読み取ったり、ソシオメトリーなどを活用して交友関係を

a viewpoint of each person as an actual feeling. In a role play of non-school attendance, a student plays a position of the person who cannot attend school, a position of a teacher in charge, a position of parents, a position of a classmate worrying about the person who cannot attend school, and the part of an onlooker. A student can have a sense to think about non-school attendance from various aspects as well as understanding of knowledge in this para-experience.

■ Constitution Encounter Group

The word "encounter" has a meaning of chance encounter as well as a meaning to face difficulty and disturbance. In school education, we carry out a warm-up, an exercise, making an encounter with another person to encounter intentionally with the inside of self, and others as a method of preventive and developmental counseling for groups. And various programs to raise desirable human relations are done to deepen the understanding of oneself and others, acceptance of oneself and experiences of mutual reliance. For examples of the exercise, there is the making of class groups, and the making of friend relationships. We can expect that absenteeism could be decreased as a positive effect by carrying out this exercise in student guidance.

(5) **Student Guidance for an Individual**

■ Student Understanding

In recent years a study of individual guidance has been conducted for the purpose of promoting development learning and supplementary learning in subject domains such as mathematics or science. Student guidance has concentrated on individual guidance from an earlier stage compared to subject guidance. As the purpose of student guidance is human being formation of an individual student, it is indispensable to give guidance based on appropriate student understanding when conducting individual guidance. For appropriate student understanding, you should utilize the observation method, an interview, a questionnaire method, inspection method, composition and writing a diary, a method of student understanding through communication with his/her friends

調査したりして、複合的に児童生徒理解を図ることが正確な理解につながる。

■教育相談

　学校での教育相談は、学級担任やホームルーム担任が担当することも多いが、学校にスクールカウンセラーが配置されている場合には、スクールカウンセラーが中心となって教育相談体制が確立していることもある。

　ここでは、従来から個別相談を実施している担任教師の場合について説明する。個別相談を実施するためにはさまざまな機会があるが、おおむね、「呼び出し相談」、「定期相談」、「チャンス相談」、「自発相談」に分けて考えることができる。「呼び出し相談」は特定の児童生徒を呼び出して面接する方法である。「定期相談」は全児童生徒を対象として順番を決めて計画的に実施する面接である。「チャンス相談」は教師側が児童生徒の学校生活の中で偶発的な接触の機会をとらえて実施する方法である。「自発相談」は児童生徒からの自発的な申し出により実施する面接である。なお、新しい動きとしては、スクールカウンセラー活用事業、スクールソーシャルワーカー活用事業、全国統一の「24時間いじめ相談ダイヤル」の設置などが始まっている。

and acquaintances.

Teachers make action observations of a student and carry out an interview and grasp the inside of a student from the results of a questionnaire investigation and read the feelings of a student expressed in a composition and a diary and utilize sociometry and investigate friends and acquaintances of a student. In this way a compound method leads to our correct understanding of the student.

■ Education Consultation

There are many cases that a homeroom and a classroom teacher are in charge of education consultation in a school. However, when a school counselor is arranged in a school, an education consultation system is established, because he/she plays an important role.

The following is an example of a teacher case having carried out an individual consultation. There are various means of conducting individual consultation, but those are divided into "summons consultation", "fixed period consultation", "chance consultation" and "spontaneous consultation". In the method of "summons consultation" a teacher or a counselor call a certain student, and have an interview with him/her. The "periodical consultation" is intended for all students, takes place in order of students, and is implemented premeditatedly. In the method of "chance consultation" a teacher or a counselor utilizes an opportunity of the contact that the teacher has accidently made in school life. The "spontaneous consultation" is carried out by a voluntary proposal from a student. In addition, there are the following new activities: a practical use activity of a school counselor, a practical use activity of a school social worker, and a "24-hour bullying consultation dial" which is used by the students in the whole country.

(6) 生徒指導上の諸問題
■暴力行為

文部科学省は年度別に児童生徒の問題行動等の状況を調査している。その中で校内暴力の発生件数も調査している。年度別の調査での暴力行為の区分は、対教師暴力、生徒間暴力、対人暴力、器物損壊である。学校内で暴力行為が発生した件数は表7-18の通りである。この表から、2007年（平成19年）度の場合、暴力行為の発生件数は、小・中・高等学校のすべての学校種で過去最高の件数に上ることがわかる。

表7-18 学校内における暴力行為発生件数の推移
（文部科学省、2008年11月20日発表）

	58年度	59年度	60年度	61年度	62年度	63年度	元年度	2年度	3年度	4年度	5年度	6年度	7年度	8年度
小学校														
中学校	3,547	2,518	2,441	2,148	2,297	2,858	3,222	3,090	3,217	3,656	3,820	4,693	5,954	8,169
高等学校	768	647	642	653	774	1,055	1,194	1,419	1,673	1,594	1,725	1,791	2,077	2,406
合計	4,315	3,165	3,083	2,801	3,071	3,913	4,416	4,509	4,890	5,250	5,545	6,484	8,031	10,575

	9年度	10年度	11年度	12年度	13年度	14年度	15年度	16年度	17年度
小学校	1,304	1,528	1,509	1,331	1,465	1,253	1,600	1,890	2,018
中学校	18,209	22,991	24,246	27,293	25,769	23,199	24,463	23,110	23,115
高等学校	4,108	5,152	5,300	5,971	5,896	5,002	5,215	5,022	5,150
合計	23,621	29,671	31,055	34,595	33,130	29,454	31,278	30,022	30,283

	18年度	19年度
小学校	3,494	4,807
中学校	27,540	33,525
高等学校	8,985	9,603
合計	40,019	47,935

(6) Many Problems in Student Guidance
■ A Violent Act

The Ministry of Education, Culture, Sports, Science and Technology has investigated the situation of problem actions of students in each year. It has covered the number of school violence outbreaks. The violence actions by investigation in the year are divided into anti-teacher violence, violence among students, violence towards other people, and instrument destruction. The number of violent actions occurred in schools is shown in the following Table.

Table 7-18 Transition of the Number of School Violent Acts from 1983 to 2007.
(Announcement of the Ministry of Education, Culture, Sports, Science and Technology, November 20, 2008)

	1983	84	85	86	87	89	90	91	92	93	94	95	96	97
Primary school														
Lower secondary school	3,547	2,518	2,441	2,148	2,297	2,858	3,222	3,090	3,217	3,656	3,820	4,693	5,954	8,169
Upper sec school	768	647	642	653	774	1,055	1,194	1,419	1,673	1,594	1,725	1,791	2,077	2,406
Sum total	4,315	3,165	3,083	2,801	3,071	3,913	4,416	4,509	4,890	5,250	5,545	6,484	8,031	10,575

	97	98	99	2000	01	02	03	04	05
Primary school	1,304	1,528	1,509	1,331	1,465	1,253	1,600	1,890	2,018
Lower secondary school	18,209	22,991	24,246	27,293	25,769	23,199	24,463	23,110	23,115
Upper sec school	4,108	5,152	5,300	5,971	5,896	5,002	5,215	5,022	5,150
Sum total	23,621	29,671	31,055	34,595	33,130	29,454	31,278	30,022	30,283

	6	7
Primary school	3,494	4,807
Lower secondary school	27,540	33,525
Upper sec school	8,985	9,603
Sum total	40,019	47,935

■いじめ

　「冷やかし・からかい」、「言葉での脅し」、「仲間はずれ」や「集団による無視」、「身体的・心理的攻撃」、「金品のたかり」、「ものを隠す」などのいじめは暴力行為とともに深刻な人権問題である。最近では、インターネットや携帯電話を利用した「ネット上のいじめ」が増加し、新しい形のいじめとして社会において大きく取りあがられてきている。さらに、いじめによる自殺は深刻な社会問題となっている。

　各学校での日常的ないじめ問題への対応策としては、「職員会議等を通じて、いじめ問題について教職員間で共通理解を図った」や、「道徳や学級活動の時間にいじめにかかわる問題を取り上げ、指導を行った」などが多いことが明らかになっている。今日では、多くの学校において、いじめを早期に発見し、早期に解決することや、いじめのない学級集団や学校をつくることが生徒指導上の重要な課題として取り上げられ、さまざまな取組が展開されている。

　従来、中学校に多いが、最近では、小学校にも増えてきており、低年齢化が進んでいる。近年数値化が急上昇したのは、いじめの定義を「当該児童生徒が、一定の人間関係のある者から、心理的、物理的な攻撃を受けたことにより、精神的な苦痛を感じているもの。なお、起こった場所は学校の内外を問わない。」としたことに関係する。

This table shows that the generating number of violent acts in school went up to the highest in all the primary, lower secondary and upper secondary schools in 2007.

■ Bullying

Bullying, such as "ridicule and teasing", "a threat by language", "alienation", "disregard by a group", "physical / mental attack", "extortion of money and goods", and "hiding a thing", is the problem of serious human rights invasion. In recent years, bullying of a new form using the Internet or cellular phones has increased, which has been considered seriously as a new type of bullying in society. Furthermore, suicide caused by teasing has become a serious social problem.

For measures against everyday bullying problems in schools, it is clear "common understanding was aimed toward school staff about bullying problems through staff meetings and other opponntunities, "or that" in the time of morality or classroom activities the problems in connection with bullying were taken up and taught" etc. Nowadays, in many schools, it is considered an important issue of student guidance to discover and solve bullying at an early stage and to establish class groups and schools without bullying with various measures taken.

Although so far there were many bullying cases in lower secondary schools, it is increasing in primary schools recently. And the abrupt increasing tendency of younger age children was found in recent years. It is related to the new definition of bullying evaluation which is shown in the following terms.

"By having received the mental and physical attack from those to whom a juvenile student concerned has some association, he/she has felt a mental pain and the place where it happened can occur either inside or outside of school."

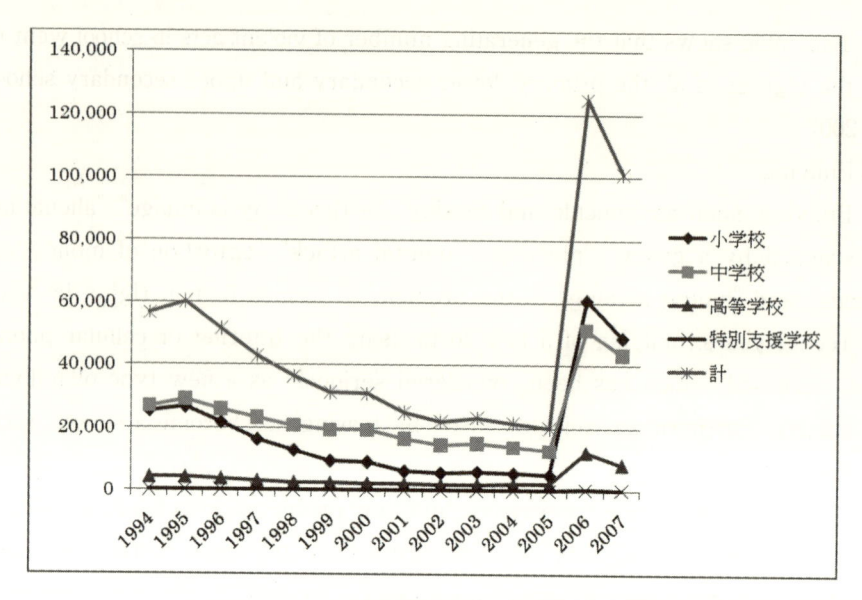

図7-4 いじめの認知（発生）件数の推移
（文部科学省、2008年11月20日発表）

■不登校

　不登校は具体的には、国立、公立、私立の小学校、中学校、高等学校で病気や経済的な理由以外で30日以上欠席した状態にあることである。

　不登校の要因としては、心理的要因、情緒的要因、身体的要因、社会的要因などが指摘されている。「不登校となったきっかけと考えられる状況」としては、2008（平成20）年度の文部科学省調査では、「その他本人に関わる問題」（41.2％）、「いじめを除く友人関係をめぐる問題」（18.5％）、「親子関係をめぐる問題」（11.1％）、「学業の不振」（10.1％）などが多い。また、「指導の結果登校する又はできるようになった児童生徒」に特に効果のあった学校の措置としては、「家庭訪問を行い、学業や生活面での相談に乗るなど様々な指導・援助を行った」（9,374校）、「登校を促すため、電話をかけたり迎えに行くなどした」（9,253校）などが多い。

　図7-5に見る通り、平成21年度学年別不登校児童生徒数からは、小学校よりも中学校に不登校が多いこと、小学校と中学校の間で大幅に不登校児童

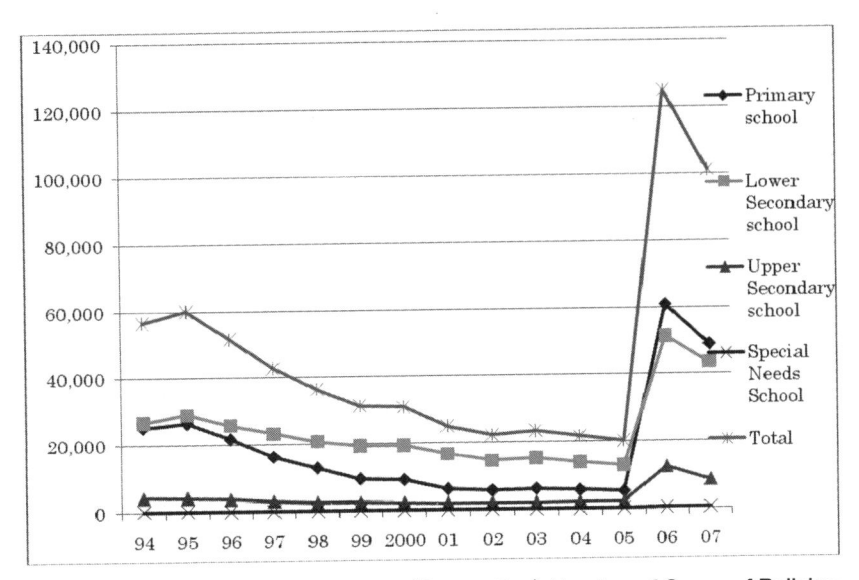

Figure 7-4 Transition of the Cognitive (Generating) Number of Cases of Bullying
(Announcement of the Ministry of Education, Culture, Sports, Science and Technology, November 20, 2008)

■ Truancy

Truancy is found in national, public and private primary schools, lower secondary schools, and upper secondary schools. It is classified as having been absent more than 30 days per year besides illness and financial reasons.

As a factor of truancy, the psychological, affective, physical, and the social factors, are pointed out. As "the situation considered to be a cause of truancy", the Ministry of Education, Culture, Sports, Science and Technology investigation of 2008 pointed out "the problem in connection with the person himself/herself" (41.2%), "the problem involving the relationships with friends except bullying" (18.5%), "the problem involving child-parent relationship" (11.1%), and "the studies of depression " (10.1%). Moreover, the effective measures taken by the school, especially for "the juvenile students who went to school or were able to come to school as a result of guidance" were "the home visit was performed and various instruction and assistance, such as giving study and life advice, were offered" (9,374

生徒数が増加することなどがわかる。中学校第1学年では小学校第6学年のときに比べると不登校の生徒の数が約3.1倍に増えており、「中1ギャップ」という名で呼ばれている。この現象を解消するための小・中連携教育の必要性が指摘されている。

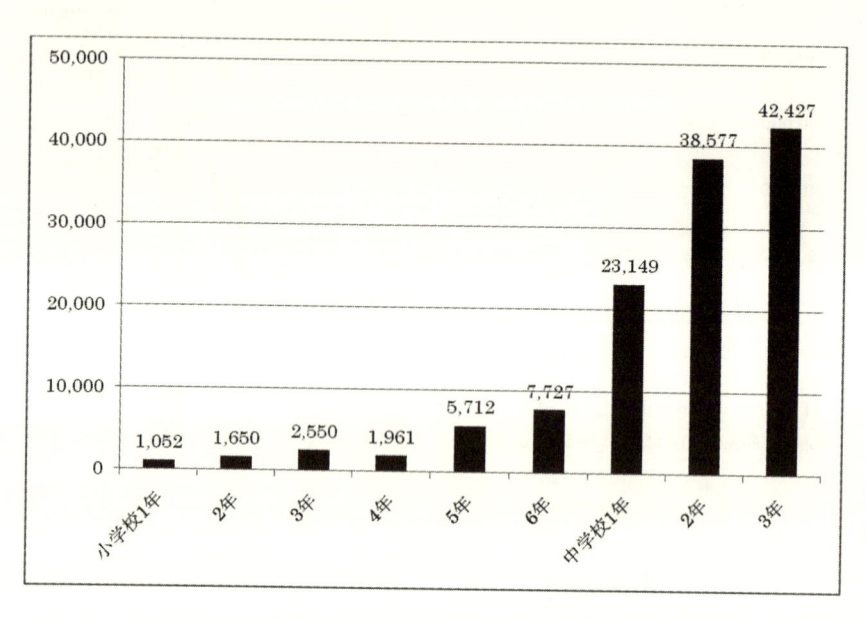

図7-5 2009年度（平成21年度）学年別不登校児童生徒数
（文部科学省、2009年8月発表）

schools), "in order to urge going to school, teachers telephoned students and went to meet them at their homes, etc." (9,253 schools).

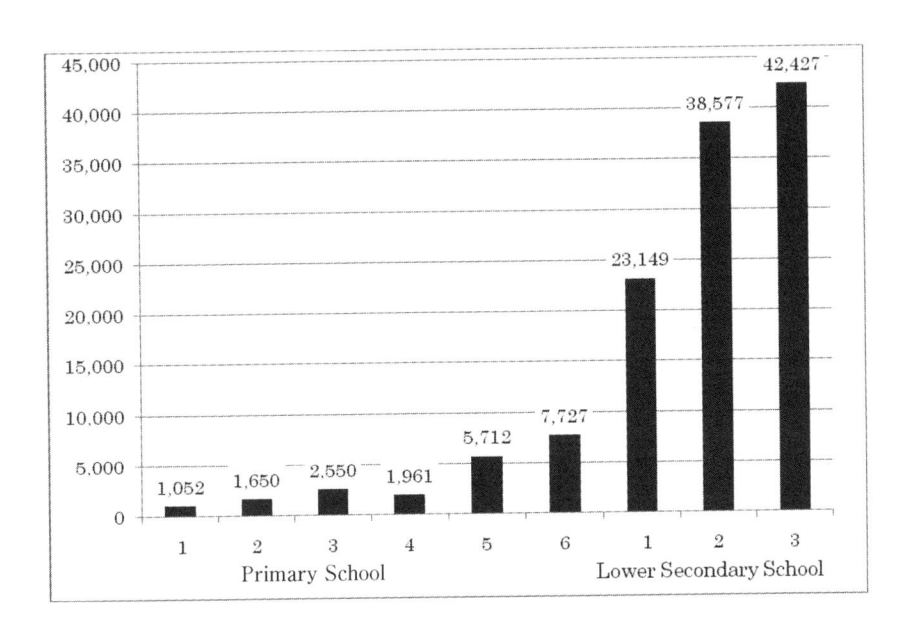

[Bar chart showing values: Primary School — 1: 1,052; 2: 1,650; 3: 2,550; 4: 1,961; 5: 5,712; 6: 7,727. Lower Secondary School — 1: 23,149; 2: 38,577; 3: 42,427.]

Figure 7-5 Number of Juvenile Students Absent from School for an Extended Period by Grade in 2009
(Announcement of the Ministry of Education, Culture, Sports, Science and Technology, August, 2009)

As for the number of juvenile students absent from school for an extended period according to grade in 2009, Figure7-5 shows that lower secondary schools have more truancy than primary schools, and that the number of juvenile students absent from school has increased sharply between primary schools and lower secondary schools. In the lower secondary school, 1st grade students, were compared with 6th grade primary school, and the number of students absent from school has increased about 3.1 times more, and is called by the name of "the 1st grade gap of lower secondary school." For solving this problem the cooperative relation between the primary schools and lower secondary schools is pointed out to be necessary.

■高等学校中途退学

　文部科学省の調査では、学校生活、進路変更、病気・けがなどの理由で高等学校を中途退学する生徒の数が明らかになっている。2008（平成20）年度の場合、国・公・私立高等学校における中途退学者数は66,226人である。国・公・私立別にみると、国立では52人(中退率0.5%)、公立では45,742人(中退率1.9%)、私立では20,432人（中退率2.0%）となる。[3] 中途退学自体の意味はそれぞれの生徒で異なるものの、不本意な退学を避けるためには、これらの高校生への生徒指導の充実が大切である。具体的には、「学校生活」については、学業指導、個人的適応指導、社会性指導の充実が、「進路変更」については進路指導の充実が、「病気・けが」には健康安全指導の充実が有効であろう。

■学校と家庭との連携

　生徒指導は学校でのみ実施しても十分な成果が得られるとは限らず、子どもの学業や生活に大きく影響する家庭との連携が必要である。青少年の問題行動の背景には、基本的な生活習慣や倫理観等が十分にしつけられていない家庭状況がある。そのため、PTA総会、学校だより、学級通信等を有効活用して家庭と連携して基本的な生活習慣や倫理観等の指導を充実させることが生徒指導の効果を高めるためにも効果的である。そして、児童生徒の家族が気軽に学校に相談できる体制づくりが必要である。

■地域社会との連携協力

　児童生徒は学校と家庭のみで生活しているのではなく、学校と家庭の往復において、あるいは休日には地域社会と関わり、地域社会で過ごす時間も多い。そのため、生徒指導は学校と家庭だけではなく、地域社会との連携協力も必要となる。

　特に不登校については、学校・家庭・関係機関が連携した地域ぐるみのサ

■ Drop out from upper secondary school

An investigation by the Ministry of Education, Culture, Sports, Science and Technology, showed the number of the students who leave upper secondary schools for the reasons of school life, course change, illness, an injury, etc.. In the case of 2008, the number of dropouts in national, public and private high schools was 66,226 persons. In national schools, there were 52 students (0.5% of dropout rate) and in public schools 45,742 students (1.9% of dropout rate)[3], and in private schools 20,432 students (2.0% of dropout rate). Although it differs by each student, substantial student guidance to these high school students is important in order to avoid unwilling withdrawal from school. For "school life", studies guidance, individual adaptation guidance, and social substantial guidance to be effective, substantial course guidance will be effective about "course change", and substantial healthy safe guidance will be effective in "an illness and an injury."

■ Cooperation with schools and homes

Even if student guidance is carried out only in school, sufficient results are not necessarily obtained. Cooperation with the homes which influence children's studies and life greatly, is required. The home situation where a fundamental lifestyle, a fundamental sense of ethics, etc. are not fully based serves as a backdrop to youth's difficult behavior. Therefore, it is an appropriate means for enriching instruction of a fundamental lifestyle and a sense of ethics, etc, to use PTA general meetings, school communications, and class communications, cooperating with homes, in order to heighten the effect of student guidance. Therefore, the formulation of the structure on which juvenile students' families can consult with schools freely is required.

■ Cooperation with communities

Juvenile students are not living only at schools and homes, they have many occasions to communicate with the community in the round trip to and from schools and homes and on holidays. Therefore, student guidance is not carried out only at schools and homes, but the cooperation with communities is also needed.

ポートシステムを整備するスクーリング・サポート・ネットワーク整備活動（ＳＳＮ）が展開されている。
　また、暴力行為や非行など、問題行動を起こす個々の児童生徒の状況に応じて学校、教育委員会、関係機関が連携、協力して対応するためのサポート・チームなど、ネットワークを活用した取組が進められている。

■学校と警察との連携
　文部科学省と警察庁は連携して児童生徒の規範意識を育むために非行防止教室を実施している。全国の学校での非行防止教室の展開は、学校や家庭内で通用する規範意識だけではなく、実社会でも通用する規範意識を育むことを目指している。

■携帯電話・インターネット
　近年、生徒指導上の諸問題のきっかけとして携帯電話やインターネットが着目されている。携帯電話をよく使う子どもは就寝時間など生活面への影響も見られることが指摘されており、また、インターネット利用におけるフィルタリングの普及促進及び適切な利用のための啓発活動も行われている。

注
1　生徒指導の歴史については、江川玟成『生徒指導の理論と方法改訂版』学芸図書、2000年、p.7の区分を参照した。
2　生徒指導の内容の区分については、江川玟成『生徒指導の理論と方法改訂版』学芸図書、2000年、pp.11-13の区分を参照した。
3　文部科学省『平成20年度児童生徒の問題行動等生徒指導上の諸問題に関する調査』、http://www.mext.go.jp/b_menu/houdou/ 21/08/__icsFiles/afieldfile/2009/08/06/1282877_1_1.pdf、2009年11月27日確認。

Especially about truancy, the schooling support network activities (SSN) which establish the support system for the cooperation of the whole community including schools, homes, and the organizations concerned are put into practice.

Moreover, the situation of each juvenile student who causes difficult behavior, such as using force and wrongdoing, is embraced, and the measure which utilized networks, such as a support team for schools, the boards of education, and the organizations concerned with cooperation and correspondence in cooperation, has advanced.

■ Cooperation with schools and the police

The Ministry of Education, Culture, Sports, Science and Technology and the National Police Agency are carrying out delinquency prevention classrooms, in order to cherish juvenile students' normative consciousness. Deployment of the delinquency prevention classrooms in schools all over the country aims at cherishing the normative consciousness which is accepted not only at schools or homes but also in actual society.

■ Cellular phones and the Internet

In recent years, peoples' attention is paid to cellular phones or the Internet and is a cause of many problems indicated in student guidance. The children that often use cellular phones, are inclined to get a negative influence in their life, such as inadequate sleep. Moreover, the education activities for spreading and promotion of filtering Internet usage and its suitable use have also been tried.

Note:
1 Concerning the history of student guidance, I referred to the following book: Binsei Egawa, "Theory and Method of Student Guidance, Revised Edition", Gakugei-Tosho Publisher, 2000, p.7
2 Concerning the content classification of student guidance, I referred to the following book: Binsei Egawa, "Theory and Method of Student Guidance, Revised Edition", Gakugei-Tosho Publisher, 2000, p.11-13
3 The Ministry of Education, Culture, Sports, Science and Technology,

658　第Ⅶ章　教科教育等の特色

集団の規律　Group Discipline

VII. The Characteristics of Courses 659

"A Survey of the Problem Actions and Guidance Problems of Students in 2008 http://www.mext.go.jp/b_menu/houdou/21/08/__icsFiles/afieldfile/2009/08/06/1282877_1_1.pdf, November 27, 2009

子ども110番　Emergency Number for Children

かたづけ　Arranging for Class

第Ⅷ章

教育内容・方法の課題

The Issues of Educational Contents and Methods

集団行動　A Group Line - up

1. 学校週五日制と教育課程・方法

■日本では、週5日制（週休2日制）の社会を実現することの一環として、2002年4月から、完全学校週五日制が実施されている。

■学校週五日制の実施は学校教育のいろいろなところに、さまざまな影響を与え、新しい問題を投げかけている。年間の総授業日数は200日前後に減少し、総授業時数は、2007年現在、小学校第4～6学年の各学年で945時間、中学校では各学年で980時間となっている。総授業時数が最も多かった時期（小学校は1968年学習指導要領の改訂、中学校は1969年学習指導要領の改訂）と比較するとそれぞれ13％、16％減となっている。

■学力を維持し、豊かな人間形成の実現を図るためには、一定の教育内容と授業時数を確保することが必要である。総授業日数と総授業時数を確保するために、2学期制の導入、学校行事の精選・見直し、授業の1単位時間の弾力的な運用、モジュール方式による時数の確保、始業式や終業式の授業実施等、実にさまざまな工夫が行われている。

■土曜日の活用も進められている。小・中学校では地域等と連携した体験的な学習機会の提供、中学校では基礎学力向上や補充・発展的学習のための学習機会の提供、高等学校では進学や資格取得のための学習機会の提供が土曜日を利用して行われている。

■2008年3月に学習指導要領が改訂された。小学校については2011年4月から、中学校については2012年4月から全面実施される。改訂学習指導

1. The Five-Day Week School System and Curriculum / Method

■ The five-day week school system has been fully introduced in Japan since April 2002 as a part of schemes to realize a five-day work week society (two-day weekend).
■ The five-day week school system has created various impacts on school education and has presented new challenges. The total days of instruction reduced to approximately 200 days in a year, and total hours of instruction as of 2007 is 945 hours in each grade from 4 to 6 in primary schools and 980 hours in each grade of lower secondary schools. The hours of instruction reduced by 13% for primary schools and by 16% for lower secondary schools compared to when the Course of Study was revised in 1968 for primary schools and in 1969 for lower secondary schools.
■ It is necessary to secure certain contents of education and hours of instruction to maintain scholastic abilities and realize rich character-building. In order to secure the total days and hours of instruction, various efforts have been made, such as introducing the two-semester school system, careful selection and reexamination of school events, flexible operation of one-unit length of a class, securing hours of instruction by applying a module system, and conduction of classes on term opening days and closing ceremonies.
■ Saturdays have been effectively used. In primary and lower secondary schools, hands-on learning collaboration with local communities are provided. In lower secondary schools, learning opportunities to improve basic scholastic abilities and supplemental and developmental studies are provided. In upper secondary school, learning opportunities to proceed to higher education and acquisition of qualifications are provided on Saturdays.
■ The Course of Study was revised in March 2008. The changes will be fully implemented from April 2011 in primary schools and from April 2012 in lower

要領によると、小学校の年間総授業時数は第4～6学年の各学年で980時間、中学校では各学年1015時間に改められる。小、中学校のいずれについても、授業時数は各学年35時間、週当たり1時間増加された。

■学校週五日制の下での授業時数の確保、教育課程・方法のあり方を工夫することが重要な課題となっている。

secondary schools. The total hours of instruction in a school year for each grade from 4 to 6 in primary schools will be changed to 980 hours, and it will be 1015 hours for each lower secondary school grade. The class hours were increased by one hour per week or 35 hours per school year for each grade in both primary and lower secondary schools.

■ Under such a five-day week school system, securing hours of instruction and showing ingenuity in curriculum and the way of education are important issues now.

2. 学力問題とカリキュラム

■日本では、21世紀を迎える前後の頃から、生徒の学力の低下が起きているのではないかという問題が深刻な社会問題になり、学校教育改革の重要な課題として取り上げられてきた。
■学力低下の指摘は、経済協力開発機構（OECD）の「生徒の学習到達度調査（PISA）」や国際教育到達度評価学会（IEA）の「国際数学・理科教育動向調査（TIMSS）」によって、日本の生徒の学力は国際的に上位にあるものの、応用力に問題があること、読解力や記述式問題に課題があること、成績中位層が減り、低位層が増加していること、学習意欲や学習習慣に課題があることなどの実態が明らかにされたことに基づいて行われた。

■大学教員によって、大学生の基礎学力低下の実態が指摘されたことも、大きなインパクトを与えることになった。
■文部科学省はそれまでの「ゆとり」の教育から「学力向上」を重視する教育への転換を図り、2008年3月に、「確かな学力」の確立を目指す学習指導要領の改訂を行った。それによって、国語、算数・数学、理科、社会、外国語、体育・保健体育の授業時数が増加され、教育内容の見直しが行われた。また、2007年度から各地域における生徒の学力の実態を把握するための全国学力テストが実施された。

■日本の学校教育では、学力の内容をどのようなものとしてとらえるかという問題（学力観）について、基本的な考え方を異にする2つの系譜がある。その一つは、知ること（認識能力）を重視し、知識や技能など客観的に測定

2. The Issues of Scholastic Ability and Curriculum

■ In Japan, since around the time entering the 21st century, a concern about a decline in scholastic abilities of students became a serious social problem and has been taken up as an important issue of school education reform.

■ The program for International Student Assessment (PISA), Organization for Economic and Co-operation and Development (OECD) and Trends in International Mathematics and Science Study (TIMSS) of International Association for the Evaluation of Educational Achievement (IEA) revealed various facts indicating that Japanese students are weak in applied skills, reading comprehension, and descriptive questions. In addition, medium segments of scores are decreasing and low segments of scores are increasing while their academic performance ranks high on an international basis. Moreover, it was explained that motivation for learning and study habits need to be improved. The decline in scholastic abilities of Japanese students was pointed out based on these reports.

■ University teachers pointed out that basic scholastic ability of university students also declined which has a major impact on society.

■ The Ministry of Education, Culture, Sports, Science and Technology revised the Course of Study to ensure "Solid academic capabilities" in March 2008, aiming to transform education from relaxed education to the one placing emphasis on improving scholastic ability. In so doing, class hours of Japanese language, arithmetic/mathematics, science, social studies, foreign language, health and physical education were increased and the contents of education were reviewed. Moreover, since 2007, national achievement tests were conducted in order to assess the actual academic level of students in each area.

■ In the Japanese school education system, there are two different basic views of scholastic ability (perspective of academic ability). One focuses on knowing (cognitive ability) and considers the importance of abilities to viewing knowledge and skills

することができる能力を学力の中心に位置付ける学力観である。他の一つは、興味や関心、意欲や態度、思考力、応用力、表現力、実践力等（機能的な学力）を重視する学力観である。認識能力を重視する立場では、基礎的な知識や技能を習得させるための系統学習を重視することになる。態度や応用力を重視する立場では、総合的な問題解決学習を重視することになる。

■今日では、「生きる力」をはぐくむという観点から、基礎的・基本的な知識・技能の習得を重視するとともに、「自ら学び自ら考える力」の育成を図ることが重視されており、バランスのとれたカリキュラムを編成し、実施することが学校の課題となっている。

■生徒の学力の実態には、高い学力の生徒と低い学力の生徒とが2極に分かれ、極端な学力の格差が見られるという問題点も指摘されている。学力の2極分解の現象は「学力格差」と呼ばれ、深刻な社会的課題になっている。少人数指導や個別指導を効果的に導入することによって、学力が低い生徒の学力を高め、格差を解消し、全体の学力を高めるようにする取り組みが力強く進められている。

in an objective manner. The other focuses on functional academic abilities such as interest, willingness, attitude, cogitation, applied skill, expressiveness, and power of execution. The former puts priority on the systematic study according to academic sequence which allows students to gain basic knowledge and skills, and the latter puts priority on comprehensive problem-solving study.

■ Today, from an aspect to foster "zest for living", acquisition of primary and basic knowledge is considered to be important as well as aiming to promote student abilities to learn and think by themselves. It is important for schools to draw up and conduct a well-balanced curriculum.

■ It is pointed out that excessive disparity is seen among those students. They are polarized with those who show high scholastic abilities and those who show low scholastic abilities. This phenomenon of polarization is called "disparities in academic achievement" and is considered as a critical social issue. By introducing small-group teaching and private tutorial programs effectively, efforts to improve scholastic ability of the students whose ability is low, eliminates the disparities, and improves overall scholastic abilities, which have been advanced.

3.「総合的な学習の時間」に関する問題

■既にⅦ章の「総合的な学習の時間」のところで指摘したように、小学校、中学校および高等学校では、1998年の学習指導要領の改訂によって「総合的な学習の時間」が新しく設けられ、2002年4月から本格的に実施され、現在に至っている。

■「総合的な学習の時間」は「知識基盤社会」に求められる自ら学び、自ら考える主体的な能力を育てるとともに、楽しく、充実した学校生活を実現するうえで、大きな成果を上げている。創設当初のねらいどおり、日本の学校を大きく変えることになった。しかし、その一方で、さまざまな問題点があることが指摘されており、今後に課題を残している。

■「総合的な学習の時間」の実施については、発足の当初から、期待どおりの成果を得ることができるかどうか、心配する声が少なくなかった。その最も大きい理由は、日本の教師は教科を横断し、教科の枠を越えた総合的なテーマに取り組ませる学習（クロスカリキュラム）の指導に必ずしも習熟していないということであった。特に中学校、高等学校の教師について、このことが心配された。また、学習指導要領では、教科等とは異なり、総合的な学習のための「時間」の枠が示されただけであり、指導内容や学習活動について具体的に示されなかった。教科書も作られていない。それぞれの学校の特色を活かした特色ある総合的な学習を構想し、実施することが期待されており、指導内容等については学校に任されていた。それがかえって不安や心配をもたせることになった。

■文部科学省は2006年6月に「総合的な学習の時間」に関する全国調査を実施した。その結果を表8-1・8-2に示した。

3. The Issues of Period for Integrated Study

■ As indicated in the Chapter VII, "Period for Integrated Study", the resulting revision of the Course of Study in 1998, the period for integrated study has been newly introduced to primary schools, lower secondary schools, and upper secondary schools. This program was fully implemented from April 2002 and has been continued up to the present day.

■ The period for integrated study has been producing significant results in realizing enjoyable and fruitful school life as well as developing independent-minded abilities: learning and thinking by students themselves, which are required in the knowledge-based society. Introduction of period for integrated study has substantially changed Japanese schools as targeted from the beginning. Meanwhile, various issues are pointed out and there are still issues to be tackled.

■ There were some voices of concern from the beginning whether the period for integrated study would be able to successfully achieve results as expected. The main reason was that Japanese teachers were not necessarily proficient in teaching Cross Curriculum, whereby teachers teach students across the subjects and allow students to try to learn theme comprehensively beyond subjects. Particularly lower and upper secondary school teachers were of special concern regarding this matter. Moreover, only the time frame for the integrated study was indicated in the Course of Study unlike subject studies, and detailed contents of instruction and learning activities were not, in addition to no textbooks being used. The period for integrated study was set up with expectations that schools would plan and implement it by taking advantage of their characteristics, and the contents of instruction were entrusted to each school. This increased worries and uneasiness among teachers.

■ The Ministry of Education, Culture, Sports, Science, and Technology conducted a nationwide survey in June 2006 regarding the period for integrated

表 8-1 「総合的な学習の時間」に対する小学生・中学生の意識

	好き	どちらともいえない	好きでない
小学生	60.0%	26.2%	11.2%
中学生	46.2%	37.7%	14.3%

表 8-2 「総合的な学習の時間」に対する教師の意識:「総合的な学習の時間」はなくした方がよい

	そう思う	そう思わない	よくわからない
小学校担任	38.3%	53.7%	6.2%
中学校担任	57.2%	34.0%	7.7%

出典:文部科学省、「総合的な学習の時間」に関する全国調査結果、2006年

　表 8-1 によると、「総合的な学習の時間」の授業は、小学生には好まれているが、中学生には小学生に比べると、好まれていないという傾向が明らかにされている。
　また、「総合的な学習の時間」はなくした方がよいかどうか、という問いに対しては表 8-2 の通り、小学校担任教師の 38％が「そう思う」と答えている。中学校担任教師の 57％が「そう思う」と答えている。このデータは日本の教育界に大きな衝撃を与えた。
　これらのデータから浮かび上がってくるのは、「総合的な学習の時間」が生徒に満足を与え、教師からも歓迎されることが大変に難しいという実態にあることである。多くの課題をもった教育活動として行われているということを率直に認めないわけにはいかない。
■2008 年 3 月に学習指導要領の改訂が行われ、「総合的な学習の時間」の授業時数は小学校、中学校および高等学校のいずれについても、大幅に縮減されることになった。小、中学校については、週当たり約 1 時間の縮減である。今日の教育改革では、学力の充実を図ることが最も重要な課題として取り上げられている。教科の基礎・基本を重視することが大切であるとみなされている。そうした状況の中で、教科横断的で、自ら学ぶ力を育てることを意図

study. The results are shown in Table 8-1 and 8-2.

Table 8-1. Perception of primary school and lower secondary school students towards the period for integrated study

	Like	Neutral	Do not like
Primary school students	60.0%	26.2%	11.2%
Lower Secondary school students	46.2%	37.7%	14.3%

Table 8-2. Perception of teachers towards the period for integrated study: "Should the period for integrated study be cancelled?"

	Yes	No	Do not know
Primary school students	38.3%	53.7%	6.2%
Lower Secondary school students	57.2%	34.0%	7.7%

Resource: The Ministry of Education, Culture, Sports, Science, and Technology, Japan, The Result of a Nationwide Survey Regarding the Period for Integrated Study, 2006

As seen in Table 8-1, the survey result shows that the period for integrated study was preferred by primary school students, but secondary school students were not.

From the results show in Table 8-2, 38% of the primary school class teachers agreed to call off the period for integrated study as did 57% of the lower secondary school class teachers. This data had a major impact on Japanese educational circles.

The data shows the fact it is very difficult for the period for integrated study to satisfy students and to be welcomed by teachers. We have to give frank recognition that the period for integrated study has been conducted as an educational activity with many issues to be tackled.

■ The Course of Study was revised in March 2008 and the class hours of the period for integrated study were considerably reduced. Approximately one hour per week was reduced in primary schools and lower secondary schools. In today's educational reform, making efforts to enrich scholastic abilities is said to be the most important issue. It is considered highly important to focus on basics and fundamentals of the subjects. Objectives of the period for integrated study

するという、一見したところそのねらいや指導内容、指導のポイントなどが分かりにくい「総合的な学習の時間」の位置付けや意義、役割が改めて問われているのである。

■総合的な学習については、理念は正しいが、実際の指導が難しく、成果が上がりにくいと言われている。教科、道徳、特別活動と重複するところが多く、関連が分かりにくいという批判も行われている。これらの問題の解決を含めて、効果的な指導の方法を実践的に明らかにしていくことが今後の重要な課題になっている。

are to teach students cross curriculum and foster self-learning ability. Its aim, contents and points of instruction are hard to understand simply. The meanings, significance, and function of the period for integrated study may be questioned again under such circumstances.

■ The period for integrated study claims to have correct philosophy but it is difficult to realize it when it comes to actual teaching and hard to see visible results. There are also criticisms that it overlaps much with other subjects, moral education, and special activities, and the relationship with them is difficult to understand. The important issues from now on are to solve these problems as well as practically clarifying effective teaching methods.

4. 教育内容・指導方法の一貫性・接続性

■現在、日本の教育界では、幼児教育と小学校、小学校と中学校、中学校と高等学校との連携や接続をどのように図るかということが、重要な課題となっている。小学校第1学年に入学した児童が集団生活に適応できず、"荒れる"現象は「小1プロブレム」と呼ばれているが、その原因の一つは教育内容や指導方法における幼・小連携が不十分であることに求められている。

■新しく中学校に入学した生徒の中に「不登校」が増える（「中1ギャップ」と呼ばれる）原因の一つは、小・中教育の連携、接続が適切に行われていないことに求められる。教科の学習や人間関係、部活動等における円滑なつながりを可能にする適切な配慮が求められている。

■現在、高等学校進学率は98％に達している。ほとんどすべての生徒が高校に進学している。しかし、高校での学習と生活に適応できずに中途で退学する者の数は例年約10万人、全体の約3％に達している。中学校との接続や連携を重視するとともに、生徒の多様な実態に対応した多様で、柔軟性に富むカリキュラムや指導方法の開発が課題となっている。

■小学校6年間、中学校3年間、合わせて9年間の義務教育の全体を通した体系的で一貫性のあるカリキュラムのあり方を探求することが課題となっている。

4. Consistency and Articulation of Educational Contents and Teaching Methods

■ At present, in Japanese education circles, the important issue is how to coordinate and connect educations of infant school (3 to 6 years old.) and primary school, primary school and lower secondary school, lower secondary school and upper secondary school. Pupils who enter the 1st grade of primary school cannot adapt to group life and become disorderly. This phenomenon is called "Shoichi Problem (problem of 1st graders of primary school)". One of the causes is found to be inadequate coordination of educational content and teaching method between infant school and primary school.

■ Truancy increases among students who are newly enrolled in lower secondary schools. This phenomenon is called "Chuichi Gap" (lower secondary school 1st graders feel a significant gap between school life on primary school and lower secondary school). One of the causes is found in the inadequate coordination and connection between primary school and lower secondary school. Appropriate focus which enables smooth coordination in subject studies, human relationships, and club activities is required.

■ Currently, the percentage of students who go on to upper secondary school is 98%. This means most lower secondary school students proceed to upper secondary education. However, the number of and students who cannot adapt to class study and life in upper secondary school to drop out of school is approximately 100,000 every year, or about 3% of the total. The issues to be tackled are developing a diverse and flexible curriculum and teaching method to respond to the actual diverse conditions of students as well as the emphasis on connection and coordination with lower secondary school.

■ An additional need is also to seek a systematic and consistent curriculum through 6 years of primary school and 3 years of lower secondary school, a total of 9 years of compulsory education.

5. 体験活動の充実

■体験は子どもの体力や運動能力、知識や考える力、社会規範や道徳性などをはぐくむ基盤となる役割をする。「なすことによって学ぶ」(ラーニング・バイ・ドゥイング)とは「なすこと」(行動、体験活動)と「考えること」(思考、知的活動)とが一体になって働き、子どもの確かな学びと成長を促すことを簡潔に述べたものである。

■日本の社会では、都市化や情報化、少子化や人間関係の希薄化が進む中で、子どもたちの生活環境が変わり、自然、地域の人々や出来事、より広い社会などに直接に触れることができる実体験を得る機会や場面が失われてきている。

手伝いや勤労、地域での異年齢の子どもたちとの遊びなどの機会も失われてきている。それに代って、テレビやインターネット等による間接体験や擬似体験、バーチャル(仮想)な体験が多くなってきている。子どもたちに直接体験あるいは実体験の機会と場を取り戻してやることが重要な課題になっている。

■学校における体験活動の充実は、教科、道徳、特別活動、総合的な学習の時間、外国語活動等、教育活動全体を通して行われている。特に道徳教育、特別活動および総合的な学習の時間の指導では直接体験に基づく学習が重視され、豊かな体験活動、体験学習の場を提供することにさまざまな工夫が行われている。

■キャリア教育の一環としての職場体験活動や就業体験活動、公共の精神や社会参画の態度を育てるためのボランティア活動や奉仕体験活動等の充実を図ることも重要な課題としてそれぞれの学校で取り組まれている。

■高等学校では、職業教育の一環として、職場体験活動や就業体験活動が重視され、その充実に大きな努力が払われている。

5. Enhancement of Hands-on Activities

■ Hands-on activities play a roll as a base to develop children's physical ability, knowledge and thinking ability, and foster a sense of social norms and morality. "Learning by Doing", as the saying simply indicates "Doing" (activities and hands-on studies) and "Thinking" (cogitation and intellectual activity) function in unison and promote learning and growth of the children.

■ In Japanese society, with the advance of urbanization, informatization, fewer children, and attenuation of human relationship, children's life environment has changed and they are losing opportunities to have real experiences, exposure to nature, local people and events, and wider societies.

Children are losing opportunities to help and work in society, and play with different age groups of children as well. Instead, they have more opportunities of indirect and simulated experiences, and virtual experiences through television and the internet. An important issue is to bring back opportunities and places of direct experience or real experience for children.

■ Hands-on activities in schools are enhanced through subjects, moral education, extracurricular activities, period for integrated study, foreign language activities, and whole-education activities. In moral education, extracurricular activities, and period for integrated study, In particular, teachers instruct students by focusing on real experiences and make efforts to provide them with an abundance of real activities and hands-on studies.

■ Each school acknowledges the importance of attaining valuable work experience or work place experience as a part of career education and volunteer activities to foster public-mindedness and a positive attitude for social participation.

■ Upper secondary schools attach importance of experiencing a job or work place as a part of vocational education and make much effort to enhance these

■体験活動や体験学習の問題点として、「体験、活動あって学習なし」と言われることが多い。体験活動や体験学習を通して何を身に付けさせるのか、何を身に付けさせたのかということを明確にすることが求められている。その意味で、体験と理論とが往復運動を繰り返す学習の展開が基本となる。重要な課題として意識されており、教育方法の重点的な課題として取り組まれている。

体験学習　Hands - on Learning

experiences.

■ In many cases, it is often said that a problem of hands-on studies or activities is that "hands-on studies provide only the opportunity of activities and there is nothing to learn". What teachers want students to gain and what teachers actually enable students to gain through hands-on studies or activities are required to be shown clearly. In that sense, basically, experience and theory should be provided to students in reciprocal motion. This is recognized as an important issue and addressed as a priority of educational method.

6. 少人数教育と少人数指導

■日本の小学校および中学校の学級は、1学級40人の児童・生徒を基準として編成される。この基準に基づいて算定された学級数に応じて、教員定数が定められ、一定数の教員が配置される。このことは「公立義務教育諸学校の学級編成及び教職員定数の標準に関する法律」によって定められている。

■文部科学省が公表しているデータによれば、少し古いデータになるが、2004年度の1学級当たりの児童生徒数は小学校で26.2人、中学校で30.6人である。これは全国の平均である。実際には、人口が少なく、児童生徒の数が少ない農村等と人口が多く、児童生徒数が多い都市とでは、著しい差がある。人口が集中している都市部や都市近郊の住宅密集地帯では、40人に近い多人数学級から成る小学校や中学校が数多くあり、少人数教育や少人数指導をどのように進めるかということが深刻な問題になっている。

■少人数教育の実現を図るためには、学級編成の基準を改定することが必要である。1学級35人あるいは30人を基準にした学級編成を行い、教員を配置すればよい。しかし、このことは、多くの教員と多額の経費を必要とする。教室の数を増やす必要がある。そのため、長い間、日本における教育施策の課題となってきた。

■少人数教育の実現を図り、少人数指導を行うために、国や自治体によるさまざまな施策が行われてきた。例えば、都道府県の判断で40人を下回る学級編成が可能になったこと、少人数指導を行うために国の負担による教員(加

6. Small Class Education and Small Class Teaching

■ Japanese primary school and lower secondary school classes are basically composed of 40 students per class. A Quota of teachers is determined on the number of classes assessed according to this rule, and fixed numbers of teachers are assigned to each school. This is regulated in "the Act on Standards for Class Formation and Fixed Number of School Personnel of Public Compulsory Education Schools".

■ According to the data publicized by the Ministry of Education, Culture, Sports, Science and Technology, although dated from 2004, indicates, the number of students in one class as 26.2 in primary schools and 30.6 in lower secondary schools. This is a national average. In fact, the situation is substantially different between rural areas and urban areas: the former have less population and fewer students, and the latter have a greater population and many students. There are many primary and lower junior high schools composed of classes with nearly 40 students in populated urban areas and residential areas in urban neighborhoods. The method of conducting small group instruction and guidance is a critical issue.

■ It is necessary to amend the standard of class composition in order to realize small class education and conduct small class teaching. An improved method would be to compose classes with a maximum of 30 to 35 students as a standard and assign teachers to the classes. This, however, requires more teachers and huge cost. The number of classrooms also should be increased. For these reasons, realization of small class education has been an educational agenda in Japan.

■ The national government and municipal governments have been implementing various measures to realize small class education and conduct small class teaching. For example, composing classes with less than 40 students are allowed

配教員）を特別に増やすこと、非常勤（パートタイム）の教員の採用を国の負担でできるようにしたことなどの措置が行われた。

■都道府県や市町村の独自の判断によって、35人学級、30人学級、あるいは児童生徒の実態に応じた少人数教育等、弾力的な学級編成を実施するケースが増えている。小学校低学年の学級に補助教員を配置するケース、国語、算数・数学、理科、英語等の授業には少人数指導やティーム・ティーチングを実施するケース、習熟の程度に応じた指導を実施するケースなど、少人数教育と少人数指導が大きな広がりをみており、それらの充実を図ることが重要な課題として意識され、実践的に取り組まれている。

■児童生徒一人ひとりの能力や特性、ニーズや個性に応じたきめ細かな指導の充実を図るために少人数教育の実現を図ることが日本の教育の重要な課題になっている。

少人数指導　Small - Group Teaching

at the prefectural government's discreation; increasing the number of teachers (additional teachers) exceptionally at the expense of the national government and enabling recruitment of part-time teachers at the expense of the national government.

■ Recently, by independent judgment of prefectural and municipal government, there are more examples of flexible class composition such as a class of 35 students, a class of 30 students, and small class education in response to actual needs of the students. There are cases such as assigning an assistant teacher in lower grade classes of primary schools; conducting small class teaching or team teaching for Japanese language, arithmetic/mathematics, science, and English classes and conducting proficiency-dependent teaching. Small class education and small class teaching such as these have been greatly increasing, and promoting these are considered as an important issue and have been practically addressed.

■ In order to enhance carefully-crafted executed based on characteristics, needs and individuality of each student, realizing small class education is a critical issue of Japanese education.

7. キャリア教育

■「キャリア」という言葉は、「経歴」「職業」などの意味で使われている。したがって「キャリア教育」とは、職業に就き、経歴をつくるための準備教育という意味になるが、現在、日本の学校教育の重要な課題として取り組まれている「キャリア教育」は、もう少し広い意味で理解され、使われている。

■すなわち、文部科学省が 2009 年 3 月に刊行している「自分に気付き、未来を築くキャリア教育」と題する小冊子によれば、「キャリア教育」とは、「児童生徒一人一人のキャリア発達を支援し、それぞれにふさわしいキャリアを形成していくために必要な意欲・態度や能力を育てる教育」と定義されており、「端的には『児童生徒一人一人の勤労観、職業観を育てる教育』とも言われています」と説明されている。こうした定義にもあらわれているように、「キャリア発達の支援」、「キャリア形成」が「キャリア教育」の本質を正しく理解するためのキーワードである。以下に、「キャリア教育」の目標と具体的な内容について文部科学省が発表している例を紹介する。

■文部科学省が 2005 年 11 月に出している『中学校職場体験ガイド』によれば、「小学校・中学校・高等学校におけるキャリア発達と職場体験等の関連（例）」は、表 8-3 のように示されている。ここでは、キャリア教育の目標と具体的な活動の例が、小学校段階から高等学校段階にいたる＜キャリア発達段階＞ごとに明らかにされている点に注目していただきたい。キャリア教育の指導に当たっては、教師は児童生徒のキャリア形成に関する発達的な視点を重視しなければならないことに留意していただきたい。

7. Career Education

■ The word "career" refers to "background," "occupation," and the like. Therefore, "career education" generally means an education in preparation for a job and to build one's career. However, "career education," which is addressed as an important issue in Japanese school education, is understood and applied in a broader sense.

■ More specifically, in a booklet titled "Career Education for Self-awareness and Future-Building" issued by the Ministry of Education, Culture, Sports, Science and Teachnology in March 2009, "career education" is defined as "an education to support the career development of each student and cultivate the willingness, attitude, and ability that are necessary to build a suitable career for each of them." It is also explained "In short, career education is understood as an education to cultivate an idea of the work habits and occupation." As seen in these definitions, the key words for correctly understanding the principle of career education are "support for career development" and "career-building." The aim of career education and its detailed content as declared by the Ministry of Education, Culture, Sports, Science and Teachnology is given below.

■ The following Table 8-3 titled "Examples of the Relationship between Career Development and Work Experience in Primary, Lower Secondary, and Upper Secondary School Stages," contained in the Work Experience Guide for Lower Secondary School was issued by the Ministry of Education, Culture, Sports, Science and Teachnology in November 2005. This table clearly states the objectives of career education with detailed examples of the activities involved therein. When teachers provide career education to their students, they should lay emphasis on the developmental perspective of career building for students.

表 8-3　小学校・中学校・高等学校におけるキャリア発達と職場体験等の関連（例）

小学校	中学校	高等学校
＜　キ　ャ　リ　ア　発　達　課　題　＞		
進路の探索・選択にかかる基盤形成の時期	現実的探索と暫定的選択の時期	現実的探索・試行と社会的移行準備の時期
・自己及び他者への積極的関心の形成・発展 ・身のまわりの仕事や環境への関心・意欲の向上 ・夢や希望、憧れる自己のイメージの獲得 ・勤労を重んじ目標に向かって努力する態度の形成	・肯定的自己理解と自己有用感の獲得 ・興味・関心等に基づく勤労観、職業観の形成 ・進路計画の立案と暫定的選択 ・生き方や進路に関する現実的探索	・自己理解の深化と自己受容 ・選択基準としての勤労観、職業観の確立 ・将来設計の立案と社会的移行の準備 ・進路の現実的吟味と試行の参加
体験的活動（例）		
・街の探検 ・家族の仕事調べ ・インタビュー ・商店街での職場見学・体験	・身近な職業聞き取り調査 ・連続した5日間の職場体験 ・職場の特定の人と行動を共にする職場見学 ・上級学校の体験入学	・インターンシップ（事業所、大学、行政機関、研究所等における就業体験） ・学校での学びと職場実習を組み合わせて行うデュアルシステム ・上級学校の体験授業 ・企業訪問

出典：文部科学省『中学校職場体験ガイド』2005年11月

■上掲の表8-3によって確かめることができるように、キャリア教育は小学校低学年から始められ、高校3年生までの12年間を通して継続される。従来行われてきた「進路指導」は主に中・高校で実施されてきた。また、職業教育は高校で行われるのが一般的であった。小学校段階から自分の個性の発見や伸長、社会への関心や参画、生き方と結びつけて学ばれるという点にキャリア教育の特色がある。

■キャリア教育は、「勤労観・職業観」の育成ということを軸にして、すべての教科等に内在するキャリア形成支援の機能を統合し、体系化を図るという方針で展開される。すべての教育活動を通して行われるという点に、進路

Table 8-3. Examples of the Relationship between Career Development and Work Experience in Primary, Lower Secondary, and Upper Secondary School Stages

Primary School	Lower Secondary School	Upper Secondary School
\multicolumn{3}{c}{Issues to be tackled in career development}		
Period to form the basis for searching and choosing a career	Period to actually search for and tentatively choose a career	Period to actually search for and experience the transition from school life to society
· Have and develop a positive interest in oneself and others · Develop interest in familiar work and environment, and enhance willingness · Cherish dreams and hopes, and visualize what one wants to be · Develop an attitude to value work and make efforts to achieve one's goal	· Have a feeling of positive self-awareness and self-esteem · Develop views on work and occupation on the basis of one's interests · Formulate a career plan and settle on a tentative idea for a career · Develop a realistic way of life and career path	· Deepen the feeling of self-awareness and develop a feeling of self-acceptance · Develop views on work and occupation on the base of which one can select a career as one of the choices · Make future plans and prepare to adapt from school life to one in society · Examine one's career realistically and treat career as a trial
\multicolumn{3}{c}{Examples of Hands-on Activities}		
· Explore a town. · Find out family members' occupations · Conduct interviews · Conduct an observation tour of the workplace and develop hands-on experience in a shopping arcade	· Conduct interviews in familiar work environments · Develop hands-on experience in a workplace for five consecutive days · Conduct an observation tour with one particular person at the workplace · Get a trial enrollment in an upper education school	· Take up an internship at a company, university, administrative institution, research laboratory, and so on · Work out a dual system, combining study in school and an internship · Attend a class at an upper education school on a trial basis · Visit various companies

Resource: The Ministry of Education, Culture, Sports, Science and Technology, Japan, "Work Experience Guide for Lower Secondary Schools", 2005.

■ As confirmed by the above chart, career education begins in lower grades in primary school and continues through 12 years until the third grade of secondary school. Conventional "course guidance" used to be provided mainly in lower and upper secondary schools. In addition, career education was generally provided in upper secondary school. A characteristic of career education is that it is introduced from primary school itself with a view to discover and enhance one's individuality, develop his/her interest in societal matters and participation in addition to connecting school experiences with future life.

■ Focusing on gaining a good understanding of work and occupation, career education is provided in such a way as to integrate and systemize a function of career-building support, which is inherent in every subject. Career education is

指導・職業教育との違いがある。

■日本の学校教育の重要な課題として「キャリア教育」ということが初めて取り上げられたのは、1999年12月の中央教育審議会の答申においてのことであった。それ以後、教育基本法の改正(2006年12月)、学校教育法の改正(2007年6月)、学習指導要領の改訂（小・中学校は2008年3月、高等学校は2009年3月）等において、「勤労を重んずる態度」、「将来の進路を選択する能力」、「キャリア教育」などを重視するという方針が示され、小・中・高校を通して取り組むべき共通な教育課題として意識され、実践されてきた。

■「キャリア教育」の充実と発展を図るということが学校教育の重要な課題として取り上げられることになった背景としては、1990年初頭のバブル崩壊後の日本の産業構造が大きな変化をするなかで、200万人に及ぶフリーター、60万人を越える若年無業者（ニート）が存在し、新卒者の早期離職が問題になるなど、若者の職業をめぐる問題が深刻な社会問題となり、学校教育の、しかも早い段階から自立した社会人・職業人となるための基礎的な教育の充実を図る必要があることが明らかになってきたという事情を指摘することができる。

■先に指摘したように、日本におけるキャリア教育は、2008年3月の小・中学校の学習指導要領の改訂（高校は2009年3月）などを契機にして急速な進展をみている教育活動であり、その本格的な取組はスタートラインについたばかりである。その内容や方法、指導法や評価の方法など、今後の充実と発展に向けて実践的に解明されるべき課題は多い。

different from course guidance and vocational education in that it forms a part of every educational activity.

■ Career education was picked up as an important issue in Japanese school education unprecedentedly in the report of the Central Education Council in December 1999. Since then, the revised Fundamental Law of Education (December 2006), the revised School Education Law (June 2007), and the revised Course of Study (March 2003 for primary and lower secondary schools and March 2009 for upper secondary school) developed a policy to value "an attitude to value work, an ability to choose one's future career," and "career education." This policy has been perceived as a common educational issue to be tackled throughout primary, lower, and upper secondary schools and put into practice.

■ Making efforts toward enhancing and developing career education is taken up as a vital issue in school education owing to the following reason. After the bubble economy burst in the early 1990s, the Japanese industrial structure underwent a drastic transformation, which generated some 2 million "freeters" (job-hoppers) and over 600 thousand "NEETs" (young people not in education, employment, or training) ; further, the early turnover of new graduates became a problem. These posed as critical social problems. As a result, enhancing basic education in order to enable an individual to become an independent member of society and a professional was necessary, right from the early stages of school education.

■ As previously pointed out, career education is one of the educational activities that has rapidly developed in Japan as a result of the revision of Course of Study for primary and lower secondary schools in March 2008 (revision for upper secondary school was done in March 2009). However, the full-fledged effort toward the wider implementation of career education is still in its initial stages. There are many issues and its instruction and evaluation methods that need to be resolved practically in order to enhance and develop career education henceforth.

あとがき

　今回の『バイリンガル・テキスト：日本の教育－制度と内容－』刊行が予定よりかなり遅れてしまい、本書の刊行を期待されていた方々に対し申し訳なく思っている。

　遅れた理由として、第1に、学習指導要領が改訂されるということで、2008年（小・中学校レベル）、2009年（高等学校レベル）の改訂内容を本テキストに反映させようとしたためである。2008年の初めまでには教科関係の原稿はほとんど届いていたが、それらは前の学習指導要領に基づいていたので、新学習指導要領に従って修正してもらうことにした。

　第2には、前回のバイリンガル・テキスト発行の際は、文部省より補助を得て、筑波大学学生に英訳を含むアルバイトを依頼することができた。今回は残念ながらそのような補助がなく編集作業に手間取ったことがあげられる。その点では、編集のお世話をいただいた上田学先生（京都女子大学）、堤正史先生（大阪成蹊大学）、ならびに作業や英訳を手伝ってくれた京都女子大学の院生・学部生に改めて感謝の意を表したい。

　なお、このバイリンガル・テキストの出版に対し、幸いに京都女子大学から平成21年度出版助成として経費の一部を補助していただいた。ここに厚くお礼申し上げる次第である。

　本書が、日本にいる外国人留学生や研究者、ならびに日本や外国の教育関係者、教育専攻学生等に広く購読、活用され、日本の教育に関する国際的理解、国際的情報発信の促進に役立てば、編者にとってこの上ない喜びである。

　なお、本書に掲載した写真は、筑波大学教育開発国際協力研究センターが2006年に開発した「日本の教育制度と教育実践」に関するCDから取ったものであることを断っておく。

　　2010年　3月

村田翼夫
山口　満

Postscript

As the Bilingual Text: Contemporary Education in Japan has been delayed in publishing, we regret to those people who wanted to buy and read the book. As for the reasons why the Text publication has been late, we may raise two points.

First, the Course of Study was revised in 2008 (those of primary and lower secondary school) and in 2009 (that of upper secondary school). We tried to introduce the contents in the manuscripts of each subject. Though the manuscripts had been sent to us in the beginning of 2008, we asked the authors to correct and update those in reference to the new Course of Study after it was revised.

Second, when the former Bilingual Text was published in 1998, we received a considerable grant from the Ministry of Education, Culture, Sports and Science, Japan enabling us to ask the students from the University of Tsukuba to help with work, including English translation from Japanese. Unfortunately this time we could not get a grant and could not employ part-time workers. Therefore, it has taken considerable time to arrange and edit the manuscripts. In this respect we are grateful to Prof. Manabu Ueda of Kyoto Women's University and Prof. Masashi Tsutsumi of Osaka Seikei University who helped us in editing the Text. We also express thanks to the graduate and undergraduate students of Kyoto Women's University who have assisted by making figures, tables and providing some English translation.

Fortunately Kyoto Women's University has provided us a part of the expenditure as a grant from the 2009 academic year for the Text publication, which we are very grateful for.

We would be so pleased if this Bilingual Text could be broadly read and used by foreign students, foreign researchers, Japanese and foreign people who work in educational institutions, students who major in education and so on. Furthermore we hope it will prove to be beneficial to deepen international understanding and to provide Japanese education information to the world.

694 あとがき

The photos which have been shown in this Textbook are taken from a comprehensive - study CD based on the educational system and practice in Japan which was developed by the Center for Research on International Cooperation in Education Development, University of Tsukuba in 2006.

March, 2010

Yokuo Murata
Mitsuru Yamaguchi

索引

あ

ICT	624
IT 教育	624, 630, 632
アイデンティティ	316

い

e-Japan 戦略	624, 630
生きる力	462, 534, 564, 668
いじめ	648
一斉指導	348, 352
一斉授業	188, 348, 350
異文化理解の教育	298
インターナショナル・スクール	290

う

運動	496, 498, 500, 502
運動部活動	496, 502, 504

え

ALT	542
英語活動	212, 544, 546
映像メディア表現	468, 470
エスノセントリズム	298, 316
遠足	340, 592, 594, 596

お

音楽	450, 456

か

海外児童生徒の教育	282, 284
外国語	542
外国語活動	542
外国語教育	542
外国語指導助手	542
外国人教員研修留学生	268, 288
外国人教師	288
外国人児童生徒	282, 284, 286
外国人留学生	266, 270, 294
開発教育	300
開発のためのアジア地域教育革新事業計画	308
科学と人間生活	332, 430, 432, 434, 436
学位取得	276
学芸員	138, 158, 320, 338
学習指導要領	328
学力格差	668
学力観	666
歌唱共通教材	458, 460
学級活動	188, 584
学級担任	72, 78, 346, 544, 546, 644
学校運営協議会	76, 194, 218
学校経営	76, 184, 188, 218
学校行事	592
学校週五日制	662

学校と家庭との連携	654	教育長	170, 172, 240, 250
学校評価	192, 218, 252, 354	教育勅語	518
学校評議員	76, 190, 192	教育費	198, 200, 202
学校評議員制度	192, 218	教育評価	354, 359
学校歴	340	教員給与	200, 254
家庭科	476, 484	教員研修制度	242
カリキュラム	324	教員採用制度	238
環境教育	300	教員職能団体	258, 260
完全習得学習（マスター・ラーニング）	358	教員団体	258
		教員任用	248, 252
		教員評価制度	252
		教員俸給表	254

き

企業内教育・研修	140, 606	教員免許状	234, 236, 238, 348
帰国児童生徒の教育	282, 284	教員免許制度	216, 232
規制の緩和	212	教員養成制度	232
技術・家庭科	476, 484	教科書	338
義務教育	22, 28, 32, 58, 62, 70, 72	教科書の検定	156
義務教育費国庫負担金	212	教科書無償制度	198
キャリア教育	638, 678, 686	教職員組合	258, 260
教育の自主性尊重主義	148	教職大学院	98, 216, 234, 244
教育委員会	166, 170, 172, 174, 180	共通一次試験	92
教育課程	324	教頭	186, 222, 256
教育課程の編成	324		
教育基本法	26, 32, 34, 36, 130, 148, 150		

く

教育公務員	246, 248, 256	クラブ活動	576, 582, 590
教育公務員特例法	68, 248		

け

教育指導行政	176	経験主義	334, 386
教育実習	236, 238	芸術教育	450
教育職員免許法	68, 232, 236, 238	系統学習	390, 424, 668
教育専門職	140, 222	系統性	396, 408, 424, 426, 430
教育相談	236, 644	系統理科	424, 426

原級留置	188	国際数学・理科教育動向調査		358, 442, 666
健康・安全	496, 498, 508, 584, 596	国際大学		294, 296
健康診断	190, 256, 594, 596	国際理解教育	292, 298, 544, 564
言語活動	370, 372, 374	国費留学生	266, 268, 272, 278
言語生活	366	国民教育制度		22
言語体系	366, 368, 532	国連大学		310
言語文化	366, 368	心の教育		512
		心のノート		536, 538
		個に応じた指導		348, 424
		コミュニケーション能力		550

こ

後期中等教育	58, 78
公共職業訓練施設	604
公共の精神	398
工芸	462, 468
高校三原則	80
構造改革特区制度	88, 214
校長	186, 188, 192, 222
高等学校	58, 78, 80
高等教育	28, 60, 84, 86
高等専門学校	60, 78
校内研修	242
校内暴力	74, 512, 646
公民科	332, 380, 384, 394
公民館	44, 130, 132, 138
国語	22, 364, 368
国語科	364
国際化・グローバル化社会	26
国際教育	282, 284, 296, 314, 318
国際教育行政	304, 306, 312, 320
国際教育到達度評価学会	442, 666
国際高校	292
国際主義	304, 312

さ

算数	400

し

時間割	340
司書	138
持続可能な開発のための教育	300, 308
持続可能な社会	398
指導教諭	186, 222, 636, 638
指導主事	176
指導・助言	140, 150, 178, 186
指導要録	356
児童会活動	588
児童生徒中心カリキュラム	424
児童生徒理解	642
私費留学生	272, 274
社会科	380
社会教育	128, 132
社会教育関係団体	136
社会教育主事	138, 176

社会教育審議会	128	職業指導	236, 482, 634, 638
社会教育法	128, 132, 136	書写	470
社会参画	398	初任者研修	240, 242, 244
社会体育施設	134, 138	自立への基礎	446
就学義務	70, 72	進路指導	638
就学奨励	204	進路指導主事	224, 636, 638
宗教教育	32, 46, 150, 530	人格の完成	576
修身	382, 516, 520	人権教育	282, 298
集団指導	640	人権尊重主義	306
主幹教諭	186, 222		
授業	346	**す**	
授業研究	416, 420	スーパーサイエンスハイスクール	438
10年経験者研修	244	スクール・カウンセラー	74, 644
小1プロブレム	676	数学科	400, 412, 414
唱歌	454, 456	数学的リテラシー	402
生涯学習社会	52, 132	図画工作	462
障害児教育	100, 104, 124		
小学校	58, 70, 72, 76	**せ**	
条件整備主義	150	生活	446
少子高齢化社会	26, 28, 492, 614	生活デザイン	488, 492
少人数教育	682	生活理科	422, 426
少人数指導	682	生徒会活動	588
少年自然の家	134	生徒指導	634
書道教育	470	生徒指導主事	224, 242, 636
情報化社会	26, 28, 52, 424, 624	生徒の学習到達度調査（PISA）	358, 666
情報活用能力	626	青年の家	134
情報通信技術（ICT）	624	世界史	386
食育	492, 586	世界青年の船	280
職員会議	186	専修学校	58, 60
職業教育	600	全日制	58, 60, 78
職業教育機関	604	全面主義道徳教育	520, 522, 532
		専門学科	58, 80, 450, 542, 608, 612

そ

総合学科	58, 80, 542, 608, 610
総合的な学習の時間	564, 670

た

体育	132, 136, 496
体験活動	678
大学	62, 84, 86, 88, 90, 94
大学院	62, 84, 96, 98
大学入試センター	92
短期大学	60, 84, 86, 90
短期留学制度	268
探究学習	424
探求的活動	570
男女共学	32, 80

ち

地域センター	310
地球市民教育	316
知識基盤社会	26, 28, 350, 670
地方分権化	166, 180, 212, 214
地方分権主義	32, 152
中1ギャップ	652, 676
中央教育審議会	34, 64, 162, 216
中学校	56, 58, 72, 74, 78
中途退学	614, 654, 676
中等教育学校	56, 82, 204
中立主義	150
地理歴史科	382, 394, 396

つ

通級による指導	106, 112, 118
通信制	58, 60, 86

て

手当	252, 256
定時制	58, 78
適応指導	640, 654
デザイン	324, 462, 466, 468
デューイ	580

と

道徳教育	512
道徳教育推進教員	524
道徳の時間	520, 522, 524, 532
道徳的実践力	532, 536
東南アジア青年の船	280
東南アジア文部大臣機構	310
読解リテラシー	364, 376
図書館	44, 130, 134, 138, 586
特別活動	576
特別支援学級	106, 112, 118, 120
特別支援学校	62, 102, 112, 114, 116
特別支援教育	100, 102, 110, 112

な

南南教育協力	280

に

21世紀への留学生政策	270
日本語・日本文化留学生制度	268
日本語教育	274, 276, 284, 316

日本史	386, 398	法律主義	148, 154, 306
日本私学振興財団	206	暴力行為	512, 646, 656
日本人学校	282, 284	保健	236, 256, 300, 506, 666
日本の教育経験	318, 320	保健体育	496
認定こども園	68, 214	補習授業校	282
		ポートフォリオ	358
		ホームルーム活動	584, 586

は

博物館　　　　　　　　　44, 134, 138

ひ

PISA	358, 364, 376, 402, 442
PTA	190
美術	462, 466, 468
美術教育	462
標準授業時数	328, 330
標準単位数	332

ふ

部活動	576, 592
副校長	186, 188, 222
福利厚生	136, 256
普通科	58, 80
不登校	74, 78, 650
ブルーム	358

へ

平和教育	282, 296, 298
ペスタロッチ	580
ヘルバルト	634

ほ

保育所	58, 66, 68, 70
訪問教育	112, 118

み

自ら学び、自ら考える能力	350, 568
民主行政主義	148
民族学校	290

め

メディア・リテラシー　　　　　　378

も

問題解決学習	384, 422, 424, 520, 668
問題解決の指導	416, 418, 420
文部科学省	60, 156, 198, 216
文部科学大臣	60, 156, 158, 178, 180, 324

ゆ

ユネスコ	254, 298, 304, 306, 308, 314
ユネスコ・アジア文化センター	308
ユネスコ憲章	296, 306

よ

幼稚園　　　　　　　　58, 66, 68, 70, 76

り

理科	422
理科教育	422, 436, 440

理科ネットワーク 438
留学生フェア 278
臨時教育審議会
　　　　26, 64, 162, 164, 348, 614

ろ

ロールプレイング 640

Index

A

ability to learn and think for oneself(自ら学び、自ら考える能力) 351, 569
ability to practice morality(道徳的実践力) 533, 537
admitting exceptional treatment by the local authority(構造改革特区制度) 89
aging society with fewer children(少子高齢化社会) 27, 29, 493, 615
allowances(手当) 253, 257
ALT(Assistant Language Teachers:外国語指導助手) 543
Arithmetic(算数) 401
Arts Education(芸術教育、美術教育) 451, 463
Arts and Handicraft(図画工作) 463
Asian Cultural Center for UNESCO(ACCU)(ユネスコ・アジア文化センター) 309
Asian Program of Educational Innovation for Development(APEID)(開発のためのアジア地域教育革新事業計画) 309
assistant language teachers(外国語指導助手) 543
authorization of textbooks(教科書の検定) 157
authorized kids center(認定こども園) 69, 215

B

Basic Act on Education(教育基本法) 27, 33, 35, 37, 131, 149, 151
Bloom(B. ブルーム) 359
board of education(教育委員会) 167, 171, 173, 175, 181
bullying(いじめ) 649

C

calligraphy education(書道教育) 471
career councelor(進路指導主事) 225, 637, 639
career education(キャリア教育) 639, 679, 687
career guidance(進路指導) 639
Central Council for Education(中央教育審議会) 35, 65, 163, 217
Chief supervising teacher(指導教諭) 187, 223, 637, 639
child society activities(児童会活動) 589
child-centered curriculum(児童生徒中心カリキュラム) 425
Children's nature house(少年自然の家) 135
citizen's public hall(公民館) 45, 131, 133, 139
Civics(公民科) 333, 381, 385, 395
class activities(学級活動) 189, 585
class hour(授業) 347
classroom teacher(学級担任) 73, 79, 347, 545, 547, 645
club activities(クラブ活動) 577, 583, 591
club activities(部活動) 577, 593
co-education(男女共学) 33, 81
common entrance exam(共通一次試験) 93
common singing materials(歌唱共通教材) 459, 461
communication ability(コミュニケーション能力) 551
company in-service training(企業内教育・研修) 141, 607
completion of character(人格の完成) 577
comprehensive course(総合学科) 59, 81, 543, 609, 611

compulsory education（義務教育）
　　　　　　　　　　　23, 29, 33, 59, 63, 71, 73
compulsory school attendance（就学義務）　71, 73
cooperation with schools and homes（学校と家庭との連携）　655
correspondence course（通信制）　59, 61, 87
Course of Study（学習指導要領）　329
Craft Production（工芸）　463, 469
cumulative guidance record（指導要録）　357
curriculum（教育課程）　325

D

day care centers（保育所）　59, 67, 69, 71
decentralization（地方分権化）　167, 181, 213, 215
deputy vice principal（教頭）　187, 223, 257
deregulation of the control（規制の緩和）　213
Design（デザイン）　325, 463, 467, 469
designated special zone for structural reform（構造改革特区）　215
development education（開発教育）　301
Dewey（John Dewey）（デューイ）　581
dietary education（食育）　493, 587
disparities in academic achievement（学力格差）　669
Drawing and Manual Arts（図画工作）　463
drawing up of curriculum（教育課程の編成）　325
drop out（中途退学）　615, 655, 677

E

education consultation（教育相談）　237, 645
education for children staying in foreign countries（海外児童生徒の教育）　283, 285
education for children with disabilities（障害児教育）　101, 105, 125
education for global citizens（地球市民教育）　317
education for human rights（人権教育）　283, 299
education for international understanding（国際理解教育）　293, 299, 545, 565

education for peace（平和教育）　283, 297, 299
education for sustainable development（持続可能な開発のための教育）　301, 309
education for the returning children（帰国児童生徒の教育）　282, 285
education for understanding different cultures（異文化理解の教育）　299
education of mind（心の教育）　513
Education Rescript（教育勅語）　519
educational evaluation（教育評価）　355, 359
educational expenditure（教育費）　199, 201, 203
educational guidance（教育指導行政）　177
Educational Personnel Certification Law（教育職員免許法）　69, 233, 237, 239
educational public service personnel（教育公務員）
　　　　　　　　　　　　　　　　　　247, 249, 257
e-Japan Strategy（e-Japan戦略）　625, 631
empiricism（経験主義）　335, 387
English Activities（英語活動）　213, 545, 547
Entrance Exam Center（大学入試センター）　93
environmental education（環境教育）　301
ethnic school（民族学校）　291
ethnocentrism（エスノセントリズム）　299, 317
excursions（遠足）　341, 593, 595, 597
exercises（運動）　497, 499, 501, 503
Extracurricular Activities（特別活動）　577

F

Fine Arts（美術）　463, 467, 469
1st grade gap of lower secondary school（中1ギャップ）　653, 677
Five-Day Week School System（学校週五日制）　663
foreign children（外国人児童生徒）　283, 285, 287
Foreign Language（外国語）　543
Foreign Language Activities（外国語活動）　543
foreign language education（外国語教育）　543
foreign students（外国人留学生）　267, 271, 295

foreign students obtained scholarships from the Ministry of Education, Culture, Sports, Science and Technology of Japan(国費留学生) 267, 269, 273, 279
foreign students with their own expenses(私費留学生) 273, 275
foreign teachers(外国人教師) 289
Foundation for the Promotion of Japanese Private Schools(日本私学振興財団) 207
Free distribution system of textbooks(教科書無償制度) 199
full time course(全日制) 59, 61, 79
Fundamental Law of Education(教育基本法) 57, 217

G

general course(普通科) 59, 81
Geography and History(地理歴史科) 383, 395, 397
graduate school(大学院) 63, 85, 97, 99
graduate school for the education of teachers(教職大学院) 99, 217, 235, 245
group guidance(集団指導) 641
guidance and advice(指導・助言) 141, 151, 179, 187, 637, 639

H

Handicraft(図画工作) 463
hands-on activities(体験活動) 679
Handwriting(書写) 471
Health and Physical Education(保健体育) 497
health and safety(健康・安全) 497, 499, 509, 585, 597
Health Education(保健) 237, 257, 301, 507, 667
Herbart(Johann Friedrich Herbart)(ヘルバルト) 634
higher education(高等教育) 29, 61, 85, 87
History of Japan(日本史) 387, 399
Home Economics(家庭科) 477, 485
Homemaking(家庭科) 477, 485
homeroom activities(ホームルーム活動) 585, 587

house for youth(青年の家) 135

I

ICT(情報通信技術) 625
identity(アイデンティティ) 317
image media expression(映像メディア表現) 469, 471
individualized instruction(個に応じた指導) 349, 425
Industrial Arts and Homemaking(技術・家庭科) 477, 485
Information Fair of Japanese Universities for Foreign Peoples(留学生フェア) 279
information literacy(情報活用能力) 627
information-oriented society(情報化社会) 27, 29, 53, 425, 623
initial training(初任者研修) 241, 243, 245
inquiry activities(探求的な活動) 573
in-service training for teachers(教員研修制度) 243
In-service Training Program for Overseas Teachers(外国人教員研修留学生制度) 269, 289
institutions of vocational education(職業教育機関) 605
International Association for the Evaluation of Educational Achievement(国際教育到達度評価学会) 443, 667
international education(国際教育) 283, 285, 297, 315, 319
international educational administration(国際教育行政) 305, 307, 313, 321
International School(インターナショナル・スクール) 291
International University(国際大学) 295, 297
International Upper Secondary School(国際高校) 293
internationalism(国際主義) 305, 313
internationalized and globalized society(国際化・グローバル化社会) 27
IT Education(IT教育) 625, 631, 633

J

Japanese educational experiences(日本の教育経験)　319, 321
Japanese Language(国語)　23, 365, 369
Japanese Language(国語科)　365
Japanese Language and Japanese Culture Program(日本語・日本文化留学生制度)　269
Japanese language education(日本語教育)　275, 277, 285, 317
junior colleges(短期大学)　61, 85, 87, 91

K

kindergarten(幼稚園)　59, 67, 69, 71, 77
knowledge-based society(知識基盤社会)　27, 29, 351, 671
Kokugo(Japanese Language)(国語)　23, 365, 369

L

language activities(言語活動)　371, 373, 375
language culture(言語文化)　367, 369
language life(言語生活)　367
language system(言語体系)　367, 369, 533
learning through inquiry(探求学習)　425
lessons according to individual needs(個に応じた指導)　349
lesson study(授業研究)　417, 421
librarian(司書)　139
library(図書館)　45, 131, 135, 139, 587
Life Environment Studies(生活)　447
lifelong learning society(生涯学習社会)　53, 133
Living Design(生活デザイン)　489, 493
lower secondary school(中学校)　57, 59, 73, 75, 79

M

mass instruction(一斉指導)　349, 353
mass teaching(一斉授業)　189, 349, 351
mastery learning(完全習得学習)　359
mathematical literacy(数学的リテラシー)　403
Mathematics(数学科)　401, 413, 415
media literacy(メディア・リテラシー)　379
Minister of Education, Culture, Sports, Science and Technology(文部科学大臣)　61, 157, 159, 179, 181, 325
Ministry of Education, Culture, Sports, Science and Technology(文部科学省)　61, 157, 199, 217
moral education(道徳教育)　513
moral education class(道徳の時間)　521, 523, 525, 533
museum(博物館)　45, 135, 139
Music(音楽)　451, 457

N

national education system(国民教育制度)　23
National Task Force for Educational Reform(臨時教育審議会)　27, 65, 163, 165, 349, 617
National Treasury Share of Compulsory Education Expenditure(義務教育費国庫負担金)　213
Neutralism(中立主義)　151
note of the heart(心のノート)　537, 539

O

obtaining degrees in universities(学位取得)　277
overall moral education(全面主義道徳教育)　521, 523, 533

P

part time course(定時制)　59, 79
Period for Integrated Study(総合的な学習の時間)　565, 671
personal adaptation guidance(適応指導)　641, 655
perspective of academic ability(学力観)　667
Pestalozzi(Johann Heinrich Pestalozzi)(ペスタロッチ)　581
Physical check-up(健康診断)　191, 257, 595, 597
Physical Education(体育)　133, 137, 497

PISA(PISA) 359, 367, 377, 403, 443
Policy on Acceptance of Foreign Students toward the 21st Century(21世紀への留学生政策) 271
portfolio(ポートフォリオ) 359
primary school(小学校) 59, 71, 73, 77
principal(校長) 187, 189, 193, 223
Principle of Providing and Maintenance of Education Conditions(条件整備主義) 151
Principle of Decentralization(地方分権主義) 33, 153
Principle of Democratic Administration(民主行政主義) 149
Principle of Legalism(法律主義) 149, 155, 307
Principle of Respect for Human Rights(人権尊重主義) 307
Principle of Respect for Independency of Education(教育の自主性尊重主義) 149
problem of 1st graders of primary school(小1プロブレム) 677
problem solving approach(問題解決の指導) 417, 419, 421
problem solving method(問題解決学習) 385, 423, 425, 521, 669
Program for International Student Assessment (PISA)(生徒の学習到達度調査) 359, 667
promoter of moral education(道徳教育推進教師) 525
PTA(PTA) 191
Public facilities for Vocational training 607
public-mindedness(公共の精神) 399

R

reading literacy(読解リテラシー) 365, 377
Regional Center(地域センター) 311
religious education(宗教教育) 33, 47, 151, 531
repeat(原級留置) 189
role playing(ロールプレイング) 641

S

salaries of teachers(教員給与) 201, 255
salary scale of teachers(教員俸給表) 255
school-based training(校内研修) 243
school calendar(学校歴) 341
school council(学校評議員) 77, 191, 193
School Councilor System(学校評議員制度) 193, 219
school counselor(スクール・カウンセラー) 75, 645
school evaluation(学校評価) 193, 219, 253, 355
school events(学校行事) 593
school for Japanese(日本人学校) 283, 285
school management(学校経営) 77, 185, 189, 219
school management board(学校運営協議会) 77, 195, 219
school violence(校内暴力) 75, 513, 647
science and human life(科学と人間生活) 333, 431, 433, 435, 437
Science(理科) 423
science education(理科教育) 423, 437, 441
Science for Daily Life(生活理科) 423, 427
Science Network(理科ネットワーク) 439
secondary school containing six year courses(中等教育学校) 57, 83, 205
self-sustainability(自立への基礎) 447
senior teacher(主幹教諭) 187, 223
sequence(系統性) 397, 409, 425, 427, 431
Ship for South-East Asian Youth(東南アジア青年の船) 281
short term study course(短期留学制度) 269
Singing(唱歌) 455, 457
Ship for World Youth(世界青年の船) 281
Shusin(Moral Education)(修身) 383, 517, 521
small class education(少人数教育) 683
small class teaching(少人数指導) 683
social education(社会教育) 129, 133
Social Education Council(社会教育審議会) 129

Social Education Law（社会教育法） 129, 133, 137
social educational organization（社会教育関係団体）
　　　　　　　　　　　　　　　　　　137
social participation（社会参画） 399
social physical institution（社会体育施設） 135, 137
Social Studies（社会科） 381
Southeast Asian Ministers of Education Organization (SEAMEO)（東南アジア文部大臣機構） 311
South-South education cooperation（南南教育協力）
　　　　　　　　　　　　　　　　　　281
special needs classes（特別支援学級）
　　　　　　　　　　　107, 113, 119, 121
special needs education（特別支援教育）
　　　　　　　　　　　101, 103, 111, 113
special needs schools（特別支援学校）
　　　　　　　　　　　63, 103, 113,115, 117
special needs support in resource rooms（通級による指導） 107, 113, 119
specialized training college（専修学校） 59, 61
specialized course（専門学科）
　　　　　　　59, 81, 451, 543, 609, 613
sports club activity（運動部活動） 497, 503, 505
standard hours of class sessions（標準授業時数）
　　　　　　　　　　　　　　　　329, 331
standard numbers of credits（標準単位数） 333
student council activities（生徒会活動） 589
student counselor（生徒指導主事） 225, 243, 637
student enrollment promotion（就学奨励） 205
student guidance（生徒指導） 635
student understanding（児童生徒理解） 643
super science high schools（スーパーサイエンスハイスクール） 439
superintendent（教育長） 171, 173, 241, 251
supervisor for social education（社会教育主事）
　　　　　　　　　　　　　　　　139, 177
supervisor（指導主事） 177
supplementary education school（補習授業校） 283

sustainable society（持続可能な社会） 399
systematic learning（系統学習） 391, 425, 669
systematic science（系統理科） 425, 427

T

teacher adoption system（教員採用制度） 239
teacher appointment（教員任用） 249, 251
teacher certification system（教員免許制度） 217, 233
teacher evaluation system（教員評価制度） 253
teacher training system（教員養成制度） 233
teachers' meeting（職員会議） 187
teachers' organization（教員団体） 259
teachers' professional organization（教員職能団体）
　　　　　　　　　　　　　　　　259, 261
teachers' union（教職員組合） 259, 261
teaching as a profession（教育専門職） 223
teaching certificate（教員免許状） 235, 237, 239, 349
teaching practice（教育実習） 237, 239
technical colleges（高等専門学校） 61, 79
technical staff of museum（学芸員） 139, 159, 321, 339
textbook（教科書） 339
three upper secondary principles（高校三原則） 81
timetable（時間割） 341
TIMSS (Trends in International Mathematics and Science Study)（国際数学・理科教育動向調査）
　　　　　　　　　　　　　　　359, 443, 667
training for teachers with 10 years of experience（10年経験者研修） 245
truancy（不登校） 75, 79, 651

U

UNESCO（ユネスコ） 255, 299, 305, 307, 309, 315
UNESCO Charter（ユネスコ憲章） 297, 307
universities（大学） 63, 85, 87, 89, 91, 95
University of the United Nations（国連大学） 311
upper secondary education（後期中等教育） 59, 79
upper secondary school（高等学校） 59, 79, 81

V

vice-principal（副校長）	185, 189, 223
violent act（暴力行為）	513, 647, 657
visiting teacher instruction（訪問教育）	113, 119
vocational education（職業教育）	601
vocational guidance（職業指導）	237, 483, 635, 639

W

welfare benefits（福利厚生）	137, 257
World History（世界史）	387

Z

zest for living（生きる力）	463, 535, 565, 669

編者紹介

村田翼夫（むらた　よくお）

1941年、富山県生まれ。京都大学教育学部卒業。国立教育研究所主任研究官、筑波大学教育学系教授、同大学名誉教授、大阪成蹊大学教授を経て、現在、京都女子大学発達教育学部教授。博士（教育学）。専攻は比較・国際教育学。

主要著書

『バイリンガル・テキスト　日本の教育（Education in Japan）』共編著、学習研究社、1998年。『東南アジア諸国の国民統合と教育－多民族社会における葛藤－』編著、東信堂、2001年。『多文化共生社会の教育』共編著、玉川大学出版部、2001年。『タイにおける教育発展－国民統合・文化・教育協力－』単著、東信堂、2007年。

山口　満（やまぐち　みつる）

1937年、京都府生まれ。東京教育大学教育学部卒業。秋田大学助教授、奈良教育大学助教授を経て筑波大学教授（教育学系）。同大学名誉教授。びわこ成蹊スポーツ大学名誉教授。中部学院大学特任教授。専攻はカリキュラム研究。

主要著書

『教育の個別化』共著、明治図書、1998年。『現代カリキュラム研究』編著、学文社、2001年。『改訂新版・特別活動と人間形成』編著、学文社、2010年。

バイリンガルテキスト
現代日本の教育－制度と内容－

＊定価はカバーに表示してあります

2010年6月1日　初　版第1刷発行

〔検印省略〕

編者 Ⓒ 村田翼夫、山口満／発行者 下田勝司　　印刷／製本 中央精版印刷

東京都文京区向丘1-20-6　郵便振替 00110-6-37828
〒113-0023　TEL (03)3818-5521　FAX (03)3818-5514

発 行 所
株式会社 東信堂

Published by TOSHINDO PUBLISHING CO., LTD
1-20-6, Mukougaoka, Bunkyo-ku, Tokyo, 113-0023, Japan
E-mail : tk203444@fsinet.or.jp　http://www.toshindo-pub.com

ISBN978-4-88713-979-4 C3037　Ⓒ Y.Murata, M.Yamaguchi

東信堂

比較教育学——越境のレッスン 伝統・挑戦・新しいパラダイムを求めて	M・ブレイ編著／馬越徹・大塚豊監訳	三六〇〇円
比較教育学	馬越徹著	三八〇〇円
世界の外国人学校	末藤美津子・大塚豊・平治編著	三八〇〇円
ヨーロッパの学校における市民的社会性教育の発展——フランス・ドイツ・イギリス	福田誠治著	三八〇〇円
世界のシティズンシップ教育——グローバル時代の国民/市民形成	嶺井明子編著	二八〇〇円
市民性教育の研究——日本とタイの比較	平田利文編著	四二〇〇円
多様社会カナダの「国語」教育（カナダの教育3）	関口礼子編著	三八〇〇円
国際教育開発の再検討——途上国の基礎教育 普及に向けて	澤田克己・小川啓一・西村幹子編著	二四〇〇円
中国教育の文化的基盤	顧明遠著／大塚豊監訳	二九〇〇円
中国大学入試研究——変貌する国家の人材選抜	大塚豊著	三六〇〇円
中国高等教育独学試験制度の展開	新井浅典子著	三二〇〇円
大学財政——世界の経験と中国の選択	南部広孝著	三四〇〇円
中国の民営高等教育機関——社会ニーズとの対応	鮑威著／龍瀬夫監訳	四六〇〇円
「改革・開放」下中国の教育の動態——江蘇省の場合を中心に	阿部洋編著	五四〇〇円
中国の職業教育拡大政策——背景・実現過程・帰結	劉文君著	五〇四八円
中国の後期中等教育の拡大と経済発展パターン——江蘇省と広東省の比較	呉琦来著	三八二七円
中国高等教育の拡大と教育機会の変容	王傑著	三九〇〇円
バングラデシュ農村の初等教育制度受容	日下部達哉著	三六〇〇円
オーストラリア学校経営改革の研究——自律的学校経営とアカウンタビリティ	佐藤博志著	三八〇〇円
オーストラリアの言語教育政策——多文化主義における「多様性と」「統一性」の揺らぎと共存	青木麻衣子著	三八〇〇円
マレーシア青年期女性の進路形成	鴨川明子著	四七〇〇円
「郷土」としての台湾——郷土教育の展開にみるアイデンティティの変容	林初梅著	四六〇〇円
戦後台湾教育とナショナル・アイデンティティ	山﨑直也著	四〇〇〇円

〒113-0023 東京都文京区向丘1-20-6　TEL 03-3818-5521　FAX 03-3818-5514　振替 00110-6-37828
Email tk203444@fsinet.or.jp　URL:http://www.toshindo-pub.com/
※定価：表示価格（本体）＋税